Lecture Notes in Computer Science 12962

More information about this series at https://link.springer.com/bookseries/558

Alessandro Crimi · Spyridon Bakas (Eds.)

Brainlesion:
Glioma, Multiple Sclerosis, Stroke and Traumatic Brain Injuries

7th International Workshop, BrainLes 2021
Held in Conjunction with MICCAI 2021
Virtual Event, September 27, 2021
Revised Selected Papers, Part I

 Springer

Editors
Alessandro Crimi ⓘ
Sano Centre for Computational Personalized
Kraków, Poland

Spyridon Bakas ⓘ
University of Pennsylvania
Philadelphia, PA, USA

ISSN 0302-9743 ISSN 1611-3349 (electronic)
Lecture Notes in Computer Science
ISBN 978-3-031-08998-5 ISBN 978-3-031-08999-2 (eBook)
https://doi.org/10.1007/978-3-031-08999-2

In loving memory of Prof. Christian Barillot

Preface

This volume contains articles from the 7th International Brain Lesion Workshop (BrainLes 2021), as well as the RSNA-ASNR-MICCAI Brain Tumor Segmentation (BraTS 2021) Challenge, the Federated Tumor Segmentation (FeTS 2021) Challenge, the Cross-Modality Domain Adaptation (CrossMoDA 2021) Challenge, and the challenge on Quantification of Uncertainties in Biomedical Image Quantification (QUBIQ 2021). All these events were held in conjunction with the Medical Image Computing and Computer Assisted Intervention (MICCAI) conference on September 27, 2021, in Strasbourg, France, taking place online due to COVID-19 restrictions.

The presented manuscripts describe the research of computational scientists and clinical researchers working on glioma, multiple sclerosis, cerebral stroke, traumatic brain injuries, vestibular schwannoma, and white matter hyper-intensities of presumed vascular origin. This compilation does not claim to provide a comprehensive understanding from all points of view; however, the authors present their latest advances in segmentation, disease prognosis, and other applications in the clinical context.

The volume is divided into five chapters: the first chapter comprises invited papers summarizing the presentations of the keynotes during the full-day BrainLes workshop and the FeTS challenge, the second includes the accepted paper submissions to the BrainLes workshop, and the third through the sixth chapters contain a selection of papers regarding methods presented at the RSNA-ASNR-MICCAI BraTS, FeTS, CrossMoDA, and QUBIQ challenges, respectively.

The content of the first chapter with the invited papers covers the current state-of-the-art literature on federated learning applications for cancer research and clinical oncology analysis, as well as an overview of the deep learning approaches improving the current standard of care for brain lesions and current neuroimaging challenges.

The aim of the second chapter, focusing on the accepted BrainLes workshop submissions, is to provide an overview of new advances of medical image analysis in all the aforementioned brain pathologies. It brings together researchers from the medical image analysis domain, neurologists, and radiologists working on at least one of these diseases. The aim is to consider neuroimaging biomarkers used for one disease applied to the other diseases. This session did not have a specific dataset to be used.

The third chapter focuses on a selection of papers from the RSNA-ASNR-MICCAI BraTS 2021 challenge participants. BraTS 2021 made publicly available the largest ever manually annotated dataset of baseline pre-operative brain glioma scans from 20 international institutions in order to gauge the current state of the art in automated brain tumor segmentation using skull-stripped multi-parametric MRI sequences (provided in NIfTI file format) and to compare different methods. To pinpoint and evaluate the clinical relevance of tumor segmentation, BraTS 2021 also included the prediction of the MGMT methylation status using the same skull-stripped multi-parametric MRI sequences but provided in the DICOM file format to conform to the clinical standards (https://www.rsna.org/education/ai-resources-and-training/ai-image-challenge/brain-tumor-ai-challenge-2021).

The fourth chapter contains a selection of papers from the Federated Tumor Segmentation (FeTS 2021) challenge participants. This was the first computational challenge focussing on federated learning, and ample multi-institutional routine clinically-acquired pre-operative baseline multi-parametric MRI scans of radiographically appearing glioblastoma were provided to the participants, along with splits on the basis of the site of acquisition. The goal of the challenge was two-fold: i) identify the best way to aggregate the knowledge coming from segmentation models trained on the individual institutions, and ii) find the best algorithm that produces robust and accurate brain tumor segmentations across different medical institutions, MRI scanners, image acquisition parameters, and populations. Interestingly, the second task was performed by actually circulating the containerized algorithms across different institutions, leveraging the collaborators of the largest real-world federation to date (www.fets.ai).

The fifth chapter contains a selection of papers from the CrossMoDA 2021 challenge participants. CrossMoDA 2021 was the first large and multi-class benchmark for unsupervised cross-modality domain adaptation for medical image segmentation. The goal of the challenge was to segment two key brain structures involved in the follow-up and treatment planning of vestibular schwannoma (VS): the VS tumour and the cochlea. The training dataset provides annotated T1 scans (N = 105) and unpaired non-annotated T2 scans (N = 105). More information can be found on the challenge website (https://crossmoda-challenge.ml/).

The sixth chapter contains a selection of papers from the QUBIQ 2021 challenge participants. QUBIQ 2021 continued the success of the first challenge on uncertainty quantification in medical image segmentation (QUBIQ 2020). The goal of the challenge was to model the uncertainty in diverse segmentation tasks in which the involved images include different modalities, e.g., CT and MRI scans and varied organs and pathologies. QUBIQ 2021 included two new 3D segmentation tasks, pancreas segmentation and pancreatic lesion segmentation.

We heartily hope that this volume will promote further exciting computational research on brain related pathologies.

December 2021

Alessandro Crimi
Spyridon Bakas

Organization

BrainLes Organizing Committee

Spyridon Bakas   University of Pennsylvania, USA
Alessandro Crimi   Sano Science, Poland

BrainLes Program Committee

Bhakti V. Baheti   University of Pennsylvania, USA
Ujjwal Baid   University of Pennsylvania, USA
Florian Kofler   Technical University of Munich, Germany
Hugo Kuijf   University Medical School of Utrecht,
                                   The Netherlands
Jana Lipkova   Technical University of Munich, Germany
Andreas Mang   University of Houston, USA
Raghav Mehta   McGill University, Canada
Sarthak Pati   University of Pennsylvania, USA
Szymon Plotka   Warsaw University of Technology, Poland
Zahra Riahi Samani   University of Pennsylvania, USA
Aristeidis Sotiras   Washington University at St. Louis, USA
Siddhesh Thakur   University of Pennsylvania, USA
Benedikt Wiestler   Technical University of Munich, Germany

Challenges Organizing Committees

Brain Tumor Segmentation (BraTS) Challenge

Ujjwal Baid   University of Pennsylvania, USA
Spyridon Bakas (Lead Organizer)   University of Pennsylvania, USA
Evan Calabrese   University of California San Francisco, USA
Christopher Carr   Radiological Society of North America, USA
Errol Colak   Unity Health Toronto, Canada
Keyvan Farahani   National Cancer Institute, National Institutes of
                                         Health, USA
Adam E. Flanders   Thomas Jefferson University Hospital, USA
Felipe C. Kitamura   Diagnósticos da América SA and Universidade
                                         Federal de São Paulo, Brazil
Bjoern Menze   University of Zurich, Switzerland
Luciano Prevedello   The Ohio State University, USA

| Jeffrey Rudie | University of California, San Francisco, USA |
| Russell Taki Shinohara | University of Pennsylvania, USA |

Federated Tumor Segmentation (FeTS) Challenge

Ujjwal Baid	University of Pennsylvania, USA
Spyridon Bakas (Task 1 Lead Organizer)	University of Pennsylvania, USA
Yong Chen	University of Pennsylvania, USA
Brandon Edwards	Intel, USA
Patrick Foley	Intel, USA
Alexey Gruzdev	Intel, USA
Jens Kleesiek	University Hospital Essen, Germany
Klaus Maier-Hein	DKFZ, Germany
Lena Maier-Hein	DKFZ, Germany
Jason Martin	Intel, USA
Bjoern Menze	University of Zurich, Switzerland
Sarthak Pati	University of Pennsylvania, USA
Annika Reinke	DKFZ, Germany
Micah J. Sheller	Intel, USA
Russell Taki Shinohara	University of Pennsylvania, USA
Maximilian Zenk (Task 2 Lead Organizer)	DKFZ, Germany
David Zimmerer	DKFZ, Germany

Cross-Modality Domain Adaptation (CrossMoDA) Challenge

Spyridon Bakas	University of Pennsylvania, USA
Jorge Cardoso	King's College London, UK
Reuben Dorent (Lead Organizer)	King's College London, UK
Ben Glocker	Imperial College London, UK
Samuel Joutard	King's College London, UK
Aaron Kujawa	King's College London, UK
Marc Modat	King's College London, UK
Nicola Rieke	NVIDIA, Germany
Jonathan Shapey	King's College London, UK
Tom Vercauteren	King's College London, UK

Quantification of Uncertainty in Biomedical Image Quantification (QUBIQ) Challenge

Spyridon Bakas	University of Pennsylvania, USA
Anton Becker	Memorial Sloan Kettering Cancer Center, USA
Andras Jakab	University Children's Hospital Zürich, University of Zürich, Switzerland

Leo Joskowicz   The Hebrew University of Jerusalem, Israel
Ender Konukoglu   ETH Zürich, Switzerland
Hongwei (Bran) Li   Technical University of Munich, Germany
Bjoern Menze   University of Zurich, Switzerland

Contents – Part I

BraTS

Contents – Part II

CrossMoDA

Invited Papers

A Review of Medical Federated Learning: Applications in Oncology and Cancer Research

Alexander Chowdhury[1], Hasan Kassem[3], Nicolas Padoy[3,4],
Renato Umeton[1,2,5,6], and Alexandros Karargyris[3,4(✉)]

[1] Dana-Farber Cancer Institute, Boston, MA, USA
renato_umeton@dfci.harvard.edu
[2] Massachusetts Institute of Technology, Cambridge, MA, USA
[3] ICube, University of Strasbourg, CNRS, Strasbourg, France
[4] IHU Strasbourg, Strasbourg, France
alexandros.karargyris@ihu-strasbourg.eu
[5] Weill Cornell Medicine, New York, NY, USA
[6] Harvard T.H. Chan School of Public Health, Boston, MA, USA

Abstract. Machine learning has revolutionized every facet of human life, while also becoming more accessible and ubiquitous. Its prevalence has had a powerful impact in healthcare, with numerous applications and intelligent systems achieving clinical level expertise. However, building robust and generalizable systems relies on training algorithms in a centralized fashion using large, heterogeneous datasets. In medicine, these datasets are time consuming to annotate and difficult to collect centrally due to privacy concerns. Recently, Federated Learning has been proposed as a distributed learning technique to alleviate many of these privacy concerns by providing a decentralized training paradigm for models using large, distributed data. This new approach has become the defacto way of building machine learning models in multiple industries (e.g. edge computing, smartphones). Due to its strong potential, Federated Learning is also becoming a popular training method in healthcare, where patient privacy is of paramount concern. In this paper we performed an extensive literature review to identify state-of-the-art Federated Learning applications for cancer research and clinical oncology analysis. Our objective is to provide readers with an overview of the evolving Federated Learning landscape, with a focus on applications and algorithms in oncology space. Moreover, we hope that this review will help readers to identify potential needs and future directions for research and development.

Keywords: Federated learning · Cancer research · Clinical oncology · Privacy-preserving computation · Healthcare informatics · Distributed learning

A. Chowdhury and H. Kassem - Joint first authors,
R. Umeton and A. Karargyris - Joint senior authors.

A. Crimi and S. Bakas (Eds.): BrainLes 2021, LNCS 12962, pp. 3–24, 2022.
https://doi.org/10.1007/978-3-031-08999-2_1

Highlights

- Federated learning (FL) has the potential to become the primary learning paradigm for distributed cancer research, but specific hurdles have slowed its adoption in the clinical setting.
- Labeled medical data is still extremely scarce; this problem also affects federated learning. A plethora of cancer datasets exist (e.g. TCIA, TCGA, Gene Expression Omnibus, etc.), but few of them are labeled for supervised learning. The ones that are labeled (i.e., the Wisconsin Breast Cancer dataset - for classification, the BraTS dataset - for image segmentation, the Kaggle datasets for skin cancer) are the ones most commonly seen being used in FL.
- The largest majority of papers we found use cancer datasets for benchmarking purposes: very few federated learning works solve an actual clinically relevant question. Many of the papers we reviewed propose new software frameworks, and virtually none follow-up with a clinical trial. This leaves FL absent from the field of clinical oncology, based on our literature review.
- The compliance and security aspect of healthcare still poses the largest hurdle. Commercial entities such as EHR vendors (e.g., Epic Systems, Cerner, Meditech, Allscripts, etc.), PACS vendors (e.g., GE, Philips, Hitachi, Siemens, Canon, etc.), and other hardware manufacturers (e.g., Nvidia, Intel, etc.) seem to be the best positioned to start pulling together resources, data, and models that use FL to improve patient outcomes.

1   Introduction

Over the past decade, machine learning has witnessed rapid growth due to the proliferation of deep learning. Fueled by large-scale training databases [1], these data driven methods have gained significant popularity. Thanks to rapidly evolving architectures, (e.g., AlexNet [2], GoogLeNet [3], ResNet [4]) convolutional neural networks (CNNs) have demonstrated consistent improvement on difficult computer vision tasks including classification, object detection, and segmentation. Other areas of machine learning, such as natural language understanding, recommendation systems and speech recognition, have also seen outstanding results in their respective applications through the introduction of novel approaches such as transformers [5,6], DLRM [7] and RNN-T [8].

Such advancements in artificial intelligence and machine learning have already disrupted and transformed healthcare through applications ranging from medical image analysis to protein sequencing [9–12]. And yet, while there are over 150 AI-based interventions that are approved by the FDA (an updated list with a focus on radiology can be reviewed at https://aicentral.acrdsi.org), many open questions persist about how to best deploy existing AI solutions in healthcare environments [13]. In addition to getting existing solutions deployed, there are many challenges that must be overcome during the training process. A consistent bottleneck has been the need for large amounts of heterogeneous data to train accurate, robust and generalizable machine learning models. However, most healthcare organizations rarely carry data in such large quantities, especially in the case of homogeneous populations or rare diseases with scarce amounts of cases.

A common way data scientists attempt to overcome this issue is by first pre-training a model on large, generic datasets (e.g., ImageNet [1]), and then fine-tuning them on specific medical tasks of interest. However, even with this approach, underperformance or generalizability issues [14] may persist. This is often the case for medical tasks where there exists a large domain shift between medical data (e.g., brain MRI, abdomen CT, genomics) and general purpose public datasets such as ImageNet [1], MIMIC-CXR [15], ChexPert [16], etc. More recently, Self Supervised Learning (SSL) approaches have demonstrated promising results in performance using large unlabelled datasets, thus alleviating the need for annotations; however, even with such SSL approaches, the need for access to large amounts of heterogeneous medical data is still necessary to train robust medical ML algorithms [17,18].

In addition to large, heterogeneous datasets, the other most common bottleneck for ML algorithm training is computational power. The need for access to considerably efficient computing resources (e.g., processing power, memory, storage space) led to the field of distributed systems [19]. Within this area, distributed machine learning has evolved as a setting where algorithms are implemented and run on multiple nodes, leveraging larger amounts of data and computational resources, thus improving performance and efficiency. The core concept of distributed learning lies in the parallelization of algorithms across computational nodes [19], but these processes are run without considering any constraints that might need to be imposed by these nodes (e.g., considering that data used across these nodes comes from different distributions). Because of this, the majority of practical applications in collaborative learning fail to keep the assumption of Independent-and-Identically-Distributed (IID) data across nodes, such as user data from mobile devices or healthcare data from different geographic and demographic properties. Federated Learning emerged as a distributed learning paradigm that takes into account several practical challenges, and differentiates itself from traditional distributed learning settings, as noted by Google [20], by addressing four main themes: statistical heterogeneity of data across nodes, data imbalance across nodes, limited communication in the distributed network (e.g., loss of synchronization, variability of communication capabilities), and the possibility of a large number of nodes relative to the amounts of data.

In the Federated Learning setting, a "federation" of client sites with their own datasets train models locally and then send their updates to a server. The weights are the only information passed over lines of communication aiming at preserving privacy. The model weights are then aggregated in the server from the client updates, and the resulting aggregated model weights are sent back to the clients for the next round of training. Because of its strong potential to preserve privacy with client sites, such as hospitals, by keeping their data in-house, Federated Learning has seen a rise in popularity over the last several years, especially in the medical domain.

Specifically, large-scale projects have been developed for facilitating collaboration of medical institutions around the globe with the aid of Federated Learning, in both academic and industrial areas [21]. Trustworthy Federated Data Analytics [22], German Cancer Consortium's Joint Imaging Platform [23], and the Melloddy project [24] were developed to improve academic research in various healthcare applications by combining multiple institutions' efforts. In industry, the HealthChain project [25] aims to develop and deploy a Federated Learning framework across four hospitals in France to help determine effective treatments for melanoma and breast cancer patients. Additionally, the Federated Tumour Segmentation initiative (FeTS) [26,27] is an international collaboration between 30 healthcare institutions aimed at enhancing tumor boundary detection, for example, in breast and liver tumors. In another international effort [28], researchers trained ML models for mammogram assessment across a federation of US and Brazilian healthcare providers.

In light of all these efforts, and given the growing adoption of Federated Learning in healthcare, we believe that the cancer research community is lacking a much needed review of the current state-of-the-art. Therefore, with this review we aim at providing an comprehensive list of Federated Learning algorithms, applications and frameworks proposed for cancer analysis. We envision that this review can function as a quick reference for Federated Learning's applications in cancer and oncology, and provide a motivation for research in specific directions.

The review is structured as follows. In Sect. 2 we give an overview of Federated Learning to introduce the reader to related concepts. The main body of this review is found in Sect. 3, which we begin by providing the search query along with the inclusion/exclusion criteria for papers. After this, we provide a summary of the current literature for: 1) Federated Learning algorithms in cancer analysis, 2) Federated Learning frameworks developed for cancer research, and 3) Algorithms developed to preserve privacy under Federated Learning settings. Finally, we conclude this review by offering our thoughts on the needs and potential future directions for Federated Learning in the cancer research and clinical oncology space.

2   Federated Learning Overview

Federated Learning was first introduced as a decentralized distributed machine learning paradigm by Google [20]. The standard Federated Learning paradigm that is outlined in this paper is as follows: i) Multiple client sites, each containing a local dataset that remains at the client site during the entirety of training, connect to a global server; ii) A global model is initialized in the global server, and the weights from this global model are passed to each of the local client sites; iii) Each client site trains a local version of the global model on their respective dataset, and then sends the updated model weights to the global server; iv) The global server updates the global model by aggregating the weights it receives from the local clients, and then passes a copy of the updated global model to each of the clients. The process that occurs between steps i–iv is called a round, and during federated training, steps i–iv are repeated for multiple rounds until the global model converges to a local minima. The most important aspect of this process is step iii. During this step, all data used for training is kept strictly on the local clients' machines. The only information that is passed between the clients and the server are weight updates. This enables multiple sites to pool their data for training of a global model while still maintaining data privacy. During step iv, the authors use an algorithm that they coin federated averaging to aggregate the weights. In this algorithm, each weight updated is weighted by the size of the client dataset from which it comes, relative to the size of the other client datasets. The aforementioned clients-server topology is known as Centralized Federated Learning. One other topology has been found in research [29], Decentralized Federated Learning, in which clients communicate peer-to-peer without a central server.

Federated Learning can be broken down into three main subtypes [30]: Horizontal Federated Learning, Vertical Federated Learning, and Federated Transfer Learning. All three of these subtypes follow the core Federated Learning paradigm, which is decentralized data pooling through the use of weight sharing and aggregation between multiple clients and a global server. They are distinguished by the way in which their data sources differ. In Horizontal Federated Learning, every client site has different users in their data, but all of these users share similar features that are extracted by the networks. In Vertical Federated Learning, users are the same across all client sites, but each client sites' data consists of different features, so the same user will be analyzed through different modalities depending on the client site. In Transfer Federated Learning, the client sites don't have users or features in common, but the tasks in their datasets are still marginally related, so pooling them together typically leads to more robust network training. For a more general review of Federated Learning, readers are referred to [29, 31, 32]. Here we also list common Federated Learning platforms: OpenFL [33], PySyft[1], Tensorflow-Federated[2], FedML [34], Flower[3], NVIDIA Clara[4], Personal Health Train (PHT[5]).

3 Review

3.1 Search Design

The literature review was conducted in October 2021 by searching Google Scholar for papers published between 2019 and 2021 that matched the query: *federated AND (cancer OR cancers OR tumor OR tumors OR oncology)*.

We chose this time period for our search query due to the fact that Google didn't publish their seminal Federated Learning paper [35] until 2017, so we didn't see a large amount of medical applications until than. A visual representation of the split of the material reviewed is presented in Fig. 1 and our review process is shown in Fig. 2.

---

[1] https://github.com/OpenMined/PySyft.
[2] https://medium.com/tensorflow/introducing-tensorflow-federated-a4147aa20041.
[3] https://flower.dev/.
[4] https://developer.nvidia.com/clara.
[5] https://pht.health-ri.nl/.

Through our review process we identified two main categories of Federated Learning applications related to cancer and oncology: whether the study was designed exclusively with cancer as its intended use-case, or whether cancer datasets were used for benchmarking a general method (Fig. 1-Category). Every

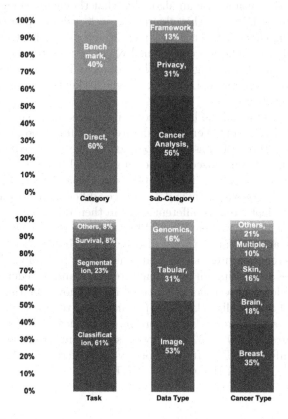

Fig. 1. Split of the papers reviewed: **Category** and **Sub-Category** represent the paper scope. **Task** refers to the machine learning task, while **Data Type** and **Cancer Type** relate to the FL input data.

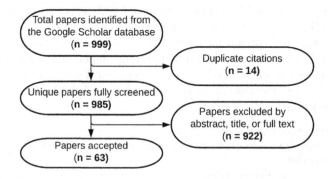

Fig. 2. A visual representation of our process for including papers for this review.

category is also further divided into three sub-categories: the first one contains the Federated Learning feasibility studies and methods that have been applied to the analysis of cancer datasets (i.e., 'Framework' in Fig. 1-Sub-Category). The second contains Federated Learning frameworks proposed or developed for 'Cancer Analysis', although almost all fail to secure relevant and novel cancer datasets and hence resort to open-access data. Finally, the third sub-category contains Federated Learning studies that address and analyze 'Privacy' of cancer data and computation.

3.2   Federated Learning Algorithms

Algorithms Designed for Cancer: Based on our literature search we identified that Federated Learning has been explored in many cancer studies, where the aim is either comparing Federated Learning to conventional centralized data analysis approaches in terms of performance, or developing novel methods to solve various challenges faced when using Federated Learning (e.g., domain shift, label deficiency, ...). In the most common training scenario, researchers simulate a Federated Learning environment by taking an existing dataset and dividing it into subsets using a partitioning scheme, where each subset represents a client in a Federated Learning group.

Federated Learning has been applied on detecting brain tumors in several studies [36–39]. In [36], the authors used the 'Brain MRI Segmentation' dataset from Kaggle for low-grade glioma segmentation [40], dividing the dataset into 5 "client" sites. The authors designed a network that achieves state-of-the-art results on the task of glioma segmentation, and those results remained consistent when they applied it to a Federated Learning setting. In [37], two separate Federated Learning environments for brain tumor segmentation were simulated using the BraTS dataset [41]. In both environments, the Federated Learning model was compared against two other collaborative learning techniques, and outperformed both. It also achieved nearly 99% of the DICE score obtained by a model trained on the entire dataset with no decentralization. Similarly, [38] demonstrated comparable performance between federated averaging and data sharing for brain tumor segmentation on the BraTS dataset [41]. Sheller et al. also showed how Federated Learning improves the learning of each participating institution both in terms of performance on local data and performance on data from unseen domains. In [39], the authors presented a comparison between a Federated Learning approach and individual training of a 3D-Unet model to segment glioblastoma in 165 multi-parametric structural MRI (mpMRI) scans. The Federated Learning approach is shown to yield superior quantitative results.

Additional studies have explored Federated Learning on a variety of other cancers, including less common types. Some of the types covered in the uses cases we reviewed included: skin cancer [42,43], breast cancer [44,45], prostate cancer [46], lung cancer [47], pancreatic cancer, anal cancer, and thyroid cancer. [42] used the ISIC 2018 dataset [48] to simulate a Federated Learning environment for classifying skin lesions. They first partitioned the dataset among multiple mock client sites, then used a Dual-GAN [49] to augment each clients' dataset. A classifier was then trained in a federated environment on the augmented datasets.

In [43], the authors use the ISIC 2019 Dermoscopy dataset [48] to demonstrate proof-of-concept for a skin lesion detection device trained using federated learning. In Roth et al. [44], a real-world experiment of federated breast density classification was performed using NVIDIA's Clara framework. The authors developed a breast density classification model with mammography data from 7 different institutions. The global federated model showed significant improvements over the locally trained models when validated against their own data as well as external site validation. In [50] and [45], the authors demonstrate the ability to successfully apply vertical federated learning (VFL) to cancer analysis, using VFL to create a survival prediction model for breast cancer. [46] performed prostate image segmentation in a federated setting. They showed how Federated Learning improves model performance on local datasets. [47] described a large experiment on 20K lung cancer patients across 8 institutes and 5 countries. They trained a logistic regressor on these distributed data. To train the LR coefficients in a distributed manner they used the Alternating Direction Method of Multipliers (ADMM). The data included tumor staging and post-treatment survival information.

In [51], the authors tackle the task of pancreas segmentation for patients with pancreatic cancer. Advanced tools to correctly identify pancreatic cancer are extremely important since pancreatic cancer is normally only detectable once it is late-stage, leading to extremely low survival rates [52]. They used two datasets obtained from hospitals in Japan and Taiwan to simulate a Federated Learning environment. The resulting model was able to better identify pancreas from both datasets than models trained only on one site and validated on the other. Concluding with similar results, [53] tested several deep learning architectures for federated thyroid images classification, and Choudhury et al. [54] used data from 3 different sites to create a prediction model for patients with anal cancer, an extremely rare form of cancer, who received radical chemoradiotherapy. The large and diverse group of examples given here demonstrates the robustness and versatility of the Federated Learning paradigm, as well as its ability to improve automated analysis on more rare cancer cases [51,53,54].

In addition to having many use cases with specific cancer types, Federated Learning's applications in genomics have also been a popular focal point for research [55,56]. [55] performed federated gene expression analysis on breast cancer and skin cancer data. [56] adapted the Cox proportional hazards (PH) model [57] in a Federated Learning setting for survival analysis. Noting that adapting this method in a distributed manner is non-trivial due to its non-separable loss function, they implemented a discrete time extension of this model with a separable loss function, and validated their method on the Genome Atlas Data (TCGA)[6], showing comparable performance to the centralized approach.

While the bulk of the papers we've reviewed so far focus purely on designing federated algorithms that can predict different aspects of cancer with high degrees of accuracy, a large sub-group of the papers in our review also aim at addressing challenges federated learning currently faces. For many papers, that challenge is either data heterogeneity [58–65], a common barrier in the medi-

---

[6] https://www.cancer.gov/tcga.

cal field where patients can be subject to different geographic and demographic conditions, or label deficiency [66,67], where it is not always guaranteed that clients' sites will have access to labeled data.

Addressing label deficiency, [66] introduced a new Federated Semi-Supervised Learning (FSSL) approach for skin lesion classification. Their method is inspired by knowledge distillation [68], where they model disease relationships in each client by a relation matrix calculated from the local model output, then aggregate the relation matrices from all clients to form a global one that is used locally in each round to ensure that clients will have similar disease relationships. In [67], the authors proposed a semi-supervised Federated Learning method, FedPerl. The method was inspired by peer learning from educational psychology and ensemble averaging from committee machines and aims to gain extra knowledge by learning from similar clients i.e. peers. This encouraged the self-confidence of the clients by sharing their knowledge in a way that did not expose their identities. Experimental setup consisted of 71,000 skin lesion images collected from 5 publicly available datasets. With little annotated data, FedPerl outperformed state-of-the-art FSSL methods and the baselines by 1.8% and 15.8%, respectively. It also generalized better to an unseen client while being less sensitive to noisy ones.

Another challenge that frequently occurs in Federated Learning is domain shift, which is caused by heterogeneity in datasets due to different scanners and image acquisition protocols at different sites. Many papers modify the original FL algorithm to account for this. Jimenez et al. [58] designed a novel weight aggregation algorithm designed to address the problem of domain shift between data from different institutions. This study utilized one public and two private datasets, and the final global model outperformed previous Federated Learning approaches. Similarly, [59] introduced a new weight aggregation strategy and showed its efficiency on pancreas CT image segmentation. [60] built on the work of [51] by developing a Federated Learning algorithm that can learn multiple tasks from heterogeneous datasets, making use of a training paradigm the authors call dynamic weight averaging (DWA). Specifically, they trained a model on the binary-classification problem of segmenting the pancreas from background as well the multi-label classification problem of segmenting healthy and tumorous pancreatic tissue and background. During the global aggregation step, the weight value for each client update was adjusted based on the variation of loss values from the previous rounds. DWA outperforms federated averaging (FedAvg) and FedProx [69], another federated weight aggregation scheme designed to handle heterogeneous networks.

In Guo et al. [61], the authors addressed the problem of domain shift while applying their algorithm to the task of MRI reconstruction, using 4 different MRI datasets; FastMRI, BraTS, IXI, and HPKs. Their algorithm, Federated Learning-based Magnetic Resonance Imaging Reconstruction with Cross-site Modeling (FL-MRCM), uses an adversarial domain identifier to align latent features taken from the encoders of 2 different sites, avoiding sharing of data while taking advantage of multiple sites' data. In all experiments, FL-MRCM came closest to reaching the upper-bound score of training a network on the entire dataset. In the same space, to alleviate domain shift performance impact, [62] proposed a new method to train deep learning algorithms in Federated Learning settings based on the disentanglement of the latent space into shape and appearance information. Their method only shared the shape parameters to mitigate domain shifts between individual clients. They presented promising results on multiple brain MRI datasets.

Researchers in [63] proposed a method to address domain shift issues in terms of performance and stability based on sharing the parameters of batch normalization across clients but keeping the batch norm statistics local. Given that these statistics are not shared with the central server they argued that there is better protection from privacy attacks. They demonstrated their algorithm on breast histopathology image analysis (Camelyon 2016[7] and Camelyon 2017[8] datasets). In [64] a key-problem of digital pathology is addressed via federated learning: stain normalization across multiple laboratories and sites. They apply GANs in a Federated Learning environment to solve the problem of color normalization that arises due to different staining techniques used at different sites. Here, a central discriminator is trained to be extremely robust by making use of several decentralized generators.

Domain shift in Federated Learning has been also studied in Neural Architecture Search (NAS). [65] applied AutoML, a NAS approach, in a federated setting for prostate image segmentation. To address domain shift, they trained a 'supernet' consisting of several deep learning modules in a federated setting, then personalize this supernet in each client by searching for the best path along the supernet components according to each client.

General Algorithms Benchmarked on Cancer Datasets: Cancer datasets are also commonly used as benchmarks for evaluating general Federated Learning approaches. BraTS [41], HAM10000 [70], Wisconsin Breast Cancer dataset [71], and TCGA[9] were the most common datasets used in the papers we sourced for this review.

The BraTS dataset is an imaging dataset used to train computer vision models for brain tumor segmentation. It is frequently used as a benchmark for state-of-the-art image analysis algorithms. Chang et al. [72] performed a Federated Learning experiment on BraTS [41] using GANs in a similar setting to [64]. They use several decentralized discriminators, placed at mock client sites, to train a centralized discriminator at the client. Receiving synthetic images from a large amount of generators allowed the authors to augment the dataset in a decentralized fashion and train the discriminator to achieve very high accuracy. In some cases the classifier was able to outperform non-Federated Learning trained models, using Area Under the Curve (AUC) as a performance metric. In [73], the authors address the problem of domain shift while benchmarking on BraTS. They partition the network, and place a copy of each partition at each client site. They then place the rest of the network on a centralized server. Lower-level features taken from each client site are aggregated and passed as input to the

---

[7] https://camelyon16.grand-challenge.org/.

[8] https://camelyon17.grand-challenge.org/.

[9] https://www.cancer.gov/tcga.

central network, which learns to be robust against domain shift. This paradigm leads to extremely strong training results, especially as the domain shift becomes more pronounced.

The HAM10000 dataset is a multi-source dermatoscopic image dataset of pigmented lesion used for skin lesion detection and segmentation. Similar to BraTS, it frequently appears in many computer vision applications, such as [74], where the authors proposed a new server aggregation method addressing statistical heterogeneity that may be present between the participating datasets. The weights are calculated to be inversely proportional to the difference between the corresponding client model distribution and the global model distribution. They validated their new method on several benchmarks, including HAM10000 [70]. In [75] a new Federated Learning strategy was introduced for tackling non iid-ness in data. Training one epoch on each local dataset was done over several communication rounds. The approach was evaluated on various datasets, including HAM10000, and showed superior results to similar methods, such as FedAVG.

The Wisconsin Breast Cancer dataset [71] is another versatile dataset that is used for benchmarking many different classification algorithms. It is a simple dataset that is easy to integrate into most ML workflows, consisting of positive and negative breast cancer samples, and several numerical features describing those samples. Salmeron et al. [76] used this dataset to simulate a Federated Learning environment. The authors then used this environment to train a Fuzzy Cognitive Map (FCM) [77] classifier that outperformed clients that were trained individually as well as a model trained on the entire dataset. Researchers in [78] extended SQL-based training data debugging (RAIN method) for Federated Learning. They demonstrated this extension on multiple datasets, including the Wisconsin Breast Cancer dataset [71]. [79] introduced a new Federated Learning strategy that showed comparable performance to federated averaging while giving two benefits: communication efficiency and trustworthiness, via Stein Variational Gradient Descent (SVGD) which is a non-parametric Bayesian framework that approximates a target posterior distribution via non-random and interacting particles. They performed extensive experiments on various benchmarks, including binary classification of breast cancer data. [80] introduced a new federated setup that requires less communication costs and no centralized model sharing; clients learn collaboratively and simultaneously without the need of synchronization. They validated their setup, termed gradient assisted learning, on various datasets including breast cancer, and showed comparable performance with state-of-the-art methods but with less communications costs. [81] investigated how to mitigate the effects of model poisoning, a scenario where one or more clients upload intentionally false model parameters (or are forced to do so, e.g. by being hacked). They introduced new model-poisoning attacks, and showed that the methods of mitigating the effects of these attacks still need development. In [82], a method for building a global model under the Federated Learning setting was proposed by learning the data distribution of each client and building a global model based on these shared distributions.

The Cancer Genome Atlas (TCGA) is a public consortium of cancer data created for the purpose of benchmarking healthcare analysis algorithms. In [83] a method was proposed for matrix factorization under Federated Learning settings. Specifically, they extended the FedAvg method to allow for robust matrix factorization. They benchmarked this method on the Cancer Genome Atlas (TCGA). Benchmarking on the same data, [84] introduced two Federated Learning algorithms for matrix factorization and applied them to a data clustering task.

3.3   Federated Learning Frameworks

Frameworks Developed for Cancer Analysis: In [85], the authors designed a decentralized framework which they coined Braintorrent. This framework removes the global server from the traditional FL paradigm, and instead allows sites to communicate their weights with one another directly. The framework was tested on the task of whole-brain segmentation, and demonstrates impressive results, outperforming traditional Federated Learning with a global server and achieving performance close to that of a model trained using pooled data. [86] designed an open source framework to facilitate analysis of local data between institutions in order to create a model for oral cavity cancer survival rates using data from multinational institutions. [87] introduced a framework, GenoPPML, that is a combination of Federated Learning and multiparty computation. The framework utilizes differential privacy and homomorphic encryption for guaranteeing preserved privacy, and it was mainly built for regression for genomics data. In [88] the authors proposed a framework to train on skin lesion images using IoT devices (smartphones). They further utilized Transfer Learning in this Federated Learning framework to circumvent the need of large, labelled data. The German National Cancer Center, an initiative whose primary goal is to foster multiclinical trials for development of improved diagnosis and treatment tools for cancer, recently released the Joint Imaging Platform (JIP) [89], a platform designed to build a foundation for Federated Learning scenarios. JIP provides containerized tools for Federated Learning, and many institutions have committed to testing JIP for use cases in the coming years. [90] provides another framework with multiple objectives and use cases. Here, the authors proposed a "marketplace" approach to federated learning: it provides the infrastructure and other computational resources for 3rd party applications to run in a Secure Multiparty Computation system; there, for sake of example, multiple computational tasks related to cancer research (from data normalization to Kaplan-Mayer analysis and COX regression) are treated as "Apps" and deployed into a secure and distributed environment.

General Frameworks: Because decentralized analysis of medical data is one of the most natural use cases for federated learning, cancer datasets are frequently included when benchmarking general federated learning frameworks. [91] introduced a framework for federated meta learning; a library for fast and efficient algorithm selection. They evaluated a prototype on various datasets including breast cancer dataset, showing better efficiency of their framework in finding the best algorithm for a given dataset against the ordinary grid search approach. In

[92], the authors design a classification framework for breast cancer that incorporates differential privacy. Similarly, [50] uses the Wisconsin Breast Dataset as once of their use cases for a privacy-verification FL framework.

3.4 Privacy Protection in Federated Learning Settings

One important benefit of Federated Learning for healthcare is its potential to mitigate privacy concerns. Although Federated Learning allows for multiple sites to train ML models on their data safely, there are still ways that this paradigm can be exploited. One very common exploitation is that dataset labels can be reconstructed from the gradients used during model training [93, 94].

In this section we discuss research that addresses privacy concerns of Federated Learning in cancer. We present papers that either benchmark their privacy-concerned investigations and methods on cancer data, or those which study Federated Learning privacy exclusively for cancer applications.

Privacy Methods for Cancer: In [95], the authors proposed a combination of meta-heuristic methods to operate the whole mechanism of aggregation, separation of models as well as evaluation. They analyzed the results in terms of the accuracy of the general model as well as for security against poisoning attacks. [96] implemented differentially privacy SGD training in a cyclic Federated Learning setting of two clients, and did an extensive study on the trade-off between privacy and accuracy. They achieved an acceptable trade-off between accuracy and privacy, and tested their experiments on classification of tumorous genes. In [97] the authors benchmarked various differential privacy methods against skin lesion classification in Federated Learning settings. [98] demonstrated an approach to prevent access to intermediate model weights by using a layer for privacy protection. The aggregation server prevented direct connections between hosts so that interim model weights cannot be viewed during training.

In [99], the authors studied the effect that two different techniques to preserve privacy had on a Federated Learning environment: injecting samples with noise or sharing only a fraction of the model's weights. Using the BraTS dataset [41] for brain tumor segmentation, they found that leaving out up to 40% of the model's weights only affected accuracy by a negligible amount. Using the BraTS dataset [41] the authors in [100] extended Private Aggregation of Teacher Ensembles (PATE) [101] which is used as an aggregation function using the teacher-student paradigm to enable privacy preserving training: teacher models are trained on private datasets and the student model (global) is trained on a public dataset using those teacher models. This extension applied a dimensionality reduction method to increase sensitivity for segmentation tasks. They validated their approach on three (2) common dimensionality reduction methods to assess differential privacy: PCA, Autoencoder and Wavelet transforms. [102] used noise injection as a successful privacy preservation technique for analyzing gigapixel whole slide images. [103] created a hybrid environment for encryption of medical data using blockchain technologies, Federated Learning, and homomorphic encryption. Homomorphic encryption is also used in [104], where it is leveraged to show secure and accurate computation of essential biomedical analysis tasks, including Kaplan-Meier survival analysis in oncology and genome-wide association studies (GWAS) in medical genetics. The authors demonstrate this through the use of their framework, FAMHE. GWAS data was also at the center of the SAFETY framework [105], where a hybrid deployment of both homomorphic encryption and secure hardware (Intel SGX) provides a good trade-off in terms of efficiency and computational support for secure statistical analysis. Rrajotte et al. [106] developed a framework called FELICIA (Federated Learning with a Centralized Adversary), which uses the PrivGAN architecture [107] to make use of data from multiple institutions and create higher-quality synthetic training data without sharing data among sites. [108] used differential privacy and demonstrated how the performance was still comparable to the centralized experiments despite the privacy-performance trade-off. They also showed empirically how the model with differential privacy became immune against adversarial attacks, and evaluated all their approaches on liver image segmentation.

General Privacy-Preserving Methods Benchmarked on Cancer Data sets: [109] introduced Federboost, a Federated Learning method for gradient boosting decision trees (GDBT). Their method can be applied for vertical and horizontal Federated Learning, and is characterized by the ease of ensuring secure model sharing. They demonstrated security and comparable performance to centralized settings using various datasets including breast cancer gene data from TCGA. [110] introduced a new Federated Learning approach for mitigating possible privacy breaches when sharing model weights. Their method was evaluated on various benchmark datasets including breast cancer data, and showed comparable performance to the conventional Federated Learning approaches while being more robust to gradient leaks, i.e. more privacy-preserving. [111] developed a homomorphic encryption framework on FPGA, aiming to accelerate the training phase under Federated Learning with the most possible encryption. They demonstrated performance improvement in speed benchmarking on multiple datasets including the Wisconsin Breast Cancer dataset.

In [112], the authors proposed attacks for two machine learning algorithms, logistic regression and XGBoost, in a Federated Learning setting. In this study the adversary does not deviate from the defined learning protocol, but attempts to infer private training data from the legitimately received information. In [113], the authors proposed an approach, self-taught Federated Learning, to address the limitations of current methods when handling heterogeneous datasets (e.g. a slow training speed, impractical for real-world applications). It exploited unsupervised feature extraction techniques for Federated Learning with heterogeneous datasets while preserving data privacy. In [114] a method is proposed to identify malicious poisoning attacks by having the server itself bootstrap trust. Specifically, the server collects a small, clean training dataset (called the root dataset) for the learning task and maintains a model (called server model) based on this to bootstrap trust. In each iteration, the server first assigns a trust score to each local model update from the clients, where a local model update has a lower trust score. They benchmarked their method against CH-MNIST; a medical image classification dataset consisting of 5,000 images of histology tiles collected from colorectal cancer patients. Where privacy is concerned, quantum cryptography is probably the next frontier of the security battleground, and some authors have started developing in this direction while using cancer datasets for benchmarking their secure federated learning frameworks [115]. Figure 1 presents an overall synopsis of all the studies reviewed in this paper based on AI tasks, cancer type, data type and category of work.

4   Conclusion and Discussion

Data decentralization is a crucial setting for developing data-driven models in healthcare due to the sensitive nature of medical data. Federated Learning, while still a new research field, has already demonstrated its potential use to support a distributed learning setup for healthcare. While the general field of Federated Learning research is very active with a focus on improving model aggregation and efficient communication between nodes, model and data privacy is a very challenging and open problem [32]. The data privacy aspect is very important especially in healthcare where legal, ethical and regulatory constraints impose tremendous restrictions and pressure to data providers (e.g., healthcare networks, research institutions)

While the Federated Learning research community is engaged in addressing the aforementioned open problems, in this paper we aimed at presenting the current status of Federated Learning in the domain of cancer and oncology because we believe that the machine learning community in this particular space can benefit from a quick review and perhaps direct research efforts in specific subareas. Our review highlighted that although a lot of works have been developed for Federated Learning only 56% of them have been exclusively proposed for cancer research or clinical oncology. This demonstrates the need for solutions designed specifically within this space. For example, privacy preserving methods may need to be researched and explored under the scope of the cancer field given that privacy requirements and guarantees can be significantly different from other areas (e.g., finance). In a similar fashion, while data heterogeneity is an open challenge in the general machine learning community, cancer and oncology datasets manifest unique properties which may require deeper clinical and medical device expertise involvement when developing methods that aim at overcoming model degradation in largely heterogeneous medical data.

Although there are quite a few frameworks developed specifically for cancer analysis (i.e., 13% Fig. 1), there is the potential risk of a fragmented platform landscape. This is true when it comes to the general Federated Learning community in which a large number of frameworks are currently being developed and maintained. Indeed, such efforts can lead to improved solutions but it is usually collaborative efforts that can achieve better adoption. In the cancer domain data scientists can benefit from platforms that aim at developing tools for distributed annotation, distributed model training workflows, and moreover the adoption of data standardization and thus better integration of Federated Learning into the clinical workflow.

When it comes to tasks (Fig. 1) we observed that the majority of algorithms are related to classification and segmentation, and use images (either from radiology or pathology) as input data type. This highlights the need for a broader exploration of other important tasks in cancer analysis such as survival prediction, genomics expression, precision medicine, patient treatment planning, and advanced patient diagnosis/prognosis through multi-modal data. Furthermore, within the context of cancer type we identified that almost 70% of the studies were addressing only a specific type of cancer: either brain tumor, or breast cancer, or skin lesions. This reaffirms our previous statement that Federated Learning should expand its application on multiple cancer types. Perhaps the reason for this increased focus on these three specific cancer types comes from the fact that these three areas have been well-established through the release of large public datasets. This emphasizes the overall need for large medical datasets being available to the research community. Ideally, federations that are currently being developed to support distributed learning (e.g., Federated Learning) will provide support in the future for secure remote machine learning development on geographically distributed data providers through robust privacy-preserving layers.

As with any new research field, Federated Learning for healthcare and in particular for cancer and oncology is still in its early days. However, whether the studies were simulating Federated Learning environments or conducting small experiments across hospitals with real private data, they constitute solid basis for future work. Federated Learning infrastructures are continuously being developed specifically for healthcare and cancer research to facilitate true collaboration between healthcare institutions across the world.

Acknowledgments. NP and AK were supported by French State Funds managed by the "Agence Nationale de la Recherche (ANR)" - "Investissements d'Avenir" (Investments for the Future), Grant ANR-10-IAHU-02 (IHU Strasbourg). NP and HK received support from the French ANR National AI Chair program (ANR-20-CHIA-0029-01, Chair AI4ORSafety).

References

1. Deng, J., et al.: ImageNet: a large-scale hierarchical image database. In: 2009 IEEE Conference on Computer Vision and Pattern Recognition, pp. 248–255. IEEE (2009)
2. Krizhevsky, A., Sutskever, I., Hinton, G.E.: ImageNet classification with deep convolutional neural networks. Adv. Neural. Inf. Process. Syst. **25**, 1097–1105 (2012)
3. Szegedy, C., et al.: Going deeper with convolutions. In: Proceedings of the IEEE Conference on Computer Vision and Pattern Recognition, pp. 1–9 (2015)
4. He, K., Zhang, X., Ren, S., Sun, J.: Deep residual learning for image recognition. In: Proceedings of the IEEE Conference on Computer Vision and Pattern Recognition, pp. 770–778 (2016)

5. Vaswani, A., et al.: Attention is all you need. In: Advances in Neural Information Processing Systems, pp. 5998–6008 (2017)
6. Devlin, J., Chang, M.-W., Lee, K., Toutanova, K.: BERT: pre-training of deep bidirectional transformers for language understanding. arXiv preprint arXiv:1810.04805 (2018)
7. Naumov, M., et al.: Deep learning recommendation model for personalization and recommendation systems. CoRR abs/1906.00091 (2019). https://arxiv.org/abs/1906.00091
8. Graves, A.: Sequence transduction with recurrent neural networks. arXiv preprint arXiv:1211.3711 (2012)
9. Suzuki, K.: Overview of deep learning in medical imaging. Radiol. Phys. Technol. **10**(3), 257–273 (2017). https://doi.org/10.1007/s12194-017-0406-5
10. Biswas, M., et al.: State-of-the-art review on deep learning in medical imaging. Front. Biosci. (Landmark Ed) **24**, 392–426 (2019)
11. Korfiatis, P., et al.: Residual deep convolutional neural network predicts MGMT methylation status. J. Digit. Imaging **30**, 622–628 (2017)
12. Jumper, J., et al.: Highly accurate protein structure prediction with AlphaFold. Nature **596**, 583–589 (2021)
13. Karargyris, A., et al.: MedPerf: open benchmarking platform for medical artificial intelligence using federated evaluation. arXiv preprint arXiv:2110.01406 (2021)
14. Chang, K., et al.: Distributed deep learning networks among institutions for medical imaging. J. Am. Med. Inform. Assoc. **25**, 945–954 (2018)
15. Johnson, A.E., et al.: MIMIC-CXR, a de-identified publicly available database of chest radiographs with free-text reports. Sci. Data **6**, 1–8 (2019)
16. Irvin, J., et al.: CheXpert: a large chest radiograph dataset with uncertainty labels and expert comparison. In: Proceedings of the AAAI Conference on Artificial Intelligence, vol. 33, pp. 590–597 (2019)
17. Chowdhury, A., Rosenthal, J., Waring, J., Umeton, R.: Applying self-supervised learning to medicine: review of the state of the art and medical implementations. Informatics **8**, 59 (2021)
18. Doersch, C., Zisserman, A.: Multi-task self-supervised visual learning. In: 2017 IEEE International Conference on Computer Vision (ICCV), pp. 2070–2079 (2017)
19. Van Steen, M., Tanenbaum, A.: Distributed systems principles and paradigms. Network **2**, 28 (2002)
20. McMahan, B., Moore, E., Ramage, D., Hampson, S., Agüera y Arcasy, B.: Communication-efficient learning of deep networks from decentralized data. In: Artificial Intelligence and Statistics, pp. 1273–1282. PMLR (2017)
21. Rieke, N., et al.: The future of digital health with federated learning. NPJ Digit. Med. **3**, 1–7 (2020)
22. Trustworthy federated data analytics (TFDA) (2020). https://tfda.hmsp.center/
23. Joint Imaging Platform (JIP) (2020). https://jip.dktk.dkfz.de/jiphomepage/
24. Machine learning ledger orchestration for drug discovery (2020). https://cordis.europa.eu/project/id/831472
25. Healthchain consortium (2020). https://www.substra.ai/en/healthchain-project
26. The federated tumor segmentation (FeTS) initiative (2020). https://www.fets.ai
27. Pati, S., et al.: The federated tumor segmentation (FeTS) challenge. arXiv preprint arXiv:2105.05874 (2021)
28. Medical institutions collaborate to improve mammogram assessment AI (2020). https://blogs.nvidia.com/blog/2020/04/15/federated-learning-mammogram-assessment/

29. Li, T., Sahu, A.K., Talwalkar, A., Smith, V.: Federated Learning: challenges, methods, and future directions. IEEE Sig. Process. Mag. **37**, 50–60 (2020)
30. Yang, Q., et al.: Federated learning. In: Synthesis Lectures on Artificial Intelligence and Machine Learning, vol. 13, pp. 1–207 (2019)
31. Li, L., Fan, Y., Tse, M., Lin, K.-Y.: A review of applications in federated learning. Comput. Ind. Eng. **149**, 106854 (2020)
32. Kairouz, P., et al.: Advances and open problems in federated learning. arXiv preprint arXiv:1912.04977 (2019)
33. Reina, G. A., et al.: OpenFL: an open-source framework for federated learning. arXiv preprint arXiv:2105.06413 (2021)
34. He, C., et al.: Fedml: a research library and benchmark for federated machine learning. arXiv preprint arXiv:2007.13518 (2020)
35. Konečný, J., et al.: Federated learning: strategies for improving communication efficiency. In: NIPS Workshop on Private Multi-Party Machine Learning (2016). https://arxiv.org/abs/1610.05492
36. Yi, L., Zhang, J., Zhang, R., Shi, J., Wang, G., Liu, X.: SU-Net: an efficient encoder-decoder model of federated learning for brain tumor segmentation. In: Farkaš, I., Masulli, P., Wermter, S. (eds.) ICANN 2020. LNCS, vol. 12396, pp. 761–773. Springer, Cham (2020). https://doi.org/10.1007/978-3-030-61609-0_60
37. Sheller, M.J., Reina, G.A., Edwards, B., Martin, J., Bakas, S.: Multi-institutional deep learning modeling without sharing patient data: a feasibility study on brain tumor segmentation. In: Crimi, A., Bakas, S., Kuijf, H., Keyvan, F., Reyes, M., van Walsum, T. (eds.) BrainLes 2018. LNCS, vol. 11383, pp. 92–104. Springer, Cham (2019). https://doi.org/10.1007/978-3-030-11723-8_9
38. Sheller, M.J., et al.: Federated learning in medicine: facilitating multi-institutional collaborations without sharing patient data. Sci. Rep. **10**, 1–12 (2020)
39. Sheller, M., Edwards, B., Reina, G. A., Martin, J., Bakas, S.: NIMG-68. Federated learning in neuro-oncology for multi-institutional collaborations without sharing patient data. Neuro-oncology **21**, vi176 (2019)
40. Mazurowski, M.A., et al.: Radiogenomics of lower-grade glioma: algorithmically-assessed tumor shape is associated with tumor genomic subtypes and patient outcomes in a multi-institutional study with the cancer genome atlas data. J. Neuro-oncol. **133**, 27–35 (2017)
41. Menze, B.H., et al.: The multimodal brain tumor image segmentation benchmark (BraTS). IEEE Trans. Med. Imaging **34**, 1993–2024 (2014)
42. Cai, X., et al.: A many-objective optimization based federal deep generation model for enhancing data processing capability in IOT. IEEE Trans. Ind. Inform. **99**, 1–1 (2021)
43. Hashmani, M.A., Jameel, S.M., Rizvi, S.S.H., Shukla, S.: An adaptive federated machine learning-based intelligent system for skin disease detection: a step toward an intelligent dermoscopy device. Appl. Sci. **11**, 2145 (2021)
44. Roth, H.R., et al.: Federated learning for breast density classification: a real-world implementation. In: Albarqouni, S., et al. (eds.) DART/DCL -2020. LNCS, vol. 12444, pp. 181–191. Springer, Cham (2020). https://doi.org/10.1007/978-3-030-60548-3_18
45. Rooijakkers, T.: Convinced-enabling privacy-preserving survival analyses using multi-party computation (2020)
46. Sarma, K.V., et al.: Federated learning improves site performance in multicenter deep learning without data sharing. J. Am. Med. Inf. Assoc. **28**, 1259–1264 (2021)
47. Deist, T.M., et al.: Distributed learning on 20 000+ lung cancer patients-the personal health train. Radiother. Oncol. **144**, 189–200 (2020)

48. Codella, N. C., et al.: Skin lesion analysis toward melanoma detection: a challenge at the 2017 international symposium on biomedical imaging (ISBI), hosted by the international skin imaging collaboration (ISIC). In: 2018 IEEE 15th International Symposium Biomedical imaging (ISBI 2018), pp. 168–172. IEEE (2018)
49. Yi, Z., Zhang, H., Tan, P., Gong, M.: DualGAN: unsupervised dual learning for image-to-image translation. In: Proceedings of the IEEE International Conference on Computer Vision, pp. 2849–2857 (2017)
50. Zhang, C., Zhang, J., Chai, D., Chen, K.: Aegis: a trusted, automatic and accurate verification framework for vertical federated learning. arXiv preprint arXiv:2108.06958 (2021)
51. Wang, P., et al.: Automated pancreas segmentation using multi-institutional collaborative deep learning. In: Albarqouni, S., Bakas, S., Kamnitsas, K., Cardoso, M.J., Landman, B., Li, W., Milletari, F., Rieke, N., Roth, H., Xu, D., Xu, Z. (eds.) DART/DCL -2020. LNCS, vol. 12444, pp. 192–200. Springer, Cham (2020). https://doi.org/10.1007/978-3-030-60548-3_19
52. McGuigan, A., et al.: Pancreatic cancer: a review of clinical diagnosis, epidemiology, treatment and outcomes. World J. Gastroenterol. **24**, 4846 (2018)
53. Lee, H., et al.: Federated learning for thyroid ultrasound image analysis to protect personal information: validation study in a real health care environment. JMIR Med. Inform. **9**, e25869 (2021)
54. Choudhury, A., et al.: Predicting outcomes in anal cancer patients using multi-centre data and distributed learning-a proof-of-concept study. Radiother. Oncol. **159**, 183–189 (2021)
55. Zolotareva, O., et al.: Flimma: a federated and privacy-preserving tool for differential gene expression analysis. arXiv preprint arXiv:2010.16403 (2020)
56. Andreux, M., Manoel, A., Menuet, R., Saillard, C., Simpson, C.: Federated survival analysis with discrete-time Cox models. arXiv preprint arXiv:2006.08997 (2020)
57. Cox, D.R.: Regression models and life-tables. J. R. Stat. Soc. Ser. B (Methodological) **34**, 187–220 (1972). http://www.jstor.org/stable/2985181
58. Jiménez-Sánchez, A., Tardy, M., Ballester, M.A.G., Mateus, D., Piella, G.: Memory-aware curriculum federated learning for breast cancer classification. arXiv preprint arXiv:2107.02504 (2021)
59. Xia, Y., et al.: Auto-FedAvg: learnable federated averaging for multi-institutional medical image segmentation. arXiv preprint arXiv:2104.10195 (2021)
60. Shen, C., et al.: Multi-task federated learning for heterogeneous pancreas segmentation. arXiv preprint arXiv:2108.08537 (2021)
61. Guo, P., Wang, P., Zhou, J., Jiang, S., Patel, V.M.: Multi-institutional collaborations for improving deep learning-based magnetic resonance image reconstruction using federated learning. In: Proceedings of the IEEE/CVF Conference on Computer Vision and Pattern Recognition, pp. 2423–2432 (2021)
62. Bercea, C. I., Wiestler, B., Rueckert, D., Albarqouni, S.: FedDis: disentangled federated learning for unsupervised brain pathology segmentation. arXiv preprint arXiv:2103.03705 (2021)
63. Andreux, M., du Terrail, J.O., Beguier, C., Tramel, E.W.: Siloed federated learning for multi-centric histopathology datasets. In: Albarqouni, S., et al. (eds.) DART/DCL -2020. LNCS, vol. 12444, pp. 129–139. Springer, Cham (2020). https://doi.org/10.1007/978-3-030-60548-3_13
64. Ke, J., Shen, Y., Lu, Y.: Style normalization in histology with federated learning. In: 2021 IEEE 18th International Symposium on Biomedical Imaging (ISBI), pp. 953–956. IEEE (2021)

65. Roth, H.R., et al.: Federated whole prostate segmentation in MRI with personalized neural architectures. In: de Bruijne, M., et al. (eds.) MICCAI 2021. LNCS, vol. 12903, pp. 357–366. Springer, Cham (2021). https://doi.org/10.1007/978-3-030-87199-4_34

66. Liu, Q., Yang, H., Dou, Q., Heng, P.-A.: Federated semi-supervised medical image classification via inter-client relation matching. arXiv preprint arXiv:2106.08600 (2021)

67. Bdair, T., Navab, N., Albarqouni, S.: Peer learning for skin lesion classification. arXiv preprint arXiv:2103.03703 (2021)

68. Seo, H., Park, J., Oh, S., Bennis, M., Kim, S.-L.: Federated knowledge distillation. arXiv preprint arXiv:2011.02367 (2020)

69. Li, T., et al.: Federated optimization in heterogeneous networks. arXiv preprint arXiv:1812.06127 (2018)

70. Tschandl, P., Rosendahl, C., Kittler, H.: The HAM10000 dataset, a large collection of multi-source dermatoscopic images of common pigmented skin lesions. Sci. Data 5, 1–9 (2018)

71. Blake, C.: UCI repository of machine learning databases (1998). http://www.ics.uci.edu/~mlearn/MLRepository.html

72. Chang, Q., et al.: Synthetic learning: learn from distributed asynchronized discriminator GAN without sharing medical image data. In: Proceedings of the IEEE/CVF Conference on Computer Vision and Pattern Recognition, pp. 13856–13866 (2020)

73. Zhang, M., Qu, L., Singh, P., Kalpathy-Cramer, J., Rubin, D. L.: SplitAVG: a heterogeneity-aware federated deep learning method for medical imaging. arXiv preprint arXiv:2107.02375 (2021)

74. Yeganeh, Y., Farshad, A., Navab, N., Albarqouni, S.: Inverse distance aggregation for federated learning with Non-IID data. In: Albarqouni, S., et al. (eds.) DART/DCL -2020. LNCS, vol. 12444, pp. 150–159. Springer, Cham (2020). https://doi.org/10.1007/978-3-030-60548-3_15

75. Nasirigerdeh, R., et al.: Federated multi-mini-batch: an efficient training approach to federated learning in Non-IID environments. arXiv preprint arXiv:2011.07006 (2020)

76. Salmeron, J.L., Arévalo, I.: A privacy-preserving, distributed and cooperative FCM-based learning approach for cancer research. In: Bello, R., Miao, D., Falcon, R., Nakata, M., Rosete, A., Ciucci, D. (eds.) IJCRS 2020. LNCS (LNAI), vol. 12179, pp. 477–487. Springer, Cham (2020). https://doi.org/10.1007/978-3-030-52705-1_35

77. Kosko, B.: Fuzzy cognitive maps. Int. J. Man Mach. Stud. 24, 65–75 (1986)

78. Liu, Y., Wu, W., Flokas, L., Wang, J., Wu, E.: Enabling SQL-based training data debugging for federated learning. arXiv preprint arXiv:2108.11884 (2021)

79. Kassab, R., Simeone, O.: Federated generalized Bayesian learning via distributed stein variational gradient descent. arXiv preprint arXiv:2009.06419 (2020)

80. Diao, E., Ding, J., Tarokh, V.: Gradient assisted learning. arXiv preprint arXiv:2106.01425 (2021)

81. Fang, M., Cao, X., Jia, J., Gong, N.: Local model poisoning attacks to byzantine-robust federated learning. In: 29th Security Symposium Security 2020, pp. 1605–1622 (2020)

82. Kasturi, A., Ellore, A.R., Hota, C.: Fusion learning: a one shot federated learning. In: Krzhizhanovskaya, V.V., Závodszky, G., Lees, M.H., Dongarra, J.J., Sloot, P.M.A., Brissos, S., Teixeira, J. (eds.) ICCS 2020. LNCS, vol. 12139, pp. 424–436. Springer, Cham (2020). https://doi.org/10.1007/978-3-030-50420-5_31

83. Wang, S., Suwandi, R. C., Chang, T.-H.: Demystifying model averaging for communication-efficient federated matrix factorization. In: ICASSP 2021–2021 IEEE International Conference on Acoustics, Speech and Signal Processing (ICASSP), pp. 3680–3684. IEEE (2021)

84. Wang, S., Chang, T.-H.: Federated matrix factorization: algorithm design and application to data clustering. arXiv preprint arXiv:2002.04930 (2020)

85. Roy, A. G., Siddiqui, S., Pölsterl, S., Navab, N., Wachinger, C.: BrainTorrent: a peer-to-peer environment for decentralized federated learning. arXiv preprint arXiv:1905.06731 (2019)

86. Geleijnse, G., et al.: Prognostic factors analysis for oral cavity cancer survival in the Netherlands and Taiwan using a privacy-preserving federated infrastructure. Sci. Rep. **10**, 1–9 (2020)

87. Carpov, S., Gama, N., Georgieva, M., Jetchev, D.: GenoPPML-a framework for genomic privacy-preserving machine learning. Cryptol. ePrint Arch. (2021)

88. Elayan, H., Aloqaily, M., Guizani, M.: Deep federated learning for IOT-based decentralized healthcare systems. In: 2021 International Wireless Communications and Mobile Computing (IWCMC), pp. 105–109. IEEE (2021)

89. Scherer, J., et al.: Joint imaging platform for federated clinical data analytics. JCO Clin. Cancer Inform. **4**, 1027–1038 (2020)

90. Matschinske, J., et al.: The featurecloud AI store for federated learning in biomedicine and beyond. arXiv preprint arXiv:2105.05734 (2021)

91. Arambakam, M., Beel, J.: Federated meta-learning: democratizing algorithm selection across disciplines and software libraries. In: 7th ICML Workshop on Automated Machine Learning (AutoML) (2020)

92. Chen, X., Wang, X., Yang, K.: Asynchronous blockchain-based privacy-preserving training framework for disease diagnosis. In: 2019 IEEE International Conference on Big Data (Big Data), pp. 5469–5473. IEEE (2019)

93. Zhu, L., Han, S.: Deep leakage from gradients. In: Yang, Q., Fan, L., Yu, H. (eds.) Federated Learning. LNCS (LNAI), vol. 12500, pp. 17–31. Springer, Cham (2020). https://doi.org/10.1007/978-3-030-63076-8_2

94. Wei, W., et al.: A framework for evaluating gradient leakage attacks in federated learning. arXiv preprint arXiv:2004.10397 (2020)

95. Połap, D., Woźniak, M.: Meta-heuristic as manager in federated learning approaches for image processing purposes. Appl. Soft Comput. **113**, 107872 (2021)

96. Beguier, C., Terrail, J. O. d., Meah, I., Andreux, M., Tramel, E. W.: Differentially private federated learning for cancer prediction. arXiv preprint arXiv:2101.02997 (2021)

97. Shah, M.M., et al.: Distributed machine learning on differentially private skin cancer data. Solid State Technol. **63**, 1777–1786 (2020)

98. Zhang, C., et al.: Feasibility of privacy-preserving federated deep learning on medical images. Int. J. Radiat. Oncol. Biol. Phys. **108**, e778 (2020)

99. Li, W., et al.: Privacy-preserving federated brain tumour segmentation. In: Suk, H.-I., Liu, M., Yan, P., Lian, C. (eds.) MLMI 2019. LNCS, vol. 11861, pp. 133–141. Springer, Cham (2019). https://doi.org/10.1007/978-3-030-32692-0_16

100. Fay, D., Sjölund, J., Oechtering, T. J.: Decentralized differentially private segmentation with pate. arXiv preprint arXiv:2004.06567 (2020)

101. Papernot, N., Abadi, M., Erlingsson, U., Goodfellow, I., Talwar, K.: Semi-supervised knowledge transfer for deep learning from private training data. arXiv preprint arXiv:1610.05755 (2016)

102. Lu, M. Y., et al.: Federated learning for computational pathology on gigapixel whole slide images. arXiv preprint arXiv:2009.10190 (2020)

103. Cheng, W., et al.: A privacy-protection model for patients. Secur. Commun. Networks **2020**, 12 (2020)
104. Froelicher, D., et al.: Truly privacy-preserving federated analytics for precision medicine with multiparty homomorphic encryption. bioRxiv (2021)
105. Sadat, M.N., et al.: SAFETY: secure gwAs in federated environment through a hYbrid solution. IEEE/ACM Trans. Comput. Biol. Bioinform. **16**, 93–102 (2018)
106. Rajotte, J.-F., et al.: Reducing bias and increasing utility by federated generative modeling of medical images using a centralized adversary. arXiv preprint arXiv:2101.07235 (2021)
107. Mukherjee, S., Xu, Y., Trivedi, A., Patowary, N., Ferres, J.L.: PrivGAN: protecting GANs from membership inference attacks at low cost to utility. Proc. Priv. Enhancing Technol. **2021**, 142–163 (2021)
108. Ziller, A., et al.: Differentially private federated deep learning for multi-site medical image segmentation. arXiv preprint arXiv:2107.02586 (2021)
109. Tian, Z., Zhang, R., Hou, X., Liu, J., Ren, K.: FederBoost: private federated learning for GBDT. arXiv preprint arXiv:2011.02796 (2020)
110. Wei, W., Liu, L., Wut, Y., Su, G., Iyengar, A.: Gradient-leakage resilient federated learning. In: 2021 IEEE 41st International Conference on Distributed Computing Systems (ICDCS), Washington DC, pp. 797–807 (2021)
111. Yang, Z., Hu, S., Chen, K.: FPGA-based hardware accelerator of homomorphic encryption for efficient federated learning. arXiv preprint arXiv:2007.10560 (2020)
112. Weng, H., et al.: Privacy leakage of real-world vertical federated learning. arXiv preprint arXiv:2011.09290 (2020)
113. Chu, K.-F., Zhang, L.: Privacy-preserving self-taught federated learning for heterogeneous data. arXiv preprint arXiv:2102.05883 (2021)
114. Cao, X., Fang, M., Liu, J., Gong, N. Z.: FLTrust: byzantine-robust federated learning via trust bootstrapping. arXiv preprint arXiv:2012.13995 (2020)
115. Li, W., Lu, S., Deng, D.-L.: Quantum federated learning through blind quantum computing. Sci. China Phys. Mech. Astron. **64**(10), 1–8 (2021). https://doi.org/10.1007/s11433-021-1753-3

Opportunities and Challenges for Deep Learning in Brain Lesions

Jay Patel[1,2], Ken Chang[1,2], Syed Rakin Ahmed[1,3,4], Ikbeom Jang[1,5],
and Jayashree Kalpathy-Cramer[1,5(✉)]

[1] Athinoula A. Martinos Center for Biomedical Imaging, Department of Radiology,
Massachusetts General Hospital, Boston, MA, USA
jkalpathy-cramer@mgh.harvard.edu
[2] Massachusetts Institute of Technology, Cambridge, MA, USA
[3] Harvard Graduate Program in Biophysics, Harvard Medical School, Harvard
University, Cambridge, MA, USA
[4] Geisel School of Medicine at Dartmouth, Dartmouth College, Hanover, NH, USA
[5] Department of Radiology, Harvard Medical School, Boston, MA, USA
https://qtim-lab.github.io/

Abstract. In recent years, deep learning techniques have shown potential for incorporation in many facets of the medical imaging pipeline, from image acquisition/reconstruction to segmentation/classification to outcome prediction. Specifically, these models can help improve the efficiency and accuracy of image interpretation and quantification. However, it is important to note the challenges of working with medical imaging data, and how this can affect the effectiveness of the algorithms when deployed. In this review, we first present an overview of the medical imaging pipeline and some of the areas where deep learning has been used to improve upon the current standard of care for brain lesions. We conclude with a section on some of the current challenges and hurdles facing neuroimaging researchers.

Keywords: Deep learning · Imaging · Neuro-oncology

1 Introduction

The advent of noninvasive imaging technologies such as magnetic resonance imaging (MRI) and computed tomography (CT) has revolutionized medicine, enabling clinicians to make informed decisions for diagnosis, surgical planning, and treatment response assessment. In recent years, access to larger and more comprehensive repositories of patient imaging data along with advances in computational resources has closed the gap between machine and human. Specifically, artificial intelligence (AI) based algorithms can now interpret imaging scans at the level of expert clinicians.

While the majority of current research is focused on the interpretation of medical imaging, upstream aspects of the imaging pipeline are primed to be improved via AI as well. Briefly, the imaging pipeline can be broken into three steps: 1) acquisition/reconstruction, 2) analysis, and 3) interpretation (Fig. 1). The first step in the pipeline is image acquisition, wherein raw data that is not visually interpretable by a human is gathered. This raw data must then be reconstructed into an anatomical image. For example, when performing an MRI, data is acquired at specific frequency bands in the Fourier domain and is then reconstructed into the spatial domain for human interpretation. The next step is image analysis, wherein both qualitative and quantitative information regarding the pathology of interest is gleaned. Finally, the last step is image interpretation, wherein a trained clinician makes judgments regarding tasks such as diagnosis or treatment planning. For instance, given a tumor's volume and location in the brain, a clinician may decide to utilize radiation in lieu of surgery. This general workflow is shown in Fig. 1.

Even though imaging has been used in clinical practice for many decades, problems still persist that hamper its efficacy. For example, patient motion during image acquisition may render a scan unreadable since most reconstruction algorithms are incapable of correcting for motion blur. Even when a scan is perfectly acquired, the complete manual analysis may be too time-consuming to be feasible, resulting in metrics such as the response assessment in neuro-oncology (RANO) criteria [49] to be used as a proxy measure for full volumetric tumor burden. In the following sections, we will discuss some of the problems that arise in the standard imaging pipeline and the opportunities that exist to utilize advanced deep learning techniques to improve the efficiency of each of these steps.

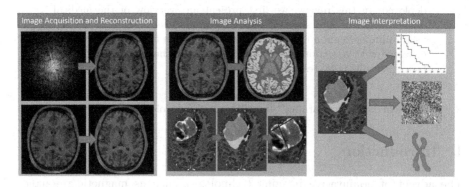

Fig. 1. The imaging pipeline is made up of three main components: 1) acquisition/reconstruction, 2) analysis, and 3) interpretation. Image acquisition and reconstruction entails converting sensor domain data into the spatial domain. Image enhancement/super-resolution can either be done in parallel with reconstruction, or as a separate step. Image analysis for brain lesions includes anatomical and tumor segmentations, along with automatic RANO measures. Finally, image interpretation includes survival prediction, tumor histopathologic grading, and radiogenomic correlations, among other applications.

2   Opportunities in Image Acquisition and Reconstruction

The first step in the imaging pipeline is acquisition and reconstruction. When an image is acquired, it is encoded into an intermediate representation of the image target known as the sensor domain. For this intermediate representation to lead to an image, the function or encoding method used to encode the image into the sensor domain must be inverted in a process known as reconstruction. Image reconstruction is required for many kinds of medical imaging, including MRI, CT, and positron emission tomography. Existing approaches for reconstruction are incomplete since noisy, real-world data often precludes knowledge of an exact inverse transform. To overcome the problems with conventional image reconstruction methods, researchers have in recent years begun testing deep learning-based approaches.

One example of a unified framework for deep learning-based image reconstruction is Automated Transform by Manifold Approximation (AUTOMAP) [54]. AUTOMAP is implemented with a deep neural network architecture composed of fully connected layers followed by convolutional layers. Zhu et al. generated training data by taking a large set of images from a natural scene and inverse encoding them into the sensor domain with the desired encoding function to create a paired dataset. The network was then trained in a supervised learning manner, enabling the network to learn the optimal strategies for image reconstruction. The trained neural network was then applied to MRI images of the human brain. Surprisingly, they found that training on images of objects such as animals and plants (rather than MRI of the brain) still allowed for accurate reconstruction of brain MRI images for three of the four commonly used encoding schemes they tested, which implies the robustness of their approach. Moreover, AUTOMAP implicitly learned how to denoise imaging, removing common artifacts such as zipper artifacts that would have persisted if the image had been reconstructed by conventional methods. When tested against simulated data using known ground truth, AUTOMAP reconstructed images were thus more accurate and had a higher SNR. The study opened opportunities for adopting deep learning approaches for image reconstruction of a wide range of different imaging modalities without having to learn complex, modality-specific physics.

Another groundbreaking reconstruction model for accelerated MRI is the Variational Network (VN) [21]. One of the biggest concerns about using learning-based reconstruction methods in the clinical workflow was that they may not preserve pathology-related features that are rare or specific to certain patients. For efficient and accurate reconstruction of MRI data, they proposed a trainable formulation for accelerated parallel imaging-based MRI reconstruction inspired by variational methods and deep learning. VN incorporates key concepts from compressed sensing, formulated as a variational model within a deep learning approach. This approach is designed to learn a complete reconstruction procedure for complex multi-channel MRI data, including all free parameters that need to be established empirically. Hammernik et al. train the model on a complete clinical protocol for musculoskeletal imaging, evaluate its performance on various accelerating factors, and train on both normal and pseudo-random Cartesian

2D sampling. Using clinical patient data, they investigated the ability of the VN approach to preserve unique pathologies not included in the training dataset. Surprisingly, it was able to preserve important features not present in the training data, outperforming conventional reconstructions for a range of pathologies while providing unprecedented reconstruction speeds.

3   Opportunities in Image Analysis

The second step in the imaging pipeline is analysis. Here, information necessary for downstream tasks is either manually or automatically extracted. Medical image analysis covers a wide span of topics, including but not limited to anatomical segmentation and volumetric quantification, extraction of parameter maps from diffusion/perfusion imaging, and groupwise population analyses. In this section, we will specifically look at examples involving brain tumor segmentation.

Primary and metastatic brain tumors account for nearly 200,000 new cases in the US every year, and imaging plays a crucial role in optimizing patient care [43,48]. Segmentation of tumor boundaries is a necessary component for successful surgical and radiotherapy treatment planning [14]. Unfortunately, tumor segmentation is a challenging task requiring substantial domain expertise. Furthermore, as many studies have shown, motion artifacts, field inhomogeneities, and differences in imaging protocols both within and across medical institutions lead to non-negligible amounts of human error as well as significant amounts of intra- and inter-rater variability [31].

To combat these issues, researchers have turned to deep learning as it has the potential to produce accurate and reproducible results many orders of magnitude faster than can be accomplished manually. The shift to trainable AI is being further encouraged by the release of open-source datasets with high-quality annotations such as that from the Multimodal Brain Tumor Segmentation Challenge (BraTS) [4,6–8,33].

Variations of 3D U-Nets [46] have provided state-of-the-art results for segmentation of primary brain tumors. For example, Myronenko won the 2018 BRATS challenge utilizing an asymmetrical residual U-Net, where most of the trainable parameters of the model resided in the encoder. Furthermore, in contrast to the standard U-Net framework which uses four or five downsampling operations in the encoder, he applied only three in order to preserve spatial context [36]. Other modifications to the U-Net structure have also been used with success. Jiang et al. won the 2019 challenge using a two-stage cascaded asymmetrical residual U-Net, where the second stage of their cascade was used to refine the coarse segmentation maps generated by the first stage [27]. The second place that year was awarded to Zhao et al., who utilized dense blocks along with various optimization strategies such as variable patch/batch size training, heuristic sampling, and semi-supervised learning [52]. It is important to note that while architectural modifications to the U-Net can provide performance boosts, they are not always necessary. Indeed, Isensee et al. won the 2020 challenge with their architecture coined "No New-Net", highlighting that a vanilla U-Net coupled with excellent training and optimization strategies can still achieve state-of-the-art results. Moreover, they achieved an average testing set dice score of 88.95% for whole tumor segmentation, achieving segmentation performance indistinguishable from human experts [25].

Similar strategies have been shown to work for metastatic brain tumors, which present additional hurdles compared to primary brain tumors. Patients with metastases often present with more than one target lesion along with micro-metastases spread systemically across the brain parenchyma. Micro-metastases are particularly challenging to segment due to their size and limited contrast enhancement. Various approaches have been proposed, from two-stage detection/segmentation pipelines to modifications of the loss function. While these approaches have yielded some improvement in performance, much work is still needed. For example, Zhou et al. developed a two-stage pipeline consisting of a detection stage followed by a segmentation stage. While they reported an excellent dice score of 87% on large metastases ($\geq$6 mm), their results dropped to just 17% for micro-metastases (<3 mm) [53]. This trend is seen in other studies as well [11,47], indicating the strong need for better segmentation algorithms for brain metastases cases.

Longitudinal measurement of lesion burden is the basis for treatment response assessment. While volumetric measurement would be the ideal metric for lesion burden, the aforementioned issues with manual tumor segmentation necessitate the use of proxy measures such as RANO. RANO for gliomas is defined as the product of the maximum bidimensional diameters of the largest axial cross-section of the tumor on MRI [49]. Even this metric is subject to inter-rater variability, since different raters may choose differing slices based on their subjective assessment of which axial slice has the largest tumor area. To automate this process, Chang et al. developed a tool called AutoRANO which used the outputs of a segmentation model capable of running on post-operative imaging to derive RANO measurements. He noted that AutoRANO had a higher correlation with manual contrast-enhancing volume than did manual RANO measures performed by expert radiologists, suggesting that AutoRANO may be a more accurate measure of tumor burden than manual RANO [14]. Similar work has been done to automate bi-directional measurements for other tumor types, with equally promising results [40].

4 Opportunities in Image Interpretation

The final step in the imaging pipeline is interpretation. From a machine learning standpoint, this is often framed as a classification problem. For example, with regards to brain tumors, image classification tasks include but are not limited to identifying subtypes, predicting pseudo-progression versus true progression, ascertaining tumor malignancy status, and identifying treatment responders. Indeed, two key facets in which the rise of AI has been particularly exciting include radiogenomics and survival prediction.

Radiogenomics refers to the correlation between imaging features and specific gene expression patterns/molecular profiles of tumors. Such approaches have mainly been studied for primary gliomas, but interest is accruing to replicate such studies for brain metastases and spinal cord tumors as well. The ability to predict molecular marker status noninvasively is important since a priori knowledge of the mutational status of key genes together with radiographic suspicion of a neoplasm might favor early intervention and/or mutation-specific therapeutic interventions. In the case of gliomas, the MGMT gene, which codes for an enzyme responsible for DNA repair following alkylating agent chemotherapy, may be silenced by methylation of its promoter during tumor development, thereby preventing repair of DNA damage. This increases the potential effectiveness of alkylating agent chemotherapy for these patients [23]. In order to demonstrate that a deep learning model could predict MGMT methylation status from imaging without the need for explicitly providing a tumor segmentation, Korfiatis et al. [30] trained three deep residual neural networks of varying sizes on a training dataset of 110 patients with T2-weighted MRI, artificially increasing the size of this dataset by splitting all 3D imaging into 2D axial slices. Here, the authors found that deeper, more parametrized networks produce better results, with their ResNet50 model achieving an accuracy of 94.9% on the test set (45 patients with 2612 slices). Another key gene conferring longer survival in glioma patients is IDH, which in its wild-type form codes for an enzyme responsible for the conversion of isocitrate to a-ketoglutarate in the Krebs cycle. Gliomas harboring the IDH1/2 mutation carry a significantly increased overall survival than the corresponding wild type [12]. Chang et al. [12] used a similar methodology as Korfiatis et al. [30] for the prediction of IDH status, utilizing a residual neural network with 2D inputs. In this case, the network required a predefined tumor segmentation, since it was trained on cropped tumor images only. The authors performed exceptional multi-institutional evaluation, acquiring data from three different sites, and reporting a final accuracy and AUC on a testing set of 147 patients of 87.6% and 0.95, respectively. Similarly, Akkus et al. [2] focused on the prediction of 1p19q co-deletion, a highly prognostic molecular marker associated with longer survival in low-grade glioma (LGG) patients. With only 387 slices in the training data, the authors noted extreme overfitting, initially seeing perfect training sensitivity, specificity, and accuracy. To mitigate this, they made use of data augmentation techniques such as random translations, rotations, and flips, resulting in an increased final test set accuracy from 63.3% to 87.7%. Additionally, Chang et al. [16] aimed to integrate prediction of MGMT methylation status, IDH mutation status, and 1p19q codeletion into a single residual network. After five-fold cross-validation on their dataset of 259 patients (5259 slices), they achieved mean accuracy of 83%, 94%, and 92%, respectively, on the three tasks. Finally, MGMT methylation status prediction from MRI was a key component of the BraTs 2021 challenge, in which many teams utilized machine learning techniques for non-invasive assessment.

Survival analysis is a technique employed in cohort and other longitudinal studies to predict the time it takes for a particular event to occur. In these studies, individuals are followed from an initial observation (e.g. study enrollment, time of diagnosis/treatment) until the occurrence of a subsequent event (e.g., death, disease, relapse) or until follow-up is no longer possible. Depending on what event is used, the time between the two is denoted as progression-free survival or overall survival (OS) [39]. Survival analyses of brain tumors have utilized both radiomics based approaches and deep learning, as well as an integration of the two. Ujjwal et al. [5] proposed a three-step framework for OS prediction which involved segmentation, radiomic feature extraction, and a survival prediction model to stratify patients into three survival groups (short-, mid-, and long-term survivors) and to predict OS. This approach achieved accuracy scores of 0.571 and 0.558 on validation and testing cohorts of 53 and 130 cases respectively. Finally, Han et al. [22] incorporated both hand-crafted radiomics features and deep features generated by a pretrained CNN on a dataset of 178 high-grade glioma patients (50 local, and 128 from TCGA), applying feature selection and Elastic Net-Cox modeling to classify patients into short- and long-term survivors. This combined feature analysis framework resulted in a log-rank test p-value of <0.001 for the 50 patient local cohort, and a corresponding value of 0.014 for the 128 patient TCGA cohort.

5 Challenges

As mentioned in the previous sections, there are significant opportunities to improve clinical decision-making and patient management using AI. However, it is important to keep in mind certain caveats and challenges to developing effective deep learning models for healthcare applications. First, it is important to acknowledge the brittleness of deep learning models, or in other words, the lack of generalizability across different acquisition settings and patient populations [15,18]. For example, different hospitals may have MRI scanners with different field strengths or use different scanning protocols. Different hospitals may also admit patients of different age groups or racial backgrounds. These institutional differences are further exacerbated by the fact that many medical datasets are small, either due to rare pathology, costly human annotations, or simply due to difficulty in extracting data from antiquated electronic medical record systems. Indeed, empirical studies have shown that there is a drop in the performance of deep learning models for brain lesions when evaluated at institutions different from the ones in which they were trained [3,44]. One approach to handle the issue of generalizability is to accumulate large quantities of diverse, multi-institutional patient data. However, logistical issues, as well as patient privacy concerns may render this impractical. Another approach involves fine-tuning the existing model on a small quantity of new data when there is dataset shift [44]. More generally, continuous learning methods allow models to be "living" and to be refined as the data changes [42]. Other approaches include methods to adapt either the data or the model itself to be able to handle new domains with approaches under the umbrella of domain adaptation [28,51]. If large quantities of data are available, but not shareable between institutions, distributed learning approaches can be used to train models without the need to share patient data, overcoming patient privacy barriers [13,45].

Another major challenge facing trainable AI models is the lack of definitive ground truth. For example, for the segmentation of brain lesions, there is often subjectivity involved in determining tumor boundaries, especially for lesions that are diffusely edematous. Similarly, the boundaries of contrast enhancement may be ambiguous as well due to the presence of necrotic regions. This subjectivity is primarily due to the spatial resolution limitations of MRI, which makes categorizing tumor components into discrete bins of necrosis, enhancing, or edema difficult. Thus, it is unsurprising that there is significant intra- and inter-rater variability for neuroimaging related segmentation [10,17,34]. In the case of radiogenomic prediction using ground truth from a single biopsy site, there is also uncertainty stemming from regional intra-lesional genetic heterogeneity of tumors [37,38,41,50]. This is further compounded by multi-focal lesions, which can also display genetic heterogeneity across lesions from the same patient [1]. For other prediction tasks, such as prognostic assessment, there may be significant confounders that are not incorporated into the inputs, such as degree of resection and chemotherapeutic regimen. Taken together, the clinical utility and efficacy of machine learning models may be limited if there is no way to handle uncertainty within the data. One way to potentially mitigate this problem is to utilize deep learning methods that can estimate uncertainty to provide multiple possible outputs, mimicking variability by different clinicians [29]. Another viable approach is to train networks to directly report a measure of uncertainty, thus allowing clinicians to stratify network outputs by the degree of confidence [24,32]. This would enable flagging of highly uncertain cases for further manual expert review.

A final challenge that should be mentioned is the reproducibility of deep learning studies for neuroimaging. With the rapid pace of advances within the field, new research often builds upon previous work to yield improvements in performance. However, without the release of code, much effort would need to be devoted to reproducing previously published results for further evaluation and development [20]. As such, there has been a growing trend towards the release of open-source frameworks for medical AI to allow for greater collaboration within the research and clinical communities [9,19,26]. On a similar front, the public release of code is increasingly becoming the expectation for publication [35]. However, this is not without potential concerns of its own, since it may result in the accidental leaking of protected patient health information or may deter the commercialization of research.

6   Conclusion

Significant progress has been made in the last few years to automate and increase the efficiency of all steps in the imaging pipeline via the use of deep learning. Specifically, greater accessibility to large-scale multi-institutional datasets and better computational resources together have led to advances in image reconstruction, analysis, and interpretation. Our review has highlighted some of the exciting AI research being performed at each of these steps in the imaging pipeline, and some challenges and pitfalls that all researchers working with neuroimaging data must acknowledge.

References

1. Abou-El-Ardat, K., et al.: Comprehensive molecular characterization of multifocal glioblastoma proves its monoclonal origin and reveals novel insights into clonal evolution and heterogeneity of glioblastomas. Neuro Oncol. **19**(4), 546–557 (2017)
2. Akkus, Z., et al.: Predicting deletion of chromosomal arms 1p/19q in low-grade gliomas from MR images using machine intelligence. J. Digit. Imaging **30**(4), 469–476 (2017). https://doi.org/10.1007/s10278-017-9984-3, https://pubmed.ncbi.nlm.nih.gov/28600641, https://www.ncbi.nlm.nih.gov/pmc/articles/PMC5537096/
3. AlBadawy, E.A., Saha, A., Mazurowski, M.A.: Deep learning for segmentation of brain tumors: Impact of cross-institutional training and testing. Med. Phys. **45**(3), 1150–1158 (2018)
4. Baid, U., et al.: The RSNA-ASNR-MICCAI BraTS 2021 benchmark on brain tumor segmentation and radiogenomic classification. arXiv preprint arXiv:2107.02314 (2021)
5. Baid, U., et al.: Overall survival prediction in glioblastoma with radiomic features using machine learning. Front. Comput. Neurosci. **14**, 61 (2020). https://doi.org/10.3389/FNCOM.2020.00061/BIBTEX
6. Bakas, S., et al.: Segmentation labels for the pre-operative scans of the TCGA-GBM collection (2017)
7. Bakas, S., Akbari, H., Sotiras, A., et al.: Segmentation labels for the pre-operative scans of the TCGA-GBM collection. The Cancer Imaging Archive (2017)
8. Bakas, S., et al.: Advancing the cancer genome atlas glioma MRI collections with expert segmentation labels and radiomic features. Sci. Data **4**(1), 1–13 (2017)
9. Beers, A., et al.: DeepNeuro: an open-source deep learning toolbox for neuroimaging. Neuroinformatics **19**(1), 127–140 (2021)
10. Bø, H.K., Solheim, O., Jakola, A.S., Kvistad, K.A., Reinertsen, I., Berntsen, E.M.: Intra-rater variability in low-grade glioma segmentation. J. Neuro-oncol. **131**(2), 393–402 (2017)
11. Bousabarah, K., et al.: Deep convolutional neural networks for automated segmentation of brain metastases trained on clinical data. Radiat. Oncol. **15**(1) (2020). https://doi.org/10.1186/s13014-020-01514-6
12. Chang, K., et al.: Residual convolutional neural network for the determination of IDH status in low- and high-grade gliomas from MR imaging. Clin. Cancer Res. **24**(5), 1073–1081 (2018). https://doi.org/10.1158/1078-0432.CCR-17-2236, https://clincancerres.aacrjournals.org/content/24/5/1073
13. Chang, K., et al.: Distributed deep learning networks among institutions for medical imaging. J. Am. Med. Inform. Assoc. **25**(8), 945–954 (2018)
14. Chang, K., et al.: Automatic assessment of glioma burden: a deep learning algorithm for fully automated volumetric and bidimensional measurement. Neuro-oncology **21**(11), 1412–1422 (2019). https://doi.org/10.1093/neuonc/noz106
15. Chang, K., et al.: Multi-institutional assessment and crowdsourcing evaluation of deep learning for automated classification of breast density. J. Am. Coll. Radiol. **17**(12), 1653–1662 (2020)

16. Chang, P., et al.: Deep-learning convolutional neural networks accurately classify genetic mutations in gliomas. Am. J. Neuroradiol. **39**, 1201–1207 (2018). https://doi.org/10.3174/ajnr.A5667, http://www.ajnr.org/content/early/2018/05/10/ajnr.A5667

17. Deeley, M., et al.: Comparison of manual and automatic segmentation methods for brain structures in the presence of space-occupying lesions: a multi-expert study. Phys. Med. Biol. **56**(14), 4557 (2011)

18. Finlayson, S.G., et al.: The clinician and dataset shift in artificial intelligence. N. Engl. J. Med. **385**(3), 283 (2021)

19. Gibson, E., et al.: NiftyNet: a deep-learning platform for medical imaging. Comput. Methods Programs Biomed. **158**, 113–122 (2018)

20. Haibe-Kains, B., et al.: Transparency and reproducibility in artificial intelligence. Nature **586**(7829), E14–E16 (2020)

21. Hammernik, K., et al.: Learning a variational network for reconstruction of accelerated MRI data. Magn. Reson. Med. **79**(6), 3055–3071 (2018). https://doi.org/10.1002/mrm.26977

22. Han, W., et al.: Deep transfer learning and radiomics feature prediction of survival of patients with high-grade gliomas. Am. J. Neuroradiol. **41**(1), 40–48 (2020). https://doi.org/10.3174/AJNR.A6365, http://www.ajnr.org/content/41/1/40, http://www.ajnr.org/content/41/1/40.abstract

23. Hegi, M.E., et al.: MGMT gene silencing and benefit from temozolomide in glioblastoma. N. Engl. J. Med. **352**(10), 997–1003 (2005). https://doi.org/10.1056/NEJMOA043331/SUPPL_FILE/997SA1.PDF, https://www.nejm.org/doi/full/10.1056/nejmoa043331

24. Hoebel, K., et al.: An exploration of uncertainty information for segmentation quality assessment. In: Medical Imaging 2020: Image Processing, vol. 11313, p. 113131K. International Society for Optics and Photonics (2020)

25. Isensee, F., Jaeger, P.F., Full, P.M., Vollmuth, P., Maier-Hein, K.H.: nnU-Net for brain tumor segmentation (2020)

26. Isensee, F., Jaeger, P.F., Kohl, S.A., Petersen, J., Maier-Hein, K.H.: nnU-Net: a self-configuring method for deep learning-based biomedical image segmentation. Nat. Methods **18**(2), 203–211 (2021)

27. Jiang, Z., Ding, C., Liu, M., Tao, D.: Two-stage cascaded U-Net: 1st place solution to BraTS challenge 2019 segmentation task. In: Crimi, A., Bakas, S. (eds.) BrainLes 2019. LNCS, vol. 11992, pp. 231–241. Springer, Cham (2020). https://doi.org/10.1007/978-3-030-46640-4_22

28. Kamnitsas, K., et al.: Unsupervised domain adaptation in brain lesion segmentation with adversarial networks. In: Niethammer, M., Styner, M., Aylward, S., Zhu, H., Oguz, I., Yap, P.-T., Shen, D. (eds.) IPMI 2017. LNCS, vol. 10265, pp. 597–609. Springer, Cham (2017). https://doi.org/10.1007/978-3-319-59050-9_47

29. Kohl, S., et al.: A probabilistic U-Net for segmentation of ambiguous images. In: Advances in Neural Information Processing Systems, vol. 31 (2018)

30. Korfiatis, P., Kline, T.L., Lachance, D.H., Parney, I.F., Buckner, J.C., Erickson, B.J.: Residual deep convolutional neural network predicts MGMT methylation status. J. Digit. Imaging **30**(5), 622–628 (2017). https://doi.org/10.1007/s10278-017-0009-z

31. Mazzara, G.P., Velthuizen, R.P., Pearlman, J.L., Greenberg, H.M., Wagner, H.: Brain tumor target volume determination for radiation treatment planning through automated MRI segmentation. Int. J. Radiat. Oncol. Biol. Phys. **59**(1), 300–312 (2004). https://doi.org/10.1016/j.ijrobp.2004.01.026

32. Mehta, R., et al.: Qu-BraTS: MICCAI BraTS 2020 challenge on quantifying uncertainty in brain tumor segmentation-analysis of ranking metrics and benchmarking results. arXiv preprint arXiv:2112.10074 (2021)
33. Menze, B.H., et al.: The multimodal brain tumor image segmentation benchmark (BRATS). IEEE Trans. Med. Imaging **34**(10), 1993–2024 (2015). https://doi.org/10.1109/TMI.2014.2377694
34. Menze, B.H., et al.: The multimodal brain tumor image segmentation benchmark (BRATS). IEEE Trans. Med. Imaging **34**(10), 1993–2024 (2014)
35. Mongan, J., Moy, L., Kahn, C.E., Jr.: Checklist for artificial intelligence in medical imaging (claim): a guide for authors and reviewers. Radiol. Artif. Intell. **2**(2), e20029 (2020)
36. Myronenko, A.: 3D MRI brain tumor segmentation using autoencoder regularization (2018)
37. Parker, N.R., et al.: Intratumoral heterogeneity identified at the epigenetic, genetic and transcriptional level in glioblastoma. Sci. Rep. **6**(1), 1–10 (2016)
38. Parker, N.R., Khong, P., Parkinson, J.F., Howell, V.M., Wheeler, H.R.: Molecular heterogeneity in glioblastoma: potential clinical implications. Front. Oncol. **5**, 55 (2015)
39. Peacock, J., Peacock, P.: Oxford Handbook of Medical Statistics. Oxford University Press, New York (2010) https://doi.org/10.1093/MED/9780199551286.001.0001
40. Peng, J., et al.: Deep learning-based automatic tumor burden assessment of pediatric high-grade gliomas, medulloblastomas, and other leptomeningeal seeding tumors. Neuro Oncol. **24**(2), 289–299 (2022)
41. Pfisterer, W.K., et al.: Diagnostic and prognostic significance of genetic regional heterogeneity in meningiomas. Neuro Oncol. **6**(4), 290–299 (2004)
42. Pianykh, O.S., et al.: Continuous learning AI in radiology: implementation principles and early applications. Radiology **297**(1), 6–14 (2020)
43. Porter, K.R., McCarthy, B.J., Freels, S., Kim, Y., Davis, F.G.: Prevalence estimates for primary brain tumors in the United States by age, gender, behavior, and histology. Neuro-oncology **12**(6), 520–527 (2010). https://doi.org/10.1093/neuonc/nop066
44. Rauschecker, A.M., et al.: Interinstitutional portability of a deep learning brain MRI lesion segmentation algorithm. Radiol. Artif. Intell. **4**(1), e200152 (2021)
45. Rieke, N., et al.: The future of digital health with federated learning. NPJ Digit. Med. **3**(1), 1–7 (2020)
46. Ronneberger, O., Fischer, P., Brox, T.: U-Net: convolutional networks for biomedical image segmentation. CoRR abs/1505.0 (2015) http://arxiv.org/abs/1505.04597
47. Rudie, J.D., et al.: Three-dimensional U-Net convolutional neural network for detection and segmentation of intracranial metastases. Radiol. Artif. Intell. **3**(3), e200204 (2021). https://doi.org/10.1148/ryai.2021200204
48. Tabouret, E., Chinot, O., Metellus, P., Tallet, A., Viens, P., Goncalves, A.: Recent trends in epidemiology of brain metastases: an overview. Anticancer Res. **32**(11), 4655–4662 (2012). https://ar.iiarjournals.org/content/32/11/4655
49. Wen, P.Y., et al.: Updated response assessment criteria for high-grade gliomas: response assessment in neuro-oncology working group. J. Clin. Oncol. **28**(11), 1963–1972 (2010)
50. Wenger, A., Ferreyra Vega, S., Kling, T., Bontell, T.O., Jakola, A.S., Carén, H.: Intratumor DNA methylation heterogeneity in glioblastoma: implications for DNA methylation-based classification. Neuro Oncol. **21**(5), 616–627 (2019)

51. Yan, W., et al.: MRI manufacturer shift and adaptation: increasing the generalizability of deep learning segmentation for MR images acquired with different scanners. Radiol. Artif. Intell. **2**(4), e190195 (2020)
52. Zhao, Y.-X., Zhang, Y.-M., Liu, C.-L.: Bag of tricks for 3D MRI brain tumor segmentation. In: Crimi, A., Bakas, S. (eds.) BrainLes 2019. LNCS, vol. 11992, pp. 210–220. Springer, Cham (2020). https://doi.org/10.1007/978-3-030-46640-4_20
53. Zhou, Z., et al.: MetNet: computer-aided segmentation of brain metastases in post-contrast T1-weighted magnetic resonance imaging. Radiother. Oncol. **153**, 189–196 (2020). Physics Special Issue: ESTRO Physics Research Workshops on Science in Development, https://doi.org/10.1016/j.radonc.2020.09.016, https://www.sciencedirect.com/science/article/pii/S016781402030788X
54. Zhu, B., Liu, J.Z., Cauley, S.F., Rosen, B.R., Rosen, M.S.: Image reconstruction by domain-transform manifold learning. Nature **555**(7697), 487–492 (2018). https://doi.org/10.1038/nature25988

Brain Lesions

EMSViT: Efficient Multi Scale Vision Transformer for Biomedical Image Segmentation

Abhinav Sagar[(✉)]

Vellore Institute of Technology, Vellore, India
abhinavsagar4@gmail.com

Abstract. In this paper, we propose a novel network named Efficient Multi Scale Vision Transformer for Biomedical Image Segmentation (EMSViT). Our network splits the input feature maps into three parts with 1×1, 3×3 and 5×5 convolutions in both encoder and decoder. Concat operator is used to merge the features before being fed to three consecutive transformer blocks with attention mechanism embedded inside it. Skip connections are used to connect encoder and decoder transformer blocks. Similarly, transformer blocks and multi scale architecture is used in decoder before being linearly projected to produce the output segmentation map. We test the performance of our network using Synapse multi-organ segmentation dataset, Automated cardiac diagnosis challenge dataset, Brain tumour MRI segmentation dataset and Spleen CT segmentation dataset. Without bells and whistles, our network outperforms most of the previous state of the art CNN and transformer based models using Dice score and the Hausdorff distance as the evaluation metrics.

1 Introduction

Deep Convolutional Neural Networks has been highly successful in medical image segmentation. U-Net (Ronneberger et al. 2015) based architectures use a symmetric encoder-decoder network with skip-connections. The limitation of CNN-based approach is that it is unable to model long-range relation, due to the regional locality of convolution operations. To tackle this problem, self attention mechanism was proposed (Schlemper et al. 2019) and (Wang et al. 2018). Still, the problem of capturing multi-scale contextual information was not solved which leads not so accurate segmentation of structures with variable shapes and scales (e.g. brain lesions with different sizes). An alternative technique using Transformers are better suited at modeling global contextual information.

Vision Transformer (ViT) (Dosovitskiy et al. 2020) splits the image into patches and models the correlation between these patches as sequences with Transformer, achieving better speed-performance trade-off on image classification than previous state of the art image recognition methods. DeiT (Touvron

A. Crimi and S. Bakas (Eds.): BrainLes 2021, LNCS 12962, pp. 39–51, 2022.
https://doi.org/10.1007/978-3-031-08999-2_3

et al. 2020) proposed a knowledge distillation method for training Vision Transformers. An extensive study was done by Bakas et al. (2018) to find the best algorithm for segmenting tumours in brain. Medical images from CT and MRI are in 3 dimensions, thus making volumetric segmentation important. Çiçek et al. (2016) tackled this problem using 3d U-Net. Densely-connected volumetric convnets was used (Yu et al. 2017) to segment cardiovascular images. A comprehensive study to evaluate segmentation performance using Dice score and Jaccard index was done by (Eelbode et al. 2020).

2   Related Work

2.1   Convolutional Neural Network

Earlier work for medical image segmentation used some variants of the original U-shaped architecture (Ronneberger et al. 2015). Some of these were Res-UNet (Xiao et al. 2018), Dense-UNet (Li et al. 2018) and U-Net++ (Zhou et al. 2018). These architectures are quite successful for various kind of problems in the domain of medical image segmentation.

2.2   Attention Mechanism

Self Attention mechanism (Wang et al. 2018) has been used successfully to improve the performance of the network. Schlemper et al. (2019) used skip connections with additive attention gate in U-shaped architecture to perform medical image segmentation. Attention mechanism was first used in U-Net (Oktay et al. 2018) for medical image segmentation. A multi-scale attention network (Fan et al. 2020) was proposed in the context of biomedical image segmentation. Jin et al. (2020) used a hybrid deep attention-aware network to extract liver and tumor in CT scans. Attention module was added to U-Net module to exploit full resolution features for medical image segmentation (Li et al. 2020). A similar work using attention based CNN was done by Liu et al. (2020) in the context of schemic stroke disease. A multi scale self guided attention network was used to achieve state of the art results (Sinha and Dolz 2020) for medical image segmentation.

2.3   Transformers

Transformer first proposed by Vaswani et al. (2017) have achieved state of the art performance on various tasks. Inspired by it, Vision Transformer (Dosovitskiy et al. 2020) was proposed which achieved better speed-accuracy tradeoff for image recognition. To improve this, Swin Transformer (Liu et al. 2021) was proposed which outperformed previous networks on various vision tasks including image classification, object detection and semantic segmentation. (Chen et al. 2021), (Valanarasu et al. 2021) and (Hatamizadeh et al. 2021) individually proposed methods to integrate CNN and transformers into a single network for medical image segmentation. Transformer along with CNN are applied in multi-modal brain tumor segmentation (Wang et al. 2021) and 3D medical image segmentation (Xie et al. 2021).

Our main contributions can be summarized as:

- We propose a novel network incorporating attention mechanism in transformer architecture along with multi scale module name EMSViT in the context of medical image segmentation.
- Our network outperforms previous state of the art CNN based as well as transformer based architectures on various datasets.
- We present the ablation study showing our network performance is generalizable hence can be incorporated to tackle other similar problems.

2.4 Background

Suppose an image is given $x \in R^{H \times W \times C}$ with a spatial resolution of $H \times W$ and C number of channels. The goal is to predict the pixel-wise label of size $H \times W$ for each image. We start by performing tokenization by reshaping the input x into a sequence of flattened 2D patches $x_p^i \in R(i = 1, .., N)$, where each patch is of size $P \times P$ and $N = (H \times W)/P^2$ is the number of patches present in the image. We convert the vectorized patches x_p into a latent D-dimensional embedding space using a linear projection vector. We use patch embeddings to make sure the positional information is present as shown below:

$$\mathbf{z}_0 = \left[\mathbf{x}_p^1 \mathbf{E}; \mathbf{x}_p^2 \mathbf{E}; \cdots ; \mathbf{x}_p^N \mathbf{E} \right] + \mathbf{E}_{pos} \tag{1}$$

where $E \in R^{(P^2 C)} \times D$ denotes the patch embedding projection, and $E_{pos} \in R^{N \times D}$ denotes the position embedding.

After the embedding layer, we use multi scale context block followed by a stack of transformer blocks (Dosovitskiy et al. 2020) made up of multiheaded self-attention (MSA) and multilayer perceptron (MLP) layers as shown in Eq. 2 and Eq. 3 respectively:

$$\mathbf{z}_i' = \text{MSA} \left(\text{Norm} \left(\mathbf{z}_{i-1} \right) \right) + \mathbf{z}_{i-1} \tag{2}$$

$$\mathbf{z}_i = \text{MLP} \left(\text{Norm} \left(\mathbf{z}_i' \right) \right) + \mathbf{z}_i' \tag{3}$$

where Norm represents layer normalization, MLP is made up of two linear layers and i is the individual block. A MSA block is made up of n self-attention (SA) heads in parallel. The structure of Transformer layer used in this work is illustrated in Fig. 1:

3 Method

3.1 Dataset

1. Synapse multi-organ segmentation dataset - We use 30 abdominal CT scans in the MICCAI 2015 Multi-Atlas Abdomen Labeling Challenge, with 3779 axial contrast-enhanced abdominal clinical CT images in total.

2. Brain Tumor Segmentation dataset - 3D MRI dataset used in the experiments is provided by the BraTS 2019 challenge (Menze et al. 2014) and (Bakas et al. 2018).

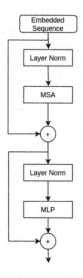

Fig. 1. Schematic of the transformer layer used in this work.

3.2   Network Architecture

The output sequence of Transformer $z_L \in R^{d \times N}$ is first reshaped to $d \times H/8 \times W/8 \times D/8$. A convolution block is used to reduce the channel dimension from d to K. This helps in reducing the computational complexity. Upsampling operations and successive convolution blocks are the used to get back a full resolution segmentation result $R \in R^{H \times W \times D}$. Skip-connections are used to fuse the encoder features with the decoder by concatenation to get more contextual information. In the encoder part, the input image is split into patches and fed into linear embedding layer. The feature map is splitted into N parts along with the channel dimension. The individual features are fused before being passed to the transformer blocks. The decoder block is comprised of transformer blocks followed by a similar split and concat operator. Linear projection is used on the feature maps to produce the segmentation map. Skip connections are used between the encoder and decoder transformer blocks to provide an alternative path for the gradient to flow thus speeding up the training process.

Two different types of convolutional operations are applied to the encoder features F_{en} to generate the feature maps $F_1 \in R_1$ and $F_2 \in R^{c \times h \times w}$ respectively. Subsequently, F is reshaped into the matrixes of feature maps F_1 and F_2. Then, a matrix multiplication operation with softmax normalization is performed in the permuted version of M and N, resulting in the position attention map $B \in R(h \times w) \times (h \times w)$, which can be defined as:

$$B_{i,j} = \frac{\exp\left(\boldsymbol{M}_i \cdot \boldsymbol{N}_j\right)}{\sum_{i=1}^{n} \exp\left(\boldsymbol{M}_i \cdot \boldsymbol{N}_j\right)} \qquad (4)$$

where $B_{i,j}$ measures the impact of ith position on j^{th} position and n = h × w is the number of pixels. After that, W is multiplied by the permuted version of B, and the resulting feature at each position can be formulated as:

$$GSA(\boldsymbol{M}, \boldsymbol{N}, \boldsymbol{W})_j = \sum_{i=1}^{n} \left(\boldsymbol{B}_{i,j} \boldsymbol{W}_j\right) \qquad (5)$$

Similarly, we reshape the resulting features to generate the final output of our vision transformer.

3.3   Residual Connection

The input feature maps of each decoder block are up-sampled to the resolution of outputs through bilinear interpolation, and then concatenated with the output feature maps as the inputs of the subsequent block, which is defined as:

$$\boldsymbol{F}_n = f_n\left(\boldsymbol{F}_{n-1}\right) \oplus v_n\left(\boldsymbol{F}_{n-1}\right) \qquad (6)$$

The detailed architecture of our network as well as the intermediate skip-connections is shown in Fig. 2:

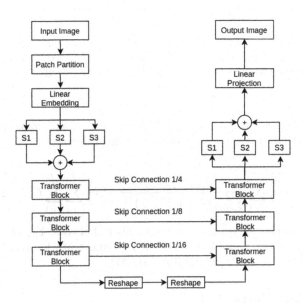

Fig. 2. Overview of our model architecture. Output sizes demonstrated for patch dimension N = 16 and embedding size C = 768. We extract sequence representations of different layers in the transformer and merge them with the decoder using skip connections.

Similar to the previous works (Hu et al. 2019), self-attention is computed as defined below:

$$\text{MSA}(Q, K, V) = SoftMax\left(\frac{QK^T}{\sqrt{d}} + B\right) V \tag{7}$$

where $Q, K, V \in R^{M^2 \times d}$ denote the query, key and value matrices. M^2 and d denotes the number of patches in a window and the dimension of the query. The values in B are taken from the random bias matrix denoted by $B \in R^{(2M-1) \times (2M+1)}$

The output of MSA is defined below:

$$\text{TMSA}(\mathbf{z}) = [\text{MSA}_1(z); \text{MSA}_2(z); \ldots; \text{MSA}_n(z)] \mathbf{W}_{tmsa} \tag{8}$$

where W_{tmsa} represents the learnable weight matrices of different heads (SA).

3.4 Loss Function

Commonly used Binary Cross Entropy and Dice Loss terms are used for training our network as defined in Eq. 9 and Eq. 10 respectively:

$$\mathcal{L}_{BCE} = \sum_{i=1}^{t} (y_i \log(p_i) + (1 - y_i) \log(1 - p_i)) \tag{9}$$

$$\mathcal{L}_{\text{Dice}} = 1 - \frac{\sum_{i=1}^{t} y_i p_i + \varepsilon}{\sum_{i=1}^{t} y_i + p_i + \varepsilon} \tag{10}$$

where t is the total number of pixels in each image, y_i represents the ground-truth value of the ith pixel, p_i the confidence score of the ith pixel in prediction results. The above two loss functions can be combined to give:

$$L_{total} = L_{BCE} + L_{Dice} \tag{11}$$

The complete loss function is a combination of dice and cross entropy terms which is calculated in voxel-wise manner as defined below:

$$L_{total} = 1 - \alpha \frac{2}{J} \sum_{j=1}^{J} \frac{\sum_{i=1}^{I} G_{i,j} Y_{i,j}}{\sum_{i=1}^{I} G_{i,j}^2 + \sum_{i=1}^{I} Y_{i,j}^2} + \beta \frac{1}{I} \sum_{i=1}^{I} \sum_{j=1}^{J} G_{i,j} \log Y_{i,j} \tag{12}$$

where I is the number of voxels, J is the number of classes, $Y_{i,j}$ and $G_{i,j}$ denote the probability output and one-hot encoded ground truth for voxel i of class j. In our experiment, $\alpha = \beta = 0.5$, and $\epsilon = 0.0001$.

3.5 Evaluation Metrics

The segmentation accuracy is measured by the Dice score and the Hausdorff distance (95%) metrics for enhancing tumor region (ET), regions of the tumor core (TC), and the whole tumor region (WT).

3.6 Implementation Details

Our model is trained using Pytorch deep learning framework. The learning rate and weight decay values used are 0.00015 and 0.005, respectively. We use batch size value of 16 and ADAM optimizer to train our model. We use a random crop of 128 × 192 × 192 and mean normalization to prepare our model input. The input image size and patch size are set as 224 × 224 and 4, respectively. As a model input, we use the 3D voxel by cropping the brain region. The following data augmentation techniques are applied:

1. Random cropping of the data from 240 × 240 × 155 to 128 × 128 × 128 voxels;
2. Flipping across the axial, coronal and sagittal planes by a probability of 0.5
3. Random Intensity shift between $[-0.05, 0.05]$ and scale between $[0.5, 1.0]$.

4 Results

We report the average DSC and average Hausdorff Distance (HD) on 8 abdominal organs (aorta, gallbladder, spleen, left kidney, right kidney, liver, pancreas, spleen, stomach) with a random split of 20 samples in training set and 10 sample for validation set using Synapse multi-organ CT dataset in Table 1. Our network clearly outperforms previous state of the art CNN as well as transformer networks.

Table 1. Comparison on the Synapse multi-organ CT dataset (average dice score %, average Hausdorff distance in mm, and dice score % for each organ). The best results are highlighted in bold.

Encoder	Decoder	DSC	HD	Aorta	GB	Kid (L)	Kid (R)	Liver	Panc	Spleen	Stomach
V-Net	V-Net	68.81	–	75.34	51.87	77.10	80.75	87.84	40.05	80.56	56.98
DARR	DARR	69.77	–	74.74	53.77	72.31	73.24	94.08	54.18	89.90	45.96
R50	U-Net	74.68	36.87	84.18	62.84	79.19	71.29	93.35	48.23	84.41	73.92
R50	AttnUNet	75.57	36.97	55.92	63.91	79.20	72.71	93.56	49.37	87.19	74.95
EMSViT	None	61.50	39.61	44.38	39.59	67.46	62.94	89.21	43.14	75.45	69.78
EMSViT	CUP	67.86	36.11	70.19	45.10	74.70	67.40	91.32	42.00	81.75	70.44
R50-EMSViT	CUP	71.29	32.87	73.73	55.13	75.80	72.20	91.51	45.99	81.99	73.95
TransUNet	TransUNet	77.48	31.69	87.23	63.13	81.87	77.02	94.08	55.86	85.08	75.62
SwinUnet	SwinUnet	79.13	21.55	85.47	66.53	83.28	79.61	94.29	56.58	90.66	76.60
EMSViT	EMSViT	**80.45**	**21.24**	**86.41**	**66.80**	**83.59**	**80.12**	**94.56**	**56.90**	**91.28**	**76.82**

We conduct the five-fold cross-validation evaluation on the BraTS 2019 training set. The quantitative results is presented in Table 2. Our network again outperforms previous state of the art CNN as well as transformer networks using most of the evaluation metrics except Hausdorff distance on ET and WT.

We compare the performance of our model against CNN based networks for the task of brain tumour segmentation in Table 3. Again, our network outperforms previous state of the art CNN as well as transformer networks.

Table 2. Comparison on the BraTS 2019 validation set. DS represents Dice score and HD represents Hausdorff distance. The best results are highlighted in bold.

Method	ET (DS%)	WT (DS%)	TC (DS%)	ET (HD mm)	WT (HD mm)	TC (HD mm)
3D U-Net	70.86	87.38	72.48	5.062	9.432	8.719
V-Net	73.89	88.73	76.56	6.131	6.256	8.705
KiU-Net	73.21	87.60	73.92	6.323	8.942	9.893
Attention U-Net	75.96	88.81	77.20	5.202	7.756	8.258
Li et al.	77.10	88.60	81.30	6.033	6.232	7.409
TransBTS w/o TTA	78.36	88.89	81.41	5.908	7.599	7.584
TransBTS w/ TTA	78.93	90.00	81.94	**3.736**	**5.644**	6.049
EMSViT	**79.24**	**90.28**	**82.23**	3.706	5.621	**7.129**

Table 3. Cross validation results of brain tumour segmentation task. DSC1, DSC2 and DSC3 denote average dice scores for the Whole Tumour (WT), Enhancing Tumour (ET) and Tumour Core (TC) across all folds. For each split, average dice score of three classes are used. The best results are highlighted in bold.

Fold	Split-1	Split-2	Split-3	Split-4	Split-5	DSC1	DSC2	DSC3	Avg.
VNet	64.83	67.28	65.23	65.2	66.34	75.96	54.99	66.38	65.77
AHNet	65.78	69.31	65.16	65.05	67.84	75.8	57.58	66.50	66.63
Att-UNet	66.39	70.18	65.39	66.11	67.29	75.29	57.11	68.81	67.07
UNet	67.20	69.11	66.84	66.95	68.16	75.03	57.87	70.06	67.65
SegResNet	69.62	71.84	67.86	68.52	70.43	76.37	59.56	73.03	69.65
EMSViT	**70.92**	**73.84**	**71.05**	**72.29**	**72.43**	**79.52**	**60.90**	**76.11**	**71.98**

In Table 4, We compare the performance of our network against previous state of the art for the task of spleen segmentation. Except on Split-4 and Split-5, our network outperforms both state of the art CNN and transformer networks.

The visualization of the validation set prediction is illustrated in Fig. 3:

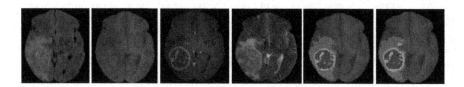

Fig. 3. All the four modalities of the brain tumor visualized with the ground-truth and predicted segmentation of tumor sub-regions for BraTS 2019 crossvalidation dataset. red label: Necrosis, yellow label: Edema and green label: Edema.

Table 4. Cross validation results of spleen segmentation task. For each split, we provide the average dice score of fore-ground class. The best results are highlighted in bold.

Fold	Split-1	Split-2	Split-3	Split-4	Split-5	Avg.
VNet	94.78	92.08	95.54	94.73	95.03	94.43
AHNet	94.23	92.10	94.56	94.39	94.11	93.87
Att-UNet	93.16	92.59	95.08	94.75	95.81	94.27
UNet	92.83	92.83	95.76	95.01	96.27	94.54
SegResNet	95.66	92.00	95.79	94.19	95.53	94.63
UNETR	95.95	94.01	96.37	**95.89**	**96.91**	95.82
EMSViT	**96.14**	**94.52**	**96.52**	95.76	96.78	**96.14**

The segmentation results of our model on the Synapse multi-organ CT dataset is shown in Fig. 4:

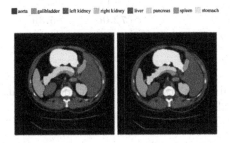

Fig. 4. The segmentation results of our network on the Synapse multi-organ CT dataset. Left depicts ground truth, while the right one depicts predicted segmentation from our network.

4.1 Ablation Studies

We conduct the experiments of our model with bilinear interpolation and transposed convolution on Synapse multi-organ CT dataset as shown in Table 6. The experiment shows that our network using transposed convolution layer achieves better segmentation accuracy.

Table 5. Ablation study on the impact of the up-sampling. Here BI denotes bilinear interpolation, TC denotes transposed convolution. The best results are highlighted in bold.

Up-sampling	DSC	Aorta	Gallbladder	Kidney (L)	Kidney (R)	Liver	Pancreas	Spleen	Stomach
BI	77.24	82.04	67.18	80.52	73.79	94.05	55.74	86.71	72.50
TC	**78.53**	**84.55**	**68.02**	**82.46**	**74.41**	**94.59**	**55.91**	**89.25**	**73.96**

We explore our network at various model scales (i.e. depth (L) and embedding dimension (d)) using BraTS 2019 validation dataset. We show ablation study to verify the impact of Transformer scale on the segmentation performance. Our network with d = 384 and L = 4 achieves the best scores of ET, WT and TC. Increasing the depth and decreasing the embedding dimension gives better results. However, the impact of depth on performance is much more than that of embedding dimension as shown in Table 8:

Table 6. Ablation study demonstrating the effect of depth and embedding dimension on our vision transformer using BraTS 2019 validation dataset. DS represents Dice score. The best results are highlighted in bold.

Depth (L)	Embedding dim (d)	ET (DS%)	WT (DS%)	TC (DS%)
1	384	69.24	84.16	70.18
1	512	69.05	83.87	69.92
2	384	70.59	84.88	72.51
2	512	70.13	84.15	71.99
4	384	**72.06**	**85.39**	**73.67**
4	512	71.55	85.06	73.05

Using the set of ablation studies, it can be inferred that the performance of our network is generalizable.

5   Conclusions

Biomedical image segmentation is a challenging problem in medical imaging. Recently deep learning methods leveraging both CNN and transformer based architectures have been highly successful in this domain. In this paper, we propose a novel network named Efficient Multi Scale Vision Transformer (EMSViT) for Biomedical Image Segmentation. We use multi scale mechanism to split the features employing different convolutions and concatenating those individual feature maps produced before being passed to transformer blocks in encoder. The decoder also uses similar mechanism with skip connections connecting the encoder and decoder transformer blocks. The output feature map after split and concat operator is passed through a linear projection block to produce the output segmentation map. Using Dice Score and the Hausdorff Distance on multiple datasets, our network outperforms most of the previous CNN as well as transformer based architectures. In the future, we would like to use Efficient Multi Scale Vision transformer to tackle other problems in computer vision like depth estimation.

References

Bakas, S., et al.: Identifying the best machine learning algorithms for brain tumor segmentation, progression assessment, and overall survival prediction in the brats challenge. arXiv preprint arXiv:1811.02629 (2018)

Cao, H., et al.: Swin-UNet: UNet-like pure transformer for medical image segmentation. arXiv preprint arXiv:2105.05537 (2021)

Chen, J., et al.: TransUNet: transformers make strong encoders for medical image segmentation. arXiv preprint arXiv:2102.04306 (2021)

Çiçek, Ö., Abdulkadir, A., Lienkamp, S.S., Brox, T., Ronneberger, O.: 3D U-Net: learning dense volumetric segmentation from sparse annotation. In: Ourselin, S., Joskowicz, L., Sabuncu, M.R., Unal, G., Wells, W. (eds.) MICCAI 2016. LNCS, vol. 9901, pp. 424–432. Springer, Cham (2016). https://doi.org/10.1007/978-3-319-46723-8_49

Dosovitskiy, A., et al.: An image is worth 16x16 words: transformers for image recognition at scale. arXiv preprint arXiv:2010.11929 (2020)

Eelbode, T., et al.: Optimization for medical image segmentation: theory and practice when evaluating with dice score or Jaccard index. IEEE Trans. Med. Imaging 39(11), 3679–3690 (2020)

Fan, T., Wang, G., Li, Y., Wang, H.: MA-Net: a multi-scale attention network for liver and tumor segmentation. IEEE Access 8, 179656–179665 (2020)

Fu, S., et al.: Domain adaptive relational reasoning for 3D multi-organ segmentation. In: Martel, A.L., et al. (eds.) MICCAI 2020. LNCS, vol. 12261, pp. 656–666. Springer, Cham (2020). https://doi.org/10.1007/978-3-030-59710-8_64

Gibson, E., et al.: Automatic multi-organ segmentation on abdominal CT with dense V-Networks. IEEE Trans. Med. Imaging 37(8), 1822–1834 (2018)

Hatamizadeh, A., Yang, D., Roth, H., and Xu, D.: UNETR: transformers for 3D medical image segmentation. arXiv preprint arXiv:2103.10504 (2021)

Hu, H., Zhang, Z., Xie, Z., Lin, S.: Local relation networks for image recognition. In: Proceedings of the IEEE/CVF International Conference on Computer Vision, pp. 3464–3473 (2019)

Isensee, F., Jaeger, P.F., Kohl, S.A., Petersen, J., Maier-Hein, K.H.: nnU-Net: a self-configuring method for deep learning-based biomedical image segmentation. Nat. Methods 18(2), 203–211 (2021)

Jin, Q., Meng, Z., Sun, C., Cui, H., Su, R.: RA-UNet: a hybrid deep attention-aware network to extract liver and tumor in CT scans. Front. Bioeng. Biotechnol. 8, 1471 (2020)

Li, C., et al.: ANU-Net: attention-based nested U-Net to exploit full resolution features for medical image segmentation. Comput. Graph. 90, 11–20 (2020)

Li, X., Chen, H., Qi, X., Dou, Q., Fu, C.-W., Heng, P.-A.: H-DenseUNet: hybrid densely connected UNet for liver and tumor segmentation from CT volumes. IEEE Trans. Med. Imaging 37(12), 2663–2674 (2018)

Liu, L., Kurgan, L., Wu, F.-X., Wang, J.: Attention convolutional neural network for accurate segmentation and quantification of lesions in ischemic stroke disease. Med. Image Anal. 65, 101791 (2020)

Liu, Z., et al.: Swin transformer: hierarchical vision transformer using shifted windows. arXiv preprint arXiv:2103.14030 (2021)

Menze, B.H., et al.: The multimodal brain tumor image segmentation benchmark (BraTS). IEEE Trans. Med. Imaging 34(10), 1993–2024 (2014)

Myronenko, A.: 3D MRI brain tumor segmentation using autoencoder regularization. In: Crimi, A., Bakas, S., Kuijf, H., Keyvan, F., Reyes, M., van Walsum, T. (eds.) BrainLes 2018. LNCS, vol. 11384, pp. 311–320. Springer, Cham (2019). https://doi.org/10.1007/978-3-030-11726-9_28

Ni, J., Wu, J., Tong, J., Chen, Z., Zhao, J.: GC-Net: global context network for medical image segmentation. Comput. Methods Program. Biomed. **190**, 105121 (2020)

Oktay, O., et al.: Attention U-Net: learning where to look for the pancreas. arXiv preprint arXiv:1804.03999 (2018)

Parmar, N., et al.: Image transformer. In: International Conference on Machine Learning, pp. 4055–4064. PMLR (2018)

Ronneberger, O., Fischer, P., Brox, T.: U-Net: convolutional networks for biomedical image segmentation. In: Navab, N., Hornegger, J., Wells, W.M., Frangi, A.F. (eds.) MICCAI 2015. LNCS, vol. 9351, pp. 234–241. Springer, Cham (2015). https://doi.org/10.1007/978-3-319-24574-4_28

Sagar, A.: Bayesian multi scale neural network for crowd counting. arXiv preprint arXiv:2007.14245 (2020)

Sagar, A.: Monocular depth estimation using multi scale neural network and feature fusion. arXiv preprint arXiv:2009.09934 (2020)

Sagar, A.: DMSANet: dual multi scale attention network. arXiv preprint arXiv:2106.08382 (2021)

Sagar, A., Soundrapandiyan, R.: Semantic segmentation with multi scale spatial attention for self driving cars. arXiv preprint arXiv:2007.12685 (2020)

Schlemper, J., et al.: Attention gated networks: learning to leverage salient regions in medical images. Med. Image Anal. **53**, 197–207 (2019)

Simpson, A.L., et al.: A large annotated medical image dataset for the development and evaluation of segmentation algorithms. arXiv preprint arXiv:1902.09063 (2019)

Sinha, A., Dolz, J.: Multi-scale self-guided attention for medical image segmentation. IEEE J. Biomed. Health Inf. **25**(1), 121-130 (2020)

Touvron, H., Cord, M., Douze, M., Massa, F., Sablayrolles, A., Jégou, H.: Training data-efficient image transformers & distillation through attention. arXiv preprint arXiv:2012.12877 (2020)

Valanarasu, J.M.J., Oza, P., Hacihaliloglu, I., Patel, V.M.: Medical transformer: gated axial-attention for medical image segmentation. arXiv preprint arXiv:2102.10662 (2021)

Vaswani, A., et al.: Attention is all you need. arXiv preprint arXiv:1706.03762 (2017)

Wang, W., Chen, C., Ding, M., Li, J., Yu, H., Zha, S.: TransBTS: multimodal brain tumor segmentation using transformer. arXiv preprint arXiv:2103.04430 (2021)

Wang, X., Girshick, R., Gupta, A., He, K.: Non-local neural networks. In: Proceedings of the IEEE Conference on Computer Vision and Pattern Recognition, pp. 7794–7803 (2018)

Xiao, X., Lian, S., Luo, Z., Li, S.: Weighted Res-UNet for high-quality retina vessel segmentation. In 2018 9th International Conference on Information Technology in Medicine and Education (ITME), pp. 327–331. IEEE (2018)

Xie, Y., Zhang, J., Shen, C., Xia, Y.: CoTr: efficiently bridging CNN and transformer for 3D medical image segmentation. arXiv preprint arXiv:2103.03024 (2021)

Yu, L., et al.: Automatic 3D cardiovascular MR segmentation with densely-connected volumetric ConvNets. In: Descoteaux, M., Maier-Hein, L., Franz, A., Jannin, P., Collins, D.L., Duchesne, S. (eds.) MICCAI 2017. LNCS, vol. 10434, pp. 287–295. Springer, Cham (2017). https://doi.org/10.1007/978-3-319-66185-8_33

Zhang, Y., Liu, H., Hu, Q.: Transfuse: fusing transformers and CNNs for medical image segmentation. arXiv preprint arXiv:2102.08005 (2021)

Zhou, Z., Rahman Siddiquee, M.M., Tajbakhsh, N., Liang, J.: UNet++: a nested U-Net architecture for medical image segmentation. In: Stoyanov, D., et al. (eds.) DLMIA/ML-CDS -2018. LNCS, vol. 11045, pp. 3–11. Springer, Cham (2018). https://doi.org/10.1007/978-3-030-00889-5_1

CA-Net: Collaborative Attention Network for Multi-modal Diagnosis of Gliomas

Baocai Yin[1,2(✉)], Hu Cheng[2], Fengyan Wang[2], and Zengfu Wang[1]

[1] University of Science and Technology of China, Hefei, China
zfwang@ustc.edu.cn
[2] iFLYTEK Research, Hefei, China
{bcyin,hucheng,fywang6}@iflytek.com

Abstract. Deep neural network methods have led to impressive break-throughs in the medical image field. Most of them focus on single-modal data, while diagnoses in clinical practice are usually determined based on multi-modal data, especially for tumor diseases. In this paper, we intend to find a way to effectively fuse radiology images and pathology images for the diagnosis of gliomas. To this end, we propose a collaborative attention network (CA-Net), which consists of three attention-based feature fusion modules, multi-instance attention, cross attention, and attention fusion. We first take an individual network for each modality to extract the original features. Multi-instance attention combines different informative patches in the pathology image to form a holistic pathology feature. Cross attention interacts between the two modalities and enhances single modality features by exploring complementary information from the other modality. The cross attention matrixes imply the feature reliability, so they are further utilized to obtain a coefficient for each modality to linearly fuse the enhanced features as the final representation in the attention fusion module. The three attention modules are collaborative to discover a comprehensive representation. Our result on the CPM-RadPath outperforms other fusion methods by a large margin, which demonstrates the effectiveness of the proposed method.

Keywords: Multi-modal · Cross attention · Gliomas

1 Introduction

Gliomas are the most common primary intracranial tumors, accounting for 40% to 50% of all cranial tumors. World Health Organization (WHO) grading system grade the gliomas from 1 (least malignant and best prognosis) to 4 (most malignant and worst prognosis). According to the pathological malignancy of the tumor cells, brain gliomas are also divided into low-grade gliomas (including astrocytoma, oligodendroglioma) and high-grade gliomas (glioblastoma). Magnetic resonance imaging (MRI) is the common examination method for gliomas, which is mainly used to identify low-grade gliomas and high-grade gliomas.

A. Crimi and S. Bakas (Eds.): BrainLes 2021, LNCS 12962, pp. 52–62, 2022.
https://doi.org/10.1007/978-3-031-08999-2_4

Due to the limitation of MRI in the identification of astrocytoma and oligo-dendroglioma, pathology images are also used. Hence, the diagnosis of gliomas in clinical practice is based on multiple modalities of medical images, which requires the doctors to have a rich experience. Computer aided diagnosis (CAD) systems are in demand to facilitate the diagnosis process.

Convolutional neural network (CNN) is the most widely used deep learning model to learn complex discriminative features of images and various architectures of CNN have been proposed, such as VGG16 [1], ResNet [2], and Densenet [3]. These networks achieve human-level performance on many tasks in the natural image field. Moreover, deep learning methods also bring significant progress in the medical field. For instance, the U-Net [4] architecture was proposed for the segmentation of neuronal structures and performed well on a variety of biomedical segmentation tasks. However, most models only focus on single modality data, such as X-ray images [5], CT images [6], or MRI images [7].

In order to obtain more information for better decision, learning methods on multi-modal data has been a growing trend. Incorporating visual information on many speech tasks has achieved great gains, such as speech enhancement [8], speech separation [9,10]. Pretraining on vision and language data quickly become a popular task after the advent of BERT [11]. In the medical image field, multi-modal data refers to the images taken by different inspection methods and non-image data [36]. Although there are some public multi-modal datasets like BraTs [12,37–39], CHAOS [13], CPM-RadPath [14,40], the methods of fusing the multi-modal data are still deficient. To the best of our knowledge, most fusion methods on medical images are limited to direct fusion by concatenating or linear weighting at the input-level [15–17], feature-level [18–20,28], or decision-level [21–23]. Pandya et al. [24] introduced a multi-channel MRI embedding strategy to improve the result of deep learning-based tumor segmentation models. This method linearly fused four modalities at the input-level. Neubauer et al. [18] improved the performance of tumor delineation by merging the features of MRI and PET/CT data after two modality-specific encoders. Kamnitsas et al. [22] trained three networks separately and averaged the confidence of each network as the final result.

MRI images and pathology images are the most common inspection methods for gliomas diagnoses. CPM-Radpath [14,40] provided both modalities to evaluate the performance of computer-aided systems. This task is difficult as the two modalities are totally different. MRI images are 3D scanning data of the brain, while pathology images are 2D microscopy data of the sliced tissue. Ma et al. [25] fused the final results of the two modalities by logistic regression. Xue et al. [26] proposed a dual path model and fused the features before the last fully connected layer directly. However, due to the great difference between the two modalities, the relation between them is quite complicated and it can not be captured by these simple fusion methods. In this work, we adopt the powerful modeling capability of the attention mechanism and propose a collaborative attention network (CA-Net). It consists of three attention based feature fusion modules. Multi-instance attention combines different pathology patch features.

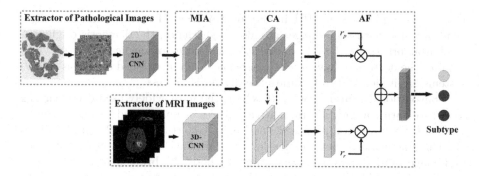

Fig. 1. The pipeline of the proposed framework. Features from the pathology image and the MRI image are fused by three modules, Multi-Instance Attention (MIA), Cross Attention (CA), Attention Fusion (AF) to identify three subtypes of gliomas.

Cross attention implicitly captures the relation between the two modalities and enhances both features by the complementary information from the other modality. Attention fusion fuses the two features according to the reliability of each feature, which is computed based on the learned cross attention matrixes, and obtain the final feature representation.

2   Method

Based on pathology images and MRI images, our task is to identify the subtypes of gliomas. The pipeline of the proposed CA-Net is shown in Fig. 1, including five parts, two feature extractors of pathological images and MRI images, three collaborative attention-based feature fusion modules, i.e. Multi-Instance Attention (MIA), Cross Attention (CA), Attention Fusion (AF).

2.1   Features Extraction

The resolution of pathological images is around 100000×100000, which is too huge for computation devices to process. A typical solution is extracting patches from the whole slide image. We exclude the white background regions and crop patches sized 256×256 without overlap. Then we filter out the patches that have low entropy. The extracted patches are then fed to a Densenet [3] structure network which consists of four stages and the number of dense blocks in each stage is 4, 8, 12, and 24.

The MRI images of each patient contain four types of scans, including T1, T2, T1-CE, and Flair. In order to reduce the useless information, extraction of the lesion is first performed by a U-Net structured lesion segmentation model with 23 layers, which is pre-trained on BraTS2019 [12,37–39]. Lesion regions are then cropped and resized to $128 \times 128 \times 128$. The four types of scans are concatenated to form a 4D tensor. The feature extractor is a 3D-Densenet [3],

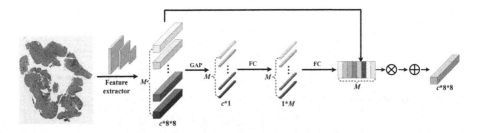

Fig. 2. The architecture of the Multi-instance Attention module (MIA). Features from different patches are fused by adaptively learned coefficients to form a holistic feature.

which consists of four stages and the number of dense blocks in each stage is 4, 8, 12, and 12.

Both the pathology image and MRI image feature extractors are trained with a cross-entropy loss. Since the pathological images are only annotated with image labels, we have no label for each patch. Thereby, we directly assign the whole image label to the sampled patches, as most studies [27] do.

2.2   Multi-instance Attention

There are multiple patches and multiple features in each pathology image, which is unbalanced when fusing with the radiology feature. So we should combine the features of all the patches to form a holistic feature, which is similar to the setting in multi-instance learning (MIL). The extracted patch is regarded as an instance and we shall build a bag feature to represent the pathology image. To this end, we propose a multi-instance attention module, as illustrated in Fig. 2.

For the convenience of parallel training, we only sample a fixed number (500 in this paper) of instances for training and inference. All the sampled instances with a feature size of $c \times 8 \times 8$ are sent to a global average pooling (GAP) layer, result in a feature size of $c \times 1$. c is the channel number. Then the attention coefficient is computed by Eq. 1.

$$a_j = \frac{\exp(w^T \tanh(vg_j))}{\sum_{j=1}^{M} \exp(w^T \tanh(vg_j))} \tag{1}$$

g_j is the feature of the jth instance after GAP. M is the number of instances. $w \in R^{M \times 1}, v \in R^{M \times c}$ are the parameters of two fully connected layers. Tanh is employed as the activation function. The learned attention coefficients are further utilized to accumulate all the instances' features and get the bag-level feature.

2.3   Cross Attention

Pathology features and radiology features have plenty of complementary information. Previous feature fusion methods including concatenation and linear

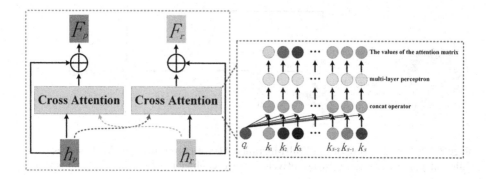

Fig. 3. The architecture of the cross-attention module.

fusion can not effectively explore the relation between the two modalities. In this work, we propose a cross-attention module to deeply learn their relations, which is illustrated in Fig. 3.

Attention is a popular mechanism in deep learning models, especially after the introduction of self-attention [29]. The most frequently used attention is scaled dot-product attention, which computes the relation by the dot product of the feature vector. The dot-product attention implies that similar features have a close relation. However, in our task, the features come from two totally different modalities, therefore, it's not a valid way to adopt the dot-product attention. We adopt additive attention [30] to explore the relationship between different modalities, which is formulated as follows:

$$e_{ij} = f(q_i, k_j), \tag{2}$$

$$\alpha_{ij} = \frac{\exp(e_{ij})}{\sum_{k=1}^{N} \exp(e_{ik})}, \tag{3}$$

$$g_i = \sum_{j=1}^{N} \alpha_{ij} k_j. \tag{4}$$

The pathology feature size is $c \times 8 \times 8$ and the radiology feature size is $c \times 4 \times 4 \times 4$. Both of them are reshaped to $c \times 64$ before sent to the attention module. c is the channel number, i.e. feature length. Attention is computed at every position. q_i is the query feature from one modality and k_j is the key feature from the other modality. N is the number of positions (64 in our setting). A shared multi-layer perceptron (MLP) followed by a softmax normalization is employed to learn their relation. Note that q_i and k_j are concatenated before sent to the MLP, which means e_{ij} will be different when the modality of the query feature changes. Then the complementary feature from the other modality can be obtained by a simple linearly weighted summation. The complementary feature g_i is added to the original query feature q_i to enhance the feature of each modality, obtaining F_p and F_r.

2.4   Attention Fusion

The last step is to fuse the features from the two modalities. Although the enhanced feature of each modality has contained the information of both modalities, we believe that the representational ability, i.e. reliabilities, of them are still different. An easy solution is to learn an adaptive linear coefficient for each modality. But this will bring in extra parameters, which will lead to overfitting. We notice that the attention matrix in the cross-attention module refers to the relation between two modalities. Thereby, we attempt to explore the reliability according to the attention matrix. Actually, when e_{ij} in Eq. 2 is bigger, it means the query feature q_i is more dependent on the key feature k_j, implying that the query feature is less reliable. Although the query feature is enhanced by the cross attention module, the complementary feature is scaled by a normalized coefficient α_{ij} for the sake of stable training. Hence, the enhanced feature still does not contain sufficient complementary information. Thus we can infer the feature reliability according to e_{ij}. We compute the reliability as in Eq. 5.

$$ r = \frac{1}{\sum_{i=1}^{N} \sum_{j=1}^{N} \sigma(e_{ij})} \tag{5} $$

σ is a measure function, which is sigmoid in this work. The final feature representation is obtained by Eq. 6.

$$ F = \frac{r_p F_p + r_r F_r}{r_p + r_r} \tag{6} $$

F_p and F_r are the enhanced pathology feature and radiology feature. r_p and r_r are the corresponding reliabilities calculated by Eq. 5 when taking pathology features and radiology features as the query feature, respectively. The higher the reliability is, the higher the weight is.

The final feature representation is sent to the classifier to be classified into three subtypes of gliomas. The loss function is cross entropy. The three attention based feature modules are jointly trained, while the feature extractors of the two modalities are trained independently.

3   Results

3.1   Experiment Setup

Dataset. CPM-RadPath [14,40] consists of 221 paired radiology images and histopathology images for training. Since we can not obtain the validation data and test data, we only utilized its training data for experiments. Due to the limited number of images in medical tasks, all the experiments were evaluated by 3-folder cross-validation. The MRI images of each patient contain four types of scans, Flair, T1, T1-Ce, and T2. Due to the differences in the staining process of slices, pathology images have a big variance in color, we converted the RGB pathology images into gray images. CPM-RadPath aims to distinguish between three subtypes of brain tumors, namely astrocytoma, oligodendroglioma, and glioblastoma. The number of each subtype is shown in Table 1.

Table 1. Data distribution of different subtypes in CPM-RadPath.

Subtype	A	O	G	Total
Number	54	34	133	221

A: astrocytoma, O: oligodendroglioma, G: glioblastoma

Implementation Details. Feature extractors of pathology images and radiology images were trained with a batch size of 400 and 20 respectively, and the number of feature channel was set to 64. Xavier initialization was adopted in all the models. Parameters were optimized by SGD [31], and the weight decay and momentum were set as 1e−4 and 0.95 respectively. The learning rate was initially set to 0.001 and was divided by 10 at 50% and 75% of the total training epochs. All the models were trained based on MXNet [32] for 200 epochs on a TeslaV100 GPU. For the pathology images, the same augmentation methods as the study [35] were used, including random brightness and contrast, random saturation and hue, flip, and rotation. Random crop and flip were adopted as data augmentation for the radiology images.

The feature extractors of the two modalities were first trained with a cross-entropy loss. Then we frozen the feature extractors and jointly trained the three attention modules.

3.2   Results of Gliomas Classification

The same evaluation metrics of the CPM-RadPath challenge [14,40] were employed to evaluate the effectiveness of the proposed method in this paper.

Results on a Single Modality. The dataset consists of pathology images and radiology images (MRI). We first evaluated the performance on single modality data. Results are displayed in Table 2. Compared with the pathology image, the results of the radiology image are much worse. The reason is that astrocytoma and oligodendroglioma only have a slight difference in radiology images, so it is difficult for models to learn a discriminative feature. And that is also why we need pathology images in this task.

When evaluated on the pathology images, we compared our multi-instance attention with another common feature fusion method, max-out [33]. Max-out selects the biggest value among all the extracted patches as the output for each feature element. We do not use concatenation because the patch number is too much, i.e. 500, leading to a higher feature length, which is hard to fuse with the radiology feature. Compared with max-out, our multi-instance attention achieved higher performance, indicating that different patches have different importance and our attention mechanism can effectively incorporate all the patches.

Table 2. Results on a single modality.

Data	Balanced-acc	F1-micro	Kappa
Radio	0.722	0.818	0.683
Patho (Max-out)	0.877	0.917	0.852
Patho (MIA)	**0.887**	**0.925**	**0.866**

Results on Multiple Modalities. Then we evaluated our methods on the multiple modality data. Since the training of feature extraction and feature fusion are independent, we directly used the output feature of the single modality model as the input feature of the fusion stage. Particularly, the pathology feature refers to the feature obtained by our proposed multi-instance attention. We compared our methods with other feature fusion methods and the results are displayed in Table 3. Simply concatenating the features is treated as the baseline. Xue et al. [26] fused the two features by a learned linear weight, while Ma et al. [25] fused the scores of each modality by logistic regression. We reimplemented them on the proposed framework.

Table 3. Comparison of different methods on multi-modal data.

Method	Balanced-acc	F1-micro	Kappa
Concat	0.866	0.917	0.851
Linear Feature Fusion	0.886	0.932	0.878
Linear Score Fusion	0.886	0.933	0.876
Ours w/o Attention Fusion	0.891	0.940	0.892
Ours	**0.912**	**0.948**	**0.906**

As pathology features and radiology features focus on different characteristics of gliomas, simple concatenation can not capture the relation between the two modalities. So when we concatenated pathology features and radiology features, the results got even worse compared with the single pathology feature. Linear feature fusion and score fusion introduce extra parameters to capture the relation between the two modalities, thus they got an improvement and were higher than every single modality. The results show that the two modalities are complementary and can benefit from each other.

The linear fusion method is a simple linear combination of two features and there is no interaction between the two modalities. So we propose the cross attention module to interact between the two modalities and intend to enhance single modality features by digging complementary information from the other modality. The enhanced features are further fused by two linear weights which are derived from the attention matrix, i.e. attention fusion. As Table 3 shows, our results outperform other methods by a large margin. We also conducted an ablation experiment that replaced the attention fusion module with a concatenation operation. The performance is also higher than other methods, which further demonstrates that the cross-attention module can explore complementary information from each other and form a comprehensive feature representation.

4   Conclusion

In this paper, we propose a collaborative attention network to utilize multiple modality data for the diagnosis of gliomas. The network consists of three attention-based feature fusion modules. The multi-instance attention combines different patch features from the pathology images to construct a holistic pathology feature. Then the pathology feature and radiology feature are fused by the cross attention module. The final feature representation is obtained by the attention fusion module. Experimental results on CPM-RadPath demonstrate the effectiveness of the proposed method.

The proposed attention fusion module recovers the reliability of different features according to their cross-attention matrices. No additional parameters are introduced in this module and it can be implemented with one line of code. Thereby, it can be served as a plug-and-play module and used in other multi-feature fusion tasks.

Acknowledgements. This work was supported by the National Key Research and Development Program of China (2020AAA0107900).

References

1. Simonyan, K., Zisserman, A.: Very deep convolutional networks for large-scale image recognition. arXiv preprint arXiv: 1409.1556
2. He, K., Zhang, X., Ren, S., Sun, J.: Deep residual learning for image recognition. In: Proceedings of the IEEE Conference on Computer Vision and Pattern Recognition (ICCV), pp. 770–778 (2016)
3. Huang, G., Liu, Z., et al.: Densely connected convolutional networks. In: Proceedings of the IEEE Conference on Computer Vision and Pattern Recognition (CVPR), pp. 2261–2269 (2016)
4. Ronneberger, O., Fischer, P., Brox, T.: U-Net: convolutional networks for biomedical image segmentation. In: Navab, N., Hornegger, J., Wells, W.M., Frangi, A.F. (eds.) MICCAI 2015. LNCS, vol. 9351, pp. 234–241. Springer, Cham (2015). https://doi.org/10.1007/978-3-319-24574-4_28
5. Frid-Adar, M., Ben-Cohen, A., Amer, R., Greenspan, H.: Improving the segmentation of anatomical structures in chest radiographs using U-Net with an ImageNet pre-trained encoder. In: Stoyanov, D., et al. (eds.) RAMBO/BIA/TIA -2018. LNCS, vol. 11040, pp. 159–168. Springer, Cham (2018). https://doi.org/10.1007/978-3-030-00946-5_17
6. Fan, D., Zhou, T., Ji, G., et al.: Inf-Net: automatic COVID-19 lung infection segmentation from CT images. IEEE Trans. Med. Imaging **39**, 2626–2637 (2020)

7. Quande, L., Lequan, Y., Pheng, A.: MS-Net: multi-site network for improving prostate segmentation with heterogeneous MRI data. IEEE Trans. Med. Imaging **39**(9), 2713–2724 (2020)
8. Gu, R., Zhang, S., Xu, Y., et al.: Multi-modal multi-channel target speech separation. IEEE J. Sel. Top. Signal Process. **14**, 530–541 (2020)
9. Wang, W., Xing, C., Wang, D., et al.: A robust audio-visual speech enhancement model. In: IEEE International Conference on Acoustics, Speech and Signal Processing (ICASSP), pp. 7529–7533 (2020)
10. Sadeghi, M., Alameda-Pineda, X.: Robust unsupervised audio-visual speech enhancement using a mixture of variational autoencoders. In: IEEE International Conference on Acoustics, Speech and Signal Processing (ICASSP) (2020)
11. Devlin, J., Lee, K., et al.: BERT: pre-training of deep bidirectional transformers for language understanding. In: Computation and Language (2018)
12. BraTS2019. https://www.med.upenn.edu/cbica/brats2019.html
13. Kavur, A.E., Gezer, N.S., Bar, M.M., et al.: CHAOS challenge - combined (CT-MR) healthy abdominal organ segmentation. In: Image and Video Processing (2020)
14. CPM-RadPath. https://www.med.upenn.edu/cbica/cpm2020.html
15. Kamnitsas, K., Ledig, C., Newcombe, V.F.J., et al.: Efficient multi-scale 3D CNN with fully connected CRF for accurate brain lesion segmentation. Med. Image Anal. **36**, 61–78 (2016)
16. Clèrigues, A., Valverde, S., Bernal, J., et al.: SUNet: a deep learning architecture for acute stroke lesion segmentation and outcome prediction in multimodal MRI. arXiv preprint arXiv: 1810.13304 (2018)
17. Shaoguo, C., Lei, M., Jingfeng, J., et al.: Automatic semantic segmentation of brain gliomas from MRI images using a deep cascaded neural network. J. Healthcare Eng. 1–14 (2018)
18. Neubauer, T., et al.: Soft tissue sarcoma co-segmentation in combined MRI and PET/CT data. In: Syeda-Mahmood, T., et al. (eds.) CLIP/ML-CDS -2020. LNCS, vol. 12445, pp. 97–105. Springer, Cham (2020). https://doi.org/10.1007/978-3-030-60946-7_10
19. Chen, Yu., Chen, J., Wei, D., Li, Y., Zheng, Y.: OctopusNet: a deep learning segmentation network for multi-modal medical images. In: Li, Q., Leahy, R., Dong, B., Li, X. (eds.) MMMI 2019. LNCS, vol. 11977, pp. 17–25. Springer, Cham (2020). https://doi.org/10.1007/978-3-030-37969-8_3
20. LaLonde, R., et al.: INN: inflated neural networks for IPMN diagnosis. In: Shen, D., et al. (eds.) MICCAI 2019. LNCS, vol. 11768, pp. 101–109. Springer, Cham (2019). https://doi.org/10.1007/978-3-030-32254-0_12
21. Myronenko, A.: 3D MRI brain tumor segmentation using autoencoder regularization. In: Crimi, A., Bakas, S., Kuijf, H., Keyvan, F., Reyes, M., van Walsum, T. (eds.) BrainLes 2018. LNCS, vol. 11384, pp. 311–320. Springer, Cham (2019). https://doi.org/10.1007/978-3-030-11726-9_28
22. Kamnitsas, K., et al.: Ensembles of multiple models and architectures for robust brain tumour segmentation. In: Crimi, A., Bakas, S., Kuijf, H., Menze, B., Reyes, M. (eds.) BrainLes 2017. LNCS, vol. 10670, pp. 450–462. Springer, Cham (2018). https://doi.org/10.1007/978-3-319-75238-9_38
23. Aygün, M., Yusuf, H., et al.: Multi modal convolutional neural networks for brain tumor segmentation. arXiv preprint arXiv: 1809.06191 (2018)
24. Apurva, P., Catherine, S., Nisargkumar, P.: Multi-channel MRI embedding: an effective strategy for enhancement of human brain whole tumor segmentation. arXiv preprint arXiv: 2009.06115 (2020)

25. Ma, X., Jia, F.: Brain tumor classification with multimodal MR and pathology images. In: Crimi, A., Bakas, S. (eds.) BrainLes 2019. LNCS, vol. 11993, pp. 343–352. Springer, Cham (2020). https://doi.org/10.1007/978-3-030-46643-5_34
26. Xue, Y., et al.: Brain tumor classification with tumor segmentations and a dual path residual convolutional neural network from MRI and pathology images. In: Crimi, A., Bakas, S. (eds.) BrainLes 2019. LNCS, vol. 11993, pp. 360–367. Springer, Cham (2020). https://doi.org/10.1007/978-3-030-46643-5_36
27. Patil, A., Tamboli, D., Meena, S., et al.: Breast cancer histopathology image classification and localization using multiple instance learning. In: IEEE International WIE Conference on Electrical and Computer Engineering (WIECON-ECE) (2019)
28. Yin, B., Cheng, H., Wang, F., Wang, Z.: Brain tumor classification based on MRI images and noise reduced pathology images. In: Crimi, A., Bakas, S. (eds.) BrainLes 2020. LNCS, vol. 12659, pp. 465–474. Springer, Cham (2021). https://doi.org/10.1007/978-3-030-72087-2_41
29. Vaswani, A., Shazeer, N., Parmar, N., et al.: Attention is all you need. In: Neural Information Processing Systems, pp. 5998–6008 (2017)
30. Dzmitry, B., KyungHyun, C., Yoshua, B.: Neural machine translation by jointly learning to align and translate. In: 3rd International Conference on Learning Representations (ICLR) (2015)
31. Niu, F., Recht, B., Re, C., et al.: HOGWILD!: a lock-free approach to parallelizing stochastic gradient descent. In: Advances in Neural Information Processing Systems 24, pp. 693–701 (2011)
32. Chen, T., Li, M., Li, Y., et al.: MXNet: a flexible and efficient machine learning library for heterogeneous distributed systems. In: Statistics (2015)
33. Soumya, R., David, P.: Multiple instance regression. In: Proceedings of the Eighteenth International Conference on Machine Learning (2001)
34. Landis, J.R., Koch, G.G.: The measurement of observer agreement for categorical data. Biometrics **33**(1), 159–174 (1977)
35. Liu, Y., Gadepalli, K., Norouzi, M., et al.: Detecting cancer metastases on gigapixel pathology images. In: Proceedings of the IEEE Conference on Computer Vision and Pattern Recognition (CVPR) (2017)
36. Chen, R.J., Lu, M.Y., Wang, J., et al.: Pathomic fusion: an integrated framework for fusing histopathology and genomic features for cancer diagnosis and prognosis. IEEE Trans. Med. Imaging **41**, 757–770 (2020)
37. Bakas, S., Reyes, M., Jakab, A., et al.: Identifying the best machine learning algorithms for brain tumor segmentation, progression assessment, and overall survival prediction in the BRATS challenge. arXiv preprint arXiv: 1811.02629 (2018)
38. Bakas, S., Akbari, H., Sotiras, A., et al.: Advancing the cancer genome atlas glioma MRI collections with expert segmentation labels and radiomic features. Nat. Sci. Data **4**, 170117 (2017)
39. Menze, B.H., Jakab, A., Bauer, S., et al.: The multimodal brain tumor image segmentation benchmark (BRATS). IEEE Trans. Med. Imaging **34**(10), 1993–2024 (2015)
40. Kurc, T., Bakas, S., Ren, X., et al.: Segmentation and classification in digital pathology for glioma research: challenges and deep learning approaches. Front. Neurosci. **14**, 27 (2020)

Challenging Current Semi-supervised Anomaly Segmentation Methods for Brain MRI

Felix Meissen[1,2(✉)], Georgios Kaissis[1,2,3], and Daniel Rueckert[1,2,3]

[1] Technical University of Munich (TUM), Munich, Germany
{felix.meissen,g.kaissis,daniel.rueckert}@tum.de
[2] Klinikum Rechts der Isar, Munich, Germany
[3] Imperial College London, London, UK

Abstract. In this work, we tackle the problem of Semi-Supervised Anomaly Segmentation (SAS) in Magnetic Resonance Images (MRI) of the brain, which is the task of automatically identifying pathologies in brain images. Our work challenges the effectiveness of current Machine Learning (ML) approaches in this application domain by showing that thresholding Fluid-attenuated inversion recovery (FLAIR) MR scans provides better anomaly segmentation maps than several different ML-based anomaly detection models. Specifically, our method achieves better Dice similarity coefficients and Precision-Recall curves than the competitors on various popular evaluation data sets for the segmentation of tumors and multiple sclerosis lesions. (Code available under: https://github.com/FeliMe/brain_sas_baseline)

Keywords: Semi-supervised Anomaly Segmentation · Anomaly detection · Brain MRI

1 Introduction

The medical imaging domain is characterized by large amounts of data, but their usability for machine learning is limited due to the challenges in sharing the data and the difficulties in obtaining labels, which requires annotations by expert radiologists and is time-consuming and costly. Especially pixel- or voxel-wise segmentation of different diseases in medical images is a tedious task. semi-supervised machine learning seems like a natural fit to gain insights into the analysis of medical images for diagnosis as it requires no annotations and can easily utilize the large amounts of data available. Especially valuable in this domain is Semi-Supervised Anomaly Segmentation (SAS). Here, unlabelled imaging data is used to build a system that can automatically detect anything that deviates from the "norm" when presented with unseen data. In medical images, this technique is particularly helpful as anomalies here often indicate morphological manifestations of pathology.

Recently, SAS achieved impressive successes in automatic industrial defect detection [9,13,17,25] on the MVTec-AD data set [8]. In the medical imaging

A. Crimi and S. Bakas (Eds.): BrainLes 2021, LNCS 12962, pp. 63–74, 2022.
https://doi.org/10.1007/978-3-031-08999-2_5

domain, most works have focused on the detection of pathologies in brain images. Here, mostly autoencoder-based approaches have been applied so far [1, 4, 5, 11, 12, 26, 27]. These techniques use only images from healthy subjects as training data to learn the distribution of "normal" brain anatomies. During inference, most of the approaches compute a so-called anomaly map as the pixel-wise residual between the input image and a predicted "normal" version of the same image generated by the model, that is closer to the training distribution. Common anomaly types in brain MRI are tumors and lesions from specific diseases such as multiple sclerosis (MS). In fact, all of the aforementioned works evaluate their performance by detecting either of them or both. In clinical routine, MR images are typically acquired using different sequences or weightings in which the tissues appear in specific intensities. Among the most common ones are T1, T2, Fluid-attenuated inversion recovery (FLAIR), or Proton density (PD)-weighting. In FLAIR images – a standard protocol for routine clinical imaging in neurology – lesions are hyperintense compared to the rest of the tissue and also tumors are usually brighter. Because of this, FLAIR images are often used in SAS of brain MRI [1, 4, 5, 20].

In our work, we leverage this prior knowledge to build a baseline that performs anomaly segmentation of brain MRI via simple thresholding of the input FLAIR image. In particular, the main contributions of our work are:

- We show that learning the distribution of "normal" anatomies in FLAIR images using existing autoencoder-based approaches does not provide better segmentation maps of common anomalies in the brain than the input images themselves binarized at a certain threshold intensity.
- We provide a simple baseline that requires no learning and outperforms most state-of-the-art SAS methods on common evaluation data sets containing brain tumors and MS lesions.

2   Related Work

Several methods for SAS in brain images have been introduced in recent years. Most of them are based on semi-supervised training of Autoencoders. The principle is depicted in Fig. 1. The model is trained on images without anomalies only to learn a distribution of healthy brain images. During inference, the newly presented image is processed by the model to obtain a "healthy" version of the same image. Usually, an anomaly map is then obtained by computing the residual between the input image and its "healthy" version. Pixels of the anomaly map above a threshold are then considered anomalous.

In [19], the authors trained a Bayesian Autoencoder to perform anomaly segmentation on CT images. Chen and Konukoglu [11] built an Adversarial Autoencoder with an additional constraint forcing the input image and its reconstruction to be close in latent space. Another reconstruction-based technique was proposed in [5], where Baur *et al.* built a VAEGAN to increase reconstruction fidelity and realism of the reconstructed images. Zimmerer *et al.* [26, 27] added gradient information from the loss-function of Variational Autoencoders (VAEs) to the reconstruction error, offering superior anomaly maps.

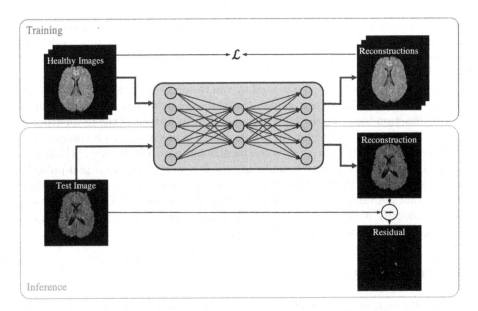

Fig. 1. Overview of Autoencoder- and GAN-based SAS. During training, the model learns the distribution of normal anatomies using only images of healthy patients. At inference time, the model generates a "healthy" version of the input image. The anomalies can be determined from the residual image. Image adapted from [4].

Restoration methods use the trained model to perform gradient optimization on the input image to construct an image that is both similar to the input and close to the distribution of normal anatomies learned by the model. Anomaly maps are again computed as the residual between the input- and the optimized image. An early example of this technique was proposed by Schlegl *et al.* [22]. They retrieve the closest version to an image that a Generative Adversarial Network (GAN) – trained on images of healthy patients only – can produce. Chen *et al.* [12] also used restoration by maximizing the evidence lower bound (ELBO) of an image on a Gaussian Mixture VAE (GMVAE).

Recently, Baur *et al.* published a comparative study [4], comparing all the methods above on the same data sets with a unified architecture. We use their results in this work to compare our baseline against all of these techniques. We use the same data sets for evaluation and use a similar pre- and post-processing pipeline. In [6], Baur *et al.* proposed to use a U-Net-like Autoencoder with skip-connections and in [7], the same authors introduced a multi-scale Autoencoder utilizing a laplacian pyramid. While [6] and [7] were both trained on the same data and used identical pre-processing as [4], only [7] was evaluated on one public data set and can be compared in this work. Pinaya *et al.* [20] achieved impressive results in SAS of brain MRI. They trained a Vector Quantised VAE (VQ-VAE) on a large cohort of FLAIR images of healthy subjects and later trained an ensemble of autoregressive Transformers in its latent space. The Transformers provide an explicit probability distribution of pixels in the latent space. Pixels with low posterior probability are considered anomalous. Since this method is not included in the comparative study by Baur *et al.* [4], we compare our results to theirs in a separate experiment.

Lastly, anomaly detection was used by van Hespen *et al.* [23] to detect chronic brain infarcts on MRI. They made a patch-based detection approach using a scoring function based on the latent space distances instead of the reconstructed image. The anomaly score for the whole image is calculated as a combination of all patches, resulting in a coarse segmentation map. We did not include this method in our experiments, because the models were trained on non-publicly available data and the model parameters are not open-source. However, they showed that SAS methods are able to spot unseen anomalies. Their system was able to identify anomalies missed in the annotation of an expert radiologist, proving the usefulness of such approaches.

3   Experiments

In the following, we present the data sets we used to evaluate our baseline, pre- and post-processing steps and evaluation metrics.

3.1   Datasets

We compare our baseline to all the publicly available data sets used for evaluation in Baur *et al.* [4] and Pinaya *et al.* [20].

To evaluate brain tumor detection, we use the training set of the 2020 version of the Multimodal Brain Tumor Image Segmentation Benchmark (BraTS) [2,3,18]. It contains T1, T2, and FLAIR scans of 371 subjects acquired across 19 institutions with multimodal, 3 T MRI scanners. It also contains manual segmentations of the tumor regions by up to four raters. The BraTS images are already skull stripped. The MSLUB [16] data set consists of T1, T2, and FLAIR images of 30 subjects with multiple sclerosis (MS). They have been acquired at the University Medical Center Ljubljana (UMCL) with a 3 T Siemens Magnetom Trio MR system. The consensus of three experts on white matter lesion segmentation is also included. As in [20], we evaluate on the White Matter Hyperintensities Segmentation Challenge (WMH) [15]. For this data set, T1 and FLAIR scans of 60 patients were acquired at three different sites in the Netherlands and Singapore. The sites used 3 T MRI scanners from Philips, Siemens, and GE. Manual segmentation of the lesions was conducted by an expert radiologist. Lastly, we use the training data of the 2015 Longitudinal MS Lesion Segmentation Challenge [10]. This dataset has 21 T1, T2, PD, and FLAIR weighted MRI scans from 5 subjects recorded at the John Hopkins MS Center with a 3 T Philips scanner. Manual lesion segmentations are available from two raters. We use the ratings of rater one (as indicated by the filename "mask1.nii") for our evaluation.

Tumors are usually much larger anomalies than MS lesions. We evaluated the exact distribution of anomaly sizes by performing a 3D connected component analysis on the segmentation maps of all data sets (Table 1). MSLUB has the smallest anomalies and also the largest number of anomalies per scan.

Table 1. Results of the 3D connected component analysis of the segmentation maps of all data sets after being registered to SRI space [21] and binarized with threshold 0.9 (See Sect. 3.2).

	BraTS	MSLUB	WMH	MSSEG2015
Avg. anomalies per scan	5	107	65	35
Avg. anomaly size (voxels)	18027	106	194	224

3.2 Pre-processing

Our pre-processing pipeline closely follows Baur *et al.* [4]. First, we skull strip the FLAIR scans using ROBEX [14]. Subsequently, we register them to the SRI space [21]. Specifically, since [21] does not contain a FLAIR Atlas, we register the T1-weighted images of all data sets and apply the same transformation to the FLAIR images and the ground truth segmentation masks. This is possible, as T1- and FLAIR images and the segmentation files are co-registered in all the data sets used. Performing registration before skull stripping resulted in failed registrations in early experiments. The registration step is not vital for our algorithm but was purely done to ensure comparability with other methods. Figure 2 shows samples of pre-processed images from all four data sets.

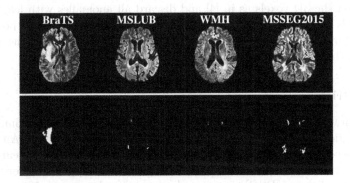

Fig. 2. Pre-processed samples and histogram-equalized (top row) and their corresponding ground truth segmentations (bottom row) from the four data sets.

During the registration process, aliasing effects occur in the – initially binary – ground truth segmentation masks that cause these masks to also have non-binary voxel values between 0 and 1 after registration. When loading the data, a decision needs to be made at which threshold a voxel in the segmentation map belongs to the segmented region. We consulted an expert radiologist and visually found 0.4 to be an acceptable threshold, but finally decided to follow Baur *et al.* [4] in using 0.9, to ensure better comparability. Note that altering this threshold has large effects on the performance of the evaluated models, especially on data sets with many small anomalies like lesions. A low threshold favors models that overestimate the true size of the anomalies, while a high threshold does the opposite.

3.3   Method

While other SAS methods usually compute anomaly maps using Neural Networks, we propose to only perform histogram equalization on the pre-processed input images and use the results directly as anomaly maps since lesions and tumors often are hyperintense in FLAIR images anyway. Histogram equalization is necessary to compensate for contrast variations among different scanner types and allows to define a global (or at least dataset-wise) threshold for binarization of the anomaly maps. We used the `equalize_hist` function of scikit-image [24] with the default value of 256 bins and a binary mask considering only pixels belonging to the brain and excluding the background. Using FLAIR images is a fair comparison since Baur *et al.* [4] and Pinaya *et al.* [20] also trained and evaluated on FLAIR images only. Our method does not require any training data or learning procedure and scales trivially to arbitrary resolutions.

3.4   Post-processing

As our only post-processing step, we perform a connected component analysis per scan on the 3D voxels as in [4] and discard all anomalies with less than 20 voxels. This value was found empirically and causes our algorithm to potentially miss very small anomalies. However, it greatly reduces the noise in the anomaly maps and thereby enhances their readability.

3.5   Metrics

We quantitatively assess the anomaly segmentation performance of our method using a variety of metrics also frequently found in related works. All metrics are produced dataset-wise. Initially, we compute Precision-Recall curves and report the area under it (AUPRC). We also provide an upper limit for the Dice similarity coefficient ($\lceil DSC \rceil$), computed using a search over $n = 100$ thresholds. Lastly, we also provide the area under the receiver operating characteristics curve (AUROC).

Table 2. Comparison of our proposed baseline to selected models of Baur *et al.* [4] and [7]. We used slices 15 to 125 of the registered FLAIR images and a resolution of 128 × 128.

Method	MSLUB			MSSEG2015		
	⌈DSC⌉	AUPRC	AUROC	⌈DSC⌉	AUPRC	AUROC
AE (dense) [4]	0.271	0.163	0.794	0.185	0.080	0.879
AE (spatial) [4,5]	0.154	0.065	0.732	0.106	0.037	0.781
VAE (rest.) [4,12]	0.333	**0.275**	0.839	0.272	0.202	0.905
GMVAE (rest.) [4,12]	0.332	0.271	0.836	0.280	0.199	0.909
f-AnoGAN [4,22]	0.283	0.221	0.856	0.342	0.255	0.923
SSAE (spatial) [7]	0.301	0.222	–	–	–	–
Ours	**0.374**	0.271	**0.991**	**0.431**	**0.262**	**0.996**

4 Results

We evaluate our method in two experiments. First, we report the performance when using slices 15 to 125 on a resolution of 128 × 128 as in the experiments of Baur *et al.* [4] and [7]. These slices contain most of the brain region in the SRI space [21] and tests did not show significant differences in the quantitative evaluation compared to the full volumes. The results of experiment one are shown in Table 2. Although for [4] the code is available online, we did not re-train the models but used the values reported in the respective papers because the training data used is not publicly available. We only report the numbers of a subset of the best performing models, the others can be inspected in the original paper. In our experiments, our proposed baseline outperforms all other methods in terms of DSC and AUROC and is competitive in AUPRC. While all models in [4] use a unified architecture, the detailed architecture of [7] is unknown, and the two papers report significantly different performances for the same models on the same data sets, indicating volatility of these methods (Table 3).

Table 3. Comparison of our proposed baseline to Pinaya *et al.* [20]. We used slices 84, 85, 86, and 87 of the registered FLAIR images and a resolution of 224 × 224.

Method	⌈DSC⌉		
	BraTS	MSLUB	WMH
Transformer [20]	**0.759**	0.465	0.441
Ours	0.738	**0.613**	**0.557**

In our second experiment, we compare to Pinaya *et al.* [20] at a resolution of 224 × 224. In this experiment, there are some differences regarding pre- and post-processing. Pinaya *et al.* [20] evaluate on data that was not skull stripped,

except for BraTS. They also did not perform any post-processing on the BraTS
data set. They registered to MNI space that has 189 slices instead of SRI with
155 slices. We therefore used slices 84, 85, 86, and 87 instead of 89 to 92 to still
ensure a fair comparison. Lastly, they used the older 2017-version of the BraTS
dataset, whereas we used the latest 2020-version. Our baseline outperforms the
Transformer strongly on the MSLUB and WMH data sets and performs only
slightly worse on the BraTS data set.

Figure 3 shows the qualitative results of our proposed baseline. The visual
segmentation quality based on image-hyperintensities is decent and shows the
approximate localization of anomalies.

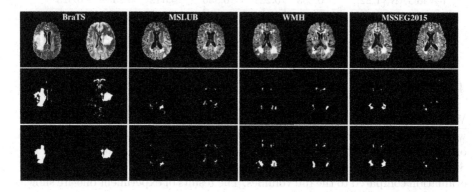

Fig. 3. Qualitative results of our baseline. Two samples are shown for each data set.
Top row: input image. Middle row: predicted anomaly map, binarized using the threshold that yields the best DSC for each data set. Bottom row: ground truth anomaly
segmentation.

We also present the quantitative results of the two experiment settings for all
data sets using all metrics in Table 4. In experiment one, our proposed method
performs best on the BraTS data set which has the largest anomalies, and worst
on MSLUB with the smallest anomalies. This can partly be attributed to our
post-processing where we discard connected components with less than 20 voxels.
Datasets with smaller anomalies are more affected by this. Also in experiment
two, BraTS is the data set with the highest ⌈DSC⌉ and AUPRC.

5   Discussion

The results in Sect. 4 show that a simple baseline can outperform or compete
with even the strongest related Machine Learning (ML) techniques. These findings challenge the effectiveness of current ML approaches for SAS. The results
of Baur *et al.* [4] also show that DSC does not correlate well with reconstruction quality. Especially, one can see in Fig. 4, that the best performing models
(VAE with restoration, dense GMVAE with restoration, and f-AnoGAN) produce very textureless reconstructions. They can detect the largest connected

Table 4. Full results of our proposed baseline on the two experimental settings. Experiment I: using slices 15 to 125 of the registered FLAIR images and a resolution of 128×128. Experiment II: using slices 84, 85, 86, and 87 of the registered FLAIR images and a resolution of 224×224.

	⌈DSC⌉	AUPRC	AUROC
Experiment I			
BraTS	0.666	0.671	0.988
MSLUB	0.374	0.278	0.991
WMH	0.457	0.339	0.979
MSSEG2015	0.431	0.262	0.996
Experiment II			
BraTS	0.738	0.762	0.985
MSLUB	0.613	0.571	0.993
WMH	0.557	0.504	0.984
MSSEG2015	0.593	0.536	0.996

anomaly located at the dorsal aspect of the right lateral ventricle (note that the images are oriented such that the patients' right ventricle is on the left side of the image) only because it is hyperintense in the input image. We refer to the original paper for a higher-resolution version of this figure. Hence, we hypothesize that the models in Baur et al. [4] do not perform anomaly segmentation by learning the normal anatomy of the data, but that the necessary information to perform anomaly segmentation with the performance presented in our work is already present in the input image. The quantitative evaluation of our experiments indicates that using the residual between the model output and the input image actually degrades the segmentation quality of the resulting anomaly map.

While we are aware that our baseline can only detect anomalies that are hyperintense, we argue that other techniques – especially those using residual maps between the input image and a reconstructed or restored version as anomaly maps – are not assumption-free, but also impose strong biases on the types of anomalies they can detect. For example, Alzheimer's disease, where one of the symptoms is atrophy of regions of the brain, cannot reliably be detected using pixel-wise residuals. Some of the existing works [4,20] leverage the same prior knowledge by considering only positive residuals as anomalies for MS lesions. However, our approach appears to make better use of this knowledge.

We point out that there exist anomaly segmentation methods like [23] that have shown to be able to detect anomalies that are not necessarily hyperintense. These methods, however, do not base their anomaly score on the reconstruction error but have other inductive biases. Van Hespen et al. [23] limit the receptive field of their model with the patch size used.

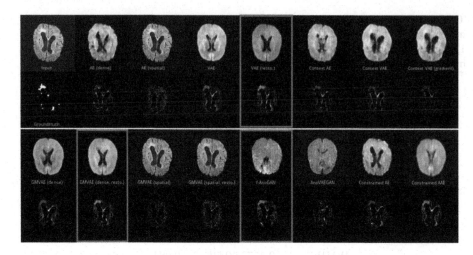

Fig. 4. Reconstructions (top row) and residuals (bottom row) of different ML-based SAS techniques. The best performing models are highlighted in red. Image from and best viewed in [4]. (Color figure online)

6   Conclusion

In this work, we advanced the current state-of-the-art in SAS of brain MRI by introducing a simple method that requires no learning. Our findings challenge the effectiveness of existing ML-based SAS approaches. While our work outperforms competing methods, the results still lack behind the ones of expert radiologists and supervised methods presented in [10,15] and [3]. This provides evidence for the need to explore alternative methods that overcome current limitations. These could include new scoring functions or multi-modal approaches. We also encourage the use of prior knowledge to build these models. While this seems counter-intuitive at first – given the promise of SAS being able to detect any kind of anomalies – we argue that current methods are also severely limited by their scoring functions in the types of anomalies they are theoretically able to detect. To this regard, we will explore the use of artificial anomalies in anomaly segmentation. We hypothesize that through careful creation and selection of artificial anomalies, models can generalize to real anomalies. Our work also highlights the requirement for a benchmark data set to better compare different techniques against each other. This benchmark should contain relevant real-world anomalies of brain MRI, but should also not be sufficiently solved via non-ML methods. Another disadvantage of the presented models is their limited spatial scope. Current SAS methods process the 2D slices of a 3D volume individually. We suspect that making better use of the 3D information of MRI will improve the anomaly detection performance of the models. We plan to explore the use of 3D machine learning models in future work as they can fully incorporate 3D information, while humans can only process volumes – such as MRI – slice-wise.

References

1. Atlason, H.E., Love, A., Sigurdsson, S., Gudnason, V., Ellingsen, L.M.: Unsupervised brain lesion segmentation from MRI using a convolutional autoencoder. In: Medical Imaging 2019: Image Processing, March 2019. https://doi.org/10.1117/12.2512953
2. Bakas, S., et al.: Advancing the cancer genome atlas glioma MRI collections with expert segmentation labels and radiomic features. Sci. Data **4**, 2052–4463 (2017). https://doi.org/10.1038/sdata.2017.117
3. Bakas, S., et al.: Identifying the best machine learning algorithms for brain tumor segmentation, progression assessment, and overall survival prediction in the BRATS challenge (2019)
4. Baur, C., Denner, S., Wiestler, B., Navab, N., Albarqouni, S.: Autoencoders for unsupervised anomaly segmentation in brain MR images: a comparative study. Med. Image Anal. **69**, 101952 (2021). https://doi.org/10.1016/j.media.2020.101952. https://www.sciencedirect.com/science/article/pii/S1361841520303169
5. Baur, C., Wiestler, B., Albarqouni, S., Navab, N.: Deep autoencoding models for unsupervised anomaly segmentation in brain MR images. In: Crimi, A., Bakas, S., Kuijf, H., Keyvan, F., Reyes, M., van Walsum, T. (eds.) BrainLes 2018. LNCS, vol. 11383, pp. 161–169. Springer, Cham (2019). https://doi.org/10.1007/978-3-030-11723-8_16
6. Baur, C., Wiestler, B., Albarqouni, S., Navab, N.: Bayesian skip-autoencoders for unsupervised hyperintense anomaly detection in high resolution brain MRI. In: 2020 IEEE 17th International Symposium on Biomedical Imaging (ISBI), pp. 1905–1909 (2020). https://doi.org/10.1109/ISBI45749.2020.9098686
7. Baur, C., Wiestler, B., Albarqouni, S., Navab, N.: Scale-space autoencoders for unsupervised anomaly segmentation in brain MRI. In: Martel, A.L., et al. (eds.) MICCAI 2020. LNCS, vol. 12264, pp. 552–561. Springer, Cham (2020). https://doi.org/10.1007/978-3-030-59719-1_54
8. Bergmann, P., Fauser, M., Sattlegger, D., Steger, C.: MVTec AD - a comprehensive real-world dataset for unsupervised anomaly detection. In: 2019 IEEE/CVF Conference on Computer Vision and Pattern Recognition (CVPR), pp. 9584–9592 (2019). https://doi.org/10.1109/CVPR.2019.00982
9. Bergmann, P., Löwe, S., Fauser, M., Sattlegger, D., Steger, C.: Improving unsupervised defect segmentation by applying structural similarity to autoencoders. In: Proceedings of the 14th International Joint Conference on Computer Vision, Imaging and Computer Graphics Theory and Applications (2019). https://doi.org/10.5220/0007364503720380
10. Carass, A., et al.: Longitudinal multiple sclerosis lesion segmentation: resource and challenge. NeuroImage **148**, 77–102 (2017). https://doi.org/10.1016/j.neuroimage.2016.12.064, https://www.sciencedirect.com/science/article/pii/S1053811916307819
11. Chen, X., Konukoglu, E.: Unsupervised detection of lesions in brain MRI using constrained adversarial auto-encoders. In: MIDL 2018 Conference book. MIDL, July 2018. https://doi.org/10.3929/ethz-b-000321650
12. Chen, X., You, S., Tezcan, K.C., Konukoglu, E.: Unsupervised lesion detection via image restoration with a normative prior. Med. Image Anal. **64**, 101713 (2020). https://doi.org/10.1016/j.media.2020.101713. https://www.sciencedirect.com/science/article/pii/S1361841520300773

13. Dehaene, D., Frigo, O., Combrexelle, S., Eline, P.: Iterative energy-based projection on a normal data manifold for anomaly localization. In: International Conference on Learning Representations (2020)
14. Iglesias, J.E., Liu, C.Y., Thompson, P.M., Tu, Z.: Robust brain extraction across datasets and comparison with publicly available methods. IEEE Trans. Med. Imaging **30**, 1617–1634 (2011). https://doi.org/10.1109/TMI.2011.2138152
15. Kuijf, H.J., et al.: Standardized assessment of automatic segmentation of white matter hyperintensities and results of the WMH segmentation challenge. IEEE Trans. Med. Imaging **38**(11), 2556–2568 (2019). https://doi.org/10.1109/tmi.2019.2905770
16. Lesjak, Ž, et al.: A novel public MR image dataset of multiple sclerosis patients with lesion segmentations based on multi-rater consensus. Neuroinformatics **16**(1), 51–63 (2017). https://doi.org/10.1007/s12021-017-9348-7
17. Liu, W., et al.: Towards visually explaining variational autoencoders. In: 2020 IEEE/CVF Conference on Computer Vision and Pattern Recognition (CVPR), pp. 8639–8648 (2020). https://doi.org/10.1109/CVPR42600.2020.00867
18. Menze, B.H., et al.: The multimodal brain tumor image segmentation benchmark (BRATS). IEEE Trans. Med. Imaging **34**(10), 1993–2024 (2015). https://doi.org/10.1109/TMI.2014.2377694
19. Pawlowski, N., et al.: Unsupervised lesion detection in brain CT using Bayesian convolutional autoencoders. In: MIDL 2018 Conference Book. MIDL, April 2018
20. Pinaya, W.H.L., et al.: Unsupervised brain anomaly detection and segmentation with transformers (2021)
21. Rohlfing, T., Zahr, N.M., Sullivan, E.V., Pfefferbaum, A.: The SRI24 multichannel atlas of normal adult human brain structure. Hum. Brain Mapp. **31**, 798–819 (2010). https://doi.org/10.1002/hbm.20906
22. Schlegl, T., Seeböck, P., Waldstein, S.M., Langs, G., Schmidt-Erfurth, U.: f-AnoGAN: fast unsupervised anomaly detection with generative adversarial networks. Med. Image Anal. **54**, 30–44 (2019). https://doi.org/10.1016/j.media.2019.01.010
23. vanHespen, K.M., Zwanenburg, J.J.M., Dankbaar, J.W., Geerlings, M.I., Hendrikse, J., Kuijf, H.J.: An anomaly detection approach to identify chronic brain infarcts on MRI. Sci. Rep. **11**, 7714 (2021). https://doi.org/10.1038/s41598-021-87013-4. https://doi.org/10.1038/s41598-021-87013-4
24. van der Walt, S., et al.: The scikit-image contributors: scikit-image: image processing in Python. PeerJ **2**, e453 (2014). https://doi.org/10.7717/peerj.453
25. Yi, J., Yoon, S.: Patch SVDD: patch-level SVDD for anomaly detection and segmentation. In: Proceedings of the Asian Conference on Computer Vision (ACCV), November 2020
26. Zimmerer, D., Isensee, F., Petersen, J., Kohl, S., Maier-Hein, K.: Unsupervised anomaly localization using variational auto-encoders. In: Shen, D., et al. (eds.) MICCAI 2019. LNCS, vol. 11767, pp. 289–297. Springer, Cham (2019). https://doi.org/10.1007/978-3-030-32251-9_32
27. Zimmerer, D., Petersen, J., Isensee, F., Maier-Hein, K.: Context-encoding variational autoencoder for unsupervised anomaly detection. In: International Conference on Medical Imaging with Deep Learning - Extended Abstract Track. London, United Kingdom, 08–10 July 2019

Small Lesion Segmentation in Brain MRIs with Subpixel Embedding

Alex Wong[1(✉)], Allison Chen[1], Yangchao Wu[1], Safa Cicek[1], Alexandre Tiard[1], Byung-Woo Hong[2], and Stefano Soatto[1]

[1] University of California, Los Angeles, CA, USA
alexw@cs.ucla.edu
[2] Chung-Ang University, Seoul, Korea

Abstract. We present a method to segment MRI scans of the human brain into ischemic stroke lesion and normal tissues. We propose a neural network architecture in the form of a standard encoder-decoder where predictions are guided by a spatial expansion embedding network. Our embedding network learns features that can resolve detailed structures in the brain without the need for high-resolution training images, which are often unavailable and expensive to acquire. Alternatively, the encoder-decoder learns global structures by means of striding and max pooling. Our embedding network complements the encoder-decoder architecture by guiding the decoder with fine-grained details lost to spatial down-sampling during the encoder stage. Unlike previous works, our decoder outputs at $2\times$ the input resolution, where a single pixel in the input resolution is predicted by four neighboring subpixels in our output. To obtain the output at the original scale, we propose a learnable down-sampler (as opposed to hand-crafted ones e.g. bilinear) that combines subpixel predictions. Our approach improves the baseline architecture by $\approx 11.7\%$ and achieves the state of the art on the ATLAS public benchmark dataset with a smaller memory footprint and faster runtime than the best competing method. Our source code has been made available at: https://github.com/alexklwong/subpixel-embedding-segmentation.

1 Introduction

A stroke occurs when a lack of blood flow prevents brain tissue from receiving adequate oxygen and nutrients. This condition affects over 795,000 people annually [28]. The severity of the outcome, including disability and paralysis, depends on the location and intensity of the stroke, as well as the time of diagnosis [2,30]. Preserving cognitive and motor functions, therefore, hinges on localizing stroke

---

A. Wong and A. Chen—Authors with equal contributions.

Supplementary Information The online version contains supplementary material available at https://doi.org/10.1007/978-3-031-08999-2_6.

A. Crimi and S. Bakas (Eds.): BrainLes 2021, LNCS 12962, pp. 75–87, 2022.
https://doi.org/10.1007/978-3-031-08999-2_6

lesions quickly and precisely. However, doing so manually requires expert knowledge, is time consuming, and is ultimately subjective [11,13].

We focus on automatically segmenting ischemic stroke lesions, which account for 87% of all strokes [28], from T1-weighted anatomical magnetic resonance imaging (MRI) brain scans. These lesions are characterized by high variability in location, shape, and size – the latter two are problematic for conventional convolutional neural networks (CNNs) where precision of irregularly shaped lesion boundaries and recall of small lesions are critical measures of success. Due to aggressive spatial downsampling (i.e. max pooling, strided convolutions) customary in CNNs, details of local structures are lost in the process. Yet, the spatial downsampling is necessary for obtaining a global representation of the input while using fixed-size filters with limited receptive fields. The outcome of which are segmentations with ambiguous boundaries between lesion and normal tissues and missed lesions that occupy small number of voxels in the MRIs.

We propose to retain small local structures by learning an embedding that maps the input to high dimensional feature maps of *twice* the input resolution. Unlike the typical CNN, we do not perform lossy downsampling on this representation; hence, the embedding preserves local structures, but lacks global context. When combined with the standard encoder-decoder e.g. U-Net [19], the embedding complements the encoder-decoder by supplying the decoder with fine-grained detail information to guide segmentation. Our network also outputs at twice the resolution of the input, representing each element in the input with a 2×2 neighborhood of predictions. The final output is obtained by combining the four predictions (akin to an ensemble) as a weighted sum where the contribution of each prediction is learned from the data. Our design not only enables the network to produce robust segmentations but also localize small lesions (Fig. 3).

Our contributions include (i) an embedding function that preserves fine-grained details of the input by mapping it to larger spatial dimensions, (ii) a neural network architecture that leverages the complementary strengths of the proposed embedding and an encoder-decoder to produce predictions at twice the input resolution, and (iii) a learnable downsampler that combines local predictions in an ensemble fashion to yield robust segmentations at the input resolution. Our approach improves the baseline U-Net architecture by $\approx 11.7\%$ and achieves the state of the art on the ATLAS [11,12] dataset with lower computational burden than the best competing method.

2   Related Work

Lesion Segmentation. Early works [4] aggregated classification results for the center pixel of patches sampled from an image. However, [4] lacked global context, so [21] addressed this with multi-stage cascaded hierarchical models. More recent works build upon the U-Net [19], a 2D fully-convolutional network with skip connections and up-convolutions. For example, [14] used a Dual Path Network [3] encoder while [26] leveraged dilated convolutions to inexpensively increase receptive fields. Furthermore, [1] fused the U-net with other high-performing modules, the BConvLSTM [24] and the SENet [8], and [18] introduced X-blocks to the U-Net, leveraging depthwise separable convolutions to reduce computational load. [31] used skip connections between successive encoder resolutions to prevent the loss of features and ConvLSTM [23] modules to maintain localization.

Recent works also leveraged 3D architectural backbones to improve localization. [32] performed 3D convolutions on a subsection of the scan and fused the results with 2D convolutions. [9] proposed an attention gate to combine 2D segmentations along the axial, sagittal, coronal planes into a 3D volume. However, these works use significantly larger memory footprints and 3D convolutions are computationally expensive – limiting the models' practicality. We note that while conventional architectures perform well globally (i.e. recovering the coarse shape of lesions) they struggle to segment small lesions that blend into the background.

Super-Resolution. There is an abundance of works in natural images super-resolution [5,6,22,25,29] and a growing number in medical imaging. [20] proposed to map MRI images from low to high-resolution with an overcomplete dictionary. [16] leveraged SRCNN [5] for super-resolving 2D MRI images and fused them to obtain a 3D volume. [17] handled arbitrary scaling factors with a 3D architecture for multi-modal 3D data. However, these works require low and high-resolution image pairs for training and are limited to the super-resolution task while our method does not rely on a larger resolution ground truth. More recently, [27] introduced Kite-Net, an upsampling encoder that outputs a latent at 8× resolution followed by a max-pooling decoder to downsample back to the original resolution. Kite-Net is used in parallel with a U-Net for lesion segmentation. Our approach draws inspiration from super resolution and latent over-representations as methods to retain local structure that are often lost in spatial downsampling. However, unlike [27], we avoid downsampling the latent with pooling (which discards information), and instead employ lossless space-to-depth and depth-to-space [22] operations to retain fine-grained details. Furthermore, we propose to learn a subpixel embedding at 2× the original resolution to guide our segmentation, which uses a much smaller memory footprint than [27]. We show that our approach can capture small lesions that are missed by [18,19,27,31,32].

3   Method

We propose a method to partition a 3D MRI volume $X \in \mathbb{R}^{C \times H \times W}$ into lesion (positive, 1) and normal (negative, 0) classes. Our method takes, as input, a 3D slice of c consecutive 2D images $x \in \mathbb{R}^{c \times H \times W}$ (c is an odd integer) from X and predicts the binary segmentation for the image $\bar{x} \in \mathbb{R}^{1 \times H \times W}$, the $\frac{c+1}{2}$-th image of x. In other words, x is a sliding window of c images centered at a target image $\bar{x}$. To avoid sampling out of bounds, we perform mean padding of size $\frac{c-1}{2} \times H \times W$ on both sides of X before sampling x (see Sec. 1 of Supp. Mat. for more details). To segment a single image $\bar{x}$, we propose to learn a deep

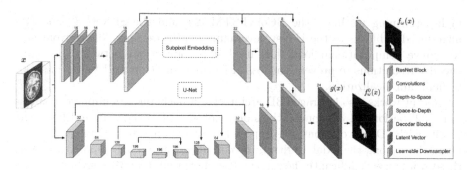

Fig. 1. *Network architecture.* SPiN is comprised of (i) a U-Net based encoder-decoder that produces subpixel predictions $f_\omega^0(x)$ at $2\times$ the input resolution, which are guided by (ii) a subpixel embedding that captures local structure. The final output $f_\omega(x)$ is achieved by combining local predictions in a 2×2 neighborhood as a weighted sum based on the per element contribution predicted by a (iii) learnable downsampler.

neural network f_ω, parameterized by ω, where $f : \mathbb{R}^{c \times H \times W} \mapsto [0,1]^{1 \times H \times W}$ is a function that takes the 3D slice x as an input and outputs the sigmoid response $f_\omega(x)$, a confidence map corresponding to lesions in $\bar{x}$. To obtain the binary segmentation of X, we aggregate our predictions by running f_ω for all x and setting any response greater than a threshold of 0.5 to the lesion class. We note that our method can be extended to multi-class segmentation simply by expanding our output to $[0,1]^{K \times H \times W}$ for K classes, and choosing the class with highest response, i.e. $\arg\max f_\omega(\cdot)$, to yield the segmentation.

3.1   Network Architecture

Our network f_ω (Fig. 1) is composed of two modules: (i) an encoder-decoder (based on U-Net [19]) that outputs at $2\times$ the input resolution, e.g. $2H \times 2W$, whose predictions are guided by (ii) a network that maps the input x to a high dimensional embedding space also at twice the input resolution. The result is a confidence map comprised of "subpixel" predictions – the output class for each input pixel is represented by four predictions within a 2×2 neighborhood. Rather than using hand-crafted downsampling techniques (e.g. bilinear, nearest neighbor) to obtain the output at the original ($1\times$) spatial resolution, we propose a learnable downsampler that predicts the weight, or contribution, of each subpixel prediction in a local region corresponding to the pixel in the $1\times$ resolution. For simplicity, we refer to our embedding function as a subpixel embedding and our overall architecture (f_ω) as a subpixel network or "SPiN" for short (Fig. 1).

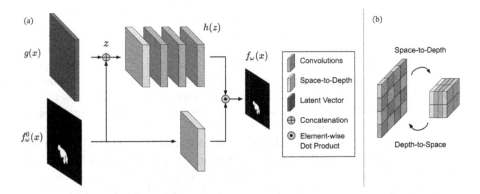

Fig. 2. *Learnable Downsampler, Space-to-Depth and Depth-to-Space.* (a): Learnable Downsampler predicts the contribution $h(z)$ of each subpixel prediction in $f_\omega^0(x)$ by conditioning on $f_\omega^0(x)$ and the latent vector $g(x)$. Subpixel predictions $f_\omega^0(x)$ are rearranged to the resolution of the input using Space-to-Depth. The final output $f_\omega(x)$ is produced by taking the element-wise dot product between $h(z)$ and the reshaped $f_\omega^0(x)$. (b) Space-to-Depth reduces resolution by rearranging elements from the spatial dimensions into the channel dimensions, where each 2×2 neighborhood is reshaped to a 4 element vector. Depth-to-Space conversely performs spatial expansion by rearranging elements from the channel dimensions to height and width dimensions.

Subpixel embedding consists of feature extraction and spatial expansion phases. Feature extraction is performed by two ResNet blocks [7] with 16 filters per layer; we also use stride of 1 and zero-padded edges to minimize spatial reduction. The extracted $16 \times H \times W$ feature maps are fed to a depth-to-space module [22] that rearranges elements from the channel dimension to the height and width dimensions (see Fig. 2-(b)). The resulting set of $4 \times 2H \times 2W$ feature maps with twice the spatial resolution then undergoes a 1×1 and a 3×3 convolution layers, with 8 filters each. The resulting $8 \times 2H \times 2W$ high dimensional feature maps, produced by our subpixel embedding function, resolve fine local details by increasing the feature map resolution and thus representing information at each pixel location with four "subpixel" feature vectors.

When used as skip connections, these embeddings complement the standard U-Net architecture that obtains a global representation of the input by spatial downsampling (striding and max pooling), which naturally discards local detail. Hence, we propose to inject these embeddings into the decoder via feature concatenation at the original ($1\times$) resolution and at the $2\times$ output resolution. To reduce the height and width dimensions of the embeddings to match the feature maps at the $1\times$ resolution, we propose a space-to-depth module, which performs the inverse operation of depth-to-space (see Fig. 2-(b)), yielding $32 \times H \times W$ feature maps. Unlike striding and pooling, the depth-to-space operation is information preserving as it rearranges feature vectors from the height and width dimensions to their channel dimension. The result is fed through a 3×3 convolutional layer with 8 filters and concatenated with the feature maps of the decoder at the $1\times$ resolution. Similarly, the embeddings at $2\times$ resolution undergo a separate 3×3 convolution to yield the output resolution guidance before being concatenated with their corresponding feature maps in the decoder. Finally, the $2\times$ decoder output $f_\omega^0(x) \in [0,1]^{1 \times 2H \times 2W}$ is produced by convolving a single 3×3 filter over the resulting latent vector $g(x) \in \mathbb{R}^{24 \times 2H \times 2W}$. We use subpixel guidance (SPG) to refer to the process of learning and injecting the embedding as skip connections, which substantially helps with localizing small lesions missed by previous works [18,19,31,32] (see Fig. 3). We note that SPG is light-weight and only uses 16K parameters.

Learnable downsampler takes the concatenation $z = [g(x); f_\omega^0(x)]$ of the latent vector $g(x)$ and the $2\times$ resolution output $f_\omega^0(x)$ and predicts $h(z)$, where $h : \mathbb{R}^{25 \times 2H \times 2W} \mapsto [0,1]^{4 \times H \times W}$. In other words, $h(z)$ is a set of $4 \times H \times W$ values that determine the contribution of each subpixel prediction in a 2×2 neighborhood of $f_\omega^0(x)$. To achieve this, we first perform space-to-depth on z to rearrange each 2×2 neighborhood into a 4 element vector. This is followed by two 3×3 convolutions of 16 filters and a 1×1 convolution with 4 filters. $h(z)$ is the softmax response of the result along the channel dimension.

To obtain the final output $f_\omega(x)$, we utilize space-to-depth to rearrange $f_\omega^0(x)$ into the shape of $4 \times H \times W$ (to match the shape of $h(z)$) and take its element-wise dot product with $h(z)$. With an abuse of notation, $f_\omega(x) = f_\omega^0(x) \cdot h(z)$. Because $h(z)$ is conditioned on the latent vector $g(x)$ of the input, the predicted weights respect lesion boundaries to yield detailed segmentations. This is unlike bilinear or nearest-neighbor downsampling where weights are predetermined and independent of the input. We note that our learnable downsampler is also lightweight and only consists of 11K parameters.

3.2 Loss Function

We assume a training set of $\{(x^{(n)}, \bar{y}^{(n)})\}_{n=1}^N$, where $\bar{y}^{(n)}$ is the ground truth corresponding to $\bar{x}^{(n)}$, the image located at the center of $x^{(n)}$. To train SPiN, we minimize the standard binary cross entropy loss,

$$\ell(y, \bar{y}) = \frac{1}{|\Omega|} \sum_{u \in \Omega} -\big(\bar{y}(u) \log y(u) + (1 - \bar{y}(u)) \log(1 - y(u))\big), \qquad (1)$$

where $\Omega \subset \mathbb{R}^2$ denotes the spatial image domain, u a pixel coordinate, and $y = f_\omega(x)$ the network output. The loss over the training set of N samples reads

$$L(\omega) = \frac{1}{N} \sum_{n=1}^N \ell(f_\omega(x^{(n)}), \bar{y}^{(n)})). \qquad (2)$$

We note that previous works [31,32] used soft Dice loss (an approximation of the true Dice score) to counter the class imbalance between normal and lesion tissues, characteristic in the lesion segmentation problem. However, a minimizer of cross entropy equivalently minimizes Dice, and empirically, we found that directly minimizing cross entropy yields better performance for our model. We

Table 1. *Evaluation metrics.* IOU denotes Intersection Over Union, and DSC denotes Dice similarity coefficient. TP, FN and FP correspond to true positive, false negative and false positive respectively.

Metric	IOU	DSC	Precision	Recall
Definition	$\frac{TP}{TP+FN+FP}$	$\frac{2\times TP}{2\times TP+FN+FP}$	$\frac{TP}{TP+FP}$	$\frac{TP}{TP+FN}$

hypothesize that our SPG allows small lesions to be recovered more easily, making our method more conducive to minimizing cross entropy, which is not prone to the noisy training signal inherent in soft Dice. We demonstrate this in row 7 of Table 4 in our ablation studies. Also, we note that our loss can be easily extended for multi-class classification to accommodate multiple lesion categories.

4   Experiments and Results

We demonstrate our method on the Anatomical Tracings of Lesion After Stroke (ATLAS) MRI dataset [11,12], using the metrics defined in Table 1. ATLAS contains 304 T1-weighted MRI scans of stroke patients with corresponding lesion annotations. The data is collected from 11 research sites worldwide, manually annotated, and post-processed (i.e. smoothing and defacing for privacy), leaving 239 patient scans with 189 2D images (197×233 resolution) each. Since no official data split is provided by [11], previous works [18,31,32] evaluated their methods using k-fold cross validation and randomly sampled data splits. However, the value of k and samples within each split varied across works. Due to the lack of consistency, the reported results are not directly comparable. Thus, we propose a training (212 patients) and a held-out testing (27 patients) split to standardize the evaluation protocol for more rigorous comparisons. We provide quantitative comparisons against [18,19,27,31,32] on the proposed training and testing split in Table 2. We also show qualitative (Fig. 3) and quantitative (Table 3) comparisons on segmenting small lesions using a subset of test set: 490 images containing *only* lesions smaller than 100 pixels (0.2% of the image). All reported results for previous works are obtained using their training procedures and open-sourced code. We also provide details on our training and testing split in Sec. 2 of Supp. Mat. and further k-fold cross validation comparisons in Sec. 3 of Supp. Mat.

Implementation Details. Our model is implemented in PyTorch [15] and optimized using Adam [10]. We used an initial learning rate of 3×10^{-4}, decreased it to 1×10^{-4} after 400 epochs, and to 5×10^{-5} after 1400 epochs for a total of 1600 epochs. We choose $c = 5$ for the number images in the input x. During training, $\bar{x}$ and its corresponding x are randomly sampled from X. Training takes ≈ 8 h on an Nvidia GTX 1080 GPU, and inference takes ≈ 11 ms per 2D image. For data augmentation, we randomly perform (i) horizontal and vertical flips, (ii) rotation between $-30°$ and $30°$, and (iii) add zero-mean Gaussian noise with

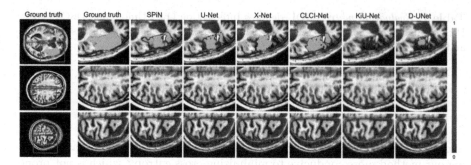

Fig. 3. *Qualitative results on ATLAS.* Columns 2–8 show (zoomed in) head-to-head comparisons across all methods for highlighted areas in column 1. Row 1 demonstrates that SPiNoutperforms existing works in capturing shape and boundary details in medium-sized, irregularly-shaped lesions. Furthermore, rows 2 and 3 demonstrate SPiN's ability to localize small lesions that are missed by other models.

Table 2. *Quantitative comparison on ATLAS.* SPiNoutperforms all methods across all performance metrics. It is also one of the least computationally expensive models, i.e. smallest test time memory footprint, second in training memory usage, and third fastest in runtime per patient (189 images).

Method	Performance metrics				Runtime (s)	Memory usage (GB)	
	DSC	IOU	Precision	Recall		Train	Test
U-Net [19]	0.584	0.432	0.674	0.558	1.375	2.291	1.181
D-UNet [32]	0.548	0.404	0.652	0.521	3.425	15.426	15.426
CLCI-Net [31]	0.599	0.469	0.741	0.536	8.860	7.853	7.853
KiU-Net [27]	0.524	0.387	0.703	0.459	1.05	23.566	1.555
X-Net [18]	0.639	0.495	0.746	0.588	5.046	11.839	11.839
SPiN(Ours)	**0.703**	**0.556**	**0.806**	**0.654**	2.145	3.273	0.803

standard deviation of 1×10^{-2} to training samples. We perform augmentation with a probability of 1 for 1400 epochs and decrease it to 0.5 thereafter so training samples will be closer to the true distribution of the dataset.

ATLAS Test Set. Table 2 shows that our approach outperforms competing methods [18,19,27,31,32] across all evaluation metrics. Specifically, we beat the best performing method X-Net [18] by an average of ≈10.4% with a 72.3% reduction in training memory and a 57.5% runtime reduction during inference. Our approach also uses a smaller memory footprint, containing only ≈5.3M parameters, compared to ≈15M in [18]. Another key comparison is with KiU-Net, which learns a representation at 8× the original input spatial resolution. Unlike us, KiU-Net [27] uses max pooling layers, which discards information, to reduce the size of their high resolution representation to the original (1×) resolution. Whereas, we maintain the 2× resolution of our embedding until the output layer, which yields subpixel predictions that are aggregated by our learnable downsam-

Table 3. *Evaluation on small lesion subset.* While [31] achieves the highest precision, we note they have the second lowest recall out of all methods – missing small lesions can negatively impact patient recovery. In contrast, our method ranks second in precision and first across all other metrics.

Method	DSC	IOU	Precision	Recall
U-Net [19]	0.368	0.225	0.440	0.316
D-UNet [32]	0.265	0.180	0.377	0.264
CLCI-Net [31]	0.246	0.178	**0.662**	0.215
KiU-Net [27]	0.246	0.255	0.466	0.206
X-Net [18]	0.306	0.213	0.546	0.268
SPiN(Ours)	**0.424**	**0.269**	0.546	**0.347**

Table 4. *Ablation study on ATLAS.* Removing ṢPG and/or LD results in performance decrease (rows 1, 2, 6), and SPG cannot be substituted with more parameters or interpolation (rows 3–5). The best results are achieved by our full model (row 8).

Method	DSC	IOU	Precision	Recall
Without SPG, LD (Baseline)	0.634	0.487	0.707	0.606
Without SPG	0.637	0.487	0.701	0.613
Replace SPG with addit. convolutions	0.627	0.475	0.721	0.596
Replace SPG w/bilinear upsampling	0.663	0.513	0.780	0.600
Replace SPG w/nearest upsampling	0.660	0.513	0.762	0.626
Replace LD with downsampling	0.670	0.526	0.786	0.625
Full model with soft Dice loss	0.684	0.546	0.729	0.672
Full model	**0.703**	**0.556**	**0.806**	**0.654**

pler to the 1× resolution. Admittedly, this comes at the cost of runtime – our method requires 2.145 s per patient and KiU-Net [27] requires 1.05 s. However, we outperform [27] by an average of 33.7% across all metrics and reduce test time memory by half. We show qualitative comparisons in row 1 of Fig. 3 where the segmentation produced by our approach better captures irregularly shaped lesions than those predicted by competing methods.

Small Lesion Segmentation. Here, we consider the task of segmenting lesions that occupy fewer than 100 pixels or 0.2% of the image. Due to the challenging nature of the task, we observe an expected drop in performance across all methods (trained on the proposed split) when segmenting small lesions (Table 3), as compared to doing so for all lesion sizes (Table 2). However, we still outperform all competing methods – by even larger margins than on the full test set. This shows that competing methods, while able to localize large and medium sized lesions, actually perform poorly on small lesions. With the exception of precision, where we tie for second with X-Net [18], we rank first in all other metrics. We note that while CLCI-Net [31] has the highest precision, it also achieved second lowest recall, meaning that it misses many small lesions, which is critical to clinical prognosis and thus patient recovery. This is also reflected in DSC and IOU where we outperform [31] by 72% and 51%, respectively. Qualitatively, rows 2 and 3 in Fig. 3 show that our method successfully localized small lesions that [18, 19, 27, 31, 32] missed entirely.

Ablation Studies. Table 4 shows the effect of each of our contributions to architectural design. Row 1 shows that our baseline, a U-Net [19] based encoder-decoder, performs significantly worse by 11.7% than the proposed approach because it lacks fine local details from SPG and uses bilinear downsampling instead of a learnable downsampler (LD). Including LD alone, but not SPG (row 2) provides no improvement as the network only learns a coarse global representation, but is still missing details lost during spatial downsampling.

In row 3, we show that solely increasing parameters (i.e. adding ResNet blocks [7] to the baseline) brings no improvement, which suggests that the performance boost is *not* a result of a larger network. In fact, SPG and the learnable downsampler marginally increase the model size as they only combine for 27K parameters. Rows 4 and 5 show that using hand-crafted 2× resolution images (from bilinear, nearest neighbor upsampling) does provide some gain. In these experiments, we replace SPG with different interpolation methods and the higher resolution images undergo 3 × 3 convolutions before being passed as skip connections to the decoder. However, because the 2× representation is not learned, as it is with SPG, the result is still ≈6% worse than our full model. Our learnable downsampler (LD) contributes 4.4% to our performance (row 6) as removing LD and replacing it with bilinear interpolation smooths lesion boundaries, resulting in loss of details. Finally, we justify the use of cross entropy for our loss function; row 7 demonstrates that minimizing a soft Dice loss, as in [31, 32], results in worse performance. The best performance is achieved with our full model using SPG and LD, and minimizing cross entropy (row 8).

5   Discussion

We propose SPiN, a network architecture that learns a spatially increasing embedding that, when used as guidance for an encoder-decoder network, helps ensure that small structures are not lost through spatial downsampling in the encoder. We note that our embedding does not create extra spatial information (data processing inequality), but serves as a means for better characterization of local regions for the downstream segmentation task. While we outperform existing works and improve on small lesion segmentation, we do cost more memory and compute than the baseline. However, the extra cost is within reason (1 GB of memory for training and ≈ 0.7 s in runtime) and does not limit applicability. Despite the improved segmentation performance, we would like to address that there is still room for improvement, especially with small lesions. The highest recall of 0.347 achieved by our model is admittedly low compared to recall metrics on the full dataset, implying that many small lesions still pass undetected. We note that this is one of the first works to study subpixel architectures in lesion segmentation, and we hope our optimistic results will motivate further exploration in this direction.

Acknowledgements. This work was supported by NIH-NEI 5R01EY029689 and R01EY030595, ARO W911NF-17-1-0304, NRF-2017R1A2B4006023 and IITP-2021-0-01341, AI Graduate School (CAU) in Korea.

References

1. Asadi-Aghbolaghi, M., Azad, R., Fathy, M., Escalera, S.: Multi-level context gating of embedded collective knowledge for medical image segmentation. arXiv preprint arXiv:2003.05056 (2020)
2. Atlantis, T., et al.: Association of outcome with early stroke treatment: pooled analysis of atlantis, ecass, and ninds rt-pa stroke trials. Lancet **363**(9411), 768–774 (2004)
3. Chen, Y., Li, J., Xiao, H., Jin, X., Yan, S., Feng, J.: Dual path networks. arXiv preprint arXiv:1707.01629 (2017)
4. Ciresan, D., Giusti, A., Gambardella, L., Schmidhuber, J.: Deep neural networks segment neuronal membranes in electron microscopy images. Adv. Neural. Inf. Process. Syst. **25**, 2843–2851 (2012)
5. Dong, C., Loy, C.C., He, K., Tang, X.: Learning a deep convolutional network for image super-resolution. In: Fleet, D., Pajdla, T., Schiele, B., Tuytelaars, T. (eds.) ECCV 2014. LNCS, vol. 8692, pp. 184–199. Springer, Cham (2014). https://doi.org/10.1007/978-3-319-10593-2_13
6. Dong, C., Loy, C.C., He, K., Tang, X.: Image super-resolution using deep convolutional networks. IEEE Trans. Pattern Anal. Mach. Intell. **38**(2), 295–307 (2015)
7. He, K., Zhang, X., Ren, S., Sun, J.: Deep residual learning for image recognition. In: Proceedings of the IEEE Conference on Computer Vision and Pattern Recognition, pp. 770–778 (2016)
8. Hu, J., Shen, L., Sun, G.: Squeeze-and-excitation networks. In: Proceedings of the IEEE Conference on Computer Vision and Pattern Recognition, pp. 7132–7141 (2018)
9. Hui, H., Zhang, X., Li, F., Mei, X., Guo, Y.: A partitioning-stacking prediction fusion network based on an improved attention u-net for stroke lesion segmentation. IEEE Access **8**, 47419–47432 (2020)
10. Kingma, D.P., Ba, J.L.: Adam: a method for stochastic gradient descent. In: ICLR: International Conference on Learning Representations, pp. 1–15 (2015)
11. Liew, S.L., et al.: A large, open source dataset of stroke anatomical brain images and manual lesion segmentations. Sci. Data **5**, 180011 (2018)
12. Liew, S.L., et al.: The anatomical tracings of lesions after stroke (atlas) dataset-release 1.1. bioRxiv, p. 179614 (2017)
13. Maier, O., et al.: Isles 2015 - a public evaluation benchmark for ischemic stroke lesion segmentation from multispectral MRI. Med. Image Anal. **35**, 250–269 (2017)
14. Manvel, A., Vladimir, K., Alexander, T., Dmitry, U.: Radiologist-level stroke classification on non-contrast CT scans with deep U-net. In: Shen, D., et al. (eds.) MICCAI 2019. LNCS, vol. 11766, pp. 820–828. Springer, Cham (2019). https://doi.org/10.1007/978-3-030-32248-9_91

15. Paszke, A., et al.: Pytorch: an imperative style, high-performance deep learning library. Adv. Neural. Inf. Process. Syst. **32**, 8026–8037 (2019)
16. Pham, C.H., Ducournau, A., Fablet, R., Rousseau, F.: Brain MRI super-resolution using deep 3D convolutional networks. In: 2017 IEEE 14th International Symposium on Biomedical Imaging (ISBI 2017), pp. 197–200. IEEE (2017)
17. Pham, C.H., et al.: Multiscale brain MRI super-resolution using deep 3D convolutional networks. Comput. Med. Imaging Graph. **77**, 101647 (2019)
18. Qi, K., et al.: X-net: brain stroke lesion segmentation based on depthwise separable convolution and long-range dependencies. In: Shen, D., et al. (eds.) X-net: brain stroke lesion segmentation based on depthwise separable convolution and long-range dependencies. LNCS, vol. 11766, pp. 247–255. Springer, Cham (2019). https://doi.org/10.1007/978-3-030-32248-9_28
19. Ronneberger, O., Fischer, P., Brox, T.: U-net: convolutional networks for biomedical image segmentation. In: Navab, N., Hornegger, J., Wells, W.M., Frangi, A.F. (eds.) MICCAI 2015. LNCS, vol. 9351, pp. 234–241. Springer, Cham (2015). https://doi.org/10.1007/978-3-319-24574-4_28
20. Rueda, A., Malpica, N., Romero, E.: Single-image super-resolution of brain MR images using overcomplete dictionaries. Med. Image Anal. **17**(1), 113–132 (2013)
21. Seyedhosseini, M., Sajjadi, M., Tasdizen, T.: Image segmentation with cascaded hierarchical models and logistic disjunctive normal networks. In: Proceedings of the IEEE International Conference on Computer Vision (ICCV), December 2013
22. Shi, W., et al.: Real-time single image and video super-resolution using an efficient sub-pixel convolutional neural network. In: Proceedings of the IEEE Conference on Computer Vision and Pattern Recognition, pp. 1874–1883 (2016)
23. Shi, X., Chen, Z., Wang, H., Yeung, D.Y., Wong, W.K., Woo, W.C.: Convolutional LSTM network: a machine learning approach for precipitation nowcasting. In: Advances in Neural Information Processing Systems, vol. 28, pp. 802–810 (2015)
24. Song, H., Wang, W., Zhao, S., Shen, J., Lam, K.M.: Pyramid dilated deeper ConvLSTM for video salient object detection. In: Proceedings of the European Conference on Computer Vision (ECCV), pp. 715–731 (2018)
25. Tang, Z., Pan, B., Liu, E., Xu, X., Shi, T., Shi, Z.: SRDA-net: super-resolution domain adaptation networks for semantic segmentation. arXiv preprint arXiv:2005.06382 (2020)
26. Tureckova, A., Rodríguez-Sánchez, A.J.: ISLES challenge: U-shaped convolution neural network with dilated convolution for 3D stroke lesion segmentation. In: Crimi, A., Bakas, S., Kuijf, H., Keyvan, F., Reyes, M., van Walsum, T. (eds.) BrainLes 2018. LNCS, vol. 11383, pp. 319–327. Springer, Cham (2019). https://doi.org/10.1007/978-3-030-11723-8_32
27. Valanarasu, J.M.J., Sindagi, V.A., Hacihaliloglu, I., Patel, V.M.: KiU-net: towards accurate segmentation of biomedical images using over-complete representations. In: Martel, A.L., et al. (eds.) MICCAI 2020. LNCS, vol. 12264, pp. 363–373. Springer, Cham (2020). https://doi.org/10.1007/978-3-030-59719-1_36
28. Virani, S.S., et al.: Heart disease and stroke statistics-2020 update: a report from the American heart association. Circulation **141**(9), e139–e596 (2020)
29. Wang, L., Li, D., Zhu, Y., Tian, L., Shan, Y.: Dual super-resolution learning for semantic segmentation. In: Proceedings of the IEEE/CVF Conference on Computer Vision and Pattern Recognition, pp. 3774–3783 (2020)
30. Chan, B.P., Albers, G.W.: Acute ischemic stroke. Curr. Treat. Options. Neurol. **1**(2), 83–95 (1999). https://doi.org/10.1007/s11940-999-0009-5

31. Yang, H., et al.: CLCI-net: cross-level fusion and context inference networks for lesion segmentation of chronic stroke. In: Shen, D., et al. (eds.) MICCAI 2019. LNCS, vol. 11766, pp. 266–274. Springer, Cham (2019). https://doi.org/10.1007/978-3-030-32248-9_30

32. Zhou, Y., Huang, W., Dong, P., Xia, Y., Wang, S.: D-Unet: a dimension-fusion u shape network for chronic stroke lesion segmentation. IEEE/ACM Trans. Comput. Biol. Bioinform. (2019)

Unsupervised Multimodal Supervoxel Merging Towards Brain Tumor Segmentation

Guillaume Pelluet[1,2]([✉]) [ID], Mira Rizkallah[1] [ID], Oscar Acosta[3] [ID],
and Diana Mateus[1] [ID]

[1] Nantes Université, École Centrale Nantes, CNRS, LS2N, UMR 6004, F-44000
Nantes, France
[2] Hera-MI, SAS, Nantes, France
guillaume.pelluet@hera-mi.com
[3] Université de Rennes 1, LTSI, UMR, 1099 Rennes, France

Abstract. Automated brain tumor segmentation is challenging given the tumor's variability in size, shape, and image intensity. This paper focuses on the fusion of multimodal information coming from different Magnetic Resonance (MR) imaging sequences. We argue it is important to exploit all the modality complementarity to better segment and later determine the aggressiveness of tumors. However, simply concatenating the multimodal data as channels of a single image generates a high volume of redundant information. Therefore, we propose a supervoxel-based approach that regroups pixels sharing perceptually similar information across the different modalities to produce a single coherent oversegmentation. To further reduce redundant information while keeping meaningful borders, we include a variance constraint and a supervoxel merging step. Our experimental validation shows that the proposed merging strategy produces high-quality clustering results useful for brain tumor segmentation. Indeed, our method reaches an ASA score of 0.712 compared to 0.316 for the monomodal approach, indicating that the supervoxels accommodate well tumor boundaries. Our approach also improves by 11.5% the Global Score (GS), showing clusters effectively group pixels similar in intensity and texture.

Keywords: Brain tumor · Supervoxel · Merging · Graph · Clustering

1 Introduction

Identifying the edges of brain tumors and observing their evolution is critical to accurately assess disease progression and thus better guide the patient's treatment plan [9].

There is a multiplicity of brain imaging techniques, starting from the different Magnetic Resonance Imaging (MRI) sequences, providing complementary information about brain tumors. However, multi-modality makes tumor segmentation, i.e., delineating the tumor's edges and quantifying the tumor's size, more complex. Commonly used sequences include T1, T2, FLAIR, and T1-weighted contrast-enhanced (T1CE). The visibility of glioma in the various sequences (modalities) is different. In the T1CE image, regions of the brain are similar to the tumor Edema region. In the T1CE, the active and necrotic regions of a tumor can be clearly distinguished. The intensities of edema and tumor regions are higher in the T2 sequence images and the FLAIR images, whereas the intensities of CerebroSpinal Fluid (CSF) are higher in the T2 and lower in FLAIR images. To sum up, one modality can present weak tumor edges but strong tumor features, while another may have strong edges but weak features. Many of the existing algorithms for brain tumor analysis focus on a single modality (e.g., a specific MRI sequence), limiting the available information to be exploited for segmentation.

Conversely, multimodal information can make the delineation and quantification more accurate, thanks to the modalities' complementarity. However, simultaneous processing different MRI sequences comprised of millions of voxels induces a significant increase in computational time. To tackle this problem, we propose to oversegment the original sequences with the idea to process supervoxels with similar information instead of the individual pixels. The concept of superpixel was originally introduced in [1] as a small homogeneous group of neighboring pixels. Hereafter, we refer to a supervoxel as an extension of a superpixel in the 3-D multi-modal setting.

We propose a two-stage unsupervised supervoxel-based approach. The first stage, performs an over-segmentation of the multimodal image with a supervoxel approach that approximates the boundaries of tumors and other objects in the multimodal image. The supervoxels are computed using an adaptation of the Scalable Simple Linear Iterative Clustering (SSLIC) algorithm [13]. Our adaption adds on a local regularity coefficient based on the variance [6] within the SSLIC algorithm. The coefficient increases the spatial constraint for supervoxels having high-intensity variances, and reduces it in areas with lower variances. Thereby, it allows supervoxel boundaries to capture perceptible objects with limited intensity variations. The second stage fuses multimodal supervoxels with a merging algorithm inspired by Fu et al. [5] to reduce the supervoxels' redundancy and their number prior to any classification task.

We evaluated our method on the publicly available multimodal BraTS 2020 dataset, which is a standard brain tumor segmentation benchmark [16]. Experiments show that the proposed merging produces highly accurate clusters compared to traditional monomodal approaches, thanks to the complementarity between modalities. We also demonstrate that using the local regularity coefficient allows generating more regular clusters on textures, better guiding the merging procedure. In the resulting segmentation after merging, the redundancy is reduced by a factor of 35 and the obtained supervoxels adhere very well to tumors boundaries.

2   Related Work

Brain tumor and lesion segmentation is often formulated as a pixel-wise semantic segmentation problem addressed with supervised learning approaches [4]. Among them, Convolutional Neural Networks (CNNs) have emerged as the current best-performing methods [15] taking different forms: 2D CCNs [2,18], 3D CNNs [3], or extended to Fully convolutional [12] or multimodal approaches [23]. Despite their good performance, pixel-wise methods suffer from high computational complexity due to the significant number of redundant pixels, particularly when dealing with multimodal images. This complexity affects both classical and learning-based algorithms. In the case of CNNs, multimodal images may require higher capacity networks, prone to overfitting if the training dataset is small. In this work, we take a step aside from pixel-wise semantic segmentation and focus on the unsupervised early fusion of multimodal information.

Compared to pixels, superpixels are more consistent with human visual cognition, contain less redundancy, and reduce noise. Superpixels generally allow to significantly improve the speed compared to pixel-based algorithms by analyzing pixels clusters [7]. These properties are useful for computationally expensive tasks, such as brain tumor segmentation in multi-sequence MRI images. Most superpixel-based algorithms cluster the image into a high number of redundant superpixels (called oversegmentation) by adding cuts to a graph or growing from predefined seeds [24]. Superpixel methods combined with conventional machine learning approaches have been used for brain tumor segmentation, demonstrating to be fast and robust to noise, initialization, and intensity non-uniformity [10,20]. However, these approaches neglect multimodal information in the superpixel step. Ignoring multimodality leads to of lack of adherence with weak boundaries, as noticed by Wang et al. [25]. Therefore, we opt for combining multimodal acquisitions, taking advantage of the complementary information to detect more detailed tumors structures and better adhere to borders.

Regarding other multimodal methods for brain tumor segmentation, Rahimpour et al. [19] compare early and late CNN fusion, favoring late fusion as it does not need an initial registration step. In our work, we opt for an early but unsupervised fusion which assumes pre-registered modalities. Soltaninejad et al. [22] also proposed an early multimodal fusion approach to produce supervoxel boundaries across multiple MR sequences, enforcing adherence to weak structures boundaries. However, similar to the monomodal case, the algorithm results in a large number of redundant superpixels, which unnecessarily increases computation time and can lead to a higher false-positive rate. For this reason, we propose two contributions to reduce supervoxels redundancy in the multimodal case. First, a variance constraint inspired by the work of Giraud et al. [6], proposed in the context of natural images to better account for textured regions; and second, a supervoxel merging step.

Outside the brain tumor segmentation literature, there has been interest in superpixel and supervoxel merging approaches. Luengo et al. [14] proposed a method that achieves high segmentation performance while reducing the number of redundant superpixels in the image, based on an iterative splitting and merg-

ing algorithm. Focusing on the scale, Fu *et al.* [5] introduced a multiscale approach for superpixel merging in the RGB color space. The method uses multiple
features to calculate a dissimilarity score between pairs of superpixels, including
color, texture, and common border length. Moreover, it simplifies the merging
graph to accelerate the merging procedure. For these two reasons, which are
relevant in our multimodal MRI case, we rely on Fu's multiscale approach for
supervoxel merging. Our experimental validation shows qualitatively and quantitatively the pertinence of our two contributions: the variance constraint and
the merging approach. Our approach combining multimodal supervoxels, the
variance constraint, and the merging step, improves tumor boundary adherence
and significantly reduces supervoxel redundancy.

3   Methods

Let multiple images of the same anatomy be acquired with different modalities
and then registered to form the multimodal image $\mathbb{I} = [I_1, I_2, \ldots, I_M]$. $\mathbb{I}$ is a 3-D
volume whose every voxel contains an M-dimensional vector. Our goal is to find a
single partition S of non-overlapping supervoxels S_i, such that, $S = \bigcup\limits_{i=1}^{n} S_i$ taking
into account intensities and borders in all modalities. To this end, we propose a
two-steps method. First, an initial oversegmentation is performed with the SSLIC
algorithm [13], refined with a variance constraint to better model the texture.
As a result we obtain an initial supervoxel clustering (See Sect. 3.1). However,
the oversegmentation can lead to a substantial number of supervoxels even for
a small tumor. This creates a burden for later tasks, such as classification. To
reduce the final number of supervoxels, a second step is necessary. Inspired by
the work of Fu *et al.* [5], we construct a graph $\mathcal{G}$ over the oversegmentation and
merge similar vertices to obtain a more meaningful segmentation (See Sect. 3.2).

3.1   Oversegmentation Based on Supervoxels

Supervoxels are irregular image blocks composed of adjacent voxels with similar texture, intensity, and brightness features. Currently, there are two common
types of supervoxel segmentation algorithms. The first one is based on graph
theory and the second on Gradient Ascent. To the later category belongs the
well-known Simple Linear Iterative Clustering (SLIC) approach [1] and its ITK
version [8]. We rely on SSLIC with multimodal features [13] to obtain a first oversegmentation of the image. By multimodal features we mean that each voxel is
characterized by an M-dimensional vector containing the intensities for that pixel
across all modalities. First, an initial clustering is given and then the clustering
is improved iteratively until convergence (refer to [13] for details).

   We propose an adaption of the SSLIC algorithm ($SSLIC_{Var}$), that modu-
lates the supervoxel compactness according to the supervoxels feature variance.
Initially introduced by Giraud *et al.* [6] in the context of natural imaging in
2D, we bring this constraint to the medical image analysis field, extending it

for the M-dimensional case. The standard SSLIC framework [13] only requires
the number of superpixels and a single parameter m. In our adapted version,
each supervoxel S_i has a different parameter m_i setting its shape regularity
(i.e. compactness). This parameter is computed according to the mean feature
(luminance in our case) variance per supervoxel across modalities:

$$m_i = m * \exp \left(\frac{\sigma_i^2(F_{\text{mod}})}{\epsilon} \right) \qquad (1)$$

where $\sigma_i^2(F_{\text{mod}})$ is the luminance variance within the supervoxel S_i in a modality,
$\bar{\cdot}$ is the mean operator and ϵ is a scaling parameter. At the output of this step,
we have an oversegmentation of our 3D multimodal volume $\mathbb{I}$.

3.2   Supervoxels Merging

The oversegmentation produced by the supervoxel-based method already reduces
some redundant information. However, the SSLIC approach is sensitive to the
seeds initialization, which constraints the final number of clusters. Flat objects
in the image, such as tumors exhibiting low texture and small intensity variation,
are still composed of redundant supervoxels. With the aim of further reducing
the redundancy, we use a method inspired from the work of Fu $et~al.$ [5] and
apply it in the context of multimodal MRI. The oversegmentation is transformed
into a Region Adjacency Graph (RAG) $\mathcal{G} = \{\mathcal{V}, \mathcal{E}\}$, with the set of vertices $\mathcal{V} = \{v_1, v_2, ..., v_n\}$ and n the number of supervoxels. Edges $\mathcal{E}$ represent connections
between adjacent supervoxels and their weights denote the dissimilarity based
on the intensity and texture features. The dissimilarity of two supervoxels i and
j, named $w_{i,j}$, is defined as Eq. 2.

$$w_{i,j} = \exp \left(- \frac{\left(\frac{\alpha \cdot D_c(i,j) + \beta \cdot D_t(i,j)}{\alpha + \beta} \right)^2}{\gamma} \right), \qquad (2)$$

where $D_c(i,j)$ and $D_t(i,j)$ are the intensity and texture dissimilarities, α and
β their respective adjustable weights, and γ governs how close to each other
features are. More specifically,

$$D_c(i,j) = \sqrt{\sum_{\text{mod}=1}^{M} \Delta Y_{\text{mod}}(i,j)}, \qquad (3)$$

where $\Delta Y_{\text{mod}}(i,j) = (Y_{\text{mod}}^i - Y_{\text{mod}}^j)^2$ and $Y_{\text{mod}}^i, Y_{\text{mod}}^j$ are the average luminance
values in the ith and j^{th} supervoxels respectively. $D_t(i,j)$ is the texture dissim-
ilarity computed in [5] as :

$$D_t(i,j) = \sqrt{\sum_{\text{mod}=1}^{M} \Delta H_{\text{mod}}(i,j)}, \qquad (4)$$

where $\Delta H_{\mathrm{mod}}(i,j)$ is the Manhattan distance between the histograms of super-voxels i and j as in [5]. The distance measures were normalized in a range of $[0;1]$ to be efficiently combined. Some brain tissues, as is the case of tumors, have lower textures and high intensity, which can result in an imbalance between intensity and texture features. Because of these complex cases, the adjustable weights from Eq. 2 were manually adjusted to better split the dissimilarity between nor-mal and tumor tissues as defined in Sect. 4.3. Once the dissimilarity measures over supervoxels and graph weights are computed, the supervoxel merging algo-rithm takes place to reduce information redundancy and achieve finer clustering. However, the Region Adjacency Graph (RAG) connects each supervoxel to all its neighbors. So, it is very computationally expensive to directly start merging the nodes with high similarity since the number of edges and nodes is still too large. To accelerate the merging process, a Nearest Neighbor Graph (NNG) [17] is determined based on the RAG. The NNG efficiently determines paired super-voxels that are the most similar. Here, the NNG is calculated using the Kruskal algorithm [11], which significantly reduces the number of edges and overall the search space, allowing for a more computationally efficient merging. The merg-ing algorithm is iteratively computed until no edges in the NNG have weights inferior to a given threshold $\mathcal{T}$ which is defined as in Eq. 5:

$$\mathcal{T} = \frac{\sum_j (\min e_j - \sigma(e_j))}{n}, \tag{5}$$

with e_j one of the edges connected to supervoxel i, that is, $e_j \in \{w_{ij}\}$, $j \in \mathcal{N}_i$ and σ denotes the standard deviation.

4 Experiments

4.1 Experimental Setup

Experiments are performed on the publicly available multimodal BraTS 2020 dataset, which is a standard brain tumor segmentation benchmark [16]. The dataset is composed of real brain MRI exams including T1, T1CE, T2, and FLAIR sequences, acquired from 19 institutions for 369 subjects. The ground truth is provided for each exam in form of contours manually delineated by experts. Three tumor subregions were annotated: contrast-enhancing tumor, non-enhancing/necrosis combined, and edema. Images are 3D volumes with a size of $[155 \times 240 \times 240]$ (DxWxH) and an isotropic resolution of 1 mm. The sequences from the dataset are co-registered to the same anatomical shape and skull-stripped by the BraTS maintainer. Images are cropped to remove the background area at the edges and normalized independently for each modal-ity between $[0;1]$.

4.2 Quality Assessment Methods

We use several reference (using ground-truth) and no-reference segmentation assessment metrics to evaluate the performance of the proposed unsupervised segmentation method in delineating tumor tissues and keeping meaningful voxels disparities. The Achievable Segmentation Accuracy (ASA) score is computed in the tumor's region to assess the accuracy of the supervoxels boundaries with respect to the ground truth. The wVar and Moran' Index (MI) quantify respectively the disparity within and between clusters. More precisely, the wVar assesses the luminance disparity of within each cluster, while MI is a spatial autocorrelation measure characterizing the degree of similarity among supervoxels. Since the SSLIC oversegmentation is highly redundant, MI is an effective measure to show the advantage of the merging approach. The best value for wVar and MI is 0 which indicates the absence of redundancy. The Global Score (GS) is defined as the average of wVar and MI and is used as a final metric with ASA. We also use the number of supervoxels in the image (Supervoxel count) to quantify the improvement brought by the merging algorithm. For the no-reference metrics, in the monomodal setting, the final results are computed as an average through all modalities for all subjects. In the multimodal setting, the final results correspond to the average across all subjects. Since the wVar et MI scores provide one measure per modality, we keep the minimal value for each supervoxel across modalites. The evaluation is done in this way to put forward the discriminative power of the different modalities. The other scores (ASA and count) directly provide a single measurement per subject.

4.3   Implementation Details

SSLIC and merging algorithms are dependent on input parameters. The quality of the output clustering with SSLIC depends on the parameters K and m. K is the number of supervoxels, which in our case is defined as the smallest desired isotropic supervoxel size $K = [10, 10, 10]$. As multimodal images are normalized independently between $[0, 1]$, the compactness factor m is defined at 0.1. This value better balances intensity and spatial features as spatial features are not normalized to the range $[0, 1]$. The variance parameter ϵ used to balance the influence of the variance on the local compactness is set to 0.01. The hyperparameters α, β, γ have been empirically defined at 0.5, 0.1, and 0.1 to balance feature importance. Several orders of values have been tested to retain the parameter set with higher ASA. The parameters used in the histogram texture similarity are set to 32 for the number of bins, 8 for the number of angles, and 10 for the histogram bin size. The whole process takes around 40s for an image of shape $[4 \times 155 \times 240 \times 240]$ with the first axis corresponding to the number of modalities M. The SSLIC algorithm and the feature extraction were computed on 12 threads with 32 GB of memory.

4.4   Experimental Results

In our experiments, we assess the benefit of exploiting multimodal information in computing supervoxels, the effectiveness of including variance as a regularity coefficient in the SSLIC and the impact of the merging algorithm relying on

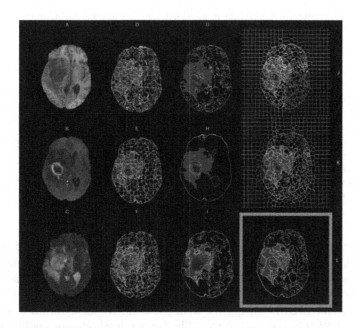

Fig. 1. The first column is an axial cross-section over 3 MRI sequences: T1 (A), T1_CE (B), T2 (C). The second column (D, E, and F) are the supervoxels computed using $Mono\_SSLIC$ on the 3 modalities independently. The third column corresponds to the result of the merging procedure applied on the previously computed supervoxels on each modality ($Mono\_SSLIC_{Merged}$). In the last column, J corresponds to the resulting segmentation of $Multi\_SSLIC$ computed on the 3D volume $\mathbb{I}$ composed of the different modalities, K is the result of SSLIC computed on $\mathbb{I}$ with the local regularity coefficient ($Multi\_SSLIC_{Var}$) and L is the proposed method including multimodal SSLIC followed by the merging procedure with the local regularity coefficient ($Multi\_SSLIC_{Var\_Merged}$). The ground-truth overlay is represented by green, red, and yellow (Edema, necrosis, and active tumor). (Color figure online)

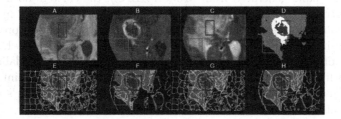

Fig. 2. (TOP) Original multimodal images zoomed in around the tumor region. Modalities are T1 (A), T1CE (B), T2 (C), and the ground truth (D). (Bottom) $Multi\_SSLIC$, $Multi\_SSLIC_{Merged}$, $Multi\_SSLIC_{Var}$ and $Multi\_SSLIC_{Var\_Merged}$ (E-H). Blue and red squares show local adaptive regularity influence on supervoxel homogeneity and compactness. The ground-truth overlay is represented by green, red, and yellow (Edema, necrosis, and active tumor). (Color figure online)

Table 1. Performance measurements computed with our own implementation of the scores added to superpixel benchmark [24]

Monomodal method	ASA	wVar	MI	GS	Supervoxel count
$Mono\_SSLIC$	.625	**.314**	.398	.356	8629.770
$Mono\_SSLIC_{Var}$	**.676**	.346	.362	.354	8233.930
$Mono\_SSLIC_{Merged}$	.290	**.314**	**.220**	**.267**	204.625
$Mono\_SSLIC_{Var\_Merged}$	.316	.348	.318	.333	203.904

Multimodal method	ASA	wVar	MI	GS	Supervoxel count
$Multi\_SSLIC$	.687	.493	.417	.455	8626.370
$Multi\_SSLIC_{Var}$	.648	.505	.383	.444	8163.21
$Multi\_SSLIC_{Merged}$	.673	.483	**.337**	.409	301.417
$Multi\_SSLIC_{Var\_Merged}$	**.712**	**.458**	.349	**.403**	298.42

colors and textures features on the segmentation accuracy. To this end, we compare 4 unsupervised segmentation methods applied in both the monomodal and the multimodal settings: SSLIC applied without ($SSLIC$) or with ($SSLIC_{Var}$) the adaptive local variance regularity coefficient, SSLIC followed by the merging step without ($SSLIC_{Merged}$) or with the adaptive local variance regularity coefficient ($SSLIC_{Var\_Merged}$, ours). The former methods are applied both in monomodal ($Mono$) and multimodal ($Multi$) settings.

Figures 1 and 2 show some qualitative results of applying the 4 segmentation methods to one subject with 4 modalities FLAIR, T1, T1CE, and T2. To further illustrate the performance of the proposed approaches, we report in Table 1 several quality metrics computed on the segmentations obtained in both the monomodal and multimodal settings.

The Benefit of Multimodality. As depicted in Fig. 1 J, applying the segmentation on multimodal images successfully takes into account the heterogeneous information from different modalities to cluster the image. On the contrary, in Fig. 1 D–F (results generated from $Mono\_SSLIC$), the clusters do not adhere completely to the ground truth tumor boundaries on the T1 and T2 modalities, since the complete information concerning the tumor is not fully present and multimodal information can not be efficiently exploited. In Fig. 1 G–I, we show the results of the merging applied independently on the three modalities with ground-truth overlay. It is clear that the T2 modality gives more information about Edema tissue whereas T1CE further characterizes the tumor's tissue. A more accurate clustering of the tumor can be seen in Fig. 1 J–L.

As shown in Table 1, the multimodal approaches i.e. $Multi\_SSLIC_{Var}$ and $Multi\_SSLIC_{Var\_Merged}$ perform better in terms of ASA compared to the monomodal approaches. Multimodal clustering exploits all the available information from different modalities and produces an accurate segmentation. We found that the best performing approach is the $Multi\_SSLIC_{Var\_Merged}$ which improves the clustering accuracy by 5.2% for the ASA Score and 25% for the GS with multimodal information. Indeed, all modalities give different complementary information about tissues. Thereby, using all available information to merge supervoxels while keeping important tissue properties, such as tumors texture, improves qualitative results as well as ASA, and GS scores.

Impact of Locally Adapting the Superpixel Regularity. Including variance inside the SSLIC algorithm allows to automatically adapt the regularity coefficient to highly textured supervoxel s and high-intensity supervoxels without manually adapting m. This makes the supervoxels more homogeneous as well as more compact, resulting in a better final clustering accuracy as shown in the Fig. 2. Blue and red squares in Fig. 2 F and H ($Multi\_SSLIC_{Merged}$ and $Multi\_SSLIC_{Var\_Merged}$), show the influence of using the local regularity coefficient on the compactness of the merged supervoxels. The resulting supervoxels are more compact and differ from their neighbors. We can see in the red square of Fig. 2 H that supervoxels have been correctly computed with more compactness and have been merged into a bigger supervoxel. Furthermore, from the quantitative results in Table 1, we can see that the local adaptive regularity coefficient $*_{Var}$ improves the results in terms of accuracy (ASA) and GS for the methods applied in both monomodal and multimodal settings (excepts for $Multi\_SSLIC$ and $Multi\_SSLIC_{Var}$). The variance of the supervoxel is an important factor to take into account in the segmentation algorithm. The MI is almost the same for both $Multi\_SSLIC_{Merged}$ and $Multi\_SSLIC_{Var\_Merged}$ demonstrating the robustness of the merging step to variance's disparity across supervoxels.

Performance of the Merging Algorithm. In the monomodal setting, in a modality where tumor tissues are not distinct, merging similar neighboring supervoxels reduces the tumor boundary accuracy. For example, in Fig. 1 H, supervoxels computed independently on the T1CE modality are not accurately merged since this modality highlights only the active tumor while other tumor tissues are not visible. This results in a poor ASA score for T1CE, therefore penalizing the final average ASA score. As such, computing the average ASA across modalities highlights the lack of the multimodal discriminant power (making use of visible tumors parts in all modalities). The merging approach applied in the multimodal setting is capable of reducing the number of supervoxels by a factor of 35 (column "Supervoxel count" in Table 1) and decreasing the redundancy (MI) by 0.21% in average compared to the initial oversegmentation). The texture homogeneity inside the merged supervoxels has been kept which demonstrates that our algorithm merges similar supervoxels. It is also interesting to note the wVar obtained on the results of applying $Mono\_SSLIC$ or $Mono\_SSLIC_{Merged}$ is approximately similar. This can be explained by the fact that the clustering was initially correct for the $Mono\_SSLIC$ step without merging.

5   Conclusion

In this work, we proposed a novel approach of merging supervoxels in a multimodal setting towards brain tumor classification. We showed that our methods applied on multimodal images are capable of exploiting the complementarity between different modalities producing very accurate clusters compared to traditional monomodal approaches. Our approach $Multi\text{-}SSLIC_{Var\text{-}Merged}$ improved the clustering accuracy by 5.2% for the ASA Score and 25% for the GS. The redundancy of supervoxels is also reduced by a factor of 35, decreasing the computational time, and making the resulting oversegmentation more suitable to be combined with a neural network classifier. Several open questions remain to be tackled in a future work. First, one drawback of the proposed approach is its dependency on prior registration of multiple modalities. Bipartite Graph Matching [21] seems to be an efficient way to alleviate this constraint. Moreover, taking into account radiomics and deep features in the computation of the supervoxels could also improve the adherence of initial over-segmentation or merged supervoxels to contrasted tissues, therefore resulting in more homogeneous final clustering.

Acknowledgments. This work was partially funded by Contract Cifre N°2020/1124. It has been also supported in part by FEDER European funds, the Pays de la Loire region and Nantes Métropole (MILCOM Project).

References

1. Achanta, R., Shaji, A., Smith, K., Lucchi, A., Fua, P., Süsstrunk, S.: Slic superpixels compared to state-of-the-art superpixel methods. IEEE Trans. Pattern Anal. Mach. Intell. **34**(11), 2274–2282 (2012). https://doi.org/10.1109/TPAMI.2012.120

2. Ahuja, S., Panigrahi, B.K., Gandhi, T.: Transfer learning based brain tumor detection and segmentation using superpixel technique. In: 2020 International Conference on Contemporary Computing and Applications, IC3A 2020, pp. 244–249 (2020). https://doi.org/10.1109/IC3A48958.2020.233306

3. Ali, M., Gilani, S.O., Waris, A., Zafar, K., Jamil, M.: Brain tumour image segmentation using deep networks. IEEE Access **8**, 153589–153598 (2020). https://doi.org/10.1109/ACCESS.2020.3018160

4. El-Melegy, M.T., El-Magd, K.M.A., Ali, S.A., Hussain, K.F., Mahdy, Y.B.: A comparative study of classification methods for automatic multimodal brain tumor segmentation. In: 2018 International Conference on Innovative Trends in Computer Engineering (ITCE). pp, 36–41 (2018). https://doi.org/10.1109/ITCE.2018.8316597

5. Fu, Z., Sun, Y., Fan, L., Han, Y.: Multiscale and multifeature segmentation of high-spatial resolution remote sensing images using superpixels with mutual optimal strategy. Remote Sens. **10**(8) (2018). https://doi.org/10.3390/rs10081289

6. Giraud, R., Ta, V., Papadakis, N., Berthoumieu, Y.: Texture-aware superpixel segmentation. In: IEEE International Conference on Image Processing (ICIP), abs/1901.11111 (2019)

7. Ibrahim, A., El-Kenawy, E.S.M.: Image segmentation methods based on superpixel techniques: a survey. J. Comput. Sci. Inf. Syst. **2020**(6), 1–10 (2020)

8. Johnson, B., Xie, Z.: Unsupervised image segmentation evaluation and refinement using a multi-scale approach. ISPRS J. Photogramm. Remote Sens. **66**(4), 473–483 (2011). https://doi.org/10.1016/j.isprsjprs.2011.02.006

9. Johnson, D.R., et al.: Glioma response assessment: classic pitfalls, novel confounders, and emerging imaging tools. Br. J. Radiol. (2019)
10. Khosravanian, A., Rahmanimanesh, M., Keshavarzi, P., Mozaffari, S.: Fast level set method for glioma brain tumor segmentation based on superpixel fuzzy clustering and lattice Boltzmann method. Comput. Methods Programs Biomed. **198**, 105809 (2021). https://doi.org/10.1016/j.cmpb.2020.105809
11. Kruskal, J.B.: On the shortest spanning subtree of a graph and the traveling salesman problem. Proc. Am. Math. Soc. **7**(1), 48–50 (1956)
12. Liqiang, Y., Erdt, M., Lipo, W.: Adaptive transfer learning to enhance domain transfer in brain tumor segmentation. In: Proceedings - International Symposium on Biomedical Imaging 2021-April, pp. 1873–1877 (2021). https://doi.org/10.1109/ISBI48211.2021.9434100
13. Lowekamp, B.C., Chen, D.T., Yaniv, Z., Yoo, T.S.: Scalable simple linear iterative clustering (SSLIC) using a generic and parallel approach. Kitware, Inc. (2018)
14. Luengo, I., Basham, M., French, A.P.: SMURFS: superpixels from multi-scale refinement of super-regions. In: British Machine Vision Conference 2016, BMVC 2016 (2016). https://doi.org/10.5244/C.30.4
15. Magadza, T., Viriri, S.: Deep learning for brain tumor segmentation: a survey of state-of-the-art. J. Imaging **7**(2) (2021). https://doi.org/10.3390/jimaging7020019
16. Menze, B.H., et al.: The multimodal brain tumor image segmentation benchmark (BRATS). IEEE Trans. Med. Imaging **34**(10), 1993–2024 (2015). https://doi.org/10.1109/TMI.2014.2377694
17. Paterson, M.S., Yao, F.F.: On nearest-neighbor graphs. In: Kuich, W. (ed.) ICALP 1992. LNCS, vol. 623, pp. 416–426. Springer, Heidelberg (1992). https://doi.org/10.1007/3-540-55719-9_93
18. Pereira, S., Pinto, A., Alves, V., Silva, C.A.: Brain tumor segmentation using convolutional neural networks in MRI images. IEEE Trans. Med. Imaging **35**(5), 1240–1251 (2016). https://doi.org/10.1109/TMI.2016.2538465
19. Rahimpour, M., Goffin, K., Koole, M.: Convolutional neural networks for brain tumor segmentation using different sets of MRI sequences. In: 2019 IEEE Nuclear Science Symposium and Medical Imaging Conference (NSS/MIC), pp. 1–3 (2019). https://doi.org/10.1109/NSS/MIC42101.2019.9059769
20. Rehman, Z.U., Naqvi, S.S., Khan, T.M., Khan, M.A., Bashir, T.: Fully automated multi-parametric brain tumour segmentation using superpixel based classification. Expert Syst. Appl. **118**, 598–613 (2019). https://doi.org/10.1016/j.eswa.2018.10.040
21. Serratosa, F.: Fast computation of bipartite graph matching. Pattern Recogn. Lett. **45**, 244–250 (2014). https://doi.org/10.1016/j.patrec.2014.04.015
22. Soltaninejad, M., et al.: Automated brain tumour detection and segmentation using superpixel-based extremely randomized trees in FLAIR MRI. Int. J. Comput. Assist. Radiol. Surg. **12**(2), 183–203 (2016). https://doi.org/10.1007/s11548-016-1483-3
23. Soltaninejad, M., et al.: Supervised learning based multimodal MRI brain tumour segmentation using texture features from supervoxels. Comput. Methods Programs Biomed. **157**, 69–84 (2018). https://doi.org/10.1016/j.cmpb.2018.01.003
24. Stutz, D., Hermans, A., Leibe, B.: Superpixels: an evaluation of the state-of-the-art. Comput. Vis. Image Underst. **166**, 1–27 (2018). https://doi.org/10.1016/j.cviu.2017.03.007
25. Wang, W., Chen, C., Ding, M., Li, J., Yu, H., Zha, S.: TransBTS: multimodal brain tumor segmentation using transformer (2021)

Evaluating Glioma Growth Predictions as a Forward Ranking Problem

Karin A. van Garderen[1]([⊠]), Sebastian R. van der Voort[1],
Maarten M. J. Wijnenga[1], Fatih Incekara[1,2], Georgios Kapsas[1],
Renske Gahrmann[1], Ahmad Alafandi[1], Marion Smits[1], and Stefan Klein[1]

[1] Department of Radiology and Nuclear Medicine,
Erasmus MC, Rotterdam, The Netherlands
k.vangarderen@erasmusmc.nl
[2] Department of Neurosurgery, Erasmus MC, Rotterdam, The Netherlands

Abstract. The problem of tumor growth prediction is challenging, but promising results have been achieved with both model-driven and statistical methods. In this work, we present a framework for the evaluation of growth predictions that focuses on the spatial infiltration patterns, and specifically evaluating a prediction of future growth. We propose to frame the problem as a ranking problem rather than a segmentation problem. Using the average precision as a metric, we can evaluate the results with segmentations while using the full spatiotemporal prediction. Furthermore, by applying a biophysical tumor growth model to 21 patient cases we compare two schemes for fitting and evaluating predictions. By carefully designing a scheme that separates the prediction from the observations used for fitting the model, we show that a better fit of model parameters does not guarantee a better predictive power.

Keywords: Glioma · Growth model · Validation · Magnetic resonance imaging · Brain

1 Introduction

As the diagnosis and delineation of glioma has improved with machine learning [4], researchers look towards the more challenging task of predicting the disease trajectory into the future [8,19]. However, the problem of tumor growth is challenging in many ways, not just by the lack of publicly available data. The variables of clinical importance, such as the speed of infiltration and proliferation, are unknown and the problem of estimating them from observations is ill-posed. Furthermore, the observations we do have are flawed as tumor cells are known to spread beyond the visible boundary on MR imaging [22].

Despite these challenges, biophysical growth models have shown promise in their ability to predict the spatial growth patterns for individual cases. They are model-driven and strongly rooted in a mechanistic understanding of tumor growth. Delineations of the tumor on MR imaging typically form the input for

A. Crimi and S. Bakas (Eds.): BrainLes 2021, LNCS 12962, pp. 100–111, 2022.
https://doi.org/10.1007/978-3-031-08999-2_8

individual model fitting, with follow-up imaging providing the gold standard of evaluation. Though other methods of evaluation exist, such as biopsy samples [10] or PET imaging [18], for most clinical cases consecutive delineations are the best approximation for a ground truth.

Due to the nature of the data, growth predictions are often framed as a segmentation problem. For example, by using an overlap metric such as the Dice Similarity Coefficient based on a sample in time [7,19]. Although this metric comes natural to the ground-truth data, it is less representative of the underlying problem. The main disadvantage of overlap-based metrics is that they treat all voxels equally, while some errors are more significant than others. Intuitively, we would want to assign more significance to false negative predictions at a large distance to the predicted tumor boundary as they represent a larger disagreement to the model and would likely require a large adjustment to predict correctly. This intuition is represented in metrics based on the segmentation boundary, such as the symmetric surface distance used in Konukoglu et al. [17]. But even a distance metric compares only to a single point in time, and using a boundary metric becomes less appropriate when the ground truth contains new disconnected lesions.

Another challenge in the evaluation of tumor growth predictions is the entanglement of model fit and prediction. All tumor growth models require an initial observation to fit model parameters. The goodness-of-fit is measured using the segmentation on this initial observation and the prediction is performed from the time of onset, through the initial observation towards the future [3]. The optimization of this inverse problem is an important topic for research, not in the least because the growth parameters can be of prognostic value by themselves [21], but often these methods are evaluated in simulated data. The clinical reality will not adhere to the strict assumptions made in the model, and therefore the predictive value of the model depends not only on the effectiveness of the model fitting but also on the correctness of the assumptions.

An ideal test of a prediction model would require a strict separation of model fitting and evaluation. However, in the problem of personalized tumor growth models this separation is not strictly possible because the initial condition used for the parameter fit is also part of the final tumor shape used for evaluation. Especially with models that simulate the full growth trajectory, there is a risk that model fit on the initial condition is strongly entangled with the prediction of growth. After all, if the shape of the initial lesion is not estimated correctly then this error will propagate to the estimation the future disease trajectory. This work explores the distinction between goodness-of-fit at the initial time-point, and predictive performance for future time-points by comparing two temporal evaluation schemes, one of which aims to strictly separate the initial condition from the predicted growth behavior.

In this work we propose the following contributions:

1. A novel framing of tumor growth as a ranking problem, with the Average Precision as the performance metric

2. The application of this evaluation framework on a biophysical tumor growth model and a dataset of 21 patient cases, to explore the relation between goodness-of-fit at the initial time-point, and predictive performance for future time-points.

2   Methods

2.1   Tumor Growth as a Ranking Problem

In this section, we propose that tumor growth prediction could be framed as a ranking problem, aimed at predicting the relative time-to-invasion of each voxel in the brain. Based on this perspective, we propose an evaluation metric for assessing the quality of the predictions (i.e., rankings) resulting from any growth model. This problem formulation is aimed at predicting infiltrative growth in a spatial sense, and simplifies the problem by disregarding the speed of growth and potential mass effect.

We assume that a growth model could produce a segmentation of the tumor $S(t)$ at any time $t > 0$. It may therefore assign to every location in the brain a time $T(x)$, which is the first time t when the tumor reaches that location. As we do not require an accurate estimation of the growth speed, we require only that the estimated $T(x)$ is a ranking of voxels in the brain, such that:

$$T(x_a) > T(x_b) \Leftrightarrow \exists t : x_a \notin S(t), x_b \in S(t). \tag{1}$$

The ranking can be evaluated by a sampling of the ground-truth segmentation S', by using the Average Precision (AP). The AP is defined as the area under the Precision-Recall (PR) curve:

$$AP = \Sigma_t (R(t) - R(t-1)) P(t), \tag{2}$$

where $R(t)$ and $P(t)$ are the recall and precision at a threshold t on the time-to-invasion ranking T, leading to the predicted segmentation $S(t) = \{x : T(x) \leq t\}$, and comparing to the reference segmentation S':

$$P(t) = \frac{|S(t) \cap S'|}{|S(t)|}, R(t) = \frac{|S(t) \cap S'|}{|S'|}. \tag{3}$$

The AP metric weighs the precision scores are with the difference in recall, so that all tumor volume predictions $S(t)$ are taken into account from the tumor onset to the time when the recall is 1. This is when the ground-truth segmentation is completely encompassed by the prediction $S(t)$. An evaluation based on a single time t would represent a point on the PR curve. If we take a volume-based sample, where the estimated tumor volume equals the observed tumor volume, i.e. $|S(t)| = |S'|$, this is the time t where $R(t) = P(t)$.

Formulating the problem as a ranking and using the AP has a number of qualitative advantages. First, the ranking T has a direct local connection to the speed of the tumor boundary. If the ranking is smooth, the gradient of the

T represents the local movement of the visible tumor boundary. It automatically assigns a larger weight to certain parts of the prediction, depending on the assigned ranking T, regardless of any assumptions on the significance of distance in space or time. We might quantify the agreement between T and S locally by using the rank of the voxel $T(x)$ as a threshold on the PR curve. A local prediction $T(x)$ is in agreement with S' if it is part of the ground-truth segmentation ($x \in S'$) and can be included with high precision $P(T(x))$, or else if it falls outside S' but can be excluded with high recall $R(T(x))$. Figure 1 illustrates the computation of the AP metric and this local measure of disagreement.

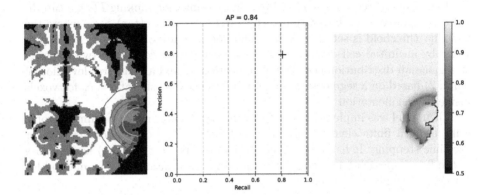

Fig. 1. Left: cross-section of tissue segmentation of a specific case with thresholds on the T map, generated by a tumor growth model, indicated as segmentation boundaries. The ground-truth segmentation S' is indicated by a red overlay. Middle: corresponding Precision-Recall curve with the same thresholds indicated. The sample with a corresponding volume is marked on the PR curve. Right: quantification of agreement by $R(T(x))$ outside S' and $P(T(x)))$ for voxels inside S'.

2.2 Example Growth Model

To illustrate the the proposed framework for evaluating tumor growth predictions, a traditional diffusion-proliferation model was used with anisotropic diffusion, informed by diffusion tensor imaging (DTI). This model is intended to illustrate the use of the evaluation framework, but it is not our aim to present a novel or improved growth model. The model is defined by a partial differential equation for the cell density c, which changes with each timestep dt according to:

$$\frac{dc}{dt} = \nabla(\mathbb{D}\nabla c) + \rho c(1 - c), \tag{4}$$

$$\mathbb{D}\nabla c \cdot n_{\delta\Omega} = 0, \tag{5}$$

where ρ is the growth factor, $n_{\delta\Omega}$ is the normal vector at the boundary between the brain and CSF, and $\mathbb{D}$ is a tensor comprising an isotropic and anisotropic component:

$$\mathbb{D} = \kappa(x)\mathbb{I} + \tau F(x)\mathbb{T}(x), \tag{6}$$

where κ and τ are parameters to weigh the two components, $\mathbb{I}$ is the identity matrix, $F(x)$ is the local Fractional Anisotropy (FA) and $\mathbb{T}$ is the normalized diffusion tensor [11].

The isotropic diffusion depends on the local tissue type [14], as defined by a separate parameter κ_w and κ_g for voxels in the white matter ($\mathcal{W}$) and grey matter ($\mathcal{G}$) respectively:

$$\kappa(x) = \begin{cases} \kappa_w & x \in \mathcal{W} \\ \kappa_g & x \in \mathcal{G} \end{cases}$$

To go from a prediction of $c(t, x)$ to a time-to-invasion ranking $T(x)$, a threshold c_v is applied at each iteration such that $T(x) = \min_t c(t, x) > c_v$, where the visibility threshold is set as $c_v = 0.5$. The initial condition of the model is provided by an initial cell density $c(t = 0)$, which can be defined in two ways: 1) as a gaussian distribution centered at a location x_s and a standard deviation of 1mm; 2) based on a segmentation by setting the cell density at $c = c_v$ for voxels inside the segmentation [7].

The model was implemented in FEniCS [1] in a cubic mesh of 1mm isotropic cells, using a finite element approach and Crank-Nicolson approximations for the time stepping. It has four unknown parameters (ρ, τ, κ_w, κ_g) and, in case of the first approach for setting $c(t = 0)$, an initial location x_s. The method for fitting x_s is explained below.

Fit of Initial Point. A fit of the point x_s is essential for the model initialization from tumor onset, and its location depends on the model parameters. Konukoglu et al. [17] have shown that an eikonal approximation can effectively mimic the evolution of the visible tumor boundary. In this work, we use an eikonal approximation that assumes the visible tumor margin moves at a speed v of $v = 4\sqrt{\rho \text{Tr}(\mathbb{D})}$, in order to estimate x_s for a given set of model parameters, by optimising the approximation of the initial tumor S_0 in terms of the Dice overlap at equal volume using Powell's method [20]. To be more robust to the optimization seed, considering that the optimization landscape may have mutliple local minima, the optimization was repeated for ten runs with different random seeds to increase the chance of finding the global optimum for x_s.

3   Experiments

3.1   Dataset

A retrospective dataset was selected from Erasmus MC of patients who a) were diagnosed with a low-grade glioma; b) were treated with surgical resection, but received no chemo- or radiotherapy; and c) had a DTI and 3D T1-weighted scan before resection, and two follow-up scans (before and after tumor progression). This resulted in data of 21 patients, after one dataset was excluded due to failed registration. Note that the time difference between the measurement of initial tumor and the two follow-up scans varied from a few months to several years.

3.2 Temporal Evaluation Schemes

In the typical timeline of fit and evaluation [14,17], described in Fig. 2 as the bidirectional scheme, the model is fitted on a tumor segmentation S_0 and then simulated from onset, through S_0, to the point of evaluation S_2. In other words, the prediction contains the behavior that it is fitted on.

We compare this method to a strictly forward evaluation scheme that separates the model fit from the prediction as much as possible. As described in Fig. 2 as the forward scheme, the parameters (in this case x_s) are fitted on an initial time-point S_0 and then used to make a prediction between two follow-up scans S_1 and S_2. By running the prediction from a segmentation S_1 instead of an initial location x_s, the potential error in fitting S_0 does not propagate to the evaluation, which is based purely on the growth behavior between S_1 and S_2 that is unknown when fitting the model.

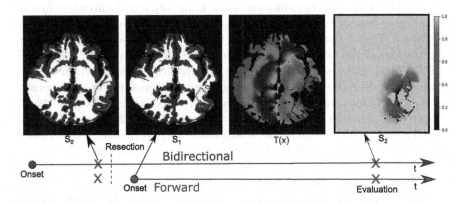

Fig. 2. Overview of two temporal evaluation schemes. Bidirectional: a growth model is fitted to the initial tumor and simulated from a seed point to generate a voxel ranking T. Forward: parameters are fitted to the initial tumor and then the model is initialized with a segmentation S_1 obtained after resection to generate the voxel ranking T. Images from left to right: example of tissue segmentation with S_0 outlined, tissue segmentation with resection cavity removed and S_1 outlined, example of final ranking T used for the evaluation with resection cavity and S_1 removed, quantification of agreement between $T(x)$ and S_2.

For our dataset, we need to consider the role of the tumor resection. In both schemes, the resection cavity as estimated by the aligment of the tissue at S_0 and S_1, is removed from the region of interest for evaluation. In the forward scheme, any voxels in the segmentation S_1 are also removed from the region of interest, leaving only the new growth visible in S_2 for evaluation. So where the bidirectional scheme evaluates predictive performance on the entirety of the remaining tumor, using S_0 only to initialize the location of onset, the forward scheme evaluates purely predictive performance based on the knowledge of S_1.

3.3   Data Preprocessing

Running a growth model from onset requires knowledge of the underlying healthy tissue. Removing pathology from an image is a research problem in itself, but commonly a registration approach with a healthy brain - often an atlas - is used [5,14,18]. In this study we used the contralateral side of the brain as a reference for healthy brain structure (similar to [6]). This is possible because in our dataset all lesions were strictly limited to one hemisphere. Using a registration of the T1-weighted image with its left-right mirrored version, all segmentations were transferred to the contralateral healthy side of the brain. To prevent unrealistic warping of the image due to image intensity changes in the tumor, while still capturing its mass effect, the b-spline registration was regularized with a bending energy penalty [16]. The weight of this penalty with the mutual information metric was tuned on a number of cases using visual inspection of the transformation.

The model input is a segmentation of the brain, separated into white matter ($\mathcal{W}$) and gray matter ($\mathcal{G}$), potentially an estimate of the local diffusion based on Diffusion Tensor Imaging (DTI), and a binary segmentation of the tumor. Segmentations of the brain and brain tissue were produced using HD-BET [13] and FSL FAST [23] respectively. For the pre-operative images, which did not include a T2W-FLAIR sequence, S_0 was segmented manually. Tumor segmentations S_1 and S_2 for consecutive images were produced using HD-GLIO [12,15] and corrected manually where necessary. Alignment with the space of S_0 was achieved with a b-spline registration, which was evaluated visually. Datasets were excluded if the registration did not produce a reasonable aligment.

As no registration or segmentation will be perfect, some inconsistencies remain that prevent a perfect prediction. To not punish the model unfairly, the voxels in S falling outside the brain were disregarded in the computation of the AP metric.

3.4   Parameters

As the variation of diffusive behavior within the brain is a defining factor for the tumor shape, and from a single observation it is impossible to estimate all parameters simultaneously, we kept the proliferation constant at $\rho = 0.01$ while using the parameters κ_w, κ_g and τ as parameters of interest. These parameters were not fitted but rather varied systematically, as listed in the legend of Fig. 3. For this range of seven growth model parameter settings, the AP performance was measured for goodness-of-fit on the baseline segmentation S_0 and predictive performance on S_2, according to the two evaluation schemes. The relation between goodness-of-fit and predictive performance was quantified using a patient-wise Spearman correlation across different growth model parameter settings. The mean of the patient-wise correlation coefficients was tested for a significant difference from zero using a one-sample t-test.

4 Results

Figure 4 shows two examples of the model input and results, in terms of the images used for tumor segmentation at the three timepoints, the segmentations and their mirrored counterparts and the results of a specfic model ($\kappa_w = 0.1$, $\kappa_g = 0.1$ and $\tau = 10$) using both the forward and bidirectional evaluation scheme. The local values of $R(T(x))$ and $P(T(x))$ indicate where the model results are most in disagreement with the ground-truth segmentation S_2.

Figure 3 shows a comparison of the goodness-of-fit, which is measured by the AP on the initial tumor segmentation S_0, and the final predictive performance on S_2.

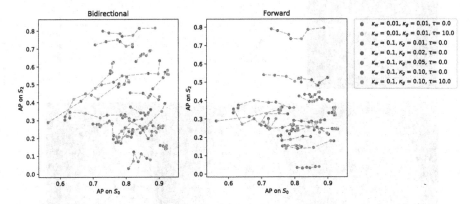

Fig. 3. Comparison of goodness-of-fit versus predictive performance for the two evaluation setups. Results for the same patient on different parameter sets are interconnected.

Comparing the performance between different growth model parameter settings, it is clear that goodness-of-fit is generally higher and more dependent on the model parameters than the predictive performance. From the growth model parameter settings, typically the best goodness-of-fit (AP on S_0) was achieved with low diffusion ($\kappa_w = 0.01$) while the worst fit was achieved when the difference in κ between white and gray matter was large ($\kappa_w = 0.1$, $\kappa_g = 0.01$ or $\kappa_g = 0.02$).

From the results of the bidirectional evaluation scheme, going from an intitial point through S_0 to S_2, it seems that there is a relation between the goodness-of-fit and the predictive performance. However, this relation disappears when using the forward evaluation scheme. These observations are confirmed by the mean patient-wise correlation coefficients, which were 0.24 (p = 0.06) for the forward scheme and -0.03(p = 0.76) for the bidirectional scheme.

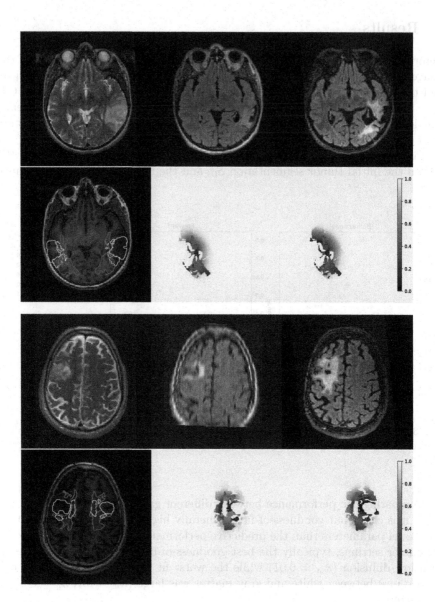

Fig. 4. Example of image processing results for two patients. Top row: T2W imaging showing the initial tumor (left) and T2W FLAIR images showing the tumor after surgery (middle) tumor and at recurrence (right). Bottom row, left: T1W imaging with boundary of resection cavity (cyan), S_1 (yellow) and S_2 (red). Both the original segmentations and the mirrored segmentations are shown. Bottom, middle: Visualization of the local quantification of agreement by $R(T(x))$ outside S_2 and $P(T(x)))$ for voxels inside S_2, for one parameter setting in the forward evaluation scheme. Bottom, right: same visualization for the bidirectional evaluation scheme, same parameter setting. (Color figure online)

5   Discussion

This work presents a formulation of the tumor growth predictions as a forward ranking problem, and describes the Average Precision metric for its evaluation. By formulating the problem in this way we can evaluate the full spatiotemporal results, even if the observations are only snapshots in the form of a segmentation. A further advantage is found in the direct link to local growth speed and quantification of the local model agreement. Though these advantages are only of a qualitative nature, and do not provide a direct benefit to the model itself, we believe it to be a useful step in the development and specifically evaluation of growth models. An important underlying assumption in this framework is that the time axis is not quantified, so the prediction does not provide information on the overall speed of growth or any potential mass effect. Predicting these factors is a highly relevant problem as well, but to predict both spatial distribution, mass effect and speed of growth would likely require at least multiple time-points for model fitting or additional clinical parameters. This is currently not feasible with the data available in clinical practice. For a model that does provide information on growth speed and mass effect, the AP metric could be combined with other metrics to separately evaluate the different factors of tumor growth.

The importance of problem formulation is further illustrated with the two temporal evaluation schemes. Specifically for personalized tumor growth models, which are fitted to an initial tumor shape, this work presents an alternative forward scheme that separates the goodness-of-fit from the evaluation of future predictions. In the forward scheme, the model is initiated with a segmentation instead of an initial point of onset, so that errors made in fitting the initial tumor do not propagate to the final prediction. The aim of this scheme is to evaluate the predictive value of the model and its parameters separately from the goodness-of-fit at the initial observation.

By comparing the bidirectional and forward evaluation schemes in a dataset of 21 patients, using a biophysical growth model, we show that the choice of evaluation greatly affects the relative performance of models. This is illustrated with different parameter setting of the same model, not with different models, but with the purpose of showing the difficulty of evaluating true predictive performance in general. In this case, for our specific model and parameter settings, the difference in performance between parameter settings can be attributed to a better fit of the initial situation, and not necessarily a prediction of unseen behavior. We must note, however, that often the goal in tumor growth modelling is to find the model that best fits the available data on a fundamental level, both initially and in the future, and overfitting is not an immediate concern with strongly model-driven research.

The dataset used in this research was a selection of patients that underwent surgical resection, but no radio- or chemotherapy. Although it is fair to assume that the diffusive behavior of the tumor is not affected during the surgery, so the model parameters would stay the same, the future growth pattern can be affected by the removal of tumor tissue. The decompression that occurs at resection also complicates the registration of post-operative imaging, which led to the exclusion of one patient due to a failed registration. However, with surgical resection being the recommended treatment for most glioma patients, this is a complicating factor that is difficult to avoid in clinical datasets and in any application in clinical practice.

As new methods of tumor growth prediction are developed, and even fully data-driven models are emerging using machine learning, comparing model performance becomes increasingly relevant. For that purpose, the framing of the problem is essential. Between the actual mechanisms of tumor growth and the segmentation is a flawed observation on MR imaging, the rather difficult problem of segmentation and registration and an estimate of the time horizon. Those factors, combined with limited data and the fact that glioma are naturally unpredictable are a major reason why tumor growth models have relied heavily on simulations [9] and qualitative observations [2] for their validation. This work is a step towards the comparison and clinical evaluation of tumor growth predictions that fits their spatiotemporal nature, and allows for localized interpretation.

Acknowledgements. This work was supported by the Dutch Cancer Society (project number 11026, GLASS-NL) and the Dutch Organization for Scientific Research (NWO).

References

1. Alnaes, M.S., et al.: The FEniCS Project Version 1.5 3(100), 9–23 (2015)
2. Angeli, S., Emblem, K.E., Due-Tonnessen, P., Stylianopoulos, T.: Towards patient-specific modeling of brain tumor growth and formation of secondary nodes guided by DTI-MRI. NeuroImage Clin. **20**, 664–673 (2018)
3. Angelini, E., Clatz, O., Mandonnet, E., Konukoglu, E., Capelle, L., Duffau, H.: Glioma dynamics and computational models: a review of segmentation, registration, and in silico growth algorithms and their clinical applications. Curr. Med. Imaging Rev. **3**(4), 262–276 (2007)
4. Bakas, S., et al.: Identifying the best machine learning algorithms for brain tumor segmentation, progression assessment, and overall survival prediction in the BRATS challenge. arXiv 124 (2018)
5. Bakas, S., et al.: GLISTRboost: combining multimodal MRI segmentation, registration, and biophysical tumor growth modeling with gradient boosting machines for glioma segmentation. In: Crimi, A., Menze, B., Maier, O., Reyes, M., Handels, H. (eds.) BrainLes 2015. LNCS, vol. 9556, pp. 144–155. Springer, Cham (2016). https://doi.org/10.1007/978-3-319-30858-6_13
6. Clatz, O., et al.: Realistic simulation of the 3-D growth of brain tumors in MR images coupling diffusion with biomechanical deformation. IEEE Trans. Med. Imaging **24**(10), 1334–1346 (2005)
7. Elazab, A., et al.: Post-surgery glioma growth modeling from magnetic resonance images for patients with treatment. Sci. Rep. **7**(1), 1–13 (2017)
8. Elazab, A., et al.: GP-GAN: brain tumor growth prediction using stacked 3D generative adversarial networks from longitudinal MR Images. Neural Netw. **132**, 321–332 (2020)

9. Ezhov, I., et al.: Neural parameters estimation for brain tumor growth modeling. In: Shen, D., et al. (eds.) MICCAI 2019. LNCS, vol. 11765, pp. 787–795. Springer, Cham (2019). https://doi.org/10.1007/978-3-030-32245-8_87

10. Gaw, N., et al.: Integration of machine learning and mechanistic models accurately predicts variation in cell density of glioblastoma using multiparametric MRI. Sci. Rep. **9**(1), 1–9 (2019)

11. Gholami, A., Mang, A., Biros, G.: Mathematical Biology An inverse problem formulation for parameter estimation of a reaction-diffusion model of low grade gliomas. J. Math. Biol. **72**, 409–433 (2016)

12. Isensee, F., Jaeger, P.F., Kohl, S.A., Petersen, J., Maier-Hein, K.H.: nnU-Net: a self-configuring method for deep learning-based biomedical image segmentation. Nat. Methods **18**, 203–211 (2020)

13. Isensee, F., et al.: Automated brain extraction of multisequence MRI using artificial neural networks. Hum. Brain Mapp. **40**(17), 4952–4964 (2019)

14. Jacobs, J., et al.: Improved model prediction of glioma growth utilizing tissue-specific boundary effects. Math. Biosci. **312**, 59–66 (2019)

15. Kickingereder, P., et al.: Automated quantitative tumour response assessment of MRI in neuro-oncology with artificial neural networks: a multicentre, retrospective study. Lancet Oncol. **20**(5), 728–740 (2019)

16. Klein, S., Staring, M., Murphy, K., Viergever, M.A., Pluim, J.P.: Elastix: a toolbox for intensity-based medical image registration. IEEE Trans. Med. Imaging **29**(1), 196–205 (2010)

17. Konukoglu, E., et al.: Image guided personalization of reaction-diffusion type tumor growth models using modified anisotropic eikonal equations. IEEE Trans. Med. Imaging **29**(1), 77–95 (2010)

18. Lipkova, J., et al.: Personalized radiotherapy design for glioblastoma: integrating mathematical tumor models, multimodal scans, and Bayesian inference. IEEE Trans. Med. Imaging **38**(8), 1875–1884 (2019)

19. Petersen, J., et al.: Deep probabilistic modeling of glioma growth. In: Shen, D., et al. (eds.) MICCAI 2019. LNCS, vol. 11765, pp. 806–814. Springer, Cham (2019). https://doi.org/10.1007/978-3-030-32245-8_89

20. Powell, M.J.D.: The BOBYQA algorithm for bound constrained optimization without derivatives. Technical report (2009)

21. Raman, F., Scribner, E., Saut, O., Wenger, C., Colin, T., Fathallah-Shaykh, H.M.: Computational Trials: unraveling motility phenotypes, progression patterns, and treatment options for glioblastoma multiforme. PLoS ONE **11**(1), e0146617 (2016)

22. Silbergeld, D.L., Chicoine, M.R.: Isolation and characterization of human malignant glioma cells from histologically normal brain. J. Neurosurg. **86**(3), 525–531 (1997)

23. Zhang, Y., Brady, M., Smith, S.: Segmentation of brain MR images through a hidden Markov random field model and the expectation-maximization algorithm. IEEE Trans. Med. Imaging **20**(1), 45–57 (2001)

Modeling Multi-annotator Uncertainty as Multi-class Segmentation Problem

Martin Žukovec, Lara Dular[(✉)], and Žiga Špiclin

Faculty of Electrical Engineering, University of Ljubljana,
Tržaška cesta 25, 1000 Ljubljana, Slovenia
lara.dular@fe.uni-j.si

Abstract. Medical image segmentation is a monotonous, time-consuming, and costly task performed by highly skilled medical annotators. Despite adequate training, the intra- and inter-annotator variations results in significantly differing segmentations. If the variations arise from the uncertainty of the segmentation task, due to poor image contrast, lack of expert consensus, etc., then the algorithms for automatic segmentation should learn to capture the annotator (dis)agreements. In our approach we modeled the annotator (dis)agreement by aggregating the multi-annotator segmentations to reflect the uncertainty of the segmentation task and formulated the segmentation as multi-class pixel classification problem within an open source convolutional neural architecture nnU-Net. Validation was carried out for a wide range of imaging modalities and segmentation tasks as provided by the 2020 and 2021 QUBIQ (Quantification of Uncertainties in Biomedical Image Quantification) challenges. We achieved high quality segmentation results, despite a small set of training samples, and at time of this writing achieved an overall third and sixth best result on the respective QUBIQ 2020 and 2021 challenge leaderboards.

Keywords: Multi-class segmentation · Noisy labels · Uncertainty aggregation · Convolutional neural networks · Challenge datasets

1 Introduction

Image segmentation is one of the fundamental tasks of medical imaging, crucial in modeling normal patient anatomy, detection of pathology, analysing patient's health status and indicating medical treatments and procedures. For instance, manual segmentation prior to surgical tumor removal and organ-at-risk contouring for radiotherapy planning is a time-consuming, mundane and thus a costly task carried out by expert annotators.

Developing automated algorithms can greatly reduce both time and money spent on medical image segmentation tasks. However, it is of extreme importance to estimate the uncertainty of output segmentation, as poor segmentation may adversely impact upon based treatments and procedures. Despite extensive expert training and experience, many researches found contours on common set of images to differ significantly between the experts [5]. These may naturally arise from the uncertainty of the segmentation task, due to poor image contrast, lack of expert consensus, etc. We therefore should expect the uncertainty of annotations to reflect in the predictions of automated algorithms.

The Quantification of Uncertainties in Biomedical Image Quantification (QUBIQ) challenge [10] aims to develop and evaluate automatic algorithms for quantification of uncertainties, arising from experts' (dis)agreement in biomedical image segmentation. In 2020 the challenge presented four different MR and CT image datasets on which a total of seven segmentation tasks were released. In 2021, the organisers added two datasets each with a single task.

This paper presents our approach to capturing multi-annotator segmentation uncertainty for nine tasks of the QUBIQ 2020 and 2021 challenges. First the multi-annotator segmentations were aggregated, considering the same performance level for each of the expert annotators, such that they approximate the segmentation task uncertainty. We advanced the state-of-the-art nnU-Net convolutional neural network (CNN) model by casting multi-annotator uncertainty estimation as multi-class segmentation problem, where aggregated segmentations were the prediction target. Thus the model was able to capture and recreate the experts' (dis)agreements. At the time of this writing[1] the proposed approach achieved the third and sixth best scores on the respective QUBIQ 2020 and 2021 leaderboards.

2   Related Work

Supervised machine learning models like the deep CNNs for image segmentation generally require large training datasets of annotated images to achieve adequate performance levels. In medical imaging domain, however, we typically obtain small datasets due to the high effort required to obtain expert annotations (i.e. manual segmentations). When training models with a single expert segmentation per image we typically consider it as ground truth (GT), despite potential annotator bias and noise. A natural strategy to reduce the impact of annotator bias and noise is to consider the annotations of multiple experts.

With the availability of multiple expert segmentations a common approach is to conceive a fusion strategy to approximate the GT [5]. The most straightforward approach is Consensus voting, annotating the area as GT if all annotators agree, and Majority voting [4,9], assigning pixel labels according to the majority rule. These definitions can be generalized by using different agreement levels. Lampert et al. [7] reported that increasing the level of agreement for forming GT increased the model's reported performance. They further noted that a higher agreement level could result in over-optimistic results, as this could be the consequence of choosing the most obvious segments of the region of interest (ROI). Further, the problem with such an approach is the loss of information about inter-annotator variability.

---

[1] September 9, 2021.

A more advanced and widely used approach to aggregating multiple expert segmentations is the Simultaneous Truth and Performance Level Estimation (STAPLE) algorithm proposed by Warfield et al. [13]. The STAPLE algorithm uses expectation-maximization to compute a probabilistic estimate of the true segmentation and the sensitivity and specificity performance characteristics for each annotator. A similar approach to STAPLE is used in SIMPLE [8] which additionally iteratively estimates the performance of segmentations and discards poorly performing segmentation before finally fusing the remaining segmentations to estimate GT. Lampert et al. [7] showed that STAPLE performs well when inter-annotator variability is low, but degrades with the increasing number of annotations and high variability of annotations. They also examined the effect of inter-annotator variance on foreground-background segmentation algorithms, in a computer vision setting. Despite not including deep neural networks, their results showed that the rank of the model is highly dependent on the chosen method used to form the GT. Furthermore, including a similar aggregation strategy into segmentation method will inevitably lead to overoptimistic results.

Training machine learning models on datasets with multiple segmentation masks in a supervised manner allows for different representations and uses of the input data for model training. Firstly, each image-segmentation pair can be treated as a separate sample. For instance Hu et al. [1] propose a segmentation model based on the Probabilistic U-Net [6], where during model training multi-annotator segmentations of each image were fed to the network in the same mini-batch. Zhang et al. [14] took into account the multi-annotator dataset in the construction of the model architecture. The so called U-Net-and-a-half was constructed from a single encoder and multiple decoders. Each decoder corresponded to an expert allowing for simultaneous learning from all masks. The loss function was computed as the aggregated loss across all decoders.

Many approaches model and/or quantify the segmentation output uncertainty. For instance, the model proposed by Hu et al. [1] based on the Probabilistic U-Net [6] uses inter-annotator variability as a training target. In this way, they were able to generate multiple diverse segmentations from each input, which represent a possible expert segmentation. Jungo et al. [4] computed uncertainty by the principle of Monte Carlo dropout. They used dropout layers at inference time to produce multiple segmentations and, by computing pixel-wise variance, estimated the model's uncertainty.

To summarize, when designing architectures for modeling annotator uncertainty on datasets with multiple annotations, we need to formulate several computational strategies: (i) a strategy to deal with multiple annotations per image in the model training input, (ii) a strategy to approximate the ground truth, and finally (iii) a strategy to model uncertainty on the model output.

In this paper, we focus on the first and third points, i.e. the strategy of handling multiple annotations per image and modeling of output uncertainty, while as for the second point we latently acknowledge that ground truth may not exist. Thus we propose to aggregate multiple annotations into a single mask and to treat each level of agreement as a separate class. Modeling multi-annotator uncertainty as multi-class segmentation problem can be simply coupled with any multi class segmentation model. According to a recent review on noisy label handling strategies [5] and our literature review, to the best of our knowledge, such a simple but effective solution to annotation aggregation and uncertainty modeling has not yet been proposed.

3   Materials and Methods

3.1   Datasets

The QUBIQ 2020 challenge data consists of four 2D CT and MR datasets of different anatomies with seven segmentation tasks, where two of the datasets, namely *Prostate* and *Brain tumor* dataset, include multiple ROIs. The QUBIQ 2021 challenge is an extension, including two additional 3D datasets, *Pancreas* and *Pancreatic lesion*, where each patient went through two scans at two time points. Each of the images was segmented by multiple trained experts, with annotator count ranging from 2 to 7, depending on the particular dataset. Additional dataset information is given in Table 1 and a few examples are visualized in Fig. 1.

Table 1. Number of given samples in training and validation dataset.

Dataset	No. samples (Train/Val.)	No. structures	No. contours	No. modalities
Prostate	55 (48/7)	2	6	1
Brain growth	39 (34/5)	1	7	1
Brain tumor	32 (28/4)	3	3	4
Kidney	24 (20/4)	1	3	1
Pancreas	58 (40/18)	1	2	1
Pancreatic lesion	32 (22/10)	1	2	1

3.2   Multi-annotation Aggregation

For segmentation of ROI given multiple annotations, we aggregated the given binary segmentation masks into a single input mask M^{in} as

$$M^{in}(x,y) = \sum_{i=1}^{N} B_i(x,y), \tag{1}$$

where N denotes the number of experts and B_i the binary value of pixel (x,y) as annotated by i-th expert. The values of the encoded mask were thus between 0 and the number of experts, where each foreground pixel value denotes the number of experts labeling the selected pixel as the ROI. In this way we encode

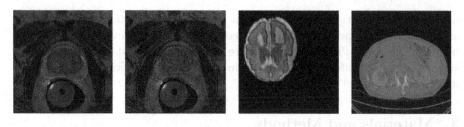

Fig. 1. Exemplary images with multi-annotator masks for segmentation tasks with single modalities (*left to right*): Prostate – Task 1, Prostate – Task 2, Brain growth and Kidney. The color notes the number of experts marking the area as segmented organ, from 0 (*blue*) to all (*red*). (Color figure online)

the three-dimensional mask input (no. of annotators, width, height) and map it into a two-dimensional space $[N\ X\ Y] \xrightarrow{M_{in}} [X\ Y]$, for image width X and image height Y, as shown in Fig. 2. By encoding multiple image masks, we transformed the problem into multi-class classification problem, with $N+1$ classes (including background), where class c marks the agreement of exactly c annotators, for $c \in \{0, 1, \ldots, N\}$.

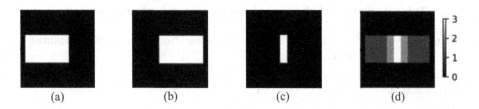

(a)   (b)   (c)   (d)

Fig. 2. Encoding of three binary segmentation masks (a), (b) and (c) into a single encoded multi-annotator mask (d), where each pixel value equals to the number of experts marking the particular pixel as the ROI.

The CNN output is a three dimensional matrix $[N + 1\ X\ Y]$, with a vector $(p_0, p_1, \ldots, p_N)$ for pixel (x, y), where p_i marks the probability that the pixel was marked as ROI by exactly c annotators. By computing $\operatorname{argmax}_c p_c$ for each pixel, we get a two dimensional output mask M^{out} with predicted regions of agreement between experts. We can further decode the output mask into three-dimensional space, as shown in Fig. 3, we obtain as many masks as there are annotators, however, this time each mask represents a quantitative agreement value. Thus, the output mask M_1^{out} represents the area where the structure of interest has been annotated by at least one annotator, whereas the marked area decreases with increasing the index j in

$$M_c^{out}(x, y) = (M^{out}(x, y) \geq c). \tag{2}$$

The output mask M_1^{out} thus represents the pixels that would be marked by at least one annotator, M_2^{out} by at least two annotators, etc. Further, dividing the output mask values with the number of annotators N results in values on the interval $[0,1]$, which can be interpreted as annotation or segmentation (un)certainty and reflects the uncertainty of the expert annotators.

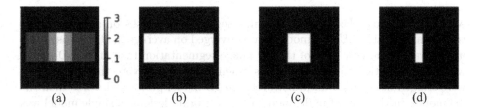

Fig. 3. Decoding of model output a) M^{out} into three binary segmentation masks b) M_1^{out}, c) M_2^{out} and d) M_3^{out}, where M_c^{out} denotes the predicted mask with ROI marked by at least c experts.

3.3   Segmentation Model

Structure segmentation and its uncertainty estimation was obtained by adapting the open-source nnU-Net [2,3]. The nnU-net framework implements a single or cascaded U-net model and, based on the input images, the particular model and its hyperparameters are chosen and configured automatically. The following subsections describe the framework and its adaptations.

Model Architecture. The nnU-Net ('no-new-Net') uses a 2D U-net or 3D U-Net [11] as a backbone architecture. The main advantage of nnU-Net is it's self configuring training pipeline and automatic adaptation of model architecture and hyperparameter tuning that considers the available hardware resources and requires little or no user input. The encoder part starts with 32 feature maps in the initial layers and doubles the number of feature maps with each downsampling and vice versa in the decoder. The number of convolutional blocks is adapted to the input patch size, assuring that downsampling does not result in feature maps smaller than $4 \times 4(\times 4)$. Compared to the original U-net, the nnU-net authors replaced the ReLU activation functions with leaky ReLU and batch normalization with instance normalization.

Loss Function. We applied the *soft Dice loss function* directly on CNN output probabilities. The output values were mapped to the $[0,1]$ interval using the softmax activation function on the output layer. For each class $c \in \{0,1,\ldots,N\}$, where class $c = 0$ represents the background without any annotations, we compute soft Dice similarity coefficient

$$sDSC_c = \frac{\sum_{x,y} p_c(x,y) \cdot M_c^{in}(x,y)}{\sum_{x,y} p_c(x,y)^2 + \sum_{x,y} M_c^{in}(x,y)^2}, \qquad (3)$$

where $p_c(x,y)$ denotes the output probability of pixel (x,y) belonging to class c, M_c^{in} the binary input mask of class c. Finally, Dice coefficient was averaged over all $N+1$ classes. For the loss function we take the negative value

$$Loss = -\frac{1}{N+1} \sum_{c=0}^{N} sDSC_c. \tag{4}$$

Model Training. For each of the nine segmentation tasks on six dataset we trained a separate nnU-Net model that converged on average in 50 epochs. A 2D model was trained for each of the 2D image segmentation task and a 3D model with full resolution for the two 3D segmentation tasks. Note that 2D models were trained also for 3D data, however, the 2D model performed worse than the 3D model. In the case of multi modal data, i.e. brain lesions, a single model was trained using all image modalities as the model input.

Based on the data fingerprint and a series of heuristic rules the image resampling and image normalization were determined. Further, the architecture of nnU-Net dynamically adapted to the dataset, selecting appropriate image input patch size and batch size [2]. To allow training on large image patches, the batch size was generally small, typically (but not less than) two images per batch.

The nnU-Net model training included various data augmentation transformations, each with certain probability p. Namely, random rotations ($p = 0.2$), scaling ($p = 0.2$), mirroring ($p = 0.2$), Gaussian noise ($p = 0.1$) and smoothing ($p = 0.2$), and additive or multiplicative inhomogeneity simulation ($p = 0.15$ or 0.15, respectively). Models were trained using stochastic gradient descent optimizer with an initial learning rate of 0.01 and Nesterov momentum of 0.99.

The nnU-Net models were trained on patches that overlapped by half of the patch size. During inference the same patch size was used as during training. The predicted patches were then combined such that the contributions of different patch predictions across the common voxels were aggregated by weighing the predictions based on the voxel location. Since accuracy was expected to drop towards the patch border, the contribution of such voxels was less then the pixels close to the patch center.

Finally, the predictions were postprocessed by first checking the training dataset samples if all classes lied within a single connected component. In this case, this property was also imposed to the test set by retaining the single largest connected component for each class.

3.4 Evaluation Metrics

Model performance was evaluated according to the provided evaluation code by the QUBIQ challenge organizers. We compared the predicted uncertainty mask M^{out}/N with the uncertainty of the GT, computed as M^{in}/N. For each image, the uncertainty masks were binarized at thresholds $0.1 \times i$; $i = 0, 1, \ldots, 9$, for which the Dice coefficient DSC_i was computed as

$$DSC_i = \frac{2TP_i}{2TP_i + FP_i + FN_i},$$

where TP denotes the true positive pixels, FP denotes the false positive pixels and FN the false negative pixels. Finally the scores were averaged across all ten values for the final performance estimation

$$\overline{DSC} = \frac{1}{10} \sum_{i=0}^{9} DSC_i.$$

4   Results

The results of our proposed model on six datasets and across nine segmentation tasks were computed on the validation datasets and are reported in Table 2 and Fig. 4. In four of the 2D segmentation tasks our approach achieved an average Dice score over 0.9, while for the other three 2D tasks it achieved a score of over 0.7. The lowest scores, significantly below the average, were achieved for the two 3D segmentation tasks introduced in QUBIQ 2021 challenge.

Table 2. Performance measure $\overline{DSC}$ per segmentation task evaluated by QUBIQ challenge organizers. The average is computed over seven tasks for QUBIQ 2020 (disregarding pancreas and pancreatic lesion) and over nine tasks for QUBIQ 2021. (Note: Evaluation metrics on QUBIQ 2020 and 2021 leaderboard are not identical. The average score of our model reported on QUBIQ 2020 leaderboard equals to 0.7476.)

Structure	$\overline{DSC}$
Brain growth	0.9336
Brain tumor - Task 1	0.9485
Brain tumor - Task 2	0.7808
Brain tumor - Task 3	0.7639
Kidney	0.9766
Prostate - Task 1	0.9610
Prostate - Task 2	0.8280
Pancreas	0.5605
Pancreatic lesion	0.3990
Average	
– QUBIQ 2020	0.8846
– QUBIQ 2021	0.7946

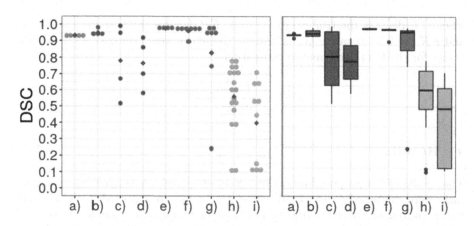

Fig. 4. Scatter plot (*left*) with marked mean values (*red*) and boxplot (*right*) of individual values of the average Dice coefficient $\overline{DSC}$ on validation images for seven tasks: *a)* Brain growth, *b)* Brain tumor - Task 1, *c)* Brain tumor - Task 2, *d)* Brain tumor - Task 3, *e)* Kidney, *f)* Prostate - Task 1, *g)* Prostate - Task 2, *h)* Pancreas, *i)* Pancreatic lesion. (Color figure online)

Due to the nature of the metric $\overline{DSC}$, the error of an incorrectly predicted pixel can accumulate when computing the DSC across multiple thresholds. In some validation images from the Brain tumor dataset (Tasks 2 and 3) the area of the annotated structures, where a fraction of the experts agree, measured only a few pixels. For such a small area an incorrect output value of even a single pixel changes the $\overline{DSC}$ metric value by a substantial amount.

Structures *a)* Brain growth, *b)* Brain tumor - Task 1, *e)* Kidney and *f)* Prostate - Task 1 were predicted consistently, without significant variation in the $\overline{DSC}$ between different cases. Due to the consistent labelling of all experts and consistent size of the structures, the neural network predictions were also consistent. In the case of the listed structures, the region of agreement of all experts was much larger than the region of disagreement, compared to the other structures. In practice, this means that the misperceived agreement pattern of a subset of annotators does not contribute to the value of metric $\overline{DSC}$ to the extent that it does in the case of small structures.

For the two 3D segmentation tasks, i.e. *h)* Pancreas and *i)* Pancreatic lesion, we observed a large variation of the $\overline{DSC}$ values. Specifically, in the cases with the value of $\overline{SDC}$ equal to 0.1, the model did not segment the ROI and instead returned an empty mask.

5   Discussion and Future Work

Intra- and inter-annotator variations result in significantly differing manual segmentations, which may be related to the uncertainty of the segmentation task; hence, the algorithms for automatic segmentation should learn to capture the annotator (dis)agreements. In our approach we modeled the annotator (dis)agreement by aggregating the multi-annotator segmentations to reflect the uncertainty of the segmentation task and formulated the segmentation as multi-class pixel classification problem within an open source nnU-Net framework [3].

Validation was carried out for a wide range of imaging modalities and segmentation tasks as provided by the 2020 and 2021 QUBIQ challenges and showed high quality segmentations according to the average Dice scores. While inspecting our results we noticed a large variation in Dice scores across validation cases for the 2D Brain tumor segmentation tasks 2 and 3 and both segmentation tasks on the 3D datasets. In part, the low $\overline{DSC}$ scores in particular cases and high variability in the score in the aforementioned tasks can be attributed to the fact that the area of agreement covers only a few pixels. This is particularly evident for Brain tumor segmentation - Task 2, as shown in Fig. 5, where one of the raters consistently segments different ROIs as the other two raters. This systematic difference is also captured by the model, that did not classify any of the pixels as the area, where all the three annotators would agree.

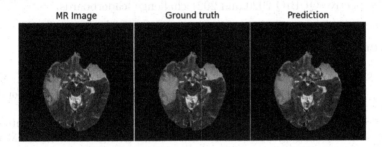

Fig. 5. Ground truth and prediction for Brain tumor - Task 2. Single annotator's ROIs marking *(blue)* significantly differ from the segmentation of the other two *(yellow)*, with a very small overlap of all three *(red)*. (Color figure online)

In 3D space, the ratio between the background and ROI becomes even larger. The poor result can therefore again be partially contributed to class imbalance. Further we can notice a large difference in input image sizes in z axis, that varies from 36 to 194 pixels on the training set. To potentially improve the results, reducing the image size around the ROI, before training the neural network could be considered.

When forming the aggregated target segmentation, we assumed, that all experts were equally trained and thus we took the sum of their segmentation masks as the ground truth. However, in the case of major disagreements in annotations, such as for Brain tumor segmentation - Task 2, a smaller weight could be given to the annotator that is not in accordance with the others. The performance might therefore be improved by the use of expert performance level estimates as obtained from the SIMPLE algorithm [8], confusion matrices as in Tanno et al. [12] or similar approaches for generating GT used as target masks.

Finally, one of the main limitations of modeling multi-annotator (dis)agreement as multi-class problem is it's sensitivity to minor changes of the softmax function, which can result in pixel misclassification. A change of argmax function by, for example, weighted sum of classes using softmax outputs as weights, could result in a more robust model.

6   Conclusion

The goal of the QUBIQ challenge was to segment nine different structures of interest, i.e. organs and pathologies, in six different datasets, for which segmentation masks of multiple experts were provided. In the context of the established nnU-Net segmentation framework, we proposed a novel strategy of handling multiple annotations per image and modeling of output uncertainty. Namely, we aggregate multiple annotations into a single mask and to treat each level of agreement as a separate class, thus modeling multi-annotator segmentation uncertainty as multi-class segmentation problem. We achieved high quality segmentation results with an overall third and sixth best overall Dice score result on the respective QUBIQ 2020 and 2021 challenge leaderboards.

References

1. Hu, S., Worrall, D., Knegt, S., Veeling, B., Huisman, H., Welling, M.: Supervised uncertainty quantification for segmentation with multiple annotations. arXiv:1907.01949 [cs, stat], July 2019. http://arxiv.org/abs/1907.01949
2. Isensee, F., Jäger, P.F., Kohl, S.A.A., Petersen, J., Maier-Hein, K.H.: Automated design of deep learning methods for biomedical image segmentation. Nat Methods 18(2), 203–211 (2021). https://doi.org/10.1038/s41592-020-01008-z, http://arxiv.org/abs/1904.08128, arXiv: 1904.08128 version: 2
3. Isensee, F., et al.: nnU-Net: self-adapting framework for U-net-based medical image segmentation. arXiv:1809.10486 [cs], September 2018. http://arxiv.org/abs/1809.10486
4. Jungo, A., Meier, R., Ermis, E., Herrmann, E., Reyes, M.: Uncertainty-driven sanity check: application to postoperative brain tumor cavity segmentation. arXiv:1806.03106 [cs], June 2018. http://arxiv.org/abs/1806.03106
5. Karimi, D., Dou, H., Warfield, S.K., Gholipour, A.: Deep learning with noisy labels: exploring techniques and remedies in medical image analysis. Med. Image Anal. 65, 101759 (2020). https://doi.org/10.1016/j.media.2020.101759
6. Kohl, S.A.A., et al.: A probabilistic U-net for segmentation of ambiguous images. arXiv:1806.05034 [cs, stat], January 2019. http://arxiv.org/abs/1806.05034
7. Lampert, T.A., Stumpf, A., Gançarski, P.: An empirical study into annotator agreement, ground truth estimation, and algorithm evaluation. IEEE Trans. Image Process. 25(6), 2557–2572 (2016). https://doi.org/10.1109/TIP.2016.2544703, http://arxiv.org/abs/1307.0426
8. Langerak, T.R., van der Heide, U.A., Kotte, A.N.T.J., Viergever, M.A., van Vulpen, M., Pluim, J.P.W.: Label fusion in atlas-based segmentation using a selective and iterative method for performance level estimation (SIMPLE). IEEE Trans. Med. Imaging 29(12), 2000–2008 (2010). https://doi.org/10.1109/TMI.2010.2057442

9. Litjens, G., Debats, O., van de Ven, W., Karssemeijer, N., Huisman, H.: A pattern recognition approach to zonal segmentation of the prostate on MRI. In: Ayache, N., Delingette, H., Golland, P., Mori, K. (eds.) MICCAI 2012. LNCS, vol. 7511, pp. 413–420. Springer, Heidelberg (2012). https://doi.org/10.1007/978-3-642-33418-4_51
10. Quantification of Uncertainties in Biomedical Image Quantification Challenge 2021. https://qubiq21.grand-challenge.org/. Accessed 11 Aug 2021
11. Ronneberger, O., Fischer, P., Brox, T.: U-net: convolutional networks for biomedical image segmentation. arXiv:1505.04597 [cs], May 2015. http://arxiv.org/abs/1505.04597
12. Tanno, R., Saeedi, A., Sankaranarayanan, S., Alexander, D.C., Silberman, N.: Learning from noisy labels by regularized estimation of annotator confusion. In: Proceedings of the IEEE/CVF Conference on Computer Vision and Pattern Recognition (CVPR), June 2019
13. Warfield, S.K., Zou, K.H., Wells, W.M.: Simultaneous truth and performance level estimation (STAPLE): an algorithm for the validation of image segmentation. IEEE Trans. Med. Imaging **23**(7), 903–921 (2004). https://doi.org/10.1109/TMI.2004.828354, https://www.ncbi.nlm.nih.gov/pmc/articles/PMC1283110/
14. Zhang, Y., et al.: U-net-and-a-half: convolutional network for biomedical image segmentation using multiple expert-driven annotations. arXiv:2108.04658 [cs], August 2021. http://arxiv.org/abs/2108.04658

Adaptive Unsupervised Learning with Enhanced Feature Representation for Intra-tumor Partitioning and Survival Prediction for Glioblastoma

Yifan Li[1], Chao Li[2], Yiran Wei[2], Stephen Price[2], Carola-Bibiane Schönlieb[3], and Xi Chen[1,4(✉)]

[1] Department of Computer Science, University of Bath, Bath, UK
{yl3548,xc841}@bath.ac.uk
[2] Division of Neurosurgery, Department of Clinical Neurosciences, University of Cambridge, Cambridge, UK
{cl647,yw500,sjp58}@cam.ac.uk
[3] Department of Applied Mathematics and Theoretical Physics, University of Cambridge, Cambridge, UK
cbs31@cam.ac.uk
[4] Department of Physics, University of Cambridge, Cambridge, UK
xc253@mrao.cam.ac.uk

Abstract. Glioblastoma is profoundly heterogeneous in regional microstructure and vasculature. Characterizing the spatial heterogeneity of glioblastoma could lead to more precise treatment. With unsupervised learning techniques, glioblastoma MRI-derived radiomic features have been widely utilized for tumor sub-region segmentation and survival prediction. However, the reliability of algorithm outcomes is often challenged by both ambiguous intermediate process and instability introduced by the randomness of clustering algorithms, especially for data from heterogeneous patients.

In this paper, we propose an adaptive unsupervised learning approach for efficient MRI intra-tumor partitioning and glioblastoma survival prediction. A novel and problem-specific Feature-enhanced Auto-Encoder (FAE) is developed to enhance the representation of pairwise clinical modalities and therefore improve clustering stability of unsupervised learning algorithms such as K-means. Moreover, the entire process is modelled by the Bayesian optimization (BO) technique with a custom loss function that the hyper-parameters can be adaptively optimized in a reasonably few steps. The results demonstrate that the proposed approach can produce robust and clinically relevant MRI sub-regions and statistically significant survival predictions.

Keywords: Glioblastoma · MRI · Auto-encoder · K-means clustering · Bayesian optimization · Survival prediction

---

C. Li—Equal contribution.

© The Author(s), under exclusive license to Springer Nature Switzerland AG 2022
A. Crimi and S. Bakas (Eds.): BrainLes 2021, LNCS 12962, pp. 124–139, 2022.
https://doi.org/10.1007/978-3-031-08999-2_10

1   Introduction

Glioblastoma is one of the most aggressive adult brain tumors characterized by heterogeneous tissue microstructure and vasculature. Previous research has shown that multiple sub-regions (also known as tumor habitats) co-exist within the tumor, which gives rise to the disparities in tumor composition among patients and may lead to different patient treatment response [9,10]. Regional differences within the tumour are often seen on imaging and may have a prognostic significance [30]. The intra-tumor heterogeneity is near ubiquitous in malignant tumors and likely to reflects cancer evolutionary dynamics [12,25]. Therefore, this intra-tumoral heterogeneity has significantly challenged the precise treatment of patients. Clinicians desire a more accurate identification of intra-tumoral invasive sub-regions for targeted therapy.

Magnetic resonance imaging (MRI) is a non-invasive technique for tumor diagnosis and monitoring. MRI radiomic features [22] provide quantitative information for both tumor partition and survival prediction [7,8]. Mounting evidence supports the usefulness of the radiomic approach in tumor characterization, evidenced by the Brain Tumor Image Segmentation (BraTS) challenge, which provides a large dataset of structural MRI sequences, i.e., T1-weighted, T2-weighted, post-contrast T1-weighted (T1C), and fluid attenuation inversion recovery (FLAIR). Although providing high tissue contrast, these weighted MRI sequences are limited by their non-specificity in reflecting tumor biology, where physiological MRIs, e.g., perfusion MRI (pMRI) and diffusion MRI (dMRI), could complement. Specifically, pMRI measures vascularity within the tumor, while dMRI estimates the brain tissue microstructure. Incorporating these complementary multi-modal MRI has emerged as a promising approach for more accurate tumor characterization and sub-region segmentation for clinical decision support.

Unsupervised learning methods have been widely leveraged to identify the intra-tumoral sub-regions based on multi-modal MRI [4,17,19,26,29,31]. Standard unsupervised learning methods, e.g., K-means, require a pre-defined class number, which lacks concrete determination criteria, affecting the robustness of sub-region identification. For instance, some researchers used pre-defined class numbers according to empirical experience before clustering [4,17]. Some other work [14,31] introduced clustering metrics, e.g., the Calinski-Harabasz (CH) index, which quantifies the quality of clustering outcomes to estimate the ideal class number. However, the CH index is sensitive to data scale [14,31], limiting its generalization ability across datasets. Some other clustering techniques, e.g., agglomerative clustering, do not require a pre-defined class number and instead require manual classification. A sensitivity hyper-parameter, however, is often needed *a priori*. The clustering results can be unstable during iterations and across datasets. Due to the above limitations, the generalization ability of clustering methods has been a significant challenge in clinical applications, particularly when dealing with heterogeneous clinical data.

Further, the relevance of clustering results is often assessed using patient survival in clinical studies [2,6,11,17]. However, existing research seldom addressed the potential influence of instability posed by the unsupervised clustering algorithms. Joint hyper-parameter optimization considering both clustering stability and survival relevance is desirable in tumor sub-region partitioning.

In this paper, we propose a variant of auto-encoder (AE), termed Feature-enhanced Auto-Encoder (FAE), to identify robust latent feature space constituted by the multiple input MRI modalities and thus alleviate the impact brought by the heterogeneous clinical data. Additionally, we present a Bayesian optimization (BO) framework [24] to undertake the joint optimization task in conjunction with a tailored loss function, which ensures clinical relevance while boosting clustering stability. As a non-parametric optimization technique based on Bayes' Theorem and Gaussian Processes (GP) [21], BO learns the representation of the underlying data distribution that the most probable candidate of the hyper-parameters is generated for evaluation in each step. Here, BO is leveraged to identify the (sub)optimal hyper-parameter set with the potential to effectively identify robust and clinically relevant tumor sub-regions. The primary contributions of this work include:

- Developing a novel loss function that balances the stability of sub-region segmentation and the performance of survival prediction.
- Developing an FAE architecture in the context of glioblastoma studies to further enhance individual clinical relevance between input clinical features and improve the robustness of clustering algorithms.
- Integrating a BO framework that enables automatic hyper-parameter search, which significantly reduces the computational cost and provides robust and clinically relevant results.

The remainder of this paper is organized as follows. Section 2 describes the overall study design, the proposed framework, and techniques. Section 3 reports numerical results, and Sect. 4 is the concluding remarks.

2   Problem Formulation and Methodology

Consider an N patients multi-modal MRI dataset Ω with M modalities defined as $\{\mathbf{X}_m\}_{m=1}^M$. $\mathbf{X}_m$ denotes the mth (pixel-wise) modality values over a collection of N patients. $\mathbf{X}_m = \{\mathbf{x}_{m,n}\}_{n=1}^N$, where $\mathbf{x}_{m,n} \in \mathbb{R}^{I_{m,n} \times 1}$ and $I_{m,n}$ denotes total pixel number of an individual MRI image for the mth modality of the nth patient.

Our goal is to conduct sub-region segmentation on MRI images and perform clinically explainable survival analysis. Instead of running unsupervised learning algorithms directly on $\mathbf{X}_m$, we introduce an extra latent feature enhancement scheme (termed FAE) prior to the unsupervised learning step to further improve the efficiency and robustness of clustering algorithms.

As shown in Fig. 1(A), FAE aims to produce a set of latent features $\{\mathbf{Z}_{m'}\}_{m'=1}^M$ that represent the original data $\{\mathbf{X}_m\}_{m=1}^M$. Unlike a standard AE that takes all modalities as input, FAE 'highlights' pairwise common features and produces $\mathbf{Z}$ through a set of encoders (denoted as E) and decoders (denoted as D). The latent features are then used in unsupervised clustering to classify tumor sub-region $\{\mathbf{P}_n\}_{n=1}^{N}$ for all patients. As an intermediate step, we can now produce spatial features $\{\mathbf{F}_n\}_{n=1}^{N}$ from the segmented figures through radiomic spatial feature extraction methods such as gray level co-occurrence matrix (GLCM) and Gray Level Run Length Matrix (GLRLM) [15].

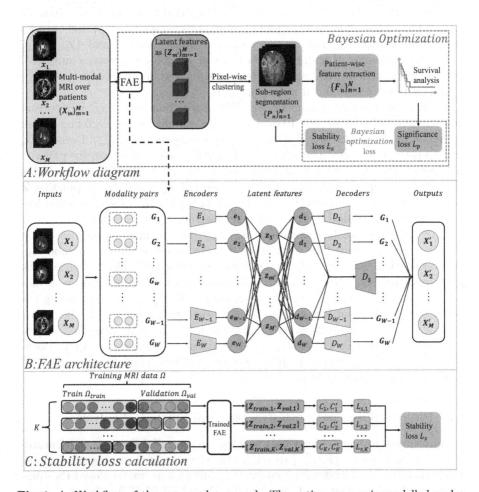

Fig. 1. A: Workflow of the proposed approach. The entire process is modelled under a Bayesian optimization framework. B: Architecture of FAE. The light orange circle represents modality $\mathbf{X}_m$ overall patients and the blue circle is the latent feature $\mathbf{Z}_{m'}$. The green dotted frame denotes the modality pair, and the green trapezoid represents feature-enhanced encoder E and decoder D. The blue trapezoid indicates the fully connected decoders D_s. C: Illustration of stability loss calculation. Circles in different colours represent individual patient MRI data, which are then randomly shuffled for K times to split into train/validation sets. (Color figure online)

2.1 Feature-Enhanced Auto-Encoder

FAE is developed on Auto-encoder (AE), a type of artificial neural network used for dimensionality reduction. A standard AE is a 3-layer symmetric network that has the same inputs and outputs. As illustrated in Fig. 1(B), FAE contains W feature-enhanced encoder layers $\{E_w\}_{w=1}^{W}$ to deal with $\{\mathbf{G}_w\}_{w=1}^{W}$ pairs of modalities, where $W = \binom{M}{2}$ pairs of modalities (from combination) given M inputs. The wth encoder takes a pair of modalities from $\{\mathbf{X}_m\}_{m=1}^{M}$ and encodes to a representation $\mathbf{e}_w$. The central hidden layer of FAE contains $\{\mathbf{Z}_{m'}\}_{m'=1}^{M}$ nodes that represents M learnt abstract features. FAE also possesses a 'mirrored' architecture similar to AE, where W feature-enhanced decoder layers $\{D_w\}_{w=1}^{W}$ are connected to the decoded representations $\{d_w\}_{w=1}^{W}$.

Unlike the standard symmetric AE, FAE has a 'dual decoding' architecture that an extra fully-connected decoder layer D_s is added to the decoding half of the networks to connect $\{d_w\}_{w=1}^{W}$ directly to the outputs $\{\mathbf{X'}_m\}_{m=1}^{M}$. Decoder D_s aims to pass all outputs information (and correlations) rather than the pairwise information from $\mathbf{G}_w$ in the back-propagation process. As a result, node weights $\{\mathbf{Z}_{m'}\}_{m'=1}^{M}$ are updated by gradients from both $\{D_w\}_{w=1}^{W}$ and D_s. In practice, $\mathbf{Z}$ and the encoders are iteratively amended by $\{D_w\}_{w=1}^{W}$ (i.e., reconstruction loss from pairwise AEs) and D_s (i.e., global reconstruction loss) in turns.

FAE enhances the latent features in every pair of input modalities before reducing the dimensionality from W to M. For instance, $\mathbf{e}_w$ is a unique representation that only depends on (and thus enhances the information of) the given input pair $\mathbf{G}_w$. Under this dual decoding architecture, FAE takes advantage of highlighting the pairwise information in $\{\mathbf{Z}_{m'}\}_{m'=1}^{M}$ while retaining the global correlation information from D_s. Another advantage of FAE lies in its flexibility to the dimensionality of input features. The FAE presented in this paper always produces the same number of latent features as the input dimension. The latent dimension might be further reduced manually depending on computational/clinical needs.

2.2 Patient-Wise Feature Extraction and Survival Analysis

We implement Kaplan-Meier (KM) survival analysis [2,17] on spatial features and sub-region counts $\{\mathbf{F}_n\}_{n=1}^{N}$ to verify the relevance of clustering sub-regions. To characterize the intratumoral co-existing sub-regions, we employed the commonly used texture features from the GLCM and GLRLM families, i.e., Long Run Emphasis (LRE), Relative mutual information (RMI), Joint Energy, Run Variance (RV) and Non-Uniformity. These features are formulated to reflect the spatial heterogeneity of tumor sub-regions. For example, LRE indicates the prevalence of a large population of tumor sub-regions. The formulas and interpretations of all these features are detailed in [27]. We next use the k-medoids technique to classify N patients into high- and low-risk subgroups based on $\{\mathbf{F}_n\}_{n=1}^{N}$ and then perform KM analysis to analyze the survival significance of the subgroups to determine the L_p, as described in Sect. 2.4 and Eq. 2.

2.3 Constructing Problem-Specific Losses

Stability Loss. We first introduce a stability quantification scheme to evaluate clustering stability using pairwise cluster distance [13,28], which will serve as part of the loss function in hyper-parameter optimization. Specifically, we employ a Hamming distance method (see [28] for details) to quantify the gap between clustering models. We first split the MRI training dataset Ω into train and validation sets, denoted as Ω_{train} and Ω_{val} respectively. We then train two clustering models C (based on Ω_{train}) and C' (based on Ω_{val}). The stability loss aims to measure the performance of model C on the unseen validation set Ω_{val}. The distance $d(\cdot)$ (also termed as L_s) is defined as:

$$L_s = d(C, C') = \min_{\pi} \frac{1}{I_{val}} \sum_{\Omega_{val}} \mathbb{1}_{\{\pi(C(\Omega_{val}) \neq C'(\Omega_{val}))\}}, \tag{1}$$

where I_{val} denotes the total number of pixels over all MRI images in the validation set Ω_{val}. $\mathbb{1}$ represents the Dirac delta function [32] that returns 1 when the inequality condition is satisfied and 0 otherwise, and function $\pi(\cdot)$ denotes the repeated permutations of dataset Ω to guarantee the generalization of the stability measure [28].

Figure 1 (C) shows the diagram for L_s calculation, where N patients are randomly shuffled for K times to mitigate the effect of randomness. K pairs of intermediate latent features $\{\mathbf{Z}_{train,k}, \mathbf{Z}_{val,k}\}_{k=1}^{K}$ are generated through FAE for training the clustering models C and C'. We then compute L_s over K repeated trials. L_s is normalized to range $[0, 1]$, and smaller values indicates more stable clusterings.

Significance Loss. We integrate prior knowledge from clinical survival analysis and develop a significance loss L_p to quantify clinical relevance between the clustering outcomes and patient survival, as demonstrated in the below equation:

$$L_p = \log(\frac{\tau}{p}) \tag{2}$$

where p represents p-value (i.e., statistical significance measure) of the log-rank test in the survival analysis and τ is a predefined threshold.

This follows the clinical practice that a lower p-value implies that the segmented tumor sub-regions can provide sensible differentiation for patient survival. In particular, given threshold τ, for p less than the threshold, the loss equation returns a increasing positive reward. Otherwise, for p greater than or equal to τ, the segmented tumor sub-regions are considered undesirable and the penalty increases with p.

2.4 Bayesian Optimization

Hyper-parameters tuning is computational expensive and often requires expert knowledge, both of which raise practical difficulties in clinical applications. In this paper, we consider two undetermined hyper-parameters: a quantile threshold $\gamma \in [0, 1]$ that distinguishes outlier data points from the majority and cluster number η for the pixel-wise clustering algorithm. We treat the entire process of Fig. 1(A) as a *black-box system*, of which the input is the hyper-parameter set $\boldsymbol{\theta} = [\gamma, \eta]$ and the output is a joint loss $\mathcal{L}$ defined as:

$$\mathcal{L} = \alpha L_s + (1 - \alpha) L_p \tag{3}$$

where α is a coefficient that balances L_s and L_p and ranges between $[0, 1]$.

Algorithm 1: Bayesian optimization for hyper-parameter tuning

---

1 Initialization of GP surrogate f and the RBF kernel $\mathcal{K}(\cdot)$
2 **while** *not converged* **do**
3 　　Fit GP surrogate model f with $\{\theta_j, \mathcal{L}_j\}_{j=1}^{J}$
4 　　Propose a most probable candidate θ_{j+1} through Equation (4)
5 　　Run **Algorithm** 2 with θ_{j+1}, and compute loss $\mathcal{L}_{j+1}$
6 　　Estimate current optimal θ_{j+2} of the constructed GP surrogate f'
7 　　Run **Algorithm** 2 with θ_{j+2}, calculate the loss $\mathcal{L}_{j+2}$
8 　　$J = J + 2$
9 **end**
10 Obtain (sub)optimal θ_* upon convergence

We address the hyper-parameter tuning issue by modelling the black-box system under BO, a sequential optimization technique that aims to approximate the search space contour of $\boldsymbol{\theta}$ by constructing a Gaussian Process (GP) surrogate function in light of data. BO adopts an *exploration-exploitation scheme* to search for the most probable $\boldsymbol{\theta}$ candidate and therefore minimize the surrogate function mapping $f : \Theta \to \mathcal{L}$ in J optimization steps, where Θ and $\mathcal{L}$ denote input and output spaces respectively. The GP surrogate is defined as: $f \sim \mathcal{GP}(\cdot|\boldsymbol{\mu}, \boldsymbol{\Sigma})$; where $\boldsymbol{\mu}$ is the $J \times 1$ mean function vector and $\boldsymbol{\Sigma}$ is a $J \times J$ co-variance matrix composed by the pre-defined kernel function $\mathcal{K}(\cdot)$ over the inputs $\{\theta_j\}_{j=1}^{J}$. In this paper, we adopt a standard radial basis function (RBF) kernel (see [3] for an overview of GP and the kernel functions).

Given training data $\Omega_B = \{\theta_j, \mathcal{L}_j\}_{j=1}^{J}$, BO introduces a so-called acquisition function $a(\cdot)$ to propose the most probable candidate to be evaluated at each step. Amongst various types of acquisition functions [24], we employ an EI strategy that seeks new candidates to maximize *expected improvement* over the current best sample. Specifically, suppose f' returns the best value so far, EI searches for a new $\boldsymbol{\theta}$ candidate that maximizes function $g(\boldsymbol{\theta}) = \max\{0, f' - f(\boldsymbol{\theta})\}$. The EI acquisition can thus be written as a function of $\boldsymbol{\theta}$:

$$a_{EI}(\boldsymbol{\theta}) = \mathbb{E}(g(\boldsymbol{\theta})|\Omega_B) = (f' - \boldsymbol{\mu})\Phi(f'|\boldsymbol{\mu}, \boldsymbol{\Sigma}) + \boldsymbol{\Sigma}\mathcal{N}(f'|\boldsymbol{\mu}, \boldsymbol{\Sigma}) \tag{4}$$

where $\Phi(\cdot)$ denotes CDF of the standard normal distribution. In practice, BO step J increases over time and the optimal θ_* can be obtained if the predefined convergence criteria is satisfied. Pseudo-code of the entire process is shown in both Algorithms 1 and Algorithm 2.

2.5   Experiment Details

Data from a total of $N = 117$ glioblastoma patients were collected and divided into training set $\Omega = 82$ and test set $\Omega_{test} = 35$, where the test set was separated for out-of-sample model evaluation. We collected both pMRI and dMRI data and co-registered them into T1C images (details in Appendix 5.1), containing approximately 11 million pixels per modality over all patients. $M = 3$ input modalities were calculated, including rCBV (denoted as $\mathbf{r}$) from pMRI, and isotropic/anisotropic components (denoted as $\mathbf{p}/\mathbf{q}$) of dMRI, thus $\mathbf{X} = \{\mathbf{p}, \mathbf{q}, \mathbf{r}\}$. Dataset Ω was used for stability loss calculation with $\Omega_{train} = 57$, $\Omega_{val} = 25$. L_s was evaluated over $K = 10$ trials for all following experiments. The BO is initialized with $J = 10$ data points Ω_B, $\gamma \in [0,1]$ and η is an integer ranges between 3 and 7. The models were developed on Pytorch platform [18] under Python 3.8. Both encoder E and decoder D employed a fully connected feed-forward NN with one hidden layer, where the hidden node number was set to 10. We adopted *hyperbolic tangent* as the activation function for all layers, *mean squared error (MSE)* as the loss function, and *Adam* as the optimiser.

Algorithm 2: Pseudo-code of the workflow as a component of BO

    // Initialization
1 Prepare MRI data Ω with N patients and M modalities, perform data filtering with quantile threshold γ
    // FAE training follows Figure 1(B)
2 Compose W pairs of modalities $G_{w=1}^W$, where $W = \binom{M}{2}$
3 Train FAE on $\{\mathbf{X}_m\}_{m=1}^M$ to generate latent features $\{\mathbf{Z}_{m'}\}_{m'=1}^W$
    // Stability loss calculation follows Figure 1(C)
4 **for** $k = 1,2,...,K$ **do**
5 | Randomly divide Ω into train (Ω_{train}) and validation (Ω_{val}) sets
6 | Produce latent pairs $\{\mathbf{Z}_{train,k}, \mathbf{Z}_{val,k}\}_{k=1}^K$
      | // Pixel-wise clustering
7 | Obtain C_k and C_k' through standard K-means with η clusters
8 | Compute kth stability loss $L_{s,k}$ by Eq (1)
9 **end**
10 Compute stability score L_s by averaging over $\{L_{s,k}\}_{k=1}^K$
    // Sub-region segmentation
11 Obtain patient-wise sub-region segments $\{\mathbf{P}_n\}_{n=1}^N$
    // Patient-wise feature extraction
12 Extract $\{\mathbf{F}_n\}_{n=1}^N$ for all N patients
    // Survival analysis
13 Cluster patients into high/low risk subgroups based on $\{\mathbf{F}_n\}_{n=1}^N$ using a standard K-Medoids algorithm. Perform survival analysis and obtain p
    // BO loss calculation
14 Compute clinical significance score L_p by Eq (2)
15 Compute joint loss L follows Eq (3)

---

3   Results and Discussions

We first present the clustering stability of the models incorporating FAE architecture, which contains 1 hidden layer with 10 hidden nodes. The hyper-parameter choice of FAE architecture, which is simple to be compared in numerical experiments, are determined by empirical experiences. Other AE variants against the baseline model and then compare the performance of the proposed methodology under different experimental settings. We finally demonstrate the results of survival analysis and independent test.

3.1   Evaluation of FAE Based Clustering

The results comparing the models are detailed in Table 1. One sees that all three AE variants show better stability performance than that of the baseline model in the varying cluster numbers. Of note, our proposed FAE architecture, which incorporates both standard AE and ensemble AE, outperforms other models in majority comparisons.

Table 1. Stability performance of cluster algorithms under different AE variants. Baseline represents the original model without AE. The standard AE represents a standard 3-layer (with 1 hidden layer) feed-forward network and the ensemble AE is the FAE without dual decoder D_s. The hidden layer contains 10 nodes for all AE variants.

Clusters	3	4	5	6
Stability score				
Baseline	0.761±0.026	0.890±0.04	0.744±0.027	0.761±0.035
Standard AE	0.909±0.024	0.896±0.063	0.859±0.06	0.836±0.061
Ensemble AE	**0.972±0.013**	0.921±0.028	0.872±0.046	0.881±0.046
FAE	0.909±0.048	**0.923±0.029**	**0.911±0.038**	**0.891±0.048**
Calinski-Harabasz (CH) score				
Baseline (10^6)	4.12±0.00003	5.16±0.00013	4.82±0.00003	4.73±0.00009
Standard AE (10^6)	5.94±0.63	5.74±0.51	5.50±0.41	5.36±0.28
Ensemble AE (10^6)	10.43±0.67	10.99±0.52	10.98±0.89	11.09±1.00
FAE (10^6)	**13.85±4.45**	**14.85±4.49**	**15.09±4.19**	**15.34±4.14**

As expected, all AE variants enhance the clustering stability and quality, shown by the stability score and CH score. The latter is relatively sensitive to data scale but can provide reasonable evaluation for a fixed dataset. In our case, as the dimensions of the original input modalities and the latent features remain identical ($M = 3$), the considerably improved stability of the models incorporating FAE architecture suggests the usefulness of the FAE in extracting robust features for the unsupervised clustering. Additionally, our experiments show that the FAE demonstrates remarkably stable performance in the clustering when the training data is randomly selected, which further supports the resilience of the FAE in extracting generalizable features for distance-based clustering algorithms.

3.2   Adaptive Hyper-parameter Tuning

Figure 2 shows the performance of the proposed approach in 4 different α values in terms of stability score (lower score value indicates better stability). 10 initial training steps and 20 follow-up BO steps are evaluated in the experiments, all the results are averaged over 10 repeated trials. One sees significant dispersion of initial points (dots in the left half of each figure) in all figures, indicating reasonable randomness of initial points in BO training. BO proposes a new

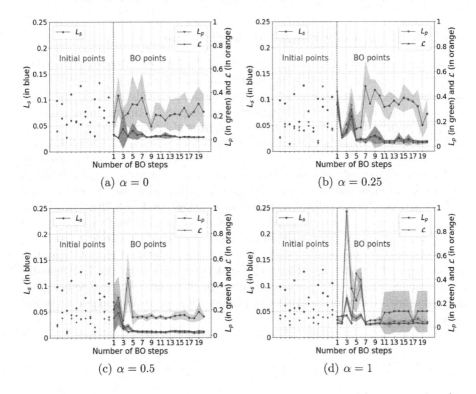

Fig. 2. Performance of the proposed approach with respect to BO step number (on x-axis). Each figure contains two y-axis: stability loss L_s (in blue) on the left y-axis, and both significant loss L_p (in green) and joint loss (in orange) on the right y-axis. All losses are normalized and the shadowed areas in different colors indicate error-bars of the corresponding curves. Figure (a)–(d) shows the performance with loss coefficient $\alpha = 0, 0.25, 0.5$ and 1, respectively. (Color figure online)

candidate θ per step after the initial training. One observes that the joint loss $\mathcal{L}$ (orange curves) converges and the proposed approach successfully estimates (sub)optimal θ_* in all α cases.

Figure 2(a) shows $\alpha = 0$ case, for which $\mathcal{L} = L_p$ according to Equation (3). In other words, the algorithm aims to optimize significance loss L_p (green curve) rather than stability loss L_s (blue curve). As a result, the orange and green curves overlap with each other, and the stability scores are clearly lower than that of L_s. A consistent trend can be observed across all four cases that the error-bar areas of L_s (blue shadowed areas) shrink as the weight of L_s increases in the joint loss. Similar observations can be seen in Fig. 2(d) where $\alpha = 1$ and $\mathcal{L} = L_s$, the error-bar area of L_p (green shadowed area) is considerably bigger than those in the rest α cases. Note that L_s and $\mathcal{L}$ also overlap with each other and the mismatch in the figure is caused by the differences of left and right y-axis scale. When $\alpha = 0.5$ (Fig. 2(c)), clustering stability can quickly converge in a few BO steps (around 6 steps in the orange curve), shows the advantage of the proposed BO integrated method in hyper-parameter optimization.

3.3   Statistical Analysis and Independent Test

Upon convergence of BO, we acquire well-trained FAE encoders to extract features from modalities, a well-trained clustering model for tumor sub-region segmentation and a population-level grouping model to divide patients into high-risk and low-risk subgroups. Eventually, we acquire 5 tumor sub-regions as $\{\mathbf{P}_n\}_{n=1}^{N}$ from features processed by the well-trained FAE, where $\mathbf{P}_n = \{\mathbf{p}_i\}_{i=1}^{I}$, $\mathbf{p}_i \in \{1, 2, 3, 4, 5\}$ denotes the sub-region labels for each pixel, and produce features $\{\mathbf{F}_n\}_{n=1}^{N}$, where $\mathbf{F}_n \in \mathbb{R}^{11 \times 1}$ represents 9 spatial features and proportion of the 2 significant sub-regions, the details of clinical features could be found in Appendix 5.2. Subsequently, we apply these well-trained models to the test set with 35 patients. The results of KM analysis are shown in Fig. 3, illustrating that the spatial features extracted from tumor sub-regions could lead to patient-level clustering that successfully separates patients into distinct survival groups in both datasets (Train: p-value $= 0.013$ Test: p-value $= 0.0034$). Figure 4 shows two case examples from the high-risk and low-risk subgroups, respectively, where different colours indicate the partitioned sub-regions. Intuitively, these sub-regions are in line with the prior knowledge of proliferating, necrotic, and edema tumor areas, respectively.

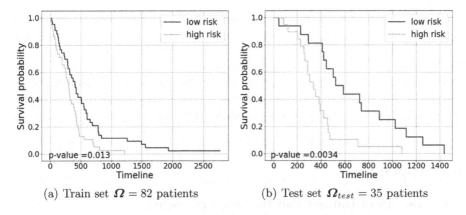

(a) Train set $\Omega = 82$ patients   (b) Test set $\Omega_{test} = 35$ patients

Fig. 3. KM survival curves for the train and test datasets.

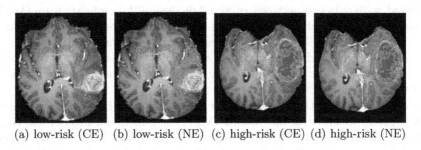

(a) low-risk (CE) (b) low-risk (NE) (c) high-risk (CE) (d) high-risk (NE)

Fig. 4. Two case examples from the high-risk (a & b) and lower-risk (c & d) group, respectively. Different colours denote the partitioned sub-regions. The two patients have significantly different proportions of sub-regions with clinical relevance, which could provide clinical decision support. (Color figure online)

4 Conclusions

The paper is an interdisciplinary work that helps clinical research to acquire robust and effective sub-regions of glioblastoma for clinical decision support. The proposed FAE architectures significantly enhance the robustness of the clustering model and improve the quality of clustering results. Additionally, robust and reliable clustering solutions can be accomplished with minimal time investment by integrating the entire process inside a BO framework and presenting a unique loss function for problem-specific multi-task optimization. Finally, the independent validation of our methodology using a different dataset strengthens its viability in clinical applications.

Although we have conducted numerous repeating trials, it is inevitable to eliminate the randomness for clustering algorithm experiments. In future work, we could include more modalities and datasets to test the framework. To enhance the clinical relevance, more clinical variables could be included into the BO framework for multi-task optimization. To summarise, the BO framework combined with the suggested FAE and mixed loss represents a robust framework for obtaining clustering results that are clinically relevant and generalizable across datasets.

5   Appendix

5.1   Details of Dataset and Imagine Processing

Patients with surgical resection (July 2010–August 2015) were consecutively recruited, with data prospectively collected by the multidisciplinary team (MDT) central review. All glioblastoma patients underwent pre-operative 3D MPRAGE (pre-contrast T1 and T1C), T2-weighted FLAIR, pMRI and dMRI sequences. All patients have a radiogical diagnosis of de novo glioblastoma, aged 18 to 75, eligible for craniotomy and radiotherapy, and all images resolution were resampled to $1 \times 1 \times 1 \, m^3$.

Co-registration of the images was accomplished using the linear registration tool (FLIRT) included in the Oxford Centre for Functional MRI of the Brain Software Library (FSL) v5.0.0 (Oxford, UK) [5,23]. NordicICE was used to process dynamic susceptibility contrast (DSC), one of the most frequently utilised perfusion methods (NordicNeuroLab). The arterial input function was automatically defined. The diffusion toolbox in FSL was used to process the diffusion images (DTI) [1]. The isotropic (p) and anisotropic (q) components were computed after normalisation and eddy current correction [20].

5.2   Details for Clinical Features

In this study, through the BO, the tumor were divided into 5 sub-regions as $\{\mathbf{P}_n\}_{n=1}^{N}$ from $\{\mathbf{Z}_{m'}\}_{m'=1}^{M}$, the features processed by the well-trained FAE, where $\mathbf{P}_n = \{\mathbf{p}_i\}_{i=1}^{I}$, $\mathbf{p}_i \in \{1, 2, 3, 4, 5\}$ denotes the sub-region labels for each pixel. Rather than representing the numerical grey value of images, the value of each $\mathbf{p}_i$ represents sub-region labels, rendering the majority of features in the GLCM and GLRLM families invalid. Finally, the Table 2 summarises the selected features which remain meaningful for the label matrix. Eventually, the clinical features $\{\mathbf{F}_n\}_{n=1}^{N}$, where $\mathbf{F}_n \in \mathbb{R}^{11 \times 1}$ include 9 spatial characteristics in Table 2 and the fraction of 2 significant sub-regions.

Table 2. Clinical features from GLCM matrix of size $N_g \times N_g$ and GLRLM matrix of size $N_g \times N_r$ family including Relative mutual information(RMI), Entropy, Joint Energy, Informational Measure of Correlation(IMC), Long Run Emphasis(LRE), Short Run Emphasis(SRE), Run Variance(RV) and Run Entropy(RE). $p(i,j|\theta)$ in the formula column describes the probability of the (i,j)th elements of matrices along angle θ, $\mu = \sum_{i=1}^{N_g} \sum_{j=1}^{N_r} p(i,j|\theta)i$ denotes the average run length of GLRLM matrix [15].

Feature name	Formula	Interpretation
RMI	$\dfrac{-(\sum_{j=1}^{N_g} p_y(j)\log_2 p_y(j)+\epsilon)+\sum_{i=1}^{N_g}\sum_{j=1}^{N_g}(p(i,j))\log_2 p(i|j)}{-\sum_{j=1}^{N_g} p_y(j)\log_2 p_y(j)+\epsilon}$	Uncertainty coefficient in landspace pattern [16]
Entropy	$-\sum_{i=1}^{N_g} p(i)\log_2(p(i)+\epsilon)$	The uncertainty/ randomness in the image values
Joint Energy	$\sum_{i=1}^{N_g}\sum_{j=1}^{N_g}(p(i,j))^2$	Energy is a measure of homogeneous patterns in the image
IMC	$\dfrac{HXY-HXY1}{\max\{HX,HY\}}$	Quantifying the complexity of the texture)
LRE	$\dfrac{\sum_{i=1}^{N_g}\sum_{j=1}^{N_r}(p(i,j))^2 j^2}{N_r(\theta)}$	LRE is a measure of the distribution of long run lengths
SRE	$\dfrac{\sum_{i=1}^{N_g}\sum_{j=1}^{N_r}\frac{(p(i,j))^2}{j^2}}{N_r(\theta)}$	SRE is a measure of the distribution of short run lengths
Non-uniformity	$\dfrac{\sum_{i=1}^{N_g}(\sum_{j=1}^{N_r} P(i,j|\theta))}{N_r(\theta)^2}$	Measures the similarity of gray-level intensity values in the image
RV	$\sum_{i=1}^{N_g}\sum_{j=1}^{N_r} p(i,j|\theta)(j-\mu)^2$	Measure of the variance in runs for the run lengths
RE	$\sum_{i=1}^{N_g}\sum_{j=1}^{N_r} p(i,j|\theta)\log_2(p(i,j|\theta)+\epsilon)$	Measures the uncertainty/randomness in the distribution of run lengths

References

1. Behrens, T.E., et al.: Characterization and propagation of uncertainty in diffusion-weighted MR imaging. Magn. Resonan. Med. Off. J. Int. Soc. Magn. Resonan. Med. **50**(5), 1077–1088 (2003)
2. Beig, N., et al.: Radiogenomic-based survival risk stratification of tumor habitat on Gd-T1w MRI is associated with biological processes in glioblastoma. Clin. Cancer Res. **26**(8), 1866–1876 (2020)
3. Brochu, E., Cora, V.M., De Freitas, N.: A tutorial on Bayesian optimization of expensive cost functions, with application to active user modeling and hierarchical reinforcement learning. arXiv preprint arXiv:1012.2599 (2010)
4. Dextraze, K., et al.: Spatial habitats from multiparametric MR imaging are associated with signaling pathway activities and survival in glioblastoma. Oncotarget **8**(68), 112992 (2017)
5. Jenkinson, M., Bannister, P., Brady, M., Smith, S.: Improved optimization for the robust and accurate linear registration and motion correction of brain images. Neuroimage **17**(2), 825–841 (2002)

6. Leone, J., Zwenger, A.O., Leone, B.A., Vallejo, C.T., Leone, J.P.: Overall survival of men and women with breast cancer according to tumor subtype. Am. J. Clin. Oncol. **42**(2), 215–220 (2019)

7. Li, C., et al.: Decoding the interdependence of multiparametric magnetic resonance imaging to reveal patient subgroups correlated with survivals. Neoplasia **21**(5), 442–449 (2019)

8. Li, C., et al.: Multi-parametric and multi-regional histogram analysis of MRI: modality integration reveals imaging phenotypes of glioblastoma. Eur. Radiol. **29**(9), 4718–4729 (2019)

9. Li, C., et al.: Intratumoral heterogeneity of glioblastoma infiltration revealed by joint histogram analysis of diffusion tensor imaging. Neurosurgery **85**(4), 524–534 (2019)

10. Li, C., et al.: Low perfusion compartments in glioblastoma quantified by advanced magnetic resonance imaging and correlated with patient survival. Radiother. Oncol. **134**, 17–24 (2019)

11. Mangla, R., et al.: Correlation between progression free survival and dynamic susceptibility contrast MRI perfusion in WHO grade III glioma subtypes. J. Neurooncol. **116**(2), 325–331 (2013). https://doi.org/10.1007/s11060-013-1298-9

12. Meacham, C.E., Morrison, S.J.: Tumour heterogeneity and cancer cell plasticity. Nature **501**(7467), 328–337 (2013)

13. Meilă, M.: Comparing clusterings by the variation of information. In: Schölkopf, B., Warmuth, M.K. (eds.) COLT-Kernel 2003. LNCS (LNAI), vol. 2777, pp. 173–187. Springer, Heidelberg (2003). https://doi.org/10.1007/978-3-540-45167-9_14

14. Meyer-Bäse, A., Saalbach, A., Lange, O., Wismüller, A.: Unsupervised clustering of fMRI and MRI time series. Biomed. Sig. Process. Control **2**(4), 295–310 (2007)

15. Mohanty, A.K., Beberta, S., Lenka, S.K.: Classifying benign and malignant mass using GLCM and GLRLM based texture features from mammogram. Int. J. Eng. Res. Appl. **1**(3), 687–693 (2011)

16. Nowosad, J., Stepinski, T.F.: Information theory as a consistent framework for quantification and classification of landscape patterns. Landscape Ecol. **34**(9), 2091–2101 (2019). https://doi.org/10.1007/s10980-019-00830-x

17. Park, J.E., Kim, H.S., Kim, N., Park, S.Y., Kim, Y.H., Kim, J.H.: Spatiotemporal heterogeneity in multiparametric physiologic MRI is associated with patient outcomes in IDH-wildtype glioblastoma. Clin. Cancer Res. **27**(1), 237–245 (2021)

18. Paszke, A., et al.: Pytorch: an imperative style, high-performance deep learning library. Adv. Neural. Inf. Process. Syst. **32**, 8026–8037 (2019)

19. Patel, E., Kushwaha, D.S.: Clustering cloud workloads: K-means vs gaussian mixture model. Procedia Comput. Sci. **171**, 158–167 (2020)

20. Pena, A., Green, H., Carpenter, T., Price, S., Pickard, J., Gillard, J.: Enhanced visualization and quantification of magnetic resonance diffusion tensor imaging using the p: q tensor decomposition. Br. J. Radiol. **79**(938), 101–109 (2006)

21. Rasmussen, C.E.: Gaussian processes in machine learning. In: Bousquet, O., von Luxburg, U., Rätsch, G. (eds.) ML -2003. LNCS (LNAI), vol. 3176, pp. 63–71. Springer, Heidelberg (2004). https://doi.org/10.1007/978-3-540-28650-9_4

22. Sala, E., et al.: Unravelling tumour heterogeneity using next-generation imaging: radiomics, radiogenomics, and habitat imaging. Clin. Radiol. **72**(1), 3–10 (2017)

23. Smith, S.M., et al.: Advances in functional and structural MR image analysis and implementation as FSL. Neuroimage **23**, S208–S219 (2004)

24. Snoek, J., Larochelle, H., Adams, R.P.: Practical Bayesian optimization of machine learning algorithms. arXiv preprint arXiv:1206.2944 (2012)

25. Sottoriva, A., et al.: Intratumor heterogeneity in human glioblastoma reflects cancer evolutionary dynamics. Proc. Natl. Acad. Sci. **110**(10), 4009–4014 (2013)
26. Syed, A.K., Whisenant, J.G., Barnes, S.L., Sorace, A.G., Yankeelov, T.E.: Multiparametric analysis of longitudinal quantitative MRI data to identify distinct tumor habitats in preclinical models of breast cancer. Cancers **12**(6), 1682 (2020)
27. Van Griethuysen, J.J., et al.: Computational radiomics system to decode the radiographic phenotype. Can. Res. **77**(21), e104–e107 (2017)
28. Von Luxburg, U.: Clustering stability: an overview. Found. Trends Mach. Learn. **2**(3), 235–274 (2010)
29. Wu, J., et al.: Unsupervised clustering of quantitative image phenotypes reveals breast cancer subtypes with distinct prognoses and molecular pathways. Clin. Cancer Res. **23**(13), 3334–3342 (2017)
30. Wu, J., Gong, G., Cui, Y., Li, R.: Intra-tumor partitioning and texture analysis of DCE-MRI identifies relevant tumor subregions to predict pathological response of breast cancer to neoadjuvant chemotherapy. J. Magn. Resonan. Imaging (JMRI) **44**(5), 1107 (2016)
31. Xia, W., et al.: Radiogenomics of hepatocellular carcinoma: multiregion analysis-based identification of prognostic imaging biomarkers by integrating gene data-a preliminary study. Phys. Med. Biol. **63**(3), 035044 (2018)
32. Zhang, L.: Dirac delta function of matrix argument. Int. J. Theor. Phys. 1–28 (2020)

Predicting Isocitrate Dehydrogenase Mutation Status in Glioma Using Structural Brain Networks and Graph Neural Networks

Yiran Wei[1], Yonghao Li[2], Xi Chen[3], Carola-Bibiane Schönlieb[4], Chao Li[1,4(✉)],
and Stephen J. Price[1]

[1] Department of Clinical Neuroscience, University of Cambridge, Cambridge, UK
[2] School of Biological Sciences, Nanyang Technological University,
Singapore, Singapore
[3] Department of Computer Science, University of Bath, Bath, UK
[4] Department of Applied Mathematics and Theoretical Physics,
University of Cambridge, Cambridge, UK
cl647@cam.ac.uk

Abstract. Glioma is a common malignant brain tumor with distinct survival among patients. The isocitrate dehydrogenase (IDH) gene mutation provides critical diagnostic and prognostic value for glioma. It is of crucial significance to non-invasively predict IDH mutation based on pre-treatment MRI. Machine learning/deep learning models show reasonable performance in predicting IDH mutation using MRI. However, most models neglect the systematic brain alterations caused by tumor invasion, where widespread infiltration along white matter tracts is a hallmark of glioma. Structural brain network provides an effective tool to characterize brain organisation, which could be captured by the graph neural networks (GNN) to more accurately predict IDH mutation.

Here we propose a method to predict IDH mutation using GNN, based on the structural brain network of patients. Specifically, we firstly construct a network template of healthy subjects, consisting of atlases of edges (white matter tracts) and nodes (cortical/subcortical brain regions) to provide regions of interest (ROIs). Next, we employ autoencoders to extract the latent multi-modal MRI features from the ROIs of edges and nodes in patients, to train a GNN architecture for predicting IDH mutation. The results show that the proposed method outperforms the baseline models using the 3D-CNN and 3D-DenseNet. In addition, model interpretation suggests its ability to identify the tracts infiltrated by tumor, corresponding to clinical prior knowledge. In conclusion, integrating brain networks with GNN offers a new avenue to study brain lesions using computational neuroscience and computer vision approaches.

Y. Wei and Y. Li—Authors are contributed equally.

A. Crimi and S. Bakas (Eds.): BrainLes 2021, LNCS 12962, pp. 140–150, 2022.
https://doi.org/10.1007/978-3-031-08999-2_11

Keywords: Glioma · MRI · Isocitrate dehydrogenase · Structural
brain network · Graph neural network

1 Introduction

1.1 Significance of Predicting IDH Mutational Status

Gliomas are common malignant brain tumors with various prognosis [16]. The
mutation status of isocitrate dehydrogenase (IDH) genes is one of the most
important biomarkers for the diagnosis and prognosis of gliomas, where IDH
mutants tend to have a better prognosis than IDH wild-types [29]. Due to the
crucial value in clinical practice, IDH mutations have been established as one of
the landmark molecular markers for glioma patients, recommended by the World
Health Organization classification of tumors of the Central Nervous System for
routine assessment in glioma patients [13].

Currently, the most widely used approaches to determine IDH mutation status, i.e., immunohistochemistry and targeted gene sequencing, rely on tumor
samples [13], which therefore cannot be assessed on those patients who are not
suitable for tumor resection or biopsy. Further, as the assays usually are time-
consuming and expensive, they are not available in some institutions.

Meanwhile, the radiogenomic approach has shown promise in predicting
molecular markers based on radiological images. Mounting evidence has supported the feasibility of predicting IDH mutation status using the pre-operative
MRI [4,6,11]. The most commonly used MRI sequences include pre-contrast
T1, post-contrast T1, T2, and T2-weighted-Fluid-Attenuated Inversion Recovery (FLAIR). Integrating the quantitative information from multi-modal MRI
promises to provide a non-invasive approach to characterize glioma and predict
IDH mutations for better treatment planning and prognostication [9,10].

1.2 Brain Structural Networks

The tissue structure of the human brain is divided into grey matter and white
matter. The grey matter, located on the brain surface, constitutes the cerebral
cortex and can be parcelled into cortical/subcortical regions based on cortical
gyri and sulci. The parcellation offers a more precise association between brain
function with cortical structure. The white matter of the cerebral cortex contains
the connecting axons among the cortical/subcortical regions. The structural network of the brain is a mathematical simplification of the connectivity of the cor-
tical/subcortical regions [3], where the nodes represent the cortical/subcortical
regions and the edges are defined as connecting white matter tracts.

Accumulating research of structural brain networks has reported significance
in neuropsychiatric diseases, including stroke, traumatic brain injury, and brain
tumors [5,12,19,27]. On the other hand, evidence shows that glioma cells tend to
invade along the white matter pathway [26] and infiltrate the whole brain [24,27].
Therefore, investigating structural brain networks could offer a tool to investigate

glioma invasion on both tumor core and normal-appearing brain regions. Further, a previous study revealed that IDH mutations could be associated with different invasive phenotypes of glioma [18]. To this end, we hypothesize that employing the structural brain networks could provide value for predicting IDH mutation status. In particular, with prior knowledge of brain structure and anatomy incorporated, a more robust prediction model could be achieved.

1.3   Graph Neural Networks

The graph neural networks (GNN) is a branch of deep learning, specialized in data formats of irregular structures, such as varying numbers of edges and random orders of nodes in graph data [14]. Unlike the traditional convolutional neural networks (CNN) that convolute elements one by one in the grid data, the GNN aggregate information into nodes from their neighbors and simultaneously learns a representation of the whole graph. By employing the GNN on structural brain networks, the topological information contained in the structural brain networks could be effectively explored, which would consequently incorporate the prior knowledge of brain organization and perceive the critical information of tumor invasion at the whole-brain level.

1.4   Related Work

Current methods of predicting IDH mutation status include radiomics/machine learning-based, deep learning-based, or a combination of both. Radiomics/ machine learning-based methods extract high dimensional handcrafted features from the MRIs, e.g., tumor intensity, shape, texture, etc., to train machine learning prediction models of molecular markers, tumor grades, or patient survival [6]. Deep learning-based approaches provide end-to-end model without pre-defined imaging features in the prediction tasks [11]. Some other methods integrated the radiomic features into a deep neural network to enhance prediction performance [4]. Albeit reasonable prediction accuracy, most of these methods are mainly driven by the computer vision tasks, without considering the systematic alteration of the brain organization during tumor invasion. Incorporating the prior knowledge from the neuroscience field shows promise to improve the prediction model.

1.5   Proposed Methods

Here we propose an approach of using GNN to predict IDH mutation status, based on the structural brain networks generated from multi-model MRI and prior human brain atlases. Our contributions include:

- A method to incorporate the prior knowledge of brain atlases with the anatomical MRI to generate structural brain networks.
- A novel architecture of GNN with specialized graph convolutional operator for aggregating multi-dimensional latent features of the multi-model MRI.
- To our best knowledge, this is the first study that leverages GNN on the multi-modal MRI to predict the IDH mutation status of glioma.

2   Methods

2.1   Datasets

This study included the pre-operative multi-modal MRI (pre-contrast T1, post-contrast T1, T2, and FLAIR) of 389 glioma patients. MRI images of 274 patients were downloaded from The Cancer Imaging Archive (TCIA) website [17,20, 21], whereas 115 patients were available from an in-house cohort. 17 of 389 patients who have missing IDH mutation status or incomplete MRI modalities were excluded. For the included patients, 103 patients are IDH mutant, and 269 are IDH wild-type.

2.2   Imaging Pre-processing

We processed the multi-modal MRI following a standard pipeline [2]. Firstly, the T1, T2, and FLAIR were co-registered to the post-contrast T1 using the FMRIB's Linear Image Registration Tool [8]. Then, brain extraction was performed on all MRI modalities to remove the skull using Brain Extraction Tool in the FMRIB Software Library (FSL) [7,22]. We also performed histogram matching [15] and voxel smoothing with SUSAN noise reduction [23]. A neurosurgeon and a researcher performed manual correction of brain masks, cross-validated using DICE score. Finally, all modalities were non-linearly co-registered using the Advanced Normalization Tools (ANTs) [1] to the MNI152 standard space, i.e., MNI-152-T1-2MM-brain provided by the FSL (Fig. 1A).

2.3   Constructing Patient Structural Brain Networks

Brain Network Template. We leveraged the brain network template derived from healthy subjects to construct brain networks in lesioned brains [19]. First, we used the prior brain atlases in healthy subjects as the template of brain networks, generating regions of interest (ROIs) for characterizing the brain networks in patients based on multi-modal MRI. Specifically, we used the Automated Anatomical Labelling (AAL) atlas [25] as the node ROIs (Fig. 1B), which includes 90 brain cortical and subcortical regions. Further, we generated a brain connectivity atlas from ten healthy subjects scanned by high-resolution diffusion MRI to derive the edge ROIs of the structural brain networks (Fig. 1C). We used a similar approach of generating brain connectivity atlas with [5,28]. In brief, firstly, pairwise tractography among the 90 regions of AAL atlas was performed in healthy subjects, then the resultant tract pathways were co-registered to the MNI152 standard space. Next, the corresponding tracts of all healthy subjects were averaged for each edge between two nodes. Finally, the top 5% voxels of the tract density were retained and binarized to generate robust edge ROIs. The generated edge atlas is shown in Fig. 1C.

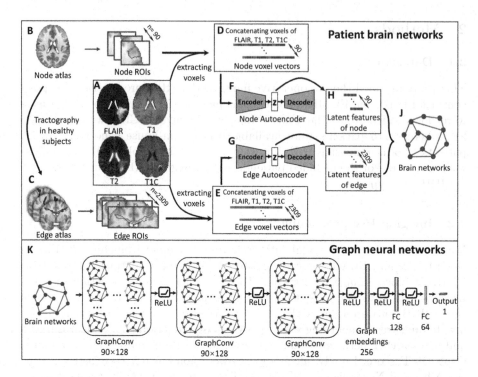

Fig. 1. Study workflow. Upper: the pipeline of constructing patient brain networks. A: Patient MRIs are pre-processed and co-registered to the atlas space. B: The AAL atlas of 90 ROIs is used as the node atlas. C: The edge atlas is generated from performing tractography among the 90 ROIs on the diffusion MRI of healthy subjects. D & E Multi-modal MRI voxels within the node/edge ROIs are extracted and concatenated to voxel vectors to characterize the node/edge. 90 node were from AAL atlas while 2309 edges are the edges that exist in 9 of 10 healthy subjects in tractography. F & G: Two autoencoders are trained using edge and node voxel vectors. H & I: Encoders of trained autoencoders are used to extract the low dimensional latent features z from the high dimensional node/edge voxels vector, respectively. J Latent node/edge features are then rearranged into graph format as the input of the GNN. K Graph convolutional neural networks consist of three hidden graph convolutional layers, one graph embedding layer, and two fully-connected (FC) layers.

Latent Features of Nodes and Edges from Autoencoders. MRI voxels within the ROIs of the node or edge atlases across the whole brain were extracted and then concatenated to voxel vectors (Fig. 1D & E). We then used two autoencoders to extract the latent features from the voxel vectors of node and edge, respectively. Vector size was set as 2500 (voxels) × 4 (modalities) = 10000. For edges and nodes with few voxels, the vectors were padding with zeros. The patient cohort was shuffled and split into a 80:20 ratio for training and testing data. Two autoencoders were trained by edge and node voxel vectors of the training data (Fig. 1F & G). Finally, the latent features of edge or node voxels were derived, with the dimension of the edge or node vectors substantially decreased from 10000 to 12 (Fig. 1H & I). The 12 latent features were used as the input of the GNN (Fig. 1J). Logistic sigmoid function was applied as transfer function for both encoder and decoder. L2 regularization with coefficient of 0.001 was used. 'msesparse' was set as the loss function.

2.4 Predicting IDH Mutation Status Using GNN

The patient brain networks constructed above were used to train the GNN, with the multi-modal MRI latent features as inputs. In addition to the 80:20 ratio of training and testing data, training data was split again into an 80:20 ratio for cross-validation. The proposed GNN consist of three graph convolutional layers similar to the one defined in [14], one node to graph embedding layers, and two fully connected feed forward layers (Fig. 1K). We used a binary cross-entropy loss, while the optimization was done using Adam optimizer.

The graph convolutional operator is defined as follow:

$$\mathbf{x}_i' = \mathbf{\Theta}_1 \mathbf{x}_i + \sum_{z=1}^{Z} \mathbf{\Theta}_2 \sum_{j \in \mathcal{N}(i)} e_{j,i,z} \cdot \mathbf{x}_j \tag{1}$$

where $\mathbf{x}_i'$ denotes the features of node i after convolution, $\mathbf{\Theta}_1$ and $\mathbf{\Theta}_2$ denote the trainable network weights. $\cdot$ is the multiply operator. $e_{j,i,z}$ represents the zth edge feature from source node j to target node i. $j \in \mathcal{N}(i)$ denotes all indices of nodes j connecting to node i with nonzero edge features. Z denotes the size of latent edge features.

The graph embedding operator is defined as follow:

$$\mathcal{G}^{\mathbf{Z}} = \sum_{i=1}^{N} \mathbf{\Theta} \mathbf{x}_i \tag{2}$$

where $\mathcal{G}^Z$ denotes the graph embedding of size Z all nodes of the graph. $\mathbf{\Theta}$ denote the trainable network weights. N denotes the number of nodes in graph. Z denotes the size of latent node features.

Random edge drop was applied to augment data during training. The weighted loss was applied in the network to mitigate the effect of data imbalance. Learning rate decay was used to stabilize the training process. Early stopping mechanism, weight decay, and dropout layers after fully connected layers were used to prevent over-fitting.

2.5 Benchmark Models

We adopted a three-dimensional Densely Connected Convolutional Networks (3D-DenseNet) (Fig. 2A) and a three-dimensional convolutional neural networks (3D-CNN) (Fig. 2B) as the benchmarks. Specifically, a classic 121-layer version of 3D-DenseNet follows the architecture described in [11] while a traditional 3D-CNN with four hidden convolutional layers with batch normalization and pooling was applied, followed by a max-pooling layer and an output layer. Data were split using the same method as the GNN model. Weighted loss, learning rate decay, and early stopping are all applied, which was similar to the GNN settings. The same loss function and optimiser were applied to the benchmark models as the GNN model. Two experiments with different input were conducted: whole-brain MRI and MRI voxels inside tumor ROIs (contrasting-enhancing tumor core and necrosis) which are generated according to [2].

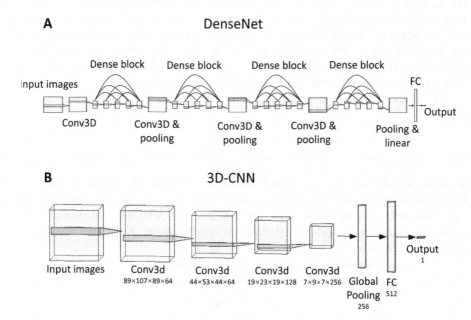

Fig. 2. Architecture of the benchmark models. A. Classic three-dimensional Densely Connected Convolutional Networks (3D-DenseNet) consist of four convolutional layers and four densely connected blocks. B. Three-dimensional convolutional neural networks (3D-CNN) consist of four hidden convolutional layers with max-pooling and batch normalization, one global pooling layer followed by dropout, and one fully connected dense layer.

3 Results and Discussion

3.1 Model Performance

Our experiments show that the proposed model performs better than the baseline models (Table 1) for both cross-validation and testing. Interestingly, the benchmark models with tumor voxels as inputs perform better than the models with the whole brain as inputs, which suggests the potential bias from the extensive brain regions beyond the local tumor. Of note, our proposed GNN model, leveraging the brain network generated based on prior atlas and whole brain MRI, performs better than all the benchmark models, which may suggest that incorporating prior knowledge of brain networks could help the deep learning models capture more informative features regarding tumor invasion over either the local tumor or the whole brain.

Table 1. Performances of IDH prediction models

Methods	Accuracy (%)	Sensitivity (%)	Specificity (%)
Cross-validation			
3D-CNN + whole brain MRI	69.1	61.2	72.1
3D-CNN + tumor ROIs	80.1	77.7	81.0
3D-DenseNet + whole brain MRI	76.1	67.0	79.6
3D-DenseNet + tumor ROIs	84.1	86.4	83.3
GNN + brain networks	87.9	97.4	88.1
Test			
3D-CNN + whole brain MRI	67.2	63.1	68.8
3D-CNN + tumor ROIs	78.2	75.7	79.2
3D-DenseNet + whole brain MRI	73.1	63.1	77.0
3D-DenseNet + tumor ROIs	83.3	83.5	83.2
GNN + brain networks	86.6	87.7	86.3

3.2 Model Interpretation

To interpret the learning process of the GNN model, we applied the GNNExplainer [30]. GNNExplainer outputs a probability score that infers the importance of the edges in the prediction task and outputs a compact subnetwork of the networks. The task was achieved by maximizing both a graph neural network's prediction and distribution of possible subnetworks. Only subnetworks with edges that have probability scores greater than 50% were retained.

Overall, we observe that the IDH wild-type is associated with a wider distribution of edge invasion, captured by the GNN model. Figure 3 presents two typical cases of IDH mutant and wild-type, respectively, which also present the distribution of key white matter tracts (edges) that are important to the prediction accuracy. In line with our prior knowledge that IDH wild-type generally causes more widespread invasion, the results of the model interpretation could further support the usefulness the proposed GNN model.

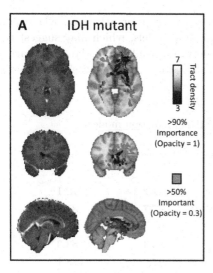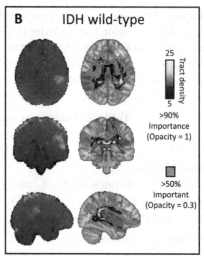

Fig. 3. Examples of IDH mutant and wild-type. A IDH mutant B. IDH wild-type. For both patients, the left panels indicate the T1-weighted images and the right panels show the output of GNNExplainer, illustrating the voxel distribution of edges that have over 50% and 90% probability of importance in IDH mutation prediction. The tract density of a voxel is defined as the number of tracts crossing the voxel.

4   Conclusion

In this paper, we propose a method to generate brain networks based on multimodal MRI and predict the IDH mutation status using GNN and the generated brain networks. Numerical results demonstrate that the proposed method outperforms benchmark methods. In future work, we could use the radiomic approach to extract representative features from the node and edge ROIs. Furthermore, special end-to-end GNN models could be developed to directly take the high dimensional multi-modal MRI voxels as inputs. To conclude, combining brain networks with GNN promises to serve as a novel powerful tool for deep learning model development in radiogenomic studies.

References

1. Avants, B.B., Tustison, N., Song, G., et al.: Advanced normalization tools (ants). Insight J. **2**(365), 1–35 (2009)
2. Bakas, S., et al.: Advancing the cancer genome atlas glioma MRI collections with expert segmentation labels and radiomic features. Sci. Data **4**(1), 1–13 (2017)
3. Bullmore, E.T., Bassett, D.S.: Brain graphs: graphical models of the human brain connectome. Annu. Rev. Clin. Psychol. **7**, 113–140 (2011)
4. Choi, Y.S., et al.: Fully automated hybrid approach to predict the IDH mutation status of gliomas via deep learning and radiomics. Neuro Oncol. **23**(2), 304–313 (2021)

5. Fagerholm, E.D., Hellyer, P.J., Scott, G., Leech, R., Sharp, D.J.: Disconnection of network hubs and cognitive impairment after traumatic brain injury. Brain **138**(6), 1696–1709 (2015)
6. Hyare, H., et al.: Modelling MR and clinical features in grade II/III astrocytomas to predict IDH mutation status. Eur. J. Radiol. **114**, 120–127 (2019)
7. Jenkinson, M., Beckmann, C.F., Behrens, T.E., Woolrich, M.W., Smith, S.M.: FSL. Neuroimage **62**(2), 782–790 (2012)
8. Jenkinson, M., Smith, S.: A global optimisation method for robust affine registration of brain images. Med. Image Anal. **5**(2), 143–156 (2001)
9. Li, C., et al.: Multi-parametric and multi-regional histogram analysis of MRI: modality integration reveals imaging phenotypes of glioblastoma. Eur. Radiol. **29**(9), 4718–4729 (2019)
10. Li, C., et al.: Characterizing tumor invasiveness of glioblastoma using multiparametric magnetic resonance imaging. J. Neurosurg. **132**(5), 1465–1472 (2019)
11. Liang, S., et al.: Multimodal 3D densenet for IDH genotype prediction in gliomas. Genes **9**(8), 382 (2018)
12. Liu, Y., et al.: Altered rich-club organization and regional topology are associated with cognitive decline in patients with frontal and temporal gliomas. Front. Hum. Neurosci. **14**, 23 (2020)
13. Louis, D.N., et al.: The 2016 world health organization classification of tumors of the central nervous system: a summary. Acta Neuropathol. **131**(6), 803–820 (2016)
14. Morris, C., et al.: Weisfeiler and leman go neural: Higher-order graph neural networks. In: Proceedings of the AAAI Conference on Artificial Intelligence, vol. 33, pp. 4602–4609 (2019)
15. Nyúl, L.G., Udupa, J.K., Zhang, X.: New variants of a method of MRI scale standardization. IEEE Trans. Med. Imaging **19**(2), 143–150 (2000)
16. Ostrom, Q.T., et al.: CBtrus statistical report: primary brain and other central nervous system tumors diagnosed in the united states in 2009–2013. Neuro-oncol. **18**(suppl_5), v1–v75 (2016)
17. Pedano, N., et al.: Radiology data from the cancer genome atlas low grade glioma [TCGA-LGG] collection. Cancer Imaging Arch. (2016). https://doi.org/10.7937/K9/TCIA.2016.L4LTD3TK
18. Price, S.J., et al.: Less invasive phenotype found in isocitrate dehydrogenase-mutated glioblastomas than in isocitrate dehydrogenase wild-type glioblastomas: a diffusion-tensor imaging study. Radiology **283**(1), 215–221 (2017)
19. Salvalaggio, A., De Filippo De Grazia, M., Zorzi, M., Thiebaut de Schotten, M., Corbetta, M.: Post-stroke deficit prediction from lesion and indirect structural and functional disconnection. Brain **143**(7), 2173–2188 (2020)
20. Scarpace, L., et al.: Radiology data from the cancer genome atlas glioblastoma multiforme [TCGA-GBM] collection [data set]. Cancer Imaging Arch. (2016). https://doi.org/10.7937/K9/TCIA.2016.RNYFUYE9
21. Shah, N., Feng, X., Lankerovich, M., Puchalski, R.B., Keogh, B.: Data from Ivy GAP [data set]. Cancer Imaging Arch. (2016). https://doi.org/10.7937/K9/TCIA.2016.XLWAN6NL
22. Smith, S.M.: Fast robust automated brain extraction. Hum. Brain Mapp. **17**(3), 143–155 (2002)
23. Smith, S.M., Brady, J.M.: Susan - a new approach to low level image processing. Int. J. Comput. Vis. **23**(1), 45–78 (1997)
24. Stoecklein, V.M., et al.: Resting-state FMRI detects alterations in whole brain connectivity related to tumor biology in glioma patients. Neuro Oncol. **22**(9), 1388–1398 (2020)

25. Tzourio-Mazoyer, N., et al.: Automated anatomical labeling of activations in SPM using a macroscopic anatomical parcellation of the MNI MRI single-subject brain. Neuroimage **15**(1), 273–289 (2002)
26. Wang, J., et al.: Invasion of white matter tracts by glioma stem cells is regulated by a notch1-sox2 positive-feedback loop. Nat. Neurosci. **22**(1), 91–105 (2019)
27. Wei, Y., et al.: Structural connectome quantifies tumor invasion and predicts survival in glioblastoma patients. bioRxiv (2021)
28. Wei, Y., Li, C., Price, S.: Quantifying structural connectivity in brain tumor patients. medRxiv (2021)
29. Yan, H., et al.: IDH1 and IDH2 mutations in gliomas. N. Engl. J. Med. **360**(8), 765–773 (2009)
30. Ying, R., Bourgeois, D., You, J., Zitnik, M., Leskovec, J.: GNNExplainer: generating explanations for graph neural networks. Adv. Neural. Inf. Process. Syst. **32**, 9240 (2019)

Optimization of Deep Learning Based Brain Extraction in MRI for Low Resource Environments

Siddhesh P. Thakur[1,2,3], Sarthak Pati[1,2,3,4], Ravi Panchumarthy[5],
Deepthi Karkada[5], Junwen Wu[5], Dmitry Kurtaev[5], Chiharu Sako[1,2],
Prashant Shah[5], and Spyridon Bakas[1,2,3(✉)]

[1] Center for Biomedical Image Computing and Analytics (CBICA),
University of Pennsylvania, Philadelphia, PA, USA
sbakas@upenn.edu
[2] Department of Radiology, Perelman School of Medicine,
University of Pennsylvania, Philadelphia, PA, USA
[3] Department of Pathology and Laboratory Medicine, Perelman School of Medicine,
University of Pennsylvania, Philadelphia, PA, USA
[4] Department of Informatics, Technical University of Munich, Munich, Germany
[5] Intel Health and Life Sciences, Intel Corporation, Santa Clara, CA, USA

Abstract. Brain extraction is an indispensable step in neuro-imaging with a direct impact on downstream analyses. Most such methods have been developed for non-pathologically affected brains, and hence tend to suffer in performance when applied on brains with pathologies, e.g., gliomas, multiple sclerosis, traumatic brain injuries. Deep Learning (DL) methodologies for healthcare have shown promising results, but their clinical translation has been limited, primarily due to these methods suffering from i) high computational cost, and ii) specific hardware requirements, e.g., DL acceleration cards. In this study, we explore the potential of mathematical optimizations, towards making DL methods amenable to application in low resource environments. We focus on both the qualitative and quantitative evaluation of such optimizations on an existing DL brain extraction method, designed for pathologically-affected brains and agnostic to the input modality. We conduct direct optimizations and quantization of the trained model (i.e., prior to inference on new data). Our results yield substantial gains, in terms of speedup, latency, throughput, and reduction in memory usage, while the segmentation performance of the initial and the optimized models remains stable, i.e., as quantified by both the Dice Similarity Coefficient and the Hausdorff Distance. These findings support post-training optimizations as a promising approach for enabling the execution of advanced DL methodologies on plain commercial-grade CPUs, and hence contributing to their translation in limited- and low- resource clinical environments.

Keywords: Low resource environment · Deep learning · Segmentation · CNN · Convolutional neural network · Brain extraction · Brain tumor · Glioma · Glioblastoma · BraTS · OpenVINO · BrainMaGe · GaNDLF

© The Author(s), under exclusive license to Springer Nature Switzerland AG 2022
A. Crimi and S. Bakas (Eds.): BrainLes 2021, LNCS 12962, pp. 151–167, 2022.
https://doi.org/10.1007/978-3-031-08999-2_12

1   Introduction

One of the most important first steps in any neuro-imaging analysis pipeline is brain extraction, also known as skull-stripping [1,2]. This process removes all non-brain portions in a brain scan and leaves the user with the portion of the image that is of maximal interest, i.e., the brain tissue and all associated pathologies. This step is an indispensable pre-processing operation that has a direct effect on subsequent analyses, and also used for de-identification purposes [3]. Enabling this to run on clinical workstations could have a tremendously positive impact on automated clinical workflows. The effects of the quality of brain extraction in downstream analyses have been previously reported, for studies on tumor segmentation [4–6] and neuro-degeneration [7].

This study specifically focuses on glioblastoma (GBM), which is the most aggressive type of adult brain tumors. GBM has poor prognosis despite current treatment protocols [8,9], and its treatment and management is often problematic with a necessity of requiring personalized treatment plans. To improve the treatment customization process, computational imaging and machine learning based assistance could prove to be highly beneficial. One of the key steps for this would be to enable a robust approach to obtain the complete region of immediate interest irrespective of the included pathologies that would result in an improved computational workflow.

While deep learning (DL) has been showing promising results in the field of semantic segmentation in medical imaging [4,10–17], the deployability of such models poses a substantial challenge, mainly due to their computational footprint. While prior work on brain extraction has focused on stochastic modeling approaches [1,2,18], modern solutions leveraging DL have shown great promise [12,15]. Unfortunately, models trained for this application also suffer from such deployment issues, which in turn reduces their clinical translation.

In recent years, well-known DL frameworks, such as PyTorch [19] and TensorFlow [20] have enabled the democratization of DL development by making the underlying building blocks accessible to the wider community. They usually require the help of moderately expensive computing with DL acceleration cards, such as Graphical Processing Units (GPUs) [21] or Tensor Processing Units (TPUs) [22]. While these frameworks will work on sites with such computational capacity (i.e., GPUs and TPUs), deploying them to locations with low resources is a challenge. Most DL-enabled studies are extremely compute intensive, and the complexity of the pipeline makes them very difficult to deploy, especially in tightly controlled clinical environments. While cloud-based solutions could be made available, patient privacy is a major health system concern, which requires multiple legal quandaries to be addressed prior to uploading data to the cloud. However, the availability of such approaches for local inexpensive compute solutions would be the sole feasible way for their clinical translation.

Quantizing neural networks can reduce the computational time required for the forward pass, but more importantly can reduce the memory burden during the time of inference. Post-quantization, a high precision model is reduced to a lower bit resolution model, thus reducing the size of the model. The final goal is to leverage the advantages of quantization and optimization, while maintaining the segmentation performance of the full precision floating point models as much as possible. Such methods can facilitate the reduction of the required memory to save and infer the generated model [23].

In this paper, we take an already published DL method, namely Brain Mask Generator (BrainMaGe)[1] [15], and make it usable for low resource environments, such as commercial-grade CPUs with low memory, and older generation CPUs by leveraging the advantages of quantization and optimization for performance improvements. We provide a comprehensive evaluation of the observed performance improvements across multiple CPU configurations and quantization methods for the publicly available TCGA-GBM dataset [6,24,25], as well as a private testing dataset.

2 Methods

2.1 Data

We identified and collected $n = 864$ multi-parametric magnetic resonance images (mpMRI) brain tumor scans from $n = 216$ GBM patients from both private and public collections. The private collections included $n = 364$ scans, from $n = 91$ patients, acquired at the Hospital of the University of Pennsylvania (UPenn). The public data is available through The Cancer Imaging Archive (TCIA) [24] and comprises of the pre-operative mpMRI scans of The Cancer Genome Atlas Glioblastoma (TCGA-GBM, $n = 125$) [6,25] collection. The final dataset (Table 1) included $n = 864$ mpMRI scans from $n = 216$ subjects with 4 structural modalities for each subject available, namely T1-weighted pre- & post-contrast (T1, & T1Gd), T2-weighted (T2) and T2 fluid attenuated inversion recovery (FLAIR). Notably, the multi-institutional data of the TCGA-GBM collection is highly heterogeneous, including scan quality, slice thickness between different modalities, scanner parameters. For the private collection data, the T1 scans were taken with high axial resolutions. The brain masks for the private collection data were generated internally and went through rigorous manual quality control, while the brain masks for the TCGA-GBM data were provided through the International Brain Tumor Segmentation (BraTS) challenge [4–6, 26–28].

2.2 Data Pre-processing

All DICOM scans were converted to the Neuroimaging Informatics Technology Initiative (NIfTI) [29] file format to facilitate computational analysis, following the well-accepted pre-processing protocol of the BraTS challenge [4–6,26–28]. Specifically, all the mpMRI volumes were reoriented to the left-posterior-superior (LPS) coordinate system, and the T1Gd scan of each patient was rigidly (6 degrees of freedom) registered and resampled to an isotropic resolution of $1mm^3$

---

[1] https://github.com/CBICA/BrainMaGe.

Table 1. The distribution of all the datasets used in the study.

Dataset	No. of subjects	No. of mpMRI scans
TCGA-GBM	125	500
UPenn	91	364
Total	**216**	**864**

based on a common anatomical atlas, namely SRI24 [30]. We chose this atlas [30] as the common anatomical space, following the convention suggested by the BraTS challenge. The remaining scans (i.e., T1, T2, FLAIR) of each patient were then rigidly co-registered to this resampled T1Gd scan by first obtaining the rigid transformation matrix to T1Gd, then combining with the transformation matrix from T1Gd to the SRI24 atlas, and resampling. For all the image registrations we used the "Greedy"[2] tool [31], which is a central processing unit (CPU)-based C++ implementation of the greedy diffeomorphic registration algorithm [32]. Greedy is integrated into the ITK-SNAP[3] segmentation software [33,34], as well as into the Cancer Imaging Phenomics Toolkit (CaPTk)[4] [35–39]. We further note that use of any non-parametric, non-uniform intensity normalization algorithm [40–42] to correct for intensity non-uniformities caused by the inhomogeneity of the scanner's magnetic field during image acquisition, obliterates the T2-FLAIR signal, as it has been previously reported [5]. Thus, taking this into consideration, we intentionally apply the N4 bias field correction approach [41] in all scans temporarily' to facilitate an improved registration of all scans to the common anatomical atlas. Once we obtain the transformation matrices for all the scans, then we apply these transformations to the non-bias corrected images. This complete pre-processing is available through CaPTk, as officially used for the BraTS challenge (Fig. 1).

2.3   Network Topology

We have used the 3D implementation [10], of the widely-used network topology of U-Net [44], with added residual connections between the encoder and the decoder, to improve the backpropagation process [10,13,15,44–46]. The actual topology used here is highlighted in Fig. 2. The U-Net topology has been extensively used in semantic segmentation of both 2D and 3D medical imaging data. The U-Net consists of an encoder, which contains convolutional layers and downsampling layers, a decoder offering upsampling layers (applying transpose convolution layers), and convolutional layers. The encoder-decoder structure contributes towards automatically capturing information at varying resolutions and scales. There is an addition of skip connections, which includes concatenated feature maps paired across the encoder and the decoder layer, to improve context

---

[2] github.com/pyushkevich/greedy, hash: 1a871c1, Last accessed: 27/May/2020.

[3] itksnap.org, version: 3.8.0, last accessed: 27/May/2020.

[4] www.cbica.upenn.edu/captk, version: 1.8.1, last accessed: 11/February/2021.

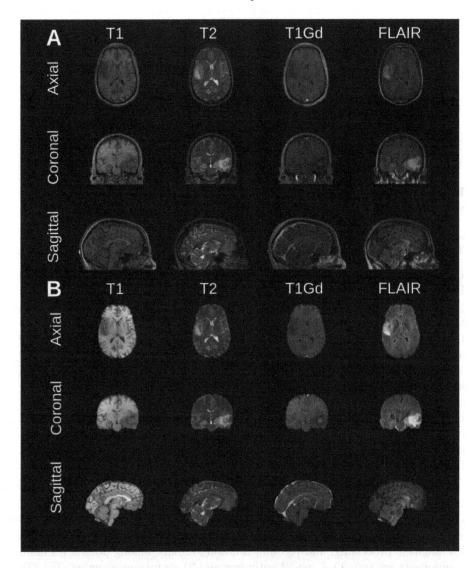

Fig. 1. Example of MRI brain tumor scan from a randomly selected subject from the test set. The Original scans (A) include the skull and other non-brain tissues, and (B) the corresponding scan slices depicting only the brain.

and feature re-usability. The residual connections utilize additional information from previous layers (across the encoder and decoder) that enable a segmentation performance boost.

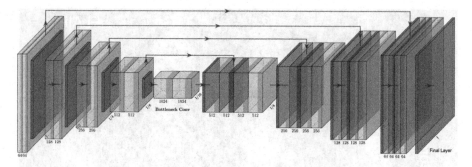

Fig. 2. The U-Net topology with residual connections from GaNDLF was used for this study. Figure was plotted using PlotNeuralNet [43].

2.4 Inference Optimizations

In this work, we used the OpenVINO toolkit (OV) for the optimizations of the BrainMaGe model. First, in order to provide estimates of scalability of the model performance in low resource environments, we conduct a comparison between the inference performance of the optimized OV model with that of the PyTorch framework. We further show a comparison of the optimized model performance across various hardware configurations typically found in such environments. We then showcase further performance improvements obtained through post-training quantization of the model and perform similar comparisons across different hardware configurations. In summary, for the BrainMaGe model, we explored both (i) conversion from PyTorch to the optimized model with an additional intermediate conversion to ONNX, which lead to an intolerable accuracy drop during the PyTorch to ONNX conversion step, and (ii) direct conversion from PyTorch to the model's optimized intermediate representation format.

2.4.1 OpenVINO Toolkit

OV is a neural network inference optimization toolkit [47], which provides inference performance optimizations for applications using computer vision, natural language processing, and recommendation systems, among others. Its main components are two: **1)** A model optimizer and **2)** an inference engine. *The OV model optimizer*, provides conversion from a pre-trained network model trained in frameworks (such as PyTorch and TensorFlow) into an intermediate representation (IR) format that can be consumed by its second main component, i.e., its inference engine. Other types of formats that are supported include the ONNX format. Hence, for frameworks like TensorFlow and PyTorch, there is an intermediate conversion step that can be performed offline. While support for direct conversion from the PyTorch framework is limited, there are specific extensions [48] that enable this. *The OV inference engine*, provides optimized implementations for common operations found in neural networks, such as convolutions, and pooling operations. OV also provides graph level optimizations, such as operator fusion and optimizations for common neural network patterns through the

Ngraph library [49]. These optimizations can provide direct improvements in the execution time of the model, enabling the latter for low- (or limited-) resource environments with tight compute constraints.

2.5   Network Quantization

Quantization is an optimization technique that has been adopted in recent times, to improve inference performance of neural network models [50,51]. It involves a conversion from a high precision datatype to a lower-precision datatype. In this study, we specifically discuss the quantization of a 32-bit floating point (FP32) model to an 8-bit integer (INT8) model as provided by Eq. 1:

$$Out_{INT8} = round(scale * In_{FP32} + zero_{offset}) \qquad (1)$$

where the *scale* factor provides a mapping of the FP32 values to the low-precision range. The $zero_{offset}$ provides a representation of the FP32 zero value to an integer value [52,53].

We have explored leveraging quantization for further improvements in inference, while maintaining the model's segmentation performance. Quantization has many benefits, including (i) speedup improvements, and (ii) reduction of memory utilization. There are two popular approaches to model quantization, namely:

1. **Quantization-aware training** [54], which involves training the neural network with fake quantization operations inserted in the network graph. The fake quantization nodes are able to learn the range of the input tensors and hence this serves as a simulation of the quantization.
2. **Post-training quantization** [55], which is the idea where the quantization process is performed post-training, but prior to the actual inference. A subset of the training dataset is selected for calibration, and this dataset is used to learn the minimum and maximum ranges of the input weights and activations for tensor quantization.

In this study, we have focused on exploring post-training quantization using the OV AccuracyAware technique [56], which provides model optimizations while explicitly limiting the segmentation performance drop. The intuition of the method is that the quantization is targeted towards all eligible layers in the topology. However, if a segmentation performance drop is observed, greater than the user-specified threshold, the layers that contribute the most to the segmentation performance drop are iteratively reverted back to the original datatype, until the desired segmentation performance level is achieved.

2.5.1   Quantitative Evaluation

The segmentation performance of the model is quantitatively evaluated according to (i) the Dice Similarity Coefficient [57] (a widely used and accepted metric for quantifying segmentation results [58]), (ii) the 95th percentile of the (symmetric) Hausdorff Distance (commonly used in Biomedical Segmentation challenges) (iii) memory utilization, and (iv) inference performance (latency). We further report the model performance for each stage of optimization, i.e., for the 1) baseline PyTorch implementation, 2) OV optimized FP32 model, and 3) OV optimized model converted to INT8 format through the post-training quantization step (Table 4). It is important to note that quantization to lower precision formats, such as INT8, typically results in a small drop in segmentation performance but this is highly dependent on the dataset. In our case, we do not notice any loss in segmentation performance after converting the model to the OV optimized model format.

2.6 Experimental Design

In favor of completeness, we chose five hardware platforms from various CPU generations, to benchmark our various model configurations. We ran inference benchmarks on all five hardware platforms with $n = 132$ images from the TCGA-GBM dataset. The results are reported based on average of running inferences on these images with a batch size of $n = 1$. See Tables 2 and 3 for the detailed hardware and software configurations.

Table 2. The detailed hardware configurations used in for our experiments. Hyper-threading and turbo was enabled for all.

	Config 1	Config 2	Config 3	Config 4	Config 5
Platform	Kaby Lake	Coffee Lake	Ice Lake -U	Tiger Lake	Cascade Lake
CPU	Core(TM) i5-7400 CPU @ 3.00 GHz	Core(TM) X-GOLD 626 CPU @ 2.60 GHz	Core(TM) i7-1065G7 CPU @ 1.30 GHz	Core(TM) i7-1185G7 CPU @ 3.00 GHz	Xeon(R) Gold 6252N CPU @ 2.30 GHz
# Nodes, # Sockets	1, 1	1, 1	1, 1	1, 1	1, 2
Cores/socket, Threads/socket	4, 4	8, 16	4, 8	4, 8	24, 48
Mem config: type, slots, cap, speed	DDR4, 2, 4GB, 2133 MT/s	DDR4, 2, 8GB, 2667 MT/s	LPDDR4, 2, 4GB, 3733 MT/s	DDR4, 2, 8GB, 3200 MT/s	DDR4, 12, 16GB, 2933 MT/s
Total memory	8 GB	16 GB	8 GB	16 GB	192 GB
Advanced technologies	AVX2	AVX2	AVX2, AVX512, DL Boost (VNNI)	AVX2, AVX512, DL Boost (VNNI)	AVX2, AVX512, DL Boost (VNNI)
TDP	90 W	95 W	15 W	28 W	150 W

Table 3. Details of the topology implementation. We used the 3D-ResU-Net architecture with 1 input channel, 2 output classes, and number of initial filters as 16.

Framework	OpenVINO 2021.4	PyTorch 1.5.1, 1.9.0
Libraries	nGraph/MKLDNN	MKLDNN
Model	Resunet_ma.xml, Resunet_ma.bin	Resunet_ma.pt
Input shape	(1, 1, 128, 128, 128)	(1, 1, 128, 128, 128)
Precision	FP32, INT8	FP32, INT8

3   Results

Of particular interest are the results obtained using the Hardware Configuration
4 (Core(TM) i7-1185G7 @ 3.00 GHz machine), which describes the current generation of hardware available in the consumer market. We further summarize the
results obtained from all hardware configurations, in Fig. 3. Table 4 shows the
summary of these metrics running on the hardware configuration 4, using the
$n = 132$ images from the public dataset. We also compare the results obtained
using PyTorch v.1.5.1 and PyTorch v.1.9.0. Notably the dynamic quantization
methodology on PyTorch v.1.9.0 did not yield any performance improvement.
With FP32 precision, the performance between the PyTorch and the OV models
is identical. Although memory utilization is slightly better with PyTorch v.1.9.0,
the inference performance (latency) is **1.89x** better with OV. When assessing
the INT8 quantized/OV model, the performance drop is negligible, with comparable memory utilization, but with a **6.2x** boost in 'latency', when compared to
PyTorch v.1.9.0. The memory utilization and the model performance are similar
across the hardware configurations, with some variations in 'latency'. On the
client hardware platforms (Configurations 1, 2, 3, and 4), with OV FP32 precision, we observed up to **2.3x** improvements in latency. The OV INT8 precision
yielded further speedups up to **6.9x**. On server hardware platforms (Configuration 5), with OV FP32 precision, we observed upto **9.6x** speedup and with
the INT8 precision we observed a speedup up to **20.5x**. Figure 3 illustrates
the speedup per configuration, and Fig. 4 highlights some example qualitative
results. The additional boost in performance with INT8 quantized model in Configurations 3, 4, and 5, is due to the hardware platform's advanced features, i.e.,
AVX512 & Intel DL Boost technology [59, 60].

Table 4. Summary of accuracy, memory utilization and performance (latency) on the
hardware configuration 4: Core(TM) i7-1185G7 @ 3.00 GHz.

DL framework	Version	Precision	Average dice score	Average Hausdorff distance	Memory utilization (normalized)	Avg. latency speedup (normalized)
PyTorch	1.5.1	FP32	0.97198	2.6577 ± 3.0	1	1
	1.9.0	FP32	0.97198	2.6577 ± 3.0	0.769	3.8
OpenVINO	2021.4	FP32	0.97198	2.6577 ± 3.0	1.285	7.1
		INT8	0.97118	2.7426 ± 3.1	0.907	23.3

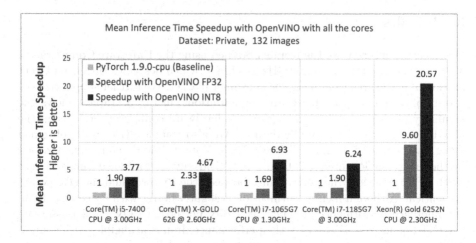

Fig. 3. Speedup across different platforms using all the cores available on a processor.

3.1 Core Scaling Improvements Across Various CPUs

Additionally, we performed a core scaling performance benchmarking to determine the scalability aspects of the model and the hardware. By limiting the number of threads to run the inference, we performed benchmarking on all the hardware configurations. Figure 5 shows a trend of increased performance with the increase in the number of threads. A slight drop in speedup can be observed if the number of threads assigned is greater than the number of physical cores. This is due to the imbalance and over-subscription of the threads. When varying the number of threads for inference, the memory utilization and accuracy are similar to running on all the threads available. The performance of both the PyTorch and the OV models improved with the increase in the number of threads allocated to the inference. However, the speedup achieved with the OV optimized FP32 and INT8 models, over PyTorch, is substantial and can be observed on all hardware configurations. Figure 5f shows the average inference time speedup achieved by limiting the number of threads on different hardware configurations.

4   Discussion

In this study, we investigated the potential contributions of mathematical optimizations of an already trained Deep Learning (DL) segmentation model, to enable its application in limited-/low-resource environments. We specifically focused on a MRI modality agnostic DL method, explicitly designed and developed for the problem of brain extraction in the presence of diffuse gliomas [14,15]. We explored these mathematical optimizations, in terms of their potential model improvements on 1) execution time, for different hardware configurations (i.e., speedup, Fig. 3), 2) speedup, as a function of increasing number of CPU cores

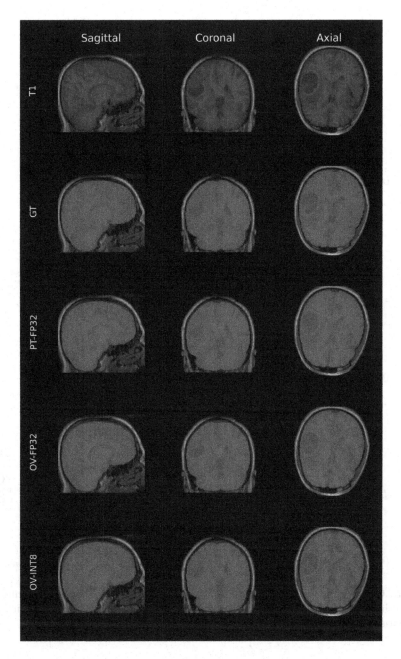

Fig. 4. Qualitative comparison of results for one of the subjects with high resolution T1 scans across the 3 visualization slices. "GT" is the ground truth mask, "PT-FP32" is the mask generated by the original PyTorch FP32 model, "OV-FP32" is the output of the optimized model in FP32, and "OV-INT8" is the output of the optimized model after quantizing to INT8.

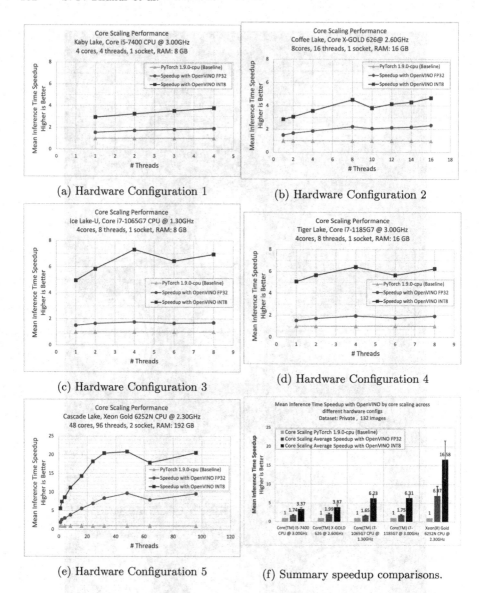

(a) Hardware Configuration 1

(b) Hardware Configuration 2

(c) Hardware Configuration 3

(d) Hardware Configuration 4

(e) Hardware Configuration 5

(f) Summary speedup comparisons.

Fig. 5. Core scaling performance improvements, across various hardware configurations, shown in (a–e). The average speedup across all hardware configurations, and comparison with the PyTorch baseline performance (f).

for all the hardware configuration we considered (Fig. 5), 3) memory requirements (Table 4), and 4) segmentation performance. Our results yield a distinct speedup, and a reduction in computational requirements, while the segmentation performance remains stable, thereby supporting the potential of the proposed solution for application in limited-/low-resource environments.

For these intended inference time optimizations (i.e., applied in the already trained model), we have particularly focused on using the post-training quantization technique. We observe that the largest improvement in terms of speedup was obtained from the post-training quantized INT8 model, which ended up being $> 23x$ faster than the native single-precision implementations, while producing a negligible segmentation performance drop as measured by both the Dice Similarity Coefficient and the Hausdorff distance (Table 4). Post training quantization is the quickest method of obtaining the quantized INT8 model and is desirable in situations where the "accuracy" (i.e., segmentation performance) drop is minimal, as well as within an acceptable threshold. In scenarios where the "accuracy" drop is greater than the acceptable threshold, quantization aware training could be an alternative approach to help in obtaining such potential improvements. However, such optimization (quantization aware training) would require model re-training.

The total number of parameters of the BrainMaGe 3D-ResU-Net model are 8.288×10^6, for which the number of Floating point operations per second (*Flops*) required for the OV FP32 model are 350.72665×10^9, whereas for the OV INT8 model the number of *Flops* required are 2.09099×10^9 and number of Integer operations per second (Iops) required are 348.63566×10^9. We observed that approximately 99.4% of *Flops* have been converted to Iops in the optimized INT8 model, resulting in two major computational benefits: (*i*) With lower precision (INT8), there is an improved data transfer speed through the memory hierarchy due to better cache utilization and reduction of bandwidth bottlenecks, thus enabling to maximize the compute resources; (*ii*) With hardware advanced features [59, 60], the number of compute operations per second (OPS) are higher, thus reducing the total compute time. These two benefits of reduced memory bandwidth and higher frequency of OPS with the lower precision model resulted in substantial improvements (Table 4).

In favor of transparency and reproducibility, we make publicly available the optimized BrainMaGe brain extraction model, through its original repository[5]. Furthermore, a more generalized solution will also be made publicly available through the Generally Nuanced Deep Learning Framework (GaNDLF)[6] [13], towards enabling scalable end-to-end clinically-deployable workflows.

We consider the immediate future work as a three-fold: 1) performance evaluation of quantization aware training compared against post-training quantization; 2) extended evaluation on a larger multi-institutional dataset [61,62], as well as evaluation of additional network topologies; 3) a comprehensive analysis covering additional hardware configurations; 4) assessment of the potential contributions of these mathematical optimizations for varying DL workloads, beyond segmentation and towards regression and classification tasks in the healthcare domain.

---

[5] https://github.com/CBICA/BrainMaGe.
[6] https://github.com/CBICA/GaNDLF.

Acknowledgments. Research reported in this publication was partly supported by the National Cancer Institute (NCI) and the National Institute of Neurological Disorders and Stroke (NINDS) of the National Institutes of Health (NIH), under award numbers NCI:U01CA242871 and NINDS:R01NS042645. The content of this publication is solely the responsibility of the authors and does not represent the official views of the NIH.

References

1. Smith, S.M.: "Bet: Brain extraction tool," FMRIB TR00SMS2b, Oxford Centre for Functional Magnetic Resonance Imaging of the Brain). Department of Clinical Neurology, Oxford University, John Radcliffe Hospital, Headington, UK (2000)
2. Smith, S.M.: Fast robust automated brain extraction. Hum. Brain Mapp. **17**(3), 143–155 (2002)
3. Schwarz, C.G., et al.: Identification of anonymous MRI research participants with face-recognition software. N. Engl. J. Med. **381**(17), 1684–1686 (2019)
4. Bakas, S., et al.: Identifying the best machine learning algorithms for brain tumor segmentation, progression assessment, and overall survival prediction in the brats challenge. arXiv preprint arXiv:1811.02629 (2018)
5. Bakas, S., et al.: Advancing the cancer genome atlas glioma MRI collections with expert segmentation labels and radiomic features. Sci. Data **4**, 170117 (2017)
6. Bakas, S., et la.: Segmentation labels and radiomic features for the pre-operative scans of the TCGA-GBM collection. Cancer Imaging Arch. (2017). https://doi.org/10.7937/K9/TCIA.2017.KLXWJJ1Q
7. Gitler, A.D., Dhillon, P., Shorter, J.: Neurodegenerative disease: models, mechanisms, and a new hope. Disease Models Mech. **10**, 499–502 (2017). 28468935[pmid]
8. Ostrom, Q.T., Rubin, J.B., Lathia, J.D., Berens, M.E., Barnholtz-Sloan, J.S.: Females have the survival advantage in glioblastoma. Neuro-oncol. **20**, 576–577 (2018). 29474647[pmid]
9. Herrlinger, U., et al.: Lomustine-temozolomide combination therapy versus standard temozolomide therapy in patients with newly diagnosed glioblastoma with methylated MGMT promoter (CeTeG/NOA-09): a randomised, open-label, phase 3 trial. Lancet **393**, 678–688 (2019)
10. Çiçek, Ö., Abdulkadir, A., Lienkamp, S.S., Brox, T., Ronneberger, O.: 3D U-net: learning dense volumetric segmentation from sparse annotation. In: Ourselin, S., Joskowicz, L., Sabuncu, M.R., Unal, G., Wells, W. (eds.) MICCAI 2016. LNCS, vol. 9901, pp. 424–432. Springer, Cham (2016). https://doi.org/10.1007/978-3-319-46723-8_49
11. Isensee, F., Jaeger, P.F., Kohl, S.A., Petersen, J., Maier-Hein, K.H.: NNU-net: a self-configuring method for deep learning-based biomedical image segmentation. Nat. Methods **18**(2), 203–211 (2021)
12. Isensee, F., et al.: Automated brain extraction of multisequence MRI using artificial neural networks. Hum. Brain Mapp. **40**(17), 4952–4964 (2019)
13. Pati, S., et al.: Gandlf: a generally nuanced deep learning framework for scalable end-to-end clinical workflows in medical imaging. arXiv preprint arXiv:2103.01006 (2021)
14. Thakur, S.P.: Skull-stripping of glioblastoma MRI scans using 3D deep learning. In: Crimi, A., Bakas, S. (eds.) BrainLes 2019. LNCS, vol. 11992, pp. 57–68. Springer, Cham (2020). https://doi.org/10.1007/978-3-030-46640-4_6

15. Thakur, S., et al.: Brain extraction on MRI scans in presence of diffuse glioma: multi-institutional performance evaluation of deep learning methods and robust modality-agnostic training. Neuroimage **220**, 117081 (2020)
16. Bhalerao, M., Thakur, S.: Brain tumor segmentation based on 3D residual U-net. In: Crimi, A., Bakas, S. (eds.) BrainLes 2019. LNCS, vol. 11993, pp. 218–225. Springer, Cham (2020). https://doi.org/10.1007/978-3-030-46643-5_21
17. Kamnitsas, K., et al.: Efficient multi-scale 3D CNN with fully connected CRF for accurate brain lesion segmentation. Med. Image Anal. **36**, 61–78 (2017)
18. Leung, K.K., et al.: Brain maps: an automated, accurate and robust brain extraction technique using a template library. Neuroimage **55**(3), 1091–1108 (2011)
19. Paszke, A., et al..: Pytorch: an imperative style, high-performance deep learning library. In: Advances in Neural Information Processing Systems, pp. 8026–8037 (2019)
20. Abadi, M., et al.: TensorFlow: a system for large-scale machine learning. In: 12th USENIX Symposium on Operating Systems Design and Implementation (OSDI), vol. 16, pp. 265–283 (2016)
21. Lin, H.W., Tegmark, M., Rolnick, D.: Why does deep and cheap learning work so well? J. Stat. Phys. **168**, 1223–1247 (2017)
22. Jouppi, N.P., et al.: In-datacenter performance analysis of a tensor processing unit (2017)
23. Hubara, I., Courbariaux, M., Soudry, D., El-Yaniv, R., Bengio, Y.: Quantized neural networks: training neural networks with low precision weights and activations (2016)
24. Clark, K., et al.: The cancer imaging archive (TCIA): Maintaining and operating a public information repository. J. Digit. Imaging **26**, 1045–1057 (2013)
25. Scarpace, L., et al.: Radiology data from the cancer genome atlas glioblastoma multiforme [TCGA-GBM] collection. Cancer Imaging Arch. **11**(4), 1 (2016)
26. Menze, B.H., et al.: The multimodal brain tumor image segmentation benchmark (brats). IEEE Trans. Med. Imaging **34**(10), 1993–2024 (2014)
27. Bakas, S., et al.: Segmentation labels and radiomic features for the pre-operative scans of the TCGA-LGG collection. Cancer Imaging Arch. (2017). https://doi.org/10.7937/K9/TCIA.2017.GJQ7R0EF
28. Baid, U., et al.: The RSNA-ASNR-MICCAI brats 2021 benchmark on brain tumor segmentation and radiogenomic classification. arXiv preprint arXiv:2107.02314 (2021)
29. Cox, R., et al.: A (sort of) new image data format standard: Nifti-1: We 150. Neuroimage **22** (2004)
30. Rohlfing, T., Zahr, N.M., Sullivan, E.V., Pfefferbaum, A.: The sri24 multichannel atlas of normal adult human brain structure. Hum. Brain Mapp. **31**, 798–819 (2009)
31. Yushkevich, P.A., Pluta, J., Wang, H., Wisse, L.E., Das, S., Wolk, D.: Fast automatic segmentation of hippocampal subfields and medial temporal lobe subregions in 3 tesla and 7 tesla t2-weighted MRI. Alzheimer's & Dementia: J. Alzheimer's Assoc. **12**(7), P126–P127 (2016)
32. Joshi, S., Davis, B., Jomier, M., Gerig, G.: Unbiased diffeomorphic atlas construction for computational anatomy. Neuroimage **23**, S151–S160 (2004)
33. Yushkevich, P.A., et al.: User-guided 3D active contour segmentation of anatomical structures: significantly improved efficiency and reliability. Neuroimage **31**(3), 1116–1128 (2006)
34. Yushkevich, P.A., et al.: User-guided segmentation of multi-modality medical imaging datasets with ITK-snap. Neuroinformatics **17**(1), 83–102 (2019)

35. Davatzikos, C., et al.: Cancer imaging phenomics toolkit: quantitative imaging analytics for precision diagnostics and predictive modeling of clinical outcome. J. Med. Imaging **5**(1), 011018 (2018)
36. Rathore, S., et al.: Brain cancer imaging phenomics toolkit (brain-CaPTk): an interactive platform for quantitative analysis of glioblastoma. In: Crimi, A., Bakas, S., Kuijf, H., Menze, B., Reyes, M. (eds.) BrainLes 2017. LNCS, vol. 10670, pp. 133–145. Springer, Cham (2018). https://doi.org/10.1007/978-3-319-75238-9_12
37. Pati, S., et al.: The cancer imaging phenomics toolkit (CaPTk): technical overview. In: Crimi, A., Bakas, S. (eds.) BrainLes 2019. LNCS, vol. 11993, pp. 380–394. Springer, Cham (2020). https://doi.org/10.1007/978-3-030-46643-5_38
38. A. Fathi Kazerooni, H. Akbari, G. Shukla, C. Badve, J. D. Rudie, C. Sako, S. Rathore, S. Bakas, S. Pati, A. Singh, et al., "Cancer imaging phenomics via captk: multi-institutional prediction of progression-free survival and pattern of recurrence in glioblastoma," JCO clinical cancer informatics, vol. 4, pp. 234–244, 2020
39. Rathore, S., et al.: Multi-institutional noninvasive in vivo characterization of IDH, 1p/19q, and egfrviii in glioma using neuro-cancer imaging phenomics toolkit (neuro-captk). Neuro-oncol. Adv. **2**(Supplement_4), iv22–iv34 (2020)
40. Sled, J.G., Zijdenbos, A.P., Evans, A.C.: A nonparametric method for automatic correction of intensity nonuniformity in MRI data. IEEE Trans. Med. Imaging **17**(1), 87–97 (1998)
41. Tustison, N.J., et al.: N4itk: improved N3 bias correction. IEEE Trans. Med. Imaging **29**(6), 1310–1320 (2010)
42. Larsen, C.T., Iglesias, J.E., Van Leemput, K.: N3 bias field correction explained as a Bayesian modeling method. In: Cardoso, M.J., Simpson, I., Arbel, T., Precup, D., Ribbens, A. (eds.) BAMBI 2014. LNCS, vol. 8677, pp. 1–12. Springer, Cham (2014). https://doi.org/10.1007/978-3-319-12289-2_1
43. Iqbal, H.: Harisiqbal88/plotneuralnet v1.0.0, December 2018
44. Ronneberger, O., Fischer, P., Brox, T.: U-net: convolutional networks for biomedical image segmentation. In: Navab, N., Hornegger, J., Wells, W.M., Frangi, A.F. (eds.) MICCAI 2015. LNCS, vol. 9351, pp. 234–241. Springer, Cham (2015). https://doi.org/10.1007/978-3-319-24574-4_28
45. Drozdzal, M., Vorontsov, E., Chartrand, G., Kadoury, S., Pal, C.: The importance of skip connections in biomedical image segmentation. In: Carneiro, G., et al. (eds.) LABELS/DLMIA -2016. LNCS, vol. 10008, pp. 179–187. Springer, Cham (2016). https://doi.org/10.1007/978-3-319-46976-8_19
46. He, K., Zhang, X., Ren, S., Sun, J.: Deep residual learning for image recognition. In: Proceedings of the IEEE Conference on Computer Vision and Pattern Recognition, pp. 770–778 (2016)
47. Openvino^{TM} toolkit overview (2021). https://docs.openvinotoolkit.org/latest/index.html
48. Pytorch extension for openvino^{TM} model optimizer (2021). https://github.com/openvinotoolkit/openvino_contrib/tree/master/modules/mo_pytorch
49. Cyphers, S., et al.: Intel nGraph: an intermediate representation, compiler, and executor for deep learning. arXiv preprint arXiv:1801.08058 (2018)
50. Wu, H., Judd, P., Zhang, X., Isaev, M., Micikevicius, P.: Integer quantization for deep learning inference: principles and empirical evaluation. CoRR, vol. abs/2004.09602 (2020)
51. Choukroun, Y., Kravchik, E., Yang, F., Kisilev, P.: Low-bit quantization of neural networks for efficient inference. In: ICCV Workshops, pp. 3009–3018 (2019)
52. Quantization algorithms. https://intellabs.github.io/distiller/algo_quantization.html

53. Int8 inference (2021). https://oneapi-src.github.io/oneDNN/dev_guide_inference_int8.html
54. Tailor, S.A., Fernandez-Marques, J., Lane, N.D.: Degree-quant: quantization-aware training for graph neural networks. arXiv preprint arXiv:2008.05000 (2020)
55. Fang, J., Shafiee, A., Abdel-Aziz, H., Thorsley, D., Georgiadis, G., Hassoun, J.H.: Post-training piecewise linear quantization for deep neural networks. In: Vedaldi, A., Bischof, H., Brox, T., Frahm, J.-M. (eds.) ECCV 2020. LNCS, vol. 12347, pp. 69–86. Springer, Cham (2020). https://doi.org/10.1007/978-3-030-58536-5_5
56. Openvino^{TM} toolkit accuracyaware method (2021). https://docs.openvinotoolkit.org/latest/workbench_docs_Workbench_DG_Int_8_Quantization.html
57. Zijdenbos, A.P., Dawant, B.M., Margolin, R.A., Palmer, A.C.: Morphometric analysis of white matter lesions in MR images: method and validation. IEEE Trans. Med. Imaging 13(4), 716–724 (1994)
58. Reinke, A., et al.: Common limitations of performance metrics in biomedical image analysis. Med. Imaging Deep Learn. (2021)
59. Arafa, M., et al.: Cascade lake: next generation intel Xeon scalable processor. IEEE Micro 39(2), 29–36 (2019)
60. Lower numerical precision deep learning inference and training (2018). https://software.intel.com/content/www/us/en/develop/articles/lower-numerical-precision-deep-learning-inference-and-training.html
61. Davatzikos, C., et al.: Ai-based prognostic imaging biomarkers for precision neuro-oncology: the respond consortium. Neuro-oncol. 22(6), 886–888 (2020)
62. Bakas, S., et al.: iGlass: imaging integration into the glioma longitudinal analysis consortium. Neuro Oncol. 22(10), 1545–1546 (2020)

BraTS

Reciprocal Adversarial Learning for Brain Tumor Segmentation: A Solution to BraTS Challenge 2021 Segmentation Task

Himashi Peiris[1]([✉]), Zhaolin Chen[1,2], Gary Egan[2], and Mehrtash Harandi[1]

[1] Department of Electrical and Computer Systems Engineering, Monash University, Melbourne, Australia
{Edirisinghe.Peiris,Zhaolin.Chen,Mehrtash.Harandi}@monash.edu
[2] Monash Biomedical Imaging (MBI), Monash University, Melbourne, Australia
Gary.Egan@monash.edu

Abstract. This paper proposes an adversarial learning based training approach for brain tumor segmentation task. In this concept, the 3D segmentation network learns from dual reciprocal adversarial learning approaches. To enhance the generalization across the segmentation predictions and to make the segmentation network robust, we adhere to the Virtual Adversarial Training approach by generating more adversarial examples via adding some noise on original patient data. By incorporating a critic that acts as a quantitative subjective referee, the segmentation network learns from the uncertainty information associated with segmentation results. We trained and evaluated network architecture on the RSNA-ASNR-MICCAI BraTS 2021 dataset. Our performance on the online validation dataset is as follows: Dice Similarity Score of 81.38%, 90.77% and 85.39%; Hausdorff Distance (95%) of 21.83 mm, 5.37 mm, 8.56 mm for the enhancing tumor, whole tumor and tumor core, respectively. Similarly, our approach achieved a Dice Similarity Score of 84.55%, 90.46% and 85.30%, as well as Hausdorff Distance (95%) of 13.48 mm, 6.32 mm and 16.98 mm on the final test dataset. Overall, our proposed approach yielded better performance in segmentation accuracy for each tumor sub-region. Our code implementation is publicly available.

Keywords: Deep learning · Brain tumor segmentation · Medical image segmentation · Generative Adversarial Network · Virtual Adversarial Training

1 Introduction

Segmentation accuracy on boundaries is essential in medical image segmentation as it is crucial for many clinical applications, such as treatment planning, disease diagnosis and image guided intervention to name a few. Tremendous progress in deep learning algorithms in dense pixel level prediction tasks has

© The Author(s), under exclusive license to Springer Nature Switzerland AG 2022
A. Crimi and S. Bakas (Eds.): BrainLes 2021, LNCS 12962, pp. 171–181, 2022.
https://doi.org/10.1007/978-3-031-08999-2_13

recently drawn attention on implementing automatic segmentation applications for brain tumor/giloma segmentation. Gliomas considered as the most common brain tumor variant in adults. Diagnosing High-Grade Gliomas (HGG) in early phases which are more malignant (since they usually grow fast and frequently destroy healthy brain tissue) is essential for treatment planning. On the other hand Low-Grade Gliomas (LGG) are slower growing tumors which can be cured if it is diagnosed in early phases. However, segmenting tumor sub regions from various medical images modalities (*e.g.*, MRI and CT) is a monotonous process which is time consuming and subjective. Medical Imaging analysis is carried out by radiologists and this manual process is tedious since the volumes are hefty in size and contains heterogeneous ambiguous sub-regions (*i.e.* edema, active tumor structures, necrotic components, and non-enhancing gross abnormality). In particular, medical image segmentation plays a cornerstone role in computer aided diagnosis. With the recent development in computer vision algorithms in deep learning, there has been many discoveries on automatic medical image segmentation. Multi-modal brain tumor segmentation challenge (BraTS) has been one of the platforms for many discoveries for many years. During the last decade, variants of Fully convolutional networks (FCN) and Convolutional Neural Network (CNN) based architectures have shown convincing performance in previous BraTS and other segmentation challenges. Recent developments in volumetric medical image segmentation networks like 3D-Unet [6] and V-Net [14] has been widely used with medical image modalities since these networks produce predictions for different planes(*i.e.* axial (divides the body into top and bottom halves), coronal (perpendicular), and sagittal (midline of the body)).

The main limitation of implementing and training these volumetric neural network architectures is out-of-memory (OOM) issues and extending these architectures are not feasible due to computational resource constraints. Many researchers have shown that, with a carefully crafted pre-processing, training and inference procedure, segmentation accuracy of 3D-UNet can improve further. By considering those factors like OOM issues, resource limitations, inference time, we propose an approach to tackle these challenges and further improve the segmentation accuracy and training process of 3D-UNet architecture [6]. In summary, **our major contributions** are,

1. Inspired by adversarial learning techniques, we propose two way adversarial learning to segment brain tumor sub regions in multi-modal MR images.
2. We introduce a volumetric discriminator model which can explicitly show the confidence towards the current prediction to impose a higher-order consistency measure of prediction and ground truth during training.
3. We introduce Virtual Adversarial Training (VAT) during model training to enhance the model's robustness to data artefacts.

2 Related Work

2.1 Medical Image Segmentation

The rapid development of deep Convolutional Neural Networks and U-shaped encoder decoder architectures have shown convincing performance in medical image segmentation. The celebrated work U-Net [18] has shown a novel direction to automatic medical image segmentation as it exploits both spatial and contextual information of images which greatly affect accuracy of segmentation models. Due to the simplicity and superior performance U-Net, many variants of U-shaped architectures are constantly emerging, such as Res-UNet [20], H-Dense-UNet [11], U-Net++ [22] and Attention-UNet [16]. Later, to handle volumetric medical image segmentation models are introduced into the field of 3D medical image segmentation, such as 3D-Unet [6] and V-Net [14].

2.2 Adversarial Learning

Generative Adversarial Networks (GANs) [8] by Goodfellow has been a major breakthrough in the image generation task. Inspired by GAN approach, many GAN based medical imaging applications were introduced recently including in the areas of medical image segmentation [12], reconstruction [17] and domain adaptation [21]. In BraTS challenge 2020, Marco *et al.* proposed 3D volume-to-volume Generative Adversarial Network for segmentation of brain tumours [7] where the discriminator is build based on PatchGAN [9] architecture style. VAT is another adversarial learning approach which has shown tremendous performance in semi-supervised learning [15]. VAT is applicable to any parametric model and it directly regularizes the output distribution by its local sensitivity of the output with respect to input [15].

Hence, inspired by above works, we propose min-max formulation with VAT for segmenting brain tumors in multi-modal MR images.

3 Methodology

We start this section by providing an overview of the BraTS dataset and proposed method as shown in Fig. 2. Then we detail out the structure of each module and the entire training pipeline.

3.1 Dataset

The Magnetic Resonance images used for the model training and evaluation are from the Multi-modal Brain tumour Segmentation Challenge (BraTS) 2021 [2–5,13]. The BraTS 2021 training dataset contains 1251 MR volumes of shape $240 \times 240 \times 155$. MRI is required to evaluate tumor heterogeneity. These MRI sequences are conventionally used for giloma detection: T1 weighted sequence (T1), T1-weighted contrast enhanced sequence using gadolinium contrast agents (T1Gd)

(T1CE), T2 weighted sequence (T2), and Fluid attenuated inversion recovery (FLAIR) sequence. From these sequences, four distinct tumor sub-regions can be identified from MRI as: The Enhancing Tumor (ET) which corresponds to area of relative hyper-intensity in the T1CE with respect to the T1 sequence, Non Enhancing Tumor (NET), Necrotic Tumor (NCR) which are both hypo-intense in T1-Gd when compared to T1, Peritumoral Edema (ED) which is hyper-intense in FLAIR sequence. These almost homogeneous sub-regions can be clustered together to compose three semantically meaningful tumor classes as, Enhancing Tumor (ET), addition of ET, NET and NCR represents the Tumor Core (TC) region and addition of ED to TC represents the Whole Tumor (WT). MRI sequences and ground truth map with three classes are shown in Fig. 1.

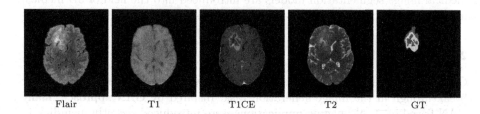

Flair   T1   T1CE   T2   GT

Fig. 1. Visual analysis of BraTs 2021 training data. In the Ground Truth (GT) Mask, green, yellow and gray represent the peritumoral edema (ED), Enhancing Tumor (ET) and non enhancing tumor/necrotic tumor (NET/NCR), respectively. (Color figure online)

3.2   Problem Formulation

Let $\mathcal{X} = \{(\mathbf{X}_i, \mathbf{Y}_i)\}_{i=1}^{m}$ be a labeled set with m number of samples, where each sample $(\mathbf{X}_i, \mathbf{Y}_i)$ consists of an image $\mathbf{X}_i \in \mathbb{R}^{C \times D \times H \times W}$ and its associated ground-truth segmentation mask $\mathbf{Y}_i \in \{0, 1, 2, 4\}^{C \times H \times W}$. Pixels with 0,1,2 and 4 in label-map represent the background/air, Necrotic (NCR) and Non-enhancing tumor core (NET), Peritumoral Edema (ED) and Enhancing Tumor (ET).

3.3   Network Architecture

The proposed network architecture consists of three modules, namely a segmentation network, a critic network and Virtual adversarial Training (VAT) block. The segmentation network (*i.e.*, $\mathcal{F}(\cdot)$) composed of down-sampling and up-sampling layers with skip pathways, making it a U like network architecture [18]. Critic is constructed as a fully convolutional adversarial network. Both networks consists 3D convolutions. The critic constructively impose the segmentation network to predict segmentation masks that are more similar to ground truth masks. The critic here, depicts Markovian PatchGAN architecture [9,10].

In the original work Markovian PatchGAN architecture enables producing confidence scores for prediction masks. Inspired by this, we adapt the similar approach to provide uncertainty information to the segmentation network. The VAT block generates adversarial examples, so that the segmentation network can learn to avoid making such incorrect predictions on new patient data and patient data with artefacts.

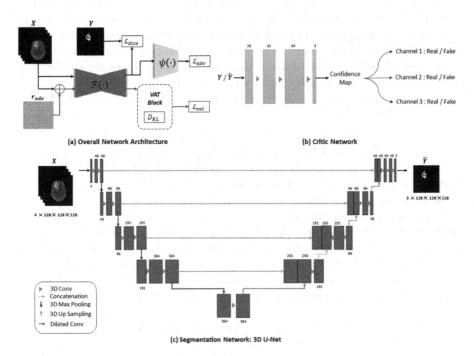

Fig. 2. Proposed overall network architecture. $\mathcal{F}(\cdot)$ and $\psi(\cdot)$ denote the Segmentation network and the Critic network. X, Y, r_{adv} and $\hat{Y}$ are input data (original patient data), ground truth segmentation masks, perturbation added on input data and the prediction generated from segmentation network. Here, Critic criticizes between prediction masks and the ground truth masks to perform the min-max game by generating a pixel-wise confidence map. VAT block improves the robustness of the model against generated adversarial examples by adding perturbation that violates the virtual adversarial direction.

3.4 Objective Function

The parameters of segmentation network is defined as θ_G and the critic network is θ_C. To encourage the segmentation network to yield predictions closer to the ground truth real masks by deceiving a critic network, we propose optimizing the following min-max problem:

$$\min_{\theta_G} \max_{\theta_C} \mathcal{L}(\theta_G; \mathcal{X}) . \tag{1}$$

We propose to train the segmentation network by minimizing a the total loss function which consists of three terms:

$$\mathcal{L}(\theta; \mathcal{X}) := \lambda_s \, \mathcal{L}_{dice}(\theta_G; \mathcal{X}) + \lambda_v \, \mathcal{L}_{vat}(\theta_G; \mathcal{X}; r_{adv}) + \lambda_c \, \mathcal{L}_{adv}(\theta_G; \theta_C; \mathcal{X}) \,, \quad (2)$$

where $\mathcal{L}_{dice}$, $\mathcal{L}_{vat}$, and $\mathcal{L}_{adv}$ denote the supervised dice loss, the virtual adversarial training loss and the critic loss respectively. Furthermore, $\lambda_s, \lambda_v, \lambda_c > 0$ are hyper-parameters of the algorithm, controlling the contribution of each loss term. It can be seen that the supervised dice loss and vat loss are only dependent on the segmentation networks while the critic loss is defined based on the parameters of the entire model. The segmentation network works robustly and shows generalization performance as long as these parameters are defined in a reasonable range. In our experiments we set $\lambda_s = 1.0$, $\lambda_v = 0.2$ and $\lambda_c = 0.3$.

As the main loss, we use dice loss and we calculate dice loss for each class (Multi-class loss function):

$$\mathcal{L}_{\text{dice}}(\theta_G; \mathcal{X}) = 1 - \mathbb{E}_{(\mathbf{X},\mathbf{Y})\sim\mathcal{X}} \left[\frac{\langle \mathbf{Y} , \hat{\mathbf{Y}} \rangle + \epsilon}{\|\mathbf{Y}\|_1 + \|\hat{\mathbf{Y}}\|_1 + \epsilon} \right], \quad (3)$$

where we use $\langle \mathbf{A}, \mathbf{B} \rangle = \sum_{i,j,k} \mathbf{A}[i,j,k]\mathbf{B}[i,j,k]$, $\|\mathbf{A}\|_1 = \sum_{i,j,k} |\mathbf{A}[i,j,k]|$ and $+\epsilon$ is the smoothing factor (set to 1 in our experiment).

VAT is an algorithm that updates the model by the weighted sum of the gradient of the regularization term which is the second loss term of our full objective function. $\mathcal{L}_{vat}$ is a non-negative function that measures the divergence between ground truth distribution and perturbed prediction distribution. Inspired by the VAT method by Takeru et al. [15], we define the divergence based Local Distributional Smoothness (LDS) as:

$$\mathcal{L}_{\text{vat}}(\theta_G; \mathcal{X}; r_{adv}) = \mathbb{E}_{(\mathbf{X},\mathbf{Y})\sim\mathcal{X}} \left[\mathcal{D}_{KL}(\mathbf{Y} \| \mathcal{F}(\theta_G, \mathbf{X} + r_{adv})) \right]. \quad (4)$$

Minimizing $\mathcal{L}_{vat}$ improves the generalization performance of the model and makes the model more robust against the adversarial examples that violates the virtual adversarial direction. Instead of having heavy data augmentation on the dataset with images perturbed by regular deformation we use adversarial perturbation which reduces the test error [19].

We denote the functionality of the critic by $\Psi : [0,1]^{H \times W} \rightarrow [0,1]^{H \times W}$ and define the normalized loss of critic for prediction distribution as:

$$\mathcal{L}_{adv}(\theta_G; \theta_C; \mathcal{X}) := \mathbb{E}_{(\mathbf{X},\mathbf{Y})\sim\mathcal{X}} \left[-\sum_{a\in H} \sum_{b\in W} \left\{ (1-\eta) \log \left(\psi(\mathbf{Y})[a,b] \right) \right. \right.$$
$$\left. \left. + \eta \log \left(1 - \psi(\hat{\mathbf{Y}})[a,b] \right) \right\} \right], \quad (5)$$

where $\eta = 0$ if the sample is generated by the segmentation network, and $\eta = 1$ if the sample is drawn from the ground truth labels. With this adversarial loss, segmentation network tries to deceive the critic by generating predictions that are more similar to ground truth masks holistically.

4   Experiments

4.1   Implementation Details

The proposed model is developed in PyTorch and trained from scratch. We use modified version of 3D UNet as the segmentation network and a 3D discriminator as the critic network. In the 3D UNet, contracting path comprises five layers including bottleneck and each consisted of two $3 \times 3 \times 3$ convolutions together with group normalization and ReLu activation. The number of feature maps in the first encoder is predefined as 48. The down-sampling layer consists a Max pooling operation with a kernel size of $2 \times 2 \times 2$ with stride 2. Blocks of expansive path consists performs up-sampling using the trilinear interpolation followed by $3 \times 3 \times 3$ convolution. Final layers consists a convolutional layer of a $1 \times 1 \times 1$ kernel with 3 output channels and a sigmoid activation. Skip connections between contracting and expansive path lead to concatenation of corresponding outputs. 3D discriminator consists 4 $3 \times 3 \times 3$ convolutions with batch normalization and leaky ReLu activation function. Discriminator here is implemented, inspired by PatchGAN [9] where cubic size is $1 \times 1 \times 1$.

Image Pre-processing. Intensities of MRI volumes are inconsistent due to various factors such as motions of patients during the examination, different manufacturers of acquisition devices, sequences and parameters used during image acquisition. To standardize all volumes, min-max scaling was performed followed by clipping intensity values. Images were then cropped to a fixed patch size of $128 \times 128 \times 128$ by removing unnecessary background pixels.

Training. For training of segmentation network we use Adam optimizer with the learning rate of $2e{-}04$ and for training of critic network, we use RMSProp optimizer with the learning rate of $5e{-}05$ as momentum based methods cause instability [1]. Training was done by splitting the original training dataset into training set (80%) and test set (20%) for 100 epochs with batch size of 2. Therefore, 1000 MR volumes are used to train the model while 251 MR volumes were used as test set.

Inference. The BraTS 2021 validation dataset contains 219 MR volumes and synapse portal conducts the evaluation. In the inference phase, the original volume re-scaled using min-max scaling followed by clipping intensity values and cropped to $240 \times 240 \times 155$ before feeding to the saved 3D UNet model.

4.2   Performance Evaluation

Segmentation accuracy of three classes (*i.e.*, ET, TC and WT) are evaluated during training and inference. Both qualitative and quantitative analysis is performed to evaluate the model accuracy.

Table 1. Validation Phase Results.

Class	Hausdorff distance	Dice score	Sensitivity	Specificity
Enhanced Tumor (ET)	21.8296	81.3898	83.3949	99.9695
Tumor Core (TC)	8.5632	85.3856	85.0726	99.9745
Whole Tumor (WT)	5.3686	90.7654	92.0858	99.9107

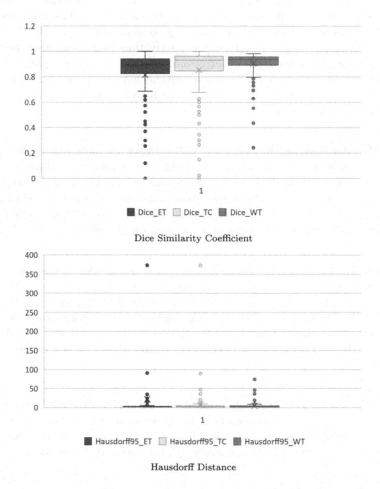

Fig. 3. The box and whisker plots of the distribution of the segmentation metrics for Validation Phase Results. The box-plot shows the minimum, lower quartile, median, upper quartile and maximum for each tumor class. Outliers are shown away from lower quartile.

Evaluation Matrices. The learning model is evaluated using four matrices (1) Dice Sørensen coefficient (DSC), (2) Hausdorff Distance, (3) Sensitivity and (4) Specificity.

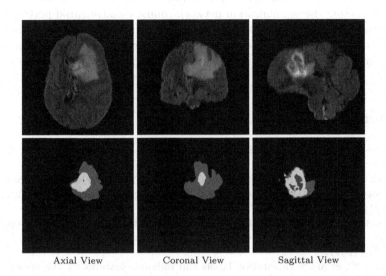

| Axial View | Coronal View | Sagittal View |

Fig. 4. Validation Phase Results for the Sample BraTS2021_00190. Here, green, yellow and gray represents the Whole tumor (WT), Enhancing Tumor (ET) and Tumor Core (TC) classes respectively. (Dice (ET) = 97.2585, Dice (TC) = 99.1492, Dice (WT) = 97.5753) (Color figure online)

Validation Phase Experimental Results. The quantitative and qualitative results during validation phase for the proposed approach is shown in Table 1 Figs. 3 and 4. It is noticeable that, the proposed framework helps in identifying fine predictions successfully.

Testing Phase Experimental Results. Our final evaluation results on the testing dataset are shown in Table 2. Compared to validation phase results, it can be seen that average of Dice Similarity Scores for tumor sub regions is improved during testing phase.

Table 2. Testing phase results.

Class	Hausdorff distance	Dice score	Sensitivity	Specificity
Enhanced Tumor (ET)	13.4802	84.5530	88.0258	99.9680
Tumor Core (TC)	16.9814	85.3010	87.7660	99.9637
Whole Tumor (WT)	6.3239	90.4583	92.1467	99.9161

5   Conclusion

In this work, we demonstrate a simple and effective way to improve training of 3D U-Net by reciprocal adversarial learning. Our approach extends the VAT method, making the segmentation network robust to adversarial perturbations, by generating adversarial examples and adapt min-max approach adapting GAN architecture. Our experiments showed that the virtual adversarial training and uncertainty guidance help to encourage the performance of the segmentation network.

References

1. Arjovsky, M., Chintala, S., Bottou, L.: Wasserstein GAN. arXiv preprint arXiv:1701.07875 (2017)
2. Baid, U., et al.: The RSNA-ASNR-MICCAI BraTs 2021 benchmark on brain tumor segmentation and radiogenomic classification. arXiv preprint arXiv:2107.02314 (2021)
3. Bakas, S., et al.: Segmentation labels and radiomic features for the pre-operative scans of the TCGA-GBM collection. Cancer Imaging Arch. Nat. Sci. Data **4**, 170117 (2017)
4. Bakas, S., et al.: Segmentation labels and radiomic features for the pre-operative scans of the TCGA-LGG collection. Cancer Imaging Arch. **286** (2017)
5. Bakas, S., et al.: Advancing the cancer genome atlas glioma MRI collections with expert segmentation labels and radiomic features. Sci. Data **4**(1), 1–13 (2017)
6. Çiçek, Ö., Abdulkadir, A., Lienkamp, S.S., Brox, T., Ronneberger, O.: 3D U-net: learning dense volumetric segmentation from sparse annotation. In: Ourselin, S., Joskowicz, L., Sabuncu, M.R., Unal, G., Wells, W. (eds.) MICCAI 2016. LNCS, vol. 9901, pp. 424–432. Springer, Cham (2016). https://doi.org/10.1007/978-3-319-46723-8_49
7. Cirillo, M.D., Abramian, D., Eklund, A.: Vox2vox: 3D-GAN for brain Tumour segmentation. arXiv preprint arXiv:2003.13653 (2020)
8. Goodfellow, I., et al.: Generative adversarial nets. In: Advances in Neural Information Processing Systems, pp. 2672–2680 (2014)
9. Isola, P., Zhu, J.Y., Zhou, T., Efros, A.A.: Image-to-image translation with conditional adversarial networks. In: Proceedings of IEEE Conference on Computer Vision and Pattern Recognition (CVPR), pp. 1125–1134 (2017)
10. Li, C., Wand, M.: Precomputed real-time texture synthesis with Markovian generative adversarial networks. In: Leibe, B., Matas, J., Sebe, N., Welling, M. (eds.) ECCV 2016. LNCS, vol. 9907, pp. 702–716. Springer, Cham (2016). https://doi.org/10.1007/978-3-319-46487-9_43
11. Li, X., Chen, H., Qi, X., Dou, Q., Fu, C.W., Heng, P.A.: H-denseunet: hybrid densely connected UNET for liver and tumor segmentation from CT volumes. IEEE Trans. Med. Imaging **37**(12), 2663–2674 (2018)
12. Mahmood, F., et al.: Deep adversarial training for multi-organ nuclei segmentation in histopathology images. IEEE Trans. Med. Imaging (2019)
13. Menze, B.H., et al.: The multimodal brain tumor image segmentation benchmark (BraTs). IEEE Trans. Med. Imaging **34**(10), 1993–2024 (2014)

14. Milletari, F., Navab, N., Ahmadi, S.A.: V-net: fully convolutional neural networks for volumetric medical image segmentation. In: 2016 Fourth International Conference on 3D Vision (3DV), pp. 565–571. IEEE (2016)
15. Miyato, T., Maeda, S.I., Koyama, M., Ishii, S.: Virtual adversarial training: a regularization method for supervised and semi-supervised learning. IEEE Trans. Pattern Anal. Mach. Intell. **41**(8), 1979–1993 (2018)
16. Oktay, O., et al.: Attention U-net: learning where to look for the pancreas. arXiv preprint arXiv:1804.03999 (2018)
17. Quan, T.M., Nguyen-Duc, T., Jeong, W.K.: Compressed sensing MRI reconstruction with cyclic loss in generative adversarial networks. arXiv preprint arXiv:1709.00753 (2017)
18. Ronneberger, O., Fischer, P., Brox, T.: U-net: convolutional networks for biomedical image segmentation. In: Navab, N., Hornegger, J., Wells, W.M., Frangi, A.F. (eds.) MICCAI 2015. LNCS, vol. 9351, pp. 234–241. Springer, Cham (2015). https://doi.org/10.1007/978-3-319-24574-4_28
19. Szegedy, C., et al.: Intriguing properties of neural networks. arXiv preprint arXiv:1312.6199 (2013)
20. Xiao, X., Lian, S., Luo, Z., Li, S.: Weighted Res-UNET for high-quality retina vessel segmentation. In: 2018 9th International Conference on Information Technology in Medicine and Education (ITME), pp. 327–331. IEEE (2018)
21. Zhang, Y., Miao, S., Mansi, T., Liao, R.: Task driven generative modeling for unsupervised domain adaptation: application to x-ray image segmentation. In: Frangi, A.F., Schnabel, J.A., Davatzikos, C., Alberola-López, C., Fichtinger, G. (eds.) MICCAI 2018. LNCS, vol. 11071, pp. 599–607. Springer, Cham (2018). https://doi.org/10.1007/978-3-030-00934-2_67
22. Zhou, Z., Rahman Siddiquee, M.M., Tajbakhsh, N., Liang, J.: UNet++: a nested U-net architecture for medical image segmentation. In: Stoyanov, D., et al. (eds.) DLMIA/ML-CDS -2018. LNCS, vol. 11045, pp. 3–11. Springer, Cham (2018). https://doi.org/10.1007/978-3-030-00889-5_1

Unet3D with Multiple Atrous Convolutions Attention Block for Brain Tumor Segmentation

Agus Subhan Akbar[1,2]([⊠]) [ID], Chastine Fatichah[1] [ID], and Nanik Suciati[1] [ID]

[1] Institut Teknologi Sepuluh Nopember, Surabaya, Indonesia
{chastine,nanik}@if.its.ac.id
[2] Universitas Islam Nahdlatul Ulama Jepara, Jepara, Indonesia
agussa@unisnu.ac.id

Abstract. Brain tumor segmentation by computer computing is still an exciting challenge. UNet architecture has been widely used for medical image segmentation with several modifications. Attention blocks have been used to modify skip connections on the UNet architecture and result in improved performance. In this study, we propose the development of UNet for brain tumor image segmentation by modifying its contraction and expansion block by adding Attention, adding multiple atrous convolutions, and adding a residual pathway that we call Multiple Atrous convolutions Attention Block (MAAB). The expansion part is also added with the formation of pyramid features taken from each level to produce the final segmentation output. The architecture is trained using patches and batch 2 to save GPU memory usage. Online validation of the segmentation results from the BraTS 2021 validation dataset resulted in dice performance of 78.02, 80.73, and 89.07 for ET, TC, and WT. These results indicate that the proposed architecture is promising for further development.

Keywords: Atrous convolution · Attention block · Pyramid features · Multiple atrous convolutions attention block · MAAB

1 Introduction

Segmentation of brain tumors using computer computing is still an exciting challenge. Several events have been held to get the latest methods with the best segmentation performance. One event that continues to invite researchers to innovate related to the segmentation method is the Brain Tumor Segmentation Challenge (BraTS Challenge). This BraTS Challenge has been held every year, starting in 2012 until now in 2021 [4].

The BraTS 2021 challenge is held by providing a larger dataset than the previous year. Until now, the dataset provided consists of training data accompanied by a label with a total of 1251 data and validation data that is not

Supported by Ministry of Education and Culture, Indonesia.

A. Crimi and S. Bakas (Eds.): BrainLes 2021, LNCS 12962, pp. 182–193, 2022.
https://doi.org/10.1007/978-3-031-08999-2_14

accompanied by a label with a total of 219 data. This validation data can be checked for correctness of labeling using the online validation tool provided on the https://www.synapse.org site [5–7,12].

Among the many current architectures, UNet has become the widely used architecture as a medical image segmentation model. Starting with use in segmenting neuronal structures in the EM Stack by [14], this architecture has been developed for segmenting 3D medical images. The development of UNet includes modifying existing blocks at each level, both in the expansion and decoder parts, modifying skip connections, and adding links in the decoder section by adding some links to form pyramid features.

One of the developments of the UNet architecture is to modify the skip connection part. Modifications are made by adding an attention gate which is intended to be able to focus on the target segmentation object. This attention-gate model is taught to minimize the influence of the less relevant parts of the input image while still focusing on the essential features for the segmentation target [15].

Other UNet architecture developments are block modification as done in [1] by creating two paths in one block. One path uses convolution with kernel size 5×5 followed by normalization and relu. The other path uses convolution with a kernel size of 3×3 followed by residual blocks. Merging the output of each path is done by concatenating the output features of each path. On the other hand, some modify the block from UNet by using atrous convolution to get a wider reception area [17].

The merging of feature maps which are the outputs of each level in the UNet decoder section, to form a feature pyramid is also carried out to improve segmentation performance as was done in [13]. The formation of this pyramid feature was inspired by the [10] research which was used to carry out the object detection process. This pyramid feature is also used in several studies to segment brain tumors [18, 21, 22].

In this study, a modification of the UNet architecture was proposed for processing brain tumor segmentation from 3D MRI images. The modifications include modifying each block with multiple atrous convolutions, adding an attention gate accompanied by a residual path to keep accelerating the convergence of the model. The skip connection portion of UNet was modified by adding an attention gate connected to the output of the lower expansion block. Moreover, the last modification is using pyramid features by combining the feature outputs from each level in the expansion section, which is connected to a convolution block to produce segmented outputs. The segmentation performance obtained is promising.

2   Methods

2.1   Dataset

The datasets used in this study are the BraTS 2021 Training dataset and the BraTS 2021 validation dataset. Each dataset was obtained with different clinical protocols and from different MRI scanners from multiple providing institutions. The BraTS 2021 Training dataset contains 1251 patient data with four modalities, T1, T1Gd, T2, and T2-Flair, accompanied by one associated segmentation label. There are four types of segmentation labels with a value of 1 indicating Necrosis/non-enhancing tumor, 2 representing edema, a value of 4 indicating tumor enhancing, and 0 for non-tumor and background. The labels provided are annotated by one to four annotation officers and are checked and approved by expert neuro-radiologists.

The BraTS 2021 Validation dataset, on the other hand, is a dataset that does not come with a label. The segmentation results must be validated online by submitting it to the provided online validation site[1] to obtain the correctness of labeling. This BraTS 2021 validation dataset contains 219 patient data with the same four modalities as the BraTS 2021 Training dataset.

2.2   Preprocessing

The 3D images of the BraTS 2021 training dataset and the BraTS 2021 validation dataset were obtained from a number of different scanners and multiple contributing institutions. The value of the voxel intensity interval of each 3D image produced will be different. So these values need to be normalized so that they are in the same interval. Each of these 3D images was normalized using the Eq. 1 similar to that done in [2].

$$I_{norm} = \frac{I_{orig} - \mu}{\sigma} \tag{1}$$

where I_{norm} and I_{orig} are the normalized image and the original image, while μ and σ are the average value and standard deviation of all non-zero voxels in the 3D image. The normalization process was carried out for each patient data and each modality-both for the BraTS 2021 training dataset during training and the BraTS 2021 validation dataset during inference.

2.3   Proposed Architecture

The architecture proposed in this study is developing the UNet architecture with a 3D Image processing approach. The proposed architecture used is shown in Fig. 1.

All modalities are used in this study, followed by a dropout layer as regularization-the use of dropout as one of the regularization models as proposed by [16]. The use of dropout as regularization is also used in several studies with a rate that varies between 0.1 to 0.5 [3,8,9,11,19,20]. In this paper, the dropout rate value used is 0.2 with the placement at the beginning of the layer.

The next layer is the Multi Atrous Attention Block (MAAB). There are several levels in this block, starting with levels 1, 2, 3 and 4. Details of the internal visualization within the block are shown in Fig. 2.

---
[1] https://www.synapse.org.

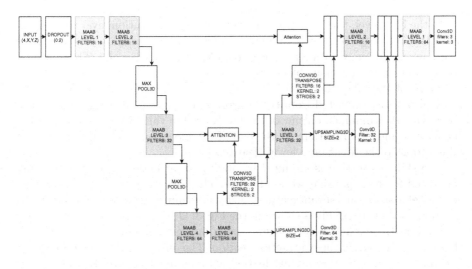

Fig. 1. Unet3D with multiple atrous convolution attention block

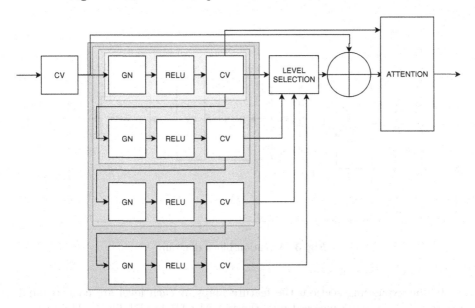

Fig. 2. Multiple Atrous Attention Block - MAAB

This MAAB block processes feature maps equipped with atrous convolutions with different dilatation factors according to their level. The atrous convolution function expands the receptive field area of the feature map without increasing the number of parameters that must be studied. The deeper the downsampling level, the greater the level of the MAAB block to increase the receptive field area that can be covered and increase architectural performance in studying feature maps.

In the first level, the MAAB block contains one convolution layer with a pre-activation strategy. For the second level, in addition to containing the first level layer, one atrous convolution layer is also added with a factor of 2. The following blocks contain the previous blocks with an increasing convolution atrous layer-the order of the dilatation factors in the convolution layers 1, 2, 4, and 8. The residual path is connected from the convolution results at the beginning of the block with the combined output of the levels used in this MAAB block by using the feature addition function. At the end of the block, an attention sub-block is added to keep the focus on relevant features.

The skip connection is modified by adding an attention block before being connected to the expansion section feature. This attention block is used to keep the model focused on relevant features such as the initiative in [15]. The attention diagram used in this study is shown in the Fig. 3. G in the figure is a feature that comes from the expansion level before being upsampled, while X is a feature of the skip connection of the contraction section. The output of this attention block is combined with the upsampling feature at an equivalent level for subsequent processing.

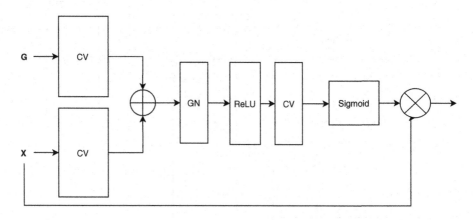

Fig. 3. Attention block diagram

In the expanding section, the feature maps at each level are concatenated together before being inserted into the last MAAB level 1 block. The feature map at the lowest level is upsampled by a factor of four, while the second level is upsampled by a factor of two to equal the size of the feature map at level one. This connection forms a feature map of the pyramid and the supervision of each lower level. The output of the last MAAB block is convoluted into three channels representing the segmentation target (ET, WT, and TC).

2.4   Loss Function

The loss function used during the training process is diceloss with the formula expressed in the Eq. 2. The objects detected in the image consist of 3 types, namely Enhanced Tumor, Tumor Core, a combination of Enhanced Tumor and Necrotic objects, and Whole Tumor, which is a combination of all tumor objects. So that the loss function used uses the combination of the three areas with the weighting as stated in the Eq. 3.

$$dloss_{obj}(P, Y) = 1 - \frac{2 \times P_{obj} \times Y_{obj} + \epsilon}{|P_{obj}| + |Y_{obj}| + \epsilon} \tag{2}$$

$$Loss = 0.34 \times dloss_{ET} + 0.33 \times dloss_{TC} + 0.33 \times dloss_{WT} \tag{3}$$

where P represents the predicted result, Y represents the segmentation target, ϵ is filled with a small value to avoid dividing by zero. Furthermore, ET, TC, and WT represent Enhanced Tumor, Tumor Core, and Whole Tumor areas.

2.5   Experiment Settings

The hardware used in this study includes an Nvidia RTX 2080i 11GB, 64GB RAM, and a Core I7 processor. While the Deep Learning framework software used is Tensorflow/Keras version 2.5.

The training was carried out using the BraTS 2021 training dataset, which contained 1251 patient data with four modalities (T1, T1Gd, T2, T2-Flair) and one ground-truth file for each patient. The data is split into two parts, with 80% as training data and 20% as local validation data. To minimize variation in training, a 5-fold cross-validation strategy is used.

The model was trained using Adam's optimizer with a learning rate of 1e-4 for 300 epochs for each fold. Data augmentation techniques used include random crop, three-axis random permutation, random replace channel with gaussian distribution, and random mirroring of each axis.

Data is trained with patches of size $72 \times 72 \times 72$ and batch size of 2 to minimize GPU memory requirements. The 3d image patches were taken from the area containing the tumor at random. During the inference process, the data is processed at size $72 \times 72 \times 72$ but with a shift of 64 voxels to each axis. Voxels from the overlapping segmentation results are averaged to get the final segmentation result.

3   Results

The time required for training and inference model using the five-fold strategy as shown in the Table 1. From the Table 1 it can be seen that the average time required for a 5-fold training with 300 epochs is 104408 s. Alternatively, per-epoch, it takes 348,027 s. This time is needed for training 1001 data and local validation for 250 data. The average inference time required is 1530 s seconds as shown in Table 1. This time is used to segment the data as much as 219 data. So that processing for each data takes an average of 6.99 s. Meanwhile, if using a combination of 5 models, it will take 10054 s so that the processing of an ensemble of 5 models for each data takes an average of 45.91 s.

Table 1. Model training time on 300 epochs

Fold	Training time (s)	Inference time (s)
Fold 1	104172	1567
Fold 2	104258	1522
Fold 3	104159	1514
Fold 4	104652	1516
Fold 5	104799	1531
Average	104408	1530

Loss obtained during training for each fold as shown in Fig. 4. From the figure, the most stable is the 3rd fold and the 5th fold with no spikes in value in the graph. While in others, there is a spike in value at certain times. As in the 1st fold, there was a spike value at the epoch between 50–100 for both training and validation loss. Likewise, in the 2nd fold and fourth fold. This condition is possible because this training uses random patches. When taking a random patch, there may not be an object, but the model detects an object so that the loss value will approach the value of 1.

From Fig. 4(f), it can be seen that the overall training of this model is convergent. The spikes in value do not exceed the initial loss value. At the end of the epoch, the loss values for training and validation also converge. In all graphs (a-e), the existing convergence pattern is close to the convergent value. The validation loss value is also not much different from the training loss value, so it can be said that the model is not overfitting.

The results of the dice score performance during training are congruent with the loss value. Assuming that the loss function used is $1 - dice$. However, because there are three objects counted in the dice, the loss value is an amalgamation of the dice scores of each object with a weight determined in the Eq. 3. The average dice value of each object during training for all folds as shown in Fig. 5. The validation scores for ET and TC objects have a good pattern, with values increasingly outperforming the training score near the end of the epoch. In comparison, the validation score for the WT object is always below the training score of the WT. However, the score pattern of each object increases until the end of the epoch.

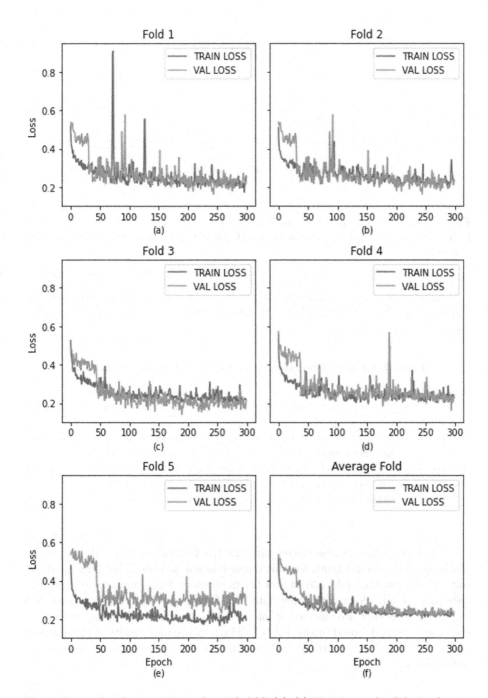

Fig. 4. Loss value during training for each fold. (a)–(e) Training and validation loss in the first fold to the fifth fold. (f) Average training and validation loss on 5-fold cross validation

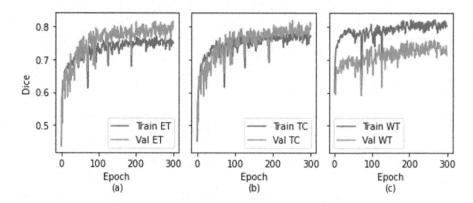

Fig. 5. Average dice score on 5-fold cross validation training: (a) Average dice score for ET Object, (b) Average dice score for TC Object, (c) Average dice score for WT Object.

Online validation of segmentation results using the 1st to fifth fold model is displayed in Table 2. Five models of training results ensembled using the average method can also be seen in the table.

Table 2. Online validation result on BraTS 2021 validation dataset

Model	Dice (%)			Sensitivity (%)			Specificity (%)			Hausdorff95		
	ET	TC	WT	ET	TC	WT	ET	TC	WT	ET	TC	WT
FOLD1	75.82	79.51	88.72	73.42	76.53	90.19	99.98	99.98	99.90	25.53	17.36	7.35
FOLD2	73.85	79.76	87.47	77.91	82.21	91.17	99.96	99.95	99.86	38.11	19.84	14.46
FOLD3	75.46	79.69	86.89	80.75	81.74	91.57	99.96	99.96	99.85	30.98	20.30	18.86
FOLD4	74.74	77.32	85.56	76.73	76.47	92.09	99.97	99.97	99.81	32.91	18.59	20.35
FOLD5	76.48	74.72	87.70	80.47	76.45	91.34	99.96	99.97	99.87	28.41	28.97	12.10
ENSEMBLE	78.02	80.73	89.07	80.51	80.55	92.34	99.97	99.97	99.88	25.82	21.17	11.78

This architecture is also tested with the BraTS 2021 testing dataset for the challenge. The ground truth for this dataset is not provided. We only send the codes that form the architecture and the mechanism for segmenting one patient data individually along with the weight file of the model in a docker format. We use five models that are ensembled into one with the same averaging method as the ensemble model used in the Table 2. The performance results of the 5 model ensemble applied to the BraTS 2021 testing dataset are outstanding, as shown in the Table 3.

Table 3. Online result on BraTS 2021 testing dataset

Model	Dice (%)			Sensitivity (%)			Specificity (%)			Hausdorff95		
	ET	TC	WT	ET	TC	WT	ET	TC	WT	ET	TC	WT
Mean	81.68	82.92	88.42	84.82	85.34	92.29	99.97	99.96	99.89	19.70	23.01	10.70
StdDev	22.30	25.52	13.29	22.50	24.45	9.87	0.05	0.07	0.15	70.71	73.63	18.54
Median	89.57	93.10	92.72	93.09	95.20	95.74	99.98	99.98	99.93	1.73	2.45	3.61
25quantile	79.84	83.86	88.13	83.51	85.34	90.66	99.96	99.97	99.88	1.00	1.00	1.73
75quantile	94.09	96.54	95.55	97.05	98.28	98.04	99.99	99.99	99.96	3.61	7.25	9.10

4 Discussion

In this study, we propose a modified Unet3D architecture for brain tumor segmentation. Modifications include modification of each block with atrous convolution, attention gate, and the addition of residual path. The skip connection section is modified by adding an attention gate that combines the features of the contraction section with the expansion section one level below its equivalent level. The pyramid feature is also added to get better segmentation performance results. Checking using the combination of 5 models on the validation dataset resulted in segmentation performance of 78.02, 80.73, and 89.07 for ET, TC, and WT objects.

In Fig. 4 especially in parts (a), (b), and (d) there is a spike in loss value in certain epochs. The alleged cause of this incident is that random patch picking will result in a volume that has no object, either ET, TC, or WT, but the model still gets its predictions, causing the loss value to spike suddenly. However, the exact cause needs further investigation.

Acknowledgements. This work was supported by the Ministry of Education and Culture, Indonesia. We are deeply grateful for BPPDN (Beasiswa Pendidikan Pascasarjana Dalam Negeri) and PDD (Penelitian Disertasi Doktor) 2020–2021 Grant, which enabled this research could be done.

References

1. Aghalari, M., Aghagolzadeh, A., Ezoji, M.: Brain tumor image segmentation via asymmetric/symmetric UNet based on two-pathway-residual blocks. Biomed. Signal Process. Control **69**, 102841 (2021). https://doi.org/10.1016/j.bspc.2021.102841

2. Akbar, A.S., Fatichah, C., Suciati, N.: Simple myunet3d for brats segmentation. In: 2020 4th International Conference on Informatics and Computational Sciences (ICICoS), pp. 1–6 (2020). https://doi.org/10.1109/ICICoS51170.2020.9299072

3. Akbar, A.S., Fatichah, C., Suciati, N.: Modified mobilenet for patient survival prediction. In: Crimi, A., Bakas, S. (eds.) Brainlesion: Glioma, Multiple Sclerosis, Stroke and Traumatic Brain Injuries, pp. 374–387. Springer, Cham (2021). https://doi.org/10.1007/978-3-030-72087-2_33

4. Baid, U., Ghodasara, S., Bilello, M., et al.: The RSNA-ASNR-MICCAI BraTS 2021 Benchmark on Brain Tumor Segmentation and Radiogenomic Classification, July 2021. http://arxiv.org/abs/2107.02314
5. Bakas, S., Akbari, H., Sotiras, A., et al.: Segmentation labels for the pre-operative scans of the tcga-gbm collection (2017). https://doi.org/10.7937/K9/TCIA.2017.KLXWJJ1Q, https://wiki.cancerimagingarchive.net/x/KoZyAQ
6. Bakas, S., Akbari, H., Sotiras, A., et al.: Segmentation labels for the pre-operative scans of the tcga-lgg collection (2017). https://doi.org/10.7937/K9/TCIA.2017.GJQ7R0EF, https://wiki.cancerimagingarchive.net/x/LIZyAQ
7. Bakas, S., Akbari, H., Sotiras, A., et al.: Advancing the cancer genome atlas glioma MRI collections with expert segmentation labels and radiomic features. Scientific Data 4(1), September 2017. https://doi.org/10.1038/sdata.2017.117
8. Chang, J., Zhang, L., Gu, N., et al.: A mix-pooling CNN architecture with FCRF for brain tumor segmentation. J. Visual Commun. Image Representation **58**, 316–322 (2019). https://doi.org/10.1016/j.jvcir.2018.11.047
9. Kabir Anaraki, A., Ayati, M., Kazemi, F.: Magnetic resonance imaging-based brain tumor grades classification and grading via convolutional neural networks and genetic algorithms. Biocybern. Biomed. Eng. **39**(1), 63–74 (2019). https://doi.org/10.1016/j.bbe.2018.10.004
10. Lin, T.Y., Dollár, P., Girshick, R., et al.: Feature pyramid networks for object detection. In: Proceedings - 30th IEEE Conference on Computer Vision and Pattern Recognition, CVPR 2017. vol. 2017-Janua, pp. 936–944. IEEE, July 2017. https://doi.org/10.1109/CVPR.2017.106. http://ieeexplore.ieee.org/document/8099589/
11. Liu, L., Wu, F.X., Wang, J.: Efficient multi-kernel DCNN with pixel dropout for stroke MRI segmentation. Neurocomputing **350**, 117–127 (2019). https://doi.org/10.1016/j.neucom.2019.03.049
12. Menze, B.H., Jakab, A., Bauer, S., et al.: The multimodal brain tumor image segmentation benchmark (BRATS). IEEE Trans. Med. Imaging **34**(10), 1993–2024 (2015). https://doi.org/10.1109/tmi.2014.2377694
13. Moradi, S., Oghli, M.G., Alizadehasl, A., et al.: MFP-Unet: a novel deep learning based approach for left ventricle segmentation in echocardiography. Phys. Medica **67**, 58–69 (2019). https://doi.org/10.1016/J.EJMP.2019.10.001. https://www.sciencedirect.com/science/article/pii/S1120179719304508
14. Ronneberger, O., Fischer, P., Brox, T.: U-Net: convolutional networks for biomedical image segmentation. In: Navab, N., Hornegger, J., Wells, W.M., Frangi, A.F. (eds.) MICCAI 2015. LNCS, vol. 9351, pp. 234–241. Springer, Cham (2015). https://doi.org/10.1007/978-3-319-24574-4_28
15. Schlemper, J., Oktay, O., Schaap, M., et al.: Attention gated networks: Learning to leverage salient regions in medical images. Med. Image Anal. **53**, 197–207 (2019). https://doi.org/10.1016/j.media.2019.01.012 https://www.sciencedirect.com/science/article/pii/S1361841518306133
16. Srivastava, N., Hinton, G., Krizhevsky, A., et al.: Dropout: a simple way to prevent neural networks from overfitting. J. Mach. Learn. Res. **15**(1), 1929–1958 (2014)
17. S. V. and I. G.: Encoder enhanced atrous (EEA) unet architecture for retinal blood vessel segmentation. Cogn. Syst. Res. **67**, 84–95 (2021). https://doi.org/10.1016/j.cogsys.2021.01.003
18. Wang, J., Gao, J., Ren, J., et al.: DFP-ResUNet: convolutional neural network with a dilated convolutional feature pyramid for multimodal brain tumor segmentation. Comput. Methods Programs Biomed., 106208, May 2021. https://doi.org/10.1016/j.cmpb.2021.106208.https://linkinghub.elsevier.com/retrieve/pii/S0169260721002820

19. Xie, H., Yang, D., Sun, N., et al.: Automated pulmonary nodule detection in CT images using deep convolutional neural networks. Pattern Recogn. **85**, 109–119 (2019). https://doi.org/10.1016/j.patcog.2018.07.031
20. Yang, T., Song, J., Li, L.: A deep learning model integrating SK-TPCNN and random forests for brain tumor segmentation in MRI. Biocybern. Biomed. Eng. **39**(3), 613–623 (2019). https://doi.org/10.1016/J.BBE.2019.06.003. https://www.sciencedirect.com/science/article/pii/S0208521618303292
21. Zhou, Z., He, Z., Jia, Y.: AFPNet: a 3D fully convolutional neural network with atrous-convolution feature pyramid for brain tumor segmentation via MRI images. Neurocomputing **402**, 235–244 (2020). https://doi.org/10.1016/j.neucom.2020.03.097. https://www.sciencedirect.com/science/article/pii/S0925231220304847
22. Zhou, Z., He, Z., Shi, M., et al.: 3D dense connectivity network with atrous convolutional feature pyramid for brain tumor segmentation in magnetic resonance imaging of human heads. Comput. Biol. Med. **121**, 103766 (2020). https://doi.org/10.1016/j.compbiomed.2020.103766

BRATS2021: Exploring Each Sequence in Multi-modal Input for Baseline U-net Performance

Polina Druzhinina[1,2(✉)], Ekaterina Kondrateva[1,2(✉)], Arseny Bozhenko[1],
Vyacheslav Yarkin[1], Maxim Sharaev[1], and Anvar Kurmukov[2]

[1] Skolkovo Institute of Science and Technology, Moscow, Russia
{Polina.Druzhinina,ekaterina.kondrateva}@skoltech.ru
[2] Artificial Intelligence Research Institute, Moscow, Russia

Abstract. Since 2012 the BraTS competition has become a benchmark for brain MRI segmentation. The top-ranked solutions from the competition leaderboard of past years are primarily heavy and sophisticated ensembles of deep neural networks. The complexity of the proposed solutions can restrict their clinical use due to the long execution time and complicate the model transfer to the other datasets, especially with the lack of some MRI sequences in multimodal input. The current paper provides a baseline segmentation accuracy for each separate MRI modality and all four sequences (T1, T1c, T2, and FLAIR) on conventional 3D U-net architecture. We explore the predictive ability of each modality to segment enhancing core, tumor core, and whole tumor. We then compare the baseline performance with BraTS 2019–2020 state-of-the-art solutions. Finally, we share the code and trained weights to facilitate further research on model transfer to different domains and use in other applications.

Keywords: brain MRI · Medical segmentation · U-Net · BRATS2021

1 Introduction

1.1 MRI-Based Models for Brain Tumor Segmentation

Following the success of computer vision-based detection systems in mammography, [2] and pulmonology [3], deep learning (DL) models application for brain MRI is extensively studied [1]. The emergence of DL solutions that outperform the standard first read of the medical image becomes possible for several reasons: the progress of hardware and software for computer vision, improvements in data management and sharing policies, but most importantly - because of massive human-labeled databases.

Brain MR imaging has several peculiarities: collected data are predominantly three-dimensional, serial, or multimodal and domain (scanner) specific. Investigated neuropathological cases are rare; data gathering and labeling are expensive, causing smaller sample sizes for research. Thus, an average sample size for DL training is restricted with hundreds of three-dimensional samples, which compromises training domain-stable solutions [4].

BraTS is the most extensive open-source collection of labeled brain MR images, which makes the dataset of the most interest in developing state-of-the-art DL solutions in neuroradiology. BraTS2021 collection includes more than a thousand annotated cases for supervised DL model training and, notably, for transfer learning to other brain diagnostics datasets and pathologies [5].

1.2 MRI Modalities in Brain Tumor Segmentation

In diagnosing brain tumors, magnetic resonance imaging (MRI) is widespread or even ubiquitous. The great diversity of imaging modalities makes it possible to explore and highlight the different tissue contrasts and unique details related to each part of the tumor. The most informative modalities, and simultaneously ones included in brain cancer treatment protocols, are T1-weighted (T1), T2-weighted (T2), T1-weighted with gadolinium contrast enhancement (T1-Gd or T1c), and T2 Fluid Attenuated Inversion Recovery (FLAIR). Each of them, under their characteristics, emphasizes different features [11]. T1 is good at distinguishing healthy tissue from malignant regions, T2 with its bright signal highlights areas of edema; T1-gd is more suitable for defining tumor boundaries; FLAIR MR images are used to differentiate edema from cerebrospinal fluid (CSF).

Yet different protocols for clinical brain tumor imaging can vary from hospital to hospital and include other biology-driven MRI methods for surgical and radiosurgical planning and assessment of treatment response. These MR modalities can include diffusion-tensor imaging (DTI), perfusion-weighted imaging (PWI), susceptibility-weighted imaging (SWI) [6] and others. Thus, there is a need to independently explore each MR sequence's predictive ability and build solutions without fixing the input set of modalities [12].

1.3 Architectures for MRI Segmentation

First DL Approaches for Image Segmentation and SOTA Solutions. First DL architectures for semantic segmentation appeared in 2015 with fully convolutional networks (FCN) [7]. Then convolutional encoder-decoder architectures of SegNet [8] and U-net [9] showed drastically better performance than just bilinear interpolation of the last layers in FCN.

Today, U-nets, being proposed in 2016, are still considered conventional for medical image segmentation tasks [10]. The original architecture has undergone modifications, for example, gained 3D convolutions (3D U-net), residual connections (Residual U-net) and incorporated DenseNet blocks (Dense U-net). nn-Unet architecture [24], proposed in 2020, is recognized as the benchmark for medical image segmentation.

Flexible architecture of the nn-Unet allows the addition of extra blocks to construct deeper network, additional channels to train multimodal input, and training on image parts (patches) for memory optimization. With data augmentation and model fine-tuning, the architecture performs good with less memory consumption than trained on full-sized images. Therefore a significant portion of today's MRI image segmentation solutions is based on the modifications of 3D U-net [13] and their ensembles.

It is worth saying that U-shaped DL architecture with up and down convolutions is not the only solution for medical image segmentation. There are lately proposed algorithms for brain tumor segmentation based on the engineering approach of MR images processing, thresholding, and binarization, which does not require extensive DL training [11]. On the opposite, more profound and heavier network architectures can outperform U-nets on distinct tasks. Recent U2-net architecture [14] showed better background separation on 2D images and exhibiting the high potential to compete with original ensembles architecture. Lately, proposed transformer architectures incorporated in U-net architecture are shown to outperform conventional ones on a small sample of abdominal images [16]. There are adversarial U-nets with a GAN-based structure. With more training, the SeGAN [15] outperforms conventional architectures.

Although the architectures above can provide more accurate predictions, at the moment, they are harder to train, fine-tune, and transfer to other domains, which is an especially important instrument in medical image analysis [17,18]. Thus, in current paper we aim to:

1. perform an ablation study to find optimal 3D U-net training setting for better convergence of lightweight model on BRATS2021 data;
2. explore the predictive ability of separate MR modalities for brain tumor segmentation;
3. share the trained weights to facilitate further research on transfer to other datasets and contrast-agnostic solutions.

2   Experiments

We choose the experiment design to find the most lightweight U-net architecture and training schema to achieve reasonable data segmentation quality on the BraTS2021 training sample. We performed an ablation study on each separate modality, as well as on multiple sequence input. Thus the shared weights could be further used for transfer learning, or pre-training on different modalities and their combinations.

2.1   Dataset

The Multi-modal Brain Tumor Segmentation Challenge (BraTS) 2021[1] dataset for segmentation task represented with a multi-parametric MRI (mpMRI) scans of glioma. Segmentation labels include glioma sub-regions - the "enhancing tumor" (ET), the "tumor core" (TC), and the "whole tumor" (WT). The

---

[1] http://braintumorsegmentation.org/.

MRI scans for subjects are provided in multiple sequences: native (T1), post-contrast T1-weighted (T1c), T2-weighted (T2), and T2 Fluid Attenuated Inversion Recovery (FLAIR) volumes.

Data preprocessing pipeline `CaPTk` include co-registration, interpolation into 1 mm^3 isotropic resolution with an image size of $240 \times 240 \times 155$, and the skull-stripping [25,26].

2.2 Baseline U-net Model

Data Preprocessing and Augmentation. The overall pipeline was written with `torchio`[2]package [20], with build in U-net and patches creation, as well as data augmentation applied to data with varying probability. Prior to training `HistogramStandardization`, `ZNormalization` were applied to the whole training sample to make zero mean, unit variance and standardize histogram of foreground.

We explored two variants of data augmentation while training, there **p** relates to the probability of transform application and **n** - to the number of artifacts produced:

1. Restricted - includes `RandomAnisotropy,p=0.25`, `RandomBlur,p=0.25`, `RandomNoise,p=0.25` (Gaussian noise), `RandomBiasField,p=0.3` (to eliminate magnetic field inhomogeneity);
2. Extensive - includes Restricted augmentations with [`RandomAffine,p=0.8`; `RandomElasticDeformation,p=0.2`] (the probability of 0.8 is set for the pair of transformations), [`RandomMotion,n=1`; `RandomSpike,n=2`; `RandomGhosting,n=2`] (the probability of 0.5 is set for three augmentations).

Training with extensive augmentations doubled the convergence time with no significant quality increase, thus all experiments with extensive augmentations were excluded from the results.

On model architecture, we explored several U-net modifications, extending the depth and width of the network and changing the normalisation and upsampling:

1. Model 1: with 3 encoding blocks and 4 out channels for first layer, patch size 64, batch normalization and ReLU activation function, linear upsampling;
2. Model 2: with 3 encoding blocks and 4 out channels for first layer, patch size 128, batch normalization and ReLU activation function, linear upsampling;
3. Model 3: with 5 encoding blocks and 4 out channels for first layer, patch size 128, batch normalization, PReLU activation function, linear upsampling;
4. Model 4: with 5 encoding blocks and 16 out channels for first layer, patch size 128, instance normalization and Leaky ReLU activation function, linear upsampling;
5. Model 5: with 5 encoding blocks and 4 out channels for first layer, patch size 128, batch normalization, PReLU activation function, trilinear upsampling and preactivation;

---

[2] https://torchio.readthedocs.io/.

6. Model 6: with 5 encoding blocks and 16 out channels for first layer, patch size 128, batch normalization, PReLU activation function, trilinear upsampling and preactivation;

Batch size was adjusted to GPU capacity. Due to the large input image size, the input patch size is $64 \times 64 \times 64$ for the first experiments and $128 \times 128 \times 128$ for deeper U-nets, and the batch size equals 32 and 16 for train, validation set, accordingly. It worth mentioning that for deeper U-net architecture, even uni-modal input model does not fit into one GPU and was paralleled to two GPU's even with drastically reduced batch size (4 for train and 2 for validation).

The ablation study was performed with the choose of optimizer, loss and different augmentations for Uni and Multi-modality image input. As optimizer we use AdamW with default parameters and Adam with learning rate 1e-3 and weight decay 1e-4. We use stochastic gradient descent optimizer (SGD) with an initial learning rate of 0.01, and momentum of 0.9 with weight decay.

2.3 Comparison with BraTS Toolkit Solutions

To compare the baseline U-net performance with State Of The Art (SOTA) networks we chose the two latest solutions implemented in BraTS Toolkit[3] [21]. BraTS Toolkit provides software for brain tumor segmentation, it incorporates state-of-the-art solutions for the past years BraTS competitions in their stable executable versions (docker containers) and a fusion of their predictions.

The latest uploads in BraTS Toolkit are `scan-2019` and `scan lite-20` implementing solution from the paper Triplanar Ensemble of 3D-to-2D CNNs with Label-Uncertainty for Brain Tumor Segmentation [23]. Additionally we compare these results to the containerized solution `xyz 2019` representing an implementation of U-net based Self-ensemble network [22].

The one subject prediction (inference) time on GPU for `scan lite-20` does not exceeded 5 min, for `xyz 2019` and `scan-2019` - 20 min. It is assumed that data preprocessing is identical to the previous years' data, and therefore the models could be applied directly. It is worth noting that these solutions are trained in previous years' BraTS data, and scoring on BraTS 2021 training data can be compromised by data leakage. Thus BraTS Toolkit solutions were scored on a blind validation set, assuming no data leak from previous years.

2.4 Experimental Settings

All the experiments were implemented on `pytorch` and trained on two NVIDIA Tesla P100 PCIe 16 GB GPU. A relatively large sample size of BraTs2021 training sample allowed to compare models on a single train/test split with a ratio of 0.7 (the same split for all models). The number of subjects in `train/test` equals 939/312, respectively (train and test sets are training sample from competition).

Thus BraTS Toolkit solutions were scored on a blind validation set 219, assuming no data leak from previous years.

---

[3] https://github.com/neuronflow/BraTS-Toolkit.

3 Results

The convergence of models on T1, T1c, T2 and FLAIR on 40 epochs for 3-block 3D U-net architecture with data augmentations, shown on Fig. 1. The experiment report is available on `Weights&Biases` page[4].

The iterations of 3D U-net ablation study represented in Table 2.

The BraTS Toolkit predictions for two models were scored on a competition blind validation set and shown in the Table 1.

Table 1. Results of two models from BraTS Toolkit on a competition blind validation set in terms of Dice coefficient, Hausdorff 95, and Sensitivity (Specificity for equals 0.999 for all table entries).

Model	Dice			Hausdorff 95			Sensitivity		
	ET	TC	WT	ET	TC	WT	ET	TC	WT
zyx 2019	0.809	0.866	0.915	14.905	6.433	4.332	0.806	0.860	0.907
scan lite-20	0.830	0.868	0.922	14.502	7.913	3.949	0.808	0.863	0.914

We show that a model based on T1c images shows better convergence than other modalities with the same training conditions. Training on all modalities simultaneously, naturally leads to better quality as it integrates information from each sequence. In addition,

First experiments on a selection of the model parameters on the T1 sequence showed that using SGD optimizer leads to smoother convergence. Adding restricted augmentations solves the fluctuating validation loss, while extended augmentations significantly raise the training process and negatively affect the quality. We show the quality increase with bigger patch size and deeper model architecture. The combination of Cross-Entropy (CE) loss with DICE loss significantly improves training of the model.

We found no significant difference in activation functions PReLU, Leaky ReLU or default ReLU. Yet, we notice the minimisation of training time while using trilinear upsampling and U-net preactivations.

The best performance achieved with the reported U-net model was acquired with multi-modal input, bigger image patches and deeper model architecture trained with data augmentations: DICE scores are 0.623, 0.791, 0.779 for ET, TC and WT respectively. This is significantly lower, than performance of last year state-of-the-art ensemble solutions: 0.830, 0.868 0.922 DICE scores for ET, TC and WT.

---

[4] `wandb.ai/polina/brats/reports/Brats--Vmlldzo5NDk5NTM?accessToken=zmj73 popy1rho9qb5lg4fh24lg9qxopkmfsuz2xccgzen5671qtqwq9buu8ccO5v.`

Table 2. Segmentation results on validation set (part of competition training samples after train-test split for fine-tuning experiments) in terms of Dice coefficient.

N	MRI sequences	Model	Optimizer	Augment	Epochs	ET	TC	WT
1	T1	1	AdamW	✗	40	0.199	0.394	0.178
2	T1	1	Adam	✗	40	0.242	0.418	0.178
3	T1c	1	Adam	✗	40	0.435	0.395	0.540
4	T1c	1	AdamW	✗	40	0.471	0.386	0.537
5	T1	1	AdamW	✗	40	0.253	0.324	0.220
6	T1	1	SGD	✗	40	0.288	0.358	0.245
7	T1	1	SGD	✓	40	0.257	0.383	0.245
8	T1	1	SGD	✓	60	0.304	0.412	0.305
9	FLAIR	1	SGD	✓	60	0.273	0.506	0.323
10	T2	1	SGD	✓	60	0.355	0.539	0.372
11	T1c	1	SGD	✓	60	0.505	0.436	0.609
12	T1, T1c, T2, FLAIR	2	SGD	✓	40	0.536	0.715	0.705
13	T1c	2	SGD	✓	60	0.560	0.500	0.679
14	T1c	3	SGD	✓	60	0.577	0.497	0.684
15	T1c, FLAIR	3	SGD	✓	40	0.608	0.753	0.757
16	T1c	4	SGD	✓	60	0.624	0.605	0.757
17	T1c, FLAIR	5	SGD	✓	60	0.616	0.778	0.763
18	T1c, FLAIR	5	SGD	✓	100	0.608	0.775	0.758
19	T1, T1c, T2, FLAIR	6	SGD	✓	30	0.621	0.785	0.766
20	T1c, FLAIR	6	SGD	✓	30	0.623	0.791	0.779

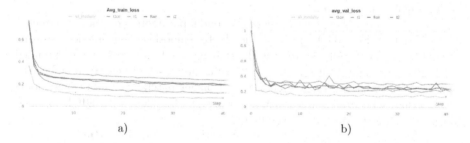

a)   b)

Fig. 1. 3D U-net lightweight architecture training on Uni and Multi-modal image input; (a) Train loss; (b) Validation loss;

4   Conclusion and Discussion

In current paper we provide a baseline segmentation accuracy for each separate MRI modality and all four sequences (T1, T1c, T2, and FLAIR) on conventional 3D U-net architecture.

We performed the ablation study and training strategy for better 3D U-net training on MR image patches.

We explored the predictive ability of each modality for the enhancing core, tumor core, and whole tumor, and find out that post-contrast T1 has more predictive ability for all tumor regions. We and compare the baseline performance with BRATS2019-2020 winning solutions `zyx 2019` and `scan lite` . Finally, we share the code and trained weights to facilitate further research on transfer to different domains and use in other applications.

Work Limitations. The BraTS toolkit solutions were scored according to the main study on the competition blind validation set. We assume that this comparison is fair if that blind validation set was not comprised of images from previous BraTS releases.

The chosen architectures are the most convenient ones, but they were shown to be outperformed by more complex variations of the U-net or their ensembles. The key idea of the current paper is to highlight the baseline accuracy for each modality instead of achieving the best performance. In the scope of this work, we were not aiming at remarkably changing the U-net architecture. Yet, it can be a valuable extension to train each modality on multiple classifier heads of the U-net and try nested structure or redesigned skip connections.

Contribution. Polina Druzhinina - conducted experiments with U-net; Ekaterina Kondrateva - experiments design and Brats Toolkit models execution; Arseny Bozhenko and Vyacheslav Yarkin - docker creation, dataset manipulations and cluster maintenance; Maxim Sharaev and Anvar Kurumkov - conducted paper camera-ready version review.

Acknowledgements. The reported study was funded by RFBR according to the research project 20-37-90149 and by RSCF grant according to the research project 21-71-10136 (creating and testing DL models on MRI data).

References

1. Pominova, M., Artemov, A., Sharaev, M., Kondrateva, E., Bernstein, A., Burnaev, E.: Voxelwise 3D convolutional and recurrent neural networks for epilepsy and depression diagnostics from structural and functional MRI data. In: IEEE International Conference on Data Mining Workshops (ICDMW), pp. 299–307. (2018). https://doi.org/10.1109/ICDMW.2018.00050
2. McKinney, S.M., Sieniek, M., Godbole, V., et al.: International evaluation of an AI system for breast cancer screening. Nature **577**, 89–94 (2020). https://doi.org/10.1038/s41586-019-1799-6
3. Ardila, D., Kiraly, A.P., Bharadwaj, S., et al.: End-to-end lung cancer screening with three-dimensional deep learning on low-dose chest computed tomography. Nat. Med. **25**, 954–961 (2019). https://doi.org/10.1038/s41591-019-0447-x
4. Kondrateva, E., Pominova, M., Popova, E., Sharaev, M., Bernstein, A., Burnaev, E.: Domain shift in computer vision models for MRI data analysis: an overview. In: Proc. SPIE 11605, Thirteenth International Conference on Machine Vision, 116050H, 4 January 2021. https://doi.org/10.1117/12.2587872
5. Cheplygina, V., de Bruijne, M., Pluim, J.P.W.: Not-so-supervised: a survey of semi-supervised, multi-instance, and transfer learning in medical image analysis. Med. Image Anal. **54**, 280–296 (2019). https://doi.org/10.1016/j.media.2019.03.009

6. Villanueva-Meyer, J.E., Mabray, M.C., Cha, S.: Current clinical brain tumor imaging. Neurosurgery **81**(3), 397–415 (2017). https://doi.org/10.1093/neuros/nyx103
7. Long, J., Shelhamer, E., Darrell, T.: Fully convolutional networks for semantic segmentation. In: Proceedings of the IEEE Conference on Computer Vision and Pattern Recognition, pp. 3431–3440
8. Badrinarayanan, V., Kendall, A., Cipolla, R.: Segnet: a deep convolutional encoder-decoder architecture for image segmentation. IEEE Trans. Pattern Anal. Mach. Intell. **39**(12), 2481–2495 (2017)
9. Ronneberger, O., Fischer, P., Brox, T.: U-Net: convolutional networks for biomedical image segmentation. In: Navab, N., Hornegger, J., Wells, W.M., Frangi, A.F. (eds.) MICCAI 2015. LNCS, vol. 9351, pp. 234–241. Springer, Cham (2015). https://doi.org/10.1007/978-3-319-24574-4_28
10. Siddique, N., Paheding, S., Elkin, C.P., Devabhaktuni, V.: U-Net and its variants for medical image segmentation: a review of theory and applications. IEEE Access **9**, 82031–82057 (2021). https://doi.org/10.1109/ACCESS.2021.3086020
11. Ranjbarzadeh, R., Bagherian Kasgari, A., Jafarzadeh Ghoushchi, S., et al.: Brain tumor segmentation based on deep learning and an attention mechanism using MRI multi-modalities brain images. Sci. Rep. **11**, 10930 (2021). https://doi.org/10.1038/s41598-021-90428-8
12. Billot, B., et al.: A Learning Strategy for Contrast-agnostic MRI Segmentation. Medical Imaging with Deep Learning. PMLR (2020)
13. Wang, F., Jiang, R., Zheng, L., Meng, C., Biswal, B.: 3D U-Net based brain tumor segmentation and survival days prediction. In: Crimi, A., Bakas, S. (eds.) BrainLes 2019. LNCS, vol. 11992, pp. 131–141. Springer, Cham (2020). https://doi.org/10.1007/978-3-030-46640-4_13
14. Qin, X., Zhang, Z., Huang, C., Dehghan, M., Zaiane, O.R., Jagersand, M.: U2-Net: going deeper with nested U-structure for salient object detection. Pattern Recogn. **106**, 107404 (2020)
15. Xue, Y., Xu, T., Zhang, H., Long, L.R., Huang, X.: Segan: adversarial network with multi-scale l 1 loss for medical image segmentation. Neuroinformatics **16**(3–4), 383–392 (2018)
16. Chen, J., et al.: Transunet: transformers make strong encoders for medical image segmentation. arXiv preprint arXiv:2102.04306 (2021)
17. Cheplygina, V., de Bruijne, M., Pluim, J.P.W.: Not-so-supervised: a survey of semi-supervised, multi-instance, and transfer learning in medical image analysis. Med. Image Analysis **54**, 280–296 (2019)
18. Chen, S., Ma, K., Zheng, Y.: Med3d: Transfer learning for 3d medical image analysis. arXiv preprint arXiv:1904.00625 (2019)
19. Menze, B.H., Jakab, A., Bauer, S., Kalpathy-Cramer, J., Farahani, K., Kirby, J., et al.: The Multimodal Brain Tumor Image Segmentation Benchmark (BRATS). IEEE Trans. Med. Imaging **34**(10), 1993–2024 (2015). https://doi.org/10.1109/TMI.2014.2377694
20. Pérez-García, F., Sparks, R., Ourselin, S.: TorchIO: a Python library for efficient loading, preprocessing, augmentation and patch-based sampling of medical images in deep learning. Computer Methods and Programs in Biomedicine, p. 106236. ISSN: 0169–2607, June 2021. https://doi.org/10.1016/j.cmpb.2021.106236
21. Kofler, F., et al.: BraTS toolkit: translating BraTS brain tumor segmentation algorithms into clinical and scientific practice. Front. Neuroscience **14** (2020). 125.0.3389/fnins.2020.00125

22. Zhao, Y.-X., Zhang, Y.-M., Song, M., Liu, C.-L.: Multi-view semi-supervised 3d whole brain segmentation with a self-ensemble network. In: Shen, D., Liu, T., Peters, T.M., Staib, L.H., Essert, C., Zhou, S., Yap, P.-T., Khan, A. (eds.) MICCAI 2019. LNCS, vol. 11766, pp. 256–265. Springer, Cham (2019). https://doi.org/10.1007/978-3-030-32248-9_29

23. McKinley, R., Rebsamen, M., Meier, R., Wiest, R.: Triplanar ensemble of 3D-to-2D CNNs with label-uncertainty for brain tumor segmentation. In: Crimi, A., Bakas, S. (eds.) BrainLes 2019. LNCS, vol. 11992, pp. 379–387. Springer, Cham (2020). https://doi.org/10.1007/978-3-030-46640-4_36

24. Isensee, F., Jäger, P.F., Full, P.M., Vollmuth, P., Maier-Hein, K.H.: nnU-Net for brain tumor segmentation. In: Crimi, A., Bakas, S. (eds.) BrainLes 2020. LNCS, vol. 12659, pp. 118–132. Springer, Cham (2021). https://doi.org/10.1007/978-3-030-72087-2_11

25. Davatzikos, C., et al.: Cancer imaging phenomics toolkit: quantitative imaging analytics for precision diagnostics and predictive modeling of clinical outcome. J Med Imaging 5(1), 011018 (2018). https://doi.org/10.1117/1.JMI.5.1.011018

26. Pati, S., et al.: The cancer imaging phenomics toolkit (CaPTk): technical overview. In: Crimi, A., Bakas, S. (eds.) BrainLes 2019. LNCS, vol. 11993, pp. 380–394. Springer, Cham (2020). https://doi.org/10.1007/978-3-030-46643-5_38

Combining Global Information with Topological Prior for Brain Tumor Segmentation

Hua Yang[1,2], Zhiqiang Shen[3], Zhaopei Li[3], Jinqing Liu[1(✉)], and Jinchao Xiao[2]

[1] College of Photonic and Electronic Engineering, Fujian Normal University,
Fuzhou, China
jqliu8208@fjnu.edu.cn
[2] Guangzhou Institute of Industrial Intelligence, Guangzhou, China
xiaojinchao@sia.cn
[3] College of Physics and Information Engineering, Fuzhou University, Fuzhou, China

Abstract. Gliomas are the most common and aggressive malignant primary brain tumors. Automatic brain tumor segmentation from multi-modality magnetic resonance images using deep learning methods is critical for gliomas diagnosis. Deep learning segmentation architectures, especially based on fully convolutional neural network, have proved great performance on medical image segmentation. However, these approaches cannot explicitly model global information and overlook the topology structure of lesion regions, which leaves room for improvement. In this paper, we propose a convolution-and-transformer network (COTRNet) to explicitly capture global information and a topology aware loss to constrain the network to learn topological information. Moreover, we exploit transfer learning by using pretrained parameters on ImageNet and deep supervision by adding multi-level predictions to further improve the segmentation performance. COTRNet achieved dice scores of 78.08%, 76.18%, and 83.92% in the enhancing tumor, the tumor core, and the whole tumor segmentation on brain tumor segmentation challenge 2021. Experimental results demonstrated effectiveness of the proposed method.

Keywords: Brain tumor segmentation · Convolutional neural network · Transformer

1 Introduction

Gliomas are the most common and aggressive malignant primary brain tumors with the highest mortality rate and prevalence [16]. Magnetic resonance imaging (MRI) is one of the most effective tools for gliomas diagnosis in clinical practice. Multi-modal MRI can provide complementary information for the anatomical structure of tumors, where T1 weighted (T1) and T1 enhanced contrast (T1ce) images highlight the necrotic and non-enhancing tumor core, while T2 weighted

(T2) and fluid attenuation inverted recovery (Flair) images enhance the peritu-moral edema [17].

Accurate segmentation of brain tumors using MRI plays an important role in gliomas treatment and operative planning [6]. However, manual segmenta-tion of brain tumor is time-consuming and resource-intensive. The segmentation results relies on the experience of doctors and influences by inter- and intra-observer errors [19]. Therefore, automatic segmentation is required. Recently, deep learning-based methods, especially fully convolutional neural networks (FCN) have demonstrated dominant performance both in natural [2,15] and medical image segmentation [9,20,25]. Nevertheless, automatic brain tumor seg-mentation is still a challenge due to the extreme intrinsic heterogeneity in appear-ance, shape, and histology [17]. Examples of gliomas are shown in Fig. 1.

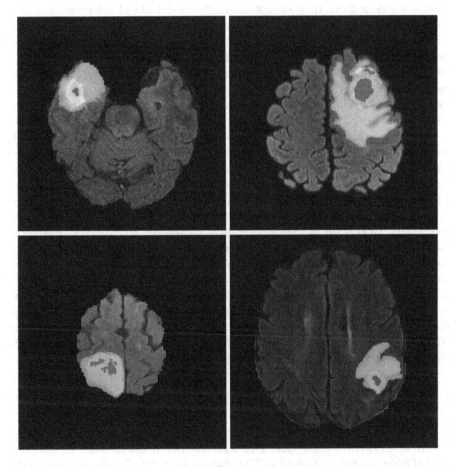

Fig. 1. Examples of gliomas with various locations, appearances, shapes, and histology in MRI. Necrotic tumor cores, peritumoral edematous, and GD-enhancing tumor are highlighted by red, green, and yellow respectively. (Color figure online)

Many studies have been proposed to solve the challenge of brain tumor segmentation [1,10,14,19,22]. Pereira et al. firstly investigated the potential of using CNN with small convolutional kernels for brain tumor segmentation [19]. Havaei et al. exploited two-pathway CNN to extract both local and more global contextual features simultaneously, and combined them to accurately segment gliomas [10]. More recently, Liu et al. proposed a multi-modal tumor segmentation network with a fusion block based on spatial and channel attention to aggregate multi-modal features for gliomas delineation [14]. Ahmad et al. designed a context-aware 3D U-Net by using densely connected blocks in both en-coder and decoder paths to extract multi-contextual information from the concept of feature reusability [1]. Wacker et al. employed pretrained model to constructed U-Net encoder to stabilize the training process and to improve prediction performance [22]. Even though the above methods achieved favorable performance on gliomas segmentation, they cannot explicitly model global information. Long-range dependency, i.e., large receptive field, is crucial of a model to perform accurate segmentation [23]. These approaches implicitly aggregated global information by stacking several local operations, i.e., convolutional layers interlaced with down-sampling operators, where large amount of convolution layers stacking in a model may influence its efficiency and cause the gradient vanish by impeding the back-propagation process. Moreover, the topological information which can be prior knowledge to simplify the segmentation task is not considered.

In this paper, we propose a convolution-and-transformer network (COTR-Net) combined with a topology-aware (TA) loss to not only explicitly model global information but also leverage topological prior to regularize network training process. In addition, we exploit transfer learning by using pretrained ResNet [11] to initialize the encoder of COTRNet. Furthermore, we employ deep supervision mechanism [13] into the decoder of COTRNet for predictions refinement. Specifically, COTRNet is improved from a U-Net-like architecture, where the encoder derives from ResNet and the decoder is the same as that of U-Net except the additional deep supervision outputs. TA loss is a weighted combination of cross entropy loss and dice loss. To exploited topological prior, we modify the one hot coding by transforming each lesion region as the single connectivity domain (SCD). The difference between the single connectivity domain coding and one hot coding is illustrated in Fig. 4. We evaluation the proposed method on brain tumor segmentation (BraTS) Challenge 2021 [3–6,17]. Experiment results demonstrate the effectiveness of the proposed method.

2   Method

In general, the COTRNet is represented by the combination of the network architecture of COTRNet itself, and TAL loss. We detail the network architecture of COTRNet on Sect. 2.1 and the TAL loss on Sect. 2.2. Finally, we specify the implementation details on Sect. 3.

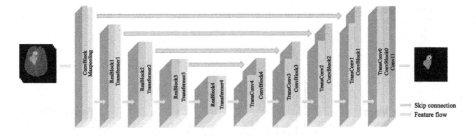

Fig. 2. Network architecture of COTRNet.

2.1   Network Architecture

Global information, i.e., long range dependency, is critical for medical image segmentation. Previous methods gradually capture long range dependencies by stacking local operators. Inspired by the detection transformer (DETR) [7] that used transformer to model global information explicitly of the input features, we propose COTRNet to model global information for brain tumor segmentation. The network architecture of COTRNet are illustrated in Fig. 2. COTRNet takes as input slices of size $4 \times 224 \times 224$ where channel $= 4$ refers to the four modality and outputs the probability map of size $1 \times 224 \times 224$.

Overall, COTRNet is a U-Net-like architecture consisting of an encoder for feature extraction, a decoder for segmentation prediction, and several skip path for feature reuse. Specifically, the encoder is composed of an input convolutional block, and four residual blocks interleaved with transformer encoder layers [21] and max-pooling layers. The convolutional layers are initialized by the parameters of ResNet18 pretrained on ImageNet. Four transformer encoder layers are inserted into the encoder for explicitly modeling global information. The diagram of the transformer encoder are shown in Fig. 3. A convolution feature map are flattened as a sequence. Then, the sequence is inputted into a transformer encoder for modelling global information. Finally, we reshape the sequence to a matrix with the shape the same as the input feature map. COTRNet includes four skip paths where the feature maps from the encoder are transfer to the decoder for concatenation with those of the decoder. The decoder is the same as that of the vanilla U-Net except four addition output layers added for deep supervision. Each convolution layer is followed by a batch normalization layer and ReLU activation except the output layers. Each output layer is a convolution layer with kernel size of one to transform the channels of the feature maps to the number of target classes.

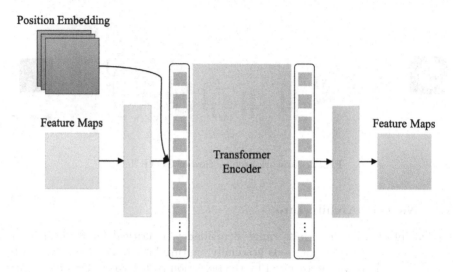

Fig. 3. Diagram of transformer encoder.

2.2 Loss Function

To leverage topology prior of segmentation objects, we modify the one hot coding to the SCD coding and combined the coding mechanism with improved weighted cross-entropy and dice loss, which refers to topology-aware loss. The difference of one hot coding and SCD coding is illustrated in Fig. 4. One hot coding translates the region of a target label to the corresponding channel, while SCD coding considers the inclusion relation between labels and translates the region of a target label to a single connection domain. This coding mechanism is appreciated for the topology structure having the inclusion relation layer-by-layer.

Formally, TA loss is formulated as,

$$\mathcal{L}_{TA}(Y,\hat{Y}) = \lambda \mathcal{L}_{WCE}\left(Y,\hat{Y}\right) + (1-\lambda)\mathcal{L}_{WDCE}\left(Y,\hat{Y}\right) \tag{1}$$

where λ controls the contribution of the $\mathcal{L}_{WCE}$ and $\mathcal{L}_{WDCE}$ to the total loss $\mathcal{L}_{TA}$. Experientially, $\lambda = 0.5$ in our experiments. Y is the ground truth and $\hat{Y}$ the predicted mask.

Further, the $\mathcal{L}_{WCE}$ is defined as

$$\mathcal{L}_{WCE}\left(Y,\hat{Y}\right) = \frac{1}{C}\sum_{c=1}^{C} w_c \sum_{j=1}^{M} [y_{j_c} \log \hat{y}_{j_c} + (1-y_{j_c})\log(1-\hat{y}_{j_c})] \tag{2}$$

The $\mathcal{L}_{DCE}$ is denoted as

$$\mathcal{L}_{WDCE}\left(Y,\hat{Y}\right) = \frac{1}{C}\sum_{c=1}^{C} w_c(1 - \frac{2\sum_{j=1}^{M} y_{jc} * \hat{y}_{jc}}{\sum_{j=1}^{M} y_{jc} + \hat{y}_{j_c}}) \tag{3}$$

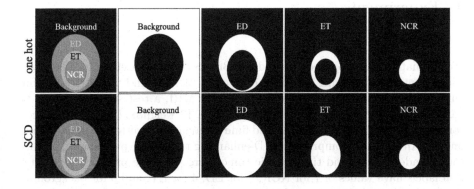

Fig. 4. Illustration of one hot coding and the single connectivity domain coding.

where M refers to the total number of pixels of the input slice and C refers the total number of classes which is equal to four (NCR, ED, ET, and the background) in our task. w_c denotes the weighted coefficient of the c_{th} class, which are set as $w_1 = 1, w_2 = 5, w_3 = 4, w_4 = 5$ in our experiments. y_{j_c} is j_{th} ground truth pixel of class c, and $\hat{y}_{j_c}$ is the corresponding predicted probability.

Deep supervision is adopted by taking into account five levels outputs of the decoder with output size of $14 \times 14, 28 \times 28, 56 \times 56, 112 \times 112, 224 \times 224$ in the back-propagation. Therefore, For a batch containing N images, the loss function J becomes,

$$J = \frac{1}{N} \sum_{i=1}^{N} \sum_{d=1}^{D} \alpha_d \mathcal{L}_{TA} \left(Y_{i_d}, \hat{Y}_{i_d} \right) \tag{4}$$

where Y_{i_d} is the d_{th} level of the i_{th} ground truth in a batch of input images, and $\hat{Y}_{i_d}$ is the corresponding prediction. $\alpha_1 = 0.05, \alpha_2 = 0.05, \alpha_3 = 0.2, \alpha_4 = 0.3, \alpha_5 = 0.4$ in the experiments.

3 Implementation Details

Pre-processing. We normalize the intensity of an MRI into $[0, 1]$. In training, slices contained foreground labels are extracted and resample to $4 \times 224 \times 224$ as network input. Data augmentation including random flip, random rotation, random crop is utilized in training process. In test, all slices of an MRI case are orderly inputted into the model to obtain predicted mask, and the overall prediction of a case are obtained by combining all the predicted mask of the slices.

Post-processing. In testing phrase, predicted masks are resampled to the original size of the input MRI. Since a glioma is an entity in an MRI, we conduct the maximum connected domain operation to the whole predicted mask.

4   Experiments

4.1   Dataset

We evaluated the proposed method on BraTS 2021 dataset with 2000 cases which contains a training set with 1251 cases of MRI and the corresponding annotations, a validation set with 219 cases of MRI, a test set no available to participants. All MRI cases are multimodal data T1 weighted (T1), T1 enhanced contrast (T1ce), T2 weighted (T2) and fluid attenuation inverted recovery (Flair) images. Annotations comprise the GD-enhancing tumor, the peritumoral edematous/invaded tissue, and the necrotic tumor core [17]. The provided segmentation labels have values of 1 for NCR, 2 for ED, 4 for ET, and 0 for background. We first evaluated the proposed method on training set through five-fold cross entropy and obtained preliminary results in unseen data of validation set. The final results on BraTS 2021 challenge will be obtained on the unseen testing data.

4.2   Metrics

Following the BraTS 2021 challenge, We adopted the Dice similarity coefficient (DSC) and Hausdorff distance (HD) to quantitatively evaluate the segmentation performance. DSC calculates the similarity between two sets, which is defined as follows,

$$DSC(A, B) = \frac{A \cap B}{A \cup B} \tag{5}$$

HD measures how far two subsets of a metric space are from each other, which is defined as the longest distance between a point set A and the most adjacent point of set B:

$$HD(A, B) = \max \left\{ \sup_{a \in A} \inf_{b \in B} d(a, b), \sup_{a \in A} \inf_{b \in B} d(b, a) \right\} \tag{6}$$

4.3   Experimental Setting

We conduct the experiments on PyTorch [18] which is accelerated by an NVIDIA GeForce GTX 1080 with 8G GPU memory. We use the Adam optimizer [12] with the learning rate of 1e-4. The network is trained over 20 epochs with a batch size of 2.

Table 1. Quantitative results on BraTS 2021 training set through five-fold cross-validation. COTRNetw/oPT: COTRNet without using pretrained parameters. COTRNetw/oDS: COTRNet without using deep supervision.

Method	Necrotic tumor core	Pertumoral edematous	Enhancing tumor
U-Net	0.5157	0.6822	0.6721
COTRNetw/oPT	0.5698	0.7296	0.6852
COTRNetw/oDS	0.5670	0.7297	0.7010
COTRNet	0.5874	0.7309	0.7273

5 Results

In the following, we reported the results on BraTS 2021 dataset. We conducted ablation study on BraTS 2021 training set through five-fold cross validation, which is presented on Sect. 5.1. Further, the preliminary results are obtained on the validation set and reported on Sect. 5.2. The final results will be obtained by evaluating the proposed model on the test set.

5.1 Results on BraTS 2021 Training Set

We conducted the oblation study on the training set through five-fold cross validation. The train set was orderly split into five subsets according to image IDs. Note that these results were obtained on our own data split method, so that are not necessarily to comparable with other challenge submissions. Moreover, we used the DSC to evaluate the model performance and calculated the DSCs on NCR, ED, and ET, respectively. The quantitative results are presented in Table 1. COTRNet achieved DSC of 58.74%, 73.09%, and 72.73% in the necrotic tumor core (NCR), the peritumoral edematous (ED), and the GD-enhancing tumor (ET) segmentation, which is the best performance compared to other three methods. We randomly selected multiple cases to illustrate the segmentation results, as shown in Fig. 5. Intuitively, the qualitative results conforms to the quantitative ones.

5.2 Results on BraTS 2021 Validation Set

For evaluation on the validation set, we trained our model on the whole training set and submitted the segmentation results to the challenge website to acquire segmentation performance. Different from the evaluation pattern on training set in which we take into account the NCR, ED, and ET sub-regions according to the annotations, the segmentation labels of the different glioma sub-regions are considered in validation phrase. The sub-regions considered for evaluation are ET, TC, and WT. The results are listed in Table 2. COTRNet achieved DSC of 77.60%, 80.21%, and 89.34% and HD of 24.9893, 19.6241, and 7.0938 in ET, TC, and WT, respectively.

5.3   Results on BraTS 2021 Test Set

For evaluation on BraTS 2021 test set, we trained our model on the whole training set and submitted the docker container of our trained model to the challenge website for testing. The results on BraTS 2021 test set are shown in Table 3. COTRNet achieved DSC of 78.08%, 76.18%, and 83.92% and HD of 28.2266, 34.4783, and 15.6148 in ET, TC, and WT, respectively.

Table 2. Quantitative results on BraTS 2021 validation set.

Metrics	ET (DSC)	TC (DSC)	WT (DSC)	ET (HD)	TC (HD)	WT (HD)
Mean	0.7760	0.8021	0.8934	24.9893	19.6241	7.0938
Std	0.2675	0.2617	0.1171	84.7575	66.0254	14.6603
Median	0.8737	0.9174	0.9262	1.7321	3	3.1623
25quantile	0.7779	0.7836	0.8825	1	1.7320	2.2361
75quantile	0.9230	0.9516	0.9465	3.6736	9	6.1644

Table 3. Quantitative results on BraTS 2021 test set.

Metrics	ET (DSC)	TC (DSC)	WT (DSC)	ET (HD)	TC (HD)	WT (HD)
Mean	0.7808	0.7618	0.8392	28.2263	34.4783	15.6148
Std	0.2725	0.3256	0.2272	87.4218	84.5480	31.4253
Median	0.8813	0.9191	0.9221	1.4142	3	3.6056
25quantile	0.7831	0.7618	0.8511	1	1.4142	2
75quantile	0.9349	0.9609	0.9510	3.2549	15.56	9.7723

Ground Truth	U-Net	COTRNetw/oPT	COTRNetw/oDS	COTRNet

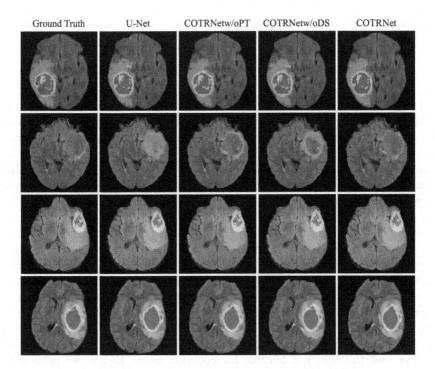

Fig. 5. Qualitative results on BraTS 2021 training set.

6 Discussion and Conclusion

In this paper, we proposed the COTRNet to solve the Brain tumor segmentation problem. COTRNet leveraged the transformer encoder layers to explicitly capture global information and adopted the topology prior of brain tumors by introducing topology constraints to the network training process. Moreover, transfer learning and deep supervision mechanism were also used to improve the segmentation performance. Experimental results on BraTS 2021 challenge demonstrated the effectiveness of the proposed method.

Table 1 summarized the results on BraTS training set through five-fold cross validation. Analysing these results, we can draw three conclusions as follows.

Effectiveness of Transformer Encoder Layers. COTRNet and two abolated methods, i.e., COTRNetw/oPT, COTRNetw/oDS, outperformed U-Net by a large margin, which demonstrated the effectiveness of transformer encoder layers to capture global information.

Effectiveness of Transfer Learning. COTRNet exceeded COTRNetw/oPT by the DSC of 1.76%, 0.13%, and 4.21% in NCR, ED, and ET, respectively. This superiority is obtained by using pretrained parameters which facilitated the model to converge to optimal.

Effectiveness of Deep Supervision. The performance between COTRNet and COTRNetw/oDS is very close. This is because deep supervision is exploited to gradually refine the segmentation details, as shown in Fig. 5. Although these details is crucial for tumor delineation, they contribute relatively few to the DSC compared with masses of tumor.

Our method inserted transformer encoder layers to the encoder-decoder architecture to explicitly capture the global information of input images for image segmentation. Since transformer is effective to model long range dependencies, a more efficient approach is to directly use transformer as feature encoder without convolution operations. However, transformer require large-scale of GPU memory and this is indispensable to achieve when the transformer layer directly takes images as input. Therefore, we first adopted several CNN layers for feature dimension reduction, as did in DETR [7]. On the other hand, transformer takes sequence data as input, which can disentangle the image structure. Therefore, the subsequent CNN layers is employed to recover the image structure. Recently, transformer has been widely exploited in medical image processing [8,24]. Zhang et al. presented a two-branch architecture, which combines transformers and CNNs in a parallel style for polyp segmentation [24]. Chen et al. proposed a TransUNet in which the transformer encodes tokenized image patches from a convolution neural network (CNN) feature map as the input sequence for extracting global contexts [8]. However, these methods need large-scale GPU memory and this will not feasible for common users. Hence, we proposed a lighted transformer-based segmentation framework which needs only 8G GPU memory for network training. We will focus on simplify the transformer network and developed more efficient segmentation architectures in our future works.

References

1. Ahmad, P., Qamar, S., Shen, L., Saeed, A.: Context Aware 3D UNet for brain tumor segmentation. In: Crimi, A., Bakas, S. (eds.) BrainLes 2020. LNCS, vol. 12658, pp. 207–218. Springer, Cham (2021). https://doi.org/10.1007/978-3-030-72084-1_19
2. Badrinarayanan, V., Kendall, A., Cipolla, R.: Segnet: a deep convolutional encoder-decoder architecture for image segmentation. IEEE Trans. Pattern Anal. Mach. Intell. **39**(12), 2481–2495 (2017)
3. Baid, U., et al.: The rsna-asnr-miccai brats 2021 benchmark on brain tumor segmentation and radiogenomic classification. arXiv preprint arXiv:2107.02314 (2021)
4. Bakas, S., et al.: Segmentation labels and radiomic features for the pre-operative scans of the tcga-gbm collection. the cancer imaging archive. Nat Sci Data **4**, 170117 (2017)
5. Bakas, S., et al.: Segmentation labels and radiomic features for the pre-operative scans of the tcga-lgg collection. The cancer imaging archive 286 (2017)
6. Bakas, S., et al.: Advancing the cancer genome atlas glioma MRI collections with expert segmentation labels and radiomic features. Sci. Data **4**(1), 1–13 (2017)
7. Carion, N., Massa, F., Synnaeve, G., Usunier, N., Kirillov, A., Zagoruyko, S.: End-to-end object detection with transformers. In: Vedaldi, A., Bischof, H., Brox, T., Frahm, J.-M. (eds.) ECCV 2020. LNCS, vol. 12346, pp. 213–229. Springer, Cham (2020). https://doi.org/10.1007/978-3-030-58452-8_13

8. Chen, J., et al.: Transunet: transformers make strong encoders for medical image segmentation. arXiv preprint arXiv:2102.04306 (2021)
9. Çiçek, Ö., Abdulkadir, A., Lienkamp, S.S., Brox, T., Ronneberger, O.: 3D U-Net: learning dense volumetric segmentation from sparse annotation. In: Ourselin, S., Joskowicz, L., Sabuncu, M.R., Unal, G., Wells, W. (eds.) MICCAI 2016. LNCS, vol. 9901, pp. 424–432. Springer, Cham (2016). https://doi.org/10.1007/978-3-319-46723-8_49
10. Havaei, M., et al.: Brain tumor segmentation with deep neural networks. Med. Image Anal. **35**, 18–31 (2017)
11. He, K., Zhang, X., Ren, S., Sun, J.: Deep residual learning for image recognition. In: Proceedings of the IEEE Conference on Computer Vision and Pattern Recognition, pp. 770–778 (2016)
12. Kingma, D.P., Ba, J.: Adam: A method for stochastic optimization. arXiv preprint arXiv:1412.6980 (2014)
13. Lee, C.Y., Xie, S., Gallagher, P., Zhang, Z., Tu, Z.: Deeply-supervised nets. In: Artificial Intelligence and Statistics, pp. 562–570. PMLR (2015)
14. Liu, C., Ding, W., Li, L., Zhang, Z., Pei, C., Huang, L., Zhuang, X.: Brain tumor segmentation network using attention-based fusion and spatial relationship constraint. In: Crimi, A., Bakas, S. (eds.) BrainLes 2020. LNCS, vol. 12658, pp. 219–229. Springer, Cham (2021). https://doi.org/10.1007/978-3-030-72084-1_20
15. Long, J., Shelhamer, E., Darrell, T.: Fully convolutional networks for semantic segmentation. In: Proceedings of the IEEE Conference on Computer Vision and Pattern Recognition, pp. 3431–3440 (2015)
16. Louis, D.N., et al.: The 2016 world health organization classification of tumors of the central nervous system: a summary. Acta Neuropathol. **131**(6), 803–820 (2016)
17. Menze, B.H., et al.: The multimodal brain tumor image segmentation benchmark (brats). IEEE Trans. Med. Imaging **34**(10), 1993–2024 (2014)
18. Paszke, A., et al.: Pytorch: an imperative style, high-performance deep learning library. Adv. Neural. Inf. Process. Syst. **32**, 8026–8037 (2019)
19. Pereira, S., Pinto, A., Alves, V., Silva, C.A.: Brain tumor segmentation using convolutional neural networks in MRI images. IEEE Trans. Med. Imaging **35**(5), 1240–1251 (2016)
20. Ronneberger, O., Fischer, P., Brox, T.: U-Net: convolutional networks for biomedical image segmentation. In: Navab, N., Hornegger, J., Wells, W.M., Frangi, A.F. (eds.) MICCAI 2015. LNCS, vol. 9351, pp. 234–241. Springer, Cham (2015). https://doi.org/10.1007/978-3-319-24574-4_28
21. Vaswani, A., et al.: Attention is all you need. In: Advances in Neural Information Processing Systems, pp. 5998–6008 (2017)
22. Wacker, J., Ladeira, M., Nascimento, J.E.V.: Transfer learning for brain tumor segmentation. In: Crimi, A., Bakas, S. (eds.) BrainLes 2020. LNCS, vol. 12658, pp. 241–251. Springer, Cham (2021). https://doi.org/10.1007/978-3-030-72084-1_22
23. Wang, Z., Zou, N., Shen, D., Ji, S.: Non-local u-nets for biomedical image segmentation. In: Proceedings of the AAAI Conference on Artificial Intelligence, vol. 34, pp. 6315–6322 (2020)
24. Zhang, Y., Liu, H., Hu, Q.: Transfuse: fusing transformers and CNNs for medical image segmentation. arXiv preprint arXiv:2102.08005 (2021)
25. Zheng, S., et al.: A dual-attention V-network for pulmonary lobe segmentation in CT scans. IET Image Proc. **15**(8), 1644–1654 (2021)

Automatic Brain Tumor Segmentation Using Multi-scale Features and Attention Mechanism

Zhaopei Li, Zhiqiang Shen, Jianhui Wen, Tian He, and Lin Pan[✉]

College of Physics and Information Engineering, Fuzhou University, Fuzhou, China
panlin@fzu.edu.cn

Abstract. Gliomas are the most common primary malignant tumors of the brain. Magnetic resonance (MR) imaging is one of the main detection methods of brain tumors, so accurate segmentation of brain tumors from MR images has important clinical significance in the whole process of diagnosis. At present, most popular automatic medical image segmentation methods are based on deep learning. Many researchers have developed convolutional neural network and applied it to brain tumor segmentation, and proved superior performance. In this paper, we propose a novel deep learned-based method named multi-scale feature recalibration network(MSFR-Net), which can extract features with multiple scales and recalibrate them through the multi-scale feature extraction and recalibration (MSFER) module. In addition, we improve the segmentation performance by exploiting cross-entropy and dice loss to solve the class imbalance problem. We evaluate our proposed architecture on the brain tumor segmentation challenges (BraTS) 2021 test dataset. The proposed method achieved 89.15%, 83.02%, 82.08% dice coefficients for the whole tumor, tumor core and enhancing tumor, respectively.

Keywords: Brain tumor segmentation · Convolutional neural network · Multi-scale feature

1 Introduction

Gliomas are the most common primary malignant brain tumors, which are caused by cancerous changes in glial cells in the brain and spinal cord. It is a very aggressive and deadly disease. And in highly developed industrialized countries, the incidence rate is increasing [13]. Accuracy tumor delineation could significantly improve the quality of nursing. Magnetic resonance (MR) imaging is an effective technology for brain tumors diagnosis. However, accurate diagnosis of brain tumor relays on the experience of doctors, which is time-consuming and often suffer from human error. Furthermore, due to the large amount of data, manual segmentation is very difficult. Therefore, accurate and automated segmentation of brain tumor segmentation using MR imaging is critical for the potential diagnosis and treatment of this disease. To this end, the Brain Tumor

Segmentation Challenge (BraTS) provide a platform for participants to evaluate their models and compare their results to other teams by using The BraTS 2021 dataset [1–4,12]. The BraTS 2021 has two tasks: Brain Tumor Segmentation and Prediction of the MGMT promoter methylation status in mpMRI scans. In this work, we only focus on segmentation task.

Fully Convolutional Neural Networks (FCN) greatly promotes the development of medical image segmentation. Especially, U-Net [16] and its variants [14,20,21] has achieved great achievements in the domain of medical image segmentation. At the same time, in the BraTS challenge, the segmentation of brain tumor by Network variation based on U-Net framework has also achieved very excellent results. For example, the latest submissions for MRI brain tumor segmentation literatures [7,9–11] are based on different variants of this structure. In BraTS 2019, Jiang et al. [7] proposed a end-to-end two-stage cascaded U-Net and won the first place. They divide the segmentation task into two stages. In the first stage, the variant structure of U-Net is used to obtain an initial segmentation result, and the result is concatenated with the original input image as the input of the second stage. In the second stage, the structure with two decoders is used to perform the segmentation task in parallel to improve the performance, and two different segmentation images are output. C. Liu et al. [9] proposed a novel multi-modal tumor segmentation network and designed a spatial constraint loss, which can effectively fuse complementary tumor information from multi-modal MR images. H. McHugh et al. [11] present a fully automated segmentation model based on a 2D U-Net architecture with dense-blocks. S. Ma et al. [10] proposed a new network based on U-Net, which uses residual U-shaped network as the main structure, and obtains good segmentation results. Although these methods achieved favorable performance in brain tumor segmentation, they didn't consider the multi-scale information or feature recalibration, which leaves room for further improvement.

In this paper, we propose a fully automatic brain tumor segmentation method named MSFR-Net. MSFR-Net consists of an improved encoder-decoder architecture in which multiscale feature extraction and self attention mechanism is used. Specifically, we designed a multi-scale feature extraction and recalibration (MSFER) module, which can effectively utilize the features of multi-modal MR images learned from CNNs. In addition, considering the class imbalance problem of brain tumors, we integrate the cross entropy and dice loss by adding weighted coefficients to the loss items. We evaluated the proposed method on the BraTS 2021. Experimental results shows that our method achieved dice coefficients (DSC) of 90.18%, 81.61%, 76.89% on the whole tumor (WT), tumor core (TC) and enhancing tumor (ET), respectively. The main contributions of our method are summarized as follows:

1) We design a MSFER module by cascading CNN layers to extract multiscale features and by adopting channel-spatial attention to recalibrate features.
2) We insert the MSFER module into a encoder-decoder architecture to develop MSFR-Net for accurate brain tumor segmentation.

3) To solve the class imbalance problem, we proposed an improved weighted cross entropy and dice loss, where the class distributions are considered.

2   Method

In the following, we first describe the overall network architecture on Sect. 2.1. Then the multi-scale feature extraction and recalibration (MSFER) module are specified on Sect. 2.2. Finally, we elaborate on the weighted cross-entropy and dice loss on Sect. 2.3.

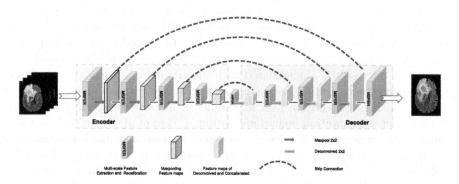

Fig. 1. The architecture of multi-scale feature recalibration network (MSFR-Net). It is compose of encoding structure (left side) and decoding structure (right side), and input is the concatenation of multi-modal MRI 2D slices.

2.1   Network Architecture

Overall, we utilize the U-Net [16] like encoder-decoder architecture as our baseline model. The encoder has four basic blocks interleaved with four down-sampling layers. The decoder includes four up-sampling layers interleaved with four basic blocks. The encoder and decoder are connected by four skip connection paths for feature concatenation. The basic block containing two CNN layers of U-Net are replaced with the MSFER module, which then construct the proposed MSFR-Net. The diagram of MSFR-Net is illustrated in Fig. 1.

The first step is the encoding stage for feature extraction. We concatenated the multi-model MR image (T1, T1ce, T2, Flair) with size of $4 \times 240 \times 240$ as the input of the network. The MSFER module includes multi-scale fusion extraction (MSFE) block and feature recalibration (FR) block. We will details this module in Sect. 2.2. The input is first flowed into a MSFER module for extracting feature information of different scales and recalibration, and then down-sampled to gradually aggregating semantic information by sacrificing spatial information. The down sampling part is realized by 2×2 max pooling. The second step is the decoding stage for spatial information recovery and pixel level classification, in which network architecture of each layer is consistent with the encoding stage. The feature maps from the encoder stage are concatenated with those from the decoder through skip connections. The final output layer of the network is a convolution layer with kernel size of one followed by a SoftMax activation for segmentation prediction.

2.2   Multi-scale Feature Extraction and Recalibration Module

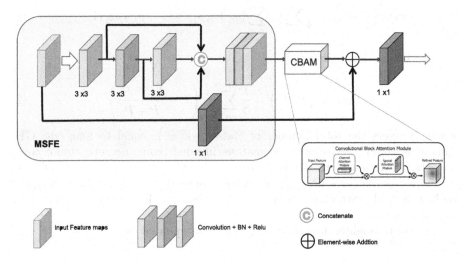

Fig. 2. The multi-scale feature extraction and recalibration (MSFER) module. Note that the subfigure of CBAM refers to [19]

In most of the existing U-Net-based methods, the features from encoder are directly connected with those from the decoder. To the best of our knowledge, the low-level features contain more details information and high-level features include more semantic information. They do not take into account the complementary information of different scale features, which will lead to performance degradation and even classification errors. In our work, we design the MSFER module, which fuse and recalibrate the features of different scales.

Figure 2 illustrates the MSFER module. A MSFER module is composed of a MSFE block with three 3 × 3 convolution layers and FR block with the convolutional block attention module (CBAM) [19]. Each output feature maps of the three convolution layers of MSFE are concatenated, and then passed through the FR block. The reason for concatenated the feature maps of different convolutions is that they have different receptive fields i.e. the feature of different scales. The concatenated features are used as the input of FR block. Moreover, the output features of FR block are added with the input features, which can improve the training efficiency [6]. Finally, we transfer the output channels to the required size using 1 × 1 convolution as the input of the subsequent network layer.

2.3   Loss Function

We propose a weighted cross-entropy (WCE) and dice (WDSC) loss for brain tumor segmentation, which can solve the problem of class imbalance. Specifically, We utilize the WCE loss to reduce the imbalance in pixel level and the WDSC loss to alleviate the problem in region level.

The WCE loss is represented as

$$\mathcal{L}_{WCE}\left(P_i, \hat{P}_i\right) = \frac{1}{s}\sum_{c=1}^{S} w_s \sum_{j=1}^{M} [p_{j_s} \log \hat{p}_{j_s} + (1 - p_{j_s}) \log (1 - \hat{p}_{js})] \qquad (1)$$

The WDSC loss is denoted as

$$\mathcal{L}_{WDSC}\left(P_i, \hat{P}_i\right) = \frac{1}{S}\sum_{s=1}^{S} w_s \left(1 - \frac{2|P \cap \hat{P}|}{P + \hat{P}}\right) \qquad (2)$$

where S refers the total number of classes which is equal to four (the GD-enhancing tumor, peritumoral edematous/invaded tissue, necrotic tumor core1 and the background) in our task, the p_{j_s} is jth ground truth pixel of class S, and $\hat{p}_{j_s}$ is the corresponding predicted probability. w_s denotes the weighted coefficient of the Sth class. M refers to the total number of pixels of the input slice in a batch.

The total weighted loss function (TW) is formulated as

$$\mathcal{L}_{TW}(P, \hat{P}) = \frac{1}{N}\sum_{i=1}^{N} \left[\theta \mathcal{L}_{WCE}\left(P_i, \hat{P}_i\right) + (1 - \theta)\mathcal{L}_{WDSC}\left(P_i, \hat{P}_i\right)\right] \qquad (3)$$

In general, the $\mathcal{L}_{TW}$ is a weighted combination of class weighted cross-entropy loss and class-weighted dice loss. P_i is the ith ground truth of a batch of input images, and $\hat{P}_i$ is the ith predicted mask of a batch of predictions. Where θ controls the contribution of the $\mathcal{L}_{WCE}$ and $\mathcal{L}_{WDSC}$ to the total loss.

3   Experiments

In this section, we introduce the dataset used in the experiment on Sect. 3.1 and explain the evaluation indicators used on Sect. 3.2. And then describe the pre-processing and post-processing methods used and the details of the experiment On Sects. 3.3 and Sect. 3.4, respectively. Finally, the implementation details are specified on Sect. 3.5.

3.1   Dataset

The BraTS 2021 dataset contains the total number of 2000 cases separated into a training set, a validation set, and a test set. Each data has multi-modal

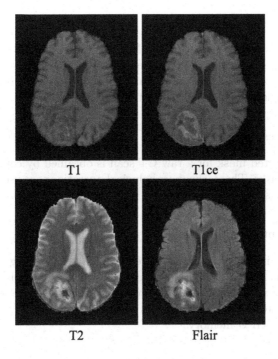

Fig. 3. An example multi-modal MRI case of the BraTS 2021 dataset.

MRI (T1, T1ce, T2, Flair) as shown in Fig. 3. All the imaging datasets have been segmented manually, by one to four raters specialists. The training set includes MR cases and the corresponding annotations GD-enhancing tumor (ET-label 4), peritumoral edematous/invaded tissue (ED-label 2), necrotic tumor core (NCR-label 1). The validation set contains 219 cases and their annotations are not provided to the participants. The test set is not publicly available to the participants.

3.2 Metrics

In our experimental results, we use DSC and Hausdorff_95 (95%HD) to assess the prediction performance. The DSC is a evaluate of similarity between the ground truth segment mask and the prediction segment mask, that the spatial overlap between the prediction results of brain tumor segmentation and the label. The difference between Hausdorff distance (HD) coefficient and Dice coefficient is that Dice coefficient is sensitive to the segmented internal filling, while Hausdorff distance is sensitive to the segmented boundary. BraTS use Hausdorff_95 that is the Hausdorff distance multiplied 95% in order to eliminate the influence of outliers in small sets.

3.3   Preprocessing

The BraTS 2021 dataset is provided in Nifti file, we sliced the data for network training according to the ground truth masks and normalized them into [0, 1] by Z-score standardization method. Data augmentation includes random rotation, random flip, random crop is utilized in training process.

3.4   Postprocessing

The whole predicted mask for a raw CT scan is obtained by combining all slice segmentation masks. Them, the morphological operations are used to refined the segmentation masks.

3.5   Implementation Details

Our experiment is conducted in PyTorch [15]. In the training, the number of epochs are set as 20 and the batch size are set as 4. The models are trained via Adam optimizer with standard back-propagation [8] with the learning rate of a fixed value of 1e−4. Our experiments are run on an NVIDIA GeForce GTX 2080Ti with 11G GPU memory.

4   Result

4.1   Results on the Training Set of BraTS 2021

We conducted ablation experiments to investigate the advantages of our model. The performance of our method was evaluated through the 5-fold Cross Validation on the training dataset. In this experiment, MSFR-Net compared with three different methods:

- 2D U-Net: Basic U-Net with muti-model MRI as input.
- 2D U-Net+M: The 2D U-Net using the proposed the MSFE block as shown in Fig. 2
- 2D U-Net+M: Replace the MSFE block of 2D U-Net+M with CBAM.

Table 1 shows the quantitative performance. MSFE-Net achieved the DSC results of 56.87%, 72.49%, and 69.55% in NCR, ED, and ET respectively. In addition, the visualization result of segmented brain tumors are shown in Fig. 4.

Table 1. Dice score (mean) of the proposed method on 5-fold Cross Validation.

Method	Necrotic tumor core	Pertumoral edematous	Enhancing tumor
2D U-Net	0.5213	0.6923	0.6847
2D U-Net+M	0.5366	0.7175	0.6624
2D U-Net+C	0.5554	0.7219	0.6940
2D MSFR-Net	0.5687	0.7249	0.6955

4.2 Results on the Validation Set of BraTS 2021

Additionally, we evaluate the 2D MSFR-Net results on the BraTS 2021 validation set. The results are listed in Table 2. For the WT, TC, and ET, our method obtained mean DSC of 90.18%, 81.61%, 76.89%, respectively. The corresponding results of the HD95 are 6.1562, 16.6548, and 30.2116, respectively.

Table 2. Quantitative results on BraTS 2021 Validation set.

Metrics	ET (DSC)	TC (DSC)	WT (DSC)	ET (HD)	TC (HD)	WT (HD)
Mean	0.7689	0.8161	0.9018	30.2116	16.6548	6.1562
Std	0.2741	0.2488	0.0911	93.5059	60.7865	9.6682
Median	0.8745	0.9228	0.9244	2	3	3
25quantile	0.7724	0.8168	0.8872	1	1.4142	1.7321
75quantile	0.9212	0.9535	0.9513	4.0923	7.3581	5.7878

4.3 Results on the Test Set of BraTS 2021

Finally, we evaluate the 2D MSFR-Net results on the BraTS 2021 test set. The results are listed in Table 3. For the WT, TC, and ET, our method obtained mean DSC of 89.15%, 83.02%, 82.08%, respectively. The corresponding results of the HD95 are 7.2793, 21.7760, and 17.0458, respectively.

Table 3. Quantitative results on BraTS 2021 Test set.

Metrics	ET (DSC)	WT (DSC)	TC (DSC)	ET (HD)	WT (HD)	TC (HD)
Mean	0.8208	0.8915	0.8302	17.0459	7.2793	21.7760
Std	0.2236	0.1405	0.2643	68.5424	13.2216	74.4397
Median	0.8912	0.9281	0.9377	1.4142	3	2.2361
25quantile	0.8133	0.8912	0.8595	1	1.7321	1.4142
75quantile	0.9393	0.9564	0.9661	2.8284	6	6.8128

GrandTruth   2D U-Net   2D U-Net+C   2D U-Net+M   Our Method

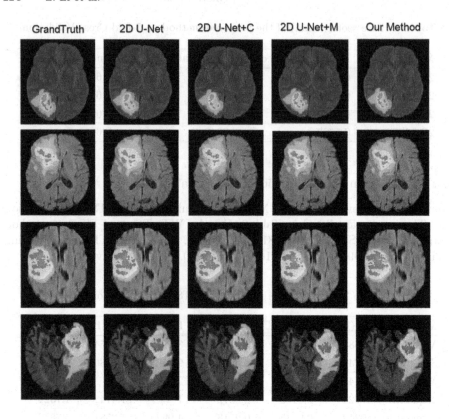

Fig. 4. The visualization result of segmented brain tumors. Different color coverage areas represent different tumors: green for WT, red for TC and yellow for ET.

5   Discussion and Conclusion

In this paper, we propose a novel network structure for brain tumor segmentation by multi-scale feature extraction and recalibration (MSFER) module. By learning the context information of multi-scale feature maps and recalibration them, it can accurately capture the complementary features of different feature maps. We performed ablation experiments on the BraTS 2021 training set and evaluated MSFR-Net on the validation set.

The major advantage of MSFR-Net is the using of multi-scale feature recalibration. In the results of cross validation shown in Table 1, the DSC of 2D U-Net in NCR and ED are 52.13% and 69.23%, respectively, while the results with the MSFE block are 53.66% and 71.75%. This comparative experiment demonstrated the effectiveness of the MSFE block which can obtain multi-scale features for context information complementary. Similarly, by introducing CBAM into U-Net, the DSC results are 55.54% and 72.19%. In particular, the score of U-Net + C network on ET has also increased from 68.47% to 69.40%, which shows that the module can effectively focus on the region of interest and recalibrate the features. Finally, we tested the MSFR-Net and obtained the best DSC of 56.87%, 72.49% and 69.55% in NCR, ED and ET segmentation, respectively. These results demonstrated the superiority of multi-scale feature recalibration. Although MSFR-Net has the superiority mentioned above, it can not explicitly model the global features which limited the segmentation performance. Inspired by the recent approaches that leveraging transformer [18] to explicitly learning global information [5,17], we will focus on integrating transformer with convolution layers to improve the segmentation framework in the future.

Acknowledgement. This work was supported by the Fujian Provincial Natural Science Foundation project (Grant No. 2021J02019, 2020J01472).

References

1. Baid, U., et al.: The rsna-asnr-miccai brats 2021 benchmark on brain tumor segmentation and radiogenomic classification. arXiv preprint arXiv:2107.02314 (2021)
2. Bakas, S., et al.: Segmentation labels and radiomic features for the pre-operative scans of the tcga-gbm collection. the cancer imaging archive. Nat. Sci. Data **4**, 170117 (2017)
3. Bakas, S., et al.: Segmentation labels and radiomic features for the pre-operative scans of the tcga-lgg collection. The cancer imaging archive 286 (2017)
4. Bakas, S., et al.: Advancing the cancer genome atlas glioma MRI collections with expert segmentation labels and radiomic features. Sci. Data **4**(1), 1–13 (2017)
5. Chen, J., et al.: Transunet: transformers make strong encoders for medical image segmentation. arXiv preprint arXiv:2102.04306 (2021)
6. He, K., Zhang, X., Ren, S., Sun, J.: Deep residual learning for image recognition. In: Proceedings of the IEEE Conference on Computer Vision and Pattern Recognition, pp. 770–778 (2016)
7. Jiang, Z., Ding, C., Liu, M., Tao, D.: Two-stage cascaded U-Net: 1st place solution to BraTS challenge 2019 segmentation task. In: Crimi, A., Bakas, S. (eds.) BrainLes 2019. LNCS, vol. 11992, pp. 231–241. Springer, Cham (2020). https://doi.org/10.1007/978-3-030-46640-4_22
8. Kingma, D.P., Ba, J.: Adam: a method for stochastic optimization. arXiv preprint arXiv:1412.6980 (2014)
9. Liu, C., Ding, W., Li, L., Zhang, Z., Pei, C., Huang, L., Zhuang, X.: Brain tumor segmentation network using attention-based fusion and spatial relationship constraint. In: Crimi, A., Bakas, S. (eds.) BrainLes 2020. LNCS, vol. 12658, pp. 219–229. Springer, Cham (2021). https://doi.org/10.1007/978-3-030-72084-1_20
10. Ma, S., Zhang, Z., Ding, J., Li, X., Tang, J., Guo, F.: A deep supervision CNN network for brain tumor segmentation. In: Crimi, A., Bakas, S. (eds.) BrainLes 2020. LNCS, vol. 12659, pp. 158–167. Springer, Cham (2021). https://doi.org/10.1007/978-3-030-72087-2_14
11. McHugh, H., Talou, G.M., Wang, A.: 2d dense-unet: A clinically valid approach to automated glioma segmentation. In: Brainlesion: Glioma, Multiple Sclerosis, Stroke and Traumatic Brain Injuries: 6th International Workshop, BrainLes 2020, Held in Conjunction with MICCAI 2020, Lima, Peru, October 4, 2020, Revised Selected Papers, Part II, vol. 12658, p. 69. Springer Nature (2021)
12. Menze, B.H., et al.: The multimodal brain tumor image segmentation benchmark (brats). IEEE Trans. Med. Imaging **34**(10), 1993–2024 (2014)

13. Ohgaki, H., Kleihues, P.: Epidemiology and etiology of gliomas. Acta Neuropathol. **109**(1), 93–108 (2005)
14. Oktay, O., et al.: Attention u-net: Learning where to look for the pancreas. arXiv preprint arXiv:1804.03999 (2018)
15. Paszke, A., Gross, S., Massa, F., Lerer, A., Bradbury, J., Chanan, G., Killeen, T., Lin, Z., Gimelshein, N., Antiga, L., et al.: Pytorch: an imperative style, high-performance deep learning library. Adv. Neural. Inf. Process. Syst. **32**, 8026–8037 (2019)
16. Ronneberger, O., Fischer, P., Brox, T.: U-Net: convolutional networks for biomedical image segmentation. In: Navab, N., Hornegger, J., Wells, W.M., Frangi, A.F. (eds.) MICCAI 2015. LNCS, vol. 9351, pp. 234–241. Springer, Cham (2015). https://doi.org/10.1007/978-3-319-24574-4_28
17. Shen, Z., Lin, C., Zheng, S.: Cotr: convolution in transformer network for end to end polyp detection. arXiv preprint arXiv:2105.10925 (2021)
18. Vaswani, A., et al.: Attention is all you need. In: Advances in Neural Information Processing Systems, pp. 5998–6008 (2017)
19. Woo, S., Park, J., Lee, J.Y., Kweon, I.S.: Cbam: convolutional block attention module. In: Proceedings of the European Conference on Computer Vision (ECCV), pp. 3–19 (2018)
20. Xiao, X., Lian, S., Luo, Z., Li, S.: Weighted res-unet for high-quality retina vessel segmentation. In: 2018 9th International Conference on Information Technology in Medicine and Education (ITME), pp. 327–331. IEEE (2018)
21. Zhou, Z., Rahman Siddiquee, M.M., Tajbakhsh, N., Liang, J.: UNet++: a nested U-Net architecture for medical image segmentation. In: Stoyanov, D., et al. (eds.) DLMIA/ML-CDS -2018. LNCS, vol. 11045, pp. 3–11. Springer, Cham (2018). https://doi.org/10.1007/978-3-030-00889-5_1

Simple and Fast Convolutional Neural Network Applied to Median Cross Sections for Predicting the Presence of MGMT Promoter Methylation in FLAIR MRI Scans

Daniel Tianming Chen[1](✉) [ID], Allen Tianle Chen[2][ID], and Haiyan Wang[3][ID]

[1] New York, NY, USA
d223chen@gmail.com
[2] KTH Royal Institute of Technology, 114 28 Stockholm, Sweden
atchen@kth.se
[3] Haiyan Consulting, Ottawa, ON, Canada

Abstract. In this paper we present a small and fast Convolutional Neural Network (CNN) used to predict the presence of MGMT promoter methylation in Magnetic Resonance Imaging (MRI) scans. Our data set is "The RSNA-ASNR-MICCAI BraTS 2021 Benchmark on Brain Tumor Segmentation and Radiogenomic Classification" by U. Baid, et al. We focus on using the median ("middle-most") cross section of a FLAIR scan and use this as the input to the neural net for training. This cross section therefore presents the most or nearly the most surface area compared to any other cross section. We are thus able to reduce the computational complexity and time of the training step while preserving the high performance extrapolation capabilities of the model on unseen data.

Keywords: MRI scans · Convolutional Neural Network · Glioblastoma · MGMT promoter methylation

1 Background

Malignant brain tumors, such as glioblastoma, are a life-threatening condition with median survival rates being less than one year. However, the presence of O-6-alkylguanine DNA alkyltransferase (MGMT) promoter methylation in the tumor can be a favorable prognostic factor for glioblastoma [1]. Analysing the brain for the presence or indication of tumors, such as MGMT promoter methylation, often involves the surgical extraction of brain tissue samples. Following this procedure, the timeline for receiving the results of the genetic characterization of the tumor can be up to several weeks. Thus there are many incentives for the development of non-invasive solutions, such as imaging techniques, which

D. T. Chen—Independent Scholar.

would ultimately lead to less invasive diagnoses and treatments for brain cancer patients and further lead to more optimal survival prospects [1].

Magnetic resonance imaging (MRI) scans are an effective non-invasive method for detecting glioblastoma through the detection of MGMT promoter methylation [1]. MRI also allows monitoring the status of a tumor in real-time [4]. FLAIR (fluid-attenuated inversion recovery) imaging is a newer and seemingly more sensitive MRI, with its images obtained with an inversion recovery sequence, characterized by having a long inversion time (TI) and a long echo time (TE) [7]. As discussed by Khademi et al. [6], FLAIR is effective for localizing pathology, achieved partly by intensifying the darkness of the cerebrospinal fluid (CSF) in contrast with white and grey matter. Khademi et al. [6] in particular discuss how FLAIR is favorable in detecting white matter lesions. One such issue with training machine learning (ML) algorithms on images is the acquisition of noise generated in the data due to misinterpretation of imaging artifacts which are generally identifiable by humans but currently a challenge for algorithms [6]. In this paper, the FLAIR dataset is chosen to train the ML algorithm for detecting MGMT promoter methylation due to the precedent seen in the papers above that FLAIR is a more rich data format than the others, leading to more effective models.

Other imaging methods have been studied, such as that of Chen et al. [4] in which a data set of T1-weighted images (CE-T1W1) was used to train the algorithm. Compared to FLAIR, CE-T1W1 had a lower Dice score [4].

Overall, ML algorithms have the potential to improve the detection of the MGMT promoter methylation and thus improving patient survival rates. One such reason is the ability for the application of the algorithm over large quantities of images which would take longer for a human to process. The key aspect to be cognizant of is the maintenance of detection accuracy of the ML algorithm compared to human judgement when searching for indicators of MGMT promoter methylation in the FLAIR images.

2 Dataset

In this section we describe our dataset fully and how we normalize it for ingestion by the net. The original dataset included 585 training samples with labels as 0 or 1, indicating the presence of MGMT methylation or not. The dataset also includes 87 test samples with no labels. Training samples 00109, 00123, 00709, all had issues with the FLAIR scan data and so we ignore them. This leaves us with 585 - 3 = 582 training samples to work with. Each sample has four types of scans associated with it, and we choose to only use the FLAIR data, which is a series of cross sectional scans [1,2]. With each sample then we choose the median cross section of the FLAIR scan (See Sect. 2.1 below on how this is done). Each cross section is a DICOM, which we convert to a PNG and then resize to a standard size of 224×224 pixels, since the sizing is not consistent between samples. We convert to an RGB PNG because a DICOM is not a numerical matrix form of data, and would be unusable with a CNN.

2.1 Selection of the Median Cross Section

Within this data set, the median (or "middle-most") cross sections of the scans are selected, as these have the most area compared to the other cross sections. This will allow for the algorithm to learn more from an individual scan and reduce the computational resource usage while preserving extrapolation capabilities of the model on unseen data. To select the desired cross-section, we sort the files by name, using a Natural Sort (aka Human Sort), since the files are labelled Image-1.dcm, Image-2.dcm, etc. where the number represents a well ordering of the images from front to back when forming a complete 3d view, and the files are not initially sorted [1,2]. We then select the median cross section by picking the median index of the sorted list of file names.

Since the image scans are in DICOM format, we convert them to PNG format.

We end up with training data like the training batch below. Here 0 indicates that the patient does not have the MGMT promoter methylation, while 1 indicates that the patient does have the MGMT promoter methylation, as labelled in the training data set:

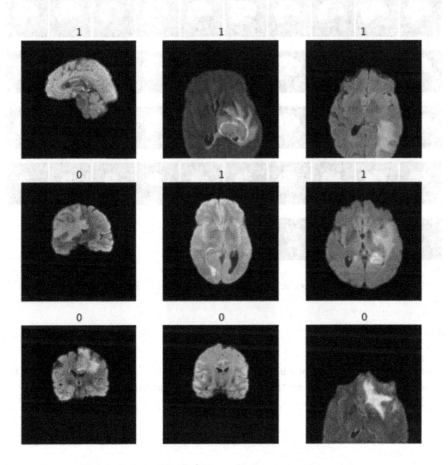

Fig. 1. Batch of 9 FLAIR median cross section scans.

Clearly we can see that our choice of the median cross section results in choosing a cross-section with nearly maximal surface area. Contrast that with the following evolution in canonical geometrical ordering as presented by Johnson [5]:

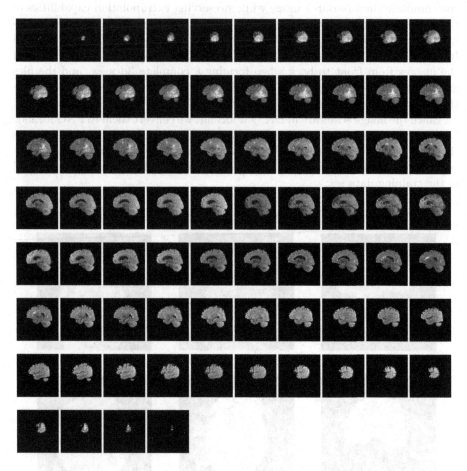

Fig. 2. The geometric evolution of one patient's FLAIR MRI [5].

3 Design

A seven-layer deep Convolutional Neural Network (CNN) is used to predict the presence of glioblastoma in the MRI scans. The training data set is based on Baid et al. [2,9–12].

3.1 Net Architecture

Below we present the string serialization of our CNN which is a modification of the architecture presented by PyTorch [8]. The padding for convolutions is **valid padding**:

```
Net(
  (conv1): Conv2d(3, 6, kernel_size=(5, 5), stride=(1, 1))
  (pool1): MaxPool2d(kernel_size=2, stride=2, padding=0, dilation=1, ceil_mode=False)
  (conv2): Conv2d(6, 16, kernel_size=(5, 5), stride=(1, 1))
  (pool2): MaxPool2d(kernel_size=2, stride=2, padding=0, dilation=1, ceil_mode=False)
  (fc1): Linear(in_features=400, out_features=120, bias=True)
  (fc2): Linear(in_features=120, out_features=84, bias=True)
  (fc3): Linear(in_features=84, out_features=10, bias=True)
)
```

Fig. 3. String serialization of the 7 layer CNN, two convolutional layers, two max pooling layers, and three linear (fully-connected) layers.

3.2 Activation Function

We apply a **Rectified Linear Unit (ReLU)** activation function to each layer, including the output layer.

3.3 Number of Outputs

Note that we emphasize that the neural net has 10 output nodes even though this is a categorical classification problem with 2 labels. We explain this in Sect. 4.3.

To better visualize this in action, we present a net graph:

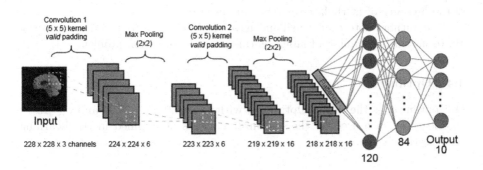

Fig. 4. Neural network architecture used in the paper.

4   Training

4.1   Software

We used the FastAI v2 package for developing the model, as well as PyTorch, python3, and pandas 1.0 [14–17]. The code used to generate all results can be found on Kaggle [18].

4.2   Hardware

We trained our neural net in a python Jupyter notebook in the Kaggle environment. The notebook's backend comes with a CPU and NVIDIA TESLA P100 GPU [13]. We trained the model with GPU acceleration.

4.3   Loss Function

Our loss function is the Categorical Cross Entropy Loss function.

$$\text{Loss} = -\sum_{i=1}^{10} y_i \cdot \log \hat{y}_i,$$

since the output vector of our net is of length 10. Note that, because we only have two ground truth labels, 0 and 1, we convert them to vectors of length 10 like so:

```
0 → [1,0,0,0,0,0,0,0,0,0]
1 → [0,1,0,0,0,0,0,0,0,0]
```

Therefore positions 3 thru 10 of each label vector is always 0.

Position 2 of the output vector of the net therefore indicates the prediction of the presence of methylation in the patient scan.

The authors note that we should have used only 2 output nodes instead of 10, to match the number of labels as this is a categorization problem.

4.4   Optimizer

Our optimizer is the Adam Optimizer, with $\beta_1 = 0.9$, $\beta_2 = 0.99$ and $\epsilon = 1e^{-5}$. The learning rate used by the optimizer i.e. α is determined in the Learning Rate section below.

4.5 Batch Size

Our batch size is 64.

4.6 Cross Validation

We hold out a random 20% of the training set as a validation set while training, unseeded. Given that there are originally 582 training samples to work with in the raw dataset, the validation set therefore contains 582 * 0.20 = 116 samples. This leaves 582 - 116 = 466 training samples to work with.

4.7 Learning Rate

We determine the ideal learning rate below. Here we plot the loss against the chosen learning rate. We employ the **LR Range test** by Smith [3] to determine the rate. We start with a learning rate of 1e−07 and end with a learning rate of 10. We iterate 100 times and stop when the loss diverges.:

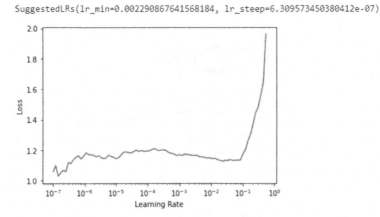

Fig. 5. Learning rate vs Loss

4.8 Training Policy

We then train the model by using the **One Cycle Policy** again by Leslie Smith [3]. We train for 10 epochs and use a max learning rate of 1e-02.

epoch	train_loss	valid_loss	error_rate	accuracy	time
0	1.179571	0.674959	0.413793	0.586207	00:02
1	1.108988	0.729703	0.586207	0.413793	00:02
2	1.076067	0.665072	0.396552	0.603448	00:02
3	1.050501	0.963969	0.586207	0.413793	00:03
4	1.027446	0.749877	0.508621	0.491379	00:02
5	1.000942	0.680456	0.405172	0.594828	00:02
6	1.002666	0.681733	0.413793	0.586207	00:02
7	0.978674	0.697218	0.474138	0.525862	00:02
8	0.965975	0.710260	0.508621	0.491379	00:02
9	0.951226	0.704067	0.517241	0.482759	00:02

Fig. 6. Training results after 10 epochs. The error_rate and accuracy are w.r.t the validation set and not the training set.

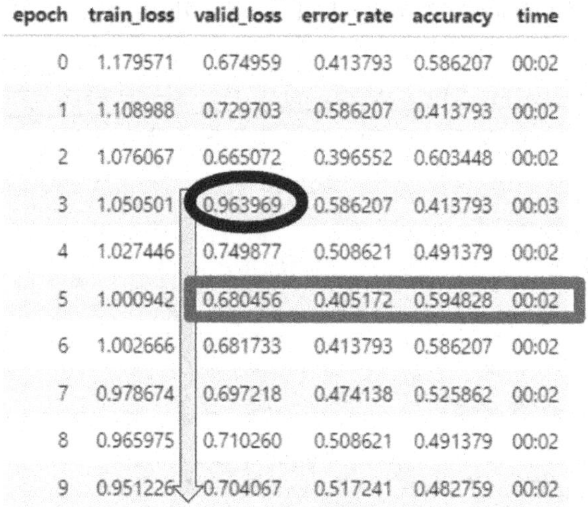

epoch	train_loss	valid_loss	error_rate	accuracy	time
0	1.179571	0.674959	0.413793	0.586207	00:02
1	1.108988	0.729703	0.586207	0.413793	00:02
2	1.076067	0.665072	0.396552	0.603448	00:02
3	1.050501	0.963969	0.586207	0.413793	00:03
4	1.027446	0.749877	0.508621	0.491379	00:02
5	1.000942	0.680456	0.405172	0.594828	00:02
6	1.002666	0.681733	0.413793	0.586207	00:02
7	0.978674	0.697218	0.474138	0.525862	00:02
8	0.965975	0.710260	0.508621	0.491379	00:02
9	0.951226	0.704067	0.517241	0.482759	00:02

Fig. 7. Same as previous figure, but we have highlighted some details.

In Fig. 7, we highlight some trends and features about Fig. 6 that are of interest to us. In red, we show that the model was able to learn, since validation loss decreases after the 3rd epoch as shown by the downward grey arrow. In blue, we show that validation error was minimized at the 5th epoch, so it may have been better to stop training at the 5th epoch. We would also like to remark that this net trained incredibly fast, with each epoch taking only 2 to 3 s.

5   Results and Discussion

At this point, we have been able to achieve an area of 0.61680 under the ROC curve between the predicted probability and the observed target, when testing on the Public Test Set as specified for the "RSNA-MICCAI Brain Tumor Radiogenomic Classification" Kaggle competition [1]. This placed our result in the top 25% of competitors on the public leaderboard in August 2021. When the private leaderboard was revealed at the end of the competition, we found that the model had achieved an area of 0.53363 under the ROC curve on the Private Test Set. We needed 170.6s of total runtime in the Kaggle notebook environment for the model to load, preprocess, train, and then predict on the dataset.

5.1   Choice of Net Architecture over Others

We are well aware of the existence more popular architectures like Resnet, and VGG. Our choice to use the architecture we chose came about due to the constraints of the competition. Unfortunately, using a pretrained model and then applying something like transfer learning was not possible due to the competition rules. We also had a constraint of around 10 h of total running time of a submitted model on the Kaggle platform, so training a Resnet or VGG from scratch would not be feasible. Therefore, it became clear to us that we needed to use a simple network architecture.

5.2   Results of Other Methods

We attempted a few other methods that performed much worse on various dimensions. One method we tried was a feature engineered solution which involved counting the number of dark points or light points, or ratios thereof, and then classifying based on the feature count. Since we converted all our images to PNGs on a 0–255 grayscale, we could basically classify a point as "dark" if its intensity was less than 100 for example, and "bright" if its intensity was brighter than 160 or so. Such decisions were made by qualitatively comparing the PNGs and the corresponding intensity values. We noticed when manually examining the PNG scans that for patients that had methylation, the methylated area would appear as a circle or ring in the brain cross section. Either the brain would appear dark, and the ring would be bright, or the brain would appear bright, and the ring would appear dark. See Fig. 8 below, which presents methylation:

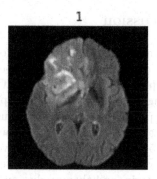

Fig. 8. This patient has methylation and shows a bright white aura against a dark brain.

In light of this, we can see that the notion of a light and dark point will become useful. Note that we also consider the entire space outside of the brain in the cross-section as dead-space points, since they are completely black and would throw off any ratio calculations if we counted them as "dark points". So exclude all of these dead-space points from being counted as "dark" points. We then tried to see if there was any clear rule that would work as a classifier, like: Out of all non-dead space points, if less than 20% of points are "dark" in a mostly "bright" brain, or vice-versa, then there must be methylation in the brain. The fundamental intuition behind this rule is to match what we were seeing in the actual methylated cross-sections with the dark ring on a bright brain, or a bright ring on a dark brain. Unfortunately, it seemed none of the attempted rules worked. The method performed very poorly with less than 0.45 area under the ROC curve on the public test set. We can see that with more exploratory data analysis, the initial intuition no longer applied and there were clear counterexamples to our rules. In Fig. 9 below we present a counterexample of a patient with no methylation, yet presenting a large white circle on a dark brain scan. We can observe Fig. 1 for more counterexamples and false positives.

Another method we tried was using 20-layer deep nets with 20+ cross sections as input, sampled at some regular interval. Thus, we were exposing more data to a larger neural net. In this sense, we basically took the method described in this paper, and just added more input data and more layers to the net, and trained for many more hours. Unfortunately, this method performed very poorly with less than 0.45 area under the ROC curve on the public test set. Therefore, it seems that training on less features is better. Our rationale for why this happened is as follows. There are only around 500 unique patient scans, each with about 500+ cross sections. So there are lots of features/dimensions per training sample but not enough training samples themselves. So the data is essentially incredibly high dimensional, making it hard for a net to learn anything when receiving the data. Sampling the middle-most cross section has a regularization effect/dimensionality reducing effect similar to Dropout layers.

0

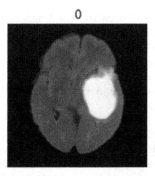

Fig. 9. This patient has no methylation and also shows a bright white circle against a dark brain.

In the end, both performed worse (less than 0.45 area under ROC curve on public test set, not scored on private test set). It should also be noted that the first alternative method was extremely fast (read - around 2 min to run the entire method and predict on the test set), while the second method was extremely slow (read - took around 9 h to run end-to-end).

6   Conclusion and Future Work

In summary, by focusing the training on the median cross sections of the FLAIR scans in the data set, the computational complexity is reduced. At the same time, the ability of the algorithm to extrapolate on this data to predict the presence of MGMT promoter methylation and glioblastoma in the FLAIR scans is preserved, thus leading to improved efficiency at this stage.

An interesting application of this design is in an embedded system or otherwise resource constrained machine performing **online learning** on real time data that the system scans and then trains the net with. Our design would provide excellent extrapolative capabilities in the system, while still being feasible due to using very little compute power relative to more data intensive methods.

For future work it would be prudent to assess the training effectiveness on including other imaging types aside from FLAIR, such as T1w, T1Gd, and T2 scans which are available in the original data set. We anticipate that the performance would improve from this due to having more data.

References

1. RSNA-MICCAI Brain Tumor Radiogenomic Classification Competition Overview. https://www.kaggle.com/c/rsna-miccai-brain-tumor-radiogenomic-classification/overview. Accessed 31 Aug 2021
2. Baid, U., et al.: The RSNA-ASNR-MICCAI BraTS 2021 Benchmark on Brain Tumor Segmentation and Radiogenomic Classification, arXiv:2107.02314 (2021)

3. Smith, L.: A disciplined approach to neural network hyper-parameters: Part 1 - learning rate, batch size, momentum, and weight decay. US Naval Research Laboratory Technical Report 5510–026 (2018)
4. Chen, X., Zeng, M., Tong, Y., Zhang, T., et al.: Automatic Prediction of MGMT Status in Glioblastoma via Deep Learning-Based MR Image Analysis. BioMed Research International, vol. 2020, Article ID 9258649, 9 pages (2020). https://doi.org/10.1155/2020/9258649
5. Johnson, N.: Initial Notebook Brain Tumour. https://www.kaggle.com/nicholasjohnson2020/initial-notebook-brain-tumour. Accessed 8 Aug 2021
6. Khademi, A., Moody, A.R., Venetsanopoulos, A.: Accurate pathology segmentation in FLAIR MRI for robust shape characterization. In: Li, S., Tavares, J.M.R.S. (eds.) Shape Analysis in Medical Image Analysis. LNCVB, vol. 14, pp. 187–227. Springer, Cham (2014). https://doi.org/10.1007/978-3-319-03813-1_6
7. Segawa, F., Kishibayashi, J., Kamada, K., Sunohara, N., Kinoshita, M.: [FLAIR images of brain diseases] No to Shinkei = Brain and Nerve. **46**(6), 531–538 (1994)
8. PyTorch: TRAINING A CLASSIFIER. https://pytorch.org/tutorials/beginner/blitz/cifar10_tutorial.html. Accessed 12 Aug 2021
9. Menze, B.H., Jakab, A., Bauer, S., Kalpathy-Cramer, J., Farahani, K., Kirby, J., et al.: The Multimodal Brain Tumor Image Segmentation Benchmark (BRATS). IEEE Trans. Med. Imaging **34**(10), 1993–2024 (2015). https://doi.org/10.1109/TMI.2014.2377694
10. Bakas, S., Akbari, H., Sotiras, A., Bilello, M., Rozycki, M., Kirby, J.S., et al.: Advancing The Cancer Genome Atlas glioma MRI collections with expert segmentation labels and radiomic features. Nature Sci. Data **4**, 170117 (2017). https://doi.org/10.1038/sdata.2017.117
11. Bakas, S., Akbari, H., Sotiras, A., Bilello, M., Rozycki, M., Kirby, J., et al.: Segmentation labels and radiomic features for the pre-operative scans of the TCGA-GBM collection. Cancer Imaging Archive (2017). https://doi.org/10.7937/K9/TCIA.2017.KLXWJJ1Q
12. Bakas, S., Akbari, H., Sotiras, A., Bilello, M., Rozycki, M., Kirby, J., et al.: Segmentation labels and radiomic features for the pre-operative scans of the TCGA-LGG collection. The Cancer Imaging Archive (2017). https://doi.org/10.7937/K9/TCIA.2017.GJQ7R0EF
13. Kaggle: Efficient GPU Usage Tips Documentation. https://www.kaggle.com/docs/efficient-gpu-usage. Accessed 18 Dec 2021
14. fast.ai: Welcome to fastai. https://docs.fast.ai/. Accessed 18 Dec 2021
15. PyTorch: Pytorch. https://pytorch.org/. Accessed 18 Dec 2021
16. pandas: pandas - Python Data Analysis Library. https://pandas.pydata.org/. Accessed 18 Dec 2021
17. Python Software Foundation: Welcome to Python.org. https://www.python.org/. Python. Org. Accessed 18 Dec 2021
18. Chen, D.T., Chen, A.T.: RSNA-MICCAI competition - Middle most FLAIR scan. https://www.kaggle.com/d223chen/rsna-miccai-competition-middle-most-flair-scan. Kaggle. Accessed 18 Dec 2021

Brain Tumor Segmentation Using Non-local Mask R-CNN and Single Model Ensemble

Zhenzhen Dai⑩, Ning Wen$^{(\boxtimes)}$⑩, and Eric Carver

Henry Ford Health System, Detroit, MI 48202, USA
nwen1@hfhs.org

Abstract. Gliomas are the most common primary malignant brain tumors. Accurate segmentation and quantitative analysis of brain tumor are critical for diagnosis and treatment planning. Automatically segmenting tumors and their subregions is a challenging task as demonstrated by the annual Multimodal Brain Tumor Segmentation Challenge (BraTS). In order to tackle this challenging task, we trained 2D non-local Mask R-CNN with 814 patients from the BraTS 2021 training dataset. Our performance on another 417 patients from the BraTS 2021 training dataset were as follows: DSC of 0.784, 0.851 and 0.817; sensitivity of 0.775, 0.844 and 0.825 for the enhancing tumor, whole tumor and tumor core, respectively. By applying the focal loss function, our method achieved a DSC of 0.775, 0.885 and 0.829, as well as sensitivity of 0.757, 0.877 and 0.801. We also experimented with data distillation to ensemble single model's predictions. Our refined results were DSC of 0.797, 0.884 and 0.833; sensitivity of 0.820, 0.855 and 0.820.

Keywords: Glioma segmentation · Non-local Mask R-CNN

1 Introduction

The incidence rate of primary brain tumors is 11–12 per 100,000 populations. Gliomas are the most common brain tumors, accounting for about 50% of the diagnosed brain tumors, and 26% of them are considered to be astrocytic tumors [1]. Glioblastoma (GBM) accounts for 50–60% of all gliomas, and it has the highest malignancy among gliomas. Gliomas exhibit different degrees of aggressiveness and variable prognosis, contain various heterogeneous histologic subregions [1]. The inherent heterogeneity of Glioma is reflected in their radiographic morphologies [2], with different intensity profiles disseminated across multi-parametric magnetic resonance imaging (mpMRI) scans, depicting different sub-regions and differences in tumor biological properties [3]. Conventionally used sequences include: T1-weighted sequence (T1), T1-weighted contrast enhanced sequence using gadolinium contrast agents (T1Gd), T2 weighted sequence (T2), and fluid attenuated inversion recovery (FLAIR) sequence. Sub-regions of Glioma can be defined from mpMRI: the appearance of enhancing

© The Author(s), under exclusive license to Springer Nature Switzerland AG 2022
A. Crimi and S. Bakas (Eds.): BrainLes 2021, LNCS 12962, pp. 239–248, 2022.
https://doi.org/10.1007/978-3-031-08999-2_19

tumor is typically hyper-intense in T1Gd when compared to T1; the non-enhancing as well as the necrotic tumor core are both hypo-intense in T1Gd when compared to T1; and the peritumoral edema is reflected by hyper-intense signal in FLAIR. The subregions of Glioma consist of three classes: Whole Tumor (WT), Tumor Core (TC), and Enhancing Tumor (ET). Example of each sequence and tumor subregions is provided in Fig. 1.

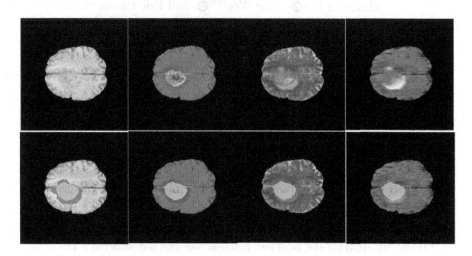

Fig. 1. Manual segmentation of brain tumor sub-regions (Red: WT; Green: ET; Yellow: NCT/NET) overlaid with different mpMRI modalities. The columns in order: T1, T1Gd, T2, FLAIR. (Color figure online)

Segmentation of brain tumors in multimodal MRI images is one of the most difficult challenges in medical image analysis because of their highly varied appearance and shape. Annotations of sub-regions of brain tumors are traditionally performed manually by radiologists; however, manual segmentation is time-consuming, subjective, and difficult to achieve repetitive segmentation [4,8]. Accurate delineation of each tumor subregion is critical to patient's disease management and provide radiologists and neuro oncologist with preoperative knowledge for appropriate therapeutic treatment guidance. There is a growing interest in computational algorithms to automatically address this task. The Brain Tumor Segmentation (BraTS) challenge [1,9–12] was launched and has now grown into an well-established competition that allows competitors to develop and evaluate their methods to address this challenge by providing a large dataset with accompanying delineations of the relevant tumor sub-regions. The sub-regions considered for evaluation are the "enhancing tumor" (ET); the "tumor core" (TC), which entails the ET, as well as the necrotic (NCR) parts of the tumor; and the "whole tumor" (WT) which entails the TC and peritumoral edematous/invaded tissue (ED).

In the past few years, many algorithms were proposed to solve this problem. Compared with other methods, deep learning has been showing the best state of the art performance for segmentation tasks in general. In this paper, we used 2D non-local Mask R-CNN to segment the sub-regions of Glioma. We experimented with the focal loss function to address the class imbalance problem from training set. We also applied data distillation to ensemble single model predictions and refined the segmentation results.

2 Methods

2.1 Dataset

The dataset provided in the BraTS 2021 training phase consists of 1251 pre-operative mpMRI scans of glioblastoma (GBM/HGG) and lower grade glioma (LGG). The mpMRI scans consist of T1, T1Gd, T2 and FLAIR, and were acquired with different clinical protocols and scanners from 19 institutions. All the imaging datasets have been segmented manually, by one to four raters, following the same annotation protocol, and their annotations were manually revised by expert board-certified neuroradiologists. The labels in the provided data are: 1 for NCR & NET, 2 for ED, 4 for ET, and 0 for everything else. The images were pre-processed with skull-stripping and co-registration to the same anatomical template and were resampled to the same resolution of 1 mm^3 and a 3D volume of $240 \times 240 \times 155$. The classes considered for object classification are WT, ET and NCR & NET.

The N4 bias field correction [13] was applied to the four mpMRI modalities to correct the low frequency intensity inhomogeneity. FLAIR, T1, T1Gd and T2 of each slice were normalized by subtracting the mean and divided by the standard deviation. Mean and standard deviation were calculated neglecting the image background. Brain patches were cropped out from images given 1-pixel (px) margin from the brain contour. Contrast stretching and histogram equalization were applied to the patches. FLAIR, T1, T1Gd and T2 patch from the same slice location made up a four-channel input and was resized to a resolution of $256 \times 256 \times 4$ px and the aspect ratio of the brain was preserved by padding with zero.

2.2 Non-local Mask R-CNN

In this paper, we experimented with region-based segmentation CNN [6] to investigate its performance in image segmentation and we experimented on 2D settings to be computational efficiency.

The Mask R-CNN network [7] is an extension of Faster R-CNN [5] with an additional branch to predict object's mask. A Region Proposal Network (RPN) is used to pick out foreground and propose candidate with bounding boxes. Features of each candidate are extracted by a RoIAlign Layer, then a segmentation CNN predicts the binary mask for each object, a classification CNN predicts the class score of masks and bounding box regression parameters which are used to further refine the bounding boxes. In our experiment, ResNet-101 plus Feature Pyramid Network was employed to extract features (F1-F4, Fig. 2) from the input images. Our method was an extension of Mask R-CNN which was a 2D non-local Mask R-CNN, as shown in Fig. 2(A).

$$I' = I + f(softmax(\theta(I_i^T)\phi(I_i))g(T)) \tag{1}$$

$$A = f(softmax(\theta(I_i^T)\phi(I_i))g(T)) \tag{2}$$

The non-local network is used to capture long-range dependencies of the four-channel input I. The new input I' is modeled in Eq. 1, where f, θ, ϕ and g are embedding functions and were implemented as 1×1 convolution. Softmax was added along both dimension i and j, which was different from [14] where softmax was added along only dimension j. Thus, the model considers not only the relationships between the ith position and other positions but also the relationships between all other position pairs when synthesizing the ith position. To reduce computation cost of the non-local network, the input I was down sampled to $128 \times 128 \times 4$. And the output of non-local network was resized to the original input size of $128 \times 128 \times 4$. An attended input A modeled in Eq. 2 was concatenated with resizing to each layer of feature pyramids to guide precise prediction. Figure 2(B) shows the architecture of non-local network.

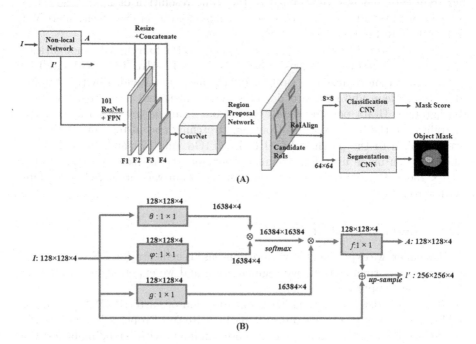

Fig. 2. (A) architecture of non-local Mask R-CNN. (B) architecture of Non-local network.

2.3 Focal Loss

The non-local Mask R-CNN network comes with two classifiers. The RPN classifies proposals into background and foreground, while the classification CNN further classifies foreground class into different objects. Though this two-stage framework achieved top accuracy on varieties of tasks, class imbalance encountered in the training data can be the central problem of misclassification of difficult examples. To tackle class imbalance, the focal loss function [15] adds a modulating term to the cross entropy loss and enables focus learning on hard negative examples. It's a dynamically scaled cross entropy loss, in which the scaling factor decreases as confidence in the proper class grows. The focal loss function is given in Eq. 3. When $\gamma = 0$, the focal loss function is the standard cross entropy criterion.

$$FL = -(1 - p_t)^\gamma log(p_t) \tag{3}$$

2.4 Single Model Ensemble

The data distillation ensembles the results from a single model run on the original unlabeled images as well as different image transformations (flipping, resizing, rotation, etc.). Such transformations are usually used as data augmentation options in training and are proved to improve single model's accuracy. In [16], it was proposed to generate new training annotations and improve over the fully-supervised baselines. In this paper, we used data distillation to ensemble results from the single model and improve the accuracy. Our ensemble function is given by Eq. 4s, where X is the input, $T_k = (T_1, ..., T_k)$ is a set of transformation functions, and T_k^{-1} is the corresponding inverse transformation function of T_k; f_θ is the segmentation branch generating object mask, f_s is the classification branch generating mask score.

$$Y = \frac{1}{1 + K}[f_\theta(X)f_s(X) + \Sigma_{k=1}^K T_k^{-1} f_\theta(T_k(X))f_s(T_k(X))] \tag{4}$$

3 Results

We randomly split the 1251 patients into 834 patients for training and 417 patients for validation. Our development was built upon [17] and models were trained on a 8X A100 GPU server. Adam optimizer was used with learning rate initiated to 0.0001, $\beta1$ to 0.9 and $\beta2$ to 0.999. Augmentation options included flipping up-down (flipud), rotation (a random angle from $-7°$ to $7°$) and Gaussian blurring (random variance from 0.7 to 1.3). Each augmentation option was applied with the probability of 0.5. We sampled model's parameters every 5000 steps for 150 epochs. Models were trained using a batch size of one. The training took about 3 days training. The best model was selected by WT dice similarity coefficient (DSC) (first criteria) and TC DSC (secondary criteria) using the validation patients. DSC is given by Eq. 5; sensitivity given by Eq. 6 is also used to evaluate the segmentation performance. TP is the true positives; FN is the false negatives and FP is the false positives.

$$DSC = \frac{2TP}{2TP + FN + FP} \tag{5}$$

$$sensitivity = \frac{TP}{TP + FN} \tag{6}$$

Our observation showed that each patient was presented with one gross tumor, therefore we generated our final predictions by keeping only the largest connected component in each volume to exclude possible false positives. Focal loss function was used both in the RPN and the classification CNN. To simplify the prediction process, we only applied the transformation of flipud in Eq. 4. Table 1 summarize our results by different methods on the 417 patients randomly selected for validation from the BraTS 2021 training phase. Figure 3 shows an example case where the sub-regions of Glioma is well predicted. Figure 4 shows an example case where the sub-regions of Glioma is hard to predict.

Table 1. DSC and sensitivity for 417 randomly selected patients from BraTS 2021.

	Non-local Mask R-CNN	+ Focal Loss	+ Ensemble
WT DSC	0.851	**0.885**	**0.884**
TC DSC	0.817	**0.829**	**0.833**
ET DSC	0.784	0.775	**0.797**
WT sensitivity	0.844	**0.877**	**0.855**
TC sensitivity	0.826	0.801	0.820
ET sensitivity	0.775	0.757	**0.820**

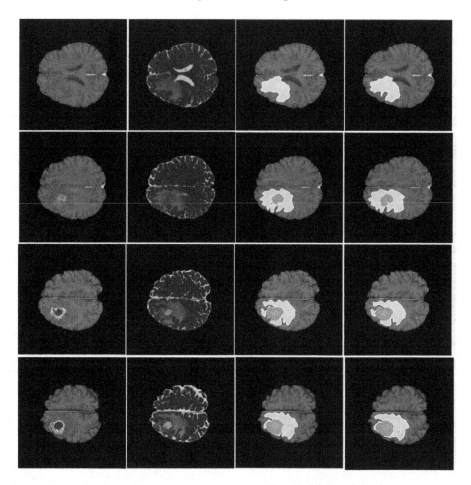

Fig. 3. A patient whose sub-regions of Glioma (Red: WT; Green: ET; Yellow: NCT/NET) is well predicted on mpMRI using the model. The columns in order: T1Gd, T2, mannal segmentation overlaid on T1Gd, model's prediction overlaid on T1Gd. (Color figure online)

4   Discussion and Conclusion

In this paper, we experimented with a 2D non-local Mask R-CNN in segmentation of sub-regions of Glioma, which includ Whole Tumor, Tumor Core, and Enhancing Tumor. The idea of implementing deep neural networks using the different types of images together (T1, T1Gd, T2 and FLAIR) resulted in a promising solution for the task of segmentation of the brain tumor. In addition, we discovered that a region-based network for semantic segmentation produced promising results with plenty of room for improvement. We found that some false positive were generated when hyper intense artifact observed on T2. One possible solution is to use FLAIR subtracting T2, and input the subtraction as

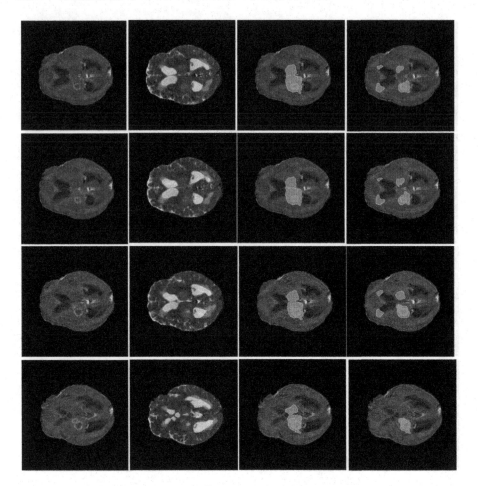

Fig. 4. A patient whose sub-regions of Glioma (Red: WT; Green: ET; Yellow: NCT/NET) is not delineated accurately from the model compared to human labels. The columns in order: T1Gd, T2, manual segmentation overlaid on T1Gd, model's prediction overlaid on T1Gd. (Color figure online)

another channel of input. It's also worthy experimenting with T1Gd subtracting T1 as well. Another solution is to use different numbers of channels with respect to the variations of the signal intensity of voxels [18].

There are some limitations of this work. We experimented with 2D network to save computational cost, which lead to discontinuities in three-dimensional z-direction in the predicted results. A 3D non-local Mask R-CNN is still worth trying in future. And a comparison with other semantic segmentation network such as U-Net may be an interesting topic.

The two classifiers from non-local Mask R-CNN suffer from class imbalance among objects. The focal loss function used in this paper was mainly aimed to address this issue. And we found the DSC of WT was largely improved. Also, by only ensembling the prediction on flipped up-down image, the DSC and sensitivity of all Glioma sub-regions (except for TC sensitivity) was improved. Ensembling predictions to filter out false predictions gives us an encouraging working direction in future.

References

1. Bakas, S., et al.: Advancing the cancer genome atlas glioma MRI collections with expert segmentation labels and radiomic features. Scientific Data **4**(1), 1–13 (2017)
2. Pallud, J., et al.: Quantitative morphological magnetic resonance imaging follow-up of low-grade glioma: a plea for systematic measurement of growth rates. Neurosurgery **71**(3), 729–740 (2012)
3. Bakas, S., et al.: Identifying the best machine learning algorithms for brain tumor segmentation, progression assessment, and overall survival prediction in the BRATS challenge, arXiv preprint arXiv:1811.02629 (2018)
4. Huang, M., Yang, W., Wu, Y., Jiang, J., Chen, W., Feng, Q.: Brain tumor segmentation based on local independent projection-based classification. IEEE Trans. Biomed. Eng. **61**(10), 2633–2645 (2014)
5. Girshick, R.: Fast R-CNN. In: Proceedings of the IEEE International Conference on Computer Vision (2015)
6. Gould, S., Gao, T., Koller, D.: Region-based segmentation and object detection. In: NIPS, vol. 1. (2009)
7. He, K., Gkioxari, G., Dollár, P., Girshick, R.: Mask R-CNN. In: Proceedings of the IEEE International Conference on Computer Vision, pp. 2961–2969 (2017)
8. Wu, Y., Zhao, Z., Wu, W., Lin, Y., Wang, M.: Automatic glioma segmentation based on adaptive superpixel. BMC Med. Imaging **19**(1), 1–14 (2019)
9. Baid, U., et al.: The RSNA-ASNR-MICCAI BraTS 2021 benchmark on brain tumor segmentation and radiogenomic classification. arXiv preprint arXiv:2107.02314 (2021)
10. Menze, B., Reyes, M., Van Leemput, K.: The multimodal brain tumor image segmentation benchmark (BRATS). IEEE Trans. Medical Imaging **34**, 1–32 (2014)
11. Bakas, S., Akbari, H., Sotiras, A., Bilello, M., Rozycki, M., Kirby, J., et al.: Segmentation labels and radiomic features for the pre-operative scans of the TCGA-GBM collection. Can. Imaging Arch. (2017). https://doi.org/10.7937/K9/TCIA.2017.KLXWJJ1Q
12. Bakas, S., Akbari, H., Sotiras, A., Bilello, M., Rozycki, M., Kirby, J., et al.: Segmentation labels and radiomic features for the pre-operative scans of the TCGA-LGG collection. Can. Imaging Arch. (2017). https://doi.org/10.7937/K9/TCIA.2017.GJQ7R0EF
13. Tustison, N.J., et al.: N4ITK: improved N3 bias correction. IEEE Trans. Med. Imaging **29**(6), 1310–1320 (2010)
14. Wang, X., Girshick, R., Gupta, A., He, K.: Non-local neural networks. In: Proceedings of the IEEE Conference on Computer Vision and Pattern Recognition 2018, pp. 7794–7803 (2018)
15. Lin, T.Y., Goyal, P., Girshick, R., He, K., Dollár, P.: Focal loss for dense object detection. In: Proceedings of the IEEE International Conference on Computer Vision 2017, pp. 2980–2988 (2017)

16. Radosavovic, I., Dollár, P., Girshick, R., Gkioxari, G., He, K.: Data distillation: towards omni-supervised learning. In: Proceedings of the IEEE Conference on Computer Vision and Pattern Recognition 2018, pp. 4119–4128 (2018)
17. Abdulla, W.: Mask R-CNN for object detection and instance segmentation on keras and tensorflow (2017)
18. Amorim, P.H., et al.: 3D u-nets for brain tumor segmentation in MICCAI 2017 brats challenge. In: Proceedings of MICCAI Workshop on Multimodal Brain Tumor Segmentation Challenge (BRATS) (2017)

EfficientNet for Brain-Lesion Classification

Quoc-Huy Trinh[1]([✉]), Trong-Hieu Nguyen Mau[1], Radmir Zosimov[2], and Minh-Van Nguyen[1]

[1] Faculty of Information Technology, University of Science, VNU-HCM, Ho Chi Minh city, Vietnam
{20120013,20120081,20127094}@student.hcmus.edu.vn
[2] SBEI School No 1228 "Lefortovo", Moscow, Russia

Abstract. In the development of technology, there are increasing cases of brain disease, there are more treatments proposed and achieved a positive result. However, with Brain-Lesion, the early diagnoses can improve the possibility for successful treatment and can help patients recuperate better. From this reason, Brain-Lesion is one of the controversial topics in medical images analysis nowadays. With the improvement of the architecture, there is a variety of methods that are proposed and achieve competitive scores. In this paper, we proposed a technique that uses efficient-net for 3D images, especially the Efficient-net B0 for Brain-Lesion classification task solution, and achieve the competitive score. Moreover, we also proposed the method to use Multiscale-EfficientNet to classify the slices of the MRI data.

Keywords: Brain-Lesion · EfficientNet · Medical image preprocessing

1 Introduction

In recent years, the number of cases that have brain lesions increasing, according to the National Brain Tumor Society, in the United States, about 700,000 people live with a brain tumour, and the figure rises by the end of 2020 [20]. Compared with other cancers such as breast cancer or lung cancer, a brain tumour is not more common, but it is the tenth leading cause of death worldwide [17]. According to United States statistics, An estimated 18,020 adults will die this year from brain cancer. Moreover, the brain lesion can have a detrimental impact on the brain of the patients and can make sequelae for the patients on the others organs or their brain. Nowadays, there are various methods to diagnose disease through medical images such as CT-scan, magnetic resonance imaging (MRI), and X-ray.

A brain lesion is the abnormal sympathy of a brain seen on a brain-imaging test, such as magnetic resonance (MRI) or computerized tomography (CT). Brain lesions appear as spots that are different from other tissues in the brain [18]. By this method, the MRI can visualize the abnormal on the slide of the brain [19].

A. Crimi and S. Bakas (Eds.): BrainLes 2021, LNCS 12962, pp. 249–260, 2022.
https://doi.org/10.1007/978-3-031-08999-2_20

The goal of the 3D-CT scans images classification task is to evaluate various methods to classify the brain lesions in the medical images correctly and efficiently [21]. Parallel to the development of Computer Vision, particularly the Deep Neural Network and Vision Transformer, multiple methods were proposed to classify the abnormal tissue in the organ through the images such as CT scans and MRIs. In recent years, significant advancement has been made in medical science as the Medical Image processing technique, which helps doctors diagnose the disease earlier and easier. Before that, the process is tedious and time-consuming. To deal with this issue, it is necessary to apply computer-aided technology because Medical Field needs efficient and reliable techniques to diagnose life-threatening diseases like cancer, which is the leading cause of mortality globally for patients [5].

In this paper, we propose a method that uses 3D EfficientNet to classify MRI images, with a new approach to using EfficientNet with Multiscale layers (MSL) to classify slices of MRI images. With the 3D EfficientNet, the model can have higher performance on feature extraction and classification task. In contrast, MSL uses the feature on the slice of image and create low-quality features to create a better feature map for the classification task. In this experiment, we use the backbones of EfficientNet B0 and EfficientNet B7 to perform an experiment and evaluation of our method.

2   Related Work

2.1   Image Classification

Image classification is a task that attempts to classify the image by a specific label. The input of the problem is the image the output is the label of this image. In recent years, the development of computing resources leads to a variety of methods in Image classification such as VGG 16, ResNet 50, and DenseNet. These architectures get the competitive result in the specific dataset. With the images sequence dataset, from the previous methods, there are various methods of Convolution Neural Network (CNN) combined with RNN or LSTM have been proposed. In a few years nearby, some Vision Transformer methods, State of the art (SOTA) architecture combined with CNN and CNN 3D have been proposed. These architecture achieve the competitive result on the task they are applied with the performance also has a competitive response on the task they are applied [2].

2.2   Transfer Learning

Transfer Learning is the method that applies the previously trained model on the large dataset we can not get access to on the new dataset. The merit of this method is we can use the previous model that has high performance to apply on feature extraction of our dataset, this is the reason why the model with the transfer learning method can achieve better accuracy while training with the small dataset [25].

2.3   Brain-Tumour Classification

Brain-Tumour classification is one the most popular tasks in medical image preprocessing [8]. The main goal of this task is to classify the brain lesions images in the set of images. With MRI images, the brain lesion is demonstrated in the dark or light spots, which are different from the others [23].

There are many methods such as segmentation model to improve the data inputs or Generative adversarial networks to increase the data numbers to improve the performance of the training process [22]. Moreover, in recent years, many network architectures have been proposed to improve the classification score of the task [6].

3   Dataset

The dataset for the experiment is from BraTS 2021, the target of the dataset is for the brain lesions classification task [14] which is from RSNA-ASNR-MICCAI BraTS 2021 challenge [4]. This dataset consists of 585 cases for training, in each case includes structural multi-parametric MRI (mpMRI) scans and is formatted in DICOM. The exact mpMRI scans included four types are:

- Fluid Attenuated Inversion Recovery (FLAIR)
- T1-weighted pre-contrast (T1w)
- T1-weighted post-contrast (T1Gd)
- T2-weighted (T2)

This dataset is seperated in two labels are 0 and 1 for the NGMT value, which is the diagnosis scale of Brain-Tumour Detection [15] (Figs. 1 and 2).

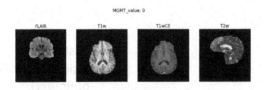

Fig. 1. Sample of NGMT value 0

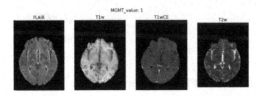

Fig. 2. Sample of sample of NGMT value 1

Regarding NGMT promoter methylation status data is defined as a binary label with 0 as unmethylated and 1 is for methylated [16]. In the challenge, this data is provided to the participants as a comma-separated value (.csv) file with the corresponding pseudo-identifiers of the mpMRI volumes [17] (study-level label).

4   Method

The method we propose in this paper is the classification method for the Brain MRI images data. The input is the Brain MRI Image data (in png, jpg or Dicom format). Then all images will be preprocessed and will be augmented before being trained by the 3D EfficientNet model. Then the model can be used to predict the NGMT value of the new Brain MRI Image data Following is the diagram of our method (Fig. 3):

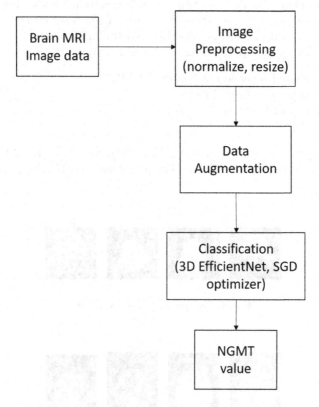

Fig. 3. Method diagram

With the 2D dataset, we create the data from slices of MRI images depend on 4 index: Flair, T1w, T1Gd and T2. These 4 index can be created to four dataset with different size for each dataset. By using CNN for the 2D images, we can ensemble and probing four data by the ratio 3:3:3:2 and 2:4:2:2 for the result of the experiment.

4.1 Data Preparation

After loading data, we resize all the images to the size (256, 256), then we split the dataset into the training set and validation set in the ratio of 0.75:0.25. After resizing and splitting the validation set, we rescale the data pixel down in the range [0, 1] by dividing by 255, in the MRI data, we can apply rescale data on the slices of the data, as the result, the scale of the data will in the range [0, 1]. Then we use the application of EfficientNet to preprocess the input. The input after preprocess is rescaled to the same input of the EfficientNet model.

4.2 Data Augmentation

Data Augmentation is vital in the data preparation process. Data Augmentation improves the number of data by adding slightly modified copies of already existing data or newly created synthetic data from existing data to decrease the probability of the Overfitting problem. We use augmentation to generate the data randomly by random flip images and random rotation with an index of 0.2. With the 2D slices, the augmentation apply on each slices of the MRI data (Fig. 4).

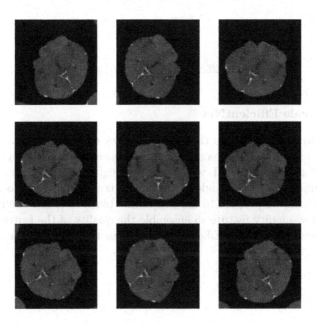

Fig. 4. The result after data augmentation process

4.3 EfficientNet 3D

EfficientNet 3D is the architecture that bases on state-of-the-art 2D EfficientNet architecture. This architecture usually is used for video classification tasks or 3D classification tasks [24]. This architecture has five main parts: Initial Convolutional Layer 3D, Mobile Inverted Residual Bottleneck Block 3D, Convolutional Layer 3D, Global Average Pooling and Fully Connected Layer. This architecture is the modified version for the architecture that uses ConvLSTM or traditional Conv3D layers and it gets competitive scores on the 3D dataset and video dataset [1]. In the experiment, we propose the method by using the input MRI images with the size $256 \times 256 \times 4$ to the input of the architecture, after passing through Convolution layer 3D, Mobile Inverted Residual Bottleneck Block 3D, and the others Convolutional layer 3D for the feature extraction, then Global Average Pooling layer will create the feature vector for the classification process (Fig. 5).

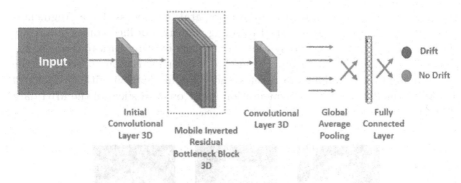

Fig. 5. EfficientNet3D B0 architecture

4.4 Multiscale EfficientNet

In the experiment, we explore that the drawback of using 3D-CNN is the mismatch of the information between the channel space. We approach a new method that uses the slices of the MRI, which are T1-weighted pre-contrast slices. However, the number of slices is adequate for the training process to achieve the well-performance, we propose to use Multiscale block to create the high-quality feature and low-quality feature to ensemble the quality of the feature, then this feature concatenate with the EfficientNet block for the output of the architecture (Fig. 6).

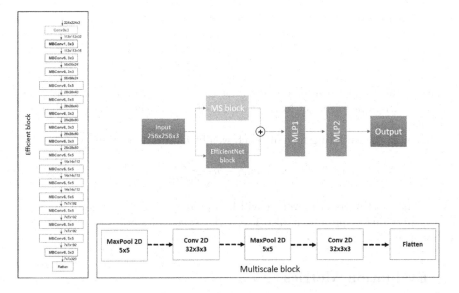

Fig. 6. Multiscale EfficientNet architecture

From the Input layers with the shape 256 × 256 × 3, there are two ways for the input is the Multiscale Block and EfficientNet Block.

We use a Multiscale block containing two Max Pooling layers with two Convolution 2D layers for creating the low-quality feature and for the feature extraction of this feature.

This feature has an integral part of the ensemble and carries more features from the first layers of the MRI slices. From this feature, when add with the high-quality feature, the model can get better performance on feature extraction. With the EfficientNet block, the high-quality feature is extracted as the traditional CNN, then the feature output of this block concatenates with the feature of Multiscale block to create the vector with shape output for the classification process.

4.5   Loss Function

To evaluate the performance of the model on the training process, we propose to use binary cross-entropy to judge the performance of the model.

$$H_p(q) = -\frac{1}{n}\sum_{i=1}^{N} y_i \cdot \log(p(y_i)) + (1 - y_i) \cdot \log(1 - p(y_i)) \tag{1}$$

Above is the formula for Binary-cross entropy, it is suitable for our binary classification problem.

4.6 Optimizer

To get the global minimum in the training process. We do various experiments with optimization such as Stochastic Gradient Descent [12], Adam [9] and Adadelta optimizer [11]. After these experiments, we decide to choose the Adam optimizer because of the merit of the Adam optimizer and the performance of this optimizer on learning rate 0.0001 and the decreasing slightly of validation loss.

Below is the updating formula each weight for Adam optimizer:

$$w_t = w_{t-1} - n\frac{m_t}{\sqrt{v_t} + \epsilon} \tag{2}$$

With adam optimizer, the weight will be updated by the average of the square of the previous slope and it also keeps the speed of slope in the previous as momentum [9].

5 Evaluation Metrics

The evaluation of the experiment is demonstrated through an area under the ROC curve (AUC), this is the scale to evaluate the binary classification. For a predictor f, an unbiased estimator of its AUC can be expressed by the Willcoxon-Mann-Whitney statistic [7]:

$$AUC(f) = \frac{\sum_{t_0 \epsilon D^0} \sum_{t_1 \epsilon D^1} 1[f(t_0) < f(t_1)]}{|D^0| \cdot |D^1|} \tag{3}$$

In this way, it is possible to calculate the AUC by using an average of a number of trapezoidal approximations, it can help to improve the fair in the evaluation phase.

6 Evaluation

The following parameters are setup for in this experiment (Table 1):

Table 1. The parameter setup for model training

Parameter	Value
Optimizer	Adam
Learning rate	0.0001
Backbone	EfficientNet B0
Loss	Binary Crossentropy
metrics	AUC

In the competition, we get an AUC score of 0.60253 on the Test dataset with 87 cases, which is a competitive score. Our methods get a competitive result when compare with the other methods on the same dataset. Below is our experimental evaluation with different optimizers with EfficientNet 3D (Table 2):

Table 2. The evaluation on each optimizer

Optimizer	Evaluation
Adam	0.60253
Adadelta	0.60124
SGD	0.60178
RMSPROP	0.60223

These evaluations are saved on 100 epochs with the best weight which is evaluated on the validation AUC metrics. After that, we use the Early Stopping method to improve the AUC score of the model by optimizing the calculation of gradient in the optimizer.

For comparison between two approaches and methods, we benchmark two methods with the same test dataset from the organizer (Table 3).

Table 3. Benchmarking for two methods

Method	AUC
EfficientNet 3D	0.60253
Multiscale EfficientNet B7	**0.67124**

From the benchmarking table, it is obvious that the performance of the Multiscale EfficientNet B7 is better than the performance of EfficientNet 3D in AUC. However, there are some drawbacks to this method in computing resources. Because creating two types of features are low-quality and high-quality features, the time for computing increases for this process, this is the drawback of this method for running on the lack of computing resources.

7   Conclusion

We demonstrated the proposal of using EfficientNet 3D to classify endoscopic images. The result of our research is competitive on the AUC evaluation metric. In our method, we use EfficientNet 3D with Adam optimizer and Early stopping method to improve the performance of the model on the training process to achieve the competitive score. Moreover, we also apply data augmentation to reduce the overfitting problem of the model on the test dataset. However, there are some drawbacks that we have to do to improve the performance of the model, such as pre-processing data, reducing the noise of the training dataset.

Furthermore, we can apply the better backbone of EfficientNet 3D, or we can use the approach of Transformer or spatial Attention modules to have a new approach to per frame of the sequence images. This new approach can get better feature extraction and better performance on the test dataset.

8   Future Work

Although our method gets a competitive score, there are some drawbacks in our methods: the training time gets long with 85s/epoch, we can custom layers in the architecture to accelerate the computing cost. We can get more layers or ensemble more backbones to achieve higher results.

Another method we can approach by classifying each frame of image in the sequence of images, by applying transfer learning methods with the previous backbone, this method can achieve the higher score and reduce the overfitting problem with the small training dataset.

References

1. Noor, A., Benjdira, B., Anmar, A., Koubaa, A.: DriftNet: aggressive driving behavior classification using 3D EfficientNet architecture
2. Havaei, M.: Brain tumor segmentation with deep neural networks. Medical Image Anal. **35**, 18–31 (2016)
3. Ruba, T., Tamilselvi, R., Parisa Beham, M., Aparna, N.: Accurate classification and detection of brain cancer cells in MRI and CT images using Nano contrast agents
4. Baid, U., et al.: The RSNA-ASNR-MICCAI BraTS 2021 benchmark on brain tumor segmentation and radiogenomic classification. arXiv:2107.02314 (2021)
5. Sultan, H., Salem, N.M., Al-Atabancy, W.: Multi-classification of brain tumor images using deep neural network. IEEE Access **7** (2019)
6. Pereira, S., Pinto, A., Alves, V., Silva, C.A.: Brain tumor segmentation using convolutional neural networks in MRI images. IEEE Trans. Med. Imaging **35**, 1240–1251 (2016)
7. Bradley, A.P.: The use of the area under the ROC curve in the evaluation of machine learning algorithms. Pattern Recognition **30**(7)
8. Işın, A., Direkoğlu, C., Şah, M.: Review of MRI-based brain tumor image segmentation using deep learning methods. Procedia Comput. Sci. (2016)
9. Zhang, Z.: Improved Adam optimizer for Deep Neural Networks. In: 2018 IEEE/ACM 26th International Symposium on Quality of Service (IWQoS), pp. 1–2 (2018). https://doi.org/10.1109/IWQoS.2018.8624183
10. Labbaf Khaniki, M.A., Behzad Hadi, M., Manthouri, M.: Feedback error learning controller based on RMSprop and Salp swarm algorithm for automatic voltage regulator system. In: 2020 10th International Conference on Computer and Knowledge Engineering (ICCKE), pp. 425–430 (2020). https://doi.org/10.1109/ICCKE50421.2020.9303718

11. Vani, S., Rao, T.V.M.: An experimental approach towards the performance assessment of various optimizers on convolutional neural network. In: 2019 3rd International Conference on Trends in Electronics and Informatics (ICOEI), pp. 331–336 (2019). https://doi.org/10.1109/ICOEI.2019.8862686
12. Wang, J., Liang, H., Joshi, G.: Overlap local-SGD: an algorithmic approach to hide communication delays in distributed SGD. In: ICASSP 2020–2020 IEEE International Conference on Acoustics, Speech and Signal Processing (ICASSP), pp. 8871–8875 (2020). https://doi.org/10.1109/ICASSP40776.2020.9053834
13. Chockler, H., Farchi, E., Godlin, B., Novikov, S.: Cross-entropy based testing. In: Formal Methods in Computer Aided Design (FMCAD 2007), pp. 101–108 (2007). https://doi.org/10.1109/FAMCAD.2007.19
14. Park, D., et al.: Automated artefact elimination in computed tomography: a preliminary report for traumatic brain injury and stroke. In: The 3rd International Winter Conference on Brain-Computer Interface, pp. 1–3 (2015). https://doi.org/10.1109/IWW-BCI.2015.7073038
15. Wulandari, A., Sigit, R., Bachtiar, M.M.: Brain tumor segmentation to calculate percentage tumor using MRI. In: 2018 International Electronics Symposium on Knowledge Creation and Intelligent Computing (IES-KCIC), pp. 292–296 (2018). https://doi.org/10.1109/KCIC.2018.8628591
16. Menze, B.H., Jakab, A., Bauer, S., Kalpathy-Cramer, J., Farahani, K., Kirby, J., et al.: The multimodal brain tumor image segmentation benchmark (BRATS). IEEE Trans. Med. Imaging 34(10), 1993–2024 (2015). https://doi.org/10.1109/TMI.2014.2377694
17. Bakas, S., et al.: Advancing the cancer genome atlas glioma MRI collections with expert segmentation labels and radiomic features. Nat. Sci. Data 4, 170117 (2017). https://doi.org/10.1038/sdata.2017.117
18. Bakas, S., et al.: Segmentation labels and radiomic features for the pre-operative scans of the TCGA-GBM collection. Can. Imaging Arch. (2017). https://doi.org/10.7937/K9/TCIA.2017.KLXWJJ1Q
19. Bakas, S., et al.: Segmentation labels and radiomic features for the pre-operative scans of the TCGA-LGG collection. Can. Imaging Arch. (2017). https://doi.org/10.7937/K9/TCIA.2017.GJQ7R0EF
20. Badža, M.M., Barjaktarovi'c, M.C.: Classification of brain tumors from MRI images using a convolutional neural network, MDPI, 14 January 2020. Accepted: 12 March 2020, Published: 15 March 2020
21. Shahriar Sazzad, T.M., Tanzibul Ahmmed, K.M., Hoque, M.U., Rahman, M.: Development of automated brain tumor identification using MRI images. In: 2019 International Conference on Electrical, Computer and Communication Engineering (ECCE), pp. 1–4 (2019). https://doi.org/10.1109/ECACE.2019.8679240
22. Somasundaram, S., Gobinath, R.: Current trends on deep learning models for brain tumor segmentation and detection - a review. In: 2019 International Conference on Machine Learning, Big Data, Cloud and Parallel Computing (COMITCon), pp. 217–221 (2019). https://doi.org/10.1109/COMITCon.2019.8862209
23. Bauer, S., May, C., Dionysiou, D., Stamatakos, G., Buchler, P., Reyes, M.: Multiscale modeling for image analysis of brain tumor studies. IEEE Trans. Biomed. Eng. 59(1), 25–29 (2012). https://doi.org/10.1109/TBME.2011.2163406

24. Yao, C., et al.: rPPG-based spoofing detection for face mask attack using efficient-net on weighted spatial-temporal representation. In: IEEE International Conference on Image Processing (ICIP) 2021, pp. 3872–3876 (2021). https://doi.org/10.1109/ICIP42928.2021.9506276

25. Cenggoro, T.W.: Incorporating the knowledge distillation to improve the EfficientNet transfer learning capability. In: International Conference on Data Science and Its Applications (ICoDSA) 2020, 1–5 (2020). https://doi.org/10.1109/ICoDSA50139.2020.9212994

HarDNet-BTS: A Harmonic Shortcut Network for Brain Tumor Segmentation

Hung-Yu Wu[(✉)] and Youn-Long Lin[(✉)]

Department of Computer Science, National Tsing Hua University, Hsinchu, Taiwan
s109062601@m109.nthu.edu.tw, ylin@cs.nthu.edu.tw

Abstract. Tumor segmentation of brain MRI image is an important and challenging computer vision task. With well-curated multi-institutional multi-parametric MRI (mpMRI) data, the RSNA-ASNR-MICCAI Brain Tumor Segmentation (BraTS) Challenge 2021 is a great bench-marking venue for world-wide researchers to contribute to the advancement of the state-of-the-art. HarDNet is a memory-efficient neural network backbone that has demonstrated excellent performance and efficiency in image classification, object detection, real-time semantic segmentation, and colonoscopy polyp segmentation. In this paper, we propose HarDNet-BTS, a U-Net-like encoder-decoder architecture with HarDNet backbone, for Brain Tumor Segmentation. We train it with the BraTS 2021 dataset using three training strategies and ensemble the resultant models to improve the prediction quality. Assessment reports from the BraTS 2021 validation server show that HarDNet-BTS delivers state-of-the-art performance (Dice_ET = 0.8442, Dice_TC = 0.8793, Dice_WT = 0.9260, HD95_ET = 12.592, HD95_TC = 7.073, HD95_WT = 3.884). It was ranked 8th in the validation phase. Its performance on the final testing dataset is consistent with that of the validation phase (Dice_ET = 0.8727, Dice_TC = 0.8665, Dice_WT = 0.9286, HD95_ET = 8.496, HD95_TC = 18.606, HD95_WT = 4.059). Inferencing an MRI case takes only 16 s of GPU time and 6GBs of GPU memory.

Keywords: Brain tumor segmentation · Medical imaging · Neural network · Deep learning

1 Introduction

A brain tumor is a mass of abnormal cells in the brain. There are many types of tumors, cancerous (malignant) or noncancerous (benign). In the treatment of brain tumors, there are usually surgical resection, radiation therapy and systemic drug therapy. When diagnosing which treatment method to use, it is necessary to be able to accurately see the location, scope and volume of the tumor, but it is not so easy to complete the above conditions, and it often requires an experienced

Supported in part by the Ministry of Science and Technology, TAIWAN.

neurosurgeon to complete it. Automatic segmentation of tumor mass region from a Magnetic Resonance Imaging (MRI) scan data is a practical approach.

Recent development in deep learning has shown remarkable progress in many computer vision tasks such as image classification, object detection or tracking, and semantic or instance segmentation. The field of medical image segmentation also benefit greatly from these progresses. For colonoscopy polyp segmentation and brain tumor segmentation, U-Net [19] employed an encoder-decoder architecture that achieved breakthrough performance and inspired many improvements [6,13].

To make a deep learning approach practical, both network architecture design and labeled dataset readiness are essential. Compared with popular ImageNet or COCO datasets, medical data is more difficult to obtain because it takes many experienced physicians long time to label, not to mention privacy, ethical and legal issues. Fortunately, the Brain Tumor Segmentation Challenge (BraTS) [1–4,15] stages a platform with expert-labeled dataset and standardized assessment metrics for fair comparison. Over the past ten years, it has greatly facilitate rapid progress of the field [11,12,21,22].

The BraTS 2021 dataset [1] consists of over 2,000 cases and is split into 1,251 for training, 219 for validation, and 570 for testing. Each data has four MRI modalities of (a) native(t1), (b) post-contrast T1-weighted (t1Gd), (c) T2-weighted (t2), and (d) T2 Fluid Attenuated Inversion Recovery (t2-FLAIR). Each case is a 3D Image of NIfTI files (.nii.gz format), the image size is $240 \times 240 \times 155$, and the ground truth tumor regions are labeled as necrotic tumor core (NCR - Label 1), peritumoral edematous (ED - Label 2), and GD-enhancing tumor (ET - Label 4). Training and validation data are available to the participants, but, only the training ground truth is given. Scoring the prediction on the validation data against unseen ground truth is done in the challenge organization's servers. Test data is hidden from the participants. Like previous BraTS challenges, participating models will be assessed with the "Dice Similarity Coefficient" and the "Hausdorff distance (95%)".

For the 2021 BraTS Challenge, we propose HarDNet-BTS based on a U-Net-like encoder-decoder architecture and a memory-efficient backbone called HarD-Net. In this paper, we will describe the network design, our training strategies, and the experiment results evaluated by the official validation server.

2   Method

We first present the proposed neural network architecture. Then we describe how we pre-process and augment the training data. Finally, we report the selection of loss function and how to train and ensemble models.

2.1   Proposed HarDNet-BTS Network Architecture

Figure 1 depicts our proposed HarDNet-BTS neural network for brain tumor segmentation. It is inspired by the encoder-decoder architecture popularized by U-Net [19] and our previous experience with FC-HarDNet [5], which was the state-of-the-art in real-time semantic segmentation on the Cityscape dataset from 2019/07–2021/01 according to PapersWithCode. After two stages of vanilla 3X3X3 convolution (colored gray), we replace all convolution pipes with HarD-Net blocks (colored blue or orange and to be elaborated later). The first stage has 32 channels while the second 64. Successively, we halve the resolution by down-sampling and double the number of channels. Skip connections are employed to transport information from the encoder side to the decoder side. The activation function is Mish [17]. All down-samplings are done with Soft-Pooling [20], and all up-samplings are done with tri-linear interpolation. Deep Supervision uses $1 \times 1 \times 1$ convolution to predict the background and number of classes before up-sampling.

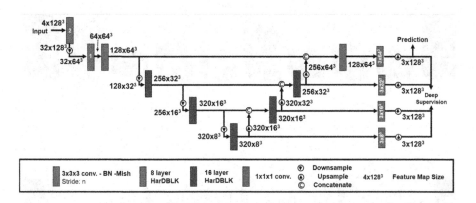

Fig. 1. HarDNet-BTS architecture overview.

Spatial information is essential to our segmentation task. After successive down-sampling operations in the encoder side, the feature map resolution is reduced to a very small size. Therefore, it is difficult to generate an accurate mask. Through three skip connections, we concatenate the feature maps from corresponding encoder and decoder stages to enhance the model's information on the spatial domain, and, hence, help integrating low and high level information to generate better masks.

A HarDNet convolution block as illustrated in Fig. 2 is an improved version of DenseNet [10]. Chao et al. [5] invented the HarDNet block based on their observation of off-chip memory traffic needed during inference. It simplifies the shortcut patterns in the Denseblock. Figure 2 shows two versions (8-layer and 16-layer) of HarDNet blocks employed in our proposed network. Unlike a Denseblock that connects every stage to every other stages, HarDNet's harmonic-wave-like connection pattern significantly reduces the amount of off-chip DRAM access. It has been open-sourced and applied to many computer vision tasks including image classification, object detection, semantic segmentation, and medical segmentation. Especially, the fully convolutional FC-HarDNet for real-time semantic segmentation and HarDNet-MSEG [9] for colonoscopy polyp segmentation both achieved state-of-the-art (SOTA) performance according to PapersWithCode.

Due to HarDNet's efficient memory usage and hence faster inference speed, we can employ many more sophisticated methods to achieve better results. For example, we can replace simple activation functions such as ReLU [18] and Leaky Relu with more sophisticated Mish [17], and AvgPooling and MaxPooling with SoftPooling [20]. Furthermore, we can use high precision 32-bit floating numbers (FP32) instead of half-precision FP16. All these lead to higher accuracy.

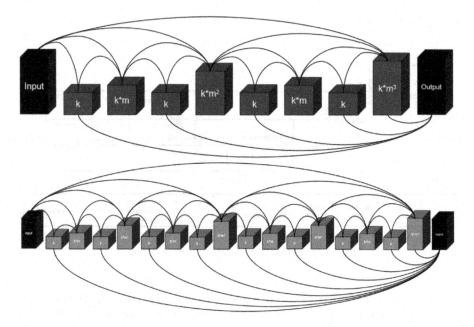

Fig. 2. A 8-layer (blue) and a 16-layer (orange) HarDNet block. Shortcut connections follow a harmonic wave pattern and channel numbers vary. (Color figure online)

2.2 Data Pre-processing

Pre-processing and normalization of the input data facilitate the model to better extract the essential features. We apply the following pre-processing suggested by Theophraste Henry et al. [8]. First, we remove the dark boundaries of the four modalities of an MRI data to cope with the problem of data imbalance and misleading prediction. Then we normalize the data values by (1) calculating the distribution of non-zero voxels in the images, (2) identifying the 1 and 99 percentile as min and max, respectively, and (3) min-max scaling the images. Finally, we employ random cropping to get the image size at $128 \times 128 \times 128$ or $144 \times 144 \times 128$ depending on the training options to be described later.

2.3   Data Augmentation

Data augmentation can increase the diversity of data, reduce the probability of over-fitting and enhance the robustness of a model. We use the following data augmentation.

- scaling each voxel to the range between 0.9 and 1.1
- adding some Gaussian noise to the images
- randomly dropping one of the four input channels
- flip and transpose

2.4   Loss Function

Commonly used loss functions for medical image segmentation networks include dice loss [7,16], cross entropy loss [11], and focal loss [14]. We employ dice loss (DL2, Eq. 1) and dice-and-cross-entropy loss (DLCEL, Eq. 4) defined below.

$$DL2 = 1 - \frac{1}{N} \sum_{i=1}^{N} \frac{A_i * B_i + e}{A_i^2 + B_i^2 + e} \tag{1}$$

$$DL = 1 - \frac{1}{N} \sum_{i=1}^{N} \frac{A_i * B_i + e}{A_i + B_i + e} \tag{2}$$

$$\text{CE} = \frac{1}{N} \sum_{i=1}^{N} -\frac{1}{\substack{\text{output} \\ \text{size}}} \sum_{j=1}^{\substack{\text{output} \\ \text{size}}} B_{ij} \cdot \log A_{ij} + (1 - B_{ij}) \cdot \log (1 - A_{ij}) \tag{3}$$

$$DLCEL = 0.8 \cdot DL + 0.2 \cdot CE \tag{4}$$

In the equations above, A is the model prediction result, B the ground truth, and e a smoothing factor. The difference between two versions of Dice Loss (DL2 of Eq. 1 and DL of 2) is in whether A and B in the denominators are squared or not. Equation 4 defines a compound loss DLCEL as a weighted combination of DL (Eq. 2) and CE (Eq. 3). N = 2 or 4 is the background and number of classes of the task. We would like the loss function to take into account these channels simultaneously. Therefore, we calculate each channel's loss separately, and use their average as the final value.

Deep supervisor produces an output for each layer of the decoder. We calculate a loss value for each layer, and optimize for their average.

2.5   Training and Model Ensemble

We train the proposed HarDNet-BTS using three strategies to obtain three model versions and their ensemble as following:

- **Version 1.** Input size: $128 \times 128 \times 128$, batch size: 6, and loss function: dice-and-cross-entropy loss (DLCEL, Eq. 4).
- **Version 2.** Input size: $144 \times 144 \times 128$, batch size: 4, and loss function: dice loss (DL2, Eq. 1).
- **Version 3.** Same as Version 1 except that we train for ET, TC, and WT separately, and merge the results afterwards.
- **Ensemble** To average the voxel confidence values of all three version's output.

2.6   Inference

To segment a test data, we first use the same data pre-processing as that of the training phase. Then, we use Test Time Augmentation (TTA) to generate 16 different data via data flipping. Each of the three versions of trained model predicts these 16 data producing totally 48 results. Finally, the average of all results is the prediction result.

Our models output are ET, TC, and WT, but the ground truth labels are in ET, NCR, and ED. So we reconstruct NCR by removing ET from TC, and ED by removing TC from WT.

In terms of speed, if only Version 1 is used and TTA is not used, an image takes about 0.25 s of GPU time and 6GBs of GPU memory. For higher accuracy requirements, with model ensembling and TTA, an image will take about 16 s.

3   Results

We have implemented the proposed HarDNet-BTS neural network in PyTorch 1.9.0 and trained it using two GPUs (NVIDIA Tesla V100 32GB). We employ the Ranger optimizer, set the initial learning rate at $1e-4$, train the network for 1,400 epochs, and fine-tuned it for 150 epochs. Figure 3 shows some sample cases of training data, ground truth, and predictions by HarDNet-BTS.

We have enrolled HarDNet-BTS into the BraTS 2021 challenge. The official evaluation metrics are: dice coefficient (Dice_ET, Dice_TC and Dice_ET) and Hausdorff distance 95% (HD95_ET, HD95_TC and HD95_WT), the former is the greater the better while the latter is the opposite. Tables 1 and 2 give the segmentation scores for the training set (1251 cases) and validation set (219 cases), respectively. In the tables, we list three values (enhancing tumor (ET), tumor core (TC), and whole tumor (WT)) of both dice coefficient (Dice) and Hausdorff distance 95% (HD95) for each of the three versions of trained models as well as their ensemble. Table 3 further show the detailed stats on the evaluation report of the validation set predicted by the ensemble model. Figure 4 gives the box plots of the same information.

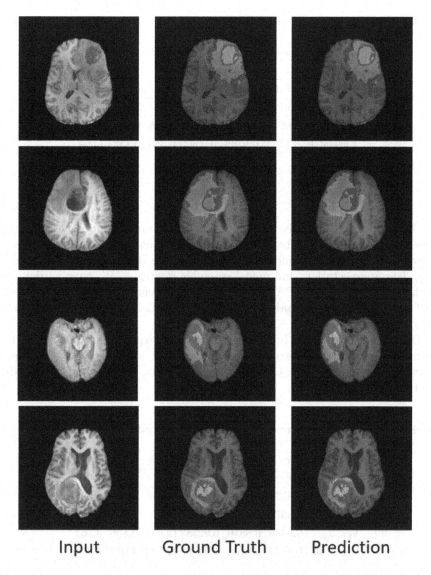

Input   Ground Truth   Prediction

Fig. 3. Sample visual results of the proposed HarDNet-BTS. The labels include NCR(red), ED(green) and ET(blue). (Color figure online)

Table 4 shows the detailed evaluation report of the test data set provided by the challenge organizer. Figure 5 compares the box plots of the dice coefficients of both validation and testing datasets. It can be seen that our model is very robust.

Table 1. The segmentation results of the BraTS 2021 training dataset (1251 cases).

Models	Dice			HD95		
	ET	TC	WT	ET	TC	WT
Ver. 1	0.9106	0.9511	0.9520	7.321	4.908	4.053
Ver. 2	0.9123	0.9557	0.9523	6.074	3.522	3.177
Ver. 3	0.9075	0.9523	0.9596	5.098	6.508	3.682
Ensemble	0.9164	0.9565	0.9593	6.385	5.132	3.064

4 Discussion

We have presented HarDNet-BTS, an encoder-decoder neural network with a memory efficient CNN backbone, for brain tumor segmentation. We have described the reasons behind network architecture design, loss function selection, data augmentation, and model ensemble strategies. We have participated in the RSNA-ASNR-MICCAI Brain Tumor Segmentation (BraTS) Challenge 2021. Validation results ranks 8th among all participants and testing results show consistent quality.

Due to GPU resource limitation, we cannot experiment with many data augmentation and training techniques. In the future, we would like to investigate more on these possibilities. Observing the box plots, we see some outliers that need further investigation.

Table 2. The segmentation results of the BraTS 2021 validation dataset (219 cases).

Models	Dice			HD95		
	ET	TC	WT	ET	TC	WT
Ver. 1	0.8375	0.8727	0.9220	15.893	8.862	4.065
Ver. 2	0.8374	0.8759	0.9229	12.555	8.630	4.108
Ver. 3	0.8386	0.8816	0.9258	12.655	7.836	3.764
Ensemble	0.8442	0.8793	0.9260	12.592	7.073	3.884

Table 3. Statistics of the prediction of the validation dataset.

	Dice			HD95		
	ET	TC	WT	ET	TC	WT
Mean	0.8442	0.8793	0.9260	12.592	7.073	3.884
StdDev	0.2084	0.1820	0.0755	60.651	35.492	7.428
Median	0.9012	0.9415	0.9467	1.414	1.732	2.236
25 quantile	0.8458	0.8848	0.9086	1.000	1.000	1.414
75 quantile	0.9534	0.9660	0.9680	2.236	4.000	3.673

Table 4. Statistics of the prediction of the testing dataset.

	Dice			HD95		
	ET	TC	WT	ET	TC	WT
Mean	0.8727	0.8665	0.9286	8.496	18.606	4.059
StdDev	0.1727	0.2457	0.0885	46.714	70.541	8.007
Median	0.9254	0.9551	0.9566	1.000	1.414	1.732
25 quantile	0.9051	0.9165	0.9086	1.000	1.000	1.000
75 quantile	0.9600	0.9774	0.9756	2.000	3.121	3.741

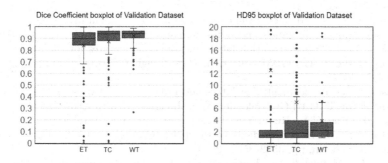

Fig. 4. Box plots of Dice and HD95 of the validation dataset (219 cases).

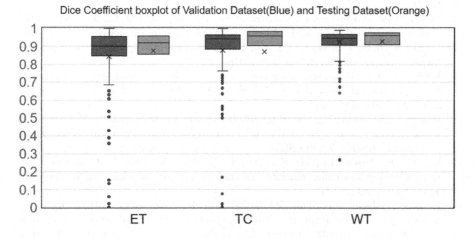

Fig. 5. Box plots of Dice coefficients of the validation dataset and testing dataset.

Acknowledgements. We would like to thank Mr. Ping Chao and Mr. James Huang for their open-sourced HarDNet and HarDNet-MSEG, respectively. We would also like to thank Mr. Wei-Xiang Kuo, Mr. Kao-chun Pan and Mr. Kuan-Ying Lai for many fruitful discussions. This research is supported in part by a grant (no. 110-2218-E-007-043) from the Ministry of Science and Technology (MOST) of Taiwan. We thank the National Center for High-performance Computing (NCHC) for providing computational and storage resources. Without it this research is impossible.

References

1. Baid, U., et al.: The RSNA-ASNR-MICCAI BraTS 2021 benchmark on brain tumor segmentation and radiogenomic classification. arXiv preprint arXiv:2107.02314 (2021)
2. Bakas, S., et al.: Advancing the cancer genome atlas glioma MRI collections with expert segmentation labels and radiomic features. Sci. Data **4**(1), 1–13 (2017)
3. Bakas, S., et al.: Segmentation labels and radiomic features for the pre-operative scans of the TCGA-GBM collection. Can. Imaging Archive. Nat. Sci. Data **4**, 170117 (2017)
4. Bakas, S., et al.: Segmentation labels and radiomic features for the pre-operative scans of the TCGA-LGG collection. Can. Imaging Archive, 286 (2017)
5. Chao, P., Kao, C.Y., Ruan, Y.S., Huang, C.H., Lin, Y.L.: Hardnet: a low memory traffic network. In: Proceedings of the IEEE/CVF International Conference on Computer Vision, pp. 3552–3561 (2019)
6. Çiçek, Ö., Abdulkadir, A., Lienkamp, S.S., Brox, T., Ronneberger, O.: 3D U-Net: learning dense volumetric segmentation from sparse annotation. In: Ourselin, S., Joskowicz, L., Sabuncu, M.R., Unal, G., Wells, W. (eds.) MICCAI 2016. LNCS, vol. 9901, pp. 424–432. Springer, Cham (2016). https://doi.org/10.1007/978-3-319-46723-8_49
7. Drozdzal, M., Vorontsov, E., Chartrand, G., Kadoury, S., Pal, C.: The importance of skip connections in biomedical image segmentation. In: Carneiro, G., et al. (eds.) LABELS/DLMIA -2016. LNCS, vol. 10008, pp. 179–187. Springer, Cham (2016). https://doi.org/10.1007/978-3-319-46976-8_19
8. Henry, T., et al.: Brain tumor segmentation with self-ensembled, deeply-supervised 3D U-net neural networks: a BraTS 2020 challenge solution. arXiv preprint arXiv:2011.01045 (2020)
9. Huang, C.H., Wu, H.Y., Lin, Y.L.: Hardnet-mseg: a simple encoder-decoder polyp segmentation neural network that achieves over 0.9 mean dice and 86 fps. arXiv preprint arXiv:2101.07172 (2021)
10. Iandola, F., Moskewicz, M., Karayev, S., Girshick, R., Darrell, T., Keutzer, K.: Densenet: Implementing efficient convnet descriptor pyramids. arXiv preprint arXiv:1404.1869 (2014)
11. Isensee, F., Jäger, P.F., Full, P.M., Vollmuth, P., Maier-Hein, K.H.: nnU-net for brain tumor segmentation. In: Crimi, A., Bakas, S. (eds.) BrainLes 2020. LNCS, vol. 12659, pp. 118–132. Springer, Cham (2021). https://doi.org/10.1007/978-3-030-72087-2_11
12. Jia, H., Cai, W., Huang, H., Xia, Y.: H2NF-Net for Brain Tumor Segmentation using Multimodal MR Imaging: 2nd Place Solution to BraTS Challenge 2020 Segmentation Task (2020)
13. Le Duy Huynh, N.B.: A U-NET++ with pre-trained efficientnet backbone for segmentation of diseases and artifacts in endoscopy images and videos (2020)

14. Lin, T.Y., Goyal, P., Girshick, R., He, K., Dollár, P.: Focal loss for dense object detection. In: Proceedings of the IEEE International Conference on Computer Vision, pp. 2980–2988 (2017)
15. Menze, B.H., et al.: The multimodal brain tumor image segmentation benchmark (BRATS). IEEE Trans. Med. Imaging **34**(10), 1993–2024 (2014)
16. Milletari, F., Navab, N., Ahmadi, S.A.: V-net: Fully convolutional neural networks for volumetric medical image segmentation. In: 2016 Fourth International Conference on 3D Vision (3DV), pp. 565–571. IEEE, October 2016
17. Misra, D.: Mish: a self regularized non-monotonic neural activation function. arXiv preprint arXiv:1908.08681 (2019). 4, 2
18. Nair, V., Hinton, G.E.: Rectified linear units improve restricted boltzmann machines. In Icml, January 2010
19. Ronneberger, O., Fischer, P., Brox, T.: U-Net: convolutional networks for biomedical image segmentation. In: Navab, N., Hornegger, J., Wells, W.M., Frangi, A.F. (eds.) MICCAI 2015. LNCS, vol. 9351, pp. 234–241. Springer, Cham (2015). https://doi.org/10.1007/978-3-319-24574-4_28
20. Stergiou, A., Poppe, R., Kalliatakis, G.: Refining activation downsampling with Softpool. arXiv preprint arXiv:2101.00440 (2021)
21. Wang, Y., et al.: Modality-Pairing Learning for Brain Tumor Segmentation. arXiv preprint arXiv:2010.09277 (2020)
22. Yuan, Y.: Automatic head and neck tumor segmentation in PET/CT with scale attention network. In: Andrearczyk, V., Oreiller, V., Depeursinge, A. (eds.) HECKTOR 2020. LNCS, vol. 12603, pp. 44–52. Springer, Cham (2021). https://doi.org/10.1007/978-3-030-67194-5_5

Swin UNETR: Swin Transformers for Semantic Segmentation of Brain Tumors in MRI Images

Ali Hatamizadeh[1(✉)], Vishwesh Nath[1], Yucheng Tang[2], Dong Yang[1], Holger R. Roth[1], and Daguang Xu[1]

[1] NVIDIA, Santa Clara, USA
ahatamizadeh@nvidia.com
[2] Vanderbilt University, Nashville, USA

Abstract. Semantic segmentation of brain tumors is a fundamental medical image analysis task involving multiple MRI imaging modalities that can assist clinicians in diagnosing the patient and successively studying the progression of the malignant entity. In recent years, Fully Convolutional Neural Networks (FCNNs) approaches have become the de facto standard for 3D medical image segmentation. The popular "U-shaped" network architecture has achieved state-of-the-art performance benchmarks on different 2D and 3D semantic segmentation tasks and across various imaging modalities. However, due to the limited kernel size of convolution layers in FCNNs, their performance of modeling long-range information is sub-optimal, and this can lead to deficiencies in the segmentation of tumors with variable sizes. On the other hand, transformer models have demonstrated excellent capabilities in capturing such long-range information in multiple domains, including natural language processing and computer vision. Inspired by the success of vision transformers and their variants, we propose a novel segmentation model termed Swin UNEt TRansformers (Swin UNETR). Specifically, the task of 3D brain tumor semantic segmentation is reformulated as a sequence to sequence prediction problem wherein multi-modal input data is projected into a 1D sequence of embedding and used as an input to a hierarchical Swin transformer as the encoder. The swin transformer encoder extracts features at five different resolutions by utilizing shifted windows for computing self-attention and is connected to an FCNN-based decoder at each resolution via skip connections. We have participated in BraTS 2021 segmentation challenge, and our proposed model ranks among the top-performing approaches in the validation phase.
Code: https://monai.io/research/swin-unetr.

Keywords: Image segmentation · Vision transformer · Swin transformer · UNETR · Swin UNETR · BRATS · Brain tumor segmentation

A. Crimi and S. Bakas (Eds.): BrainLes 2021, LNCS 12962, pp. 272–284, 2022.
https://doi.org/10.1007/978-3-031-08999-2_22

1   Introduction

There are over 120 types of brain tumors that affect the human brain [27]. As we enter the era of Artificial Intelligence (AI) for healthcare, AI-based intervention for diagnosis and surgical pre-assessment of tumors is at the verge of becoming a necessity rather than a luxury. Elaborate characterization of brain tumors with techniques such as volumetric analysis is useful to study their progression and assist in pre-surgical planning [17]. In addition to surgical applications, characterization of delineated tumors can be directly utilized for the prediction of life expectancy [32]. Brain tumor segmentation is at the forefront of all such applications.

Brain tumors are categorized into primary and secondary tumor types. Primary brain tumors originate from brain cells, while secondary tumors metastasize into the brain from other organs. The most common primary brain tumors are gliomas, which arise from brain glial cells and are characterized into low-grade (LGG) and high-grade (HGG) subtypes. High grade gliomas are an aggressive type of malignant brain tumors that grow rapidly and typically require surgery and radiotherapy and have poor survival prognosis [40]. As a reliable diagnostic tool, Magnetic Resonance Imaging (MRI) plays a vital role in monitoring and surgery planning for brain tumor analysis. Typically, several complimentary 3D MRI modalities, such as T1, T1 with contrast agent (T1c), T2 and Fluid-attenuated Inversion Recovery (FLAIR), are required to emphasize different tissue properties and areas of tumor spread. For instance, gadolinium as the contrast agent emphasizes hyperactive tumor sub-regions in the T1c MRI modality [15].

Furthermore, automated medical image segmentation techniques [18] have shown prominence for providing an accurate and reproducible solution for brain tumor delineation. Recently, deep learning-based brain tumor segmentation techniques [19,20,30,31] have achieved state-of-the-art performance in various benchmarks [2,7,34]. These advances are mainly due to the powerful feature extraction capabilities of Convolutional Neural Networks (CNN)s. However, the limited kernel size of CNN-based techniques restricts their capability of learning long-range dependencies that are critical for accurate segmentation of tumors that appear in various shapes and sizes. Although several efforts [10,23] have tried to address this limitation by increasing the receptive field of the convolutional kernels, the effective receptive field is still limited to local regions.

Recently, transformer-based models have shown prominence in various domains such as natural language processing and computer vision [13,14,37]. In computer vision, Vision Transformers [14] (ViT)s have demonstrated state-of-the-art performance on various benchmarks. Specifically, self-attention module in ViT-based models allows for modeling long-range information by pairwise interaction between token embeddings and hence leading to more effective local and global contextual representations [33]. In addition, ViTs have achieved success in effective learning of pretext tasks for self-supervised pre-training in various applications [8,9,35]. In medical image analysis, UNETR [16] is the first methodology that utilizes a ViT as its encoder without relying on a CNN-based feature extractor. Other approaches [38,39] have attempted to leverage the power of ViTs as a stand-alone block in their architectures which otherwise consist of CNN-based components. However, UNETR has shown better performance in terms of both accuracy and efficiency in different medical image segmentation tasks [16].

Recently, Swin transformers [24,25] have been proposed as a hierarchical vision transformer that computes self-attention in an efficient shifted window partitioning scheme. As a result, Swin transformers are suitable for various downstream tasks wherein the extracted multi-scale features can be leveraged for further processing. In this work, we propose a novel architecture termed Swin UNEt TRansformers (Swin UNETR), which utilizes a U-shaped network with a Swin transformer as the encoder and connects it to a CNN-based decoder at different resolutions via skip connections. We validate the effectiveness of our approach for the task of multi-modal 3D brain tumor segmentation in the 2021 edition of the Multi-modal Brain Tumor Segmentation Challenge (BraTS). Our model is one of the top-ranking methods in the validation phase and has demonstrated competitive performance in the testing phase.

2   Related Work

In the previous BraTS challenges, ensembles of U-Net shaped architectures have achieved promising results for multi-modal brain tumor segmentation. Kamnitsas et al. [21] proposed a robust segmentation model by aggregating the outputs of various CNN-based models such as 3D U-Net [12], 3D FCN [26] and Deep Medic [22]. Subsequently, Myronenko et al. [30] introduced SegResNet, which utilizes a residual encoder-decoder architecture in which an auxiliary branch is used to reconstruct the input data with a variational auto-encoder as a surrogate task. Zhou et al. [42] proposed to use an ensemble of different CNN-based networks by taking into account the multi-scale contextual information through an attention block. Zhou et al. [20] used a two-stage cascaded approach consisting of U-Net models wherein the first stage computes a coarse segmentation prediction which will be refined by the second stage. Furthermore, Isensee et al. [19] proposed the nnU-Net model and demonstrated that a generic U-Net architecture with minor modifications is enough to achieve competitive performance in multiple BraTS challenges.

Transformer-based models have recently gained a lot of attraction in computer vision [14,24,41] and medical image analysis [11,16]. Chen et al. [11] introduced a 2D U-Net architecture that benefits from a ViT in the bottleneck of the network. Wang et al. [38] extended this approach for 3D brain tumor segmentation. In addition, Xie et al. [39] proposed to use a ViT-based model with deformable transformer layers between its CNN-based encoder and decoder by processing the extracted features at different resolutions. Different from these approaches, Hatamizadeh et al. [16] proposed the UNETR architecture in which a ViT-based encoder, which directly utilizes 3D input patches, is connected to a CNN-based decoder. UNETR has shown promising results for brain tumor segmentation using the MSD dataset [1]. Unlike the UNETR model, our proposed Swin UNETR architecture uses a Swin transformer encoder which extracts feature representations at several resolutions with a shifted windowing mechanism

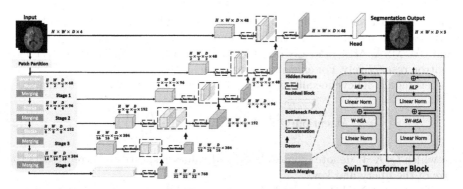

Fig. 1. Overview of the Swin UNETR architecture. The input to our model is 3D multi-modal MRI images with 4 channels. The Swin UNETR creates non-overlapping patches of the input data and uses a patch partition layer to create windows with a desired size for computing the self-attention. The encoded feature representations in the Swin transformer are fed to a CNN-decoder via skip connection at multiple resolutions. Final segmentation output consists of 3 output channels corresponding to ET, WT and TC sub-regions.

for computing the self-attention. We demonstrate that Swin transformers [24] have a great capability of learning multi-scale contextual representations and modeling long-range dependencies in comparison to ViT-based approaches with fixed resolution.

3   Swin UNETR

3.1   Encoder

We illustrate the architecture of Swin UNETR in Fig. 1. The input to the Swin UNETR model $\mathcal{X} \in \mathbb{R}^{H \times W \times D \times S}$ is a token with a patch resolution of (H', W', D') and dimension of $H' \times W' \times D' \times S$. We first utilize a patch partition layer to create a sequence of 3D tokens with dimension of $\lceil \frac{H}{H'} \rceil \times \lceil \frac{W}{W'} \rceil \times \lceil \frac{D}{D'} \rceil$ and project them into an embedding space with dimension C. The self-attention is computed into non-overlapping windows that are created in the partitioning stage for efficient token interaction modeling. Figure 2 shows the shifted windowing mechanism for subsequent layers. Specifically, we utilize windows of size $M \times M \times M$ to evenly partition a 3D token into $\lceil \frac{H'}{M} \rceil \times \lceil \frac{W'}{M} \rceil \times \lceil \frac{D'}{M} \rceil$ regions at a given layer l in the transformer encoder. Subsequently, in layer $l + 1$, the partitioned window regions are shifted by $(\lfloor \frac{M}{2} \rfloor, \lfloor \frac{M}{2} \rfloor, \lfloor \frac{M}{2} \rfloor)$ voxels. In subsequent layers of l and $l + 1$ in the encoder, the outputs are calculated as

$$
\begin{aligned}
\hat{z}^l &= \text{W-MSA}(\text{LN}(z^{l-1})) + z^{l-1} \\
z^l &= \text{MLP}(\text{LN}(\hat{z}^l)) + \hat{z}^l \\
\hat{z}^{l+1} &= \text{SW-MSA}(\text{LN}(z^l)) + z^l \\
z^{l+1} &= \text{MLP}(\text{LN}(\hat{z}^{l+1})) + \hat{z}^{l+1}.
\end{aligned}
\tag{1}
$$

Here, W-MSA and SW-MSA are regular and window partitioning multi-head self-attention modules respectively; $\hat{z}^l$ and $\hat{z}^{l+1}$ denote the outputs of W-MSA and SW-MSA; MLP and LN denote layer normalization and Multi-Layer Perceptron respectively. For efficient computation of the shifted window mechanism, we leverage a 3D cyclic-shifting [24] and compute self-attention according to

$$\text{Attention}(Q, K, V) = \text{Softmax}\left(\frac{QK^\top}{\sqrt{d}}\right)V. \tag{2}$$

In which Q, K, V denote queries, keys, and values respectively; d represents the size of the query and key.

The Swin UNETR encoder has a patch size of $2 \times 2 \times 2$ and a feature dimension of $2 \times 2 \times 2 \times 4 = 32$, taking into account the multi-modal MRI images with 4 channels. The size of the embedding space C is set to 48 in our encoder. Furthermore, the Swin UNETR encoder has 4 stages which comprise of 2 transformer blocks at each stage. Hence, the total number of layers in the encoder is $L = 8$. In stage 1, a linear embedding layer is utilized to create $\frac{H}{2} \times \frac{W}{2} \times \frac{D}{2}$ 3D tokens. To maintain the hierarchical structure of the encoder, a patch merging layer is utilized to decrease the resolution of feature representations by a factor of 2 at the end of each stage. In addition, a patch merging layer groups patches with resolution $2 \times 2 \times 2$ and concatenates them, resulting in a $4C$-dimensional feature embedding. The feature size of the representations are subsequently reduced to $2C$ with a linear layer. Stage 2, stage 3 and stage 4, with resolutions of $\frac{H}{4} \times \frac{W}{4} \times \frac{D}{4}$, $\frac{H}{8} \times \frac{W}{8} \times \frac{D}{8}$ and $\frac{H}{16} \times \frac{W}{16} \times \frac{D}{16}$ respectively, follow the same network design.

3.2 Decoder

Swin UNETR has a U-shaped network design in which the extracted feature representations of the encoder are used in the decoder via skip connections at each resolution. At each stage i ($i \in \{0, 1, 2, 3, 4\}$) in the encoder and the bottleneck ($i = 5$), the output feature representations are reshaped into size $\frac{H}{2^i} \times \frac{W}{2^i} \times \frac{D}{2^i}$ and fed into a residual block comprising of two $3 \times 3 \times 3$ convolutional layers that are normalized by instance normalization [36] layers. Subsequently, the resolution of the feature maps are increased by a factor of 2 using a deconvolutional layer and the outputs are concatenated with the outputs of the previous stage. The concatenated features are then fed into another residual block as previously described. The final segmentation outputs are computed by using a $1 \times 1 \times 1$ convolutional layer and a sigmoid activation function.

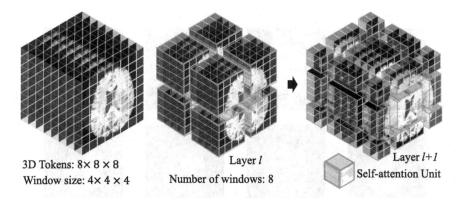

3D Tokens: 8× 8 × 8
Window size: 4× 4 × 4
Layer *l*
Number of windows: 8
Layer *l+1*
Self-attention Unit

Fig. 2. Overview of the shifted windowing mechanism. Note that $8 \times 8 \times 8$ 3D tokens and $4 \times 4 \times 4$ window size are illustrated.

Table 1. Swin UNETR configurations.

Embed dimension	Feature size	Number of blocks	Window size	Number of heads	Parameters	FLOPs
768	48	[2, 2, 2, 2]	[7, 7, 7]	[3, 6, 12, 24]	61.98M	394.84G

3.3 Loss Function

We use the soft Dice loss function [29] which is computed in a voxel-wise manner as

$$\mathcal{L}(G,Y) = 1 - \frac{2}{J} \sum_{j=1}^{J} \frac{\sum_{i=1}^{I} G_{i,j} Y_{i,j}}{\sum_{i=1}^{I} G_{i,j}^2 + \sum_{i=1}^{I} Y_{i,j}^2}. \tag{3}$$

where I denotes voxels numbers; J is classes number; $Y_{i,j}$ and $G_{i,j}$ denote the probability of output and one-hot encoded ground truth for class j at voxel i, respectively.

3.4 Implementation Details

Swin UNETR is implemented using PyTorch[1] and MONAI[2] and trained on a DGX-1 cluster with 8 NVIDIA V100 GPUs. Table 1 details the configurations of Swin UNETR architecture, number of parameters and FLOPs. The learning rate is set to 0.0008. We normalize all input images to have zero mean and unit standard deviation according to non-zero voxels. Random patches of $128 \times 128 \times 128$ were cropped from 3D image volumes during training. We apply a random axis mirror flip with a probability of 0.5 for all 3 axes. Additionally, we apply data augmentation transforms of random per channel intensity shift in the range $(-0.1, 0.1)$, and random scale of intensity in the range $(0.9, 1.1)$ to input image channels. The batch size per GPU was set to 1. All models were trained

---

[1] http://pytorch.org/.
[2] https://monai.io/.

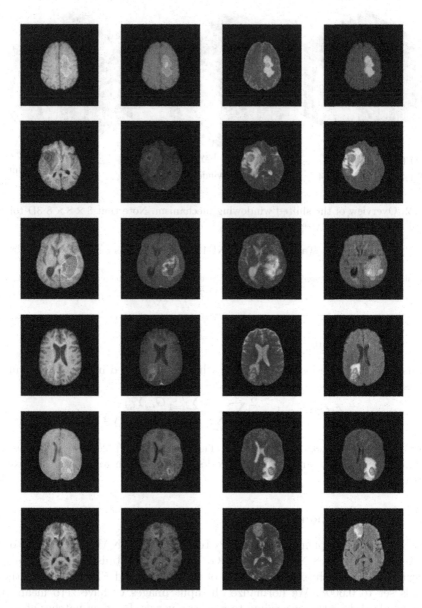

Fig. 3. A typical segmentation example of the predicted labels whic are overlaid on T1, T1c, T2 and FLAIR MRI axial slices in each row. The first two rows depict ∼75th percentile performance based on the Dice score. Rows 3 and 4 depict ∼50th percentile performance while the last two rows are at ∼25th percentile performance. The image intensities are on a gray color scale. The blue, red and green colors correspond to TC, ET and WT sub-regions respectively. Note that all samples have been selected from the BraTS 2021 validation set. (Color figure online)

for a total of 800 epochs with a linear warmup and using a cosine annealing learning rate scheduler. Fonr inference, we use a sliding window approach with an overlapping of 0.7 for neighboring voxels.

3.5 Dataset and Model Ensembling

The BraTS challenge aims to evaluate state-of-the-art methods for the semantic segmentation of brain tumors by providing a 3D MRI dataset with voxel-wise ground truth labels that are annotated by physicians [3–6,28]. The BraTS 2021 challenge training dataset includes 1251 subjects, each with four 3D MRI modalities: a) native (T1) and b) post-contrast T1-weighted (T1Gd), c) T2-weighted (T2), and d) T2 Fluid-attenuated Inversion Recovery (T2-FLAIR), which are rigidly aligned, and resampled to a $1 \times 1 \times 1$ mm isotropic resolution and skull-stripped. The input image size is $240 \times 240 \times 155$. The data were collected from multiple institutions using various MRI scanners. Annotations include three tumor sub-regions: the enhancing tumor, the peritumoral edema, and the necrotic and non-enhancing tumor core. The annotations were combined into three nested sub-regions: Whole Tumor (WT), Tumor Core (TC), and Enhancing Tumor (ET). Figure 3 illustrates typical segmentation outputs of all semantic classes. During this challenge, two additional datasets without the ground truth labels were provided for validation and testing phases. These datasets required participants to upload the segmentation masks to the organizers' server for evaluations. The validation dataset, which is designed for intermediate model evaluations, consists of 219 cases. Additional information regarding the testing dataset was not provided to participants.

Our models were trained on BraTS 2021 dataset with 1251 and 219 cases in the training and validation sets, respectively. Semantic segmentation labels corresponding to validation cases are not publicly available, and performance benchmarks were obtained by making submissions to the official server of BraTS 2021 challenge. We used five-fold cross-validation schemes with a ratio of 80:20. We did not use any additional data. The final result was obtained with an ensemble of 10 Swin UNETR models to improve the performance and achieve a better consensus for all predictions. The ensemble models were obtained from two separate five-fold cross-validation training runs.

4   Results and Discussion

We have compared the performance of Swin UNETR in our internal cross validation split against the winning metCategorylogies of previous years such as SegRes-Net [30], nnU-Net [19] and TransBTS [38]. The latter is a ViT-based approach which is tailored for the semantic segmentation of brain tumors.

Table 2. Five-fold cross-validation benchmarks in terms of mean Dice score values. ET, WT and TC denote Enhancing Tumor, Whole Tumor and Tumor Core respectively.

Dice Score	Swin UNETR				nnU-Net				SegResNet				TransBTS			
	ET	WT	TC	Avg	ET	WT	TC	Avg.	ET	WT	TC	Avg.	ET	WT	TC	Avg.
Fold 1	**0.876**	**0.929**	**0.914**	**0.906**	0.866	0.921	0.902	0.896	0.867	0.924	0.907	0.899	0.856	0.910	0.897	0.883
Fold 2	**0.908**	**0.938**	**0.919**	**0.921**	0.899	0.933	**0.919**	0.917	0.900	0.933	0.915	0.916	0.885	0.919	0.903	0.902
Fold 3	**0.891**	**0.931**	**0.919**	**0.913**	0.886	0.929	0.914	0.910	0.884	0.927	0.917	0.909	0.866	0.903	0.898	0.889
Fold 4	**0.890**	**0.937**	**0.920**	**0.915**	0.886	0.927	0.914	0.909	0.888	0.921	0.916	0.908	0.868	0.910	0.901	0.893
Fold 5	**0.891**	**0.934**	**0.917**	**0.914**	0.880	0.929	**0.917**	0.909	0.878	0.930	0.912	0.906	0.867	0.915	0.893	0.892
Avg.	**0.891**	**0.933**	**0.917**	**0.913**	0.883	0.927	0.913	0.908	0.883	0.927	0.913	0.907	0.868	0.911	0.898	0.891

Table 3. BraTS 2021 validation dataset benchmarks in terms of mean Dice score and Hausdorff distance values. ET, WT and TC denote Enhancing Tumor, Whole Tumor and Tumor Core respectively.

	Dice			Hausdorff (mm)		
Validation dataset	ET	WT	TC	ET	WT	TC
Swin UNETR	0.858	0.926	0.885	6.016	5.831	3.770

Evaluation results across all five folds are presented in Table 2. The proposed Swin UNETR model outperforms all competing approaches across all 5 folds and on average for all semantic classes (e.g. ET, WT, TC). Specifically, Swin UNETR outperforms the closest competing approaches by 0.7%, 0.6% and 0.4% for ET, WT and TC classes respectively and on average 0.5% across all classes in all folds. The superior performance of Swin UNETR in comparison to other top performing models for brain tumor segmentation is mainly due to its capability of learning multi-scale contextual information in its hierarchical encoder via the self-attention modules and effective modeling of the long-range dependencies.

Moreover, it is observed that nnU-Net and SegResNet have competitive benchmarks in these experiments, with nnU-Net demonstrating a slightly better performance. On the other hand, TransBTS, which is a ViT-based methodology, performs sub-optimally in comparison to other models. The sub-optimal performance of TransBTS could be attributed to its inefficient architecture in which the ViT is only utilized in the bottleneck as a standalone attention module, and without any connection to the decoder in different resolutions.

The segmentation performance of Swin UNETR in the BraTS 2021 validation set is presented in Table 3. According to the official challenge results[3], our benchmarks (Team: NVOptNet) are considered as one of the top-ranking methodologies across more than 2000 submissions during the validation phase, hence being the first transformer-based model to place competitively in BraTS challenges. In addition, the segmentation outputs of Swin UNETR for several cases in the validation set are illustrated in Fig. 3. Consistent with quantitative benchmarks, the segmentation outputs are well-delineated for all three sub-regions.

---

[3] https://www.synapse.org/#!Synapse:syn25829067/wiki/612712.

Table 4. BraTS 2021 testing dataset benchmarks in terms of mean Dice score and Hausdorff distance values. ET, WT and TC denote Enhancing Tumor, Whole Tumor and Tumor Core respectively.

	Dice			Hausdorff (mm)		
Testing dataset	ET	WT	TC	ET	WT	TC
Swin UNETR	0.853	0.927	0.876	16.326	4.739	15.309

Furthermore, the segmentation performance of Swin UNETR in the BraTS 2021 testing set is reported in Table 4. We observe that the segmentation performance of ET and WT are very similar to those of the validation benchmarks. However, the segmentation performance of TC is decreased by 0.9%.

5 Conclusion

In this paper, we introduced Swin UNETR which is a novel architecture for semantic segmentation of brain tumors using multi-modal MRI images. Our proposed model has a U-shaped network design and uses a Swin transformer as the encoder and CNN-based decoder that is connected to the encoder via skip connections at different resolutions. We have validated the effectiveness of our approach by in the BraTS 2021 challenge. Our model ranks among top-performing approaches in the validation phase and demonstrates competitive performance in the testing phase. We believe that Swin UNETR could be the foundation of a new class of transformer-based models with hierarchical encoders for the task of brain tumor segmentation.

References

1. Antonelli, M., et al.: The medical segmentation decathlon. arXiv preprint arXiv:2106.05735 (2021)
2. Baid, U., et al.: The RSNA-ASNR-MICCAI brats 2021 benchmark on brain tumor segmentation and radiogenomic classification. arXiv preprint arXiv:2107.02314 (2021)
3. Bakas, S., et al.: Segmentation labels and radiomic features for the pre-operative scans of the TCGA-GBM collection. The Cancer Imaging Archive (2017). https://doi.org/10.7937/K9/TCIA.2017.KLXWJJ1Q
4. Bakas, S., et al.: Segmentation labels and radiomic features for the pre-operative scans of the TCGA-LGG collection. The Cancer Imaging Archive (2017). https://doi.org/10.7937/K9/TCIA.2017.GJQ7R0EF
5. Bakas, S., et al.: Advancing the cancer genome atlas glioma MRI collections with expert segmentation labels and radiomic features. Sci. Data 4, 1–13 (2017)
6. Bakas, S., Reyes, M., et Int, Menze, B.: Identifying the best machine learning algorithms for brain tumor segmentation, progression assessment, and overall survival prediction in the BRATS challenge. In: arXiv:1811.02629 (2018)

7. Bakas, S., et al.: Identifying the best machine learning algorithms for brain tumor segmentation, progression assessment, and overall survival prediction in the brats challenge. arXiv preprint arXiv:1811.02629 (2018)
8. Bao, H., Dong, L., Wei, F.: Beit: Bert pre-training of image transformers. arXiv preprint arXiv:2106.08254 (2021)
9. Caron, M., et al.: Emerging properties in self-supervised vision transformers. In: Proceedings of the IEEE/CVF International Conference on Computer Vision (2021)
10. Chen, C., Liu, X., Ding, M., Zheng, J., Li, J.: 3D dilated multi-fiber network for real-time brain tumor segmentation in MRI. In: Shen, D., et al. (eds.) MICCAI 2019. LNCS, vol. 11766, pp. 184–192. Springer, Cham (2019). https://doi.org/10.1007/978-3-030-32248-9_21
11. Chen, J., et al.: Transunet: transformers make strong encoders for medical image segmentation. arXiv preprint arXiv:2102.04306 (2021)
12. Çiçek, Ö., Abdulkadir, A., Lienkamp, S.S., Brox, T., Ronneberger, O.: 3D U-Net: learning dense volumetric segmentation from sparse annotation. In: Ourselin, S., Joskowicz, L., Sabuncu, M.R., Unal, G., Wells, W. (eds.) MICCAI 2016. LNCS, vol. 9901, pp. 424–432. Springer, Cham (2016). https://doi.org/10.1007/978-3-319-46723-8_49
13. Devlin, J., Chang, M.W., Lee, K., Toutanova, K.: Bert: pre-training of deep bidirectional transformers for language understanding. arXiv preprint arXiv:1810.04805 (2018)
14. Dosovitskiy, A., et al.: An image is worth 16x16 words: Transformers for image recognition at scale. In: International Conference on Learning Representations (2020)
15. Grover, V.P., Tognarelli, J.M., Crossey, M.M., Cox, I.J., Taylor-Robinson, S.D., McPhail, M.J.: Magnetic resonance imaging: principles and techniques: lessons for clinicians. J. Clin. Exp. Hepatol. 5(3), 246–255 (2015)
16. Hatamizadeh, A., et al.: UNETR: transformers for 3d medical image segmentation. arXiv preprint arXiv:2103.10504 (2021)
17. Hoover, J.M., Morris, J.M., Meyer, F.B.: Use of preoperative magnetic resonance imaging t1 and t2 sequences to determine intraoperative meningioma consistency. Surg. Neurol. Int. 2, 142 (2011)
18. Huo, Y., et al.: 3D whole brain segmentation using spatially localized atlas network tiles. Neuroimage 194, 105–119 (2019)
19. Isensee, F., Jäger, P.F., Full, P.M., Vollmuth, P., Maier-Hein, K.H.: nnU-Net for brain tumor segmentation. In: Crimi, A., Bakas, S. (eds.) BrainLes 2020. LNCS, vol. 12659, pp. 118–132. Springer, Cham (2021). https://doi.org/10.1007/978-3-030-72087-2_11
20. Jiang, Z., Ding, C., Liu, M., Tao, D.: Two-stage cascaded U-Net: 1st place solution to BraTS challenge 2019 segmentation task. In: Crimi, A., Bakas, S. (eds.) BrainLes 2019. LNCS, vol. 11992, pp. 231–241. Springer, Cham (2020). https://doi.org/10.1007/978-3-030-46640-4_22
21. Kamnitsas, K., et al.: Ensembles of multiple models and architectures for robust brain tumour segmentation. In: Crimi, A., Bakas, S., Kuijf, H., Menze, B., Reyes, M. (eds.) BrainLes 2017. LNCS, vol. 10670, pp. 450–462. Springer, Cham (2018). https://doi.org/10.1007/978-3-319-75238-9_38
22. Kamnitsas, K., et al.: Efficient multi-scale 3D CNN with fully connected CRF for accurate brain lesion segmentation. Med. Image Anal. 36, 61–78 (2017)

23. Liu, D., Zhang, H., Zhao, M., Yu, X., Yao, S., Zhou, W.: Brain tumor segmentation based on dilated convolution refine networks. In: 2018 IEEE 16th International Conference on Software Engineering Research, Management and Applications (SERA), pp. 113–120. IEEE (2018)
24. Liu, Z., Lin, Y., Cao, Y., Hu, H., Wei, Y., Zhang, Z., Lin, S., Guo, B.: Swin transformer: Hierarchical vision transformer using shifted windows. In: Proceedings of the IEEE/CVF International Conference on Computer Vision (2021)
25. Liu, Z.,et al.: Video swin transformer. arXiv preprint arXiv:2106.13230 (2021)
26. Long, J., Shelhamer, E., Darrell, T.: Fully convolutional networks for semantic segmentation. In: Proceedings of the IEEE Conference on Computer Vision and Pattern Recognition, pp. 3431–3440 (2015)
27. Louis, D.N., et al.: The 2007 who classification of tumours of the central nervous system. Acta Neuropathol. **114**(2), 97–109 (2007)
28. Menze, B.H., et al.: The multimodal brain tumor image segmentation benchmark (brats). IEEE Trans. Med. Imaging **34**(10), 1993–2024 (2015)
29. Milletari, F., Navab, N., Ahmadi, S.A.: V-net: fully convolutional neural networks for volumetric medical image segmentation. In: 2016 Fourth International Conference on 3D Vision (3DV), pp. 565–571. IEEE (2016)
30. Myronenko, A.: 3D MRI brain tumor segmentation using autoencoder regularization. In: Crimi, A., Bakas, S., Kuijf, H., Keyvan, F., Reyes, M., van Walsum, T. (eds.) BrainLes 2018. LNCS, vol. 11384, pp. 311–320. Springer, Cham (2019). https://doi.org/10.1007/978-3-030-11726-9_28
31. Myronenko, A., Hatamizadeh, A.: Robust semantic segmentation of brain tumor regions from 3D MRIs. In: Crimi, A., Bakas, S. (eds.) BrainLes 2019. LNCS, vol. 11993, pp. 82–89. Springer, Cham (2020). https://doi.org/10.1007/978-3-030-46643-5_8
32. Nie, D., Zhang, H., Adeli, E., Liu, L., Shen, D.: 3D deep learning for multi-modal imaging-guided survival time prediction of brain tumor patients. In: Ourselin, S., Joskowicz, L., Sabuncu, M.R., Unal, G., Wells, W. (eds.) MICCAI 2016. LNCS, vol. 9901, pp. 212–220. Springer, Cham (2016). https://doi.org/10.1007/978-3-319-46723-8_25
33. Raghu, M., Unterthiner, T., Kornblith, S., Zhang, C., Dosovitskiy, A.: Do vision transformers see like convolutional neural networks? Adv. Neural. Inf. Process. Syst. **34**, 12116–12128 (2021)
34. Simpson, A.L., et al.: A large annotated medical image dataset for the development and evaluation of segmentation algorithms. arXiv preprint arXiv:1902.09063 (2019)
35. Tang, Y., et al.: Self-supervised pre-training of swin transformers for 3D medical image analysis. arXiv preprint arXiv:2111.14791 (2021)
36. Ulyanov, D., Vedaldi, A., Lempitsky, V.: Instance normalization: the missing ingredient for fast stylization. arXiv preprint arXiv:1607.08022 (2016)
37. Vaswani, A., et al.: Attention is all you need. In: Advances in Neural Information Processing Systems, pp. 5998–6008 (2017)
38. Wang, W., Chen, C., Ding, M., Yu, H., Zha, S., Li, J.: TransBTS: multimodal brain tumor segmentation using transformer. In: de Bruijne, M., et al. (eds.) MICCAI 2021. LNCS, vol. 12901, pp. 109–119. Springer, Cham (2021). https://doi.org/10.1007/978-3-030-87193-2_11
39. Xie, Y., Zhang, J., Shen, C., Xia, Y.: COTR: efficiently bridging CNN and transformer for 3D medical image segmentation. arXiv preprint arXiv:2103.03024 (2021)
40. Zacharaki, E.I., et al.: Classification of brain tumor type and grade using MRI texture and shape in a machine learning scheme. Magnetic Resonance Med. Off. J. Int. Soc. Magnetic Resonan. Med. **62**(6), 1609–1618 (2009)

41. Zheng, S., et al.: Rethinking semantic segmentation from a sequence-to-sequence perspective with transformers. In: Proceedings of the IEEE/CVF Conference on Computer Vision and Pattern Recognition, pp. 6881–6890 (2021)
42. Zhou, C., Chen, S., Ding, C., Tao, D.: Learning contextual and attentive information for brain tumor segmentation. In: Crimi, A., Bakas, S., Kuijf, H., Keyvan, F., Reyes, M., van Walsum, T. (eds.) BrainLes 2018. LNCS, vol. 11384, pp. 497–507. Springer, Cham (2019). https://doi.org/10.1007/978-3-030-11726-9_44

Multi-plane UNet++ Ensemble for Glioblastoma Segmentation

Johannes Roth[1], Johannes Keller[2], Stefan Franke[2], Thomas Neumuth[2], and Daniel Schneider[2(✉)]

[1] Center for Scalable Data Analytics and Artificial Intelligence (ScaDS.AI), University of Leipzig, Leipzig, Germany
[2] Innovation Center Computer Assisted Surgery (ICCAS), University of Leipzig, Leipzig, Germany
daniel.schneider@uni-leipzig.de

Abstract. Glioblastoma multiforme (grade four glioma, GBM) is the most aggressive malignant tumor in the brain and usually treated by combined surgery, chemo- and radiotherapy. The O-6-methylguanine-DNA methyltransferase (MGMT) promoter methylation status was shown to be predictive of GBM sensitivity to alkylating agent chemotherapy and is a promising marker for personalized treatment. In this paper we propose to use a multi-plane ensemble of UNet++ models for the segmentation of gliomas in MRI scans, using a combination of Dice loss and boundary loss for training. For the prediction of MGMT promoter methylation, we use an ensemble of 3D EfficientNet (one per MRI modality). Both, the UNet++ ensemble and EfficientNet are trained and validated on data provided in the context of the Brain Tumor Segmentation Challenge (BraTS) 2021, containing 2.000 fully annotated glioma samples with four different MRI modalities. We achieve Dice scores of 0.792, 0.835, and 0.906 as well as Hausdorff distances of 16.61, 10.11, and 4.54 for enhancing tumor, tumor core and whole tumor, respectively. For MGMT promoter methylation status prediction, an AUROC of 0.577 is obtained.

Keywords: Medical image segmentation · Ensemble learning · Glioma · MGMT promoter methylation

1 Introduction

Gliomas comprise roughly 80% of all malignant brain tumors [7]. Particularly the grade four glioma, referred to as glioblastoma multiforme (GBM), indicates poor medical prognosis. GBM are usually treated with combined surgery, radiotherapy and chemotherapy. Treatment is often complicated by the strong morphological and histological heterogeneity of gliomas, consisting of distinct regions such as active tumor, cystic and necrotic structures, and edema/invasion. Automated and accurate methods for semantic segmentation of gliomas from multiparametric magnetic resonance imaging (mpMRI) scans are critical to diagnosis and

© The Author(s), under exclusive license to Springer Nature Switzerland AG 2022
A. Crimi and S. Bakas (Eds.): BrainLes 2021, LNCS 12962, pp. 285–294, 2022.
https://doi.org/10.1007/978-3-031-08999-2_23

therapy. In recent years, genomic studies identified molecular glioma subtypes exhibiting correlation to prognosis and treatment response. So it was shown that the O-6-methylguanine-DNA methyltransferase (MGMT) promoter methylation status is predictive of GBM sensitivity to alkylating agent chemotherapy [18]. Molecular genetic markers may lead to more specialized and personalized treatment of glioma patients. The field of radiomics aims to predict similar disease characteristics via automated feature extraction from medical images.

In the context of the brain tumor segmentation challenge (BraTS), a large-scale mpMRI dataset of patients with glioma is provided annually to evaluate state-of-the-art methods for automatic tumor segmentation and classification [1–4, 13]. Specifically, the challenge consists of two tasks - the accurate segmentation of gliomas into the three subregions enhancing tumor, tumor core and whole tumor and the prediction of the MGMT promoter methylation marker from mpMRI scans.

In this paper, we present image processing pipelines for both the segmentation and classification task. For segmentation, we propose a multi-plane UNet++ [19] ensemble with a combination of Dice and boundary loss for accurate tumor border prediction. Fully convolutional networks such as UNet [14] are the current method of choice for medical image segmentation. Their hierarchical encoder-decoder structure captures spatial context in the input images and produces high resolution segmentation masks. The UNet++ considered in this work uses nested dense skip pathways instead of the vanilla skip connections, increasing semantic similarity between the encoder and decoder feature maps. Aggregating the output of ensembles of deep neural networks is a common technique shown to increase performance in various prediction tasks [8]. For classification, we use a 3D EfficientNet [16] ensemble consisting of four models - one per MRI modality. The EfficientNet architecture enables the training of lightweight classification models without loss in performance compared to larger models such as ResNet [9].

The work at hand is structured as follows: Sect. 2 describes the dataset used for training and validation, as well as the details of our model ensembles and training procedures. In Sect. 3 we present the preliminary results of our methods on the provided test datasets. Ultimately, in Sect. 4 we draw conclusions and provide ideas for future research.

2 Methods

2.1 Data

The data used for training and validation of the models presented in this paper is provided by the BraTS Challenge 2021 [1]. The data for the segmentation task contains 2.000 GBM cases, each providing four MRI modalities - T1-weighted (T1), post gadolinium T1-weighted (T1-Gd), T2-weighted (T2) and T2-weighted-fluid-attenuated inversion recovery (T2-FLAIR) (see Fig. 1 for example slices).

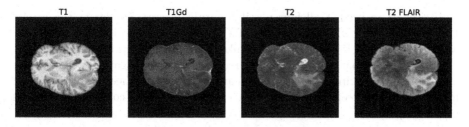

Fig. 1. Example scans of the four MRI modalities T1, T1-Gd, T2 and T2-FLAIR (from left to right) provided by the BRATS data.

The image data was preprocessed by co-registration to the same anatomical template, skull stripping and interpolation to a resolution of $1\,mm^3$. Each GBM sample was manually annotated by up to four raters. The annotations include the Gd-enhancing tumor (ET), the peritumoral edematous/invaded tissue (ED), and the necrotic tumor core (NCR). The union of ET and NCR is called tumor core (TC). Last, the whole tumor (WT) is comprised of the TC and ED regions. The classification task provides largely the same cases and the corresponding MGMT promoter methylation information, but without any preprocessing or information about the location of the tumor.

2.2 Brain Glioblastoma Segmentation

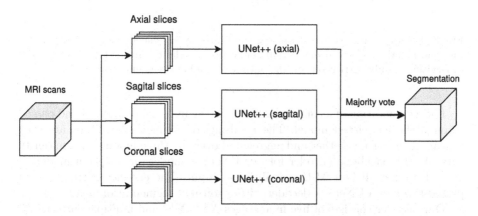

Fig. 2. Overview of the proposed segmentation pipeline. Each mpMRI scan is sliced to create axial, sagital and coronal 2D images. All four modalities are concatenated and passed through the respective UNet++ model, producing a segmentation for each slice. The resulting segmentation maps are then concatenated back into cubes, which are then aggregated by a majority vote.

An overview of our segmentation pipeline is shown in Fig. 2. We trained an individual UNet++ [19] on 2D MRI slices in each anatomical plane (axial, sagital, and coronal) to predict all four possible output classes. Similar to the vanilla UNet architecture, UNet++ consists of a pathway through hierarchical encoder and decoder subsections additionally linked by skip connections to retain information at higher spatial resolutions. To reduce the semantic gap between encoder and decoder, the skipping feature maps are gradually enriched by incorporating information from deeper layers through a number of nested convolutional blocks (see Fig. 3).

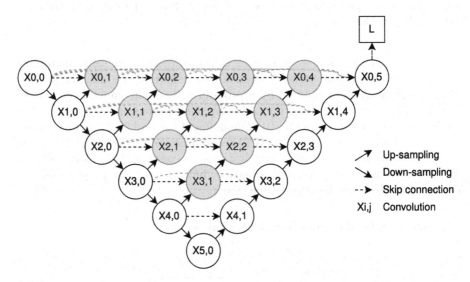

Fig. 3. UNet++ architecture, featuring the typical UNet encoder and decoder pathway and a series of nested dense skip connections, adapted from [19]. In this work, supervision is only carried out on the output of the final segmentation head.

For segmentation of a complete MRI scan, the image data is sliced and passed through the associated model. The resulting 2D segmentation maps are then concatenated back together and aggregated over the three models by a majority vote. As the backbone encoder for our UNet++ models, a Xception model [5] is used, taking all four MRI modalities as input. The encoder output is then passed through a UNet++ decoder with a softmax segmentation head.

Our decoder consists of five final stages $X^{4,1}$–$X^{0,5}$ and multiple corresponding intermediate stages. Each stage consists of two convolutional blocks, made up by a convolutional layer with kernel size 3, followed by a batch normalization layer and a ReLU activation. The number of feature maps of the convolutional layers in each stage $j \in \mathbb{N}_{[1,5]}$ is 2^{j+3}, i.e. 16, 32, 64, 128, and 256, respectively. For a forward pass through $X^{i,j}$, the logits of $X^{i+1,j-1}$, upsampled via nearest neighbour interpolation when necessary and concatenated with the logits of intermediate $X^{i,k}, k \in \mathbb{N}_{[0,j)}$, are used as input. Segmentation masks are obtained by passing the logits of $X^{0,5}$ through a softmax layer.

The model was trained to minimize the following loss function;

$$L = (1 - \alpha)L_{Dice} + \alpha L_{Boundary},$$

where L_{Dice} is the dice loss, $L_{Boundary}$ refers to the boundary loss [11], and α is a weight parameter. The binary dice loss is defined as

$$L_{Dice} = 1 - \frac{2 \sum_{i \in X} y_i p_i}{\sum_{i \in X}(y_i + p_i)},$$

where i refers to the index over pixels provided X is the set of all pixels in a slice, while y_i and p_i indicate the corresponding true class label and the predicted class softmax output, respectively. The boundary loss is used to improve segmentation accuracy at the periphery of the different tumor regions. For binary class segmentation it is defined as

$$L_{Boundary} = \sum_{i \in X} p_i f_S(i)$$

with $f_S(i) : X \rightarrow \mathbb{R}$ being a pre-computed level set function encoding the Euclidean distance of i to the boundary of the compact region S of the positive target class. Equation (2.2) becomes minimal, when the boundaries of the ground truth and prediction region are aligned (for more details, see [11]). To obtain the total multi-class loss, as necessary for the segmentation task, we use the macro average of the losses for each tumor class in a one-versus-all manner. We slowly shift the total loss towards the boundary loss by initializing α with 0.01 and then linearly increasing by $\Delta\alpha = 0.01$ each epoch. During preprocessing, we resized every slice to 256×256 pixels and used random image transformations such as flipping, rotations, as well as Gaussian or Poisson noise (with $\mu = 0, \sigma = 0.2$ for both) in order to mitigate overfitting. We trained our models using the Adam optimizer [12] with a learning rate of $1e - 4$ and betas $(0.9, 0.999)$ for 50 epochs, using a batch size of 16. During training, the learning rate is reduced by a factor of 0.1 whenever the validation loss stopped decreasing for more than two epochs. For this purpose, a hold out validation set comprising 20% of the available training data was used. Ultimately, the model with the best validation score was used for inference.

2.3   Prediction of MGMT Promoter Methylation Status

For the prediction of the MGMT promoter methylation marker a classifier ensemble was used (see Fig. 4 for a schematic representation of the pipeline).

Since for this task the mpMRI data was not co-registered, we used each modality independently to train a corresponding 3D EfficientNet [16]. The models architecture followed the 2D EfficientNet-B0 architecture with a width and depth coefficient of 1.0 and a dropout probability of 0.2, but with 3D convolutions to enable processing of complete MRI scans (see Table 1).

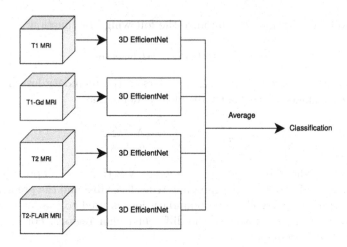

Fig. 4. Overview of the proposed classification pipeline. Each MRI modality scan is passed into a 3D EfficientNet and scores are averaged to obtain the final class prediction.

Table 1. EfficientNet-B0 architecture: Information flows through successive convolutional stages in a feed-forward manner (increasing the level of feature abstraction while reducing spatial resolution), then is aggregated via 1×1 convolution and pooling, and finally processed by a fully connected classifier. Each row describes a stage in the network with the number of layers and output channels. MBConv refers to the mobile inverted bottleneck block from [15]).

Stage	Operator	#Channels	#Layers
1	Conv, 3×3	32	1
2	MBConv1, 3×3	16	1
3	MBConv6, 3×3	24	2
4	MBConv6, 5×5	40	2
5	MBConv6, 3×3	80	3
6	MBConv6, 5×5	112	3
7	MBConv6, 5×5	192	4
8	MBConv6, 3×3	320	1
9	Conv, 1×1 & Pooling & FC	1280	1

For inference, we averaged over the class scores of all trained models. The models are optimized using binary cross entropy loss

$$L_{BCE} = -\frac{1}{N} \sum_{i=1}^{N} \left[y_i \cdot \log(p) + (1 - y_i) \cdot \log(1 - p) \right],$$

where $y_i \in \{0, 1\}$ denotes the class label of sample i and p_i refers to the predicted output probability of the positive class. To obtain those class pseudo-probabilities, we used a sigmoid on the model logits. Similarly to the segmentation task, the models were trained using Adam optimizer with a learning rate of

0.001 and betas $(0.9, 0.999)$ for 10 epochs. During training, 20% of the available data was held out for validation. For data augmentation, random rotations were applied to the MRI scan volumes.

3   Results

The final leaderboard evaluation was carried out with a hidden test set provided by the BraTS 2021 challenge. Using the UNet++ ensemble for glioma segmentation we achieved average dice scores of 0.792, 0.835 and 0.906 and average

Table 2. Preliminary evaluation scores for the UNet++ ensemble for enhancing tumor (ET), tumor core (TC) and whole tumor (WT). The scores were computed on a hidden test set provided by the BraTS 2021 challenge.

Metric	ET	TC	WT
Dice	0.79185	0.83494	0.90638
95% Hausdorff distance	16.60631	10.11467	4.53913
Sensitivity	0.79693	0.80568	0.88333
Specificity	0.99975	0.99984	0.99948

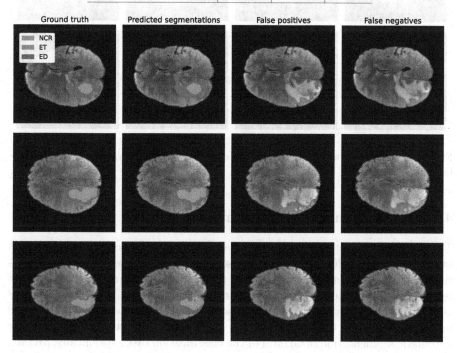

Fig. 5. Glioma segmentation example slices obtained using the UNet++ ensemble. The columns from left to right show the ground truth segmentations, predicted segmentations, as well as the false positive and the false negative regions for Gd-enhancing tumor (ET, blue), the peritumoral edematous/invaded tissue (ED, green), and the necrotic tumor core (NCR, yellow). (Color figure online)

95%-Hausdorff distances of 16.606, 10.115 and 4.549 for enhancing tumor, tumor core and whole tumor, respectively. Table 2 shows all evaluation scores, averaged over all samples in the hidden test set. Figure 5 features a few example annotated MRI slices for qualitative assessment, while Fig. 6 shows exemplary prediction failures. The MGMT promoter methylation classification model achieved an AUROC score of 0.577 on the hidden test set.

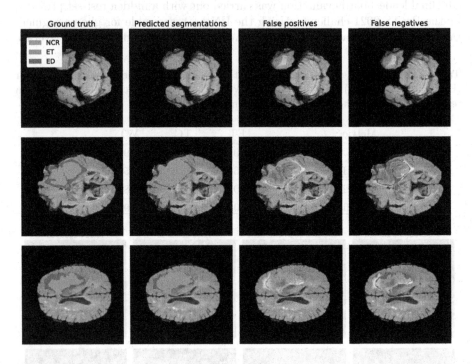

Fig. 6. Examples of low accuracy predictions during segmentation obtained using the UNet++ ensemble.

4   Discussion and Conclusion

This work presented our solutions to the tumor segmentation and classification tasks of the BraTS 2021 challenge. For segmentation, we used an ensemble consisting of three UNet++ models - one per anatomical plane - for the task of segmenting GBM and their subregions in the human brain. The combination of ensemble majority voting and training with boundary loss achieved fairly good performance on the test data and thus turned out to be a valid approach for automatic segmentation of GBM. For the classification task - specifically, MGMT promoter methylation marker prediction - we chose to omit any preprocessing or feature extraction. Instead we use an ensemble of 3D EfficientNets on the raw MRI image series - one EfficientNet per MRI modality. Here, our approach resulted in acceptable results.

Various means of improving the performance of our methods in both BraTS tasks exist. The segmentation ensemble used could be expanded or its models replaced with other FCN architectures, potentially including techniques such as feature map competition or attention mechanisms. Deep supervision may be used with the UNet++ models. Additionally, we plan to use boundary refinement with a post-processing pipeline similar to BPR [17]. The observed segmentation failures may suggest decreased performance for outlier cases. Here, advanced techniques to improve generalization such as adversial learning schemes may be beneficial. For our approach to the classification task, segmentation of the tumor regions and cropping during preprocessing is planned in future work. Also registration of the mpMRI modalities and subsequent use of multichannel input to the EfficentNet might be of benefit. Most importantly, virtually no hyperparameter tuning was conducted in this work and would potentially promote the performance of both segmentation and classification task.

For adoption in clinical practice, automated methods should be able to provide realistic estimates of their (un)certainty. While this work focuses on point estimation, the presented methods may be further extended by recent techniques for epistemic uncertainty estimation such as hypermodels [6] or ensemble knowledge distillation [10] as well as uncertainty calibration methods.

Acknowledgements. Computations for this work were done (in part) using resources of the Leipzig University Computing Centre. This work was funded by the German Federal Ministry of Education and Research (BMBF) grant number 1IS18026B (Johannes Roth - ScaDS.AI Dresden/Leipzig) and 03Z1L512 (Johannes Keller, Stefan Franke, and Daniel Schneider - ICCAS).

References

1. Baid, U., et al.: The RSNA-ASNR-MICCAI BraTS 2021 benchmark on brain tumor segmentation and radiogenomic classification. CoRR abs/2107.02314. arXiv: 2107.02314 (2021). http://arxiv.org/abs/2107.02314
2. Bakas, S., et al.: Advancing the cancer genome atlas glioma MRI collections with expert segmentation labels and radiomic features. Sci. Data **41** (2017). https://doi.org/10.1038/sdata.2017.117
3. Bakas, S., et al.: Segmentation Labels for the Pre-operative Scans of the TCGA-GBM collection (2017). https://doi.org/10.7937/K9/TCIA.2017.KLXWJJ1Q. https://wiki.cancerimagingarchive.net/x/KoZyAQ
4. Bakas, S., et al.: Segmentation Labels for the Pre-operative Scans of the TCGA-LGG collection (2017). https://doi.org/10.7937/K9/TCIA.2017. GJQ7R0EF. https://wiki.cancerimagingarchive.net/x/LIZyAQ
5. Chollet, F.: Xception: deep learning with depthwise separable convolutions. CoRR abs/1610.02357 (2016). arXiv: 1610.02357. http://arxiv.org/abs/1610.02357
6. Dwaracherla, V., et al.: Hypermodels for Exploration. 2020. eprint. arXiv:2006.07464
7. Goodenberger, M.L., Jenkins. R.B.: Genetics of adult glioma. Can. Gen. **205**(12), 613–621 (2012). https://doi.org/10.1016/j.cancergen.2012.10.009
8. Hansen, L.K., Salamon, P.: Neural network ensembles. IEEE Trans. Pattern Anal. Mach. Intell. **12**(10), 993–1001 (1990). https://doi.org/10.1109/34.58871

9. He, K., et al.: Deep Residual Learning for Image Recognition. CoRR abs/1512.03385 (2015). arXiv: 1512.03385 (2015). http://arxiv.org/abs/1512.03385
10. Hinton, G., Vinyals, O., Dean, J.: Distilling the knowledge in a neural network. eprint: arXiv:1503.02531 (2015)
11. Kervadec, H., et al.: Boundary loss for highly unbalanced segmentation. Med. Image Anal. **67**, 101851 (2021). https://doi.org/10.1016/j.media.2020.101851. ISSN: 1361-8415
12. Kingma, D.P., Ba, J.: Adam: a method for stochastic optimization. arXiv: 1412.6980 [cs.LG] (2017)
13. Menze, B.H., et al.: The multimodal brain tumor image segmentation benchmark (BRATS). IEEE Trans. Med. Imaging **34**(10), 1993–2024 (2015). https://doi.org/10.1109/tmi.2014.2377694
14. Ronneberger, O., Fischer, P., Brox, T.: U-Net: convolutional networks for biomedical image segmentation. CoRR abs/1505.04597. arXiv: 1505.04597 (2015).http://arxiv.org/abs/1505.04597
15. Sandler, M., et al.: Inverted residuals and linear bottlenecks: mobile networks for classification, detection and segmentation. CoRR abs/1801.04381, arXiv: 1801.04381 (2018). http://arxiv.org/abs/1801.04381
16. Tan, M., Le, Q.V.: EfficientNet: rethinking model scaling for convolutional neural networks. CoRR abs/1905.11946. arXiv: 1905.11946 (2019). http://arxiv.org/abs/1905.11946
17. Tang, C., et al.: Look closer to segment better: boundary patch refinement for instance segmentation. arXiv preprint arXiv:2104.05239 (2021)
18. Weller, M., et al.: MGMT promoter methylation in malignant gliomas: ready for personalized medicine? Nat. Rev. Neurol. **6**(1), 39–51 (2009). https://doi.org/10.1038/nrneurol.2009.197
19. Zhou, Z., et al.: UNet++: a nested U-Net architecture for medical image segmentation. CoRR abs/1807.10165. arXiv: 1807.10165 (2018). http://arxiv.org/abs/1807.10165

Multimodal Brain Tumor Segmentation Using Modified UNet Architecture

Gaurav Singh and Ashish Phophalia[✉]

Indian Institute of Information Technology Vadodara,
Gandhinagar, Gujarat 382028, India
{201851044,ashish_p}@iiitvadodara.ac.in

Abstract. Segmentation of brain tumor is challenging due presence of
healthy or background region more compared to tumor regions and also
the tumor region itself divided in edema, tumor core and non enhancing regions makes it hard to segment. Given the scarcity of such data, it
becomes more challenging. In this paper, we built a 3D-UNet based architecture for multimodal brain tumor segmentation task. We have reported
results on BraTS 2021 Validation and Test Dataset. We achieved a Dice
value of 0.87, 0.76 and 0.73 on whole tumor region, tumor core region and
enhancing part respectively for Validation Data and 0.73, 0.67 and 0.63
on whole tumor region, tumor core region and enhancing part respectively for Test Data.

Keywords: Convolutional Neural Network · Unet · Brain Tumor ·
Segmentation · Magnetic Resonance Imaging

1 Introduction

Gliomas is a very common type of tumor develops in the brain. In the brain
tumors about 33% contains gliomas, originates from glial cells that covers and
support neurons in the brain. It is being classified as either High Grade Gliomas
(HGG) or Low Grade Gliomas (LGG). High Grade Gliomas is more aggressive
growth leading to death. The tumor region itself comprises of sub-regions of Gd-
enhancing tumor, the peritumoral edematous/invaded tissue, and the necrotic
tumor core.

The automated method must have sense of depiction of tumor region and
differentiate it from healthy tissue regions. However, due to high variance in
tumor regions in terms intensity, texture, appearance, location, etc. one need to
be careful while doing segmentation with incorporating these challenges [1,2].

Clinically, multiple image volumes are being acquired for the brain. Each
image is corresponds to a sequence. In general, there is a 4 image sequence is
obtained T1, T1-contrast enhanced, T2, FLAIR because certain components of
tumor regions are clearly visible in certain image sequences.

The tumor constitutes of Edema which constitutes of fluid and water, can
be best seen in FLAIR, T2 modality. Necrosis (NCR) which is accumulation

© The Author(s), under exclusive license to Springer Nature Switzerland AG 2022
A. Crimi and S. Bakas (Eds.): BrainLes 2021, LNCS 12962, pp. 295–305, 2022.
https://doi.org/10.1007/978-3-031-08999-2_24

of dead cells this can be best seen T1 contrast enhanced. Enhancing Tumor indicated breakdown of blood brain barriers which can seen clearly T1ce. There are different modality of brain scans with varies in different intensity.

The MICCAI BraTS Challenge have seen many methods in recent years and it aims to give accurate segmentation of tumors [3]. UNet [4] based architecture has been used as one of the successful architecture with having accurate results for tumor segmentation. The best performing methods have used UNets (an encoder-decoder framework) as their segmentation achitecture [5–9]. Some methods tried to levearge advantage of 3D and 2D based architecture through triplanar ensembles of CNNs [10].

In this paper, we have built a 3D-Unet [4] based model for brain tumor segmentation task by leveraging more contextual information while decoding via bottleneck layer at each encoder's block output.

2   Methods

2.1   Data Pre-processing and Augmentation

In this work, original size for every patient's MRI images was $240 \times 240 \times 155$ with 4 modality (Flair, T1, T1Gd, T2). We have removed some background pixel from each dimension of MRI image and reduced it to size of $160 \times 192 \times 128$ to have portion around its center, considering that only brain tissue will be extracted. The intensity normalization step is applied to each modality while keeping background as 0. We extracted random patch of patch size of $128 \times 128 \times 128$ from every patient's MRI images after combining each modality as channel [11].

From the work of [12], we used elastic deformation with square deformation grid with displacements sampled from a normal distribution with standard deviation 2 voxels with probability being 0.75.

2.2   Model Architecture

UNet [4] is being one of the successful model in medical domain in terms of architecture. It does image segmentation based on pixels produced by convolutions layers of the neural network.

In this work, we have built a 3D-UNet based architecture having residual connections [13] in it and have some modification on Vox2Vox's Generator [11]. It does by concatenating previous block output with current block output in bottleneck layer (forces model to only contain the useful information to be able to reconstruct the segmentation map) and have passed each encoder output (Downward) through one another Conv Block (Horizontal1) as can be seen in Fig. 1. This helps to refine the encoder each block's output to produce more accurate segmentation.

Our model takes input of 3D volume having channels as Flair, T1, T1ce, T2 makes it size of $128 \times 128 \times 128 \times 4$. It outputs the same size of input having predicted segmentation, where each channel corresponds to one of the labels(NCR, ED, ET, everything else).

Our model consists of following blocks:

Downward: four down sampling block, each followed by Conv3D with kernel size $4 \times 4 \times 4$, strides 2 after that Instance Norm is applied and LeakyReLU with negative slope is 0.3.

Horziontal1: four horizontal block, each followed by Conv3D with kernel size $4 \times 4 \times 4$, strides 1 and padding same after that Instance Norm is applied and LeakyReLU with negative slope is 0.3.

Horziontal2: three horizontal block, each followed by Conv3D with kernel size $4 \times 4 \times 4$, strides 1 and padding same after that Instance Norm is applied, dropout with 0.2 is added and LeakyReLU with negative slope is 0.3. Each of its input in this block is concatenation of current input and its previous output from horizontal layer.

Upward1: three upward block, each followed by ConvTranspose3D with kernel size $4 \times 4 \times 4$, strides 2 after that Instance Norm is applied, and LeakyReLU with negative slope is 0.3. Each of them is concatented to corresponding 'Horizontal2' block layer.

Upward2: one output block followed by ConvTranspose3D with kernel size $4 \times 4 \times 4$, strides 2 after that Instance Norm is applied, and Softmax.

2.3 Training

For brain tumor segmentation, we have trained the network for 25 epochs. We used Adam optimizer (combines adaptive learning rate and gradient descent with momentum property) for our network with the learning rate being 0.00005, $\beta_1 = 0.9$ and $\beta_2 = 0.999$.

For the loss, we used Generalized Dice loss [14] which helps to deal with the class imbalanced situation that always occurs in brain tumor segmentation task where background region dominating over tumor regions, this loss helps us to comes out from this situation by penalizing less to network with the majority class with lower weight and penalizing high for minority classes with high weights. The weights of each class is given by the inverse of its volume. All the experiments are being conducted on Google Colab Pro using an 16 GB NVIDIA P100 GPU with 13.6 GB RAM.

The entire network is being trained from scratch and do not use other training data other than BraTS 2021 Dataset [3, 15–18]. It took around 48 hrs to completely train the network. We trained with batch size of 8 and validated with batch size of 4. For the training purpose, we randomly split BraTS training dataset into two parts 85% for training set and 15% for evaluation set for our own experiments to validate model performance.

During Inference time, we can take $160 \times 192 \times 128$ patch size from each modality after removing some background pixels from each dimension and mostly around its center portion because convolution operation is being not affected having different size of input in this case and then applied intensity normalization. Then it passes input through the network and get the predicted segmentation of

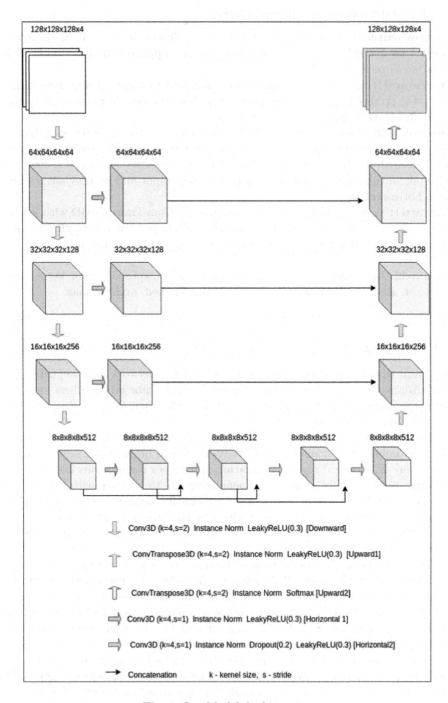

Fig. 1. Our Model Architecture

the same size of input ($160 \times 192 \times 128 \times 4$) and then we padded it zero so that it can have size of $240 \times 240 \times 155$.

3 Results

3.1 Dataset

We have used BraTS 2021 dataset in this work. Each patient has 4 modalities, namely, i) T1 and ii) contrast-enhanced T1-weighted (T1-Gd), iii) T2, and iv) Fluid Attenuated Inversion Recovery (FLAIR), and associated ground truth label, each of size $240 \times 240 \times 155$.

The sub-regions are: i) the "Enhancing Tumor" (ET), ii) the "Necrotic Tumor Core" (TC), and iii) the "Whole Tumor" (WT). The segmented class labels are: 1 for NCR, 2 for ED (Edema), 4 for ET, and 0 for everything else. All input scans are rigidly registered to the same anatomical atlas using the Greedy diffeomorphic registration algorithm [19], ensuring a common spatial resolution of ($1 \, mm^3$). We have 1251 samples in training set, 219 samples in validation set and 570 samples in testing set for our experiment [3,15–18].

3.2 Performance Analysis

We have reported results based on below metric as provided by BraTS Challenge:

$$(i) \; Dice \; Score = \frac{2TP}{FN + FP + 2TP},$$

$$(ii) \; Sensitivity = \frac{TP}{FN + TP},$$

$$(iii) \; Specificity = \frac{TN}{FP + TN},$$

and (iv) 95th percentile of Hausdorff Distance (H95)

where FP, FN, TP, and TN are number of false positive, false negative, true positive and true negative voxels respectively.

Figure 2 shows comparison of Ground Truth Segmentation (Top) and Predcited Segmentation from our model (Bottom) on specific slice of MRI Image. Figure 3 shows Predicted Segmentation from our model. Figure 4 shows Box Plot of Dice Coefficient score on each tumor regions. Figure 5 shows histogram of whole tumor region on BraTS Validation Data. Figure 6 shows Robust Hausdorff Distance on BraTS Validation Data. Figure 7 shows histogram Sensitivity on BraTS Validation Data. Figure 8 shows Specificity on BraTS Validation Data.

The mean value of Dice coefficient score for whole tumor, tumor core and enhance tumor regions are 0.87, 0.76 and 0.73 respectively as can be seen in Table 1 on Validation Data. Sensitivity and Specificity of each tumor region for Validation Data shows respectively in Table 2. The mean value of Dice coefficient score for whole tumor, tumor core and enhance tumor regions are 0.73, 0.67 and 0.63 respectively as can be seen in Table 3 on Test Data. Sensitivity and Specificity of each tumor region for Test Data shows respectively in Table 4.

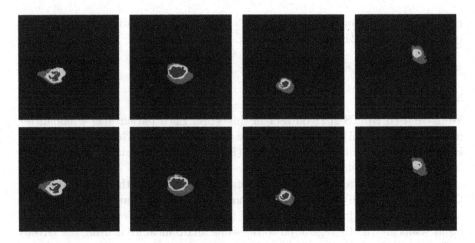

Fig. 2. Ground Truth segmentation (Top) and Predicted segmentation (Bottom) Left-to-Right: BraTS2021_00000 patient ID on slice 80 BraTS2021_00003 patient ID on slice 100, BraTS2021_00045 patient ID on slice 50, BraTS2021_00046 patient ID on slice 100.

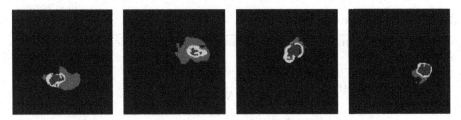

Fig. 3. Predicted segmentation on BraTS 2021 Validation Dataset Left-to-Right: BraTS2021_00001 patient ID on slice 70 BraTS2021_00013 patient ID on slice 70, BraTS2021_00015 patient ID on slice 90, BraTS2021_00027 patient ID on slice 80.

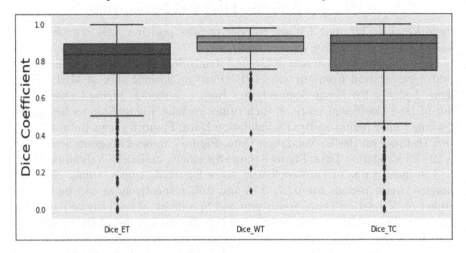

Fig. 4. The dice coefficient on BraTS 2021 validation data.

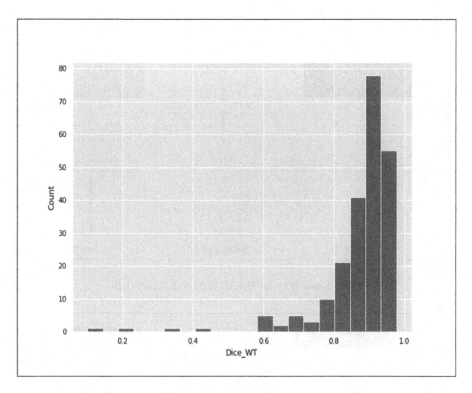

Fig. 5. The performance graph of dice coefficient on whole tumor region on BraTS 2021 validation data.

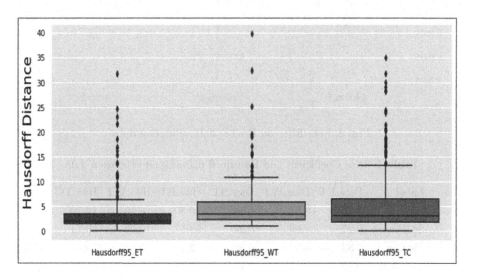

Fig. 6. Hausdorff distance on BraTS 2021 validation data.

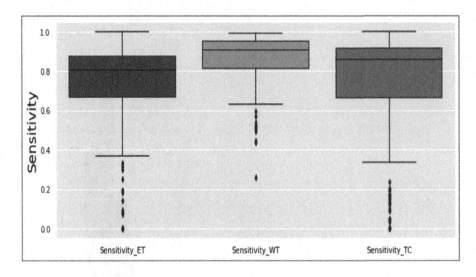

Fig. 7. Sensitivity on BraTS 2021 validation data.

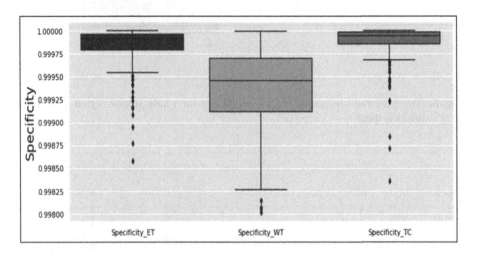

Fig. 8. Specificity on BraTS 2021 validation data.

Table 1. Dice Coefficient and Hausdorff distance on validation data

Label	Dice_ET	Dice_WT	Dice_TC	H95_ET	H95_WT	H95_TC
Mean	0.73	0.87	0.76	30.50	6.29	14.70
StdDev	0.27	0.09	0.28	93.57	10.29	50.74
Median	0.83	0.90	0.89	2.23	3.31	3.16
25quantile	0.73	0.85	0.74	1.41	2.23	1.73
75quantile	0.89	0.93	0.93	5.0	6.0	8.77

Table 2. Sensitivity and specificity on validation data

Label	Sens_ET	Sens_WT	Sens_TC	Spec_ET	Spec_WT	Spec_TC
Mean	0.70	0.86	0.72	0.99	0.99	0.99
StdDev	0.26	0.12	0.28	0.0003	0.0008	0.0003
Median	0.80	0.90	0.85	0.99	0.99	0.99
25quantile	0.66	0.81	0.65	0.99	0.99	0.99
75quantile	0.87	0.95	0.91	0.99	0.99	0.99

Table 3. Dice Coefficient and Hausdorff distance on test data

Label	Dice_ET	Dice_WT	Dice_TC	H95_ET	H95_WT	H95_TC
Mean	0.65	0.73	0.69	72.69	63.26	72.79
StdDev	0.34	0.33	0.37	143.42	132.37	141.81
Median	0.83	0.88	0.89	2.23	4.30	3.60
25quantile	0.58	0.75	0.61	1.41	2.44	1.73
75quantile	0.90	0.92	0.94	11.07	12.24	16.79

Table 4. Sensitivity and Specificity on Test Data

Label	Sens_ET	Sens_WT	Sens_TC	Spec_ET	Spec_WT	Spec_TC
Mean	0.63	0.71	0.67	0.84	0.84	0.84
StdDev	0.34	0.33	0.36	0.35	0.35	0.35
Median	0.80	0.87	0.86	0.99	0.99	0.99
25quantile	0.52	0.68	0.52	0.99	0.99	0.99
75quantile	0.88	0.93	0.92	0.99	0.99	0.99

4   Discussion

In this paper, we have built a 3D-UNet based architecture which allows more contextual information to produce segmentation map for multimodal brain tumor segmentation task. Our model achieves mean value of Dice coefficient for whole tumor, tumor core and enhance part are 0.87, 0.76 and 0.73 respectively on validation set and 0.73, 0.67 and 0.63 respectively on test set.

For further work, we can do ensemble on different set of dataset and can achieve better results, and also post processing can be applied to remove smaller volume class labels to decrease false positives.

References

1. Despotović, I., Goossens, B., Philips, W.: MRI segmentation of the human brain: challenges, methods, and applications. In: Computational and Mathematical Methods in Medicine, vol. 2015 (2015)
2. Gordillo, N., Montseny, E., Sobrevilla, P.: State of the art survey on MRI brain tumor segmentation. Magn. Reson. Imaging **31**(8), 1426–1438 (2013)
3. Baid, U., et al.: The RSNA-ASNR-MICCAI brats 2021 benchmark on brain tumor segmentation and radiogenomic classification (2021)
4. Ronneberger, O., Fischer, P., Brox, T.: U-Net: convolutional networks for biomedical image segmentation. In: Navab, N., Hornegger, J., Wells, W.M., Frangi, A.F. (eds.) MICCAI 2015. LNCS, vol. 9351, pp. 234–241. Springer, Cham (2015). https://doi.org/10.1007/978-3-319-24574-4_28
5. Isensee, F., Jäger, P.F., Full, P.M., Vollmuth, P., Maier-Hein, K.H.: nnU-Net for brain tumor segmentation. In: Crimi, A., Bakas, S. (eds.) BrainLes 2020. LNCS, vol. 12659, pp. 118–132. Springer, Cham (2021). https://doi.org/10.1007/978-3-030-72087-2_11
6. Jiang, Z., Ding, C., Liu, M., Tao, D.: Two-stage cascaded U-Net: 1st place solution to BraTS challenge 2019 segmentation task. In: Crimi, A., Bakas, S. (eds.) BrainLes 2019. LNCS, vol. 11992, pp. 231–241. Springer, Cham (2020). https://doi.org/10.1007/978-3-030-46640-4_22
7. Isensee, F., Kickingereder, P., Wick, W., Bendszus, M., Maier-Hein, K.H.: No new-net. In: Crimi, A., Bakas, S., Kuijf, H., Keyvan, F., Reyes, M., van Walsum, T. (eds.) BrainLes 2018. LNCS, vol. 11384, pp. 234–244. Springer, Cham (2019). https://doi.org/10.1007/978-3-030-11726-9_21
8. Kim, G.: Brain tumor segmentation using deep fully convolutional neural networks. In: Crimi, A., Bakas, S., Kuijf, H., Menze, B., Reyes, M. (eds.) BrainLes 2017. LNCS, vol. 10670, pp. 344–357. Springer, Cham (2018). https://doi.org/10.1007/978-3-319-75238-9_30
9. Isensee, F., Kickingereder, P., Wick, W., Bendszus, M., Maier-Hein, K.H.: Brain tumor segmentation and radiomics survival prediction: contribution to the BRATS 2017 challenge. In: Crimi, A., Bakas, S., Kuijf, H., Menze, B., Reyes, M. (eds.) BrainLes 2017. LNCS, vol. 10670, pp. 287–297. Springer, Cham (2018). https://doi.org/10.1007/978-3-319-75238-9_25
10. McKinley, R., Rebsamen, M., Meier, R., Wiest, R.: Triplanar ensemble of 3D-to-2D CNNs with label-uncertainty for brain tumor segmentation. In: Crimi, A., Bakas, S. (eds.) BrainLes 2019. LNCS, vol. 11992, pp. 379–387. Springer, Cham (2020). https://doi.org/10.1007/978-3-030-46640-4_36
11. Cirillo, M.D., Abramian, D., Eklund, A.: Vox2Vox: 3D-GAN for brain tumour segmentation. In: Crimi, A., Bakas, S. (eds.) BrainLes 2020. LNCS, vol. 12658, pp. 274–284. Springer, Cham (2021). https://doi.org/10.1007/978-3-030-72084-1_25
12. Cirillo, M.D., Abramian, D., Eklund, A.: What is the best data augmentation for 3D brain tumor segmentation? (2021)
13. He, K., Zhang, X., Ren, S., Sun, J.: Deep residual learning for image recognition (2015)
14. Sudre, C.H., Li, W., Vercauteren, T., Ourselin, S., Jorge Cardoso, M.: Generalised dice overlap as a deep learning loss function for highly unbalanced segmentations. In: Cardoso, M.J., et al. (eds.) DLMIA/ML-CDS -2017. LNCS, vol. 10553, pp. 240–248. Springer, Cham (2017). https://doi.org/10.1007/978-3-319-67558-9_28

15. Bakas, S., et al.: Segmentation labels for the pre-operative scans of the TCGA-LGG collection (2017)
16. Bakas, S., et al.: Segmentation labels for the pre-operative scans of the TCGA-GBM collection (2017)
17. Bakas, S., et al.: Advancing the cancer genome atlas glioma MRI collections with expert segmentation labels and radiomic features. Sci. Data **4**, 1–13 (2017)
18. Menze, B.H., et al.: The multimodal brain tumor image segmentation benchmark (BRATS). IEEE Trans. Med. Imaging **34**, 1993–2024 (2015)
19. Yushkevich, P.A., Pluta, J., Wang, H., Wisse, L.E., Das, S., Wolk, D.: Fast automatic segmentation of hippocampal subfields and medial temporal lobe subregions in 3 tesla and 7 tesla t2-weighted MRI. Alzheimer's Dementia **7**(12), P126–P127 (2016)

A Video Data Based Transfer Learning Approach for Classification of MGMT Status in Brain Tumor MR Images

D. M. Lang[1,2,3](✉) ⓘ, J. C. Peeken[1,2,4] ⓘ, S. E. Combs[1,2,4] ⓘ,
J. J. Wilkens[2,3] ⓘ, and S. Bartzsch[1,2] ⓘ

[1] Institute of Radiation Medicine, Helmholtz Zentrum München, Munich, Germany
[2] Department of Radiation Oncology,
School of Medicine and Klinikum rechts der Isar,
Technical University of Munich (TUM), Munich, Germany
daniel.lang@tum.de
[3] Physics Department, Technical University of Munich, Garching, Germany
[4] Deutsches Konsortium für Translationale Krebsforschung (DKTK),
Partner Site Munich, Munich, Germany

Abstract. Patient MGMT (O^6 methylguanine DNA methyltransferase) status has been identified essential for the responsiveness to chemotherapy in glioblastoma patients and therefore depicts an important clinical factor. Testing for MGMT methylation is invasive, time consuming and costly and lacks a uniform gold standard. We studied MGMT status assessment by multi-parametric magnetic resonance imaging (mpMRI) scans and tested the ability of deep learning for classification of this task. To overcome the limited number of training examples we used a transfer learning approach based on the video clip classification network C3D [30], allowing for full exploitation of three dimensional information in the MR images. MRI sequences were fused using a locally connected layer. Our approach was able to differentiate MGMT methylated from unmethylated patients with an area under the receiver operating characteristics curve (AUC) of 0.689 for the public validation set. On the private test set AUC was given by 0.577. Further studies for assessment of clinical importance and predictive power in terms of survival are needed.

Keywords: MGMT status · Glioblastoma · Transfer learning · Deep learning

1 Introduction

Glioblastoma (GB) represents a very aggressive form of malignant brain tumor with a relative 5-year survival rate less than 8% [21]. The standard therapy approach includes surgery followed by radiotherapy subsidized by concurrent and adjuvant chemotherapy with an alkylating agent, i.e. temozolomide (TMZ) [26].

A. Crimi and S. Bakas (Eds.): BrainLes 2021, LNCS 12962, pp. 306–314, 2022.
https://doi.org/10.1007/978-3-031-08999-2_25

TMZ leads to disruption of DNA replication by addition of a methyl group to the O^6 position of guanine, ultimately resulting in apoptosis. However, the MGMT gene encodes a DNA repair protein that is able to remove alkyl groups, which inhibits the effects of TMZ. [27] Therefore, high levels of MGMT are an important determinant of treatment failure, making MGMT status an essential clinical factor. [8]

MGMT status is typically determined using tissue sample based polymerase chain reaction (PCR) methods, but *Han and Kamdar* [7] have proven the ability of deep learning models to predict patients MGMT status based on multi-parametric magnetic resonance imaging (mpMRI) scans, allowing for non-invasive and fast testing. Task of the Brain Tumor Segmentation (BraTS) Challenge 2021 [1–4,20] was the development of such a mpMRI scan based MGMT promoter methylation status prediction for glioblastoma patients.

The training data set of the challenge involved 585 independent patients, with information about four different MRI sequences. Deep learning models typically require data sets of larger size. We tested the ability of transfer learning to overcome this need for large data set sizes by following the approach developed previously [15]. The video clip classification network C3D [30] was used as a feature extractor. Video data is available in large data set sizes and has the same three dimensional structure as MR images, with the third dimension being time. This allows for full exploitation of three dimensional information in the MR images. C3D processes its input data by 3D convolutional layers, i.e. handling all three dimensions in the same manner, which makes it a perfect fit as baseline model used for feature extraction. Feature vectors of the different MRI sequences were fused using a locally connected layer.

2   Material and Methods

The data set included three cohorts: training, validation and testing. The training cohort involved 585 cases with available mpMRI scans and MGMT status, for the 87 validation cohort cases only mpMRI scans were publicly accessible and the testing set was completely hidden. Data acquisition involved multiple institutions, scanners and imaging protocols [1].

MRI sequences were given in the form of fluid-attenuated inversion recovery (FLAIR), T1 weighted with contrast enhancement (T1wCE), T1 weighted (T1w) and T2 weighted (T2w) acquisition. Not all sequences were available for all patients, for missing sequences arrays filled with zeros were used.

MGMT status was given as a binary label (methylated vs. unmethylated) with testing performed based on different assays including pyrosequencing and next generation quantitative bisulfite sequencing of promoter cytosine-phosphate-guanine sites [1]. The fraction of methylated/unmethylated cases in the training set was given by 307/278.

2.1 Preprocessing

We performed a stratified split, based on patient MGMT status, to separate the training cohort into a train set of 497 cases and a tuning set with 88 cases. Re-orientation to the LPS (Lateral-Posterior-Superior) coordinate system was applied, all cases were resampled to a uniform voxel size of $1\,\text{mm} \times 1\,\text{mm} \times 3\,\text{mm}$, a minimum image size of $126\,\text{mm} \times 126\,\text{mm} \times 150\,\text{mm}$ was provided using zero padding and voxel values v_i were normalized following

$$\hat{v}_i = \frac{v_i - \mu}{\sigma} \times 255/8 + 255/3, \tag{1}$$

with μ and σ the mean voxel value and standard deviation per image.

In order to identify regions in the images that contain air only a binary voxel wise mask was generated based on MRI image voxel values using a threshold value of 1:

$$m_i = \begin{cases} 1 & \text{if } v_i > 1 \\ 0 & \text{else} \end{cases}, \tag{2}$$

with m_i the voxel value of the mask and v_i the respective MRI voxel value.

Images were then cropped based on bounding boxes defined by the binary mask, under consideration of the minimal image size mentioned before. Voxels lying outside the mask were set to zero.

2.2 Model

Following the transfer learning approach [15], the video classification model C3D [30] pretrained on the Sports-1M data set [12] was used as feature extractor. C3D consists of 3D convolutional and max-pooling layers followed by dense layers, a scheme can be seen in Fig. 1. Application of the C3D video classification model as a feature extractor allows for full utilization of 3 dimensional information in the downstream task. This would not be possible for a model pretrained on imaging data (e.g. ImageNet [6]) which could only be trained on slices of the MR images.

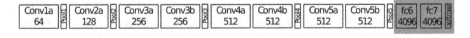

Fig. 1. C3D model, taken from *Tran et al.* [30]. Convolutional layers, denoted *Conv*, feature kernels of size $3 \times 3 \times 3$ and stride 1 for all dimensions, respective filter sizes are shown in the image. Max-pooling layers, denoted *Pool*, feature kernels of size $2 \times 2 \times 2$, except for *Pool1* with a kernel size of $1 \times 2 \times 2$. Fully connected layers *fc*, highlighted in gray, were removed from the network and weights of the convolutional layers were kept fix.

The advantage of using C3D instead of another video classification network lies in the uniform handling of all dimensions in the input data by application of 3D convolution and pooling layers. Usually, newer video classification models handle the time dimension of the video data in a separate way (e.g. *Xie et al.* [32]), which does not fit the structure of medical imaging data in the downstream task.

The model was trained to classify video clips of the Sports-1M data set, containing 1.1 million videos of 487 sports activities. Weights of the trained C3D model are available online [29].

We removed all dense layers of the pretrained model and kept weights of the convolutional layers fixed during training, i.e. no fine tuning was performed for the convolutional layers. A feature vector f^j for each image j of the mpMRI sequence was generated by passing them through the convolutional layers of the C3D model. Input size of $112 \times 112 \times 48$ voxels was chosen, resulting in feature vectors of size 8192.

We then combined all feature vectors using a locally connected layer. Each neuron g_i of the locally connected layer was only connected to one neuron f_i from each of the four feature vectors $f^{1,\cdots,4}$ by

$$g_i = \sum_j^4 f_i^j w_i^j + b, \tag{3}$$

with w and b denoting the weights and bias of the layer.

The locally connected layer was followed by dense layers of size 256 and 128, resulting in one output neuron. Dropout [25] with a probability of 0.5 followed by a ReLU activation layer was applied after the locally connected layer and all the dense layers. Dropout layers randomly set some of their neurons to zero with a given probability, it was shown that this technique helps to prevent the network from overfitting [11]. Sigmoid activation was used after the final output neuron. A scheme of the model can be seen in Fig. 2.

During training augmentation methods included: flipping on the sagittal and coronal plane, rotation by a multiple of $90°$ and addition of gaussian noise with standard deviation of 5 and zero mean. Training cases were randomly cropped to the desired input size, validation cases were center cropped.

The Adam optimizer [13] with a learning rate of 10^{-4} was used to optimize the binary crossentropy loss and batch size was 16. All models were trained locally (on a Nvidia Tesla M60 graphics card) for 150 epochs. The best performing models were chosen based on the minimal tuning set loss and selected to be evaluated on the public validation set. Finally, the two best performing models, based on the public validation set AUC score, were submitted to be evaluated on the private test set.

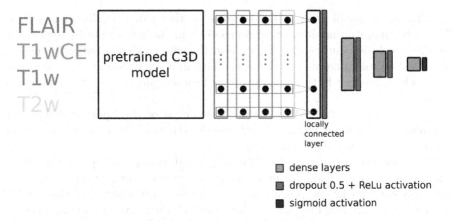

FLAIR
T1wCE
T1w
T2w

pretrained C3D
model

locally
connected
layer

■ dense layers
■ dropout 0.5 + ReLu activation
■ sigmoid activation

Fig. 2. MGMT classification model. Feature extraction is performed using the convolutional part of the pretrained C3D model. The four resulting feature vectors are combined by the locally connected layer. The locally connected layer is followed by dense layers ending in one output neuron. Dropout with a rate of 0.5 and ReLU activation is applied after the locally connected layer and all dense layers. The final output neuron is followed by a sigmoid activation layer.

3   Results

The best performing model achieved a training and tuning loss of 0.638 (0.623–0.653) and 0.649 (0.608–0.692), and an AUC score of 0.699 (0.660–0.737) and 0.685 (0.589–0.781). Errors were computed using bootstrap re-sampling of 10,000 samples and computation of 5% and 95% percentiles. A receiver operating characteristics curve plot for the tuning set can be seen in Fig. 3. For a

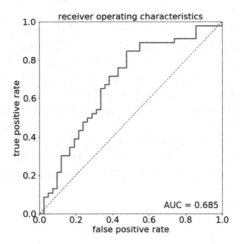

Fig. 3. Tuning set results. Receiver operating characteristics curve plot with a area under the curve of 0.685.

threshold value of 0.5 in the sigmoid output layer the network achieved a sensitivity and specificity of 0.674 and 0.619 on the tuning set. Negative and positive predictive values were given by 0.634 and 0.660.

For the public validation set the algorithm achieved an AUC score of 0.689 and performance on the final private test set was given by 0.577.

4 Discussion

We presented a video data based transfer learning approach for classification of MGMT status in brain tumors based on mpMRI data. MRI sequences were processed by pretrained convolutional layers and then fused using a locally connected layer followed by dense layers. The network was able to discriminate MGMT methylated from unmethylated cases with an AUC of 0.685 and 0.689 for the tuning and public validation set. However, the final AUC score on the private test set achieved only 0.577.

Features of medical imaging data are affected by the application of different scanners and scan protocols [16,18]. Deep learning models are sensitive to such domain shifts between training and test set [9,14,22]. Therefore, the inclusion of different image acquisition procedures can lead to strong performance drops [31]. *Li et al.* [17] trained a radiomics model for prediction of ATRX gene mutation status in lower-grade glioma patients and experienced a decline from 0.925 validation AUC to 0.725 when tested on external data. Hence, the multi-institutional property of the data set, involving several different scanners and imaging protocols, may explain the reduced performance on the test set. Furthermore, medical cohorts are typically several orders of magnitude smaller than data sets usually encountered in the domain of deep learning. The tuning/validation set of the problem at hand involved 88/87 cases. For such data set sizes at least small overfitting on the validation set is inevitable, also leading to a drop between tuning/validation and testing performance. However, for in depth analysis of mechanisms causing the inferior predictive power on the test set image acquisition information would be needed.

The fusion of different imaging modalities by a locally connected layer allowed for construction of a model with relatively small number of trainable weights. For general verification of applicability, the method has to be tested on other classification problems.

Typical AUC scores reached by machine and deep learning models on the task of MRI based MGMT status determination are ranging between 0.60 and 0.90 [5,7,23,33]. *Tixier et al.* [28] showed that combination of mpMRI imaging features obtained by radiomics analysis and patient MGMT status has the power to better stratify patient into survival subcohorts than MGMT status alone. However, results of the BraTS Challenge 2021 demonstrated that improvements in robustness are inevitable for successful MRI based MGMT status determination. For deep learning, transfer learning is known to improve robustness [10], but no sufficient result could be achieved for the problem at hand. *Rebuffi et al.* [24] showed that, when combined with model weight averaging, data augmentation can also improve model robustness, but the method has to be tested in the medical domain.

For clinical applicability, improvements in robustness have to be achieved and mechanisms leading to inferior performance on external data have to be identified. Current MGMT methylation status assays lack uniform methods and definitions, with no gold standard test at hand [19]. This prohibits direct comparison with other testing methods. Determination of predictive power in terms of survival would be one possible way to circumvent this problem, but no ground truth survival data is available in the study data set.

5   Conclusion

We have tested the ability of video clip transfer learning in combination with image sequence fusion by a locally connected layer for MGMT status prediction in glioblastoma patients based on mpMRI data. Sufficient results could be achieved on the public validation set, for the private test set a drop in performance was encountered. Mechanisms leading to performance decline have to be analyzed and model robustness has to be improved for clinical applicability. For further verification, correlation with survival data is needed.

References

1. Baid, U., et al.: The RSNA-ASNR-MICCAI BraTS 2021 benchmark on brain tumor segmentation and radiogenomic classification. arXiv:2107.02314 (2021)
2. Bakas, S., et al.: Segmentation labels and radiomic features for the pre-operative scans of the TCGA-GBM collection. Cancer Imaging Arch. Nat. Sci. Data **4**, 170117 (2017)
3. Bakas, S., et al.: Segmentation labels and radiomic features for the pre-operative scans of the TCGA-LGG collection. Cancer Imaging Arch. **286** (2017)
4. Bakas, S., et al.: Advancing the cancer genome atlas glioma MRI collections with expert segmentation labels and radiomic features. Sci. Data **4**(1), 1–13 (2017)
5. Chen, X., et al.: Automatic prediction of MGMT status in glioblastoma via deep learning-based MR image analysis. In: BioMed Research International 2020 (2020)
6. Deng, J., Dong, W., Socher, R., Li, L.J., Li, K., Fei-Fei, L.: ImageNet: a large-scale hierarchical image database. In: 2009 IEEE Conference on Computer Vision and Pattern Recognition, pp. 248–255. IEEE (2009)
7. Han, L., Kamdar, M.R.: MRI to MGMT: predicting methylation status in glioblastoma patients using convolutional recurrent neural networks. In: Pacific Symposium on Biocomputing 2018: Proceedings of the Pacific Symposium, pp. 331–342. World Scientific (2018)
8. Hegi, M.E., et al.: MGMT gene silencing and benefit from temozolomide in glioblastoma. N. Engl. J. Med. **352**(10), 997–1003 (2005)
9. Hendrycks, D., Dietterich, T.: Benchmarking neural network robustness to common corruptions and perturbations. arXiv preprint arXiv:1903.12261 (2019)
10. Hendrycks, D., Lee, K., Mazeika, M.: Using pre-training can improve model robustness and uncertainty. In: International Conference on Machine Learning, pp. 2712–2721 (2019)

11. Hinton, G.E., Srivastava, N., Krizhevsky, A., Sutskever, I., Salakhutdinov, R.R.: Improving neural networks by preventing co-adaptation of feature detectors. arXiv preprint arXiv:1207.0580 (2012)
12. Karpathy, A., Toderici, G., Shetty, S., Leung, T., Sukthankar, R., Fei-Fei, L.: Large-scale video classification with convolutional neural networks. In: Proceedings of the IEEE Conference on Computer Vision and Pattern Recognition, pp. 1725–1732 (2014)
13. Kingma, D.P., Ba, J.: Adam: a method for stochastic optimization. arXiv preprint arXiv:1412.6980 (2014)
14. Kurakin, A., Goodfellow, I., Bengio, S.: Adversarial examples in the physical world. arXiv preprint arXiv:1607.02533 (2016)
15. Lang, D.M., Peeken, J.C., Combs, S.E., Wilkens, J.J., Bartzsch, S.: Deep learning based HPV status prediction for oropharyngeal cancer patients. Cancers 13(4), 786 (2021)
16. Lee, J., et al.: Radiomics feature robustness as measured using an MRI phantom. Sci. Rep. 11(1), 1–14 (2021)
17. Li, Y., et al.: Genotype prediction of ATRX mutation in lower-grade gliomas using an MRI radiomics signature. Eur. Radiol. 28(7), 2960–2968 (2018). https://doi.org/10.1007/s00330-017-5267-0
18. Lu, L., Ehmke, R.C., Schwartz, L.H., Zhao, B.: Assessing agreement between radiomic features computed for multiple CT imaging settings. PLoS ONE 11(12), e0166550 (2016)
19. Mansouri, A., et al.: MGMT promoter methylation status testing to guide therapy for glioblastoma: refining the approach based on emerging evidence and current challenges. Neuro Oncol. 21(2), 167–178 (2019)
20. Menze, B.H., et al.: The multimodal brain tumor image segmentation benchmark (BRATS). IEEE Trans. Med. Imaging 34(10), 1993–2024 (2014)
21. Ostrom, Q.T., Patil, N., Cioffi, G., Waite, K., Kruchko, C., Barnholtz-Sloan, J.S.: CBTRUS statistical report: primary brain and other central nervous system tumors diagnosed in the United States in 2013–2017. Neuro Oncol. 22(Supplement_1), iv1–iv96 (2020)
22. Quiñonero-Candela, J., Sugiyama, M., Lawrence, N.D., Schwaighofer, A.: Dataset Shift in Machine Learning. MIT Press, Cmabridge (2009)
23. Rathore, S., et al.: Non-invasive determination of the O6-methylguanine-DNA-methyltransferase (MGMT) promoter methylation status in glioblastoma (GBM) using magnetic resonance imaging (MRI) (2018)
24. Rebuffi, S.A., Gowal, S., Calian, D.A., Stimberg, F., Wiles, O., Mann, T.A.: Data augmentation can improve robustness. In: Advances in Neural Information Processing Systems, vol. 34 (2021)
25. Srivastava, N., Hinton, G., Krizhevsky, A., Sutskever, I., Salakhutdinov, R.: Dropout: a simple way to prevent neural networks from overfitting. J. Mach. Learn. Res. 15(1), 1929–1958 (2014)
26. Tan, A.C., Ashley, D.M., López, G.Y., Malinzak, M., Friedman, H.S., Khasraw, M.: Management of glioblastoma: state of the art and future directions. CA Cancer J. Clin. 70(4), 299–312 (2020)
27. Thomas, R.P., Recht, L., Nagpal, S.: Advances in the management of glioblastoma: the role of temozolomide and MGMT testing. Clin. Pharmacol. Adv. Appl. 5, 1 (2013)
28. Tixier, F., et al.: Preoperative MRI-radiomics features improve prediction of survival in glioblastoma patients over MGMT methylation status alone. Oncotarget 10(6), 660 (2019)

29. Tran, D., Bourdev, L., Fergus, R., Torresani, L., Paluri, M.: C3D: Generic features for video analysis. http://vlg.cs.dartmouth.edu/c3d/
30. Tran, D., Bourdev, L., Fergus, R., Torresani, L., Paluri, M.: Learning spatiotemporal features with 3D convolutional networks. In: Proceedings of the IEEE International Conference on Computer Vision, pp. 4489–4497 (2015)
31. Ugurlu, D., et al.: The impact of domain shift on left and right ventricle segmentation in short axis cardiac MR images. arXiv preprint arXiv:2109.13230 (2021)
32. Xie, S., Sun, C., Huang, J., Tu, Z., Murphy, K.: Rethinking spatiotemporal feature learning: speed-accuracy trade-offs in video classification. In: Proceedings of the European Conference on Computer Vision (ECCV), pp. 305–321 (2018)
33. Yogananda, C., et al.: MRI-based deep-learning method for determining glioma MGMT promoter methylation status. Am. J. Neuroradiol. **42**(5), 845–852 (2021)

Multimodal Brain Tumor Segmentation Using a 3D ResUNet in BraTS 2021

Linmin Pei[1]([✉]) and Yanling Liu[2]

[1] Imaging and Visualization Group, ABCS, Frederick National Laboratory for Cancer Research, Frederick, MD 21702, US
linmin.pei@nih.gov

[2] Integrated Data Science Section, Research Technology Branch, National Institute of Allergy and Infectious Disease, Rockville, US
yanling.liu@nih.gov

Abstract. In this paper, we propose a multimodal brain tumor segmentation using a 3D ResUNet deep neural network architecture. Deep neural network has been applying in many domains, including computer vision, natural language processing, etc. It has also been used for semantic segmentation in medical imaging segmentation, including brain tumor segmentation. In this work, we utilize a 3D ResUNet to segment tumors in brain magnetic resonance image (MRI). Multimodal MRI is prevailing in brain tumor analysis due to providing rich tumor information. We apply the proposed method to the Multimodal Brain Tumor Segmentation Challenge (BraTS) 2021 validation dataset for tumor segmentation. The online evaluation of brain tumor segmentation using the proposed method offers the dice score coefficient (DSC) of 0.8196, 0.9195, and 0.8503 for enhancing tumor (ET), whole tumor (WT), and tumor core (TC), respectively.

Keywords: Deep neural network · Tumor segmentation · Multimodal MRIs

1 Introduction

Glioblastoma (GB), and diffuse astrocytic glioma with molecular features of GBM (WHO IV astrocytoma), are the most common and aggressive malignant primary tumor in central nervous system (CNS), with extreme intrinsic heterogeneity in appearance, shape, and histology [1]. In each year, 23 out of 100,000 people are diagnosed with CNS brain tumors in the US [2]. According to the revised CNS tumors classification of world health organization (WHO), brain tumors are classified in considering of the integration of histology and molecular features, including glioblastoma, IDH-wildtype/-mutant, diffuse astrocytoma, IDH-wildtype/-mutant, etc. [3]. It is believed that the survival period of glioma patients is highly associated with tumor type [4]. Proper tumor classification is helpful for tumor treatment management. However, the median survival period of patients with glioblastoma (GBM) remains 12–16 months [5], even with modern treatment advancement. Brain tumor segmentation is of importance for brain tumor prognosis, treatment planning, and follow-up evaluation. An accurate tumor segmentation could lead to a better prognosis. Manual brain tumor segmentation by radiologists

© The Author(s), under exclusive license to Springer Nature Switzerland AG 2022
A. Crimi and S. Bakas (Eds.): BrainLes 2021, LNCS 12962, pp. 315–323, 2022.
https://doi.org/10.1007/978-3-031-08999-2_26

is tedious, time-consuming, and error-prone to raters [4]. Therefore, developing automatic computer-aided brain tumor segmentation is highly desired. Structural magnetic resonance imaging (MRI) is widely used for brain tumor study because of the noninvasiveness and soft tissue capturable ability. It is noticed that one single structural MRI is very challenging to segment all types of tumors due to imaging artifacts and complication of different tumors. Multi-parametric MRI (mpMRI) offers complementary information for different tumors. The mpMRI sequences include T1-weighted MRI (T1), T1-weighted MRI with contrast enhancement (T1ce), T2-weighted MRI (T2), and T2-weighted MRI with fluid-attenuated inversion recovery (T2-FLAIR). T1ce and T2-FLAIR are usually considered good sources to identify enhancing tumor (ET)/necrosis (NC) and peritumoral edema (ED), respectively.

There are many works on brain tumor segmentation in the literature. The proposed methods are threshold-based, region-based, conventional machine learning-based methods [6–11], etc. However, the threshold-based methods and region-based methods are out of date because setting a proper threshold is very difficult. These methods are incapable for high-quality multi-tissue separation. Tumor segmentation is also considered as a classification issue. As such, conventional machine learning-based methods have become popular for tumor classification. However, the prerequisite of hand-crafted feature extraction and follow-up feature selection is very challenging for such methods. It requires advanced knowledge of computer vision and a good understanding of radiology, which limits its applications. Recently, deep learning attracts much attention because of its success in many domains, such as computer vision [12], medical imaging analysis [13], etc. In comparison to conventional machine learning-based methods, feature extraction and selection are automatically completed by using deep learning-based methods [12, 14–17]. In addition, these deep learning-based methods are appliable for multiclass issues.

In this work, we use a 3D ResUNet for brain tumor segmentation. The 3D ResUNet architecture is composed two parts, an encoding part, and a decoding part. The encoding part extracts high dimensional convolutional features from the input. Oppositely, the decoding part transfers the extracted convolutional features to classification label maps. The weights of neurons are adjusted driven by loss between the classification label maps with the corresponding ground truth until the loss reaches a small value or defined threshold.

2 Method

2.1 Brain Tumor Segmentation

For a high-grade glioma patient, a typical brain tumor has multi-subtype tumors: enhancing tumor (ET), non-enhancing tumor (NET), necrosis (NC), and peritumoral edema (ED). However, there is difficult to distinguish the NET and ED in clinical, even for professional radiologists. These subtype tumors show on mpMRI with different appearances. T2 and T2-FLAIR are mainly used for identifying ED because it shows a strong signal, while T1ce sequence is employed for distinguishing ET. Even with mpMRI, identifying all subtype tumors is still challenging due to many factors, such as imaging artifacts, image acquisition quality, intensity inhomogeneity, etc. In general, deep learning-based methods outperform the traditional machine learning methods in many applications, such as image semantic segmentation, face detection, etc. [18].

To achieve accurate brain tumor segmentation, we propose a 3D ResUNet deep learning-based method. The proposed architecture is showing in Fig. 1. The 3D ResUNet architecture consists of two parts: an encoding part and a decoding part. The encoding part extracts high dimensional convolutional features from the input, and the decoding part oppositely transfers the extracted convolutional features to segmentation label maps. The computational loss of the label maps and ground truth drives the voting weights adjustment through an optimizer.

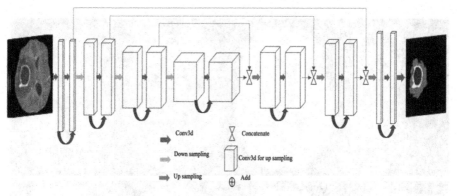

Fig. 1. The proposed ResUNet architecture.

3   Materials and Pre-processing

3.1   Data

In the experiment, there are 1251 cases with mpMRI obtained from the Multimodal Brain Tumor Segmentation Challenge 2021 (BraTS 2021) [5, 18–21]. Different from previous BraTS challenges, the BraTS 2021 has the largest dataset ever, and there is no indication of high-grade glioma (HGG)/low-grade glioma (LGG) information. Each patient case contains multi-parametric MRI (mpMRI), including T1, T1-ce, T2, and T2-FLAIR. These clinically acquired mpMRI scans are co-registered, skull-stripped, and denoised [20]. Each image has a uniform size of $240 \times 240 \times 155$ across cases. A typical brain tumor of HGG cases has multiple subtype tumors: necrotic (NC), peritumoral edema (ED), and enhancing tumor (ET). Ground truth of the training data is public for all participants. However, the ground truths of validation and testing data are privately owned by the challenge organizer and are not available for participants. The participants are allowed to submit the segmentation result online multiple times through the Synapse Evaluation Platform for evaluating their methods. It is noticed that the evaluation of the BraTS 2021 is based on three tumor subregions and Hausdorff distance. The three tumor sub-regions are enhancing tumor, tumor core (TC), and whole tumor (WT). TC is the combination of ET and NC, while the WT is all abnormal tissues. In the validation phase, there are 219 cases with the same format and type images as training data.

3.2 Pre-processing

Since the challenge data is acquired from multiple centers, the intensity scale could vary. Therefore, it is necessary to apply intensity normalization to minimize the impact of intensity variance across cases and modalities. There are several methods for intensity normalization. One popular method is z-score intensity normalization applied in brain regions in the mpMRIs. The z-score normalization ensures intensity with zero mean and unit standard deviation (std) [22]. In the experiment, we apply the z-score normalization for all cases. Figure 2 illustrates an example of image comparison before and after z-score normalization.

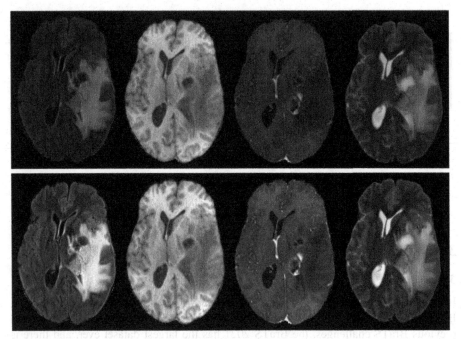

Fig. 2. An instance of intensity normalization. Top figures: raw images, and bottom figures: normalized image using z-score normalization. From left to right: T2-FLAIR, T1, T1ce, and T2. Bottom from left to right.

4 Experiments and Results

4.1 Hyper-parameter Setting

All images in the experiment have a size of $240 \times 240 \times 155$. Due to the limited graphics processing unit (GPU) resource, we randomly crop all mpMRI images with a size of 128x128x128 to fit the proposed deep neural network. To maximize the processed patch size, we set the batch size as 1 for the proposed 3D ResUNet. The loss function is computed using cross-entropy as follows:

$$L = -(y \log (p) + (1 - y) \log (1 - p)),$$

(1)

where p and y are the class prediction and ground truth (GT), respectively.

We set the training epoch as 200, and use Adam [23] optimizer with an initial learning rate of $lr_0 = 0.001$ in training phase, and the learning rate (lr_i) is gradually reduced.:

$$lr_i = lr_0 * \left(1 - \frac{i}{N}\right)^{0.9},$$

(2)

where i is epoch counter, and N is a total number of epochs in training.

4.2 Measurement Metric

In the experiment, there are two main measurement metrics: dice similarity coefficient (DSC) [24] and Hausdorff distance (HD). The DSC is computed as following:

$$DSC = \frac{2TP}{FP + 2TP + FN},$$

(3)

where TP, FP, and FN are the numbers of true positive, false positive and false negative, respectively. The HD measures the distance between the predicted segmentation with the corresponding ground truth, as following:

$$HD95 = percentile\left(max_{a \in pred} min_{b \in gt}(d(pred, gt)), 95^{th}\right)$$

(4)

4.3 Tumor Segmentation

For the brain tumor segmentation task, we utilize a 5-fold cross-validation scheme to train models. Figure 3 shows a case with segmentation using the proposed method in multiple views. In the image, the green, blue, and yellow represents necrosis (NC), enhancing tumor (ET), and edema (ED). Figure 4 demonstrates another two examples with the complete multimodal images and segmentations generated by the proposed method.

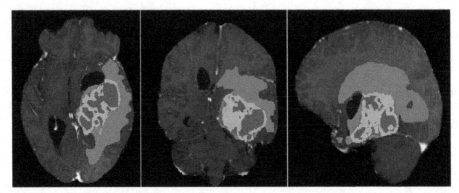

Fig. 3. An example of tumor segmentation using the proposed method. From left to right: T1ce overlaid with predicted segmentation in axis view, sagittal view, and coronal view, respectively. Color code: green, blue, and yellow represents NC, ET, and ED, respectively.

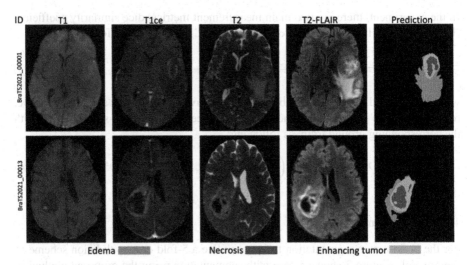

Fig. 4. Two cases of BraTS2021. Each case has four image modalities (from left to right): T1, T1ce, T2, and T2-FLAIR. The predicted label using our deep learning model is showing in the last column. Color code on the predicted label: yellow, green, and blue represents edema, necrosis, and enhancing tumor, respectively.

4.4 Online Evaluation

After we obtained models from the training phase, we then apply the trained models to BraTS 2021 validation dataset and evaluate the performance through the online portal. There are 219 cases with unknown tumor grade. The online evaluation of our segmentation achieves average DSC as 0.8196, 0.8503, and 0.9195 for ET, WT, and TC, respectively. Hausdorff distance (HD), a matric measuring the spacing distance between segmentation and ground truth, is also provided by the online evaluation. A smaller

HD indicates a better segmentation. The average of HD at 95 percentiles is 17.89 mm, 9.89 mm, and 4.3 mm for ET, WT, and TC, respectively.

Table 1. Brain tumor segmentation performance using the online evaluation of BraTS 2021 validation and testing dataset.

Phase	Dice_ET	Dice_WT	Dice_TC	Hausdorff95_ET	Hausdorff95_WT	Hausdorff95_TC
Validation	0. 8196	0. 899	0. 8503	17.89	4.3	9.89

The online evaluation performance shows the proposed method has good performances, with high DSC and low HD in validation phase. The Hausdorff distances are smaller in ET and TC in testing phase comparing to validation phase.

4.5 Online Testing Evaluation

To participate the BraTS 2021 challenge, instead of submitting the segmentation results, all participants are required to submit the models/methods wrapped with Docker via the online submission portal. The challenge organizer applies the models/methods to the testing data to evaluate the performance.

Phase	Dice_ET	Dice_WT	Dice_TC	Hausdorff95_ET	Hausdorff95_WT	Hausdorff95_TC
Testing	0. 859	0. 916	0. 862	12.62	6.17	18.22

Comparing to the performance in validation phase, the dices of enhancing tumor (ET), whole tumor (WT), and tumor core (TC) are higher in the testing phase. However, the Hausdorff distances of WT and TC are worse.

5 Conclusion

In the paper, we utilize a deep learning-based method, namely ResUNet for brain tumor segmentation. The ResUNet is composed of an encoding and a decoding part. The online evaluation suggests a promising performance on both brain tumor segmentation and overall survival prediction.

Acknowledgements. This project has been funded in part with federal funds from the National Cancer Institute, National Institutes of Health, under contract HHSN26120080001E. The content of this publication does not necessarily reflect the views or policies of the Department of Health and Human Services, nor does the mention of trade names, commercial products, or organizations imply endorsement by the U.S. Government.

References

1. Baid, U., et al.: The RSNA-ASNR-MICCAI BraTS 2021 Benchmark on Brain Tumor Segmentation and Radiogenomic Classification (2021). arXiv preprint arXiv:2107.02314
2. Ostrom, Q.T., Gittleman, H., Truitt, G., Boscia, A., Kruchko, C., Barnholtz-Sloan, J.S.: CBTRUS statistical report: primary brain and other central nervous system tumors diagnosed in the United States in 2011–2015. Neurooncology **20** (suppl_4), iv1-iv86 (2018)
3. Louis, D.N., et al.: The 2016 world health organization classification of tumors of the central nervous system: a summary. Acta Neuropathol. **131**(6), 803–820 (2016)
4. Shboul, Z.A., Alam, M., Vidyaratne, L., Pei, L., Elbakary, M.I., Iftekharuddin, K.M.: Feature-guided deep radiomics for glioblastoma patient survival prediction (in English). Front. Neurosci. Original Res. **13**(966), 20 September 2019 (2019). https://doi.org/10.3389/fnins.2019.00966
5. Menze, B.H., et al.: The multimodal brain tumor image segmentation benchmark (BRATS). IEEE Trans. Med. Imaging **34**(10), 1993–2024 (2014)
6. Mustaqeem, A., Javed, A., Fatima, T.: An efficient brain tumor detection algorithm using watershed & thresholding based segmentation. Int. J. Image Graph. Sign. Process. **4**(10), 34 (2012)
7. Pei, L., Bakas, S., Vossough, A., Reza, S.M., Davatzikos, C., Iftekharuddin, K.M.: Longitudinal brain tumor segmentation prediction in MRI using feature and label fusion. Biomed. Sign. Process Control **55**, 101648 (2020)
8. Pei, L., Reza, S.M., Li, W., Davatzikos, C., Iftekharuddin, K.M.: Improved brain tumor segmentation by utilizing tumor growth model in longitudinal brain MRI. In: Medical Imaging 2017: Computer-Aided Diagnosis. International Society for Optics and Photonics, vol. 10134, p. 101342L (2017)
9. Pei, L., Reza, S.M., Iftekharuddin, K.M.: Improved brain tumor growth prediction and segmentation in longitudinal brain MRI. In: 2015 IEEE International Conference on Bioinformatics and Biomedicine (BIBM), pp. 421–424. IEEE (2015)
10. Prastawa, M., Bullitt, E., Ho, S., Gerig, G.: A brain tumor segmentation framework based on outlier detection. Med. Image Anal. **8**(3), 275–283 (2004)
11. Ho, S., Bullitt, E., Gerig, G.: Level-set evolution with region competition: automatic 3-D segmentation of brain tumors. In: null, Citeseer, p. 10532 (2002)
12. LeCun, Y., Bengio, Y., Hinton, G.: Deep learning. Nature **521**, 436, 05/27/online (2015). https://doi.org/10.1038/nature14539
13. Pereira, S., Meier, R., Alves, V., Reyes, M., Silva, C.A.: Automatic brain tumor grading from MRI data using convolutional neural networks and quality assessment. In: et al. Understanding and Interpreting Machine Learning in Medical Image Computing Applications. MLCN DLF IMIMIC 2018. LNCS, vol. 11038, pp. 106–114. Springer, Cham (2018). https://doi.org/10.1007/978-3-030-02628-8_12
14. Goodfellow, I., Bengio, Y., Courville, A.: Deep Learning. MIT Press (2016)
15. Mohsen, H., El-Dahshan, E.-S.A., El-Horbaty, E.-S.M., Salem, A.-B.M.: Classification using deep learning neural networks for brain tumors. Future Comput. Inform. J. **3**(1), 68–71 (2018)
16. He, K., Zhang, X., Ren, S., Sun, J.: Deep residual learning for image recognition. In: Proceedings of the IEEE Conference on Computer Vision and Pattern Recognition, pp. 770–778 (2016)
17. Ronneberger, O., Fischer, P., Brox, T.: U-net: convolutional networks for biomedical image segmentation. In: International Conference on Medical image computing and computer-assisted intervention, pp. 234–241. Springer (2015)
18. Bakas, S., et al.: Identifying the best machine learning algorithms for brain tumor segmentation, progression assessment, and overall survival prediction in the BRATS challenge. arXiv preprint arXiv:1811.02629 (2018)

19. Bakas, S., et al.: Segmentation labels and radiomic features for the pre-operative scans of the TCGA-GBM collection. The Cancer Imaging Archive (2017) ed, (2017)
20. Bakas, S., et al.: Advancing the cancer genome atlas glioma MRI collections with expert segmentation labels and radiomic features. Scientific data **4**, 170117 (2017)
21. Bakas, S., et al.: Segmentation labels and radiomic features for the pre-operative scans of the TCGA-LGG collection. The Cancer Imaging Archive, vol. 286, (2017)
22. Kreyszig, E.: Advanced Engineering Mathematics, 10th (ed.), Wiley (2009)
23. Kingma, D.P., Ba, J.: Adam: a method for stochastic optimization, arXiv preprint arXiv:1412. 6980 (2014)
24. Dice, L.R.: Measures of the amount of ecologic association between species. Ecology **26**(3), 297–302 (1945)

3D MRI Brain Tumour Segmentation with Autoencoder Regularization and Hausdorff Distance Loss Function

Vladimir S. Fonov[1]($\boxtimes$) (iD), Pedro Rosa-Neto[2] (iD), and D. Louis Collins[1]($\boxtimes$) (iD)

[1] McConnell Brain Imaging Centre, Montreal Neurological, Institute, McGill University, Montreal, Canada
{vladimir.fonov,louis.collins}@mcgill.ca
[2] Translational Neuroimaging Laboratory, The McGill University Research Centre for Studies in Aging, Douglas Hospital, McGill University, Montreal, Quebec, Canada

Abstract. Manual segmentation of the Glioblastoma is a challenging task for the radiologists, essential for treatment planning. In recent years deep convolutional neural networks have been shown to perform exceptionally well, in particular the winner of the BraTS challenge 2019 uses 3D U-net architecture in combination with variational autoencoder, using Dice overlap measure as a cost function. In this work we are proposing a loss function that approximates Hausdorff Distance metric that is used to evaluate performance of different segmentation in the hopes that it will allow achieving better performance of the segmentation on new data.

Keywords: Brain tumor · U-Net · Variational autoencoder · Hausdorff distance

1 Introduction

Brain and other nervous system tumors were the leading cause of cancer death among men younger than 40 years and women younger than 20 years in the USA in 2017 [1]. Glioblastoma (GBM) is the most common malignant primary brain tumor making up 54% of all gliomas and 16% of all primary brain tumors, with an incidence rate of 3.19 per 100,000 persons in the USA [2]. GBM Treatment is complex, consisting of tumor resection, followed up by radiation therapy and chemotherapy. Delineation and segmentation of the tumor and its subregions is a complicated and time-consuming manual task essential for treatment planning. The RSNA ASNR MICCAI Brain Tumor Segmentation (BraTS) 2021 challenge is set up to evaluate performance of various methods of automatic delineation of the tumor boundaries and sub-regions based on a large collection of MRI scans of patients with various brain tumors [3].

Since the MRI signal is dependent on proton density and tissue relaxation parameters, it is an ideal imaging modality to study brain tumors. By changing the acquisition parameters, the signal intensity can be associated with different characteristics of the tumor. For example, oedema surrounding the tumor has a medium to dark intensity on T1 and T1c, and is often brighter than GM or WM in FLAIR and T2. The tumor itself can be broken up roughly into core, enhancing, necrotic and cystic regions. The non-enhancing core is brighter than CSF and often darker than GM or WM on T1 and T1c, but can be sometimes brighter if the tumor has high protein, fat, cholesterol or melanin levels. With FLAIR contrast, the non-enhancing core is often darker than GM or WM, but not as dark as CSF. In T2, it is brighter than GM or WM due to higher water content, but not as bright as CSF. The active part of the tumor, the enhancing core, is very bright in T1 contrast images due to gadolinium-based contrast agents leaking through the weakened blood brain barrier in new blood vessels feeding the tumor cells. With less nutrients and oxygen, cells die and form the solid necrotic region of the tumor that is darker than non-enhancing tumor in T1, T1c and FLAIR images, and may have a speckled appearance in T2. The necrotic cystic regions of a tumor are filled with liquid, and thus have an intensity similar to CSF in T1, T1c, T2 and FLAIR images. We note that in BRATS data, the necrotic region is not differentiated from the tumour core in the training labels.

With their ability to represent very complex distributions, deep convolutional neural nets are ideal to model the intensities of the different brain tumor regions.

Results from the previous BraTS competitions [4, 5] showed that the best performing methods used various forms of convolutional neural networks (CNN). In particular, the winner of the segmentation part of BraTS 2019 challenge used a U-net architecture combined with variational auto-encoder regularization [5, 6].

The design of our network is inspired by the one published by Myronenko et al. [6]. The main difference between that work and ours is in the loss function where we integrate a combination of both the Dice kappa overlap metric [7] and a multi-label Hausdorff-like distance approximation, inspired by the single label Hausdorff approximation suggested by Karimi et al. [8].

2   Methods

Our deep learning convolutional neural network is based on a 3D version of the U-NET architecture [9] which is frequently used for semantic segmentation of 3D medical images. This architecture consists of two parts: an encoder, where image features of different levels of details are extracted and a decoder, which combines features to produce segmentation results. In addition to the encoder and decoder branches, our network includes a variational auto-encoder (VAE) branch, similar to the work of Myronenko [6], that is designed to re-create the input image, with the idea that it provides additional regularization to the network parameters.

Overall design of the proposed network is shown on Fig. 1.

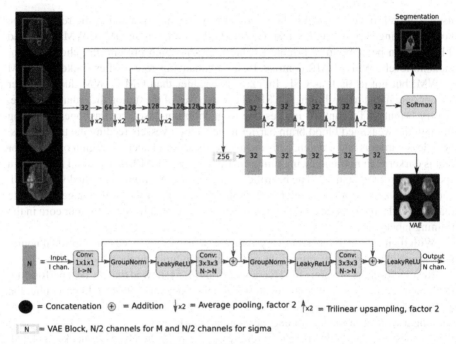

Fig. 1. DNN architecture

2.1 Loss Functions

The common measure of the goodness of anatomical region segmentation is the Dice kappa overlap measure; many methods use this metric directly as a loss function for CNN training. However, in case of multiple labels weighted sum of separate Dice overlap measurements are often used. In our approach we decided to use the cross-entropy loss function instead, since it produces smoother gradients needed for training.

The common problem with either Dice overlap or cross-entropy loss functions is that they don't geometrically localize the errors in segmentation, whereas accurate tracing of the border of the tumor is very important in planning surgery or radiotherapy. The Hausdorff distance measure is another metric used to estimate quality of the segmentation results, which is sensitive to the geometric properties of the segmentation results, but it is difficult to use as a loss function to train DNNs, since it is not differentiable in its classic form, and in addition, is not stable in case of noisy data [8]. Previously, a method suitable for use in DNN was proposed in [8], however it was formulated for a single label problem. We propose a modification to the one-sided distance-transform loss function, described in [8], to extend it to the multi-label case.

$$Loss_{DT-OS}(q, p) = \frac{1}{|\Omega|} \sum_{\Omega} \left((p - q)^2 \cdot d_p^{\alpha} \right) \tag{1}$$

Equation 1, shows the one-sided Hausdorff-like distance loss function, as introduced in [8], where Ω denotes volume of interest, p denotes binary labels for the ground-truth segmentation, q denotes probability labels for the DNN output and d_p is unsigned bi-directional distance from the border of p, and α is an adjustable parameter. Since d_p does not depend on the current estimation of the segmentation, this value is precomputed in advance, and computation of the loss function carries similar numerical complexity as cross-entropy or Dice kappa. In our methods we used the "Exact Euclidean distance transform" from scipy [12].

To extend the loss function to multilabel segmentation problem we propose two loss functions, given set of labels L (including background label), and $u_{l,p}$ - the unidirectional distance from the border of the structure with label l outside the structure, and zero inside the structure. It's easy to see that in case of two labels (background and foreground), and $\beta = 2$, this loss is equivalent to the loss in Eq. 1

$$Loss_{mean}(q, p, L) = \frac{1}{|L|} \sum_{l \subset L} \frac{1}{|\Omega|} \sum_{\Omega} \left(q_l^{\beta} \cdot u_{l,p}^{\alpha} \right) \qquad (2)$$

The goal of the second loss function is to mimic the sparse nature of the real Hausdorff distance more closely:

$$Loss_{max}(q, p, L) = \frac{1}{|L|} \sum_{l \subset L} max_{\Omega} \left(q_l^{\beta} \cdot u_{l,p}^{\alpha} \right) \qquad (3)$$

In our experiment we used parameters $\alpha = 1$, $\beta = 1$, but it's possible to find better parameters using cross-validation.

Our total loss function was following:

$$Loss = W_{CE} \cdot Loss_{CE} + W_{mean} \cdot Loss_{mean} + W_{max} \cdot Loss_{max} + W_{VAE} \cdot Loss_{VAE} + W_{KL} \cdot Loss_{KL} \qquad (4)$$

where $Loss_{CE}$- cross-entropy loss, $Loss_{VAE}$- L2 norm of the variational autoencoder reconstruction error, $Loss_{KL}$- Kulback-Leibler norm of the difference of VAE parameters from the normal distributions with zero mean and unit standard deviation, as described in [4].

The weights of each loss were chosen empirically, based on [4] and our internal experiments: $W_{CE} = 1.0$, $W_{mean} = 0.1$, $W_{max} = 0.01$, $W_{VAE} = 0.1$, $W_{KL} = 0.1$

2.2 Data Preprocessing

To normalize intensity ranges for all MRI scans, we used histogram matching to calculate the intensity scaling coefficient to match the reference subject BraTS2021_00000 intensity distribution within brain mask.

2.3 Data Augmentation

In order to make segmentation robust with respect to the possible perturbations seen in MRI scans, we used two kinds of data augmentation: (i) offline geometric transformation, where random affine transformations were applied to each dataset, and results and distance transformations needed for Hausdorff-like cost function were pre-computed; (ii) online signal augmentation where random signal shift, amplification and voxel-level additive noise were added (after signal intensity Z-transformation) to the images each time data was used for training the DNN. We generated 32 offline-augmented datasets for each original dataset.

Table 1. Data augmentation parameters

Geometric shift	$\mu = 0.0$ mm, $\sigma = 2.0$ mm
Rotation around X,Y,Z	$\mu = 0.0$ deg, $\sigma = 10$ deg
Geometric scaling X,Y,Z	$\mu = 1.0$, $\sigma = 0.03$
Intensity shift	$\mu = 0.0$, $\sigma = 0.1$
Intensity amplification	$\mu = 1.0$, $\sigma = 0.1$
Voxel level additive noise	$\mu = 0.0$, $\sigma = 0.1$

2.4 Model Training

For the final training before submission, we split off-line augmented datasets into two sets: training (datasets corresponding to 1241 subjects) and validation (10 unique subjects).

To train DNN we used AdamW: variant of the Adam optimization algorithm [10] with Decoupled Weight Decay Regularization [11]. We used 100 warm up iterations with learning rate of 1e−7, followed by regular training with learning rate 1e−4, we used weight decay (L2 regularization weight) of 1e−4. Training was done for 100 epochs.

During training we extracted random patches of $144 \times 144 \times 144$ voxels from each dataset. Four available imaging modalities were concatenated as four input channels to the DNN. The output of the DNN was a four-channel probability map (after softmax) corresponding to the Background (BKG), enhancing tumor (ET), the tumor core (TC) and necrosis, and the whole tumor (WT). After the end of each epoch DNN was applied to the online validation subset to calculate generalized overlap kappa and symmetric Hausdorff-distance. Models corresponding to the best performance in terms of kappa overlap and HD were stored to be used for the final submission. For the final result, we used the weights of DNN corresponding to the epoch that achieved the best generalized Dice overlap ratio.

2.5 Inference

For the inference, the DNN was applied to the patches of $144 \times 144 \times 144$ voxels that were extracted from the MRI scans, with 4 channels corresponding to the 4 available imaging modalities. Patches were extracted from the MRI scans with a stride of 64 voxels, resulting tissue probability maps were center-cropped to $128 \times 128 \times 128$ voxels to minimize edge effects; overlapping areas were merged using exponential averaging, and final segmentation was created by choosing the label with highest probability.

3 Results

DNN was implemented using pytorch version 1.9.0 [14], using the BraTS-2021 training dataset (1251 subjects) [3, 15–18], we didn't use any additional data. We split the BraTS 2021 training dataset into two subsets: 1241 training and 10 on-line validation. We evaluated the impact of several parameters: offline data augmentation, use of mean and max distance loss, and regularizing effect of variational autoencoder.

DNN training was performed on two systems: (i) the Nvidia DGX-1 system, consisting of 8× Nvidia Tesla V100 GPU with 16 Gb of RAM each and (ii) a cluster of two workstations with Nvidia RTX-3090 (24 Gb RAM) connected via 10 Gb Ethernet link. In both cases a distributed data parallel scheme was used to utilize all available GPUs. Batch size was adjusted based on the available RAM for each system: DGX-1 used batch size of 8 × 2 samples and cluster with RTX-3090 used 3 × 2 samples.

Training one epoch after offline data augmentation took 2.5 h on DGX-1, because the number of data samples was increased by a factor of 32, without offline augmentation one epoch took 7.5 min on the cluster with two RTX-3090.

In order to estimate the effect of using different loss functions as and offline data augmentation, we performed five experiments: (i) with offline data augmentation and all loss functions described above; (ii) without offline data augmentation but with all loss functions; (iii) without offline data augmentation and without $Loss_{max}$; (iv) without offline data augmentation, without $Loss_{max}$, without $Loss_{mean}$; (v) without offline data augmentation and without VAE regularization.

The resulting DNN was used to segment the validation dataset that was uploaded to the BraTS 2021 online evaluation system. Performance is shown on Fig. 2. Overall, use of offline data augmentation, VAE regularization and $Loss_{mean}$, seem to improve performance of the DNN.

Performance of the submitted model on the testing dataset is shown in Table 2.

Table 2. Performance on the testing dataset

	Mean	StdDev	Median	25th quantile	75th quantile
Dice_ET	0.8145	0.2151	0.8829	0.8017	0.9269
Dice_WT	0.9060	0.1266	0.9432	0.8981	0.9646
Dice_TC	0.8463	0.2520	0.9408	0.8783	0.9681
Sensitivity_ET	0.8437	0.2357	0.9345	0.8542	0.9665
Sensitivity_WT	0.8959	0.1399	0.9370	0.8757	0.9723
Sensitivity_TC	0.8441	0.2547	0.9460	0.8703	0.9757
Specificity_ET	0.9996	0.0004	0.9997	0.9995	0.9999
Specificity_WT	0.9995	0.0008	0.9997	0.9994	0.9999
Specificity_TC	0.9997	0.0006	0.9999	0.9997	1.0000
Hausdorff95_ET	19.5828	75.9712	2.2361	1.4142	3.3166
Hausdorff95_WT	7.3669	31.8179	2.2361	1.4142	4.8990
Hausdorff95_TC	22.3228	80.1173	2.0000	1.0000	4.1231

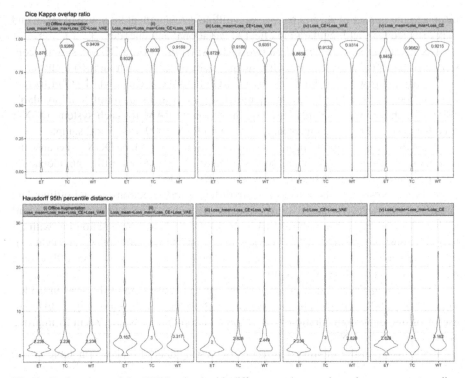

Fig. 2. Performance of the DNN trained with different settings, red numbers represent median values.

4 Discussion and Conclusion

In this paper we proposed a modification of previously-published semantic segmentation DNN for brain tumor segmentation. Our contributions are use of the cost function which is more closely related to the clinical requirements and use of a data augmentation scheme that more closely mimics potential variations of the clinical data.

Our experiments with different combinations of loss functions and data augmentation, showed that extensive data augmentation has a similar impact on the final performance as any of the proposed additional loss function, and that there is a small but noticeable improvement of the performance when using $Loss_{mean}$ function in addition to the cross-entropy and variational autoencoder regularization.

Since we do not have access to the test labels, we can only suggest interpretations of the test results. For example, the mean Dice_ET is much smaller than the median, and the StdDev is high. This might be due to cases where no manual ET labs exist, but the proposed technique finds some labels or vice versa.

The median Hausdorff metrics are very good (all <2.25 mm), however the mean values are quite large - this would indicate that a post-processing step would be useful to remove extra voxels, those disconnected from the main regions.

Acknowledgments. Data used in this publication were obtained as part of the RSNA-ASNR-MICCAI Brain Tumor Segmentation (BraTS) Challenge project through Synapse ID (syn25829067).

References

1. Siegel, R.L., Miller, K.D., Jemal, A.: Cancer statistics, 2020. CA Canc. J. Clin. **70**(1), 7–30 (2020). https://doi.org/10.3322/caac.21590. Epub 2020 Jan 8 PMID: 31912902

2. Ostrom, Q.T., Gittleman, H., Farah, P., Ondracek, A., Chen, Y., Wolinsky, Y., et al.: CBTRUS statistical report: primary brain and central nervous system tumors diagnosed in the United States in 2006–2010. Neuro. Oncol. **15** Suppl:2ii–56 (2013)

3. Baid, U., et al.: The rsna-asnr-miccai brats 2021 benchmark on brain tumor segmentation and radiogenomic classification (2021). arXiv:2107.02314

4. Bakas, S., et al.: Identifying the Best Machine Learning Algorithms for Brain Tumor Segmentation, Progression Assessment, and Overall Survival Prediction in the BRATS Challenge (2018). arXiv:1811.02629

5. Tiwari, A., Srivastava, S., Pant, M.: Brain tumor segmentation and classification from magnetic resonance images: review of selected methods from 2014 to 2019. Pattern Recogn. Lett. **131**, 244–260 (2020). ISSN 0167-8655

6. Myronenko, A.: 3D MRI brain tumor segmentation using autoencoder regularization arXiv: 1810.11654

7. Taha, A.A., Hanbury, A.: Metrics for evaluating 3D medical image segmentation: analysis, selection, and tool. BMC Med Imaging **15**, 29 (2015). https://doi.org/10.1186/s12880-015-0068-x

8. Karimi, D., Salcudean, S.E.: Reducing the hausdorff distance in medical image segmentation with convolutional neural networks. IEEE Trans. Med. Imaging, **39**(2), 499–513 (2019). arXiv:1904.10030

9. Ronneberger, O., Fischer, P., Brox, T.: U-Net: convolutional networks for biomedical image segmentation. In: Navab, N., Hornegger, J., Wells, W.M., Frangi, A.F. (eds.) MICCAI 2015. LNCS, vol. 9351, pp. 234–241. Springer, Cham (2015). https://doi.org/10.1007/978-3-319-24574-4_28

10. Kingma, D.P., Ba, J.: Adam: A Method for Stochastic Optimization arXiv:1412.6980

11. Loshchilov, I., Hutter, F.: Decoupled Weight Decay Regularization (2017). arXiv:1711.05101

12. Scipy exact distance transform: https://docs.scipy.org/doc/scipy/reference/generated/scipy.ndimage.distance_transform_edt.html

13. Crum, W.R., Camara, O., Derek, L.G.H.: Generalized overlap measures for evaluation and validation in medical image analysis. IEEE Trans. Med. Imag. **25**(11), 1451–1461 (2006)https://doi.org/10.1109/TMI.2006.880587

14. Ketkar, N.: Introduction to PyTorch. In: Deep Learning with Python, pp. 195–208. Apress, Berkeley, CA (2017). https://doi.org/10.1007/978-1-4842-2766-4_12

15. Menze, B.H., et al.: The multimodal brain tumor image segmentation benchmark (BRATS). IEEE Trans. Med. Imaging **34**(10), 1993–2024 (2015). https://doi.org/10.1109/TMI.2014.2377694

16. Bakas, S., et al.: Advancing The Cancer genome Atlas glioma MRI collections with expert segmentation labels and radiomic features. Nat. Sci. Data **4**, 170117 (2017). https://doi.org/10.1038/sdata.2017.117

17. Bakas, S., et al.: Segmentation labels and radiomic features for the pre-operative scans of the TCGA-GBM collection. Canc. Imaging Arch. (2017). https://doi.org/10.7937/K9/TCIA.2017.KLXWJJ1Q
18. Bakas, S., et al.: Segmentation labels and radiomic features for the pre-operative scans of the TCGA-LGG collection. Canc. Imaging Arch. (2017). https://doi.org/10.7937/K9/TCIA.2017.GJQ7R0EF

3D CMM-Net with Deeper Encoder for Semantic Segmentation of Brain Tumors in BraTS2021 Challenge

Yoonseok Choi[✉], Mohammed A. Al-masni[✉], and Dong-Hyun Kim[✉]

Department of Electrical and Electronic Engineering, College of Engineering,
Yonsei University, Seoul, Republic of Korea
{yunseok4444,m.almasani,donghyunkim}@yonsei.ac.kr

Abstract. We propose a 3D version of the Contextual Multi-scale Multi-level Network (3D CMM-Net) with deeper encoder depth for automated semantic segmentation of different brain tumors in the BraTS2021 challenge. The proposed network has the capability to extract and learn deeper features for the task of multiclass segmentation directly from 3D MRI data. The overall performance of the proposed network gave Dice scores of 0.7557, 0.8060, and 0.8351 for enhancing tumor, tumor core, and whole tumor, respectively on the local-test dataset.

Keywords: Brain tumor segmentation · Pyramid pooling module · U-Net · Glioblastoma · 3D semantic segmentation · Multimodal MRI

1 Introduction

The incidence rate of primary brain tumors is 11–12 per 100,000 populations. Gliomas are the most common brain tumors, accounting for about 50% of the diagnosed brain tumors, and 26% of them are considered to be astrocytic tumors [1]. In particular, glioblastoma (GBM) accounts for 50–60% of all gliomas, and it has the highest malignancy among gliomas. Therefore, it is important to accurately segment brain tumors in order to improve the diagnosis and hence and the appropriate treatment.

Magnetic Resonance Imaging (MRI) plays an important role in diagnosing brain tumors. Since 2011, the Brain Tumor Segmentation (BraTS) challenge has led to the development of automated segmentation networks to segment brain tumors using 3D multimodal MRI data. The data provided by BraTS have different contrasts and include T1, T2, Fluid-Attenuated Inversion Recovery (FLAIR), and T1 Contrast-Enhanced (T1CE) [2–6]. Figure 1 shows examples of these four images along with the brain tumor mask. In the BraTS2021 challenge, a total of 1,251 patient data were provided with their brain tumor masks for training. However, 219 additional data without their mask labels were given for validation. The input image size for all data is 240 × 240 × 155 voxels. The label mask consisted of three classes: Edema (ED), Enhancing Tumor (ET), and Necrosis (NE) where the Tumor Core (TC) is defined as the sum of ET and NE, and the Whole Tumor (WT) is composed of the sum of ED, ET and NE. In the

© The Author(s), under exclusive license to Springer Nature Switzerland AG 2022
A. Crimi and S. Bakas (Eds.): BrainLes 2021, LNCS 12962, pp. 333–343, 2022.
https://doi.org/10.1007/978-3-031-08999-2_28

rightmost image of Fig. 1, the green part indicates ED, the yellow part indicates the ET, and the red part means NE.

In this work, we propose a 3D version of the Contextual Multi-scale Multi-level Network (3D CMM-Net) [7] with deeper encoder depth for automated semantic segmentation of different sub-regions of brain tumors in the BraTS2021 challenge. The proposed network involved multiple pyramid pooling modules which have the possibility to get multi-scale feature maps in each level of the encoder and the capability to extract and learn deeper features for the task of multi-class segmentation directly from 3D MRI data.

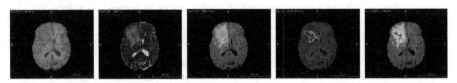

Fig. 1. Example of BraTS2021 dataset. From left, T1, T2, FLAIR, T1CE, and brain tumor mask

2   Method

2.1   Data Preprocessing and Augmentation

To reduce the computation complexity during training and improve the overall performance, we applied some preprocessing procedures to our dataset. First, we normalize all input images using zero mean and unit standard deviation. Then, we cropped all dataset using the center spatial crop from $240 \times 240 \times 155$ to $128 \times 128 \times 128$ voxels. This cropping process enables to reduce the size of input images and hence maintaining lower computation cost during training. It is of note that all the cropped data still includes the structure of brain tissue as well as the tumors. In order to take the advantage of the presence of four different image modalities (i.e., T1, T2, FLAIR, and T1CE), we concatenated all four types and utilized them as an input to our network. This could help in extracting various spatial features during training and enhance the overall segmentation of brain tumors.

Moreover, we use different data augmentation techniques to enlarge our training data. We randomly flip all input images with a probability of 0.4 and rotate them multiple times in the x-y axis with a probability of 0.4 between 90 and 270°. Finally, we randomly adjust the contrast of the input images, which is a kind of gamma correction, with a probability of 0.5.

2.2   Dilated Convolution

Dilated convolution is a method of forcibly increasing the receptive field by adding zero padding inside the filter [8]. The advantage of using dilated convolution compared to the conventional standard convolution is its ability to increase the receptive field with maintaining the same number of weights in the convolution kernel. Basic convolution and the dilated convolution are defined as:

$$f[x] * w[x] = \sum_{k=-\infty}^{\infty} f[k] \cdot w[x - k] \tag{1}$$

$$f[x] *_r w[x] = \sum_{k=-\infty}^{\infty} f[k] \cdot w[r(x - k)] \tag{2}$$

where f[x] and w[x] are a discrete input image and a discrete filter or kernel, respectively. In (1) and (2), the $'*'$ means convolution and the $'\cdot'$ indicates multiplication operator. Dilated rate $'r'$ in (2) means the gap of the weights' location in the convolution kernel. The larger the $'r'$ value implies the larger the size of the receptive field, where the loss of information in spatial dimension is small. Figure 2(a) demonstrates how the dilated convolution works when r = 2 and kernel size is 3 × 3. Due to the characteristic of maintaining spatial information, dilated convolution is particularly used for segmentation.

2.3 Pyramid Pooling Module

The primary advantage of the Pyramid Pooling Module (PPM) is that it can obtain both local and global features at the same time [9]. Here, we explain step by step how the PPM proceeds. A pooling kernel of a different size is applied to each pyramid. As shown in Fig. 2 (b), the spatial size of the feature maps for each pyramid after pooling is 2 × 2 × 2, 4 × 4 × 4, 8 × 8 × 8, and 16 × 16 × 16. After that, using 1 × 1 × 1 convolution reduces the number of channels in the feature map for each pyramid by dividing it by the number of pyramids (i.e., four in this work). For example, Fig. 2 (b) shows four pyramids. So, the number of channels in the feature map after convolution is reduced to a quarter compared to the previous feature maps. Then, through upsampling, the feature maps in each pyramid are resized to be equal to their original size just before applying the PPM. Finally, all these feature maps are concatenated with the original one. Then the number of channels on output from PPM is going to be double compared to the input of PPM.

The Half Pyramid Pooling Module (HPPM) located in the bottleneck of the proposed network as shown in Fig. 3 has little difference from the PPM. HPPM only concatenates the feature maps in each pyramid without adding the previous original input feature maps. This is due to the number of channels of feature maps in the bottleneck of the proposed network being very large and causing GPU memory limitation if PPM is used.

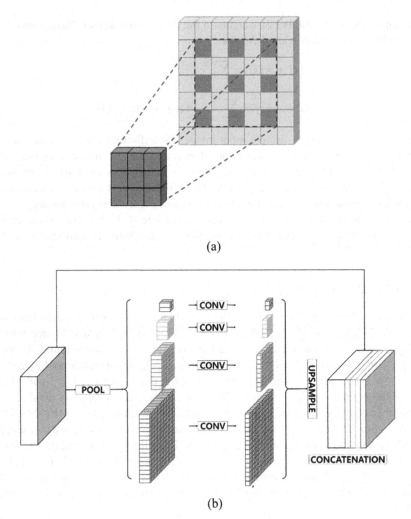

Fig. 2. (a) Description of the dilated convolution with dilated rate r = 2 of 3 × 3 kernel, (b) The pyramid pooling module with four pyramids where each pyramid has a size of 2 × 2 × 2, 4 × 4 × 4, 8 × 8 × 8, and 16 × 16 × 16

2.4   Network Architecture

We use the CMM-Net [7] as our backbone since it has an attractive advantage of segmentation tasks in the medical domain. In this work, we develop a 3D version of the existing 2D CMM-Net and enlarge the depth of the encoder with two HPPM blocks in the bottleneck of the network as shown in Fig. 3. We apply dilated convolution to the whole convolution blocks in our network in order to enlarge the receptive field without increasing the number of weights in the convolution kernel as well as use the PPM in the encoder part to get the multiscale feature map at once. We tabulate thoroughly the structure of our model in Table 1.

2.4.1 Loss

The proposed 3D CMM-Net is optimized by minimizing the dice loss [9]. Dice loss is computed as:

$$L_{dice} = \frac{2 \cdot \sum P_{true} \cdot P_{pred}}{\sum P_{true}^2 + \sum P_{pred}^2 + \epsilon} \tag{3}$$

where P_{ture} and P_{pred} indicate the label mask provided from BraTS and the predicted mask of our model, respectively. Summation in (3) is computed as voxel-wise and ϵ prevents from zero division. Since the output of the proposed network has 3 channels for TC, WT, and ET except for the background class, we have applied the dice loss per each channel of the output.

2.4.2 Optimization

We use Adam optimization algorithm when we train the model with initial learning rate $\alpha_0 = 1e^{-4}$ and make it gradually decrease as:

$$\alpha = \alpha_0 \cdot \left(1 - \frac{e}{N_e}\right)^{0.9} \tag{4}$$

where $'e'$ counts the current epochs and $'N_e'$ is the total number of epochs. We use 100 epochs in our case. We implement our network using Pytorch [10] and train it on one NVIDIA GeForce RTX 3090 24 GB GPU.

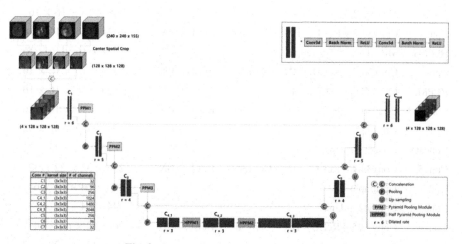

Fig. 3. Proposed 3D CMM-Net architecture

3   Result

To train the proposed network, we used the BraTS2021 training dataset that contains 1,251 patients without additional data. Before releasing the validation dataset from the

338   Y. Choi et al.

BraTS, we randomly selected 51 patients among the BraTS2021 training dataset as a test dataset to evaluate the performance of the proposed network. We call this subset

Table 1. Detailed Architecture of the proposed 3D CMM-Net where BN stands for Batch Normalization, Conv3d-r: 3 × 3 × 3 convolution with dilated rate r, MP: Multiscale Pooling in PPM as shown in Fig. 2(b), Conv: 1 × 1 × 1 convolution, Up: 3D linear spatial upsampling

Name	Contents	Output size
Input	Cropped & Concatenated 4ch image	4 × 128 × 128 × 128
Conv1	Conv3d-6 – ReLU – BN – Conv3d-6 – ReLU – BN	32 × 128 × 128 × 128
PPM1	MP – Conv – Upsample – Concat	64 × 128 × 128 × 128
Concat1	Conv1 + PPM1	96 × 128 × 128 × 128
Pool1	Max Pooling	96 × 64 × 64 × 64
Conv2	Conv3d-5 – ReLU – BN – Conv3d-5 – ReLU – BN	96 × 64 × 64 × 64
PPM2	MP – Conv – Upsample – Concat	192 × 64 × 64 × 64
Concat2	Conv2 + PPM2	288 × 64 × 64 × 64
Pool2	Max Pooling	288 × 32 × 32 × 32
Conv3	Conv3d-4 – ReLU – BN – Conv3d-4 – ReLU – BN	256 × 32 × 32 × 32
PPM3	MP – Conv – Upsample – Concat	512 × 32 × 32 × 32
Concat3	Conv3 + PPM3	768 × 32 × 32 × 32
Pool3	Max Pooling	768 × 16 × 16 × 16
Conv4–1	Conv3d-3 – ReLU – BN – Conv3d-3 – ReLU – BN	1024 × 16 × 16 × 16
HPPM1	MP – Conv – Upsample	1024 × 16 × 16 × 16
Conv4–2	Conv3d-3 – ReLU – BN – Conv3d-3 – ReLU – BN	1400 × 16 × 16 × 16
HPPM2	MP – Conv – Upsample	1400 × 16 × 16 × 16
Conv4–3	Conv3d-3 – ReLU – BN – Conv3d-3 – ReLU – BN	2048 × 16 × 16 × 16
Up1	Upsample	2048 × 32 × 32 × 32
Concat4	Concat3 + Up1	2816 × 32 × 32 × 32
Conv5	Conv3d-4 – ReLU – BN – Conv3d-4 – ReLU – BN	256 × 32 × 32 × 32
Up2	Upsample	256 × 64 × 64 × 64
Concat5	Concat2 + Up2	544 × 64 × 64 × 64
Conv6	Conv3d-5 – ReLU – BN – Conv3d-5 – ReLU – BN	96 × 64 × 64 × 64
Up3	Upsample	96 × 128 × 128 × 128
Concat6	Concat1 + Up3	192 × 128 × 128 × 128
Conv7	Conv3d-6 – ReLU – BN – Conv3d-6 – ReLU – BN	32 × 128 × 128 × 128
Conv-out	Conv	4 × 128 × 128 × 128
Output	Predicted masks with 4 different classes for each channel	4 × 128 × 128 × 128

a 'local-test'. On the local-test dataset, the proposed 3D CMM-Net obtained the dice scores per class of ET: 0.7557, TC: 0.8060, and WT:0.8351 as shown in Table 2.

We proceed with the ablation study by changing the structure of 3D CMM-Net in order to figure out whether HPPM works well or not.

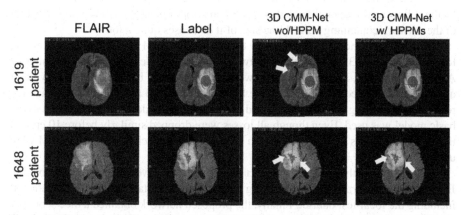

Fig. 4. Prediction result of two different models for ablation study on some patients among local-test datasets. The green area indicates ED, the yellow subregion means ET, and the red one is NE. (Color figure online)

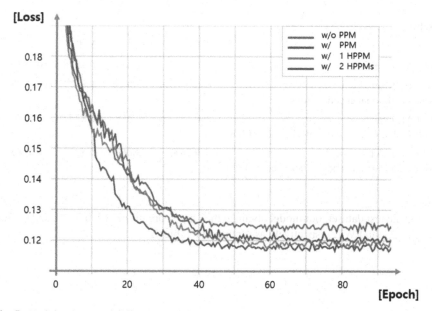

Fig. 5. Training losses of different conditions where the basic model structure is 3D CMM-Net with two additional encoders.

So, we examined two different models where one is 3D CMM-Net with only two additional encoder blocks and the other is 3D CMM-Net with two additional encoder blocks and two HPPMs. An example result is shown in Fig. 4. In the first row of Fig. 4, the predicted mask of the model without HPPM has the wrong ED area indicated with the yellow arrow. However, in the case of using the HPPM, we can find out that the wrongly predicted ED sub-region was disappeared in the predicted mask. In the second row of Fig. 4, for the network without HPPM there is wrongly predicted NE as pointed by the yellow arrow. Even though there is still an error of prediction of NE for the output of the network containing HPPM, the size of it decreases quite a lot.

We conducted another ablation study to find out how PPM and HPPM affect training loss where we used 3D CMM-Net with two additional encoder blocks as a basic model. As shown in Fig. 5, all training losses were dropped stably but in the case of without using PPM, indicated by green line, the loss was converged at a higher value than the rest. In case of using HPPM, orange and brown lines, a model with PPM added to the basic model was used. Even though all losses were dropped similarly before 10 epochs the training loss was dropped faster than others after 10 epochs when two HPPM were used.

After releasing the validation dataset which does not have the label mask from the BraTS2021, we retrain our model using all the training datasets (i.e., 1,251 patients) including the local-test dataset. Finally, the proposed network obtained a dice score per class of ET: 0.7321, TC: 0.7514, and WT: 0.8743 as shown in Table 3.

Table 2. Dice score per each class on the local-test dataset of different models

Network	Dice			
Class	ET	TC	WT	Avg
3D CMM-Net	0.7450	0.8049	0.8076	0.7859
3D CMM-Net with 2 additional encoder blocks	0.7502	0.8053	0.8077	0.7877
3D CMM-Net with 2 additional encoder blocks and 1HPPM	0.7556	0.8055	0.8347	0.7986
3D CMM-Net with 2 additional encoder blocks and 2HPPMs	**0.7557**	**0.8060**	**0.8351**	**0.7989**

On the test dataset, our model obtained the Dice score of 0.7212, 0.7410, and 0.7702 for ET, TC, and WT, respectively as reported in Table 4.

Table 3. Dice score and Hausdorff distance per each class on the validation dataset of proposed model

Metric	Dice			Hausdorff (mm)		
Class	ET	TC	WT	ET	TC	WT
Mean	**0.7321**	**0.7514**	**0.8743**	35.0074	24.6376	10.1613
Sd	0.5987	0.3070	0.1823	101.6312	77.2684	36.5176
Median	0.8521	0.9023	0.9320	2.2361	3.4641	2.8284
25 quantile	0.7180	0.7068	0.8785	1.1414	2	1.7321
75 quantile	0.9075	0.9430	0.9532	5.4312	10.8166	5.7549

Table 4. Dice score and Hausdorff distance per each class on the test dataset of proposed model

Metric	Dice			Hausdorff (mm)		
Class	ET	TC	WT	ET	TC	WT
Mean	**0.7212**	**0.7410**	**0.7702**	31.6602	34.8666	22.8658
Sd	0.2950	0.3174	0.2544	95.4076	97.0577	69.2853
Median	0.8399	0.8898	0.8755	2.2361	5.4772	4
25 quantile	0.7036	0.7047	0.7495	1.4142	3	2
75 quantile	0.9094	0.9489	0.9240	7.0152	13.5089	11.7045

4 Discussion

In this work, we propose a 3D deep learning network for semantic segmentation of brain tumors from 3D multimodal MRI data. There are a total of three tumor classes that we have to segment: ET, TC, and WT, respectively. During the experiment with the local-test dataset, we found that ET was the most difficult class to be segmented throughout all local-test sets. This is due to that ET occupied the smallest part of the total tumor area [11]. At first, we added two more encoder blocks in order to solve this issue. Even though the dice score of ET is slightly increased from 0.7450 to 0.7502. However, increasing the number of encoders to extract deeper features causes another problem. As illustrated in Fig. 4, the network with adding only two additional encoders compared to the 3D CMM-Net incorrectly predicted the ED region or the NE part.

Thus, we added an HPPM block between the two added encoders to solve this problem. The proposed network in this study can further extend the receptive field by adding the HPPM block and at the same time obtaining multi-scale feature maps. The prediction output of our model with two additional encoders and HPPMs is shown in the rightmost of Fig. 4. When we try to extend the number of encoders and add HPPM in the bottleneck of our network, the performance was enhanced. Our proposed 3D CMM-Net with deeper encoder and HPPM results in the dice scores of 0.7321, 0.7514, and 0.8743 for ET, TC, and WT, respectively on the validation dataset. The results of the validation data on WT were higher than the results of the local-test dataset. On the test dataset, our model obtained the lower Dice score than local-test and validation sets as shown in Table 4. However, this trend is common when looking at the winner case from 2017 to last year.

We also looked into the training loss on different conditions where we could find out that in the case of 3D CMM-Net with two additional encoders and two HPPMs the loss was dropped faster than others after 10 epochs. That graph shows that HPPM helps the model to be learned efficiently on the given data because HPPM could extract the local feature and global one at the same time from the given data.

However, there is still a limit to add infinite encoder blocks for further improving the segmentation performance due to the restricted GPU memory we can utilize. Recently, there is a trend to improve the performance by exploiting the Vision Transformer [12–14]. In the future, we plan to properly adopt the Vision Transformer to our proposed network.

Acknowledgements. This work was supported by the Korea Medical Device Development Fund grant funded by the Korea government (the Ministry of Science and ICT, the Ministry of Trade, Industry and Energy, the Ministry of Health & Welfare, Republic of Korea, the Ministry of Food and Drug Safety) (Project Number: 202011D23).

References

1. Holland, E.C.: Glioblastoma multiforme: the terminator. Proc. Natl. Acad. Sci. **97**, 6242–6244 (2000)
2. Baid, U., et al.: The rsna-asnr-miccai brats 2021 benchmark on brain tumor segmentation and radiogenomic classification. arXiv preprint arXiv:2107.02314 (2021)
3. Menze, B.H., et al.: The multimodal brain tumor image segmentation benchmark (BRATS). IEEE Trans. Med. Imaging **34**, 1993–2024 (2014)
4. Bakas, S., et al.: Advancing the cancer genome atlas glioma MRI collections with expert segmentation labels and radiomic features. Sci. Data **4**, 1–13 (2017)
5. Bakas, S., et al.: Segmentation labels and radiomic features for the pre-operative scans of the TCGA-LGG collection. Canc. Imaging Arch. **286** (2017)
6. Bakas, S., et al.: Segmentation labels and radiomic features for the pre-operative scans of the TCGA-GBM collection. the cancer imaging archive. Nat. Sci. Data **4**, 170117 (2017)
7. Al-Masni, M.A., Kim, D.-H.: CMM-Net: Contextual multi-scale multi-level network for efficient biomedical image segmentation. Sci. Rep. **11**(10191), 1–18 (2021)
8. Yu, F., Koltun, V.: Multi-scale context aggregation by dilated convolutions. arXiv preprint arXiv:1511.07122 (2015)
9. Zhao, H., Shi, J., Qi, X., Wang, X., Jia, J.: Pyramid scene parsing network. In: Proceedings of the IEEE Conference on Computer Vision and Pattern Recognition, pp. 2881–2890 (2017)
10. Paszke, A., et al.: Pytorch: An imperative style, high-performance deep learning library. Adv. Neural. Inf. Process. Syst. **32**, 8026–8037 (2019)
11. Badrinarayanan, V., Kendall, A., Cipolla, R.: Segnet: a deep convolutional encoder-decoder architecture for image segmentation. IEEE Trans. Pattern Anal. Mach. Intell. **39**, 2481–2495 (2017)
12. Xie, E., Wang, W., Yu, Z., Anandkumar, A., Alvarez, J.M., Luo, P.: SegFormer: Simple and Efficient Design for Semantic Segmentation with Transformers. arXiv preprint arXiv:2105.15203 (2021)

13. Dosovitskiy, A., et al.: An image is worth 16×16 words: Transformers for image recognition at scale. arXiv preprint arXiv:2010.11929 (2020)
14. Hatamizadeh, A., Yang, D., Roth, H., Xu, D.U.: Transformers for 3D Medical Image Segmentation. arXiv 2021. arXiv preprint arXiv:2103.10504

Multi Modal Fusion for Radiogenomics Classification of Brain Tumor

Timothy Sum Hon Mun[1](✉)(iD), Simon Doran[1](✉)(iD), Paul Huang[1](✉)(iD),
Christina Messiou[1,2](✉)(iD), and Matthew Blackledge[1](✉)(iD)

[1] Institute of Cancer Research, 123 Old Brompton Road, South Kensington,
London, UK
{timothy.sumhonmun,simon.doran,paul.huang,christina.messiou,
matthew.blackledge}@icr.ac.uk
[2] Royal Marsden Hospital, 203 Fulham Road, Chelsea, London, UK
christina.messiou@rmh.nhs.uk

Abstract. Glioblastomas are the most common and aggressive malignant primary tumor of the central nervous system in adults. The tumours are quite heterogeneous in its shape, texture, and histology. Patients that have been diagnosed with glioblastoma typically have low survival rates and it can take weeks to perform a genetic analysis of an extracted tissue sample. If an effective way to diagnose glioblastomas have been discovered through the use of imaging and AI techniques, this can lead to quality of life improvement for patients through better planning of therapy and surgery required. This work is part of the Brain Tumor Segmentation BraTS 2021 challenge. The challenge is to predict the MGMT promotor methylation status from multi-modal MRI data. We propose a multi-modal late fusion 3D classification network for brain tumor classifcation on 3D MRI images by using all 4 different modalities (T1w, T1wCE, T2w, FLAIR) and also can be extended to include radiomics features or other external features into the network. We also then compare it against 3D classification models trained on each image modality on its own and then ensembled together during inference.

Keywords: Brain tumor · Medical imaging · Multi-modal classification

1 Introduction

Glioblastoma are the aggressive malignant primary tumor of the central nervous system in adults. Patients typically have very poor prognosis, and the current gold standard for treatment composes of surgery, followed by chemotherapy and/or radiotherapy. MGMT (O[6]-methylguanine-DNA methyltransferase) is a DNA repair enzyme that the methylation of its promoter in newly diagnosed glioblastoma has been identified as a favorable prognostic factor and a predictor of chemotherapy response. Thus determination of MGMT promoter methylation status in newly diagnosed glioblastoma can influence treatment decision making.

A. Crimi and S. Bakas (Eds.): BrainLes 2021, LNCS 12962, pp. 344–355, 2022.
https://doi.org/10.1007/978-3-031-08999-2_29

The presence of the MGMT promoter methylation has some evidence that it is a strong predictor of responsiveness to chemotherapy. Therefore, it will introduce new treatment and management strategies that can help brain cancer patients to have less invasive treatment options if techniques are able leverage this feature.

MRI data of different modality such as T1w, T1wCE, T2w and FLAIR has been provided by the challenge to predict the MGMT promoter methylation status. The intrinsic features of the biological tissue contribute to its signal intensity on an MR image and hence image contrast. The proton determines the maximum signal that can be obtained from a given tissue. The T1 time of a tissue is the time it takes for the excited spins to recover and be available for the next excitation. It affects signal intensity indirectly and can be changed at random. It can only be contrast enhanced. Images with contrast that is mainly determined by T1 are called T1-weighted images (T1w). The T2 time mostly determines how quickly an MR signal fades after excitation. The T2 contrast of an MR image can be controlled by the operator as well. Images with contrast that is mainly determined by T2 are called T2-weighted images (T2w). FLAIR is a also considered a T2-weighted technique but it dampens ventricular CSF signal compared to normal T2w images.

The use of features generated by radiomics and genomics which leads to the term radiogenomics in model development process are also active areas of research in this area. Although it requires a dataset that is annotated with the ground truth segmentation masks of the location of the tumour in order to be able to extract the features from the tumor which was not provided along with this challenge.

This year, BraTS 2021 training dataset consisted of 585 cases - each with four different 3D MRI modalities (T1w, T1wCE, T2 and FLAIR) which are not rigidly aligned to the same space. The validation dataset (81 cases) is used to calculate the public leaderboard ranking on Kaggle.

In this work, we describe our multi-modality fusion approach for 3D brain MGMT classification from multimodal 3D MRI images.

2   Related Work

The BraTS challenge has been ongoing for many years and has produced plenty of research onto the state of art for segmentation, uncertainty classification, survival prediction and others. For example, past iterations have investigated many different techniques in the area of segmentation [27]. A lot of great work has been possible due to this challenge and the datasets provided [2–5,10].

Large quantities of annotated datasets are not as readily available in the medical imaging domain compared to other domains. Therefore, using augmentation techniques to generate more data has been shown to improve the performance of networks in [13,14]. The two papers provided a lot of ideas on data augmentation to try while manipulating the data for the challenge. GANs [6] which is a state of the art technique used for generating synthetic data to increase the amount of data for modelling. [7] has provided a review of the use of GANs in medical imaging and the results have been promising.

Radiomics [8] is the high-throughput feature extraction process that allows us to extract mineable data from images and the subsequent analysis of these data for decision support. It can contain first, second, and higher-order statistics. These data are combined with other demographics data and are mined with sophisticated bioinformatics tools to develop models that may potentially improve diagnostic, prognostic, and predictive accuracy At this point in time, the field of radiomics research are concentrated on the improvement of models to provide the most accurate possible diagnoses which will leads to better patient care and outcomes. It has also been used in problems relating to brain tumours and survival prediction such as in [9].

3   Method and Experiments

3.1   Data Description

The BraTS dataset [10] consists of retrospective brain tumor mpMRI scans acquired from multiple different institutions under standard clinical conditions although with different equipment and imaging protocols. Therefore, the imaging quality is heteregeneous due to the diverse clinical practice across different institutions. Inclusion criteria for the Task 2 challenge's dataset comprised pathologically confirmed diagnosis available MGMT promoter methylation status. The data have been updated since the previous iteration of BraTS challenge and the total number of cases has increased from 660 to 2,000. The MGMT methylation status was based on the laboratory assessment of the surgical brain tumor specimen.

The mpMRI scans consist of 4 different modalities acquired with various protocols and difference scanners from multiple institutions.

Standardized pre-processing has been applied to all the BraTS mpMRI scans. Specifically, the applied pre-processing routines include conversion of the DICOM files to the NIFTI file format, re-orientation to a common orientation system such as RAI, co-registration to the same anatomical template, resampling to a uniform isotropic resolution ($1\,mm^3$) and finally skull-stripping. The pre-processing pipeline is publicly available through the Cancer Imaging Phenomics Toolkit (CaPTk) [11] and Federated Tumor Segmentation (FeTS) [12]. Conversion to NIFTI strips the DICOM metadata from the images and essentially removes all Protected Health Information (PHI) from the DICOM headers. Furthermore, skull stripping mitigates potential facial reconstruction/recognition of the patient.

For Task 2 (Radiogenomic Classification), all the imaging volumes were converted from NIFTI to DICOM files while preserving the original patient space. Each MRI sequence and its associated DICOM scan in the patient space are required for this conversion process. The DICOM scans were read as ITK images and the skull-stripped volume is rigidly registered to it, providing a transformation matrix that defines the spatial mapping between the two volumes.

The acquired transformation matrix is applied to all skull-stripped volume and its corresponding segmentation labels to translate them both to that patient space. These transformed volumes are then passed through CaPTk's NIFTI to DICOM conversion engine to generate DICOM image volumes for the skull-stripped image. Once all MRI sequences were converted back to the DICOM file format, the dataset was anonymized further using two steps involved the RSNA Clinical Trials Processor Anonymizer and whitelisting of DICOM files.

The data is provided by the competition has three cohorts: Training, Validation (Public), and Testing (Private). The training and the validation cohorts are provided to the participants and the participants will not have access to the "Testing" cohort at all times, during and after the competition. The training dataset was sourced from 18 institutions internationally where some of the data comes from the Cancer Imaging Archive (TCIA) but the majority has not previously been made publicly available.

The private test set included a significant proportion of cases from organizations not represented in the training dataset to simulate real-world clinical environment and evaluate the generalization ability of the models with this data obtained at different sites as revealed by the organizers after the competition has ended.

3.2 Data Pre-processing and Augmentation

Data augmentation techniques have been shown to implicity regularize and improve generalization of deep neural networks to unseen datasets. It is vital in scenarios where the amount of high-quality ground-truth data is limited because acquiring and annotating new data is costly and time-consuming. [13,14] both show that data augmentation significantly improves the performance of the neural network through their experiments with BraTS datasets. Elastic deformations and brightness adjustment seem to be best combination of augmentation to be applied to the data. It can be useful to train the network on brain scans that are oriented differently so that the model does not overfit to the training data and this is also enabled by the fact that all subjects in BraTS have been co-registered to a common space.

The types of data pre-processing and augmentation that have been performed on the mpMRI scans so far are as shown below.

Data Pre-processings:

- Perform resampling and alignment of the planes of different MRI imaging modalities (the planes are different even for the same patient between different modalities) to one reference patient
- Create sub-volumes of $64 \times 64 \times 64$ voxels and $128 \times 128 \times 128$ voxels
- Remove blank images
- Crop to focus on regions of interest
- Normalize and standardize intensity values
- Apply CLAHE for histogram equalization

Data Augmentations:

- Random Scaling
- Random Rotation
- Random Flipping
- Random Shearing
- Brightness adjustment
- N4 bias field correction which has shown in work well in [5, 28]

3.3   Single Modality Classification Networks

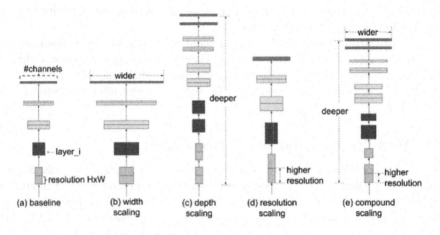

Fig. 1. Efficient net compound scaling [16]

Fig. 2. Efficient net architecture [17]

Our current baseline classification network is an EfficientNet which can arbitrarily scale network dimensions, such as depth, width, and resolution by performing a grid search to find the relationship between different scaling dimensions of the baseline network under a fixed resource constraint. This model scaling is the main idea of this network which can seen in Fig. 1. The model scaling method achieves a balance of scaling all dimensions of network width/depth/resolution by scaling each of them with a constant ratio. This scaling approach was shown to work well due to the idea that the input image is bigger, a network with more layers and more channels to capture more fine-grained patterns on a larger image will needed.

A multi objective neural architecture search (NAS) approach was used to develop the architecture of the network that balances the tradeoff between accuracy and floating point operations. There are 8 different EfficientNets ranging from B1 to B7 with the baseline model being B0. We experimented with all the B0–B7 architectures and found that a simpler model tends to perform better so the results presented in this paper will be based on the B0 architecture. An example of the underlying architecture of the baseline model is shown in Fig. 2. The building block of the MBConv block consists of the inverted residual blocks, squeeze and excitation block as well as swish activation.

Our model is trained from scratch using a 3D version of EfficientNet implemented in Pytorch. More details can be found in the original paper [16] and the code for the 3D version is from [18] (Fig. 3 and 4).

Our initial approach trains a classification network per each image modality, then use each of them to predict the MGMT value and then ensemble their predictions to be used as the final predictions as can be seen in Fig. 2.

3.4 Multi Modality Classification Network

Our next approach is to try to take advantage of all the different MRI image modalities during the training process by concatenating their feature maps before the classification head. We also explored the opportunity concatenate other features that are not from the images such as DICOM metadata into the feature map before classification which did not have meaningful improvements to the model. The late fusion may lose information on the interactions between modal-

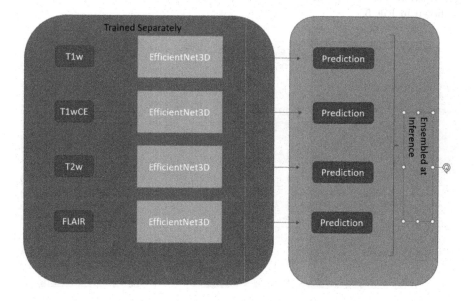

Fig. 3. Single modality and ensemble

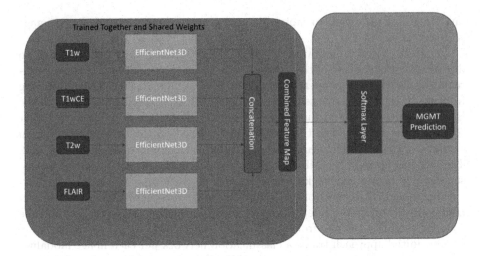

Fig. 4. Multi-modality approach with late fusion v1

ity but it is easy to train as well as has flexiblity to be extended and make predictions if one or more of the other modalities are not available.

Combining early fusion (merging 4 different MRI modalities into a single 4 channel image) with late fusion could also be promising. There are many different ways to perform multi modal fusion that can be explored and is covered in [22].

The next stage in our pipeline that we are planning to work on is to use DeepBrainSeg to predict the segmentations from each different modalites in the data and then extracting radiomic features from the volume of interest (morphological, texture, histogram-based, first/second order statistic and others). This is shown in Fig. 5.

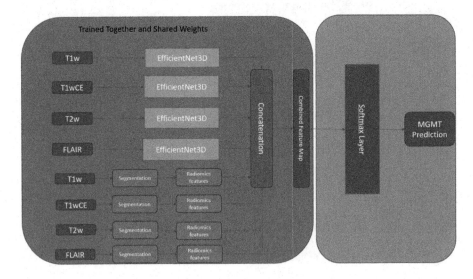

Fig. 5. Multi-modality approach with late fusion v2

4 Results

Our network is implemented mainly using PyTorch [19] while the image processing and augmentation on the dataset provided without any external data is done using a combination of SimpleITK [20,21]. The model is trained on Google Colab Pro which provides a range of GPUs such as Nvidia K80s, T4s, P4s and P100s. We compared the performance of the single modality approach (ensemble of single modality models), multi-modality approach and ensemble of the two approaches. The single modality approach takes about 8 h to train on Google Colab Pro GPUs for about 25 epochs. The multi-modality approach takes about 24 h to train on Google Colab Pro for about 8 epochs.

We report our results on the public leaderboard (validation) dataset at the time of submission of this paper. Our predictions are submitted on the Kaggle platform alongside a notebook with inference code. We also ensembled a combination of models trained using the single modality approach and the multi-modality approach to test whether there will be improvement in performance and surprisingly it did not so we believe that more data augmentation might be needed for model robustness. Our best performing classification model gives an AUC score of 0.698 on the public leaderboard (Table 1).

Table 1. Public leaderboard results for methods

Method name	AUC score
Ensemble of single modality	0.634
Multi modal late fusion	0.698
Ensemble of the two methods	0.603

Not all of our models were scored on the private testing dataset due to a submission scoring error on Kaggle which did not provide further information. Out of the models that were scored, the simpler models scored much better on the testing dataset where the AUC is only around 0.5–0.51 that is much lower than the validation dataset. Other participants has also reported much lower AUC on the testing dataset compared to the validation dataset.

5 Discussion and Conclusion

In this work, we described an initial multi-modal late fusion architecture for MGMT value using all four different modalities of 3D MRIs in the dataset that have been provided by the BraTS Challenge 2021.

We have experimented with different approaches such as training different state of the art classification architectures in 2D and 3D such as ResNets and SE-Resnets. We also tested different hyperparameters such as learning rate (with and without scheduling) and the batch size but had to keep the batch size to 4 due to GPU memory limits. We have different datasets with different voxel sizes of $64 \times 64 \times 64$ and $128 \times 128 \times 128$ that are used in training the models. The current multi-modality model is only trained with the axial plane but we plan to also train the model on sagittal and coronal planes as well.

Different data pre-processing and augmentation techniques were employed such as normalization and standardizing the intensity values in the images, removing blank images, resampling and align image planes of different modalities, cropping, N4 bias field correction and others. The N4 bias correction on MRI images seems to beneficial on some images and not all of them so further investigation have to be done to identify the images that will benefit the most from this processing.

All of the training of the models has been done on the Kaggle Notebooks and mainly Google Colab Pro which have limited VM runtime of 9 h and 24 h respectively. The GPUs provided by Google Colab Pro can vary depending on availability as well as being outside of the user's control and therefore hard to get a consistent runtime alongside a quota for GPU usage where no GPUs will be allocated once that limit is reached. So the current approach has not been fine-tuned extensively yet. Therefore, we plan to perform more in-depth fine-tuning of the final models and approach using Google AI Platform notebooks to use more powerful GPUs without runtime limit or GPU quotas.

There's a lot more room for improvement the current architecture to be extended for the remaining duration of the competition to be able to take advantage of the information available in the MRI datasets provided by the competition as well as external datasets. One of the key ideas that we would like to explore is to either segment the MRI brain images provided in the challenge by hand or to use a model pretrained on brain tumor data to automatically segment the images so that we are able to perform feature extraction using radiomics or deep learning. If we can extract the radiomics or deep learning features for each modality, then we can perform feature reduction by keeping statistically significant and uncorrelated features before possibly fuse/concatenate them alongside the combined feature vector of different MRI modalities before the classification head. This could probably improve the performance of this multi-modality approach. An example of a feature extraction pipeline can be seen in Fig. 6.

Early fusion of the 4 different image modalities into a 4-channel image and then using this new representation to train a classification network is also another possible avenue for exploration. Due to small size of training, public leaderboard and private leaderboard data, a more thorough exploration of data augmentation techniques will probably be useful to make the models more robust.

The low generalization ability of our models was also experienced by other participants in the competition and was covered by the organizers of the competition in [26]. This is can be partly attributed to the small size of the dataset (training, validation, testing) as well as the presence of multi-institutional data in the testing dataset which is not present in the training dataset. Therefore, a simpler model and greater focus on data processing was shown to be more promising as can be seen with the approach that was shared by the first place

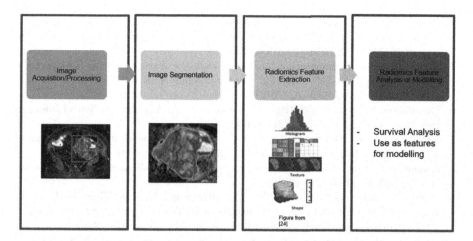

Fig. 6. Example of a feature extraction pipeline using radiomics or deep learning.

winner in [25] where ensembling and complex models performed well in the validation dataset but not on the testing dataset. The inherent difficulty in generalizing the model to an unseen data was illustrated in [27] where the paper showed a great reduction in performance when a model trained and validated using public data from the US to predict a different mutation in brain cancer (ATRX) tested poorly on testing dataset from China.

The conclusion from participating in this challenge is that more work still needs to be done before application of imaging AI can be confidently used for radiogenomics. There is not a strong enough evidence that medical imaging alone can be used to predict methylation (MGMT promoter status) or genomic features of cancer with high confidence to deliver valuable prognostic information to clinicians and patients. Additional analysis also needs to be conducted on discrepancy between the performance observed in the challenge with literatures that also looked at the prediction of MGMT status such as [28] and the factors that lead to this discrepancy.

References

1. Bakas, S., et al.: Identifying the best machine learning algorithms for brain tumor segmentation, progression assessment, and overall survival prediction in the BraTS challenge. arXiv preprint arXiv:1811.02629 (2018)
2. Menze, B.H., Jakab, A., Bauer, S., Kalpathy-Cramer, J., Farahani, K., Kirby, J., et al.: The multimodal brain tumor image segmentation benchmark (BraTS). IEEE Trans. Med. Imaging **34**(10), 1993–2024 (2015). https://doi.org/10.1109/TMI.2014.2377694
3. Bakas, S., Akbari, H., Sotiras, A., Bilello, M., Rozycki, M., Kirby, J.S., et al.: Advancing the cancer genome atlas glioma MRI collections with expert segmentation labels and radiomic features. Nat. Sci. Data **4**, 170117 (2017). https://doi.org/10.1038/sdata.2017.117

4. Bakas, S., et al.: Segmentation labels and radiomic features for the pre-operative scans of the TCGA-GBM collection. Cancer Imaging Arch. (2017). https://doi.org/10.7937/K9/TCIA.2017.KLXWJJ1Q

5. Bakas, S., et al.: Segmentation labels and radiomic features for the pre-operative scans of the TCGA-LGG collection. Cancer Imaging Arch. (2017). https://doi.org/10.7937/K9/TCIA.2017.GJQ7R0EF

6. Goodfellow, I, et al.: Generative adversarial nets. In: Advances in Neural Information Processing Systems, vol. 27 (2014)

7. Yi, X., Walia, E., Babyn, P.: Generative adversarial network in medical imaging: a review. Med. Image Anal. **58**, 101552 (2019)

8. Kumar, V., et al.: Radiomics: the process and the challenges. Magn. Resonan. Imaging **30**(9), 1234–1248 (2012)

9. Isensee, F., Kickingereder, P., Wick, W., Bendszus, M., Maier-Hein, K.H.: Brain tumor segmentation and radiomics survival prediction: contribution to the BRATS 2017 challenge. In: Crimi, A., Bakas, S., Kuijf, H., Menze, B., Reyes, M. (eds.) BrainLes 2017. LNCS, vol. 10670, pp. 287–297. Springer, Cham (2018). https://doi.org/10.1007/978-3-319-75238-9_25

10. Baid, U., et al.: The RSNA-ASNR-MICCAI BraTS 2021 benchmark on brain tumor segmentation and radiogenomic classification. arXiv:2107.02314 (2021)

11. Davatzikos, C., et al.: Cancer imaging phenomics toolkit: quantitative imaging analytics for precision diagnostics and predictive modeling of clinical outcome. J. Med. Imaging **5**(1), 011018 (2018)

12. Sheller, M.J., et al.: Federated learning in medicine: facilitating multi-institutional collaborations without sharing patient data. Sci. Rep. **10**(1), 1–12 (2020)

13. Nalepa, J., Marcinkiewicz, M., Kawulok, M.: Data augmentation for brain-tumor segmentation: a review. Front. Comput. Neurosci. **13**, 83 (2019)

14. Cirillo, M.D., Abramian, D., Eklund, A.: What is the best data augmentation for 3D brain tumor segmentation?. arXiv preprint arXiv:2010.13372 (2020)

15. Dai, L., Li, T., Shu, H., Zhong, L., Shen, H., Zhu, H.: Automatic brain tumor segmentation with domain adaptation. In: Crimi, A., Bakas, S., Kuijf, H., Keyvan, F., Reyes, M., van Walsum, T. (eds.) BrainLes 2018. LNCS, vol. 11384, pp. 380–392. Springer, Cham (2019). https://doi.org/10.1007/978-3-030-11726-9_34

16. Tan, M., Le, Q.: EfficientNet: rethinking model scaling for convolutional neural networks. In: International Conference on Machine Learning. PMLR (2019)

17. EfficientNet Google Blog. https://ai.googleblog.com/2019/05/efficientnet-improving-accuracy-and.html. Accessed 19 Aug 2021

18. EfficientNetPytorch-3D. https://github.com/shijianjian/EfficientNet-PyTorch-3D. Accessed 19 Aug 2021

19. Paszke, A., et al.: Pytorch: an imperative style, high-performance deep learning library. In: Advances in Neural Information Processing Systems, vol. 32, pp. 8026–8037 (2019)

20. Yaniv, Z., Lowekamp, B.C., Johnson, H.J., Beare, R.: SimpleITK image-analysis notebooks: a collaborative environment for education and reproducible research. J. Digit. Imaging **31**(3), 290–303 (2017). https://doi.org/10.1007/s10278-017-0037-8

21. Lowekamp, B.C., Chen, D.T., Ibáñez, L., Blezek, D.: The design of SimpleITK. Front. Neuroinform. **7**, 45 (2013). https://doi.org/10.3389/fninf.2013.00045

22. Morency, L.-P., Baltrusaitis, T.: Tutorial on multimodal machine learning CMU multimodal communication and machine learning laboratory [MultiComp Lab] (2017)

23. Hussain, S., Anwar, S.M., Majid, M.: Segmentation of glioma tumors in brain using deep convolutional neural network. Neurocomputing **282**, 248–261 (2018). https://doi.org/10.1016/j.neucom.2017.12.032

24. Crombé, A., et al.: T2-based MRI delta-radiomics improve response prediction in soft-tissue sarcomas treated by neoadjuvant chemotherapy. J. Magn. Resonan. Imaging **50**(2), 497–510 (2019)

25. Kaggle First Place Solution. https://www.kaggle.com/c/rsna-miccai-brain-tumor-radiogenomic-classification/discussion/281347. Accessed 02 Dec 2021

26. Kaggle Results Discussion about Low Model Performance by Organizers. https://www.kaggle.com/c/rsna-miccai-brain-tumor-radiogenomic-classification/discussion/284024. Accessed 02 Dec 2021

27. Li, Y., et al.: Genotype prediction of ATRX mutation in lower-grade gliomas using an MRI radiomics signature. Eur. Radiol. **28**(7), 2960–2968 (2018). https://doi.org/10.1007/s00330-017-5267-0

28. Yogananda, C.G.B., et al.: MRI-based deep-learning method for determining glioma MGMT promoter methylation status. Am. J. Neuroradiol. **42**(5), 845–852 (2021)

A Joint Graph and Image Convolution Network for Automatic Brain Tumor Segmentation

Camillo Saueressig[1,2] , Adam Berkley[1], Reshma Munbodh[3(✉)] ,
and Ritambhara Singh[1,2(✉)]

[1] Department of Computer Science, Brown University, Providence, USA
ritambhara@brown.edu
[2] Center for Computational Molecular Biology, Brown University, Providence, USA
[3] Department of Radiation Oncology, Brown Alpert Medical School, Providence, USA
reshma_munbodh@brown.edu

Abstract. We present a joint graph convolution - image convolution neural network as our submission to the Brain Tumor Segmentation (BraTS) 2021 challenge. We model each brain as a graph composed of distinct image regions, which is initially segmented by a graph neural network (GNN). Subsequently, the tumorous volume identified by the GNN is further refined by a simple (voxel) convolutional neural network (CNN), which produces the final segmentation. This approach captures both global brain feature interactions via the graphical representation *and* local image details through the use of convolutional filters. We find that the GNN component by itself can effectively identify and segment the brain tumors. The addition of the CNN further improves the median performance of the model on the validation set by 2% across all metrics evaluated.

Keywords: Graph neural networks · Brain tumor segmentation · Deep learning

1 Introduction

Tumor segmentation is a cornerstone of nearly all standard tumor treatments. It is integral for surgical and radiation planning, treatment response analysis, and longitudinal tumor monitoring, among other standard practices. However, manual tumor segmentation is notoriously time-consuming and subjective, even for highly trained radiologists. Automatic tumor segmentation can produce such segmentations in a fraction of the time in a standardized, reproducible fashion. Over the past decade, the performance of automated biomedical segmentation methods has significantly improved across multiple tumor types, and brain tumors are no exception [7,9]. The Brain Tumor Segmentation dataset (BraTS) is the largest publicly available dataset of glioma MRIs and corresponding expert segmentations and has played a pivotal role in developing and evaluating these methods [3–6,12].

The 2021 BraTS tumor segmentation challenge consists of over 2000 multi-parametric magnetic resonance images (MRIs) of tumorous brain volumes (specifically, gliomas) imaged across a wide array of institutions. While the images are compiled from a number of different institutions, they are all processed using a standard pipeline,

A. Crimi and S. Bakas (Eds.): BrainLes 2021, LNCS 12962, pp. 356–365, 2022.
https://doi.org/10.1007/978-3-031-08999-2_30

and the same four modalities are available for every volume. These are T1-weighted, T1-weighted contrast-enhanced, T2-weighted, and Fluid Attenuated Inversion Recovery (FLAIR) modalities, all of which provide complementary information on the location and shape of the tumor and its compartments. The ground truth labels are generated using an ensemble of top-performing models from previous years and are manually revised by an expert neuroradiologist for all images. The challenge aims to correctly classify each voxel of a given brain volume as either healthy tissue, edema, enhancing tumor (ET), or necrotic tumor core. These tumor sub-regions can be combined into the whole tumor (WT) and core tumor (necrotic core + enhancing tumor, CT) to further evaluate model performance on gross tumor segmentation [2].

Our submission to the BraTS 2021 challenge is a joint graph neural network (GNN) - convolutional neural network (CNN) model (summarized in Fig. 1). The GNN module aims to partition the brain into distinct regions and predict the label of each region, and the CNN component refines the predictions made by the GNN. Unlike the vast majority of BraTS competitors in recent years [6], which exclusively perform inference directly on voxel data, our model instead learns and predicts primarily on a graphical representation of the brain. We model each brain volume as composed of small, contiguous regions and connect nearby regions using edges, forming a graph. Each graph node contains information summarizing the intensity information of the brain in that region across all four modalities, and the edges allow neighboring regions to share their information with each other. This formulation greatly simplifies the representation of a brain from millions of voxels down to only thousands of nodes, while preserving nearly all the information. It also enables the modeling of explicit connectivity between different regions of the brain and potential long-range interactions between distant regions, which are difficult to capture using only CNNs. We have previously developed a similar model composed only of a graph neural network on the 2019 BraTS dataset [13]. Here, we improve on our previous work by adding a shallow CNN to the end of the model, which smooths out the model predictions at region boundaries and provides a substantial ($\geq 2\%$) improvement in both median Dice score and median Hausdorff distance on the validation set.

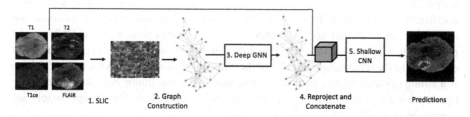

Fig. 1. GNN-CNN Model Overview. MRI Modalities are first stacked to create one 3D Image with 4 channels. 1) Combined modalities are clustered into supervoxels using SLIC. 2) Supervoxels are converted to a graph structure such that each supervoxel becomes one graph node (depicted graph is greatly simplified). 3) Graph is fed through a Graph Neural Network 4) Node prediction outputs (more specifically, logits) are overlaid back onto the supervoxels. The original input image features are concatenated with re-projected node logits. 5) The result is fed through a 2-layer CNN which produces final predictions.

2   Methods

Our GNN-CNN model is composed of two components. The core component is a graph neural network (GNN) [10, 14]. For a given input graph representing one patient sample, where each node corresponds to a collection of adjacent voxels in the original MRI image, the GNN predicts each node's label. Since the GNN can only predict the label of nodes (i.e. brain regions) atomically, its predictions are necessarily coarser than voxel-based predictions. This property can lead to incorrect predictions at the edges of tumor compartments, where created regions can contain voxels of multiple labels [13]. This shortcoming is especially pronounced in small tumors. Accordingly, we have added a second component to our model: a shallow CNN [11]. The convolutional layers receive both the GNN prediction logits (projected back into an image) and the original voxel image data. They are thus able to make fine-grained adjustments to the coarse predictions based on local voxel information. The details of the model are presented in Fig. 2.

2.1   Graph Construction from MRI Modalities

Both the input and the output of the GNN are required to be graph-structured data. Therefore, before feeding the MRI scans into our network, we transform them into graphs. Graphs are composed of nodes and edges, where both the nodes and the edges can have features associated with them. In this work, each node corresponds to one image region, and an edge between two nodes corresponds to spatial proximity of the corresponding regions. We partition the brain into regions using supervoxels. Supervoxels are the 3D analog to superpixels, i.e., collections of nearby pixels that share similar intensities.

We construct the supervoxels using the Simple Linear Iterative Clustering (SLIC) algorithm [1]. SLIC uses a combination of spatial and intensity information to partition an image into approximately a desired number of supervoxels using K-means clustering. While the input to SLIC is traditionally in either RGB or Lab color space, we find that running SLIC directly on the stacked MRI modalities still produces meaningful supervoxels. To determine the optimal hyperparameters for the SLIC algorithm, we perform a grid search across k, the number of supervoxels and m, the compactness coefficient (the weighting between spatial and intensity information), and compute the achievable segmentation accuracy (ASA). ASA measures how well the GNN would perform on a given supervoxel partitioning, given that it classifies every supervoxel according to the most common label of the constituent voxels. The ASA is high if there is a strong correspondence between supervoxel shape and tumor boundaries, resulting in supervoxels composed of voxels with the same label. It is low if supervoxels are composed of voxels with mixed labels.

After the supervoxels are generated via SLIC, we discard those supervoxels that lie outside the brain volume. Of the remaining supervoxels, each is assigned a feature vector, a label, and a set of neighbors. The feature vector summarizes the intensities of the input MRIs for its comprising voxels. We empirically found that intensity quintiles for each modality yielded the best results. The label is the majority label (mode) of its constituent voxels. The neighbors of a supervoxel are all other supervoxels which are directly adjacent to it. A graph is then constructed where each supervoxel forms one node with its associated features and label, and each supervoxel shares an unweighted and undirected edge with its neighbors.

2.2   GNN Architecture

Our graph neural network is composed of several sequential GraphSAGE-pool layers [8] alternated with the ReLU non-linearity (Fig. 2). Each layer transforms the features of each node by aggregating information from that node's neighbors, according to Eq. 1

$$h_u^{(l+1)} = \sigma(W^{(l)} \cdot (h_u^{(l)} \parallel max(\sigma(W_{pool} \cdot h_v^{(l)}) \ \forall \ v \in V(u))) \quad (1)$$

where $h_u^{(l)}$ is the features of node u at layer l, σ is a differentiable, non-linear activation function, $W^{(l)}$ is a layer specific trainable weight matrix, W_{pool} is a global trainable weight matrix, $\parallel$ is the concatenation operator, and $V(u)$ is the subset of nodes which are directly connected to u via edges, also known as the neighborhood of u.

The input layer expects 20 features (5 quintiles for each of four modalities) and the output layer outputs 4 logits (one for each label). The output logits are duplicated, where one copy is passed directly through a loss function which backpropagates only through the GNN, and the other is passed through to the CNN (Fig. 2)

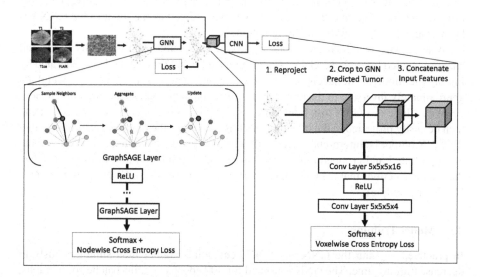

Fig. 2. Detailed view of GNN and CNN. Left: The GNN is composed of GraphSAGE layers alternated with a nonlinearity. Each GraphSAGE layer updates each node's features by sampling neighboring nodes and aggregating the features (Eq. 1). **Right**: 1) The output of the GNN is reprojected into a 3D image by assigning each voxel the output logits of its corresponding node. 2) Based on this reprojection, the approximate location of the tumor predicted by the GNN is located and cropped out. 3) The projected and cropped logits are concatenated with the image features for that same location. This volume is then fed through a two-layer CNN. Note that the output of both the GNN and CNN components have an associated loss function.

2.3 CNN Architecture

The CNN consists of two convolutional layers with a $5 \times 5 \times 5$ kernel size and a stride of 1 (Fig. 2). The first layer has 16 filters and the second 4 (one for each label) with ReLU nonlinearity between the two layers. The architecture is purposefully kept simple since it only serves to refine the predictions made by the GNN.

The input to the CNN is the concatenation of the GNN output logits ($f = 4$) and the input MRI modalities ($f = 4$) for each voxel. Therefore, the CNN receives the predictions of the GNN in addition to the image features, which allows it to correct the predictions made by the GNN. This correction is especially relevant around the edges of the tumor and its compartments, where the coarse predictions from the GNN can often result in misclassifications of strips of voxels. We feed only the tumorous tissue through the CNN to reduce the memory requirement and computation time. Specifically, we crop out a patch of the volume containing the tumor, as predicted by the GNN, and the CNN further refines only that patch.

2.4 Loss Functions

We calculate and backpropagate loss through our model at two locations. A voxel-wise cross-entropy loss is calculated from the output of the CNN and backpropagated *only* through the convolutional layers. This loss is unweighted as the input to the CNN has been cropped to the tumor-containing volume.

A node-wise weighted cross-entropy loss is calculated from the GNN logits and backpropagated through the GNN. The ground truth label for each node is generated by finding the mode of the labels in the corresponding supervoxel. This loss is weighted approximately inversely to the prevalence of each label to address the class imbalance.

We include this GNN loss function to obtain prediction logits of the nodes that can then be easily projected in the image space. It is crucial for the model's performance that the GNN output be interpretable as predictions, so that the predicted tumorous volume can be located and cropped out. Furthermore, this formulation allows us to visualize the finer corrections that the CNN layer performs over the coarse GNN predictions (see Fig. 3 for example).

2.5 Model Training

In practice, we train the GNN and CNN sequentially rather than simultaneously to decrease training time. The GNN is trained for 300 epochs on mini-batches of 6 graphs, whereas the CNN is trained for 100 epochs using only one sample at a time. The training of a full model takes approximately 2 days on an 8 GB GPU.

We used the AdamW optimizer with weight decay of 0.0001 and exponentially decrease learning rate according to Eq. 2

$$lr_e = lr_0 * \lambda^e \tag{2}$$

where lr_0 is the initial learning rate, e is the current epoch and $\lambda = 0.98$. We found that adding additional regularization, such as dropout or higher weight decay, did not improve performance.

The BraTS 2021 dataset is split into training (n = 1251), validation (n = 216), and test (n = 570) partitions. The hyperparameters for only the GNN component, i.e., GNN layer sizes, GNN depth, learning rate, and class weighting, were tuned using random search and 5-fold cross-validation on the entire training set (n = 1251). The GNN architecture with the best average performance across the 5 folds was then integrated into the full hybrid model. Three architectural replicates were trained on the entire dataset and evaluated on the validation set. The best performing replicate was then submitted for evaluation on the test dataset. We report the mean and median results of the best performing replicate on both the validation and test sets in Sect. 3.3.

2.6 Data Preprocessing

The BraTS dataset MRIs are all padded to a standard shape to facilitate image-based processing. Since our approach is primarily graph-based and does not rely on uniform input sizes, we first crop each patient sample to the tightest possible bounding box around the brain to minimize the amount of background volume prior to supervoxel creation. Subsequently, we rescale each MRI to the approximate $[0, 1]$ range by dividing by the 99.5 percentile of intensity values in that MRI. The raw MRI data is not collected in a bounded range and can vary by several orders of magnitude even between two images of the same modality. As such, this step normalizes the intensity values to be consistent across the dataset. Finally, we compute the mean and standard deviation for each modality across the entire training dataset (on non-zero voxels) and standardize each modality to have zero mean and unit variance.

3 Results

3.1 Hyperparameters

The SLIC parameters with the highest achievable segmentation accuracy (ASA) were $k = 15000$ and $m = 0.5$. The value for m differs from that in our previous work [13] as our preprocessing steps have slightly changed.

The best performing GNN model from the cross-validation phase had 6 layers with 256 neurons each and a learning rate of 0.0005. The GNN is thus deeper and has many more learnable parameters than the CNN. This is a purposeful design choice to force the GNN to do the majority of the learning.

3.2 Evaluation Metrics

The performance of the models submitted to the BraTS challenge are evaluated using two metrics, Dice score and the 95th percentile of the symmetric Hausdorff distance. Both metrics are evaluated over the whole tumor, core tumor, and active tumor sub-regions. Intuitively, the Dice score measures the overlap between the predictions and the ground truth while Hausdorff distance measures the most the predicted and ground truth segmentations diverge from each other.

$$\text{Dice} = \frac{2TP}{2TP + FP + FN}. \tag{3}$$

where TP, FP, and FN are the number of true positives, false positives, and false negatives, respectively. True positive voxels are defined as those correctly assigned as belonging to a specific tumor compartment.

$$HD95 = 95\% \ (d(\hat{Y}, Y) \| d(Y, \hat{Y})) \tag{4}$$

where d is the element-wise distance of every voxel in the first set to the closest voxel of the same label in the second, $\hat{Y}$ are the predicted labels of each voxel, Y are the ground truth labels of each voxel, and $\|$ is the concatenation operator.

3.3 Performance

Table 1. Mean results on validation set.

Metric	Dice			HD95		
Tumor subregion	WT	TC	ET	WT	TC	ET
GNN	0.874	0.782	**0.738**	6.92	16.67	**20.40**
GNN-CNN	**0.894**	**0.807**	0.734	**6.79**	**12.62**	28.20

Table 2. Median results on validation set.

Metric	Dice			HD95		
Tumor subregion	WT	TC	ET	WT	TC	ET
GNN	0.906	0.885	0.813	3.46	3.16	2.45
GNN-CNN	**0.925**	**0.908**	**0.842**	**3.00**	**3.00**	**2.24**

The mean and median results on the validation set are given in Tables 1 and 2, respectively. On the validation set, we report both the performance of the GNN model and of the joint GNN-CNN model.

The comparison of the two models shows that the addition of the convolutional layers to the model improves mean and median performance across both metrics in the whole tumor and core tumor regions, and is inconclusive for the enhancing tumor. In the case of ET, the CNN improves the average segmentation (better median), but also seems to exacerbate poor performance on outliers (worse mean). Nonetheless, the overall improved results indicate that the addition of the CNN can successfully correct misclassification errors that result from mixed-label supervoxels, even while the CNN architecture is very simple. Notably, the median improvement across all three subregions demonstrates that the joint GNN-CNN model is 1) better able to distinguish the border edema from healthy tissue, 2) better able to distinguish NET from edema, and 3) better able to distinguish ET from NET on a typical brain.

An example segmentation highlighting these improvements is provided in Fig. 3, along with two of the four input modalities. The FLAIR image provides information

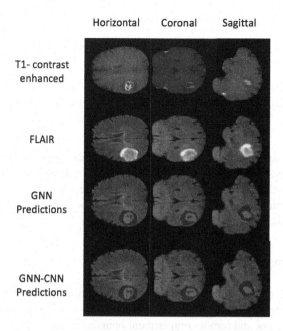

Fig. 3. Example Predictions on Validation Brain Three slices (horizontal, coronal, and sagittal) of the same brain from the validation set are shown. The first row is from the T1ce modality, and the second is from the FLAIR modality. The third shows the GNN predictions. The fourth row contains the GNN predictions refined through the CNN. Ground truth segmentations are unavailable for the validation set. Red = edema, Blue = NET/necrosis, Yellow = ET. We observe that the GNN accurately identifies the tumorous region but makes slight errors in classifying the individual compartments. The CNN, however, can refine the predictions in greater accordance with the images. (Color figure online)

on the tumor core and edema and is thus well suited for the segmentation of the whole tumor. The T1ce modality provides complementary information on NET/necrotic tissue and the enhancing tumor and is thus vital for delineation of the ET and NET subregions. The predictions that have been refined through the CNN (last row) are both smoother and correspond more closely with the shape and appearance of the tumor in the two modalities than the predictions made directly by the GNN (third row).

Given its superior performance on the validation set, we chose the joint model for evaluation on the test set. These results are provided in Table 3. The test set consists of 570 images. Of these, 87 have a different orientation than the images in the train and validation set. Unfortunately, the challenge organizers informed us that our model submission was unable to produce segmentations for these 87 images. Nonetheless, to preserve consistency across all participants, they have been included in the aggregated results with Dice scores of 0 and Hausdorff distances of 300.

On the test set, the median results approach those achieved on the validation set, but the mean scores fall far below the expected performance. We suspect that the discrepancy between mean and median scores is caused by the inclusion of the 87 failed

Table 3. Results on test set.

Metric	Dice			HD95		
Tumor subregion	WT	TC	ET	WT	TC	ET
Mean	0.747	0.680	0.560	63.15	72.63	75.74
Median	0.911	0.884	0.703	3.74	3.16	3.31

cases. The existence of such outliers would skew the mean more than the median scores, leading to the observed pattern. Nonetheless, the median results indicate that, on a typical unseen tumor, our model is effective at locating the whole and core tumor, but has difficulty delineating the enhancing tumor from surrounding regions. Possible improvements to ET prediction are considered in the discussion.

4 Discussion

We have presented a joint GNN-CNN network for automatic brain tumor segmentation. The GNN can produce good segmentations on its own, but struggles to accurately delineate exact tumor and tumor compartment boundaries due to the coarse supervoxel generation step. We show that this limitation can be at least partially circumvented by adding convolutional layers to the end of the model to smooth out predictions. While it is likely that a more complex CNN could further boost performance, this work aims to improve the feasibility of GNNs for tumor segmentation rather than to engineer an optimal CNN.

A clear direction for future work is to diagnose the failure cases of our model. In particular, our model should be able to produce a segmentation on any volume, regardless of orientation. It is likely that this issue is technical rather than a failure of the model to generalize, but it is difficult to identify without access to the testing data. Furthermore, it will be interesting to explore how segmentation of the enhancing tumor can be improved. The enhancing tumor is typically a small or set of small regions, which makes it inherently harder to accurately delineate with supervoxels. Perhaps a hierarchical segmentation scheme or more complex CNN will be able to improve model performance here. It has also been demonstrated by other participants of this year's challenge that post-processing heuristics to remove false positive ET predictions can have a meaningful impact on performance. Lastly, we also aim to incorporate a soft Dice loss in future work to improve the predictions of the composite tumor regions, rather than just the individual subtypes.

References

1. Achanta, R., Shaji, A., Smith, K., Lucchi, A., Fua, P., Süsstrunk, S.: Slic superpixels compared to state-of-the-art superpixel methods. IEEE Trans. Pattern Anal. Mach. Intell. **34**(11), 2274–2282 (2012)
2. Baid, U., et al.: The RSNA-ASNR-MICCAI BraTS 2021 benchmark on brain tumor segmentation and radiogenomic classification. arXiv preprint arXiv:2107.02314 (2021)

3. Bakas, S., et al.: Segmentation Labels and Radiomic Features for the Pre-operative Scans of the TCGA-GBM collection. The Cancer Imaging Archive (2017). https://doi.org/10.7937/K9/TCIA.2017.KLXWJJ1Q

4. Bakas, S., et al.: Segmentation Labels and Radiomic Features for the Pre-operative Scans of the TCGA-LGG collection. The Cancer Imaging Archive (2017). https://doi.org/10.7937/K9/TCIA.2017.GJQ7R0EF

5. Bakas, S., et al.: Advancing the cancer genome atlas glioma MRI collections with expert segmentation labels and radiomic features. Sci. Data **4**, 170117 (2017)

6. Bakas, S., et al.: Identifying the best machine learning algorithms for brain tumor segmentation, progression assessment, and overall survival prediction in the brats challenge. arXiv preprint arXiv:1811.02629 (2018)

7. Bi, W.L., et al.: Artificial intelligence in cancer imaging: clinical challenges and applications. CA Cancer J. Clin. **69**(2), 127–157 (2019)

8. Hamilton, W., Ying, Z., Leskovec, J.: Inductive representation learning on large graphs. In: Advances in Neural Information Processing Systems, pp. 1024–1034 (2017)

9. Haque, I.R.I., Neubert, J.: Deep learning approaches to biomedical image segmentation. Inform. Med. Unlocked **18**, 100297 (2020)

10. Kipf, T.N., Welling, M.: Semi-supervised classification with graph convolutional networks. arXiv preprint arXiv:1609.02907 (2016)

11. LeCun, Y., Bengio, Y., Hinton, G.: Deep learning. Nature **521**(7553), 436–444 (2015)

12. Menze, B.H., et al.: The multimodal brain tumor image segmentation benchmark (BRATS). IEEE Trans. Med. Imaging **34**(10), 1993–2024 (2014)

13. Saueressig, C., Berkley, A., Kang, E., Munbodh, R., Singh, R.: Exploring graph-based neural networks for automatic brain tumor segmentation. In: Bowles, J., Broccia, G., Nanni, M. (eds.) DataMod 2020. LNCS, vol. 12611, pp. 18–37. Springer, Cham (2021). https://doi.org/10.1007/978-3-030-70650-0_2

14. Zhou, J., et al.: Graph neural networks: a review of methods and applications. arXiv preprint arXiv:1812.08434 (2018)

Brain Tumor Segmentation Using Neural Network Topology Search

Alexandre Milesi[(✉)], Michal Futrega, Michal Marcinkiewicz, and Pablo Ribalta

NVIDIA, Santa Clara, CA 95051, USA
alexandrem@nvidia.com

Abstract. We apply a method from Automated Machine Learning (AutoML), namely Neural Architecture Search (NAS), to the task of brain tumor segmentation in MRIs for the BraTS 2021 challenge. NAS methods are known to be compute-intensive, so we use a continuous and differentiable search space in order to apply a DiNTS search for optimal fully convolutional architectures. Our method obtained Dice scores of 0.9161, 0.8707 and 0.8537 for whole tumor, tumor core and enhancing tumor regions respectively on the test dataset, while requiring no manual design of the network architecture, which was found automatically from the provided training data.

Keywords: BraTS · Deep Learning · AutoML · Neural Architecture Search

1 Introduction

Gliomas remain the most common primary brain tumors in humans [1]. They are characterized by different levels of aggressiveness, which directly influences prognosis. Due to the gliomas' heterogeneity (in terms of shape and appearance) manifested in multi-modal magnetic resonance imaging (MRI), their accurate delineation is an important yet challenging medical image analysis task. Manual segmentation of such brain tumors is time-consuming and prone to human errors and biases. The process also lacks reproducibility which adversely affects the effectiveness of patient's monitoring, and can ultimately lead to inefficient prognosis and treatment.

The majority of manual segmentation issues could be resolved using computer-aided automatic or semi-automatic methods of data processing. Recent advances in Deep Learning (DL), mainly in convolutional neural networks (CNNs), have allowed the DL-based models to approach or even surpass the human level performance in natural image classification [2] or microscope image segmentation [3], given sufficient amount of training data is provided.

Automatic brain tumor segmentation is one of the most challenging problems in medical image processing. Obtaining a computational model capable of surpassing a trained-human-level performance would provide valuable assistance to clinicians and would enable a more precise, reliable, and standardized approach to disease detection, treatment planning and monitoring.

Naturally, DL-based models are perfect targets for the task as long as their data-volume requirement is satisfied. The Brain Tumor Segmentation Challenge (BraTS) provides a state-of-the-art dataset of fully annotated MRI brain scans with corresponding segmentation masks, which is widely used through academia and industry.

Having a large, high-quality dataset is only the first step for training a high-quality model. One still needs to carefully design a network which will take advantage of the data within the dataset and provide accurate predictions. This task usually needs a lot of experience and trial-and-error approach, which can be suboptimal at times. So far, the state-of-the-art models in brain tumor segmentation are based on an encoder-decoder-like architectures, with the most prominent example being the U-Net [4]. Indeed, U-Net-like architectures, sometimes with modifications, have a great track record of winning the previous three challenges. In 2018, Myronenko et al. modified a U-Net model by adding a Variational Autoencoder branch for regularization [5]. In 2019, Jiang et al. employed a two-stage U-Net pipeline to segment the substructures of brain tumors from coarse to fine [6]. In 2020, Isensee et al. applied the nnU-Net framework with specific BraTS-designed modifications regarding data post-processing, region-based training, data augmentation, and minor modifications to the nnU-Net pipeline [7].

It is evident that a well-designed U-Net-based architecture performs very well on tasks such as brain tumor segmentation. However, in most cases, there is a need for manual effort of an expert to design and apply required modifications to the baseline model. In this context, the model which won BraTS 2020, nnU-Net, represents a very important step in the right direction. nnU-Net represents a framework for training (medical) segmentation models that is able to adapt the model architecture and data pipeline to the given task. There are high-level rules imposed on the framework, but the implementation of details is automated.

In this paper, we took the automated network architecture design approach to a higher level. We took advantage of a methodology of a neural network design called Neural Architecture Search (NAS). NAS was proposed by Zoph et al. [8] to automatically uncover optimal architectures contained within a given search space. NAS can be applied to optimize an architecture on multiple levels. A standard approach would be to perform a search on a topology level, which describes the high-level connections within the network, and cell level, which optimizes operations taking place at a low level (for example in particular network layers). In medical image segmentation, NAS was successfully applied in various approaches, such as NAS-UNet [9] or V-NAS [10].

The downside of the NAS algorithms is that they are both computationally expensive and take a long time to provide results; for example, C2FNAS [11] takes 333 GPU days to be trained on Medical Segmentation Decathlon [12], while Reinforced Learning [13] and evolutionary approaches can be even slower [14]. Moreover, traditional NAS algorithms suffer from *the discretization gap* problem, which arises when a continuous representation is binarized and leads to loss of performance. To solve this problem, FairDARTS [5] proposed a zero-one loss to push the continuous representation close to binary.

In this paper, we exploit DiNTS [15]—a novel bi-level NAS method that is continuous, differentiable, and integrates topology contraints during the training. Being continuous and differentiable makes the use of gradient-based optimizers possible, that are more effective than Reinforcement Learning [13] or evolutionary methods [14]. The topology-aware training allows the architecture to converge to a solution that is feasible (providing paths from the input to the output) and can easily be converted to a final discrete architecture. Due to a specifically designed topology loss, the discretization gap is largely reduced compared to methods where the training is unaware of topology constraints.

2   Methods

2.1   Data

The training data provided for the BraTS challenge [16–20] is a set of brain MRI scans along with segmentation annotations of tumor regions. For each of the 1,251 examples, four modalities are included, that were acquired with different clinical protocols and various scanners from multiple data-contributing institutions. The given modalities are native (T1), post-contrast T1-weighted (T1Gd), T2-weighted (T2), and T2 Fluid Attenuated Inversion Recovery (T2-FLAIR). The 3D volumes are skull-stripped and registered to $1\,\mathrm{mm}^3$ isotropic resolution with dimensions of $240 \times 240 \times 155$ voxels.

Segmentation labels were annotated manually by one to four experts. Annotations comprise the GD-enhancing tumor (ET), the peritumoral edematous/invaded tissue (ED), and the necrotic tumor core (NCR). Voxels that are not labeled as part of the tumor are treated as background class, as shown in Fig. 1.

In order for submissions to be evaluated on an online platform, 219 additional validation samples without associated ground truth were also released. For the final test evaluation, 530 cases were kept secret by the organizers. All volumes are provided as NIfTI files [21].

2.2   Pre-processing and Data Augmentation

The MONAI open-source framework [22] was used to load and pre-process the brain volumes from raw NIfTI files. The four modalities were concatenated together along the channels dimension. An additional binary channel was added to identify the brain region (voxels where any modality is non-zero).

Non-zero intensities were normalized channel-wise so that they follow a $\mathcal{N}(0, 1)$ distribution and volumes were aligned using the RAS orientation. For training in memory-limited environments, random crops of $128 \times 128 \times 128$ voxels were generated. The following data augmentations were applied to reduce overfitting:

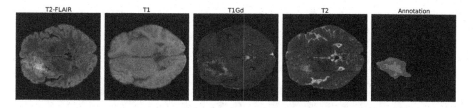

Fig. 1. Slices of a training sample with associated ground truth. Annotations classes: background (blue), necrotic tumor core (orange), peritumoral edematous/invaded tissue (green), GD-enhancing tumor (purple). (Color figure online)

- random flip around each axis independently (x, y, z) with probability 0.3.
- random intensity scaling of $[-0.1; 0.1]$
- random intensity shift of $[-0.1; 0.1]$ (brain region only)
- random gaussian noise of standard deviation up to 0.3 (brain region only)

When voxel interpolation was needed, bilinear was used for the inputs, and nearest neighbor was used for the labels.

2.3 Differentiable Neural Network Topology Search

During the DiNTS optimization, two aspects of the network architecture are searched simultaneously via gradient descent:

1. The **topology**, *i.e.* the high-level connections between layers of various feature scales
2. The **cells**, *i.e.* the specific operations applied on the feature maps

The topology search space is a multi-paths fully convolutional network containing 12 layers, each with 4 scales of feature maps (1/2, 1/4, 1/8, 1/16), as illustrated in Fig. 2. Each feature scale is only connected to adjacent scales, meaning there are in total $10 \cdot 12 = 120$ topology connections, also called cells or edges. This search space is flexible and not restrained to U-shaped or single-path architectures like previous NAS methods [11,23].

For each cell independently, 5 operation blocks are considered, as shown in Fig. 2 (right):

- skip connection
- 3D convolution $(3 \times 3 \times 3)$
- pseudo-3D convolution $(3 \times 3 \times 1)$
- pseudo-3D convolution $(3 \times 1 \times 3)$
- pseudo-3D convolution $(1 \times 3 \times 3)$

Pseudo-3D refers to the sequence of two convolutions described in [24], which has been used in V-NAS [10]. Each operation block (except for the skip connection) is also preceded by a ReLU non-linearity and followed by instance normalization [25] with a learnable affine transform. Cells that map to a higher

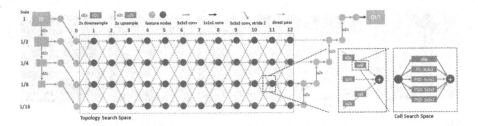

Fig. 2. Architecture (topology and cell) search space for DiNTS. Input and output stems (light blue) are fixed, while green connections are optimized during the architecture search. Figure from [15]. (Color figure online)

or lower scale have an additional 2× upsampling or 2× downsampling respectively. Downsampling is performed with $1 \times 1 \times 1$ convolutions with stride 2, while upsampling is performed with trilinear scaling followed by a $1 \times 1 \times 1$ convolution with stride 1.

Architecture Search. For each fold, an architecture search was performed to select an optimal topology and optimal cell operations. Trainable parameters were split into two groups:

- Parameters of the neural network ω_{net} (convolutions and instance normalization weights and biases)
- Parameters of the architecture ω_{arch} (topology weights and internal cell weights)

The training set (consisting of four folds) was partitioned equally into two subsets, *train_net* and *train_arch*. The first subset was used to train the network weights, while the second was used to train the architecture weights.

During this search, the stem cell at scale 1 had 16 filters and this number was doubled each time the spatial size was decreased by half. All architecture and network weights were initialized randomly as in [15].

During a warm-up period, only ω_{net} was updated using the *train_net* partition. After this warm-up, both *train_net* and *train_arch* were iterated on simultaneously, to update both ω_{net} and ω_{arch}.

The loss function used to optimize ω_{net} was an even mix of the cross-entropy loss and the multi-class smoothed Sørensen-Dice loss. This is called the segmentation loss $\mathcal{L}_{\text{seg}}$. The use of the Dice loss helps mitigate the effect of class imbalance as shown in [10]. Following Isensee *et al.* [7], we trained on the nested classes used for evaluation instead of the raw provided classes.

ω_{arch} was optimized using a loss function that integrates, in addition to $\mathcal{L}_{\text{seg}}$, a topology loss $\mathcal{L}_{\text{tp}}$ as well as losses $\mathcal{L}_{\alpha}$ and $\mathcal{L}_{\eta}$ to encourage the binarization of the architecture weights, as introduced in [15].

The architecture loss function is then $\mathcal{L}_{\text{arch}} = \mathcal{L}_{\text{seg}} + t/t_{\text{all}} \cdot (\mathcal{L}_{\text{tp}} + \mathcal{L}_{\alpha} + \mathcal{L}_{\eta})$, where t/t_{all} represent the progress of the architecture search, so that the weight given to topology losses is linearly increased with time.

Pruning. Once architecture weights ω_{arch} are found, a discretization step converts the continuous weights to binary ones, selecting a topology that prunes paths of low importance. This pruning must be done carefully, as to not create infeasible paths, *i.e.* paths where a node has an input but no output, or has an output but no input.

This step is performed by maximum likelihood estimation together with Dijsktra algorithm, as described in [15].

For selecting operations of cells, the operation with the largest weight is picked and the others are discarded.

Because the training was aware of pruning constraints via the topology loss, the discretization gap, *i.e.* the accuracy difference between the continuous and the discrete architecture, is reduced.

Retraining. For each fold, the selected discrete architecture was retrained from scratch on the remaining folds (*train_net* and *train_arch* together), this time only updating network weights ω_{net} using the $\mathcal{L}_{\text{seg}}$ loss. The number of channels was also increased compared to the architecture search step (32 for the stem at scale 1).

An initial warm-up period was used to raise to learning rate up to the selected value. During the rest of the training, the learning rate was decayed with a step schedule.

Ensemble. Final predictions on the test and validation sets are obtained by combining the predictions of the five retrained models in order to reduce variance.

Each model predicts a probability map using sliding window inference, where overlapping windows are blended using a gaussian kernel giving more weight to the center of the window. Probabilities predictions of the models are then averaged, and the class with the highest probability is picked for each voxel. Test-time augmentation was also used, where predictions for the 8 possible volumes flips were averaged. The resulting segmentation map is then saved in the NIfTI format with the same alignment as the input volumes.

2.4 Experimental Setup

The training dataset was split into 5 folds so that 5 models could be trained on 4 folds each, and evaluated on the remaining fold. Each fold contained either 250 or 251 examples, so each model was trained on around 1,000 examples.

A PyTorch [26] implementation of DiNTS was used. Training and inference were performed inside the NVIDIA NGC PyTorch 21.07 Docker container, allowing for the full encapsulation of dependencies, reproducible runs, as well as easy deployment on any system. Training and search runs were performed using Mixed Precision [27] in order to speed up the model and save memory. The architecture search and retraining were performed on a NVIDIA DGX-1V (8× V100 32 GB) system.

Hyper-parameters for the architecture search include a batch size of 1 per GPU (8 in total), the Adam optimizer for both ω_{arch} and ω_{net}, with a learning rate of 8×10^{-4}, weight decay of 4×10^{-5} and betas of (0.9, 0.999) for ω_{net}, and a learning rate of 1×10^{-3}, no weight decay, and betas of (0.5, 0.999) for ω_{arch}. Architecture search warm-up lasted 10k steps, and retraining warm-up lasted 1k steps. A full search took 30k steps, while a retraining was 31k steps (warm-up included for both).

For each fold, the architecture search took around 210 GPU-hours on a system down-clocked to 160 W per GPU, and used 26 GB of GPU memory. Retraining took 140 GPU-hours on the down-clocked system, and used 23 GB of GPU memory. In total, $5 \cdot (210 + 140) = 1,750$ GPU-hours were spent in the full pipeline, excluding the prediction on validation samples.

3   Results

3.1   Selected Topologies

The topologies resulting from the architecture searches are multi-paths and dense, using a mixture of all five proposed cell operations. The memory loss, that DiNTS can add to the topology loss in order to encourage light networks, was not used here in order to maximize the model capacity and accuracy.

An example of such a topology is illustrated in Fig. 3. We can observe two horizontal pathways through the maximum feature scale (1/2) and the minimum scale (1/16). Around 25% of the cells were pruned during the discretization step.

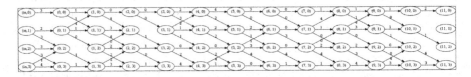

Fig. 3. Example of a selected architecture after optimization (fold 0). Numbers on the edges represent the type of cell (0: skip, 1: $3 \times 3 \times 3$ conv, 2: $3 \times 3 \times 1$ P3D, 3: $3 \times 1 \times 3$ P3D, 4: $1 \times 3 \times 3$ P3D)

3.2   Quantitative Results

Table 1 shows the best results obtained by the DiNTS method on the test data held by the BraTS organizers, as well as the cross-validation on the training data.

3.3   Qualitative Results

Score summaries like the Dice and Hausdorff distance provide a good way to compare models for a challenge, but in order to understand more precisely the

Table 1. Scores obtained on the test data (via the Synapse platform) and on our cross-validation folds. ET stands for enhancing tumor, TC stands for tumor core (ET+NCR), and WT stands for whole tumor (ET+ED+NCR).

	Dice		
	ET	TC	WT
Our submission	0.8537	0.8707	0.9161
CV (average)	0.8480	0.8856	0.9048
CV (fold 0)	0.8435	0.8867	0.9070
CV (fold 1)	0.8508	0.8788	0.9006
CV (fold 2)	0.8443	0.8897	0.8986
CV (fold 3)	0.8552	0.8886	0.9076
CV (fold 4)	0.8460	0.8844	0.9101

strengths and fallbacks of predictors, manual inspection of prediction is sometimes necessary.

Figure 4 shows an example where the DiNTS method successfully captured all relevant tumor regions identifiable from the four input modalities.

Figure 5 shows however a case where DiNTS failed to predict accurately the whole tumor region. It over-segmented seemingly healthy tissue as part of the peritumoral edematous/invaded tissue (top left of the tumor).

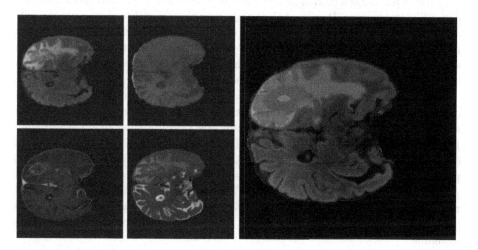

Fig. 4. Example of an accurate prediction (right) overlayed on the FLAIR modality (validation dataset).

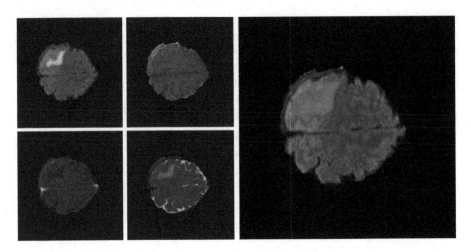

Fig. 5. Example of a problematic prediction (right) overlayed on the FLAIR modality (validation dataset).

4   Discussion

While the DiNTS method managed to get reasonable results with no manual tuning of the network architecture and very little hyperparameter search, it still suffers from some drawbacks that will need to be addressed in future research.

First of all, the selected architectures can be obscure, especially when they are dense like in our case. It is hard to explain why the algorithm chose specific cells and operations instead of others. There is no clear encoder-decoder architecture like we see in manually created topologies, and the pattern of cell operation seems arbitrary. Existing work [28] combines NAS methods with network design to yield efficient and performant architectures.

Then, even if DiNTS and differentiable NAS provide major improvements on this side, NAS methods are still relatively expensive to train. One must have access to multi-GPU systems in order for the training time to be reasonable. Each architecture fold takes around 9 GPU-days to compute, which can be quite expensive using existing cloud platforms. This would mean spending around 800$ per search using AWS, and 550$ per search using Google Cloud (on-demand pricing for NVIDIA DGX-1V 32 GB). This can prevent researchers with limited resources to apply these techniques effectively. Hopefully, we currently observe a downward trend of cloud computing prices, as the hardware becomes more available.

5   Conclusion

This paper presented our participation to the BraTS 2021 challenge. We explored the use of Automated Machine Learning (AutoML) using an efficient differentiable Neural Architecture Search to segment tumor regions out of brain MRI scans. No manual tuning of the network architecture was needed, limiting human biases and labour.

The search of an optimal architecture required a low amount of researcher-hours, while still using a significant amount of GPU-hours. In the spirit of nnU-Net, this work is a step towards a fully-automated system that would be able to perform well on any input dataset that is presented to it, underpinning the democratization of Deep Learning on medical data.

References

1. Goodenberger, M.L., Jenkins, R.B.: Genetics of adult glioma. Cancer Genet. **205** (2012). https://doi.org/10.1016/j.cancergen.2012.10.009
2. Russakovsky, O., et al.: ImageNet large scale visual recognition challenge. Int. J. Comput. Vis. **115**(3), 211–252 (2015). https://doi.org/10.1007/s11263-015-0816-y
3. Zeng, T., Wu, B., Ji, S.: DeepEM3D: approaching human-level performance on 3D anisotropic EM image segmentation. Bioinformatics **33**(16), 2555–2562 (2017). https://doi.org/10.1093/bioinformatics/btx188
4. Ronneberger, O., Fischer, P., Brox, T.: U-Net: convolutional networks for biomedical image segmentation. In: Navab, N., Hornegger, J., Wells, W.M., Frangi, A.F. (eds.) MICCAI 2015. LNCS, vol. 9351, pp. 234–241. Springer, Cham (2015). https://doi.org/10.1007/978-3-319-24574-4_28
5. Myronenko, A.: 3D MRI brain tumor segmentation using autoencoder regularization. In: Crimi, A., Bakas, S., Kuijf, H., Keyvan, F., Reyes, M., van Walsum, T. (eds.) BrainLes 2018. LNCS, vol. 11384, pp. 311–320. Springer, Cham (2019). https://doi.org/10.1007/978-3-030-11726-9_28
6. Jiang, Z., Ding, C., Liu, M., Tao, D.: Two-stage cascaded U-Net: 1st place solution to BraTS challenge 2019 segmentation task. In: Crimi, A., Bakas, S. (eds.) BrainLes 2019. LNCS, vol. 11992, pp. 231–241. Springer, Cham (2020). https://doi.org/10.1007/978-3-030-46640-4_22
7. Isensee, F., Jäger, P.F., Full, P.M., Vollmuth, P., Maier-Hein, K.H.: nnU-Net for brain tumor segmentation. In: Crimi, A., Bakas, S. (eds.) BrainLes 2020. LNCS, vol. 12659, pp. 118–132. Springer, Cham (2021). https://doi.org/10.1007/978-3-030-72087-2_11
8. Zoph, B., Le, Q.V.: Neural architecture search with reinforcement learning (2017)
9. Weng, Y., Zhou, T., Li, Y., Qiu, X.: NAS-Unet: neural architecture search for medical image segmentation. IEEE Access **7**, 44247–44257 (2019). https://doi.org/10.1109/ACCESS.2019.2908991
10. Zhu, Z., Liu, C., Yang, D., Yuille, A., Xu, D.: V-NAS: neural architecture search for volumetric medical image segmentation. In: 2019 International Conference on 3D Vision (3DV), pp. 240–248 (2019). https://doi.org/10.1109/3DV.2019.00035
11. Yu, Q., Yang, D., Roth, H., Bai, Y., Zhang, Y., Yuille, A.L., Xu, D.: C2FNAS: Coarse-to-fine neural architecture search for 3D medical image segmentation (2020)
12. Antonelli, M., et al.: The medical segmentation decathlon (2021)
13. Baker, B., Gupta, O., Naik, N., Raskar, R.: Designing neural network architectures using reinforcement learning (2017)
14. Real, E., Aggarwal, A., Huang, Y., Le, Q.V.: Regularized evolution for image classifier architecture search (2019)
15. He, Y., Yang, D., Roth, H., Zhao, C., Xu, D.: DiNTS: differentiable neural network topology search for 3d medical image segmentation, March 2021

16. Baid, U., et al.: The RSNA-ASNR-MICCAI BraTS 2021 benchmark on brain tumor segmentation and radiogenomic classification (2021)
17. Menze, B.H., et al.: The multimodal brain tumor image segmentation benchmark (BRATS). IEEE Trans. Med. Imaging **34**(10), 1993–2024 (2015). https://doi.org/10.1109/TMI.2014.2377694
18. Bakas, S., et al.: Advancing the cancer genome atlas glioma MRI collections with expert segmentation labels and radiomic features. Sci. Data **4** (2017). https://doi.org/10.1038/sdata.2017.117
19. Bakas, S., et al.: Segmentation labels and radiomic features for the pre-operative scans of the TCGA-GBM collection, July 2017. https://doi.org/10.7937/K9/TCIA.2017.KLXWJJ1Q
20. Bakas, S., et al.: Segmentation labels and radiomic features for the pre-operative scans of the TCGA-LGG collection, July 2017. https://doi.org/10.7937/K9/TCIA.2017.GJQ7R0EF
21. Cox, R., et al.: A (sort of) new image data format standard: NiFTI-1, vol. 22, January 2004
22. Consortium, M.: MONAI: Medical open network for AI, March 2020. https://doi.org/10.5281/zenodo.4323058, https://github.com/Project-MONAI/MONAI
23. Liu, C., et al.: Auto-DeepLab: hierarchical neural architecture search for semantic image segmentation (2019)
24. Qiu, Z., Yao, T., Mei, T.: Learning spatio-temporal representation with pseudo-3D residual networks (2017)
25. Ulyanov, D., Vedaldi, A., Lempitsky, V.S.: Instance normalization: the missing ingredient for fast stylization. CoRR abs/1607.08022 (2016). http://arxiv.org/abs/1607.08022
26. Paszke, A., et al.: Pytorch: an imperative style, high-performance deep learning library. In: Wallach, H., Larochelle, H., Beygelzimer, A., d' Alché-Buc, F., Fox, E., Garnett, R. (eds.) Advances in Neural Information Processing Systems 32, pp. 8024–8035. Curran Associates, Inc. (2019). http://papers.neurips.cc/paper/9015-pytorch-an-imperative-style-high-performance-deep-learning-library.pdf
27. Micikevicius, P., et al.: Mixed precision training (2018)
28. Howard, A., et al.: Searching for MobileNetV3 (2019)

Segmenting Brain Tumors in Multi-modal MRI Scans Using a 3D SegNet Architecture

Nabil Jabareen[iD] and Soeren Lukassen[(✉)][iD]

Berlin Institute of Health at Charité - Universitätsmedizin Berlin,
Charitéplatz 1, 10117 Berlin, Germany
soeren.lukassen@charite.de

Abstract. Gliomas are the most common type of primary brain tumor, and high-grade gliomas are typically treated using a combination of chemotherapy, radiation therapy, and surgical excision. For the latter two therapy options, precise knowledge about the location of the tumor and its components is required, which can be obtained using MRI scans. Manually labeling the tumor area in those 3-dimensional images is a tedious and time-consuming task, hence major efforts have been made to provide automated segmentation. We present our solution to the BraTS 2021 challenge Task1, where we segment gliomas in MRI scans using a SegNet-based approach, achieving competitive and stable performance across tumor types and components. Compared to previous solutions using UNet architectures, our model achieves improved segmentation of the peritumoral edema and comparable performance for the other classes while reducing the number of parameters.

Keywords: Brain tumors · Deep learning · Segmentation

1 Introduction

1.1 Gliomas

Gliomas are tumors arising from supporting cells of the brain and represent the most common form of primary brain tumors. Several distinct entities can be distinguished based on their cells of origin and their malignity, with the majority arising from astrocytes (astrocytomas). Among these, glioblastomas (GBMs), also known as grade IV astrocytomas, are the most common brain tumors while being associated with the worst clinical outcome. Without treatment, the median survival of patients is as low as three months, which can be extended to 15 months through combined treatment with chemotherapeutic agents, radiation, and surgery [10].

Due to the extensive capacity of GBMs to invade the surrounding healthy tissue, as well as the need to destroy as many cancer cells as possible while leaving healthy brain tissue intact, it is vital to obtain a precise localization of the tumor and its sub-regions [18]. At the core of the tumor, there is typically a necrotic zone,

A. Crimi and S. Bakas (Eds.): BrainLes 2021, LNCS 12962, pp. 377–388, 2022.
https://doi.org/10.1007/978-3-031-08999-2_32

caused by nutrient and oxygen starvation in fast-growing tumors (here abbreviated by NCR) [16]. This zone is surrounded by living and proliferating tumors cells, the enhancing tumor (ET). As GBMs compromise the integrity of the blood-brain barrier, the tumor is surrounded by an edema, caused by extravasation of fluid from leaky blood vessels in the tumor's vicinity (WT) [19]. These different tumor compartments can be distinguished by medical imaging. The gold standard for this is multi-modal magnetic resonance imaging (MRI), a technique which delivers images highlighting different structures within soft tissues.

1.2 Segmentation

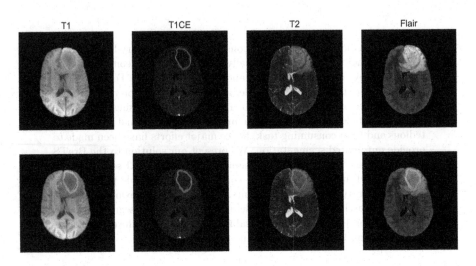

Fig. 1. Four different modalities of MRI scans used for the segmentation. Top row: modalities alone. Bottom row: superimposed ground truth for segmentation with the peritumoral edema shown in blue, enhancing tumor in red, and necrotic tumor core in green. (Color figure online)

Segmentation refers to the task of identifying regions in an image that belong to a certain class, e.g. tumor, healthy tissue, and background. In contrast to object detection, no attempt is made to separate bordering areas belonging to the same class but different entities thereof. Thus, the typical output of a segmentation is a so-called segmentation map, a tensor of the same size as the original image in terms of spatial dimensions, but with one or several channels indicating the presence of certain mutually exclusive or potentially overlapping features, respectively [20]. Due to this relationship of the input and output images, UNet architectures have been exceedingly successful [13]. These convolutional neural networks correspond to an autoencoder-like structure with skip connections between the corresponding encoder and decoder blocks, concatenating the encoder weights to the decoder ones while restoring the image size through transposed convolutions. The skip connections thus enable the preservation of spatial information [17]. Because max-pooling on the encoder is reversed using transposed convolutions, some localization information about maxima is lost during the process. Furthermore, transposed convolutions need to be learned, adding parameters to the model. SegNet architectures aim to alleviate this problem by using unpooling layers instead of transposed convolutions. In these models, the indices of the maxima identified during the max pooling are retained and passed to the unpooling layers, perfectly preserving the localization of the maxima and improving the resolution of the segmentation map [3].

For the past ten years, the annual Brain Tumor Segmentation Challenge (BraTS) has addressed the task of segmenting brain tumors and their substructures from MRI scans, reflecting the advances in the field of (medical) image processing during that time and providing large, well-annotated data sets for researchers to use.

2 Methods

2.1 Data Sources

Data used in this publication were obtained as part of the RSNA-ASNR-MICCAI Brain Tumor Segmentation (BraTS) Challenge project through Synapse ID (syn25829067) [4–7,14]. 3D NIfTI images of size $155 \times 240 \times 240$ (Depth $\times$ Height $\times$ Width) with one channel for each of the four modalities were used as input to the model, while training labels were provided as single-channel NIfTI with integer class labels. Example images are shown in Fig. 1.

2.2 Preprocessing

The data obtained were already skull-stripped, scaled, and cropped as described previously. Our implementation of a SegNet was based on the nnUNet framework, so the additional preprocessing corresponded to that described in [13]. Importantly this includes the cropping of the original input size of $155 \times 255 \times 255$ to $128 \times 128 \times 128$ (see Fig. 2).

2.3 Network Architecture

Table 1. Parameter counts for nnUNet and nnSegNet model architectures.

	nnUNet	nnSegNet
Number of parameters	31,198,176	27,663,648

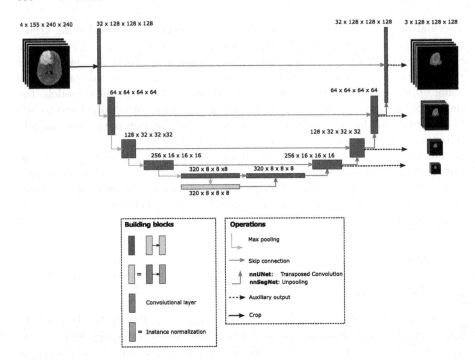

Fig. 2. Depiction of the UNet and SegNet architectures used. Both network types are largely equivalent, with the exception of transposed convolutions in the decoder of the UNet being replaced by unpooling layers in the SegNet (green arrows). (Color figure online)

The proposed nnSegNet architecture is designed to be an efficient deep convolutional neural network for pixel-wise semantic segmentation. It is based on the nnUNet framework [13].

The encoder topology of the nnSegNet consists of five max pooling operations with kernel size of $2 \times 2 \times 2$ and a stride of $2 \times 2 \times 2$. The indices of the max pooling operation are stored and later used in the unpooling operation. The unpooling operation computes a partial inverse of the max pooling operation and therefore allows to recreate the feature map size of the corresponding encoder step. For the unpooling operation we used a kernel size of $2 \times 2 \times 2$ and stride of $2 \times 2 \times 2$. The feature map of the corresponding encoder step and the unpooled feature map are concatenated in the decoder part of the network. For a visual comparison of both architectures, see Fig. 2.

2.4 Training

For training, we used the hyperparameters automatically determined by the nnUNet framework [13]. Every network architecture was trained for 1,000 epochs with 250 iterations for each epoch. The training was performed on a NVIDIA A100 40G GPU and took 37.5 h. The initial learning rate was set to 0.01 and a polynomial learning decay was used. As an optimizer we used Stochastic gradient descent with a momentum of 0.99 and weight decay of 3×10^{-5}. To train the model we used deep supervision on auxiliary outputs of different depths of the network (see Fig. 2).

As a loss function we used a sum of the dice coefficient and the binary cross entropy loss on all auxiliary outputs. The final loss was computed as the weighted sum of all auxiliary losses.

2.5 Postprocessing

To obtain the final prediction we used the computed softmax for every class in a sequential pattern. First, the output mask for the WT class was generated with a given threshold. Second, the output mask for the NCR class was generated with a given threshold and the previous mask was overwritten. Finally, this step was repeated for the ET class.

During training the thresholds for all classes were set to 0.5. To improve the final model performance, we optimized the softmax thresholds for every class (see Fig. 4) on a 5-fold cross validation. For every fold we sampled 1000 different threshold combinations. Due to the interdependence of the different classes and the resulting large search space, we decided to use a Tree-structured Parzen Estimator Approach (TPE) to optimize the thresholds [9]. Finally, we used the median thresholds for every class from all five folds. This optimization was done separately for the nnSegNet, nnUNet and their Ensemble. We used optuna [2] as optimization framework.

Our second postprocessing step, is aimed to reduce false positive ET predictions. Therefore, we used two thresholds on the predicted ET volume and the predicted NCR volume. These thresholds were computed with a decision tree algorithm with a depth of two. Finally, the ET label was suppressed in the final prediction an replaced by the next highest softmax value, if the predicted ET volume was ≤ 129.5 and the NCR volume was > 16954.0 (see Fig. 5).

2.6 Metrics

Several metrics were used in the evaluation, specifically the Dice Coefficient [11], sensitivity, specificity, and Hausdorff95 (HD95) distance [15]. The first three are calculated from overlap of sets, with TP indicating true positive, FP false positive, TN true negative, and FN false negative:

$$Dice = \frac{2TP}{2TP + FP + FN} \tag{1}$$

$$Sensitivity = \frac{TP}{TP + FN} \tag{2}$$

$$Specificity = \frac{TN}{TN + FP} \tag{3}$$

The Hausdorff95 distance is defined by the supremum sup of the distance d between two sets X and Y, made more robust to outliers by reporting the $95th$ percentile rather than the maximum:

$$d_{H95} = P_{95} \left\{ \sup_{x \in X} d(x, Y), \sup_{y \in Y} d(X, y) \right\} \tag{4}$$

3 Results

3.1 Network Architecture

To gauge the performance of existing model architectures, we first trained a UNet using the nnUNet architecture, a frontrunner in previous segmentation challenges. On the training dataset with 5-fold cross-validation, this network already outperformed top solution of the past years, likely due to the increased size of the training dataset (see Fig. 3 and [1,8]).

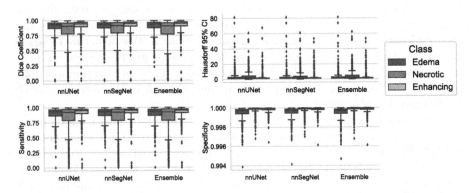

Fig. 3. Performance metrics for different model architectures. Per-image metrics are shown for images from the training dataset, using 5-fold cross-validation. Ensemble denotes a combination of nnSegNet activations for the peritumoral edema and nnUNet activations for the other classes. Horizontal lines indicate the median, boxes depict the inter-quartile range (IQR), whiskers extend to 1.5x the IQR.

As with relatively few exceptions the predicted segmentation masks were very close to the ground truth labels, we hypothesized that performance gains could be achieved via smaller adjustments to the network and postprocessing rather than through rewriting the entire architecture. Specifically, we aimed to increase the resolution of the predicted masks while reducing the risk of overfitting. To this end, we replaced the transposed convolutions in the decoder part of the network with unpooling layers, leading to a SegNet architecture (here called nnSegNet due to its integration into the nnUNet framework) which should result in a better conservation of location as shown in [3]. Simultaneously this leads to a reduction of the number of parameters in the model by roughly 10% (see Table 1). This resulted in a slight stabilization of the metrics characterized by a lower standard deviation and inter-quartile range of the individual sample scores (see Fig. 3). On the public validation dataset, the performance of the nnSegNet was slightly decreased for the tumor core and enhancing tumor classes, but increased for the peritumoral edema (see Table 2), with mean scores slightly favoring the nnUNet architecture. An ensemble method combining the predictions of the nnUNet for TC and ET and the nnSegNet for WT did not appear to achieve an overall increase in performance on the training set with cross-validation (see Fig. 3).

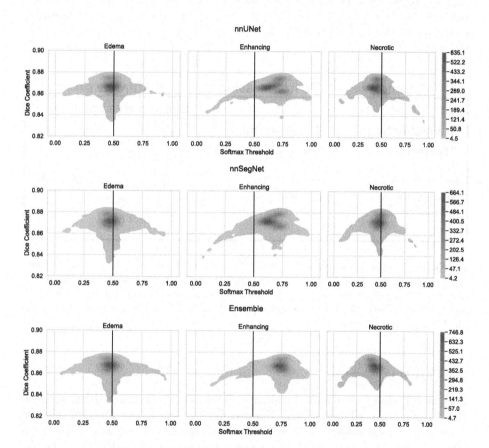

Fig. 4. Threshold optimization. Results of the parameter tuning of thresholds for assigning classes from the softmax activations of the model output. Thresholds are shown on the horizontal axis, Dice Coefficients on the vertical axis. Grey levels indicate the density of trials where a corresponding score was achieved. Top row: UNet architecture. Middle row: SegNet architecture. Bottom row: Ensemble with WT from nnSegNet and the other classes predicted from the nnUNet activations.

3.2   Postprocessing

To further improve the performance, we decided to fine-tune the class assignment. As class labels were non-overlapping, it would be possible to use the argmax along the output channels. However, as the classes are nested and predicted with different sensitivities, we took a different approach, sequentially predicting each class to be present if the softmax surpassed a certain threshold (see Sect. 2.5) [13]. To improve the performance of our model, we decided to tune the threshold for each class, revealing that the previously used threshold of 0.5 is not ideal for all classes (see Fig. 4). For ensembles of nnSegNet and nnUNet, this approach was used with the softmax activations for TC and ET from the nnUNet and WT from the nnSegNet, but this did not lead to a major improvement (see Figs. 3 and 4). In Fig. 5 an overview of the postprocessing pipeline is visualized.

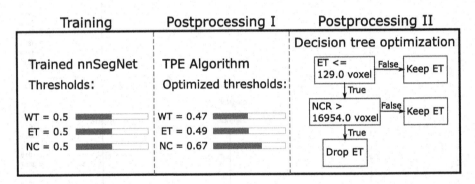

Fig. 5. Postprocessing steps of the nnSegNet added to the nnUNet postprocessing. After training, the first postprocessing step is to optimize the prediction thresholds using the TPE algorithm. The second postprocessing step is to apply a decision tree and eventually drop the ET label and replace it with the next most likely label based on the predicted softmax.

3.3   Missing Classes

For the ET class, we observed a drastic difference of the mean HD95 between the training and validation sets. Upon closer inspection, we found this to be caused by several outliers where ET area was predicted, but was absent from the ground truth annotation. In the metrics calculation for the BraTS challenge, these cases were scored with a HD95 of over 370, resulting in a strong skewing of scores considering the mean score for correctly predicted images was below 10. To address the erroneous prediction of ET voxels in images where no enhancing tumor was present, we made use of the observation that these images typically had very few voxels predicted to be ET, allowing us to set a threshold below which we could reassign the voxels to one of the other two tumor classes or background.

Table 2. Performance metrics for all classes for various model architectures. pp indicates models subjected to threshold tuning and removal of small ET predictions.

Model	Dice WT	Dice ET	Dice TC	HD95 WT	HD95 ET	HD95 TC
nnUNet	0.926	0.816	0.885	3.793	22.873	7.425
nnSegNet	**0.928**	0.808	0.877	3.483	26.232	7.571
Ensemble	0.926	0.808	0.885	3.792	26.231	7.406
nnUNet pp	0.926	**0.848**	0.886	3.783	**9.286**	5.813
nnSegNet pp	**0.928**	0.847	0.878	**3.470**	9.335	7.564
Ensemble pp	0.926	0.843	**0.887**	3.783	9.432	**5.789**

Still, overall scores were strongly influenced by poorly performing outliers, as can be seen from the discrepancy of mean and median score values of the nnSegNet (see Table 3). Similar effects were observed for the other model architectures.

Table 3. Mean vs. median performance metrics for the nnSegNet.

	Dice WT	Dice ET	Dice TC	HD95 WT	HD95 ET	HD95 TC
Mean	0.928	0.847	0.878	3.470	9.335	7.564
Median	0.948	0.903	0.944	2.236	1.414	1.732

4 Discussion

4.1 Performance

While the models presented achieve a markedly increased performance compared to previous top competitors, this is in large part due to the increase in samples (660 in 2020, 2,000 in 2021), highlighting the importance of large, well-annotated datasets for machine learning. The nnUNet without the proposed post-processing, which is identical to an architecture used for BraTS 2020 [12], already performed exceedingly well, with minor performance gains through the post-processing for the WT and TC classes. The nnSegNet architecture did not improve overall results, but achieved a comparable performance with only 88% of the parameters of the nnUNet.

Scores below a Dice Coefficient of 0.9 or a HD95 distance of above 5 were mostly attributable to outliers, indicating that the general performance of the models is exceedingly good. This is also reflected in the median scores of the nnSegNet, and is especially apparent in the HD95 there. The median HD95 are in the range of 2, which likely falls within the range of disagreement between human specialists. Penalizing the incorrect presence of even a single voxel of e.g. ET in an image where it is absent with a distance of over 370 gives these outlier cases an outsized influence. Since this is the largest possibility for improvement of the segmentation metrics, addressing these outliers above all else is the most promising way to improve the performance in future challenges. To improve the usability in a real-world setting, however, a closer look at common misclassification of e.g. anatomical structures is needed. This is currently disincentivized in challenges, but could be achieved by penalizing the classification of areas such as the choroid plexus as part of the tumor.

Previous BraTS challenges already focused on tasks such as uncertainty evaluation, which are a promising way forward in terms of real-world usability. While most images could be segmented with near-perfect accuracy, it would be beneficial to direct a human supervisor towards the cases where performance was likely poor, both on a per-image and a per-region basis. Given the exceedingly large dataset provided and the outstanding performance of models submitted by the contestants, it would certainly be of interest to revisit the uncertainty challenge again.

4.2 Further Model Size Reduction

Typically CNNs require large quantities of memory and processing time to be deployed successfully. This often makes CNNs difficult to use in real life applications. To tackle this issue we explored the influence of the number of parameters on the model performance.

The presented nnSegNet reduces the number of trainable parameters from the original nnUNet already from 31.2×10^6 parameters to 27.6×10^6 parameters. This is achieved by replacing the transposed convolutions in the nnUNet by the unpooling operation. We continued reducing the number of trainable parameters by reducing the number of stacked convolutional layers from two to one (see Fig. 2). The resulting model has 17.4×10^6 trainable parameters and reduces the multiply-accumulate operations in a forward pass more than two fold. The mean Dice Coefficient of this small model dropped from 0.928 to 0.889.

Finally, we would like to balance between the model size and model performance to improve the CNNs capabilities in real life applications. This again could very well be tuned by the quantification of uncertainty, specifying the acceptable level of quality drop in an application specific manner.

Acknowledgments. The authors thank Georgios Nikolis for his support with regard to the HPC infrastructure and Foo Wei Ten and Dongsheng Yuan for fruitful discussions. We are grateful to David Kaul for providing a clinical perspective on brain tumor segmentation. We also want to thank all members of the Berlin Institute of Health and especially Prof. Eils and Prof. Conrad for their support.

This work was supported by the German Ministry for Education and Research (BMBF, junior research group "Medical Omics", 01ZZ2001).

References

1. Brats2020 validation phase leaderboard. https://www.cbica.upenn.edu/BraTS20/lboardValidation.html. Accessed 21 Aug 2021
2. Akiba, T., Sano, S., Yanase, T., Ohta, T., Koyama, M.: Optuna: a next-generation hyperparameter optimization framework. In: Proceedings of the 25rd ACM SIGKDD International Conference on Knowledge Discovery and Data Mining (2019)
3. Badrinarayanan, V., Kendall, A., Cipolla, R.: SegNet: a deep convolutional encoder-decoder architecture for image segmentation (2016)
4. Baid, U., et al.: The RSNA-ASNR-MICCAI BraTs 2021 benchmark on brain tumor segmentation and radiogenomic classification (2021)
5. Bakas, S., et al.: Segmentation labels and radiomic features for the pre-operative scans of the TCGA-GBM collection. Cancer Imaging Arch. Nat. Sci. Data **4**, 170117 (2017)
6. Bakas, S., et al.: Segmentation labels and radiomic features for the pre-operative scans of the TCGA-LGG collection. Cancer Imaging Arch. **286** (2017)
7. Bakas, S., et al.: Advancing the cancer genome atlas glioma MRI collections with expert segmentation labels and radiomic features. Sci. Data **4**(1), 170117 (2017). https://doi.org/10.1038/sdata.2017.117, https://doi.org/10.1038/sdata.2017.117
8. Bakas, S., et al.: Identifying the best machine learning algorithms for brain tumor segmentation, progression assessment, and overall survival prediction in the brats challenge (2019)
9. Bergstra, J., Bardenet, R., Bengio, Y., Kégl, B.: Algorithms for hyper-parameter optimization. In: Shawe-Taylor, J., Zemel, R., Bartlett, P., Pereira, F., Weinberger, K.Q. (eds.) Advances in Neural Information Processing Systems, vol. 24. Curran Associates, Inc. (2011). https://proceedings.neurips.cc/paper/2011/file/86e8f7ab32cfd12577bc2619bc635690-Paper.pdf
10. Brodbelt, A., Greenberg, D., Winters, T., Williams, M., Vernon, S., Collins, V.P.: Glioblastoma in England: 2007–2011. Eur. J. Cancer **51**(4), 533–542 (2015). https://doi.org/10.1016/j.ejca.2014.12.014, https://www.sciencedirect.com/science/article/pii/S0959804915000039
11. Dice, L.R.: Measures of the amount of ecologic association between species. Ecology **26**(3), 297–302 (1945). https://doi.org/10.2307/1932409, https://esajournals.onlinelibrary.wiley.com/doi/abs/10.2307/1932409
12. Isensee, F., Jaeger, P.F., Full, P.M., Vollmuth, P., Maier-Hein, K.H.: nnu-Net for brain tumor segmentation (2020)
13. Isensee, F., Jaeger, P.F., Kohl, S.A.A., Petersen, J., Maier-Hein, K.H.: nnu-Net: a self-configuring method for deep learning-based biomedical image segmentation. Nat. Methods **18**(2), 203–211 (2021). https://doi.org/10.1038/s41592-020-01008-z
14. Menze, B.H., et al.: The multimodal brain tumor image segmentation benchmark (BraTs). IEEE Trans. Med. Imaging **34**(10), 1993–2024 (2015). https://doi.org/10.1109/TMI.2014.2377694
15. Pompeiu, D.: Sur la continuité des fonctions de variables complexes. In: Annales de la Faculté des sciences de Toulouse: Mathématiques, vol. 7, pp. 265–315 (1905)
16. Rong, Y., Durden, D.L., Van Meir, E.G., Brat, D.J.: 'Pseudopalisading' necrosis in glioblastoma: a familiar morphologic feature that links vascular pathology, hypoxia, and angiogenesis. J. Neuropathol. Exp. Neurol. **65**(6), 529–539 (2006). https://doi.org/10.1097/00005072-200606000-00001

17. Ronneberger, O., Fischer, P., Brox, T.: U-net: convolutional networks for biomedical image segmentation (2015)
18. Weller, M., et al.: EANO guidelines on the diagnosis and treatment of diffuse gliomas of adulthood. Nat. Rev. Clin. Oncol. **18**(3), 170–186 (2021). https://doi.org/10.1038/s41571-020-00447-z
19. Wolburg, H., Noell, S., Fallier-Becker, P., Mack, A.F., Wolburg-Buchholz, K.: The disturbed blood-brain barrier in human glioblastoma. Mol. Asp. Med. **33**(5), 579–589 (2012). https://doi.org/10.1016/j.mam.2012.02.003, https://www.sciencedirect.com/science/article/pii/S0098299712000180, water Channel Proteins (Aquaporins and Relatives)
20. Yang, R., Yu, Y.: Artificial convolutional neural network in object detection and semantic segmentation for medical imaging analysis. Front. Oncol. **11**, 573 (2021) https://doi.org/10.3389/fonc.2021.638182, https://www.frontiersin.org/article/10.3389/fonc.2021.638182

Residual 3D U-Net with Localization for Brain Tumor Segmentation

Marc Demoustier[1], Ines Khemir[1], Quoc Duong Nguyen[1(✉)],
Lucien Martin-Gaffé[1], and Nicolas Boutry[2]

[1] EPITA Majeure Santé, 94270 Le Kremlin-Bicêtre, France
quoc-duong.nguyen@epita.fr
[2] EPITA Research and Development Laboratory (LRDE),
94270 Le Kremlin-Bicêtre, France

Abstract. Gliomas are brain tumors originating from the neuronal support tissue called glia, which can be benign or malignant. They are considered rare tumors, whose prognosis, which is highly fluctuating, is primarily related to several factors, including localization, size, degree of extension and certain immune factors. We propose an approach using a Residual 3D U-Net to segment these tumors with localization, a technique for centering and reducing the size of input images to make more accurate and faster predictions. We incorporated different training and post-processing techniques such as cross-validation and minimum pixel threshold.

Keywords: Brain tumor segmentation · Deep learning · Convolutional neural networks · Residual 3D U-Net

1 Introduction

Gliomas or glial tumors are all brain tumors, benign or malignant, arising from the neuronal support tissue or glia. They are rare tumors, whose prognosis, which is extremely variable, is mainly related to several factors, including location, size, degree of extension and certain immune factors.

The average survival time is from 12 to 18 months. Brain tumor diagnosis and segmentation are difficult, particularly using manual segmentation.

In addition, medical image annotation experts have to manually annotate tumor segmentation, which is time consuming and difficult. Automatic segmentation of tumors allows for better diagnosis and treatment planning.

Nowadays, deep learning represents the most effective technology for many tasks such as segmentation, tracking and classification in medical image analysis. Many studies for brain tumor segmentation use deep learning techniques, especially convolutional neural networks *(CNN)*. Recent entries in the *Brain Tumor Segmentation Challenge (BraTS)* challenge are mostly based on these convolutional neural networks, specifically on the U-Net architecture [19] or similar, using an encoder and a decoder with skip-connections. They have shown very convincing performance in previous iterations of the challenge [12].

A. Crimi and S. Bakas (Eds.): BrainLes 2021, LNCS 12962, pp. 389–399, 2022.
https://doi.org/10.1007/978-3-031-08999-2_33

The *BraTS* challenge provides the largest fully annotated, openly accessible database for model development and is the primary competition for objective comparison of segmentation methods [2–5,17]. The *BraTS 2021* dataset includes 1251 training cases and 219 validation cases. Reference annotations for the validation set are not provided to participants. Instead, participants can utilize the online evaluation platform to evaluate their models and compare their results with other teams on the online leaderboard. In parallel to the segmentation task, the *BraTS 2021* competition includes the task of predicting of the MGMT promoter methylation status in mpMRI scans. In this work, we only take part in the segmentation task.

To segment these tumors, the *BraTS* dataset contains 5 images in NIfTI format for each patient. These images come from MRI (Magnetic Resonance Imaging), each of the first four images coming from different moments of the MRI. These different modalities are named T1, T1ce, T2 and FLAIR. The last image corresponds to the ground truth, i.e. the tumor and its different regions. The pixel values of this image are:

- 4 for the GD-enhancing tumor
- 2 for the peritumoral edematous/invaded tissue
- 1 for the necrotic tumor core
- 0 for everything else

Using these pixel values, we can find the different tumor regions:

- Whole Tumor (WT): 1, 2, 4
- Tumor Core (TC): 1 and 4
- Enhanced Tumor (ET): 4

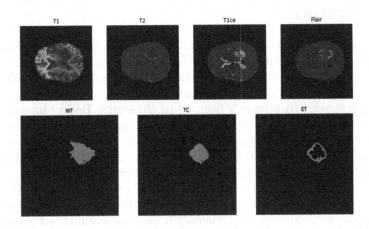

Fig. 1. Modalities and labels

In this paper, we use a residual 3D U-Net using localization with cross-validation for each region (WT, TC, ET) (Fig. 1).

2   Methods

The implementation used *PyTorch*. As a result, we describe the models with *PyTorch* keywords and methods.

2.1   Pre-processing

Images given in the BraTS dataset are in 240 (Width) × 240 (Height) × 155 (Number of slices) × 4 (FLAIR, T1, T1ce, T2), in the NIfTI format.

The goal in our approach was to keep the images as close as possible to the original data despite the limitations of GPU memory, that is, without too much pre-processing on the input images.

We chose to crop the images to 192 × 192 × 155 to remove the empty borders of the images, then added 5 empty slices to obtain a multiple of 8 on every dimension (except for the channels).

As a result, the images given as input of the model are left with as little modification as possible.

2.2   Residual 3D U-Net

The model we are using is a Residual 3D U-Net, based on Superhuman Accuracy on the SNEMI3D Connectomics Challenge [16]. Residual U-Nets have already been used for biomedical applications [18,20]. Our model is a variant of the U-Net [19] in 3D [7].

The architecture inherits the main elements from U-Net: a contracting path with convolutions and downsampling, an expansive path with convolutions and upsampling, and skip connections from the contracting path to the expansive path.

Our model differs from the 3D U-Net on different aspects, such as the use of same convolution instead of valid convolution. We also added a residual skip connection to each convolution block, it helps to solve the vanishing gradient problem and to preserve information captured in the initial layers. As we are limited by VRAM, we have to use a small batch size. We used Group Normalization as it performs better than Batch Normalization on a small batch size and it improves the ability of the network to generalize and allows the model to converge rapidly.

In a residual block, the first two convolutions are preceded by group normalization and followed by the ReLU activation function. After the last convolution layer, there is a concatenation of the residual connection, and then activation is called to include the residual information.

On the contracting path of the U-Net, we use what we call an encoding residual block (ERB), which contains a MaxPool3d with a kernel size of 2 and a residual block.

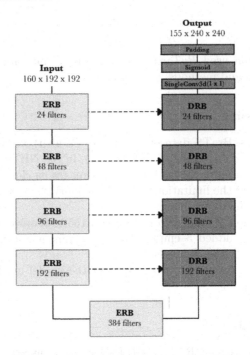

Fig. 2. Overview of the residual 3D U-Net

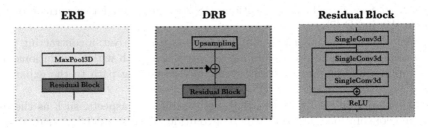

Fig. 3. Residual 3D U-Net blocks

On the expansive path of the U-Net, we use a decoding residual block (DRB), which contains a `ConvTranspose3d` layer with a kernel size of 3 and a scaling factor of size 2 to revert to the size of the encoding residual data from the same level skip connection. After the concatenation of the skip connection, the residual block is added.

At the end of this network, a 1×1 convolution is used to reduce the number of output channels to the number of labels. The number of labels will be 3 for a multi-class prediction and 1 in the case of a single-class prediction.

We have trained 3 separate single-class prediction models. One for each region WT, TC and ET which take 4 channels as input, again FLAIR, T1, T1ce and T2.

As the three models predict one label, a sigmoid has been used as final activation function.

The architecture of this network is built to recover the original shape of the data by using padding on heights and widths of the images. (see Fig. 2).

As the MRI images are quite heavy, having only 16 GB of VRAM on our GPUs, it was necessary to use 24 filters on the first layer of the network to avoid saturating the GPU memory. However, we are able to run the model with more filters using localization which we discuss in the next section (Fig. 3).

2.3 Localization

Training the models on TC and ET did not give great results. These regions are particularly small and the models could not refine the predictions correctly. That is because the "base" model only uses 24 filters on the first level of the U-Net.

Increasing the number of filters was not possible because of our VRAM limitations. We thought about an interpolation to reduce the size of our input images but this technique is too destructive.

In order to make the best out of the VRAM limits, we use localization. It consists in using the predictions on WT, center the input images around the segmented tumors and crop the input images around these segmented tumors (Fig. 4).

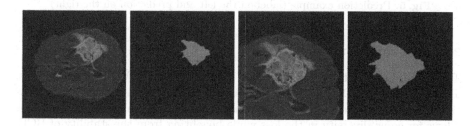

Fig. 4. FLAIR image of a brain with localization

Using this method, we are able to crop the input images into much smaller images of size $128 \times 128 \times 128$ instead of $192 \times 192 \times 160$. Whole tumors can fit inside these cropped images. As a result, the VRAM usage decreased and we were able to increase the number of filters from 24 to 64 on the first convolutional layer of the U-Net.

Once we have predicted the area of the tumor, we can run the models on WT, TC and ET with 64 filters using the cropped images as input. Note: We run the model on WT again with 64 filters to get the best results.

With a higher number of filters, the model is able to capture more complex features such as in the TC and ET regions (Fig. 5).

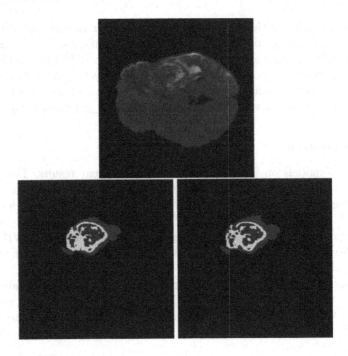

Fig. 5. Prediction example (label on the left and prediction on the right)

2.4   Loss Function

The hybrid loss function is used to train the models for the WT and TC regions. This loss combines Dice loss with the standard binary cross-entropy (BCE) loss that is generally the default for segmentation models. Summing the two methods allows for some diversity in the loss while benefiting from the stability of BCE. Both losses have the same coefficients in the hybrid loss.

$$BCE\_loss = \frac{1}{N}\sum_{n=1}^{N} H(p_n, q_n) = -\frac{1}{N}\sum_{n=1}^{N} [y_n log(\hat{y}_n) + (1 - y_n)log(1 - \hat{y}_n)] \quad (1)$$

$$Dice\_loss = \frac{2|X \cap Y|}{|X| + |Y|} \quad (2)$$

For the ET region, the standard binary cross-entropy (BCE) loss was used as it requires more stability in training.

2.5   Cross Validation

Cross-validation is a method used to train multiple models and improve predictive performance. The test set is separated beforehand.

We chose the k-fold method which consists in dividing the dataset in 5 blocks. The k-fold method allows us to create 5 different models that each have one different validation block and the 4 remaining blocks as the training set.

In order to maximize our scores, we combined the predictions of all 5 models by doing an average (Regression Voting Ensemble) of the weights then binarized the outputs. We also tried a majority vote (Classification Voting Ensemble) after the binarization.

2.6   Post-processing

The analysis of our results obtained on the validation set of BraTS shows that our predictions contained a large number of false positives, on the TC and ET regions.

In order to decrease that number, we defined a threshold for the number of pixels on an image [12]. Each prediction containing a number of pixels below this threshold is considered an empty prediction because we know that a tumor does not necessarily contain an enhanced tumor (ET). Several threshold values were tested.

3   Experiments and Results

3.1   Implementation Details

In the *BraTS 2021 Segmentation Challenge*, the training data is composed of 1251 multimodal MRI cases.

The network is implemented with *PyTorch*. The models were trained on 4 NVIDIA Tesla V100 16 GB GPUs. Each model was trained for 40 to 60 epochs with a batch size of 4, Adam optimizer with a learning rate of 0.0001 (BCE-Dice loss), 0.00003 (BCE-Dice loss), 0.003 (BCE) respectively for WT, TC and ET.

The model used to crop the input images and center on the tumor has the same learning rate as the model trained for WT and also uses the BCE-Dice loss.

We reduced the learning rate with the callback `ReduceLROnPlateau` by a factor of 0.4, with a patience and a cooldown of 2 epochs.

3.2   Performance on the Validation Set of *BraTS 2021*

The Validation Dataset of BraTS 2021 contains 219 brains MRI. For each brain, the four modality (T1, T2, T1ce and FLAIR) are used in order to predict the multi-class prediction. Predictions are evaluated thanks to the Dice coefficient, the Hausdorff distance (Hausdorff95), the sensitivity (True Positive Rate) score and a specificity (True Negative Rate) score. They are defined as follows:

$$Dice = \frac{2TP}{FP + 2TP + FN} \tag{3}$$

$$Hausdorff(T, P) = max\{sup_{t \in T} inf_{p \in P} d(t, p), sup_{p \in P} inf_{t \in T} d(t, p)\} \quad (4)$$

$$Sensitivity = \frac{TP}{TP + FN} \quad (5)$$

$$Specificity = \frac{TN}{TN + FP} \quad (6)$$

where TP, FP, TN and FN denote respectively the number of true positive, false positive, true negative and false negative voxels.

The Hausdorff distance computes the distance between the predicted regions and the ground truth regions. t and p denote respectively the pixels in the ground truth regions T and the predicted regions P. $d(t,p)$ is the function that computes the distance between the points t and p (Tables 1 and 2).

Table 1. Performance comparison using the dice coefficient on the BraTS 2021 Validation set using the online tool

Methods	WT (%)	TC (%)	ET (%)
Baseline (BCE loss)	90.98	80.24	74.07
Classification Voting Ensemble[a]	91.42	80.96	77.07
Regression Voting Ensemble (RVE)[a]	91.45	80.98	77.58
BCE-Dice loss (WT & TC)[b]	91.34	82.71	77.58
RVE[a] + Localization[d]	91.64	82.71	78.26
RVE[a] + ET threshold 100[c]	91.45	80.98	78.91
RVE + Localization[d] + ET threshold 400[c]	91.64	82.71	78.71
RVE + Localization[d] + ET threshold 600[c]	**91.64**	**82.71**	**80.22**

[a] Cross-Validation evaluation method (see Sect. 2.5)
[b] BCE-Dice loss function (see Sect. 2.4)
[c] Post processing using thresholding (see Sect. 2.6)
[d] Second network with reframing around the WT (see Sect. 2.3)

Table 2. Submission result on validation set

Tumor region	WT (%)	TC (%)	ET (%)
Dice	91.64	82.71	80.22
Hausdorff95	4.35	12.50	25.13
Sensitivity	93.61	85.74	79.14
Specificity	99.90	99.95	99.97

3.3   Performance on the test set of *BraTS 2021*

	Dice_WT (%)	Dice_TC (%)	Dice_ET (%)	HD95_WT	HD95_TC	HD95_ET
Mean	89.21	81.30	80.64	11.81	26.57	32.18
StdDev	16.87	28.79	26.52	47.15	86.49	98.98
Median	94.42	93.63	90.86	2.24	2.0	1.41
25quantile	89.92	86.17	80.48	1.41	1.0	1.0
75quantile	96.72	96.54	95.03	5.10	4.97	3.0

4   Conclusion

In this paper, we propose a segmentation method using the Residual 3D U-Net as the skeleton of the network, which uses the four modalities on an area where the tumor has been predicted. The localization method allows us to exploit the limitations of VRAM to the fullest by cropping and centering on the whole tumor without any performance loss. The evaluation of our method on the BraTS 2021 test set gives dice scores of 89.21, 81.30, 80.64 for the whole tumor, the tumor core and enhancing tumor, respectively.

Acknowledgement. We would like to thank Arnaud Renard and his team, for the access to their supercomputer ROMEO, the Regional Super Computer Center hosted by the University of Reims Champagne-Ardenne. We also would like to thank Christian Chabrerie for his support throughout the project.

References

1. Abraham, N., Khan, N.: A novel focal Tversky loss function with improved attention u-net for lesion segmentation. In: 2019 IEEE 16th International Symposium on Biomedical Imaging (ISBI 2019), pp. 683–687 (2019)
2. Baid, U., et al.: The RSNA-ASNR-MICCAI BraTs 2021 benchmark on brain tumor segmentation and radiogenomic classification. CoRR abs/2107.02314 (2021). https://arxiv.org/abs/2107.02314
3. Bakas, S., et al.: Advancing the cancer genome atlas glioma MRI collections with expert segmentation labels and radiomic features. Sci. Data **4** (2017). https://doi.org/10.1038/sdata.2017.117
4. Bakas, S., et al.: Segmentation labels and radiomic features for the pre-operative scans of the TCGA-GBM collection, July 2017. https://doi.org/10.7937/K9/TCIA.2017.KLXWJJ1Q
5. Bakas, S., et al.: Segmentation labels and radiomic features for the pre-operative scans of the TCGA-LGG collection, July 2017. https://doi.org/10.7937/K9/TCIA.2017.GJQ7R0EF
6. Caesar, H., Uijlings, J.R.R., Ferrari, V.: Region-based semantic segmentation with end-to-end training (2016). http://arxiv.org/abs/1607.07671

7. Çiçek, Ö., Abdulkadir, A., Lienkamp, S.S., Brox, T., Ronneberger, O.: 3D U-net: learning dense volumetric segmentation from sparse annotation. In: Ourselin, S., Joskowicz, L., Sabuncu, M.R., Unal, G., Wells, W. (eds.) MICCAI 2016. LNCS, vol. 9901, pp. 424–432. Springer, Cham (2016). https://doi.org/10.1007/978-3-319-46723-8_49

8. Eelbode, T., et al.: Optimization for medical image segmentation: theory and practice when evaluating with dice score or Jaccard index. IEEE Trans. Med. Imaging **39**(11), 3679–3690 (2020). https://doi.org/10.1109/TMI.2020.3002417

9. Fidon, L., et al.: Generalised Wasserstein dice score for imbalanced multi-class segmentation using holistic convolutional networks. In: Crimi, A., Bakas, S., Kuijf, H., Menze, B., Reyes, M. (eds.) BrainLes 2017. LNCS, vol. 10670, pp. 64–76. Springer, Cham (2018). https://doi.org/10.1007/978-3-319-75238-9_6

10. Guo, D., Wang, L., Song, T., Wang, G.: Cascaded global context convolutional neural network for brain tumor segmentation. In: Crimi, A., Bakas, S. (eds.) BrainLes 2019. LNCS, vol. 11992, pp. 315–326. Springer, Cham (2020). https://doi.org/10.1007/978-3-030-46640-4_30

11. Isensee, F., Kickingereder, P., Wick, W., Bendszus, M., Maier-Hein, K.H.: No new-net. In: Crimi, A., Bakas, S., Kuijf, H., Keyvan, F., Reyes, M., van Walsum, T. (eds.) BrainLes 2018. LNCS, vol. 11384, pp. 234–244. Springer, Cham (2019). https://doi.org/10.1007/978-3-030-11726-9_21

12. Isensee, F., Jäger, P.F., Full, P.M., Vollmuth, P., Maier-Hein, K.H.: nnU-Net for brain tumor segmentation. In: Crimi, A., Bakas, S. (eds.) BrainLes 2020. LNCS, vol. 12659, pp. 118–132. Springer, Cham (2021). https://doi.org/10.1007/978-3-030-72087-2_11

13. Islam, M., Vibashan, V.S., Jose, V.J.M., Wijethilake, N., Utkarsh, U., Ren, H.: Brain tumor segmentation and survival prediction using 3D attention UNet. In: Crimi, A., Bakas, S. (eds.) BrainLes 2019. LNCS, vol. 11992, pp. 262–272. Springer, Cham (2020). https://doi.org/10.1007/978-3-030-46640-4_25

14. Jiang, Z., Ding, C., Liu, M., Tao, D.: Two-stage cascaded U-net: 1st place solution to BraTS challenge 2019 segmentation task. In: Crimi, A., Bakas, S. (eds.) BrainLes 2019. LNCS, vol. 11992, pp. 231–241. Springer, Cham (2020). https://doi.org/10.1007/978-3-030-46640-4_22

15. Lee, C.Y., Xie, S., Gallagher, P., Zhang, Z., Tu, Z.: Deeply-supervised nets. In: Lebanon, G., Vishwanathan, S.V.N. (eds.) Proceedings of the Eighteenth International Conference on Artificial Intelligence and Statistics. Proceedings of Machine Learning Research, vol. 38, pp. 562–570. PMLR, San Diego, California, USA, 09–12 May 2015. http://proceedings.mlr.press/v38/lee15a.html

16. Lee, K., Zung, J., Li, P., Jain, V., Seung, H.: Superhuman accuracy on the snemi3D connectomics challenge. arXiv abs/1706.00120 (2017)

17. Menze, B.H., et al.: The multimodal brain tumor image segmentation benchmark BbraTs). IEEE Trans. Med. Imaging **34**(10), 1993–2024 (2015). https://doi.org/10.1109/TMI.2014.2377694

18. Milletari, F., Navab, N., Ahmadi, S.A.: V-net: fully convolutional neural networks for volumetric medical image segmentation (2016)

19. Ronneberger, O., Fischer, P., Brox, T.: U-net: convolutional networks for biomedical image segmentation. In: Navab, N., Hornegger, J., Wells, W.M., Frangi, A.F. (eds.) MICCAI 2015. LNCS, vol. 9351, pp. 234–241. Springer, Cham (2015). https://doi.org/10.1007/978-3-319-24574-4_28

20. Yu, L., Yang, X., Chen, H., Qin, J., Heng, P.A.: Volumetric convnets with mixed residual connections for automated prostate segmentation from 3D MR images, January 2017
21. Zhao, Y.-X., Zhang, Y.-M., Liu, C.-L.: Bag of tricks for 3D MRI brain tumor segmentation. In: Crimi, A., Bakas, S. (eds.) BrainLes 2019. LNCS, vol. 11992, pp. 210–220. Springer, Cham (2020). https://doi.org/10.1007/978-3-030-46640-4_20

A Two-Phase Optimal Mass Transportation Technique for 3D Brain Tumor Detection and Segmentation

Wen-Wei Lin[1], Tiexiang Li[2,3(✉)], Tsung-Ming Huang[4(✉)] ⓘ, Jia-Wei Lin[1], Mei-Heng Yueh[4], and Shing-Tung Yau[5]

[1] Department of Applied Mathematics, National Yang Ming Chiao Tung University, Hsinchu 300, Taiwan
[2] Nanjing Center for Applied Mathematics, Nanjing 211135, People's Republic of China
[3] School of Mathematics, Southeast University, Nanjing 211189, People's Republic of China
txli@seu.edu.cn
[4] Department of Mathematics, National Taiwan Normal University, Taipei 116, Taiwan
min@ntnu.edu.tw
[5] Department of Mathematics, Harvard University, Cambridge, USA

Abstract. The goal of optimal mass transportation (OMT) is to transform any irregular 3D object (i.e., a brain image) into a cube without creating significant distortion, which is utilized to preprocess irregular brain samples to facilitate the tensor form of the input format of the U-net algorithm. The BraTS 2021 database newly provides a challenging platform for the detection and segmentation of brain tumors, namely, the whole tumor (WT), the tumor core (TC) and the enhanced tumor (ET), by AI techniques. We propose a two-phase OMT algorithm with density estimates for 3D brain tumor segmentation. In the first phase, we construct a volume-mass-preserving OMT via the density determined by the FLAIR grayscale of the scanned modality for the U-net and predict the possible tumor regions. Then, in the second phase, we increase the density on the region of interest and construct a new OMT to enlarge the target region of tumors for the U-net so that the U-net has a better chance to learn how to mark the correct segmentation labels. The application of this preprocessing OMT technique is a new and trending method for CNN training and validation.

Keywords: Optimal mass transportation · Two-phase OMT · Volume-measure-preserving map · Irregular 3D image

1 Introduction

In recent years, the MSD2018 [1,2] and BraTS2020 [3–5] databases have provided a challenging platform for brain tumor segmentation by AI techniques and

A. Crimi and S. Bakas (Eds.): BrainLes 2021, LNCS 12962, pp. 400–409, 2022.
https://doi.org/10.1007/978-3-031-08999-2_34

attracted enormous attention and interest from researchers in this field. Furthermore, very recently, BraTS2021 [3,5–8] was jointly organized by the RSNA, the ASNR and the MICCAI society, which provides 1251 training and 219 validation brain samples with four scanned modalities, namely, fluid-attenuated inversion recovery (FLAIR), T1-weighted (T1), T1-weighted contrast-enhanced (T1CE) and T2-weighted (T2), by multiparametric magnetic resonance imaging (mp-MRI) and focuses on the evaluation of state-of-the-art methods for the task of brain tumor segmentation on the whole tumor (WT labeled by {2,1,4}), the tumor core (TC labeled by {1,4}) and the enhanced tumor (ET labeled by {4}). To address this issue, convolutional neural network (CNN) structures with two layers [9] and eight layers [10] were proposed to make good progress in brain tumor segmentation. Then, a more sophisticated multiple CNN architecture, called the U-net model, was first developed in [11] and improved in [12] by assembling two full CNNs and a U-net. The merits of applying the U-net model to the challenge of MSD2018 were first proposed by [13].

The input data are one of the key components of the CNN. Experience has shown that adding a large amount of training data and expanding the size of trillion-parameter models can effectively provide excellent prediction performance. Because of the limitation of Moore's law, the calculation of a super model can become extremely expensive and inefficient. For this reason, preprocessing for the effective representation of a large amount of input data becomes crucial. Taking an irregular 3D effective brain image from an MRI, which is generally composed of 1.5 million vertices, randomly selecting several cubes (e.g., 16 cube filters in [14]) with seamless coverage to overplay the irregular brain image is a natural way to fit the input format of tensors for the U-net system. An elegant two-stage optimal mass transportation (2SOMT) method newly proposed in [15] is designed to first transform an irregular brain image to a unit ball and then to a $128 \times 128 \times 128$ cube with minimal distortion and small conversion loss. This strategy can greatly reduce the capacity of input data, so there are more opportunities to expand various types of training data and effectively use the existing U-net algorithm to improve the expected accuracy of prediction. However, 2SOMT did not sufficiently make full usage of the density information in the brain image.

In this paper, we propose a two-phase OMT algorithm for U-Net to improve the effectiveness of tumor segmentation. First, based on the projected gradient method, we develop an OMT algorithm that maps an irregular 3D brain image to a cube directly and ensures its sublinear convergence. The characteristics of the OMT map are to preserve the local mass unchanged and minimize the distortion. With this peculiar feature, in the first phase, we construct a volume-mass-preserving OMT by FLAIR grayscales for the U-net and predict the possible region of tumors. In the second phase, we increase the density distribution of interesting regions with fine meshes in the brain image and construct a new OMT to enlarge the target region for the U-net so that the U-net learning program is similar to taking a magnifying glass to view and learn how to mark the segmentation labels. The application of this preprocessing OMT technique is indeed an innovative idea and the most streamlined method for CNN training and prediction.

2   Method

2.1   Discrete OMT as a Preprocessing for the U-Net

Let $\mathcal{M}$ be a simplicial 3-complex with a genus-zero boundary that describes an irregular 3D brain image. $\mathcal{M}$ is composed of sets of vertices $\mathcal{V}(\mathcal{M})$, edges $\mathcal{E}(\mathcal{M})$, faces $\mathcal{F}(\mathcal{M})$ and tetrahedrons $T(\mathcal{M})$. A discrete OMT problem is to find a bijective function with minimal distortion that maps $\mathcal{M}$ to a canonical simple domain such as a ball, an ellipsoid, a cube or a cuboid. Since a tensor form is a necessary input format for the U-net algorithm, in this paper, we propose an OMT algorithm to map $\mathcal{M}$ to a cube while minimizing the transport cost by the projected gradient method. Without loss of generality, in this paper, each simplicial 3-complex $\mathcal{M}$ is centralized so that the center of mass is located at the origin and the mass of $\mathcal{M}$ is normalized to one. $\mathcal{C}$ is denoted as a unit cube with a constant density of one.

Let ρ be a density map on $\mathcal{V}(\mathcal{M})$. The piecewise linear density functions of ρ on $T(\mathcal{M})$ and the volume measure are respectively defined by

$$\rho(\tau) = \frac{1}{4} \sum_{i=1}^{4} \rho(v_i), \ \tau \in T(\mathcal{M}), \ v_i \in \mathcal{V}(\tau), \tag{1a}$$

$$m_\rho(v) := \frac{1}{4}\rho(v) \sum_{v \subset \tau} |\tau|, \ \tau \in T(\mathcal{M}), \ v \in \mathcal{V}(\mathcal{M}), \tag{1b}$$

where $|\tau|$ is the volume of τ. Denote

$$\mathbb{F}_\rho = \{f : \mathcal{M} \to \mathcal{C} \mid \rho(\tau)|\tau| = |f(\tau)|, \ \forall \tau \in T(\mathcal{M})\} \tag{2}$$

as the set of all volume-measure-preserving piecewise linear maps from $\mathcal{M}$ to $\mathcal{C}$, in which the bijective maps between τ and $f(\tau)$ are determined by the barycentric coordinates on τ. The discrete OMT problem on $\mathcal{M}$ with respect to $\| \cdot \|_2$ is to find an $f_\rho^* \in \mathbb{F}_\rho$ that solves the optimal problem

$$f_\rho^* = \underset{f \in \mathbb{F}_\rho}{\mathrm{argmin}}\, c(f), \quad \text{with } c(f) = \sum_{v \in \mathcal{V}(\mathcal{M})} \|v - f(v)\|_2^2 m_\rho(v). \tag{3}$$

Suppose $g_\rho^* = \mathrm{argmin}\frac{1}{3} \sum_{\hat{v} \in \mathcal{V}(\partial\mathcal{M})} \{\|\hat{v} - g(\hat{v})\|_2^2(\rho(\hat{v}) \sum_{\hat{v} \subset \alpha} |\alpha|)\}$ over $g : \partial\mathcal{M} \to \partial\mathcal{C}$ with $\rho(\alpha)|\alpha| = |g(\alpha)|$ for all $\alpha \in \mathcal{F}(\partial\mathcal{M})$, which is computed by area-measure-preserving OMT [16]. We now propose a volume-measure-preserving OMT algorithm for solving the OMT map f^* from $\mathcal{M}$ to $\mathcal{C}$ for (3) by the projected gradient method combined with the volume stretch energy minimization VSEM algorithm [16] with g_ρ^* fixed on the boundary of $\mathcal{M}$.

We first compute a volume-measure-preserving map $\mathbf{f}^{(0)}$ by VSEM [17] with $\mathbf{f}_{\mathrm{B}}^{(0)} = \mathbf{g}_\rho^*$ as a fixed boundary map, where $\mathbf{g}^*$ is the inducing vector of g^*. For $k = 0, 1, \ldots$, we update the vector by

$$\mathbf{f}^{(k)} = \mathbf{f}^{(k)} - \eta(\nabla c(f^{(k)})), \tag{4}$$

where $\eta > 0$ is the step length determined by the line-search procedure. Then, we project $\mathbf{f}^{(k)}$ onto the convex domain $\mathbb{F}_\rho$ of (2). We fix $\mathbf{f}_{\mathsf{B}}^{(k)} = \mathbf{g}_\rho^*$ as the boundary map on $\partial\mathcal{M}$ and perform the VSEM [17] by updating the interior map $\mathbf{f}_{\mathrm{I}}$ by

$$L_{\mathrm{I,I}}\mathbf{f}_{\mathrm{I}} = -L_{\mathrm{I,B}}\mathbf{g}_\rho^*, \quad \mathrm{I} = \{1, \ldots, n\}\backslash\mathsf{B}, \ n = \#\mathcal{V}(\mathcal{M}) \tag{5}$$

using the modified volume-weighted Laplacian matrix as $L \leftarrow L(f)$ defined in [17] at each iteration until the volume-weighted stretch energy $E(f) = \frac{1}{2}(\mathbf{f}^t)^\top L\mathbf{f}^t$ converses, where $\mathbf{f} = [\mathbf{f}_{\mathrm{I}}^\top, \mathbf{g}_\rho^{*\top}]^\top = [\mathbf{f}^1, \mathbf{f}^2, \mathbf{f}^3] \in \mathbb{R}^{n\times 3}$.

Similar to the standard convergence analysis of the projected gradient method (see, e.g., [16,18]), the OMT algorithm can be proven to be convergent with a sublinear rate of $\mathcal{O}(1/k)$.

2.2 Two-Phase OMT for Training and Validation

A brain image scanned by mpMRI typically provides four modalities, FLAIR, T1, T1CE and T2, with various grayscale values ranging from 0 to 65535 on each voxel of four $240 \times 240 \times 155$ cuboids, denoted by $\{I_s\}_{s=1}^4$. For a training brain image, let $\mathcal{L}$ denote the $240 \times 240 \times 155$ labeled cuboid by $\mathrm{WT} = \{2,1,4\}$, $\mathrm{TC} = \{1,4\}$, $\mathrm{ET} = \{4\}$ and $\{0\}$ for others. In practice, the grayscale values on I_s can be normalized in $[0,1]$, denoted by $\overline{I}_s$, by (grayscale value $-$ mean)/variance with a suitable shift and scaling.

An actual brain is contained in I_s and accounts for approximately 12%–20% voxels. Suppose $\mathcal{M} \subseteq I_s$ is a simplicial 3-complex with a genus-zero boundary composed of tetrahedral meshes representing a brain image. The normalized grayscale on the voxel $\overline{I}_s(i,j,k)$ can help with defining the density map on $\mathcal{V}(\mathcal{M})$ by

$$\rho_s(v) = \exp(\overline{I}_s(i,j,k)), \ v \in \overline{I}_s(i,j,k). \tag{6}$$

Two-Phase OMT and U-Net Algorithm for Training. We now propose a two-phase OMT algorithm with estimates of density functions to construct the effective input tensor for the U-net algorithm.

Phase I. We construct a density function on $\mathcal{V}(\mathcal{M})$ by $\rho_1(v) = \exp(\overline{I}_1(i,j,k))$ for $v \in \overline{I}_1(i,j,k)$, as in (6), where $\overline{I}_1$ records the normalized FLAIR grayscales. In general, the FLAIR modality typically reflects the distribution of $\mathrm{WT} = \{2,1,4\}$. We compute the OMT map $f_{\rho_1}^*$ as in (3) from $\mathcal{M}$ to a 128^3 cube $\mathcal{N}_0$. Then, we compute four 128^3 cubes $\{\mathcal{N}_{0,s}\}_{s=1}^4$ and one 128^3 cube $\mathcal{L}_0$ corresponding to the grayscales of $\mathcal{M} \subseteq I_s$, $s = 1, \ldots, 4$, and labels in $\mathcal{M} \subseteq \mathcal{L}$, respectively, via the OMT map $f_{\rho_1}^*$. Then, we call the U-net with the input data of 4×128^3 $\{\mathcal{N}_{0,s}\}_{s=1}^4$ and one 128^3 $\mathcal{L}_0$ to train Net 0.

Net 0 is designed to detect the possible tumor region of WT and then used to construct a new density function for enlarging the tumor region for phase II.

Phase II. For a given training brain image, we expand the tumor region of WT with labeled $1 = \{2,1,4\}$ outward by 5 voxels, say $\mathcal{T} \subseteq \mathcal{M}$, and construct a new density function with fine meshes by

$$\widehat{\rho}_1(v) = \begin{cases} \exp(\overline{I}_1(i,j,k)), & v \in \overline{I}_1(i,j,k) \subset \mathcal{T}, \\ 1, & \text{otherwise.} \end{cases} \tag{7}$$

We compute the OMT map $f^*_{\widehat{\rho}_1}$ from $\mathcal{M}$ to 128^3 cube $\mathcal{N}_1$ and four 128^3 cubes $\{\mathcal{N}_{1,s}\}^4_{s=1}$ corresponding to the grayscale values of $\mathcal{M} \subseteq I_s$ via the OMT $f^*_{\widehat{\rho}_1}$. Then, we construct three 128^3 cubes $\mathcal{L}_1$, $\mathcal{L}_2$ and $\mathcal{L}_3$ associated with the labels of $\{\mathbf{0} = \{0\}, \mathbf{1} = \{2,1,4\} = \text{WT}\}$, $\{\mathbf{0} = \{0,2\}, \mathbf{1} = \{1,4\} = \text{TC}\}$, and $\{\mathbf{0} = \{0,2,1\}, \mathbf{1} = \{4\} = \text{ET}\}$, respectively. Then, we call the U-net with the input data of 4×128^3 $\{\mathcal{N}_{0,s}\}^4_{s=1}$ and $\mathcal{L}_j$, respectively, for $j = 1,2,3$, to train three nets, namely, Net 1, Net 2, and Net 3.

Net 0, Net 1–Net 3 for Validation. Once we have computed Net 0 and Net 1–Net 3 by phase I and phase II, respectively, we use Net 0 to detect the possible tumor region of WT = $\{2,1,4\}$ and expand this region outward by 5 voxels, say $\mathcal{T} \subseteq \mathcal{M}$, and construct a new density function $\widetilde{\rho}_1$ depending on $\mathcal{T}$ with fine meshes as in (7). We compute four 128^3 cubes $\{\mathcal{N}_{1,s}\}^4_{s=1}$ for grayscale values of FLAIR, T1, T1CE and T2 via OMT $f^*_{\widetilde{\rho}_1}$ and use Net 1, Net 2 and Net 3 to validate three 128^3 cubes $\mathcal{L}_1$, $\mathcal{L}_2$ and $\mathcal{L}_3$ for predicted labels.

Validation of a testing brain image:

(i) Net 1 → $\{\mathbf{0} = \{0\}, \mathbf{1} = \{2,1,4\}\}$ on $\mathcal{L}_1$;
Net 2 → $\{\mathbf{0} = \{0,2\}, \mathbf{1} = \{1,4\}\}$ on $\mathcal{L}_2$;
Net 3 → $\{\mathbf{0} = \{0,2,1\}, \mathbf{1} = \{4\}\}$ on $\mathcal{L}_3$.
(ii) According to the labels $\{\mathbf{0}, \mathbf{1}\}$ on $\mathcal{L}_1$, we mark a 128^3 cube $\mathcal{L}$ by $\{0\}$ and $\{1\}$ for labels "$\mathbf{0}$" and "$\mathbf{1}$" on $\mathcal{L}_1$, respectively;
According to the labels $\{\mathbf{0}, \mathbf{1}\}$ on $\mathcal{L}_2$, we mark $\mathcal{L}$ by $\{1\}$ for label "$\mathbf{1}$" on $\mathcal{L}_2$;
According to the labels $\{\mathbf{0}, \mathbf{1}\}$ on $\mathcal{L}_3$, we mark $\mathcal{L}$ by $\{4\}$ for label "$\mathbf{1}$" on $\mathcal{L}_3$.
(iii) Let w denote the center of a voxel v$\subset \mathcal{M}$. Voxel v is labeled by $f^*_{\widehat{\rho}_1}(w)$, where $f^*_{\widehat{\rho}_1}(w)$ is contained in some voxel of $\mathcal{L}$.

The flow chart of the two-phase OMT and the U-net algorithm for training and validation is summarized in Fig. 1.

3   Results

As in the previous sections, the OMT map transforms irregular 3D brain images into cubes while preserving the local mass and minimizing the deformation, which makes the U-net algorithm train an effective prediction function for brain tumor detection and segmentation.

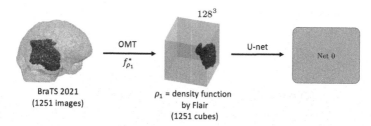

(a) 1251 OMT maps with density function ρ_1 by the grayscales of Flairs, and the Net 0 computed by the U-net algorithm.

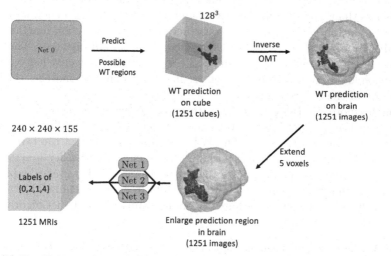

(b) Use Net 0 to do object detection of the testing data and get a possible WT region. Augment the WT region by 5 voxel outward and test it by the Net 1–Net 3 to get the segmentation labels.

Fig. 1. (a) Phase I: construct the Net 0 to predict the possible WT region; (b) Phase II: construct Net 1–Net 3 to evaluate the possible labels on the original brain image.

Conversion Loss Between Cubes and Original Brains. Let $\mathcal{A}$ and $\mathcal{B}$ denote the label sets of the ground truth labels and the conversion labels by $f^*_{\rho_1}$ on $\mathcal{M} \subseteq \mathcal{L}$ for the WT (labeled by $\{2, 1, 4\}$), TC (labeled by $\{1, 4\}$) and ET (labeled $\{4\}$), respectively. We define the conversion loss by $1 - \frac{2|\mathcal{A} \cap \mathcal{B}|}{|\mathcal{A}| + |\mathcal{B}|}$, where $|\mathcal{A}|$ denotes the cardinal number of $\mathcal{A}$. In Table 1, we illustrate the average of the conversion loss between brains and cubes for WT, TC and ET of all 1251 brain images in the BraTS 2021 Challenge dataset with typical grid sizes of 96^3 and 128^3 by the OMT map $f^*_{\rho_1}$.

Table 1. Conversion loss between brains and cubes with grid sizes of 96^3 and 128^3, respectively.

OMT-$f_{\rho_1}^*$	WT	TC	ET
Conversion loss for 96^3	0.43%	0.30%	0.65%
Conversion loss for 128^3	0.084%	0.026%	0.047%

We see that the deformation of OMT-$f_{\rho_1}^*$ from $\mathcal{M}$ to the 128^3 cube does not produce a considerable accuracy loss, and the maximal conversion loss of the WT is less than 0.084%. On the other hand, the maximal conversion loss of ET is 0.65%, which is not adequate for constructing a good prediction function, even though a cube size of 96^3 would save considerable computational cost. Therefore, the size of the cube with 128^3 is an excellent choice that not only has a smaller conversion loss between cubes and the original brains but also matches the input limitation of the U-net algorithm.

Furthermore, in Table 2, we show the average percentages of the WT, TC and ET in the original brain and in the 128^3 cube by the OMT-$f_{\bar\rho_1}^*$ with the new density function as in (7). The WT accounts for 6.49% of the raw data of the original brain. However, under the newly constructed density function and enhanced histogram equalization of the grayscale and OMT-$f_{\bar\rho_1}^*$ map in phase II of Sect. 2.2, the WT is enhanced almost twofold in cube, reaching 20.28%. This indeed helps with detecting various tumors in brains by the U-net algorithm.

Table 2. The average percentages of tumors in the raw data of size $240 \times 240 \times 155$ and cubes of size $128 \times 128 \times 128$ computed by the OMT-$f_{\bar\rho_1}^*$.

Data type	WT	TC	ET
Tumor in the raw data ($240 \times 240 \times 155$)	6.49%	2.42%	1.45%
Tumor in the cube ($128 \times 128 \times 128$)	20.28%	7.62%	4.62%

Dice Score of Validation and Testing. As in Sect. 2.2, we train Net 0, Net 1 - Net 3 by using the U-net algorithm on the 1251 brain samples from BraTS 2021 Challenge dataset [6]. BraTS 2021 dataset contains 2000 brain images. An online evaluation platform for BraTS 2021 was recently opened and provided 219 unlabeled brain image samples for validation. The others are unreleased brain image samples for testing. The feedback Dice scores of the WT, TC, and ET for validation and testing presented in Table 3 are evaluated by Net 0, Net 1 - Net 3, at 160 epochs by the U-net algorithm.

Table 3. The Dice scores of the WT, TC, and ET in the validation and testing sets with 160 epochs in the U-net algorithm.

	Validation	Testing				
		Mean	StdDev	Median	25 quantile	75 quantile
WT	0.9200	0.5205	0.4508	0.9344	0	0.9368
TC	0.8523	0.4872	0.4586	0.7070	0	0.9479
ET	0.8289	0.4722	0.4368	0.7078	0	0.9026

Other measurements of sensitivity, specificity for the voxelwise overlap in the segmented regions, and the Hausdorff dimension HD95 for the evaluation of the distance between segmentation boundaries are all calculated and shown in Table 4. The Dice scores for the testing data are unsatisfactory, probably because our executables did not recognize the types of orientations of the testing data. All the training data we use are in LPI voxel-order; however, the testing data orientations are either RAI or LPI voxel-order. As a result, the Dice scores for those testing data in RAI voxel-order would be terrible due to the wrong orientation. This issue should be remedied in our future release.

Table 4. Sensitivity, specificity and HD95 for the WT, TC, and ET for the validation and testing sets with 160 epochs in the U-net algorithm.

		Sensitivity			Specificity			HD95		
		WT	TC	ET	WT	TC	ET	WT	TC	ET
Validation		0.9259	0.8511	0.8431	0.9993	0.9998	0.9997	3.800	8.210	16.33
Testing	Mean	0.5139	0.4942	0.4732	0.5786	0.5787	0.5788	161.0	168.9	167.9
	StdDev	0.4450	0.4603	0.4420	0.4934	0.4935	0.4936	181.8	183.4	184.2
	Median	0.8117	0.7637	0.6607	0.9988	0.9995	0.9995	8.106	12.57	4.241
	25 quantile	0	0	0	0	0	0	2.236	1.732	1.414
	75 quantile	0.9239	0.9524	0.9156	0.9998	0.9999	0.9999	374	374	374

To further understand the specific advantage of the two-phase OMT maps while preserving the local mass ratios, as well as minimizing the transport cost and distortion, we randomly divide 1251 brain samples into 1000 samples for training and 251 for validation. The Dice scores of WT, TC, and ET in the cubes and brains, respectively, for training and validation shown in Table 5 are computed by Net 0, Net 1 - Net 3. Without augmenting the data and performing any postprocessing in this work, the Dice scores in Table 5 are quite satisfactory.

Table 5. The Dice scores of the WT, TC, and ET in brains in the training and validation with 160 epochs in the U-net algorithm.

Epochs	Dice score (Brains)		
160	WT	TC	ET
Training	0.9614	0.9340	0.9121
Validation	0.9317	0.8896	0.8564

4   Discussion

This work mainly introduces the 2-phase OMT technique for 3D brain tumor detection and segmentation. The OMT technique to this research area was first introduced by Lin et al. [15]. However, the density function estimates for the prediction of possible tumor regions were not sufficiently utilized in [15]. In this paper, we first use FLAIR grayscales to construct a corresponding density function for the OMT to transform an irregular 3D brain image to a 128^3 cube with minimal distortion, which is particularly beneficial to the U-net algorithm's input format for creating a predicting Net 0. Second, we use it to predict the possible tumor regions expanding outward 5 voxels and construct an associated step density function on the brain. Then, we perform U-net with this new density function to train three nets, Net 1 - Net 3, for label evaluations of the validation set. The use of the OMT map to convert an irregular 3D image to a cube with minimal transport cost and local mass ratio is a new attempt to introduce it into the medical imaging field. For a brain image that only needs to be represented by a cube, which saves considerable capacity in the computer environment for the input data of the U-net, an augmentation technique, such as rotating, mirroring, shearing, and cropping, as well as a postprocessing technique are our next research topics.

Acknowledgments. This work was partially supported by the Ministry of Science and Technology (MoST), the National Center for Theoretical Sciences, the Big Data Computing Center of Southeast University, the Nanjing Center for Applied Mathematics, the ST Yau Center in Taiwan, and the Shing-Tung Yau Center at Southeast University. W.-W. Lin, T.-M. Huang, and M.-H. Yueh were partially supported by MoST 110-2115-M-A49-004-, 110-2115-M-003-012-MY3, and 109-2115-M-003-010-MY2 and 110-2115-M-003-014-, respectively. T. Li was supported in part by the National Natural Science Foundation of China (NSFC) 11971105.

References

1. Antonelli, M., et al.: The Medical Segmentation Decathlon (2021). http://medicaldecathlon.com/. 2106.05735
2. Simpson, A.L., et al.: A large annotated medical image dataset for the development and evaluation of segmentation algorithms. arXiv 1902.09063 [cs.CV] (2019). http://arxiv.org/abs/1902.09063. 1902.09063

3. Bakas, S., et al.: Advancing the cancer genome atlas glioma MRI collections with expert segmentation labels and radiomic features. Sci. Data **4**, 170117 (2017)

4. Bakas, S., et al.: Identifying the best machine learning algorithms for brain tumor segmentation, progression assessment, and overall survival prediction in the BRATS challenge (2019). 1811.02629

5. Menze, B.H., et al.: The multimodal brain tumor image segmentation benchmark (BRATS). IEEE Trans. Med. Imag. **34**, 1993–2024 (2015)

6. Baid, U., et al.: The RSNA-ASNR-MICCAI BraTS 2021 benchmark on brain tumor segmentation and radiogenomic classification. arXiv:2107.02314 (2021)

7. Bakas, S., et al.: Segmentation labels and radiomic features for the pre-operative scans of the TCGA-GBM collection. Cancer Imaging Arch. (2017). https://doi.org/10.7937/K9/TCIA.2017.KLXWJJ1Q

8. Bakas, S., et al.: Segmentation labels and radiomic features for the pre-operative scans of the TCGA-LGG collection. Cancer Imaging Arch. (2017). https://doi.org/10.7937/K9/TCIA.2017.GJQ7R0EF

9. Zikic, D., Ioannou, Y., Criminisi, A., Brown, M.: Segmentation of brain tumor tissues with convolutional neural networks. In: Proceedings of the MICCAIBRATS 2014, pp. 36–39 (2014)

10. Randhawa, R.S., Modi, A., Jain, P., Warier, P.: Improving boundary classification for brain tumor segmentation and longitudinal disease progression. In: Crimi, A., Menze, B., Maier, O., Reyes, M., Winzeck, S., Handels, H. (eds.) BrainLes 2016. LNIP, vol. 10154, pp. 65–74 Springer, Cham (2016). https://doi.org/10.1007/978-3-319-55524-9_7

11. Ronneberger, O., Fischer, P., Brox, T.: U-Net: convolutional networks for biomedical image segmentation. In: Navab, N., Hornegger, J., Wells, W.M., Frangi, A.F. (eds.) MICCAI 2015. LNCS, vol. 9351, pp. 234–241. Springer, Cham (2015). https://doi.org/10.1007/978-3-319-24574-4_28

12. Kamnitsas, K., Bai, W., Ferrante, E., McDonagh, S., Sinclair, M., Pawlowski, N., Rajchl, M., Lee, M., Kainz, B., Rueckert, D., Glocker, B.: Ensembles of multiple models and architectures for robust brain tumour segmentation. In: Crimi, A., Bakas, S., Kuijf, H., Menze, B., Reyes, M. (eds.) BrainLes 2017. LNCS, vol. 10670, pp. 450–462. Springer, Cham (2018). https://doi.org/10.1007/978-3-319-75238-9_38

13. Isensee, F., Kickingereder, P., Wick, W., Bendszus, M., Maier-Hein, K.H.: No new-net. In: Crimi, A., Bakas, S., Kuijf, H., Keyvan, F., Reyes, M., van Walsum, T. (eds.) BrainLes 2018. LNCS, vol. 11384, pp. 234–244. Springer, Cham (2019). https://doi.org/10.1007/978-3-030-11726-9_21

14. Isensee, F., Kickingereder, P., Wick, W., Bendszus, M., Maier-Hein, K.H.: Brain tumor segmentation and radiomics survival prediction: contribution to the BRATS 2017 challenge. In: Crimi, A., Bakas, S., Kuijf, H., Menze, B., Reyes, M. (eds.) BrainLes 2017. LNCS, vol. 10670, pp. 287–297. Springer, Cham (2018). https://doi.org/10.1007/978-3-319-75238-9_25

15. Lin, W.-W., et al.: 3D brain tumor segmentation using a two-stage optimal mass transport algorithm. Sci. Rep. **11**, 14686 (2021)

16. Yueh, M.-H., Huang, T.-M., Li, T., Lin, W.-W., Yau, S.-T.: Projected gradient method combined with homotopy techniques for volume-measure-preserving optimal mass transportation problems. J. Sci. Comput. **88**(3), 1–24 (2021). https://doi.org/10.1007/s10915-021-01583-z

17. Yueh, M.-H., Li, T., Lin, W.-W., Yau, S.-T.: A novel algorithm for volume-preserving parameterizations of 3-manifolds. SIAM J. Imag. Sci. **12**, 1071–1098 (2019)

18. Parikh, N., Boyd, S.: Proximal algorithms. Found. Trends Optim. **1**, 127–239 (2014)

Cascaded Training Pipeline for 3D Brain Tumor Segmentation

Minh Sao Khue Luu[1,3(✉)] 🆔 and Evgeniy Pavlovskiy[2] 🆔

[1] Department of Mathematics and Mechanics, Novosibirsk State University, 1 Pirogova Street, Novosibirsk 630090, Russia
khue.luu@g.nsu.ru
[2] Stream Data Analytics and Machine Learning Laboratory, Novosibirsk State University, 1 Pirogova Street, Novosibirsk 630090, Russia
pavlovskiy@post.nsu.ru
[3] Innoflex Technology, Brisbane, QLD, Australia

Abstract. We apply a cascaded training pipeline for the 3D U-Net to segment each brain tumor sub-region separately and chronologically. Firstly, the volumetric data of four modalities are used to segment the whole tumor in the first round of training. Then, our model combines the whole tumor segmentation with the mpMRI images to segment the tumor core. Finally, the network uses whole tumor and tumor core segmentations to predict enhancing tumor regions. Unlike the standard 3D U-Net, we use Group Normalization and Randomized Leaky Rectified Linear Unit in the encoding and decoding blocks. We achieved dice scores on the validation set of 88.84, 81.97, and 75.02 for whole tumor, tumor core, and enhancing tumor, respectively.

Keywords: 3D U-Net · Brain tumor segmentation · Medical image segmentation

1 Introduction

Glioblastoma is the most common malignant primary brain tumor in humans. The tumor has a variety of histological sub-regions, including edema/invasion, active tumor structures, necrotic components, and non-enhancing gross abnormalities. Accurate segmentation of these intrinsic sub-regions using Magnetic Resonance Imaging (MRI) is critical for the potential diagnosis and treatment of this disease. In most clinical centers, the segmentation of whole tumor and sub-compartment is still performed manually and is considered the standard approach. However, manual segmentation takes time and requires skilled experts, hence it is crucial to employ fully automated segmentation tools capable of segmenting brain tumor sub-regions. Recently, Deep learning (DL) has been widely adopted for medical imaging thanks to its ability to learn complicated representations from raw data without requiring human engineering and domain expertise to create feature extractors. Therefore, a considerable number of studies about DL applications in brain tumor segmentation have been introduced, demonstrating its success in the field. Moreover, the Multimodal Brain Tumor Segmentation Challenge (BraTS)

A. Crimi and S. Bakas (Eds.): BrainLes 2021, LNCS 12962, pp. 410–420, 2022.
https://doi.org/10.1007/978-3-031-08999-2_35

dataset, which includes multi-institutional multimodal MRI scans of glioblastoma and lower grade glioma, has attracted many researchers to submit their fully automatic brain tumor segmentation algorithms and received significant results.

The U-Net, introduced by Ronneberger et al. [1], was the first high-impact encoder-decoder structure that was widely employed for medical image segmentation. It comprises a contracting path and an expanding path, which is similar to the fully convolutional network architecture. However, the novelty of U-Net lies in the fact that the up-sampling and down-sampling layers are joined via skip connections to connect opposing convolution and deconvolution layers. The U-Net's symmetric structure with skip connections was a perfect solution for medical imaging segmentation tasks because it can combine low-level and high-level features in medical images to recognize objects that contain noise and blurred boundaries. Several variants of U-Net that are capable of performing 3D segmentation were later introduced and achieved noteworthy advancement. For instance, Çiçek et al. [2] suggested a 3D U-Net by substituting 2D operations in 2D U-Net with 3D counterparts, while Milletari et al. [3] built a 3D-variant of U-Net architecture called V-net by employing residual blocks. Because these architectures are trained on entire images or large image patches rather than small patches, they are influenced by data scarcity, which is often handled via data transformations like shifting, rotating, scaling, or random deformations. The research of Kayalıbay et al. [4] employed a 3D U-Net liked network architecture for bone and brain tumor segmentation. They combined different segmentation maps created at various scales to speed up convergence. However, because this method used wide receptive fields in convolutional layers, it can be computationally costly. Isensee et al. [5] proposed a 3D U-Net with modifications to the up-sampling pathways, filters number, methods of normalization, and the batch size, enabling training with large image patches and capturing spatial data that leads to improvements in segmentation performance. A separable 3D U-Net made up of sparable 3D convolutions was proposed in a more recent paper by Chen et al. [6]. Using several 3D U-Net blocks, their S3D-UNet design fully utilizes the 3D volumes. It's also worth noting that the winning submissions to the BraTS 2019 and BraTS 2020 used U-Net-based designs as well. While Jiang et al. [7] utilized a two-stage cascaded U-Net, Isensee et al. [8] used the nnU-Net architecture that was originally developed as a general-purpose U-Net based network for segmentation.

In this study, we propose a chronological cascaded 3D U-Net network, which concatenates segmentation from the previous round to the next ones. Each training round is performed as a normal brain tumor segmentation training process. We also apply a customized weighted dice loss function to give weights for different losses on brain tumor sub-regions. We achieved dice scores on the validation set of 88.84, 81.97, and 75.02 for WT, TC, and ET, respectively.

2 Dataset

We use the RSNA-ASNR-MICCAI BraTS 2021 challenge training and validation datasets [9–13], which include 1251 and 219 cases respectively. Each case contains 4 volumetric MRI scans from 4 different modalities, which are a) native (T1) and b) post-contrast T1-weighted (T1Gd (Gadolinium)), c) T2-weighted (T2), and d) T2 Fluid Attenuated Inversion Recovery (T2-FLAIR) volumes. All BraTS mpMRI scans have been applied standardized pre-processing routines, such as NIFTI file format conversion, re-orientation, co-registration, resampling to 1 mm^3, and skull-tripping. Annotations in the datasets were approved by board-certified experts who have been working with glioma for more than 15 years. Each annotation includes the necrotic tumor core (NCR—label 1), the peritumoral edematous/invaded tissue (ED—label 2), and Gd-enhancing tumor (ET—label 4).

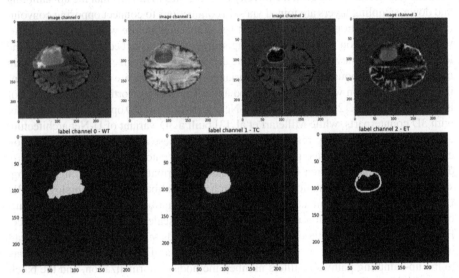

Fig. 1. Overview of the training images. The first row displays a sample input data in four channels, corresponding to four modalities. The second row shows three tumor sub-regions in a sample ground truth: WT, TC, and ET.

2.1 Tumor Distribution

From the training dataset, we found that almost every slice in an MR image might contain tumors, even some first few slices. There are only several last slices of the image that does not contain any tumor. Therefore, to keep the tumor information as much as possible, instead of reducing the depth of the 3D image to 128 slices like in other popular methods, we keep the number of slices to be 155.

Also, in order to reduce the computational cost, we want to reduce the height and width of the 3D MR images to a size that is small enough and is consistent among the dataset but at the same time preserve the tumor regions. To select a good region of interest for the training images, we analyze the tumor distribution by adding all segmentation images in the dataset together and visualizing the regions that are likely to include tumors. The background with values 0 is still black, but regions that many tumors occur contain high values and become brighter in the visualization. We examined the summary images in both 3D and 2D versions to detect regions where tumors appear crowdedly.

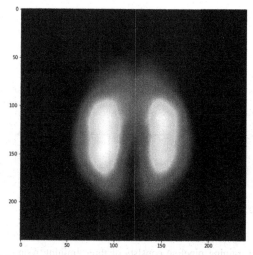

Fig. 2. A 2D plot of the tumor regions of all training data. The brighter the color is, the more likely the tumors occur in that region. (Color figure online)

Figure 2 shows that tumors appear symmetrically on both hemispheres among images in the training dataset, represented by the bright color. Overall, the areas that are more likely to contain tumors are central parts of both hemispheres. In the summary image, the hemisphere on the left side has brighter and slightly larger tumor-likely regions than the one on the right. It is represented by the larger white area on the left, which has a clearer boundary. This indicates that in the training dataset, tumors occur more on the left part of the image and their locations are concentrated.

3 Method

3.1 Overall Architecture

We propose a training architecture that consists of three training rounds, each round includes a 3D U-Net architecture inspired by [2] and [8] with some minor modifications. We call them the Modified 3D U-Net. Our network segments each brain tumor sub-regions separately, from the largest region to the smallest, then concatenate the segmentation of the current sub-region with the input data to feed to the network of the next training round. In other words, we train the volumetric images of four modalities and segment the WT in the first round of training, then combine the WT segmentation with the mpMRI images to segment TC, and finally use WT and TC segmentations to predict the ET region. Each network in a training round is fully independent. The network for WT was trained, its weights frozen and the output used for the subsequent networks. This allows flexible adjustment of hyperparameters for each network corresponding to the output tumor sub-regions. The training process is described in detail in Fig. 1 (Fig. 3).

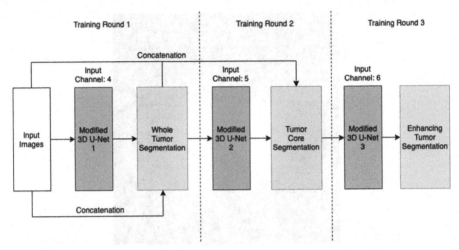

Fig. 3. Our proposed training pipeline consists of three training rounds, which are trained to segment a specific type of brain tumor sub-regions.

3.2 The Modified 3D U-Net

This section provides a complete description and explanation of the modified 3D U-net used in a training round. This is the main building block of the training process.

Like the standard U-Net and 3D U-Net, our network has an encoder and a decoder which are interconnected by skip connections. The input data is center cropped to 155 $\times$ 160 $\times$ 160. In the encoding part, each layer contains a block of double 3 $\times$ 3 $\times$ 3 convolutions and Group Normalization (GN) [14] with a group size of 8. The layers are followed by a Randomized Leaky Rectified Linear Unit (RReLU) [15] activation, with randomly sampled from a uniform distribution. After the block, a 2 $\times$ 2 $\times$ 2 max-pooling with strides of 2 is applied. In the decoding part, upsampling using the trilinear algorithm is performed. Skip connections from layers of equal resolution provide information from the low-level features. The output is applied a sigmoid nonlinearity function with a threshold of 0.5.

The training objective is the dice loss function, which is discussed in more detail in Sect. 3.4. The loss operates on three brain tumor sub-region WT, TC, and ET separately. Our network uses Adam [16] optimization function with a learning rate of 1e$-$4. The learning rate is decayed by a factor or 1e$-$2 when the metric has stopped improving for 2 epochs. The model is trained with 3 rounds for 3 sub-regions, each round with 50 epochs. The training procedure is described in Sect. 3.4 (Fig. 4).

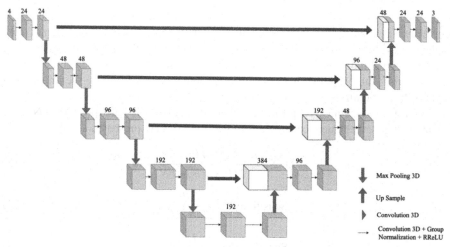

Fig. 4. The proposed U-net based architecture with minor modifications which is used in each training round.

3.3 Region-Based Training

Although the provided labels for the data are 'necrotic tumor core', 'edema', and 'enhancing tumor', the evaluation of the segmentation is performed on the three overlapping brain tumor sub-regions called enhancing tumor (ET, label 4), tumor core (TC, label 1 and 4), and whole tumor (WT, label 1, 2 and 4). We found that the network's performance improved when segmenting these tumor sub-regions directly. Therefore, we change the optimization target to the brain tumor sub-regions for the input data and apply a sigmoid function for the output of the network.

3.4 Loss Function

Dice loss originates from the Sørensen–Dice coefficient (DSC), which measures the overlapping regions between two sets. The coefficient ranges from 0 to 1, with 0 means no overlap and 1 means perfect overlap. The dice loss is set as 1 − DSC, therefore, it also ranges from 0 to 1, the smaller the better.

$$\mathcal{L}_{dice} = 1 - \frac{2 \times \sum_i^N p_i \times g_i + \varepsilon}{\sum_i^N p_i^2 + \sum_i^N g_i^2 + \varepsilon} \tag{1}$$

In the above formula, p_i and g_i represent the corresponding voxel values of prediction and ground truth respectively. $\varepsilon = 1\text{e--}6$ is a tiny number added to both numerator and denominator to avoid zero division.

In this study, DCS is used as the loss function during training and validation.

3.5 Metrics

There are several metrics used in the evaluation of this semantic segmentation network, such as DCS, sensitivity, specificity, and Hausdorff95 distance. DCS is a statistical-based metric that scores the overlapped region of the segmentation result and the ground truth. Sensitivity is the proportion of genuinely positive voxels in the 3D image that is correctly classified as positive. Meanwhile, specificity represents the proportion of truly negative voxels that are correctly classified as negative. Lastly, the Hausdorff95 is the 95th percentile of distances from the boundary points in set X to the nearest point in set Y. Using the 95th percentile instead of the maximum values eliminate the impact of a small subset of outliers.

With TP indicating true positive, TN true negative, FP false positive, FN false negative, the mathematical calculations of these metrics are presented as follows.

$$DCS = \frac{2TP}{2TP + FP + FN} \tag{2}$$

$$Sensitivity = \frac{TP}{TP + FN} \tag{3}$$

$$Specificity = \frac{TN}{TN + FP} \tag{4}$$

$$Hausdorff95 \ distance = P_{95}\left\{ \sup_{x \in X} d(x, Y), \ \sup_{y \in Y} d(X, y) \right\} \tag{5}$$

3.6 Training Procedure

The training procedure includes three training rounds. Each round is trained as a normal training process with input is volumetric data and output is the segmentation for one tumor sub-region. The later round use results from the previous concatenated with the same volumetric data as the input. The first round is to train WT segmentation, which is the largest region, then the second round is for TC, and the last round is dedicated for ET, which is the hardest sub-region to segment. This training procedure gives more information to the model to segment the smaller sub-regions and help the later training rounds converge faster.

3.7 Postprocessing

The output of the model has the dimension of $3 \times 155 \times 160 \times 160$ with three layers of tumor sub-regions are stacked together. Also, the label values of the output are 0 (background) and 1 (tumor). However, the segmentation's dimension required to be evaluated is $240 \times 240 \times 155$ with labels 0, 1, 2, 4 as described in Sect. 2. Therefore, we need to add zero paddings around the heigh and width of the model's output and change the order of dimension so that the final output's dimension becomes $240 \times 240 \times 155$.

We also need to convert the binary values of three overlapped brain tumor sub-regions into 0, 1, 2, 4 correspondingly. The output consists of 3 segmentations of brain tumor sub-regions, each segmentation contains values 0 or 1. If value 1 appears on all three tumor sub-regions, it is mapped to value 4, because the ET only occurs inside the TC, which also only occurs inside WT. If value 1 appears in 2 sub-regions, it is mapped as follows (Table 1).

Table 1. The conversion table for mapping binary values of voxels

	WT	TC	ET
WT	2	1	4
TC	2	1	4
ET	4	4	0

Tumor voxels (voxels have value 1) appear in both WT and ET, or TC and ET are converted to 4, while ones only appear in ET are changed to 0 as background. This removes extra clusters that do not belong to the brain tumor region or reduce the amount of false positive classification on ET. In addition, tumor voxels appear only on TC or will be converted to 1 as those appear on both WT and TC. This avoids the effect of the WT segmentation "eating" other brain tumor small sub-regions (Fig. 5).

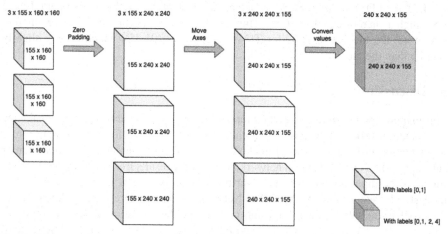

Fig. 5. Diagram of our post-processing step that converts a stack of three blocks of binary segmentation to one block of non-binary segmentation

4 Experiments and Results

The network is trained using the Pytorch framework on an Nvidia GeForce GTX 1080Ti GPU. The GPU memory allows training with a batch size of 1. All mpMRI scans in the training dataset are used in the proposed network. The BraTS 2021 training dataset is divided into a training and validation set. Then the segmentation files are evaluated by the online platform. According to the reported results, our proposed network achieves dice score and Hausdorff distance (95%) (HD95) as follows (Table 2).

Overall, performance on WT segmentation is the highest among brain tumor sub-regions, indicated by the highest DSC and lowest HD95. This agrees with the fact that

Table 2. Mean Dice Score (DSC) and Hausdorff distance (95%) (HD95), of our proposed segmentation network on the BraTS 2021 validation dataset using the online evaluation portal.

	WT	TC	ET	Mean
DSC	88.84	81.97	75.02	81.94
HD95	7.97	12.60	30.41	16.99
Sensitivity	90.32	83.40	76.94	83.55
Specificity	99.91	99.96	99.97	99.95

the WT sub-region is larger in shape and the boundary is smoother than the other sub-regions. Segmentation for ET has the lowest DSC and a very large HD95 because there are cases where there are ET voxels in the ground truth, but our proposed network failed to predict. This causes the DCS of that case to lower to 0 and the HD95 becomes maximum. In other cases, where ET is predicted, the DCS for ET is high. Specifically, the median of DSC of ET is 86.89, which means 50% of the validation cases of ET have DSC higher than or equal to 86.89. This also happens to TC but in a smaller amount. Therefore, the median of DSC for TC is a lot higher (91.35), which is only slightly smaller than the median of WT (92.50).

5 Discussion

This manuscript describes our method for our participation in the BraTS 2021 challenge segmentation task. We proposed a cascaded training pipeline for the 3D brain tumor segmentation task. Our proposed method trains a model to segment each brain tumor sub-regions in a different neural network, then use the results from the previous training round as the input for the next one. Our training starts with WT, then TC, and ET is the last to be segmented. We use 3D U-Net-inspired architecture with modifications to train each of the sub-regions. Out results obtained on the validation set are dice scores of 88.84, 81.97, and 75.02 for WT, TC, and ET respectively. Because of the timeframe of the challenge, our manuscript only covers a small number of modifications and therefore has limitations.

Data Augmentation Has not Been Applied. Data Augmentation includes techniques to increase the amount of training data by giving the model more modified copies of the existing ones. They help the model increase generalization and reduce the effect of the class imbalance issue. In this study, we haven't applied data augmentation to the training data, this may hurt the model's performance, especially on cases where ET does not appear.

The Algorithm to Map Labels from 0 and 1 to 0, 1, 2, and 4 Needs to Be Implemented Carefully. The output of our proposed model contains three layers of segmentation for each brain tumor sub-regions and we need to convert them into one layer. There are disagreements from each segmentation of brain tumor sub-regions. The algorithm to convert those disagreements into proper classification strongly affects the final segmentation results. Further analysis should be done to improve the current mapping algorithm.

Different Architectures for Each Training Round Should Have Been Experimented. Since we train the model to segment WT, TC and ET separately, there is room for experiments on different architectures for each training round. The depth of the architecture could be considered to learn more detailed information as ET has more uncertain shapes than the others.

Larger Batch Sizes have not been Experimented. Due to the limitation of our training resources, we do not implement the training pipeline with different batch sizes except for the batch size of 1. This may not help in observing and analyzing the benefit of Group Normalization. We believe that more thorough optimization of hyperparameters could result in faster convergence as well as further performance gain.

Acknowledgement. We would like to express our appreciation to the Stream Data Analytics and Machine Learning Laboratory for providing office places and computational resources to complete this research.

References

1. Ronneberger, O., Fischer, P., Brox, T.: U-Net: convolutional networks for biomedical image segmentation (2015). https://doi.org/10.1007/978-3-319-24574-4_28
2. Çiçek, Ö., Abdulkadir, A., Lienkamp, S.S., Brox, T., Ronneberger, O.: 3D U-Net: learning dense volumetric segmentation from sparse annotation. In: Ourselin, S., Joskowicz, L., Sabuncu, M.R., Unal, G., Wells, W. (eds.) MICCAI 2016. LNCS, vol. 9901, pp. 424–432. Springer, Cham (2016). https://doi.org/10.1007/978-3-319-46723-8_49
3. Milletari, F., Navab, N., Ahmadi, S.-A.: V-Net: fully convolutional neural networks for volumetric medical image segmentation (October 2016). https://doi.org/10.1109/3DV.2016.79
4. Kayalıbay, B., Jensen, G., van der Smagt, P.: CNN-based segmentation of medical imaging data (June 2017)
5. Isensee, F., Kickingereder, P., Wick, W., Bendszus, M., Maier-Hein, K.H.: Brain tumor segmentation and radiomics survival prediction: contribution to the BRATS 2017 challenge. In: Crimi, A., Bakas, S., Kuijf, H., Menze, B., Reyes, M. (eds.) BrainLes 2017. LNCS, vol. 10670, pp. 287–297. Springer, Cham (2018). https://doi.org/10.1007/978-3-319-75238-9_25
6. Chen, W., Liu, B., Peng, S., Sun, J., Qiao, X.: S3D-UNet: separable 3D U-Net for brain tumor segmentation. In: Crimi, A., Bakas, S., Kuijf, H., Keyvan, F., Reyes, M., van Walsum, T. (eds.) BrainLes 2018. LNCS, vol. 11384, pp. 358–368. Springer, Cham (2019). https://doi.org/10.1007/978-3-030-11726-9_32
7. Jiang, Z., Ding, C., Liu, M., Tao, D.: Two-stage cascaded U-Net: 1st place solution to BraTS challenge 2019 segmentation task. In: Crimi, A., Bakas, S. (eds.) BrainLes 2019. LNCS, vol. 11992, pp. 231–241. Springer, Cham (2020). https://doi.org/10.1007/978-3-030-46640-4_22
8. Isensee, F., Jäger, P.F., Full, P.M., Vollmuth, P., Maier-Hein, K.H.: nnU-Net for brain tumor segmentation. In: Crimi, A., Bakas, S. (eds.) BrainLes 2020. LNCS, vol. 12659, pp. 118–132. Springer, Cham (2021). https://doi.org/10.1007/978-3-030-72087-2_11
9. Baid, U., et al.: The RSNA-ASNR-MICCAI BraTS 2021 benchmark on brain tumor segmentation and radiogenomic classification (July 2021). http://arxiv.org/abs/2107.02314

10. Menze, B.H., et al.: The multimodal brain tumor image segmentation benchmark (BRATS). IEEE Trans. Med. Imaging **34**(10), 1993–2024 (2015). https://doi.org/10.1109/TMI.2014.2377694
11. Bakas, S., et al.: Advancing the cancer genome atlas glioma MRI collections with expert segmentation labels and radiomic features. Nat. Sci. Data **4**(1), 170117 (2017). https://doi.org/10.1038/sdata.2017.117
12. Bakas, S., et al.: Segmentation labels and radiomic features for the pre-operative scans of the TCGA-GBM collection (June 2017). https://doi.org/10.7937/K9/TCIA.2017.KLXWJJ1Q
13. Bakas, S., et al.: Segmentation labels and radiomic features for the pre-operative scans of the TCGA-LGG collection (June 2017). https://doi.org/10.7937/K9/TCIA.2017.GJQ7R0EF

NnUNet with Region-based Training and Loss Ensembles for Brain Tumor Segmentation

Jun Ma[1(✉)] and Jianan Chen[2]

[1] Department of Mathematics, Nanjing University of Science and Technology, Nanjing, China
junma@njust.edu.cn
[2] Department of Medical Biophysics, University of Toronto, Toronto, Canada
geoff.chen@mail.utoronto.ca

Abstract. Brain tumor segmentation in multi-model MRI scans is a long-term and challenging task. Motivated by the winner solution in BraTS 2020 [7], we incorporate region-based training, a more aggressive data augmentation, and loss ensembles to build the widely used nnUNet model. Specifically, we train ten cross-validation models based on two compound loss functions and select the five best models for ensembles. On the final testing set, our method achieves average Dice scores of 0.8760, 0.8843, and 0.9300 and 95% Hausdorff Distance values of 12.3, 15.3, and 4.75 for enhancing tumor, tumor core, and whole tumor respectively.

Keywords: nnUNet · Segmentation · Brain tumor · Loss function

1 Introduction

Brain tumor segmentation (BraTS) is a long-term and well-known challenge in medical image processing community, which aims to evaluate and compare different state-of-the-art brain tumor segmentation methods in multi-parametric magnetic resonance imaging (mpMRI) scans. In the recent BraTS 2021 challenge, participants were called to produce segmentation labels of three different glioma sub-regions: the enhancing tumor (ET), the tumor core (TC), and the whole tumor (WT) from pre-operative four-sequence MRI scans (T1-weighted, post-contrast T1-weighted, T2-weighted, and T2 Fluid Attenuated Inversion Recovery) which were acquired with different clinical protocols and various scanners from multiple institutions.

nnUNet [6] has been widely used in various medical image segmentation challenges. For example, nine in ten top solutions developed their solution based on nnUNet in MICCAI 2020 [11]. The winner solution [7] in BraTS 2020 also employed nnUNet and some BraTS-specific modifications were developed to further improve the performance, including region-based training, postprocessing, increasing batch size, using more data augmentation, replacing the default instance normalization with batch normalization, using batch Dice loss rather than sample Dice loss, and model selection with BraTS-like ranking. The final model is the ensembles of three top performing models, including 25 cross-validation models totally.

A. Crimi and S. Bakas (Eds.): BrainLes 2021, LNCS 12962, pp. 421–430, 2022.
https://doi.org/10.1007/978-3-031-08999-2_36

Our solution is based on the BraTS2020 winner solution with the publicly available nnUNet trainer: nnUNetTrainerV2BraTSRegions, including the region-based training and more data augmentation. The main modification is that we train two groups of models with different loss functions. Doing more ablation studies with other settings (e.g., batch Dice loss) is desired, but we do not have enough computational resources to run experiments. Due to the storage limitation (the data located on HDD rather than SSD), training one cross-validation model costs about 15 days on NVIDIA TITAN V100 GPU.

2   Methods

Loss function is an important component in modern deep learning networks. Recent study has shown that none of the popular segmentation loss functions can consistently achieve the best performance on multiple segmentation tasks and compound loss functions are the most robust and competitive losses [12]. Moreover, it has been proved that directly optimizing the partially overlapping brain tumor regions (whole tumor, tumor core, and enhancing tumor) can benefit segmentation performance in BraTS challenge [7,8,15,19,20]. Motivated by these successful solutions, we train two groups (nnUNetTrainerV2BraTSRegions) nnUNet models with DiceCE loss and Dice-TopK loss and select best models for final ensembles. The loss ensemble strategy was also employed by the winning method of intracranial aneurysms segmentation challenge [10,18], which is a highly imbalanced segmentation task as well. The loss function details are provided as follows. Let g_i and s_i denote the ground truth and the predicted segmentation, respectively. N and C denote the number of voxels and categories in the ground truth mask, respectively.

2.1   Cross Entropy Loss

$$L_{CE} = -\frac{1}{N} \sum_{i=1}^{N} \sum_{c=1}^{C} g_i^c log s_i^c, \tag{1}$$

where g_i^c is binary indicator if class label c is the correct classification for pixel i, and s_i^c is the corresponding predicted probability.

2.2   Dice Loss

Dice similarity coefficient (DSC) is the most commonly used segmentation evaluation metric and Dice loss [14] is designed to directly optimize the DSC, which is defined by

$$L_{Dice} = 1 - \frac{2 \sum_{i=1}^{N} \sum_{c=1}^{C} g_i^c s_i^c}{\sum_{i=1}^{N} \sum_{c=1}^{C} g_i^{c2} + \sum_{i=1}^{N} \sum_{c=1}^{C} s_i^{c2}}. \tag{2}$$

Unlike weighted cross entropy, it does not require class re-weighting for imbalanced segmentation tasks.

2.3 TopK Loss

TopK loss aims to force networks to focus on hard samples during training. It retains the $k\%$ worst pixels for loss, irrespective of their loss/probability values, which is defined by

$$L_{TopK} = -\frac{1}{N} \sum_{c=1}^{C} \sum_{i \in \mathbf{K}} g_i^c \log s_i^c, \tag{3}$$

where $\mathbf{K}$ is the set of the $k\%$ worst pixels. We choose $k = 10\%$ in our experiments because other percentage settings do not show remarkable improvements [12].

2.4 Compound Loss

Compound loss functions have been proven to be relatively robust [12]. Thus, we use two compound loss functions to train the nnUNet models:

(1) DiceCE loss: Dice loss plus cross entropy

$$L_{DiceCE} = L_{Dice} + L_{CE}; \tag{4}$$

(2) DiceTopK loss: Dice loss plus TopK loss

$$L_{DiceTopK} = L_{Dice} + L_{TopK}. \tag{5}$$

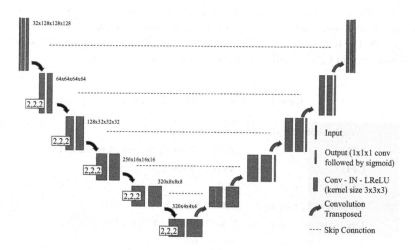

Fig. 1. An overview of network architecture.

2.5   NnUNet Network Architecture

We employ the default nnUNet [6] as the main network architecture because it has
shown very strong performance on many segmentation tasks [11]. Figure 1 presents an
overview of the network architecture. Specifically, it contains an encoder and a decoder
that are composed by plain $3 \times 3 \times 3$ convolutions, $1 \times 1 \times 1$ convolutions, $2 \times 2 \times 2$ convolutions and transposed convolutions, instance normalization, Leaky ReLU, and skip
connections. The number of channels is displayed in the encoder part of the network.
Deep supervision [5] (green box) is added to all but the two lowest resolutions in the
decoder.

Motivated by the BraTS 2020 winning solution [7], the main modification to the
default nnUNet is to replace the softmax function with a sigmoid function and change
the optimization target to the three tumor subregions (whole tumor, tumor core, and
enhancing tumor).

3   Experimental Results

3.1   Environment Setting

All the experiments are based on Multimodal Brain Tumor Segmentation Challenge
2021 (BraTS 2020) dataset [1–3, 13, 16, 17], which includes 1251 training cases and 219
validation cases. We train five cross-validation models with DiceCE loss and DiceTopK
loss, respectively. The final model is the ensemble of five best-fold models. Table 1
lists our experimental environments and requirements and Table 2 presents the training
protocols. The training time is very long (about 15 days per model) because we only
have a traditional mechanical hard disk to store the dataset and there is a bottleneck on
CPU as well. The data loading process is very slow in this setting. Using solid state disk
and more powerful CPU would significantly reduce the training time.

Table 1. Environments and requirements.

Windows/Ubuntu version	CentOS 3.10.0
CPU	Intel E5-2650 v4 Broadwell @ 2.2 GHz
GPU	NVIDIA P100 12G
CUDA version	11.0
Programming language	Python 3.8
Deep learning framework	Pytorch (Torch 1.8.0, torchvision 0.2.2)
Specific dependence	nnUNet 0.6

Table 2. Training protocols.

Data augmentation methods	Rotations, scaling, Gaussian noise, Gaussian blur, brightness, contrast, simulation of low resolution, gamma correction and mirroring
Initialization of the network	"he" normal initialization
Patch sampling strategy	More than a third of the samples in a batch contain at least one randomly chosen foreground class which is the same as nn-Unet [6].
Batch size	2
Patch size	$128 \times 128 \times 128$
Total epochs	1000
Optimizer	Stochastic gradient descent with nesterov momentum ($\mu = 0.99$)
Initial learning rate	0.01
Learning rate decay schedule	Poly learning rate policy: $(1 - epoch/1000)^{0.9}$
Stopping criteria, and optimal model selection criteria	Stopping criterion is reaching the maximum number of epoch (1000).
Training time	~15 days/model

3.2 Quantitative Results on Training Set

We trained five-fold models for DiceCE loss and DiceTopK loss, respectively. Table 3 presents the quantitative results (Dice) for each tumor component. DiceCE loss obtained better performance on fold 2–5 and DiceTopK loss obtained better performance on fold 1. Finally, we selected the model with better performance in each fold as an ensemble which was used for predicting the validation set and testing set.

Table 3. Dice scores of five-fold cross validation results on training set. In each fold, best scores are highlighted with bold numbers.

Fold	Loss Function	Enhancing Tumor	Tumor Core	Whole Tumor	Average DSC
Fold 1	DiceCE	0.8647	0.9134	0.9242	0.9008
	DiceTopK	**0.8701**	**0.9213**	**0.9327**	**0.9080**
Fold 2	DiceCE	**0.8781**	**0.9225**	**0.9341**	**0.9116**
	DiceTopK	0.8614	0.9162	0.9211	0.8996
Fold 3	DiceCE	**0.8806**	**0.9299**	**0.9416**	**0.9149**
	DiceTopK	0.8624	0.9014	0.9243	0.8960
Fold 4	DiceCE	**0.8812**	**0.9243**	**0.9416**	**0.9157**
	DiceTopK	0.8753	0.9174	0.9361	0.9096
Fold 5	DiceCE	**0.8723**	**0.9145**	**0.9289**	**0.9052**
	DiceTopK	0.8613	0.9042	0.9217	0.8957

3.3 Quantitative Results on Validation Set

Table 4 shows the quantitative results of validation dataset. The whole tumor achieved the best performance while the performance of enhancing tumor was relatively low. We also checked the per-cases performance and found that several cases obtained 0 Dice scores because the ground truth does not have enhancing tumor but the segmentation result does.

Table 4. Dice and 95% Hausdorff Distance of brain tumor segmentation on validation set.

Metric	Dice			95% Hausdorff distance		
	Enhancing Tumor	Tumor Core	Whole Tumor	Enhancing Tumor	Tumor Core	Whole Tumor
Mean	0.8217	0.8786	0.9259	21.09	9.20	3.80
Std	0.2446	0.1835	0.0803	81.04	43.66	6.28
Median	0.9032	0.9421	0.9481	1.41	1.73	2.24
25quantile	0.8249	0.8727	0.9063	1.00	1.00	1.41
75quantile	0.9530	0.9686	0.9691	2.45	3.74	3.74

We also present the sensitivity and specificity results. Our solution has nearly perfect specificity, indicating that most segmentation results are real brain tumor. The sensitivity is lower than specificity, indicating that some lesions are missed in the segmentation results (Table 5).

Table 5. Sensitivity and specificity of brain tumor segmentation on validation set.

Metric	Sensitivity			Specificity		
	Enhancing Tumor	Tumor Core	Whole Tumor	Enhancing Tumor	Tumor Core	Whole Tumor
Mean	0.8237	0.8621	0.9304	0.9998	0.9998	0.9994
Std	0.2575	0.1978	0.0894	0.0004	0.0003	0.0008
Median	0.9156	0.9383	0.9578	0.9999	0.9999	0.9996
25quantile	0.8350	0.8549	0.9165	0.9998	0.9998	0.9992
75quantile	0.9659	0.9754	0.9826	1.0000	1.0000	0.9998

3.4 Qualitative Results on Validation Set

Figure 2 and Fig. 3 show some visualized examples of well-segmented cases and poorly segmented cases, respectively. Most well-segmented cases in Fig. 2 have good contrast and the tumor boundaries are clear. However, the tumors in poorly segmented cases (as shown in Fig. 3) usually have low contrast, especially for the enhancing tumor. Moreover, some cases have different intensity distribution (e.g., the last row in Fig. 3) from the training set and the trained models cannot generalize well on such cases.

3.5 Quantitative Results on Testing Set

Table 6 presents the final results on the testing set. Overall, the performance is comparable of even better than the performance on the validation set (Table 4), indicating that our method has good generalization ability.

Table 6. Dice and 95% Hausdorff Distance of brain tumor segmentation on testing set.

Metric	Dice			95% Hausdorff distance		
	Enhancing Tumor	Tumor Core	Whole Tumor	Enhancing Tumor	Tumor Core	Whole Tumor
Mean	0.8760	0.8843	0.9300	12.3	15.3	4.75
Std	0.1853	0.2293	0.0903	59.6	65.1	17.0
Median	0.9382	0.9636	0.9582	1.00	1.41	1.73
25quantile	0.8549	0.9159	0.9166	1.00	1.00	1.00
75quantile	0.9679	0.9827	0.9782	2.00	3.00	4.12

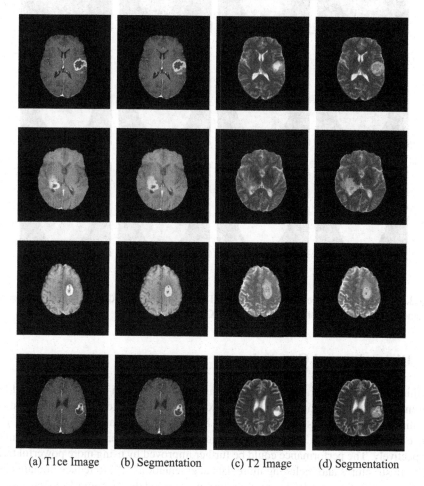

(a) T1ce Image   (b) Segmentation   (c) T2 Image   (d) Segmentation

Fig. 2. Examples of well-segmented cases. The green, yellow, and red colors denote edema, enhancing tumor and tumor core, respectively. (Color figure online)

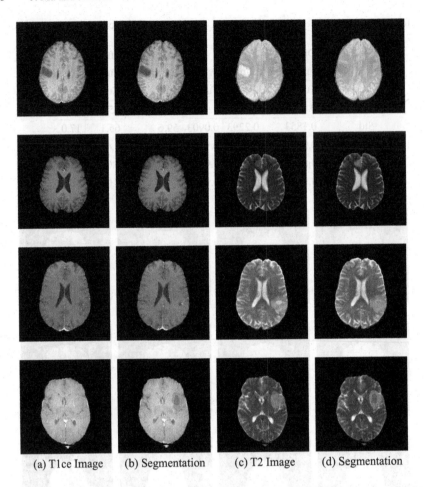

(a) T1ce Image   (b) Segmentation   (c) T2 Image   (d) Segmentation

Fig. 3. Examples of poor segmentation results. The green, yellow, and red colors denote edema, enhancing tumor and tumor core, respectively. (Color figure online)

4   Discussion and Conclusion

In this work, we have trained the popular nnUNet with region-based training and loss ensembles to segmentation brain tumor. Experiments on the testing set show that our solution achieved Dice scores of 0.8760, 0.8843, and 0.9300 and 95% Hausdorff Distance values of 12.3, 15.3, and 4.75 for enhancing tumor, tumor core, and whole tumor respectively. The performance could be further improved by using more powerful training infrastructures and including more data augmentation [4,9] to reduce domain gaps. Moreover, our final model is an ensemble of five models. It would be interesting to compare different methods with only one model because model ensembles usually cost extensive computational resources that could hindering the deployment in real clinical practice.

Acknowledgment. The authors would like to thank the BraTS 2021 challenge organizers for holding this great challenge. The authors also thank Fabian Isensee for making the code of the nnUNet and their BraTS 2020 winning solution publicly available. The authors declare that the segmentation method they implemented for participation in the BraTS 2021 challenge has not used any pre-trained models nor additional datasets other than those provided by the organizers.

References

1. Baid, U., et al.: The RSNA-ASNR-MICCAI brats 2021 benchmark on brain tumor segmentation and radiogenomic classification. arXiv preprint arXiv:2107.02314 (2021)
2. Bakas, S., et al.: Advancing the cancer genome atlas glioma MRI collections with expert segmentation labels and radiomic features. Sci. Data **4**, 170117 (2017)
3. Bakas, S., et al.: Identifying the best machine learning algorithms for brain tumor segmentation, progression assessment, and overall survival prediction in the brats challenge. arXiv preprint arXiv:1811.02629 (2018)
4. Campello, V.M., et al.: Multi-centre, multi-vendor and multi-disease cardiac segmentation: the M&MS challenge. IEEE Trans. Med. Imaging **40**(12), 3543–3554 (2021)
5. Dou, Q., et al.: 3D deeply supervised network for automated segmentation of volumetric medical images. Med. Image Anal. **41**, 40–54 (2017)
6. Isensee, F., Jaeger, P.F., Kohl, S.A., Petersen, J., Maier-Hein, K.H.: nnU-Net: a self-configuring method for deep learning-based biomedical image segmentation. Nat. Methods **18**(2), 203–211 (2021)
7. Isensee, F., Jäger, P.F., Full, P.M., Vollmuth, P., Maier-Hein, K.H.: nnU-Net for brain tumor segmentation. In: Crimi, A., Bakas, S. (eds.) BrainLes 2020. LNCS, vol. 12659, pp. 118–132. Springer, Cham (2021). https://doi.org/10.1007/978-3-030-72087-2_11
8. Jiang, Z., Ding, C., Liu, M., Tao, D.: Two-stage cascaded U-Net: 1st place solution to BraTS challenge 2019 segmentation task. In: Crimi, A., Bakas, S. (eds.) BrainLes 2019. LNCS, vol. 11992, pp. 231–241. Springer, Cham (2020). https://doi.org/10.1007/978-3-030-46640-4_22
9. Ma, J.: Histogram matching augmentation for domain adaptation with application to multi-centre, multi-vendor and multi-disease cardiac image segmentation. In: International Workshop on Statistical Atlases and Computational Models of the Heart, pp. 177–186 (2020)
10. Ma, J.: Loss ensembles for extremely imbalanced segmentation. arXiv preprint arXiv:2101.10815 (2020)
11. Ma, J.: Cutting-edge 3D medical image segmentation methods in 2020: are happy families all alike? arXiv preprint arXiv:2101.00232 (2021)
12. Ma, J., et al.: Loss odyssey in medical image segmentation. Med. Image Anal. **71**, 102035 (2021)
13. Menze, B.H., et al.: The multimodal brain tumor image segmentation benchmark (brats). IEEE Trans. Med. Imaging **34**(10), 1993–2024 (2014)
14. Milletari, F., Navab, N., Ahmadi, S.: V-net: Fully convolutional neural networks for volumetric medical image segmentation. In: 2016 Fourth International Conference on 3D Vision (3DV), pp. 565–571 (2016)
15. Myronenko, A.: 3D MRI brain tumor segmentation using autoencoder regularization. In: Crimi, A., Bakas, S., Kuijf, H., Keyvan, F., Reyes, M., van Walsum, T. (eds.) BrainLes 2018. LNCS, vol. 11384, pp. 311–320. Springer, Cham (2019). https://doi.org/10.1007/978-3-030-11726-9_28
16. Spyridon, B., et al.: Segmentation labels and radiomic features for the pre-operative scans of the TCGA-GBM collection. The Cancer Imaging Archive (2017)

17. Spyridon, B., et al.: Segmentation labels and radiomic features for the pre-operative scans of the TCGA-LGG collection. The Cancer Imaging Archive (2017)
18. Timmins, K.M., et al.: Comparing methods of detecting and segmenting unruptured intracranial aneurysms on TOF-MRAS: the Adam challenge. NeuroImage p. 118216 (2021)
19. Wang, G., Li, W., Ourselin, S., Vercauteren, T.: Automatic brain tumor segmentation using cascaded anisotropic convolutional neural networks. In: Crimi, A., Bakas, S., Kuijf, H., Menze, B., Reyes, M. (eds.) BrainLes 2017. LNCS, vol. 10670, pp. 178–190. Springer, Cham (2018). https://doi.org/10.1007/978-3-319-75238-9_16
20. Zhao, Y.-X., Zhang, Y.-M., Liu, C.-L.: Bag of tricks for 3D MRI brain tumor segmentation. In: Crimi, A., Bakas, S. (eds.) BrainLes 2019. LNCS, vol. 11992, pp. 210–220. Springer, Cham (2020). https://doi.org/10.1007/978-3-030-46640-4_20

Brain Tumor Segmentation Using Attention Activated U-Net with Positive Mining

Har Shwinder Singh[✉]

Hong Kong University of Science and Technology, Hong Kong, China
hssingh@connect.ust.hk

Abstract. This paper proposes a Deeply Supervised Attention U-Net Deep Learning network with a novel image mining augmentation method to segment brain tumors in MR images. The network was trained on the 3D segmentation task of the BraTS2021 Challenge Task 1. The Attention U-Net model improves upon the original U-Net by increasing focus on relevant feature maps, increasing training efficiency and increasing model performance. Notably, a novel data augmentation technique termed Positive Mining was applied. This technique crops out randomly scaled, positively labelled training samples and adds them to the training pipeline. This can effectively increase the discriminative ability of the Network to identify a tumor and use tumor feature-specific attention maps. The metrics used to train and validate the network were the Dice coefficient and the Hausdorff metric. The best performance on the online final dataset with the aforementioned network and augmentation technique was: Dice Scores of 0.858, 0.869 and 0.913 and Hausdorff Distance of 12.7, 16.9 and 5.43 for the Enhancing Tumor (ET), Tumor Core (TC) and Whole Tumor (WT).

Keywords: Attention U-Net · Brain tumor segmentation · Positive Mining

1 Introduction

1.1 Medical Image Segmentation

Image segmentations in the medical context have become integral in clinical practice, as medical diagnoses are frequently accompanied by scanned images. These images can then be digitally stored and labelled by a medical professional in the relevant field to highlight regions of interest for diagnosis. However, the diagnosis and segmentation of the images requires a medical specialist and can be very inefficient, time-consuming and error prone. Thus, the emergence and improvement of AI models in assisting medical professionals to perform such segmentations and automatic labelling of regions of interest holds great potential in improving the service and quality of healthcare in the modern age [1].

Specifically for medical segmentation tasks, there has been a large growth in the number and type of Deep Learning Architectures that have shown state-of-the-art performances on medical segmentation challenges. This has led to architectures that show a strong potential of out-performing medical professionals and even providing new insights into understanding disease and management [2].

A. Crimi and S. Bakas (Eds.): BrainLes 2021, LNCS 12962, pp. 431–440, 2022.
https://doi.org/10.1007/978-3-031-08999-2_37

1.2   Brain Tumor AI Challenge (2021)

The task this paper is trained on is specifically a brain-tumor segmentation task. The dataset consists of 3D multi-modal MR brain scans of brain cancer patients. This task is hosted as the Brain Tumor Segmentation Challenge (BraTS) 2021. BraTS is a long running challenge that uses multi-parametric magnetic resonance imaging (mp-MRI) scans. BraTS provides a very large and comprehensive annotated database of brain mp-MRI scans with detailed labelled segmentations [3–5, 7, 10]. The dataset [3–5, 7, 10] for the year 2021 comprises of 4 modes of MR scans: a) native (T1), b) post-contrast T1-weighted (T1Gd), c) T2-weighted (T2) and d) T2 Fluid Attenuated Inversion Recovery (T2-FLAIR). These scans were collected with different protocols and scanners from numerous institutions. Each training sample contains 4 modal MR images and 1 labelled segmentation mask. The original training set contains 3 labels: a Non Enhancing Tumor (NET), a peritumoral edematous tissue (ED), a Necrotic Tumor Core (NCR) and the background is labelled as 0. A sample of the training dataset is shown below:

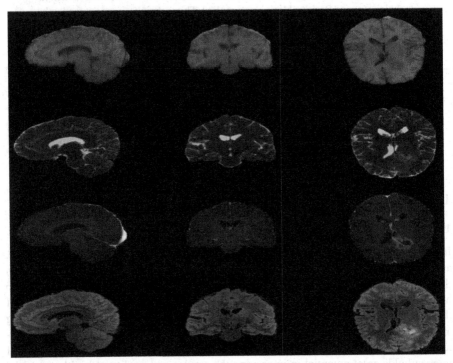

Fig. 1. A sample from the BraTS 2021 training dataset to visualize the mp-MRI MR scans **Top:** T1, **Second from Top:** T2, **Third from Top:** T1Gd, **Bottom:** T2-Flair

BraTS2021 provided 1251 training samples and 219 validation samples. The annotations for the validation are not released to the participants. The participants can only receive a score on the validation by making submissions to the official BraTS chosen platform. The scores on the platform for BraTs2021 were unranked (Fig. 1).

The winners of the most recent BraTs2020 have largely been Deep Learning Networks, with the U-Net architecture showing consistent state-of-the-art performance [6]. Additionally, previous winners use a modified labelling framework. The original labels of NET, ED and NCR are transformed into 3 new labels. The ET label is unmodified, then a new label named Whole Tumor (WT) is made by combining the label of ED with TC. Finally ET, NET and NCR are combined to create a label named Tumor Core (TC).

2   Methods

2.1   Baseline Architecture

The baseline architecture for the network was the 3-D Attention U-Net [9]. This architecture is built by adding a Convolutional Block Attention Module (CBAM) [8] to the residual skip connections of a U-Net Architecture. This architecture is shown below:

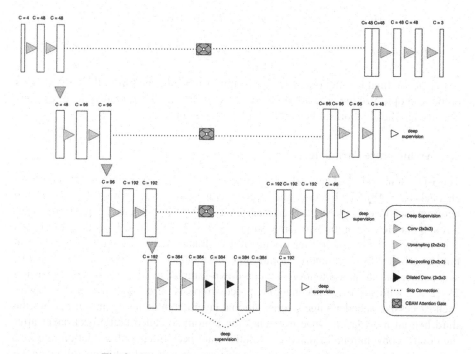

Fig. 2. 3D Attention U-Net network with CBAM module

2.2   CBAM Attention Mechanism

Specifically, the CBAM is a duo-attention module that uses a channel and spatial module to create attention maps that can increase the "focus" of the network on more relevant and discriminative features amongst the channels and the spatial domain. The CBAM achieves this by generating 2 attention maps [8]: a 1D channel attention map Mc (C × 1 × 1) that reduces, and a 2D spatial attention map Ms (1 × H × W). The Mc map uses average pooling (AvgPool) and max pooling (MaxPool) to down-sample an incoming input, which is then passed through a 1 layer Multi Later Perceptron (MLP). The Hadamard product (⊗) is calculated between the 2 pools. Finally, the output of the product is activated by a sigmoid function. This process is shown below:

$$M_C(F) = Sigmoid(MLP(AvgPool(F)) \otimes MLP(MaxPool(F)))$$

$$F' = Mc(F) \otimes F$$

Then, the next Ms map operates on F' to create space-specific attention. It applies the AvgPool and MaxPool along the Channel axis, then concatenates the output along the same axis. It is then run through a convolutional layer (Conv) and activated by a sigmoid function.

$$M_S(F') = Sigmoid\left(Conv\left(AvgPool\left(F'\right)\left(MaxPool\left(F''\right)\right)\right.\right)$$

$$F'' = Mc\left(F'\right) \otimes F'$$

Thus, the final F″ attention activated output can be obtained from the CBAM. This output can optimize the network on focus on relevant and discriminative features. This is proven in the ablation studies in the following sections.

2.3 Architecture Parameters

The 3-D Attention U-Net network's input convolutional layer was chosen to be of size 48 channels (C = 48). The Encoder and Decoder consist of 4 stages with a skip connection between each level of the stage. Starting from the left (Encoders), each input block is put through double convolutions of dimension 3 × 3 × 3 (H × W × L) with stride 1, and activated with the Rectified Linear Unit (ReLU) function. This activated output is then put through the CBAM attention module and concatenated to the opposing decoder via a skip connector. The non-attention output is down-sampled by Max Pooling of dimension 2 × 2 × 2 with stride 2. This encoding process repeats thrice as shown in Fig. 2, with each successive encoder stage's convolutional layer depth doubling until it reaches the third bottom most layer. Once it reaches the bottom so called bottle neck layer after the double convolution, 2 dilated convolutions are performed with a dilation rate of 2 without Max Pooling. Deep supervision is performed on the convolutions following the encoder and dilation layers by using a 1 × 1 × 1 convolutional layer with stride 1 and with sigmoid activation and trilinear up-sampling [9].

When it enters the decoder stage on the right, it is using a 2 × 2 × 2 up-sampling concatenated with the attention activated skip connections from the decoders. There is deep supervision performed at feature map that is then up-sampled in the decoder layer. This process is then repeated in the decoder thrice with the convolutional layer depth halving at each up-sampling. Finally, a 3-label prediction is obtained at the final decoder output by running it through a 3-channel final convolution.

2.4 Loss Function and Metrics

The loss function for training on the task is the Dice Loss [11], it is also one of the 2 metrics BraTS 2021 uses to evaluate submissions. The BraTS2021 also uses the Hausdorff [11]. However, this was not included in the loss function as the Hausdorff distance metric is very computationally expensive and slows down training significantly.

The Dice Loss is based on the Dice Metric which is defined as:

$$Dice\,Metric = \frac{2TP}{2TP + FN + FP}$$

where TP, FN and FP denote the True Positive, False Negative and False Positive predictions, this metric is computed individually for each label class ET, WT and TC.

The Dice Loss can then be defined from this metric as:

$$Dice\,Loss = 1 - \frac{1}{N} \sum \frac{Pn * Rn + \varepsilon}{Pn^2 + Rn^2 + \varepsilon}$$

where Pn is the output of the network with some input, it is the activated prediction. Rn is the ground truth label. The n subscript signifies the channel (MR modes). ε is a smoothing factor that ensures a continuous function.

There were numerous variations of the Dice Loss tested, specifically weighted Dice Loss was tried in different weightages. However, there were minimal or negative performance effects. A noted difficulty was to find an optimal weightage for performance optimization.

2.5 Image Processing and Augmentation

The input image is first cropped to C $\times$ 128 $\times$ 128 $\times$ 128, where C is the channel size at input; which is 4 for our network corresponding to the Modal MR. This size was optimal to retain performance and information. This is because larger cropping sizes considerably increased computational time, while smaller dimensions caused comparatively significant information loss. The image is limited in its intensity to 1-99th percentile of any non-zero intensity values.

Probability based augmentations were then performed in the pre-processing pipeline as follows:

- Dropout with a Probability of 0.2
- Rescaling by 1.1 or 0.9 with a Probability of 0.5
- Random flipping along chosen axis with a Probability of 0.3
- Positive Mining with a Probability of 0.1

This pre-processing was heavily inspired by [9], though the augmentations applied in this paper are less aggressive as stronger augmentations were seen to decrease accuracy, especially on lower epoch training pipelines. Positive Mining was seen to effectively improve performance. This augmentation is further explained in the next section.

2.6 Positive Mining

Positive Mining is a novel method and is defined as a type of image augmentation that extracts only the non-zero (positively) labelled regions of the training segmentation mask from the training image. This is defined below:

$$Positively\ Mined\ Sample = Ti \otimes E(T_L)$$

where Ti is the input training sample, TL is the segmented labels, E is a function that randomly resizes and interpolates the non-zero label from a scale of 0.9 to 1.1.

The actual image label is left unchanged. The E function's scaling is done to capture information about regions in and around the label, since these regions can provide potentially strong discriminative features for the network. This augmentation method corresponded to an increase in accuracy. This is hypothesized to be due to the network more effectively learning tumor isolated samples and the attention mechanisms being able to create new feature focus maps that centre on tumor spatial features (Fig. 3).

The positive mining augmentation is visualized in the figure below, where the normal sample of the brain is in the top layer and the positively mined samples are shown at the bottom.

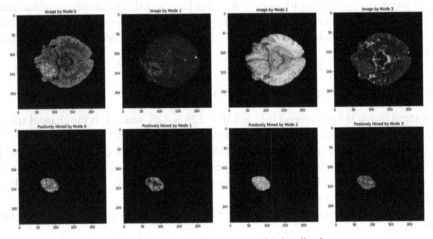

Fig. 3. Positive mining on sample visualized

As seen from the figure, this also can have a strong boosting effect on the performance time due to the input data features being highly reduced.

This method outperformed results on a dataset without any such Positive Mining, especially when training on a smaller number of epochs. There was a limited but observable impact on over-fitting when training on a cross-validation training schema. This might be due to the fact there is less irrelevant information that may cause over-fitting due to the positive mining only focusing on more relevant features.

2.7 Training

Different training schemas and pipelines were used. Namely, the training on the local training set was done on a 5-Fold Cross Validation Model. For the final submission to the platform, the network was trained on the entire dataset.

The optimizer used was Ranger, a batch size of 4 was selected and trained in parallel with the use of 4 GPUs. A global seed value was selected and the training pipeline consisted of 50 epochs due to resource and time constraints as the dataset can be very computationally demanding.

Ablation results on the cross-validation set did not include the Hausdorff due to significant performance slowdowns. The ablation results table is shown below:

Table 1. Cross validation results with different network and architectures

Models	Dice ET	Dice TC	Dice WT
Normal U-Net	73.27	79.85	76.10
Attention U-Net with CBAM	75.888	81.07	76.27
Attention U-Net with CBAM and Positive Mining	76.58	82.89	77.56

3 Results

3.1 Validation and Final Test Phase Results

The validation phase was a sample set of data that BraTS2021 released on their online platform and was used to serve as validation for a model. The Test phase was a single submission to test final model performance, for which the same architecture as the final validation was used. There were submissions of varying pipelines and the main Attention U-Net network architecture. The results for validation and test phases are show in the table below for the mean values of Dice and Hausdorff signified by H95:

Table 2. Validation results from BRaTS2021

Models	Dice ET	Dice TC	Dice WT	H95 ET	H95 TC	H95 WT
5-Fold Val. Training	0.753	0.808	0.899	21.8	12.5	6.45
Total Dataset Training	0.757	0.834	0.841	28.4	11.3	15.9
Total Dataset + Positive Mining	0.808	0.868	0.901	16.6	9.76	4.95
Total Dataset + Positive Mining + Test Time Augmentation	0.817	0.86	0.908	14.5	9.9	5.97

Table 3. Test results from BRaTS2021

Model	Dice ET	Dice WT	Dice TC	H95 ET	H95 WT	H95 TC
Final Model	0.858	0.913	0.869	12.7	5.43	16.9

For the validation phase, the 5-fold validation model served as a initial verification submission. It was then followed by a network that was trained on the entire dataset. The positive mining of 10% was combined with training this network. Lastly, the final submission included an additional Test Time Augmentation, which makes meant the input images were also augmented as pre-processing before inputting the validation data to the model (Fig. 4).

Overall, the most competitive network was the Attention U-Net with CBAM module, with a positive mining of 10% and Test Time Augmentation included. It showed strong improvements across most metrics for each tumour label. A sample of a prediction vs label is shown below:

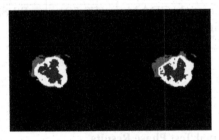

Fig. 4. **Left:** Label Prediction, **Right:** Ground Truth label

4   Discussion

The architecture of using an Attention U-Net paired with positive mining trained on the BraTS2021 training dataset, with a Dice loss function achieves competitive results to accurately segment brain tumors. Notable performance gains were from the attention mechanisms and positive mining. Positive mining augmentation has shown promising results in reducing computational load and boosting accuracy. Currently, image augmentation methods are very commonly applied in segmentation tasks and have shown great success. Such augmentations [14] can work to help a model regularize more effectively as shown by the competitive validation dataset which was unseen (Fig. 5).

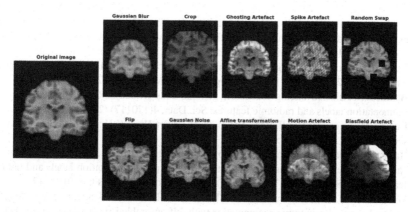

Fig. 5. Augmentation on medical segmentation tasks [15]

The parameters and pipeline chosen for the network architecture could still be further optimized and explored. As this paper focuses on the attention and positive mining, it did not explore in depth different combinations of loss functions, optimization methodologies and varying depth of U-Net encoder and decoders.

The method of positive mining could also be further explored in terms of merging it with concepts such as hard-sample mining, which picks and retrains training samples that a given neural network performs poorly on. These can be further combined into the training scheme. Augmentations of sample mining have not been explored heavily in research, these can also be further developed into pipeline training, where successively hard or positively mined samples are cycled through the models training.

Additionally, this paper's method left the original labels unchanged when applying positive mining. However, when conducting testing, scaling the label mutually showed minor improvements. This is an avenue that can be further explored, as there have been known issues with inter-observer bias, especially in the field of medical segmentation where differing medical specialists [12] segment out positive labels by hand. This can give rise to high variance and subjectivity on the labels. There have been recent efforts [13] to decrease label bias by using deep learning to regularize already existing and newly generated segmentation labels.

The major bottle neck while training on 4 modal MR images was a very high computational demand, due to a combination of the 3-D nature of the data coupled with a 4-dimensional channel and one of the largest brain tumor datasets. Ensembles were not deployed for similar reasons due to the high computational demands and short timeline for validation and training submissions.

References

1. Norouzi, A., et al.: Medical image segmentation methods. Algorithms Appl. IETE Tech. Rev. **31**(3), 199213 (2014). https://doi.org/10.1080/02564602.2014.906861
2. Razzaki, S., et al.: A comparative study of artificial intelligence and human doctors for the purpose of triage and diagnosis (2018). arXiv:1806.10698

3. Baid, U., et al.: The RSNA-ASNR-MICCAI BraTS 2021 Benchmark on Brain Tumor Segmentation and Radiogenomic Classification, arXiv:2107.02314 (2021)

4. Menze, B.H., Jakab, A., Bauer, S., Kalpathy-Cramer, J., Fara-hani, K., Kirby, J., et al.: The multimodal brain tumor image segmentation benchmark (BRATS). IEEE Trans. Med. Imaging **34**(10), 1993–2024 (2015). https://doi.org/10.1109/TMI.2014.2377694

5. Bakas, S., et al.: Advancing the cancer genome atlas glioma MRI collections with expert segmentation labels and radiomic features. Sci. Data, **4**(170117) (2017)

6. Isensee, F., Jaeger, P.F., Full, P.M., Vollmuth, P., Maier-Hein, K.H.: nnU-Net for brain tumor segmentation (2020). arXiv:2011.00848

7. Bakas, S., Akbari, H., Sotiras, A., Bilello, M., Rozycki, M., Kirby, J.S., et al.: Advancing the cancer genome atlas glioma MRI collections with expert segmentation labels and radiomic features. Nat. Sci. Data **4**, 170117 (2017). https://doi.org/10.1038/sdata.2017.117

8. Woo, S., Park, J., Lee, J., Kweon, I.S.: CBAM: convolutional block attention module (2018)

9. Henry, T., et al.: Brain tumor segmentation with self-ensembled, deeply-supervised 3D U-net neural networks: a BraTS 2020 challenge solution (2020). arXiv:2011.01045

10. Bakas, S., Akbari, H., Sotiras, A., Bilello, M., Rozycki, M., Kirby, J., et al.: Segmentation labels and radiomic features for the pre-operative scans of the TCGA-GBM collection. The Cancer Imaging Archive (2017).https://doi.org/10.7937/K9/TCIA.2017.KLXWJJ1Q

11. Jadon, S.: A survey of loss functions for semantic segmentation (2020)

12. Jungo, A., et al.: On the Effect of Interobserver Variability for a Reliable Estimation of Uncertainty of Medical Image Segmentation. Lecture Notes in Computer Science, pp. 682–690 (2018)

13. Karimi, D., Dou, H., Warfield, S., Gholipour, A.: Deep learning with noisy labels: exploring techniques and remedies in medical image analysis (2020)

14. Perez, L., Wang, J.: The Effectiveness of Data Augmentation in Image Classification using Deep Learning2 (2017)

15. Dufumier, B., Gori, P., Battaglia, I., Victor, J., Grigis, A., Duchesnay, E.: Benchmarking CNN on 3D anatomical brain MRI: architectures, data augmentation and deep ensemble learning. Neuroimage (2021)

Hierarchical and Global Modality Interaction for Brain Tumor Segmentation

Yang Yang[1], Shuhang Wei[1], Dingwen Zhang[1(✉)], Qingsen Yan[2], Shijie Zhao[1], and Junwei Han[1]

[1] School of Automation, Northwestern Polytechnical University, Xi'an, China
zhangdingwen2006yyy@gmail.com
[2] Australian Institute for Machine Learning, University of Adelaide, Adelaide, Australia
https://nwpu-brainlab.gitee.io/index_en.html

Abstract. Multi-modality brain tumor segmentation is vital for the treatment of gliomas, which aims to predict the regions of the necrosis, edema and tumor core on multi-modality magnetic resonance images (MRIs). However, it is a challenging task due to the complex appearance and diversity shapes of tumors. Considering that multi modality of MRIs contain rich biological properties of the tumors, we propose a novel multi-modality tumor segmentation network for segmenting the brain tumor based on fusing the complementary information and global semantic dependency information upon the multi-modality imaging data. Specifically, we propose a hierarchical modality interaction block to build the internal relationship between complementary modality pair, and then enhance the complementary information between the them by using the channel and spatial co-attention. To capture the long-dependency relationship of cross-modality information, we propose a global modality interaction transformer block to build the global semantic interaction between the multi-modality local features. The global modality interaction Transformer block makes up for CNN's poor perception of global semantic dependency information across modes. We evaluate our method on the validation set of multi-modality brain tumor segmentation challenge 2021 (BraTs2021). The proposed multi-modality brain tumor segmentation network achieves 0.8518, 0.8808 and 0.926 Dice score for the ET, CT and WT.

Keywords: Brain tumor segmentation · Transformer · Cross-modality information

1 Introduction

Gliomas are the most common intracranial malignant brain tumors, which arise from the neuroepithelial tissue and accounting for about 40%–50% of the central nervous system tumors. It is a malignant disease threatening human health with high recurrence rate and high mortality rate. Surgical resection is the main treatment for glioma. The principle is to remove the tumor as much as possible on the premise of preserving the nerve function. Accurate and automatic predicting the tumor regions in medical images plays a key role in the diagnosis and treatment of gliomas. It can help clinicians to speed up the identification of tumor regions and improve the efficiency of preoperative planning. However, automatically identify and segment brain tumor regions is a challenging task. For example, the shapes and appearances of gliomas are various, and there is no obvious boundary between tumor and brain tissue. The segmentation model is difficult to determine the accurate and complete silhouette of the tumor from the medical image where the discriminations between lesions and healthy tissues are unclear.

The multi-modality magnetic resonance image (MRI) can provide complementary information for highlighting the lesion regions and brain tissues and is widely used for the diagnosis and research of brain tumors. The multi-modality MRI sequences include four modality [14], i.e., T1-weighted (T1), T1 contrast-enhanced (T1c), T2-weighted (T2), and T2 Fluid Attenuation Inversion Recovery (FLAIR). The T1 and T1C modality are usually considered as good sources to visualize the anatomical structure and necrotic (enhancing tumor) region, T2 and FLAIR modality highlight the lesion and peritumoral edema regions [13,14]. For the multi-modality brain tumor segmentation task, i.e., BraTs2021 [1–4,14,18], the segmentation model aims to predict the sub-regions of brain tumor, including Whole Tumor (WT), Tumor Core (TC), and Enhancing Tumor (ET), according to the multi-modality sequences (T1, T1c, T2 and FLAIR). The complementary information across multi-modality not only enhances visual differences between the lesions and healthy tissue regions but also plays an important role to guide the segmentation model identifying each region of the brain tumor.

Recently, the convolutional neural network (CNN) based brain tumor segmentation methods [10–12,20] have achieved success in recent BraTs challenges. Specifically, the U-shape network architectures [15,19,21], i.e., the encoder-decoder architectures with skip connections, are mainly used for improving the performance of the brain tumor segmentation. The skip connections fuse the features between the encoding and decoding pathways to recover the lost spatial information caused by down-sampling. The conventional CNN based methods simply assign different modality to different channels, due to the lack of information interaction mechanism between the channels, the rich cross-modality information has not been fully explored.

To make full use of cross-modality information, in this work, we proposed a Transformer [8] and NNUnet [11] combination network for multi-modality brain tumor segmentation. Specifically, we establish a designed complementary relationship between multimodal MRIs according to the property of each modality. The important information of brain tumor sub-regions can be reasonably enhanced by using the channel-wise and spatial-wise co-attention [16] between the complementary modality pairs. To further improve the performance of multi-modality brain tumor segmentation, we introduce the Transformer [8] to our network to learn the global semantic dependency information across modality. The Transformer [8] compares the semantics of each local feature and other local features from different modalities, which can capture not only the local dependencies between local adjacent semantic features but also the global dependencies between remote cross-modality features. This global dependence helps improve the performance of brain tumor segmentation by integrating a wider range of cross-modality context information. Figure 1 shows the overall architecture of our proposed brain tumor segmentation network.

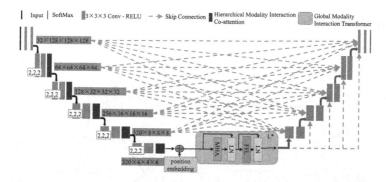

Fig. 1. Overview of the proposed network architecture. The network is U-net based architecture [11]. The hierarchical modality interaction co-attention block captures the complementary information of different modalities, the global modality interaction transformer block captures the cross-modality global semantic dependency information, the skip connection fuse the multi-scale complementary information and cross-modality global semantic dependency information for brain tumor segmentation.

2 Method

2.1 Overall Network Structure

We employ the U-net shape 3D encoder-decoder architecture [11] with skip connection as the backbone to extract the feature of each modality and predict the segmentation of the brain tumor. Four MRI modalities of each patient with size $240 \times 240 \times 155$ are concatenated into a four channel tensor following the order of T1, T1c, T2 and FLAIR, which is yielded as an input of our network with size $4 \times 240 \times 240 \times 155$. The output feature maps of each encoding block are divided equally into four sections along the channel to present the features of multi modalities. The hierarchical modality interaction co-attention block takes the multi modalities features as input to enhance the complementary information between the modality pairs by using spatial and channel common co-attention (SCCA). At the end of last encoder lock, the multi modalities features are fed to the proposed global modality interaction transformer block to learn the global semantic dependency information between the multi modality images. The decoder blocks use the skip connections to fuse the multi-scale cross-modality complementary information, the global semantic dependency information for segmenting the brain tumor sub-regions in the multi-modality MRIs. The brain tumor segmentation prediction including three channels, i.e., $3 \times 240 \times 240 \times 155$, where each channel presents the sub-region of tumor: ET, TC and WT, respectively.

2.2 Hierarchical Modality Interaction Co-attention

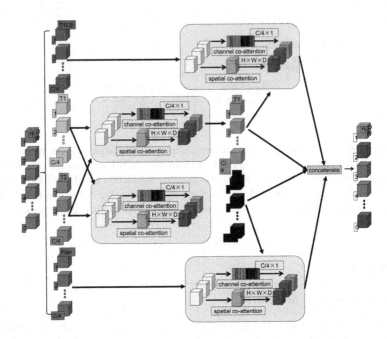

Fig. 2. Illustration of the hierarchical modality interaction co-attention block.

Multi-modality MRIs provide rich biological properties of the sub-regions of brain tumor. We proposed a hierarchical modality interaction co-attention block to capture the cross-modality complementary information, which could improve the perception sensitivity of the feature extractors for brain tumor sub-regions information. To achieve this goal, we design a cross-modality interaction strategy to guide the channel and spatial co-attention (SCCA) to capture the complementary relationships between modality pairs. The SCCA re-calibrates channel-wise feature responses and highlights the co-interesting feature between complementary modality pairs. Based on the features of T1 and T2, the hierarchical modality interaction co-attention block is progressively employed to fuse the features of the multi modality.

Figure 2 illustrates the architecture of the hierarchical modality interaction co-attention block. The block divides the output feature map $\mathbf{f}_{ei}$ with size $C \times H \times W \times D$ of the encoder block E_i into four sections with size $C/4 \times H \times W \times D$ along the channel dimension, i.e., $\mathbf{f}_{T1}$, $\mathbf{f}_{T1c}$, $\mathbf{f}_{T2}$ and $\mathbf{f}_{FLAIR}$, each of which presents the local feature map of corresponding modality. Then, the important information in the local detail feature maps $\mathbf{f}_{T1}$, $\mathbf{f}_{T1c}$, $\mathbf{f}_{T2}$ and $\mathbf{f}_{FLAIR}$ are enhanced by following strategies:

1) The T1 feature map $\mathbf{f}_{T1}$ is enhanced by T2 modality $\mathbf{f}_{T2}$, i.e., $\hat{\mathbf{f}}_{T1} = SCCA(\mathbf{f}_{T1}; \mathbf{f}_{T2})$. The T2 modality more significantly reflects the lesion region of the tumor than T1 modality, while, the T1 modality contains rich information of the

health-tissues. This strategy encourages feature extractor to learn the discriminative information of the lesion and healthy brain tissue regions.

2) We use the feature map of T1 modality $\mathbf{f}_{T1}$ to restrain the healthy tissue features in the T2 modality, i.e., $\hat{\mathbf{f}}_{T2} = SCCA(\mathbf{f}_{T2}; \mathbf{f}_{T1})$, which encourages the feature extractor to learn the information of whole lesion region including necrotic, tumor core and edema regions in T2 modality.

3) For the FLAIR modality, we use the enhanced feature map of T2 modality $\hat{\mathbf{f}}_{T2}$ to reinforce the information of edema region in the feature map $\hat{\mathbf{f}}_{FLAIR}$, i.e., $\hat{\mathbf{f}}_{FLAIR} = SCCA(\mathbf{f}_{FLAIR}; \hat{\mathbf{f}}_{T2})$.

4) For the T1c modality $\mathbf{f}_{T1c}$, we use the enhanced feature map of T1 modality $\hat{\mathbf{f}}_{T1}$ to reinforce the information of necrotic region, i.e., $\hat{\mathbf{f}}_{T1c} = SCCA(f_{T1c}; \hat{\mathbf{f}}_{T1})$.

The $SCCA(\mathbf{f}_a; \mathbf{f}_b)$ refers to the spatial and channel co-attention operation which is applied to the features of complementary modality pairs $(\mathbf{f}_a, \mathbf{f}_b)$. In this work, $SCCA(\mathbf{f}_a; \mathbf{f}_b)$ enhances the modality feature $\mathbf{f}_a$ by using the channel-wise and spatial-wise attention of the modality feature $\mathbf{f}_b$. The channel co-attention $CCA(\mathbf{f}_a; \mathbf{f}_b)$ can be formulated as:

$$CCA(\mathbf{f}_a; \mathbf{f}_b) = \sigma(\mathbf{W}^{C \times \frac{C}{2}} \delta(\mathbf{W}^{\frac{C}{2} \times C} AvgPool(\mathbf{f}_b))) \odot \mathbf{f}_a, \tag{1}$$

where, the $\odot$ is the element-wise multiplication, $AvgPool(\cdot)$ refers the 3D average pooling operation for the 4D tensor $\mathbf{f}_b \in \mathbb{R}^{C \times H \times W \times D}$, the $\mathbf{W}^{C \times \frac{C}{2}}$ and $\mathbf{W}^{\frac{C}{2} \times C}$ present the parameters of two fully connected layers. The $\delta(\cdot)$ and $\sigma(\cdot)$ refers ReLU and Sigmoid activation respectively. The spatial co-attention $SCA(\mathbf{f}_a; \mathbf{f}_b)$ can be defined as:

$$SCA(\mathbf{f}_a; \mathbf{f}_b) = \sigma(\mathbf{W}^{1 \times 1 \times 1} \mathbf{f}_b) \odot \mathbf{f}_a, \tag{2}$$

where The $\mathbf{W}^{1 \times 1 \times 1}$ refers a convolutional layer with a kernel size of $1 \times 1 \times 1$. The channel and spatial co-attention $SSCA(\mathbf{f}_a; \mathbf{f}_b)$ is defined as:

$$SCCA(\mathbf{f}_a; \mathbf{f}_b) = \delta(\mathbf{W}^{3 \times 3 \times 3}(CCA(\mathbf{f}_a; \mathbf{f}_b) + SCA(\mathbf{f}_a; \mathbf{f}_b)). \tag{3}$$

2.3 Global Modality Interaction Transformer

We present a global modality interaction transformer block to capture the cross-modality global semantic dependency information for brain tumor segmentation. The Transformer is good at to learn explicit global and long-range semantic dependency [6,7] from the input sequence. Therefore, we employ the Transformer for building the global dependency of local semantic information in each modality, which can help the brain tumor segmentation model to extract more powerful cross-modality features. Figure 3 shows the architecture of the proposed global modality interaction transformer block. The Transformer block consists of L Transformer layers ($L = 6$), each of which starts with the multi-head attention (MHA) building the global dependencies between the local features of multi modalities and enhance them by a feed-forward layer (FFL).

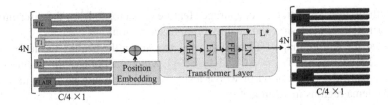

Fig. 3. Illustration of the global modality interaction transformer block. "MHA", "FFL" and "LN" refer to the Multi-head attention layer, the feed-forward layer and the normalization layer, respectively.

Given the output feature maps of the latest encoder block for the four modality: $\hat{\mathbf{f}}_{T1}$, $\hat{\mathbf{f}}_{T1c}$, $\hat{\mathbf{f}}_{T2}$ and $\hat{\mathbf{f}}_{FLAIR}$ with size $\frac{C}{4} \times \frac{H}{16} \times \frac{W}{16} \times \frac{D}{16}$. The Transformer layer expects a sequence as input. We spread the spatial dimension of each feature maps into one dimension, i.e., $\hat{\mathbf{S}}_{T1} \in \mathbb{R}^{\frac{C}{4} \times N}$, $\hat{\mathbf{S}}_{T1c} \in \mathbb{R}^{\frac{C}{4} \times N}$, $\hat{\mathbf{S}}_{T2} \in \mathbb{R}^{\frac{C}{4} \times N}$ and $\hat{\mathbf{S}}_{FLAIR} \in \mathbb{R}^{\frac{C}{4} \times N}$, where, $N = \frac{H}{16} \times \frac{W}{16} \times \frac{D}{16}$ and $C = 320$. Then, we concatenate the modality features along the dimension N to merge a feature sequence $\mathbf{S}$ with size $\frac{C}{4} \times 4N$. The input of Transformer based fusion block can be formulated as $\mathbf{S} = \{\hat{\mathbf{S}}_{T1}, \hat{\mathbf{S}}_{T1C}, \hat{\mathbf{S}}_{T2}, \hat{\mathbf{S}}_{FLAIR}\}$. The local features in each modality are treated as a token and fed into the Transformer block to learn global semantic interaction information. We also introduce the learnable position embeddings [6,7,17] $\mathbf{Pe} \in \mathbb{R}^{\frac{C}{4} \times 4N}$ and fuse them with the feature sequence for encoding the location information of each local detail features for brain tumor segmentation:

$$\mathbf{z}_0 = \mathbf{W} \times \mathbf{S} + \mathbf{Pe}, \tag{4}$$

where, $\mathbf{W}$ is the linear projection operation, $\mathbf{z}_0$ is the input feature embeddings for the first Transformer layer. The Transformer layer in this work has a standard architecture as in previous works [6,7,17], which consists of a multi-head attention (MHA) layer, a feed forward layer (FFL) and two normalization layer (LN). The output of the l-th ($l = 1, ..., 6$) Transformer layer $\mathbf{z}_l$ can be calculated by:

$$\mathbf{z}_l = FFL\left(LN\left(\mathbf{z}_l'\right) + \mathbf{z}_l'\right), \mathbf{z}_l' = MHA\left(LN\left(\mathbf{z}_{l-1}\right) + \mathbf{z}_{l-1}\right). \tag{5}$$

The of the Transformer block is divided along dimension N into four parts, and then, a reshape and a channel-wise concatenation aggregate them into a 4D feature map with size $C \times \frac{H}{16} \times \frac{W}{16} \times \frac{D}{16}$ for facilitating subsequent decoding operations.

2.4   Network Encoder Pathway

We follow the nnUnet architecture [11] to build the encoder network. It consists of five encoder blocks, each of which contains a down-sampling layer (convolutional kernel size is $3 \times 3 \times 3$, stride $= (2, 2, 2)$) and a 3D convolutional layer (convolutional kernel size is $3 \times 3 \times 3$, stride $= (1, 1, 1)$). The output of the encoder block is fed to a hierarchical modality interaction co-attention block for capturing the complementary information between multi modalities. At the end of the last cross-modality internal relationship block, the output is fed to the proposed transformer based fusion block for capturing the cross-modality global semantic interaction information.

2.5 Network Decoder Pathway

The shallow features in the encoder pathway contain rich detail information of the tumor sub-regions which is important for predict the refined segmentation result for brain tumors. In this work, we use the skip connections to fuse the multi-scale cross-modality complementary information for recovering the lost detail information are caused by down-sampling. We also integrate the cross-modal semantic dependency information into each decoder block to make full use of cross-modal information for improving the performance of the brain tumor segmentation network.

The Decoder network consists of four decoder blocks, each of which also has the same network architecture as the decoder block in nnUnet [11], i.e., a 3D deconvolutional layer (kernal size is $3 \times 3 \times 3$, stride $= (2, 2, 2)$) for up-sampling and a 3D deconvolutional layer (kernal size is $3 \times 3 \times 3$, stride $= (1, 1, 1)$) for feature recovering. For each decoder block, the skip connections fuse the multi-scale complementary information and the global semantic dependency information, and the up-sampled features. The multi-scale complementary information and the global semantic dependency information are sampled into the same size and concatenated with the up-sampled features from the previous decoder block along channel dimension. Finally, the decoder network outputs the segmentation for the sub-regions ET, TC and WT of brain tumors. Considering that there will be some noise in the segmentation result of ET, therefore, we employ the connected component-based post-processing [5,9] to remove the noise regions in segmentation results.

2.6 Training

The proposed methods were implemented in PyTorch on an PH402 SKU 200 GPU with 32 GB memory. We employ the cross-entropy loss function to train our proposed network on training data set of BraTs2021 [1–4,14]. Each sample in the training data is centered cropped to size $192 \times 160 \times 108$. This ensures that the useful information of each sample is kept within the cropping boundary while minimizing the content-free areas of the sample. We used Adam to optimize the entire network parameters from scratch with the initial learning rate 1×10^{-3} and the batch size is 1. The training process took 1000 epochs, the learning rate decreases according to the strategy of "poly" learning rate strategy[11]: $(1 - epoch/epoch_{max})^{0.9}$.

3   Results

The proposed multi-modality brain tumor segmentation network is evaluated on validation set of BraTs 2021. The segmentation results of the proposed network are reported in Table 1. The proposed method have received mean Dice scores of ET, WT and TC as 0.8518, 0.8808 and 0.926 on validation set, respectively. The Hausdorff95, sensitivity and specificity are also reported in Table 1. We also show the quantitative analysis of

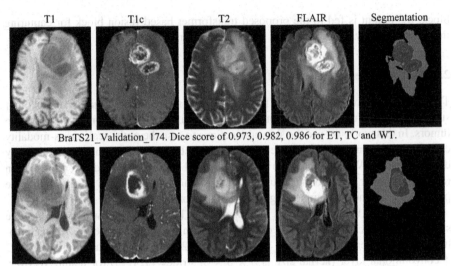

| T1 | T1c | T2 | FLAIR | Segmentation |

BraTS21_Validation_174. Dice score of 0.973, 0.982, 0.986 for ET, TC and WT.

BraTS21_Validation_190. Dice score of 0.981, 0.993, 0.990 for ET, TC and WT.

Fig. 4. Qualitative results on BraTs2021. The enhancing tumor (ET) is shown in red, tumor core (TC) in blue and edema (WT) in yellow. (Color figure online)

the comparable study of proposed work with the baseline work [11] in Table 2. Our proposed network achieves better brain tumor segmentation results in Dice scores for each class than the baseline work. This experiment demonstrates that the proposed cross-modality detail interaction information and cross-modality global semantic interaction information fusion strategy can effectively improve the performance of multi-modality brain tumor segmentation. The Fig. 4 shows the qualitative results of our method on

Table 1. Segmentation results of ET, CT and WT on BraTs 2021 Challenge Validation set in terms of the Dice score, Hausdorff95, Sensitivity and Specificity. All scores are evaluated online.

Metrics	ET	TC	WT
Dice (%)	85.178	88.079	92.605
Hausdorff95 (mm)	6.034	7.397	3.653
SensitiVITy (%)	84.374	85.932	92.821
Specificity (%)	99.982	99.982	99.936

Table 2. Comparison results of our method and Baseline [11] on the BRATS 2021 validation set in term of Dice (%). All scores are evaluated online.

Method	ET	TC	WT
Baseline [11]	79.293	87.239	92.388
Ours	85.178	88.079	92.605

the validation data set of BraTs2021. In general, the qualitative and quantitative results have proved the effectiveness of the proposed method.

4   Conclusion

In this work, we proposed a hierarchical and global modality interaction network for multi-modality brain tumor segmentation. In Each scale of encoder block, the local features of complementary modality pairs are hierarchically interacted for capturing the cross-modality complementary information by using channel-wise and spatial-wise co-attention. We also proposed global modality interaction Transformer block to extract the global cross-modality semantic dependencies information. The proposed brain tumor segmentation network has been evaluated on the validation set of BraTs 2021 Challenge and achieved high Dice scores of 0.8518, 0.8808, and 0.926 for the tumor sub-regions ET, TC, and WT, respectively.

Acknowledgment. This work was supported by the National Key R&D Program of China under Grant 2020AAA0105701, the Key-Area Research and Development Program of Guangdong Province(2019B010110001), the National Science Foundation of China (Grant Nos. 61936007, 61876140, 61806167 and U1801265), and the research funds for interdisciplinary subject, NWPU.

References

1. Baid, U., et al.: The RSNA-ASNR-MICCAI BraTs 2021 benchmark on brain tumor segmentation and radiogenomic classification. arXiv preprint arXiv:2107.02314 (2021)
2. Bakas, S., et al.: Segmentation labels and radiomic features for the pre-operative scans of the TCGA-LGG collection. Cancer Imaging Arch. **286** (2017)
3. Bakas, S., et al.: Segmentation labels and radiomic features for the pre-operative scans of the TCGA-GBM collection. Cancer Imaging Arch. Nat. Sci. Data **4**, 170117 (2017)
4. Bakas, S., et al.: Advancing the cancer genome atlas glioma MRI collections with expert segmentation labels and radiomic features. Sci. Data 4(1), 1–13 (2017)
5. Bilic, P., et al.: The liver tumor segmentation benchmark (LiTs). arXiv preprint arXiv:1901.04056 (2019)
6. Cao, H., et al.: Swin-Unet: Unet-like pure transformer for medical image segmentation. arXiv preprint arXiv:2105.05537 (2021)
7. Chen, J., et al.: TransUnet: transformers make strong encoders for medical image segmentation. arXiv preprint arXiv:2102.04306 (2021)
8. Dosovitskiy, A., et al.: An image is worth 16x16 words: transformers for image recognition at scale. arXiv preprint arXiv:2010.11929 (2020)
9. Heller, N., et al.: The state of the art in kidney and kidney tumor segmentation in contrast-enhanced CT imaging: results of the kits19 challenge. Med. Image Anal. **67**, 101821 (2021)
10. Isensee, F., Kickingereder, P., Wick, W., Bendszus, M., Maier-Hein, K.H.: Brain tumor segmentation and radiomics survival prediction: contribution to the BRATS 2017 challenge. In: Crimi, A., Bakas, S., Kuijf, H., Menze, B., Reyes, M. (eds.) BrainLes 2017. LNCS, vol. 10670, pp. 287–297. Springer, Cham (2018). https://doi.org/10.1007/978-3-319-75238-9_25

11. Isensee, F., Maier-Hein, K.H.: nnu-net for brain tumor segmentation. In: Brainlesion: Glioma, Multiple Sclerosis, Stroke and Traumatic Brain Injuries: 6th International Workshop, BrainLes 2020, Held in Conjunction with MICCAI 2020, Lima, Peru, October 4, 2020, Revised Selected Papers, Part II. vol. 12658, p. 118. Springer Nature (2021)
12. Jiang, Z., Ding, C., Liu, M., Tao, D.: Two-stage cascaded U-net: 1st place solution to BraTS challenge 2019 segmentation task. In: Crimi, A., Bakas, S. (eds.) BrainLes 2019. LNCS, vol. 11992, pp. 231–241. Springer, Cham (2020). https://doi.org/10.1007/978-3-030-46640-4_22
13. Liu, C., et al.: Brain tumor segmentation network using attention-based fusion and spatial relationship constraint. arXiv preprint arXiv:2010.15647 (2020)
14. Menze, B.H., et al.: The multimodal brain tumor image segmentation benchmark (BraTs). IEEE Trans. Med. Imaging **34**(10), 1993–2024 (2014)
15. Ronneberger, O., Fischer, P., Brox, T.: U-net: convolutional networks for biomedical image segmentation. In: Navab, N., Hornegger, J., Wells, W.M., Frangi, A.F. (eds.) MICCAI 2015. LNCS, vol. 9351, pp. 234–241. Springer, Cham (2015). https://doi.org/10.1007/978-3-319-24574-4_28
16. Roy, A.G., Navab, N., Wachinger, C.: Concurrent spatial and channel 'squeeze & excitation' in fully convolutional networks. In: Frangi, A.F., Schnabel, J.A., Davatzikos, C., Alberola-López, C., Fichtinger, G. (eds.) MICCAI 2018. LNCS, vol. 11070, pp. 421–429. Springer, Cham (2018). https://doi.org/10.1007/978-3-030-00928-1_48
17. Wang, W., Chen, C., Ding, M., Li, J., Yu, H., Zha, S.: TransBTS: multimodal brain tumor segmentation using transformer. arXiv preprint arXiv:2103.04430 (2021)
18. Zhang, D., Huang, G., Zhang, Q., Han, J., Han, J., Yu, Y.: Cross-modality deep feature learning for brain tumor segmentation. Pattern Recogn. **110**, 107562 (2020)
19. Zhang, Z., Liu, Q., Wang, Y.: Road extraction by deep residual u-net. IEEE Geosci. Remote Sens. Lett. **15**(5), 749–753 (2018)
20. Zhao, Y.-X., Zhang, Y.-M., Liu, C.-L.: Bag of tricks for 3D MRI brain tumor segmentation. In: Crimi, A., Bakas, S. (eds.) BrainLes 2019. LNCS, vol. 11992, pp. 210–220. Springer, Cham (2020). https://doi.org/10.1007/978-3-030-46640-4_20
21. Zhou, Z., Rahman Siddiquee, M.M., Tajbakhsh, N., Liang, J.: UNet++: a nested U-net architecture for medical image segmentation. In: Stoyanov, D., et al. (eds.) DLMIA/ML-CDS -2018. LNCS, vol. 11045, pp. 3–11. Springer, Cham (2018). https://doi.org/10.1007/978-3-030-00889-5_1

Ensemble Outperforms Single Models in Brain Tumor Segmentation

Jianxun Ren[1]([✉]), Wei Zhang[2], Ning An[2], Qingyu Hu[2,3], Youjia Zhang[2], and Ying Zhou[2]

[1] School of Aerospace Engineering, Tsinghua University, Beijing, China
`rjx17@mails.tsinghua.edu.cn`
[2] Neural Galaxy Inc., Beiqing Road, Changping District, Beijing, China
[3] School of Computer Science and Technology, University of Science and Technology of China, Anhui, China

Abstract. Brain tumor segmentation remains an open and popular challenge, for which countless medical image segmentation models have been proposed. Based on the platform that BraTS challenge 2021 provided for researchers, we implemented a battery of cutting-edge deep neural networks, such as nnU-Net, UNet++, CoTr, HRNet, and Swin-Unet to directly compare performances amongst distinct models. To improve segmentation accuracy, we first tried several modification techniques (e.g., data augmentation, region-based training, batch-dice loss function, etc.). Next, the outputs from the five best models were averaged using a final ensemble model, of which four models in the committee were organized in different architectures. As a result, the strengths of every single model were amplified by the aggregation. Our model took one of the best performing places in the Brain Tumor Segmentation (BraTS) 2021 competition amongst over 1200 excellent researchers from all over the world, which achieved Dice score of 0.9256, 0.8774, 0.8576 and Hausdor Distances (95%) of 4.36, 14.80, 14.49 for whole tumor, tumor core, and enhancing tumor respectively.

Keywords: Brain tumor segmentation · Ensemble learning · nnU-Net · UNet++ · CoTr · HRNet

1 Introduction

Glioma is one of the most aggressive and fatal brain tumor. The precise segmentation of glioma based on medical images plays a crucial role in treatment planning, computer-aided surgeries, and health monitoring. However, the ambiguous boundaries of tumors and their variations in shape, size and position, pose difficulties in distinguishing them from brain tissues. It is especially challenging for the traditional medical domain to accurately and automatically segment the glioma tissues.

The BraTS Challenge provides a platform which enables researchers to fairly evaluate their state-of-the-art algorithms in segmenting brain glioma. The BraTS

A. Crimi and S. Bakas (Eds.): BrainLes 2021, LNCS 12962, pp. 451–462, 2022.
https://doi.org/10.1007/978-3-031-08999-2_39

challenge has been running since 2012, attracting top research teams around the world each year. In 2021, the challenge was jointly organized by the Radiological Society of North America (RSNA), the American Society of Neuroradiology (ASNR), and the Medical Image Computing and Computer Assisted Interventions (MICCAI) society. Around 1200 researchers participated in the challenge. The number of cases collected by the BraTS committee has drastically risen from 660 to 2000 in 2021, compared to last year [15]. The dataset consists of 1251 training, and 219 validation cases, while the test data are not open to the public [1–5]. Multi-parametric magnetic resonance imaging (mpMRI) includes four modalities available for all cases: the native T1-weighted (T1), post-contrast T1-weighted (T1Gd), T2-weighted (T2), and T2-weighted Fluid Attenuated Inversion Recovery (T2-FLAIR) images [13]. BraTS evaluates brain glioma sub-regions segmentation, including the enhancing tumor (ET), the tumor core (TC), and the whole tumor (WT) [14].

Due to the rapid development of deep learning, various newly evolved deep neural networks outperformed traditional algorithms. A state-of-the-art medical image segmentation method termed U-Net was first introduced in 2015 [6]. The encoder-decoder based deep neural network with skip-connections achieved an advanced performance. Since then, numerous algorithms have been developed using the U-Net as the backbone. A self-adaptive UNet-like neural network called nnU-Net (no new U-Net) can automatically optimize multiple processes including preprocessing, network architecture, and post-processing without few manual interventions [7]. Another recently proposed cutting-edge U-shaped transformer neural network named Swin-Unet has given a demonstrated performance on multi-organ and cardiac segmentation challenges [11]. In addition to the impressive performance of these individual models, ensemble learning aggregating two or more models could achieve better and more generalizable results. The most popular ensemble methods include ensemble mean, ensemble vote, ensemble boosting, and ensemble stacking methods. Ensemble mean is a method that averages predictions across multiple models to make the most of them. Ensemble vote methods calculates the votes and accept the majority votes, which could lower result variances. Ensemble boosting methods train models based on mistakes from previous models, and ensemble stacking methods use a model to combine predictions from different types of models.

In this study, we implemented multiple different models and applied the ensemble learning to collaborate them. We used two metrics, Dice similarity coeffi-cient (Dice) and Hausdor Distance (HD), to evaluate model performance. Dice ranges from 0 to 1, which indicates the similarity between predicted and ground truth, and HD signifies the largest segmentation error. To promote model accuracy, we have added several modification methods. The final ensemble model gave an unprecedented result based on the selected top-performing models. In Sect. 2, we will briefly introduce the main model architectures that have been utilized on the BraTS dataset, then further implementation details will be introduced. In Sect. 3, we described the performances of individual model and the ensemble model. Lastly, Sect. 4 will discuss all the findings of the current research and potential improvement for future studies will be proposed.

2   Methods

2.1   Ensemble Learning

Ensemble is the most popular fusion method. Not only does it address advantages over various models, but it also improves the overall predictive performances, while increases the robustness and generalization. Ensemble mean averages the unweighted output from multiple models, whereas the ensemble vote takes the unweighted voting results from the majority models. The ensemble mean model showed a convincing performance over most individual models as well as the ensemble vote method. The detailed individual models attempted in the current study are explained as follow:

NnU-Net. F. Isensee et al. proposed a powerful automatic biomedical image segmentation, named nnU-Net (no new net), which can be trained out-of-the-box to segment diverse 3D medical datasets and requires zero manual intervention and expert knowledge. nnU-Net surpasses a broad variety of datasets in many international biomedical image segmentation competitions [8]. Due to the great success of nnU-Net has performed in the medical image segmentation competitions, we applied nnU-Net on the BraTS2021 dataset, the baseline model without any modifications has already achieved an impressive performance on this auxiliary domain. nnU-Net is well-known for its U-Net-like architecture, a symmetric encoder-decoder structure with skip-connections. The encoder completes downsampling, and the decoder upsamples the salient features passed from the bottleneck. Both encoder and decoder have five convolutional layers and are connected by a bottleneck block.

Despite the architecture itself, hyper-parameter is another key determinant in influencing the overall model performance. Data are normalized before being fed into the first layer. The input patch size is $128 \times 128 \times 128$, and uses a batch size of 2, followed by a Leaky ReLU function to handle data nonlinearities. Skip-connections collect high-resolution features from the encoder to reduce the spatial information loss caused by downsampling. At the end of the decoder, a $1 \times 1 \times 1$ filter is applied to guarantee the number of channels is 3, then the output is passed to a softmax function. Loss function sums Dice and Cross-Entropy (CE) loss during 1000 training epochs, consisting of 250 iterations per epoch, and the initial learning rate is 0.001.

U-Net++. U-Net++ is one of the popular variants that uses U-Net as the backbone. U-Net performance is hindered by its suboptimal depth design and the same level feature maps fusion through skip-connections. To overcome the shortcomings listed above, U-Net++ embedded nested U-Nets and redesigned the skip-connections. To this end, pruning is allowed to dispose the burden of unnecessary layers and parameters, while maintaining its outstanding segmenting ability [9].

The initialized input patch size is $96 \times 96 \times 96$ with a batch size of 2 and followed by an Instance Normalization (IN) layer. The 3D model has trained 320 epochs on Dice and HD95 loss and using 0.001 as the learning rate.

High-Resolution Net (HRNet). Unlike many state-of-the-art architectures, HRNet does not encode input images into low-resolution representations and then decode information from the salient features. On the contrary, HRNet keeps high-resolution representations throughout the entire process. Hence, more precised semantic and spatial information are maintained to its architecture. Brain tumor segmentation is a position-sensitive task. Comparing with other model structures, HRNet can improve the ability to capture detailed positional information [10]. Therefore, we further developed a 3D version HRNet to implement on the BraTS dataset.

The model has been trained by $128 \times 128 \times 128$ input images, with a total number of 320 epochs, where 250 iterations were performed per epoch. We adopted a small batch size equals to 2, the initial learning rate is 0.001, and the sum of Dice loss and CE are used for model evaluation.

Swin-Unet. Due to the transformer's convincing performance in the Natural Language Processing (NLP) domain, Swin-Unet is developed to draw its strength in long-term semantic segmentation and transferring to the computer vision domain. Swin-Unet is the first pure transformer-based Unet variant, with a symmetric transformer-based encoder and decoder, which are interconnected by skip-connections. According to H. Cao et al. [11], Swin-Unet effectively solves the over-segmentation problem encountered by Convolutional Neural Network(CNN)-based models.

Comparing with HRNet, it shares similar parameters with the Swin-Unet 2D model. However, its 2D performance is a lot worse than expected. Hence, the 3D model has not been completed.

CoTr. CNN has achieved a competitive performance, but its performance is still inevitably hindered by its limited receptive fields. Since Transformer can effectively address this issue, Xie et al. [12] proposed a novel architecture that combines CNN and Transformer. The introduced architecture in CoTr successfully inherits the advantages of CNN and Transformer.

The patch size of $128 \times 128 \times 128$ is fed into the three-stage-algorithm, each stage consists of one transformer and one convolutional layer. CoTr opt for Dice and CE as the loss function. The model has trained 320 epochs (250 iterations per epoch) with a learning rate of 0.001.

2.2   Data Augmentation (DA)

Limited data can seriously constrain model performance, especially on the unseen dataset. Therefore, data augmentation is necessary, as it expands the limited dataset and supports the models in gaining more insights. Each data has a 20% chance of being scaled, rotated, increased in contrast or mirrored, where the probability is randomized and independent of each other.

2.3   Batch Normalization (BN)

Batch normalization is believed in bringing benefits like faster convergence, more robustness, better generalization and mitigating overfitting.

2.4   Batch Dice (BD)

The Batch-wise Dice loss is computed over the batch. This approach avoids large targets dominating the prediction results [17]. BD processes the data as an integral sample, computed over all samples in the batch. Unlike minibatches which assume samples are independent. Hence, the model is less sensitive to the imperfect predictions [18]. However, according to our empirical results, batch dice actually degrades model performance, the implementation details are explained in Sect. 3.1.

2.5   Postprocessing

The predicted enhancing tumor (ET) are sometimes too small to be taken into consideration. In other words, when the predicted enhancing tumor volume is smaller than some thresholds, it can be replaced with necrosis labels [18]. The best threshold is selected via optimizing the ET Dice. Postprocessing may sacrifice the HD95 ET score by a small amount, but ET Dice can be improved by around 2%, or even more.

The performance of three selected models before and after postprocessing are shown in Table 1 for comparison. Obviously, the ET Dice improvement is attributed to postprocessing.

2.6   Evaluation Metrics

Evaluating model performance is an essential process. The following metrics are the main tools used to measure medical image segmentation qualities.

Dice Similarity Coefficient (Dice). Dice quantifies how closely the prediction matches the ground truth, a perfect prediction results in 1, and 0 vice versa.

Hausdorff Distance 95 (HD95). HD measures the longest distance between the predictions and the ground truth. HD95 calculates the 95th percentile of the distance, which reduce the impact caused by a small number of outliers.

Table 1. The performances of each model (before and after postprocessing) are presented in the table, the results for individual Dice and HD95 predictions are listed on the left, and the mean values are on the right. Postprocessing is specially designed to improve the Dice scores of enhancing tumors (ET). Although the postprocessing could cause slight sacrifices in the HD95 mean, but the overall results after postprocessing outperform the results original predictions.

Model	Dice			HD95			Dice mean	HD95 mean
	WT	TC	ET	WT	TC	ET		
nnU-Net	0.9322	0.9032	0.8405	4.57	4.66	14.69	0.8919	7.97
nnU-Net(Post)	0.9322	0.9032	**0.8599**	4.57	4.66	**11.47**	**0.8984**	**6.90**
UNet++	0.9292	0.9097	0.8491	4.58	7.54	13.54	0.8960	8.55
UNet++(Post)	0.9292	0.9097	**0.8593**	4.58	7.54	**13.28**	**0.8994**	**8.47**
CoTr	0.9322	0.9111	0.8501	4.41	5.97	**13.11**	0.8978	**7.83**
CoTr(Post)	0.9322	0.9111	**0.8643**	4.41	5.97	14.24	**0.9025**	8.21

Cross Entropy (CE). CE is another widely used loss function that aims to alleviate the negative influences caused by an imbalanced dataset. Hence, other class re-balancing methods or weighted class training techniques can be neglected.

Specificity and Sensitivity. Specificity and sensitivity measure how valid a test is. The sensitivity of ET measures whether the model is capable of correctly identifying the enhancing tumor. Specificity of ET measures the model's ability in correctly differentiating the surrounding brain tissues from the enhancing tumor. In other words, sensitivity demonstrates the true-positive rate and specificity demonstrates the true-negative rate of the model in terms of identifying tumors.

3 Results

3.1 Batch Dice (BD) Implementation

In the initial design, the BD modification wad expected to improve the segmentation ability, but in practice, it does the exact opposite. Our results suggest that BD implementation has the tendency of over delineating normal brain tissues as enhancing tumor. Table 2 compares two nnU-Net models that share the same hyperparameters. As seen, the one trained without BD outperforms the others.

Visual predictions are depicted in Fig. 1. Enhancing tumor areas are plotted in red, blue defines the tumor core, and the whole tumor areas are shown in green. Obviously, Fig. 1a shows that BD is prone to over delineate enhancing tumor parts, while Fig. 1b proves that predictions without BD are closer to the ground truth. BD updates Dice more frequently, resulting in its overemphasis on tiny components and neglecting the whole picture.

Table 2. Batch Dice (BD) Implementation Comparison: the whole tumor (WT), tumor core (TC), enhancing tumor (ET) Dice and HD95 score of nnU-Net are shown in the first row respectively, where the second row compares the nnU-Net model with the BD modification. Batch dice loss function degrades the nnU-Net model overall performance, especially on HD95 score.

Model	Dice			HD95			Dice mean	HD95 mean
	WT	TC	ET	WT	TC	ET		
nnU-Net	**0.9283**	**0.9074**	0.8466	**4.45**	**7.91**	**11.04**	**0.8941**	**7.80**
nnU-Net + BD	0.9237	0.9025	**0.8472**	6.31	9.43	15.06	0.8911	10.27

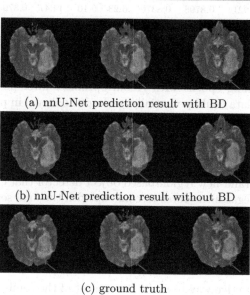

(a) nnU-Net prediction result with BD

(b) nnU-Net prediction result without BD

(c) ground truth

Fig. 1. Comparison of nnU-Net Neural Network performance before and after using Batch Dice (BD). Green indicates the whole tumor, red indicates the enhancing tumor, and blue indicates the tumor core. 1a depicts three tumor regions predicted by nnU-Net with batch dice loss function. 1b depicts three tumor regions predicted by nnU-Net without batch dice loss function. 1c displays the ground truth. As the region pointed by the arrow suggests, model with BD predicts normal brain tissues as enhancing tumor, whereas models without BD do not have this tendency.

3.2   Individual Model Comparison

All baseline models without hyperparameter tuning are summarized in Table 3, all of which achieved approximately 89% mean of Dice. Slight variations can be seen in the HD95 mean, but all results are around 8.

Since the baseline of nnU-Net already showed a convincing performance in segmenting brain tumors, we fine-tuned the baseline and further compared other combinations of hyperparameters. First, the training epoch was increased from 320 to 500. Ideally, increasing the number of times that the model learns from the

Table 3. Baseline Models Summary: all baseline models with zero hyperparemeter tuning have already achieved good performances with approximately Dice mean of 89% and HD95 mean of 8.

Model	Dice			HD95			Dice mean	HD95 mean
	WT	TC	ET	WT	TC	ET		
nnU-Net	**0.9322**	0.9032	0.8405	4.57	**4.66**	14.69	0.8919	7.97
CoTr	0.9321	**0.9108**	**0.8498**	4.42	5.99	**13.16**	**0.8976**	**7.85**
UNet++	0.9292	0.9097	0.8491	4.58	7.54	13.54	0.8960	8.55
HRNet	0.9226	0.8976	0.8404	6.75	11.58	15.44	0.8869	11.25
Swin-Unet (2D)	0.9214	0.8796	0.8370	6.23	9.10	14.47	0.8793	9.93

training set, allows the model to minimize the error. The experimental findings showed that Dice and HD95 scores were optimized to 0.9056 and 7.69 respectively in 500 training epochs with Adam optimizer after postprocessing. Second, unbalanced data could potentially mislead the model in producing severely biased results. Thus, we replaced Dice loss with Tversky loss function [19], which evolves from Dice specialized to overcome this challenge. The proposed method did not change Dice much but has improved the HD95 by 10%. In addition, brain tumor segmentation can be viewed as a pixel-wise classification task. P. Arbeláez et al. designed a brand-new region-based object detector that classifies every single pixel and aggregates the votes to come up with the final segmentation result [20]. We implemented this method along with multiple DA approaches. However, none of them surpasses the existing models.

3.3 Ensemble Model Comparison

Ensemble is an effective way to make the utmost of the combination of multiple models. To compare the ensemble models in terms of averaging and voting methods, we compare the same models with these two methods. Specifically, ensemble mean and vote models of nnU-Net, CoTr, UNet++, HRNet, and Swin-Unet are developed for comparison. The ensemble mean model slightly outperformed the vote model with 0.9036 Dice mean and 8.13 HD95 mean, whereas ensemble vote ends up with 0.9019 and 8.15 for Dice mean and HD95 mean respectively. Other comparisons are in line with the above findings. In other words, the ensemble mean consistently beats ensemble vote. For this reason, ensemble vote will not be studied further.

3.4 Overall Comparison

Amongst all of the models attempted, five best performing models on the validation set are selected for the aggregation of the final ensemble mean model. The every single model and the ensemble model validation results are presented in Table 4. As elaborated above, the ensemble model produces the highest Dice mean of 0.8783, the best HD95 score of the whole tumor and the tumor core equals to 3.65 and 7.65 respectively.

Table 4. Model Comparison on Validation Dataset: The five best-performing individual models are selected to aggregate the ensemble mean model. According to the validation results, the overall ensemble model showed highest Dice mean than each single model and acceptable HD95 mean.

Model	Dice			HD95			Dice mean	HD95 mean
	WT	TC	ET	WT	TC	ET		
nnU-Net 500 [a]	0.9230	0.8727	**0.8349**	3.83	7.73	24.18	0.8769	11.91
HRNet 320 [b]	0.9234	0.8689	0.8284	3.72	7.85	20.80	0.8734	**10.79**
nnU-Net 320 [c]	0.9195	**0.8752**	0.8372	5.61	7.70	20.91	0.8773	11.41
UNet++ 320 [d]	0.9210	0.8659	0.8217	4.13	8.15	27.65	0.8695	13.31
CoTr 320 [e]	0.9207	0.8566	**0.8349**	4.43	10.06	**19.68**	0.8707	11.39
Ensemble [f]	**0.9258**	0.8747	0.8344	**3.65**	**7.65**	24.14	**0.8783**	11.81

[a] nnU-Net with AdamW optimizer and 500 training epochs, postprocessing using optimal threshold equals to 500.

[b] HRNet with half channel, AdamW optimizer, and 320 training epochs, postprocessing using optimal threshold equals 500.

[c] nnU-Net with AdamW optimizer and 320 training epochs, postprocessing using optimal threshold equals to 500.

[d] UNet++ three stage with AdamW optimizer and 320 training epochs, postprocessing using optimal threshold equals to 500.

[e] CoTr with AdamW optimizer and 320 training epochs, postprocessing using optimal threshold equals to 500.

[f] Ensemble of the above five models, average outputs with equal weights, and postprocessing using the optimal threshold equals to 750.

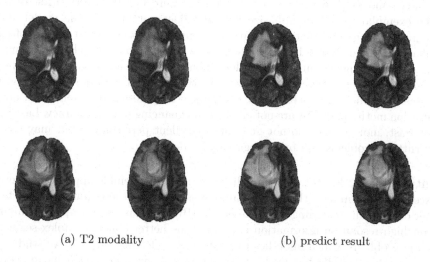

(a) T2 modality   (b) predict result

Fig. 2. A graphical example is demonstrated in this figure. Figure 2a on the left illustrates an example of input T2 modality, the high-signal gray areas are the abnormal regions; Fig. 2b visualised the predicted results by our best model. Green indicates the whole tumor(WT), red refers to the enhancing tumor(ET), and tumor core(CT) is demonstrated in blue. (Color figure online)

4 Discussion

In the current research, we have implemented numerous cutting-edge deep neural networks, in terms of individual and ensemble models with various architectures to improve segmentation of brain tumors. We found prediction Dice and HD95 were strengthened using ensemble models and the ensemble mean consistently outperformed other aggregating models. The final model was obtained from top five models according to their 5-fold cross-validation and postprocessing results. The code is written in PyTorch, and all the models were conducted on AWS p2.xlarge, Tesla K80 (12G GPU RAM), RAM 61G, 4vCPU. These models are trained with AdamW optimizer but with different number of epochs. To be specific, CoTr 320 training eopchs, three-stage unet++ with 320 epochs, nnU-Net with 320 and 500 training epochs, and HRNet with half channel 320 training epochs, which produces the best predictions on validation data with whole tumor, tumor core and enhancing tumor Dice score of 0.9256, 0.8774, 0.8576, and HD95 score of 4.36, 14.80, and 14.49 correspondingly.

By implementing deep neural networks with various architectures, like nnU-Net, UNet++, HRNet, Swin-Unet, and CoTr, our research has addressed different challenges in brain tumor segmentation. In addition, hyperparameters are further fine-tuned to obtain better performance, such as loss function, DA, postprocessing, etc. The advantages of various models are strengthened by aggregating the unweighted averages, which is in line with previously reported findings demonstrated by K. Kamnitsas et al. [21].

According to our research, a few techniques have been tried in an attempted to boost model performance, yet the results were unsatisfactory. First of all, The exemplary results emphasize that BD does not improve the model ability in depicting tiny tumors, but instead depicts the background as part of the enhancing tumor. Since BD failed to capture small tumors, we chose to remove the entire enhancing tumor if it is less than some thresholds. Indeed, postprocessing effectively optimized ET loss, but tiny enhancing tumor recognition is critical in clinical practice. Moreover, the specially designed region-based optimization method and DA are not efficient in enhancing model accuracy. Last but not least, more epochs do not guarantee excellent performance but may cause overfitting problems and bring negative effects.

Future Work. Firstly, although the predominant ensemble approach achieves excellent performance, the individual models still have the potentials to be further developed. According to our research, HRNet is capable of capturing abundant high-resolution information and may thus better handle complex segmentation problems, which underlies the potential of delving into relative studies.

Secondly, as reflected in Table 3, the lowest Dice and HD95 mean scores indicate that CoTr worth an in-depth study, which future research could extend upon the current study to make further exploration.

Finally, the ensemble mean does give reliable predictions, but the prediction accuracy of some models on the committee is slightly worse than others. In this case, reducing the corresponding model weights is expected to get better results.

References

1. Baid, U., et al.: The RSNA-ASNR-MICCAI BraTS 2021 benchmark on brain tumor segmentation and radiogenomic classification. arXiv:2107.02314 (2021)
2. Menze, B.H., Jakab, A., Bauer, S., Kalpathy-Cramer, J., Farahani, K., Kirby, J., et al.: The multimodal brain tumor image segmentation benchmark (BRATS). IEEE Trans. Med. Imaging **34**(10), 1993–2024 (2015). https://doi.org/10.1109/TMI.2014.2377694
3. Bakas, S., et al.: A dvancing the Cancer Genome Atlas glioma MRI collections with expert segmentation labels and radiomic features. Nat. Sci.ntific Data **4**, 170117 (2017). https://doi.org/10.1038/sdata.2017.117
4. Bakas, S., et al.: Segmentation labels and radiomic features for the pre-operative scans of the TCGA-GBM collection. The Cancer Imaging Archive (2017). https://doi.org/10.7937/K9/TCIA.2017.KLXWJJ1Q
5. Bakas, S., et al.: Segmentation labels and radiomic features for the pre-operative scans of the TCGA-LGG collection. The Cancer Imaging Archive (2017). https://doi.org/10.7937/K9/TCIA.2017.GJQ7R0EF
6. Ronneberger, O., Fischer, P., Brox, T.: U-net: convolutional networks for biomedical image segmentation. In: International Conference on Medical Image Computing and Computer-Assisted Intervention (2015)
7. Isensee, F., Jäger, P.F., Kohl, S.A., Petersen, J., Maier-Hein, K.H.: Automated design of deep learning methods for biomedical image segmentation. arXiv preprint arXiv:1904.08128 (2019)
8. Isensee, F., Jäger, P.F., Kohl, S.A., Petersen, J., Maier-Hein, K.H.: nnU-Net: a self-configuring method for deep learning-based biomedical image segmentation. Nat Methods **18**, 203–211 (2021). https://doi.org/10.1038/s41592-020-01008-z
9. Zhou, Z., Siddiquee, M.M.R., Tajbakhsh, N., Liang, J.: UNet++: redesigning skip connections to exploit multiscale features in image segmentation. arXiv:1912.05074v2 (2020)
10. Wang, J. et al.: Deep high-resolution representation learning for visual recognition. arXiv:1908.07919v2 (2020)
11. Cao, H., et al.: Swin-Unet: Unet-like pure transformer for medical image segmentation. arXiv:2015.05537v1 (2021)
12. Xie, Y., Zhang, J., Shen, C., Xia, Y.: CoTr: efficiently bridging CNN and transformer for 3D medical image segmentation. arXiv:2013.03024v1 (2021)
13. BraTS Challenge Data. https://www.synapse.org/#!Synapse:syn25829067/wiki/610865. Accessed 2 Aug 2021
14. BraTS Challenge Overview. https://www.synapse.org/#!Synapse:syn25829067/wiki/610863. Accessed 19 Aug 2021
15. Center for Biomedical Image Computing & Analytics. http://braintumorsegmentation.org/. Accessed 23 Dec 2021
16. Ioffe, S., Szegedy, C.: Batch normalization: accelerating deep network training by reducing internal covariate shift. arXiv:1502.03167v3 (2015)
17. Chang, Y., Lin, J., Wu, M., Chen, T., Hsu, W.H.: Batch-wise dice loss: rethinking the data imbalance for medical image segmentation. In: 33rd Conference on Neural Information Processing Systems (NeurIPS 2019), Vancouver, Canada (2019)
18. Isensee, F., Jäger, P.F., Full, P.M., Vollmuth, P., Maier-Hein, K.H.: nnU-Net for Brain Tumor Segmentation. arXiv:2011.00848v1 (2020)
19. Salehil, S.S.M., Erdogmus, D., Gholipour, A.: Tversky loss function for image segmentation using 3D fully convolutional deep networks. arXiv:1706.05721v1 (2017)

20. Arbeláez, P., Hariharan, B., Gu, C., Gupta, S., Bourdev, L., Malik, J.: Semantic segmentation using regions and parts (2012). https://doi.org/10.1109/CVPR.2012.6248077
21. Kamnitsas, K., et al.: Ensembles of multiple models and architectures for robust brain tumour segmentation (2017). ISBN: 978-3-319-75237-2

Brain Tumor Segmentation Using UNet-Context Encoding Network

Md. Monibor Rahman, Md. Shibly Sadique, Ahmed G. Temtam, Walia Farzana,
L. Vidyaratne, and Khan M. Iftekharuddin$^{(\boxtimes)}$

Vision Lab, Electrical and Computer Engineering, Old Dominion University, Norfolk, VA
23529, USA
{mrahm006,msadi002,atemt001,wfarz001,lvidy001,kiftekha}@odu.edu

Abstract. Glioblastoma is an aggressive type of cancer that can develop in the brain or spinal cord. Magnetic Resonance Imaging (MRI) is key to diagnosing and tracking brain tumors in clinical settings. Brain tumor segmentation in MRI is required for disease diagnosis, surgical planning, and prognosis. As these tumors are heterogeneous in shape and appearance, their segmentation becomes a challenging task. The performance of automated medical image segmentation has considerably improved because of recent advances in deep learning. Introducing context encoding with deep CNN models has shown promise for semantic segmentation of brain tumors. In this work, we use a 3D UNet-Context Encoding (UNCE) deep learning network for improved brain tumor segmentation. Further, we introduce epistemic and aleatoric Uncertainty Quantification (UQ) using Monte Carlo Dropout (MCDO) and Test Time Augmentation (TTA) with the UNCE deep learning model to ascertain confidence in tumor segmentation performance. We build our model using the training MRI image sets of RSNA-ASNR-MICCAI Brain Tumor Segmentation (BraTS) Challenge 2021. We evaluate the model performance using the validation and test images from the BraTS challenge dataset. Online evaluation of validation data shows dice score coefficients (DSC) of 0.7787, 0.8499, and 0.9159 for enhancing tumor (ET), tumor core (TC), and whole tumor (WT), respectively. The dice score coefficients of the test datasets are 0.6684 for ET, 0.7056 for TC, and 0.7551 for WT, respectively.

Keywords: Glioblastoma · Segmentation · Deep neural network · Uncertainty · Monte Carlo dropout · Test time augmentation

1 Introduction

Glioblastoma (GBM) is the most common and aggressive malignant primary tumor of the central nervous system (CNS) in adults, with extreme intrinsic heterogeneity in appearance, shape, and histology [1]. Patients diagnosed with the most aggressive type of brain tumor have a median survival time of two years or less [2]. Accurate brain tumor segmentation is important not only for treatment planning but also for follow-up evaluation [3]. Manual brain tumor segmentation is time-consuming, less efficient, and prone to error [4, 5]. Therefore, it is desirable to have a computer-aided

A. Crimi and S. Bakas (Eds.): BrainLes 2021, LNCS 12962, pp. 463–472, 2022.
https://doi.org/10.1007/978-3-031-08999-2_40

image-based robust automatic brain tumor segmentation system. Different strategies for brain tumor segmentation have been investigated, including threshold-based, region-based, and traditional machine learning-based methods [6–9]. However, those methods are limited because of the complex mathematic model or difficult hand-crafted feature extraction. Recent deep learning (DL) models-based automated tumor segmentation systems have demonstrated considerable performance improvements [3, 10]. DL has made it feasible to build large-scale trainable models that can learn the best features for a specific task [11]. To achieve successful tumor segmentation, DL models often require many training examples. It is a very challenging task to build an accurate deep learning model because of the lack of biomedical and bioimaging datasets. Therefore, proper regularization and hyper-parameter tuning are required for developing an efficient DL network.

Inspired by the popular deep learning architecture known as UNet [12] and the concept of context encoding designed for semantic segmentation [13], we implement a state-of-the-art deep UNet-Context Encoding (UNCE) framework for automatic brain tumor segmentation. Additionally, we compute the uncertainty using a combination of Monte Carlo dropout (MCDO) and test time augmentation (TTA) of data to improve the overall performance and to obtain a confidence measure in the brain tumor segmentation outputs [14].

2   Methods

2.1   Data Descriptions

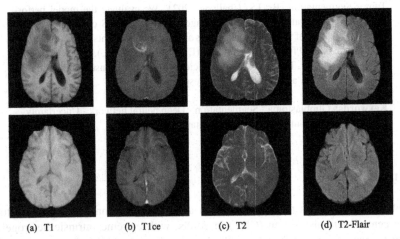

(a) T1   (b) T1ce   (c) T2   (d) T2-Flair

Fig. 1. Examples of four different MRI modalities of two different training samples: (a) T1, (b) T1ce, (c) T2 and (d) T2-FLAIR.

The RSNA-ASNR-MICCAI Brain Tumor Segmentation (BraTS) Challenge 2021 dataset is obtained from multiple different institutions under standard clinical conditions

[1]. Different institutions used different equipment and imaging protocols which resulted in a vastly heterogeneous image quality reflecting diverse clinical practices across different institutions. Ground truth annotations of every tumor sub-region for brain tumor segmentation were approved by expert neuroradiologists [15–18]. The BraTS 2021 training dataset consists of 1251 cases with the ground truth labels. In the validation phase, there are 219 cases are provided without any associated ground truth. Each patient case has four MRI modalities: T1-weighted (T1), T1-weighted contrast enhancement (T1ce), T2-weighted (T2), and T2-weighted fluid-attenuated inversion recovery (T2-FLAIR). All modality sequences are co-registered, skull-stripped, denoised, and bias-corrected [19]. Image size is 240 X 240 X 155 for each imaging modality. Tumors have different sub-tissues: necrotic (NC), peritumoral edema (ED), and enhancing tumor (ET). Figure 1 shows the images of four MRI modalities (T1, T1ce, T2 and FLAIR) of two different training examples.

2.2 Network Architecture

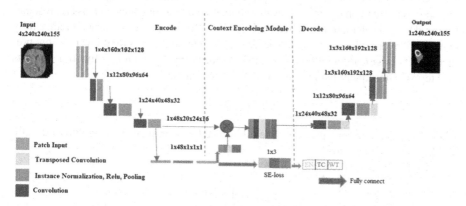

Fig. 2. Overview of the UNet-Context Encoding (UNCE) Network.

The UNet is a convolutional network architecture used for fast and precise segmentation of images. The bottleneck layer of UNet captures the global semantic context features of the scene with rich contextual information. In this work, we have implemented an UNCE network architecture that integrates multiple volumetric MRI processing tasks. Inspired by the work of context encoding network [13], the UNCE architecture is substantially augmented for brain tumor segmentation.

An overview of the UNCE deep learning method for tumor segmentation is shown in Fig. 2. The UNCE captures global texture features using a semantic loss to provide regularization in training. The architecture consists of encoding, context encoding, and decoding modules. The encoding module extracts high-dimensional features of the input. The context encoding module produces updated features and a semantic loss to regularize the model by ensuring all segmentation classes are represented. The decoding module reconstructs the feature maps to produce segmentation masks as output. Figure 2 presents a detailed architecture of the proposed UNCE model including the parameter settings used at each layer.

2.3 Implementation

The MRI scans provided for the competition are co-registered, skull-stripped, denoised and bias corrected. Since the dataset was collected from different institutions and MRI scanners, the intensities show substantial variations across examples. Consequently, we perform normalization of all examples to have zero mean and unit standard deviation. The dimension of each training sample is $240 \times 240 \times 155$. The size of the images is reduced by cropping to a size of $192 \times 160 \times 128$ to manage computational memory and cost. To generate additional training images, we augment data by adding uniform white noise with limited amplitude.

A critical feature of the proposed UNCE is the context encoding module, which computes scaling factors related to the representation of all classes. These factors are learned simultaneously in the training phase via the semantic loss error regularization, defined by L_{se}. The scaling factors capture global information of all classes, essentially learning to mitigate the training bias that may arise due to imbalanced class representation in data. To calculate the Semantic Error loss (SE-loss), we construct another fully connected layer with a sigmoid activation function upon the encoding layer, so that predict object classification in the image [13]. Accordingly, the final loss function consists of 2 terms: Subsequent paragraphs, however, are indented.

$$L = L_{dice} + L_{se} \tag{1}$$

where L_{dice} is a Dice calculated by the difference between prediction and ground truth, and L_{se} is the sematic loss.

Dice loss is computed as:

$$L_{dice} = 1 - DSC \tag{2}$$

where DSC is dice similarity coefficient [20]. The DSC is defined as,

$$DSC = \frac{2TP}{FP + 2TP + FN} \tag{3}$$

where TP, FP and FN are the numbers of true positive, false positive and false negative, respectively.

We use Adam optimizer [20] with initial learning rate of $lr_0 = 0.0001$ in training phase, and the learning rate (lr_i) is gradually reduced by following:

$$lr_i = lr_0 * (1 - \frac{i}{N})^{0.9} \tag{4}$$

where i is epoch counter, and N is a total number of epochs in training.

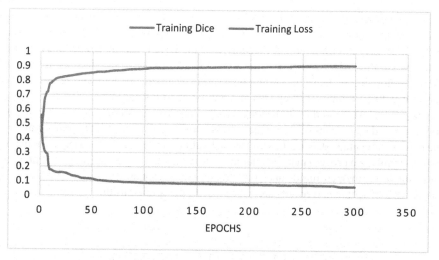

Fig. 3. Training loss and training dice vs number of epochs.

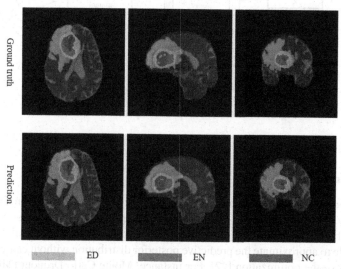

Fig. 4. T2 image overlaid with our prediction. From left to right: axial, coronal, sagittal view respectively.

2.4 Training

We implement the context-aware deep learning network in PyTorch and train the network on NVIDIA V100 HPC platform using the 2021 BraTS training dataset (1251 cases). To train the network, we use 80% of all training data and the remaining 20% of the training data is used to validate the trained model. We train the network using one of the regularization techniques known as a dropout. In this implementation, 30% of random weight was dropped to train the network. The same network was also trained without applying the dropout. The UNCE architecture is trained for over 300 epochs and the best performing versions based on the validation set are retained for testing. Figure 3 shows the training loss and training soft dice curve of the UNCE for the BraTS 2021 dataset. Effective training of the network is observed by the monotonically decreasing loss and the corresponding increase in training dice score. The network achieves an overall dice score of 0.90 by the first 110 epochs and continues to further improve performance at a slower pace. At the end of 300 epochs, we get an average training loss of 0.0701 and training soft dice reaches 0.9131. Once the network is fully trained, the performance of the network is evaluated using the BraTS 2021 validation dataset (219 cases) utilizing the online submission process made available by the challenge organizers. Figure 4 presents an example segmented tumor and the corresponding ground truth of T2 images. The trained model segmented results are very close to the ground truth.

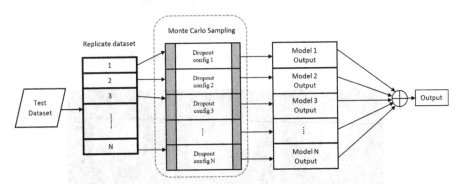

Fig. 5. Monte Carlo dropout computation framework

2.5 Uncertainty Measures

Bayesian probability theory offers mathematically grounded tools to reason about model uncertainty. However, Bayesian techniques with deep learning usually result in models with prohibitive computational costs. Therefore, it may be prudent to utilize methods that are able to approximate the predictive posterior distribution without changing either the models or the optimization [22]. For instance, Monte Carlo Dropout (MCDO) utilizes the dropout layers within a deep neural network at test time to conduct Monte Carlo sampling of the parametric posterior to obtain an approximation of the predictive posterior distribution. We adopt this technique for the UNCE as follows: 1) activate dropout layers in UNCE at test time. 2) Replicate each testing image y, N times and pass each through the dropout enabled UNCE. This essentially runs each replication through a different version of UNCE generated by random dropout masks. 3) obtain the N different predictions $P_n(y)$, where each prediction is a vector of SoftMax scores for the C classes. 4) Then we compute the average prediction score [23] for the N samples as follows.

$$P_N(y) = \frac{1}{N} \sum_{n=1}^{N} P_n(y) \tag{5}$$

In the MCDO technique, we turn on the dropout during the evaluation. Additionally, we conduct test time augmentation of inputs to further increase the sample size and to capture epistemic uncertainty in the predictions. The final segmentation results are obtained by averaging over all the outputs obtained after applying a combination of MCDO and TTA to a given testing example as shown in Eq. (5). Figure 5 shows the framework of the MCDO method. The output from each Monte Carlo sampling model is fused to get the final segmented results.

3 Results and Discussion

Table 1. Performance of the BraTS 2021 validation data for three models.

UNCE Model	Statistical parameter	Dice Score			Hausdorff95		
		ET	TC	WT	ET	TC	WT
No Dropout	Mean	0.7696	0.8281	0.9121	20.24	12.10	4.71
	std	0.2489	0.2395	0.0762	77.34	50.10	7.64
	Median	0.8532	0.9278	0.9348	2.24	2.24	2.83
	25quantile	0.7713	0.8324	0.8894	1.41	1.41	1.73
	75quantile	0.9016	0.9544	0.9547	3.16	5.15	4.64
Dropout	Mean	0.7720	0.8465	0.9141	20.51	7.03	4.07
	std	0.2555	0.2011	0.0746	77.36	26.43	5.65
	Median	0.8589	0.9291	0.9350	2.24	2.00	2.45
	25quantile	0.7870	0.8376	0.8947	1.41	1.41	1.41
	75quantile	0.9052	0.9570	0.9575	3.19	5.00	4.24
MCDO + TTA	Mean	0.7786	0.8499	0.9159	20.26	6.71	4.35
	std	0.2501	0.2031	0.0752	77.35	25.97	6.98
	Median	0.8606	0.9310	0.9366	2.00	2.00	2.45
	25quantile	0.7837	0.8321	0.8980	1.41	1.41	1.41
	75quantile	0.9084	0.9579	0.9588	3.00	5.01	4.24

We first obtain the best performing UNCE models using the training dataset provided by the RSNA-ASNR-MICCAI Brain Tumor Segmentation (BraTS) Challenge 2021 organizer. We use three models (Model without dropout, Model applying dropout and model using combined MCDO and TTA) to generate the segmented results. These models are then evaluated using the validation dataset through the online evaluation tool Table 1. Shows the DSC, and Hausdorff distance of the validation dataset of three such models for 219 examples. The DSC quantifies the similarity between tumor segmentation and ground truth and Hausdorff distance measures how far two subsets (tumor segmentation and ground truth) of a metric space are from each other. The dice scores of the model without dropout are 0.7698, 0.8281 and 0.9121 for enhancing tumor (ET), tumor core (TC) and whole tumor (WT) respectively. The hausdorff95 distances of the same model are 20.24 for ET, 12.10 for TC and 4.71 for WT. The model that is trained by applying dropout in each layer of the network show improvements in the dice scores and hausdorff95 distances for all three tumor cases. The third model uses MCDO and TTA to further improve performance through the uncertainty quantification strategy discussed in Sect. 2.5. For this experiment, we set the Monte Carlo sample number $N = 100$ and obtain the average of corresponding sample outputs to form the final segmentation results. The evaluation results show a further improvement of dice scores compared to the other two models.

The final model was tested by the BraTS challenge organizers. Following the requirement of the challenge, we prepared a Docker image of our model. In the test phase, 570 MRI images were segmented to evaluate the model performance. Note among the 570 test examples, 87 were not segmented successfully. Table 2 shows the test results for our model.

Table 2. Performance of the BraTS 2021 Test data.

UNCE Model	Statistical parameter	Dice Score			Hausdorff95		
		ET	TC	WT	ET	TC	WT
MCDO + TTA	Mean	0.6684	0.70562	0.7551	74.26	74.36	62.77
	std	0.3527	0.38792	0.3544	145.76	144.47	132.87
	Median	0.8424	0.9239	0.9262	2.23	2.23	3
	25quantile	0.6582	0.5461	0.8148	1.41	1	1.41
	75quantile	0.8984	0.9601	0.9588	6.38	14.08	11.08

4   Conclusion

In this work, we use a UNet-context encoding 3D deep learning based method for brain tumor segmentation. The model takes advantage of context encoding, which captures global context features. Semantic error loss is used to regularize the model that helps to manage the class specific sample bias that exists within the tumor tissue segmentation task. BraTS2021 training dataset is used to generate and train several versions of the proposed UNet-Context Encoding (UNCE) model and evaluate three representative versions using the validation dataset provided by the BraTS20201 organizers. The results show that the UNCE version combined with the Monte Carlo Dropout (MCDO) and Test Time Augmentation (TTA) based uncertainty quantification framework yields the best performance.

Acknowledgements. This work was partially funded through NIH/NIBIB grant under award number R01EB020683. This research was supported by the Research Computing clusters at Old Dominion University, Norfolk, VA under National Science Foundation Grant No. 1828593.

References

1. Baid, U., et al.: The RSNA-ASNR-MICCAI BraTS 2021 Benchmark on Brain Tumor Segmentation and Radiogenomic Classification, arXiv:2107.02314 (2021)
2. Ostrom, Q.T., Gittleman, H., Truitt, G., Boscia, A., Kruchko, C., Barnholtz-Sloan, J.S.: CBTRUS statistical report: primary brain and other central nervous system tumors diagnosed in the United States in 2011–2015. Neurooncology, **20**(suppl_4), iv1–iv86 (2018)
3. Pereira, S., Pinto, A., Alves, V., Silva, C.A.: Brain tumor segmentation using convolutional neural networks in MRI images. IEEE Trans. Med. Imaging **35**(5), 1240–1251 (2016)
4. Pei, L., Vidyaratne, L., Monibor Rahman, M., Shboul, Z.A., Iftekharuddin, K.M.: Multimodal brain tumor segmentation and survival prediction using hybrid machine learning. In: Crimi, A., Bakas, S. (eds.) BrainLes 2019. LNCS, vol. 11993, pp. 73–81. Springer, Cham (2020). https://doi.org/10.1007/978-3-030-46643-5_7
5. Pei, L., et al.: Deep learning with context encoding for semantic brain tumor segmentation and patient survival prediction. Proceedings Volume 11314, Medical Imaging 2020. Computer-Aided Diagnosis, 113140H (2020). https://doi.org/10.1117/12.2550693
6. Mustaqeem, A., Javed, A., Fatima, T.: An efficient brain tumor detection algorithm using watershed & thresholding-based segmentation. Int. J. Image Graph. Signal Process. **4**(10), 34 (2012)
7. Pei, L., Vidyaratne, L., Hsu, W.W., Rahman, M.M., Iftekharuddin, K.M.: Brain tumor classification using 3D convolutional neural network. Brainlesion: Glioma, Multiple Sclerosis, Stroke and Traumatic Brain Injuries, pp. 335–342, May 2020
8. Prastawa, M., Bullitt, E., Ho, S., Gerig, G.: A brain tumor segmentation framework based on outlier detection. Med. Image Anal. **8**(3), 275–283 (2004)
9. Ho, S., Bullitt, E., Gerig, G.: Level-set evolution with region competition: automatic 3-D segmentation of brain tumors. In: null, p. 10532. Citeseer (2002)
10. Myronenko, A.: 3D MRI brain tumor segmentation using autoencoder regularization. In: International MICCAI Brainlesion Workshop, pp. 311–320. Springer (2018)
11. Pei, L., Vidyaratne, L., Rahman, M.M., et al.: Context aware deep learning for brain tumor segmentation, subtype classification, and survival prediction using radiology images. Sci. Rep. **10**, 19726 (2020). https://doi.org/10.1038/s41598-020-74419-9
12. Kingma, D.P., Ba, J.: Adam: a method for stochastic optimization, arXiv preprint arXiv:1412.6980 (2014)
13. Zhang, H., et al.: Context encoding for semantic segmentation. In: Proceedings of the IEEE Conference on Computer Vision and Pattern Recognition, pp. 7151–7160 (2018)
14. Wang, G., Li, W., Aertsen, M., Deprest, J., Ourselin, S´., Vercauteren, T.: Aleatoric uncertainty estimation with test-time augmentation for medical image segmentation with convolutional neural networks. Neurocomputing, **338**, 34–45 (2019)
15. Menze, B.H., Jakab, A., Bauer, S., Kalpathy-Cramer, J., Farahani, K., Kirby, J., et al.: The multimodal brain tumor image segmentation benchmark (BRATS). IEEE Trans. Med. Imaging **34**(10), 1993–2024 (2015). https://doi.org/10.1109/TMI.2014.2377694
16. Bakas, S., Akbari, H., Sotiras, A., Bilello, M., Rozycki, M., Kirby, J.S., et al.: Advancing the cancer genome atlas glioma MRI collections with expert segmentation labels and radiomic features. Nat. Sci. Data **4**, 170117 (2017). https://doi.org/10.1038/sdata.2017.117
17. Bakas, S., et al.: Segmentation labels and radiomic features for the pre-operative Scans of the TCGA-GBM collection. The Cancer Imaging Archive (2017). https://doi.org/10.7937/K9/TCIA.2017.KLXWJJ1Q
18. Bakas, S., et al.: Segmentation labels and radiomic features for the pre-operative scans of the TCGA-LGG collection. The Cancer Imaging Archive (2017). https://doi.org/10.7937/K9/TCIA.2017.GJQ7R0EF

19. Liu, D., et al.: Imaging-genomics in glioblastoma: combining molecular and imaging signatures. Front. Oncol. **11**, 2666 (2021). https://www.frontiersin.org/article/10.3389/fonc.2021.699265

20. Dice, L.R.: Measures of the amount of ecologic association between species. Ecology **26**(3), 297–302 (1945)

21. Ronneberger, O., Fischer, P., Brox, T.: U-Net: convolutional networks for biomedical image segmentation. In: Navab, N., Hornegger, J., Wells, W., Frangi, A. (eds.) MICCAI 2015. LNIP, vol. 9351, pp. 234–241. Springer, Cham (2015). https://doi.org/10.1007/978-3-319-24574-4_28

22. Gal, Y., et al.: Dropout as a Bayesian approximation: representing model uncertainty in deep learning. In: Proceedings of the 33rd International Conference on Machine Learning, New York, NY, USA (2016)

23. Combalia, M., Hueto, F., Puig, S., Malvehy, J., Vilaplana, V.: Uncertainty estimation in deep neural networks for dermoscopic image classification. In: 2020 IEEE/CVF Conference on Computer Vision and Pattern Recognition Workshops (CVPRW), pp. 3211-3220 (2020). https://doi.org/10.1109/CVPRW50498.2020.00380

Ensemble CNN Networks for GBM Tumors Segmentation Using Multi-parametric MRI

Ramy A. Zeineldin[1,2,3]($\boxtimes$), Mohamed E. Karar[2], Franziska Mathis-Ullrich[3], and Oliver Burgert[1]

[1] Research Group Computer Assisted Medicine (CaMed), Reutlingen University, Reutlingen, Germany
Ramy.Zeineldin@Reutlingen-University.DE
[2] Faculty of Electronic Engineering (FEE), Menoufia University, Menouf, Egypt
[3] Health Robotics and Automation (HERA), Karlsruhe Institute of Technology, Karlsruhe, Germany

Abstract. Glioblastomas are the most aggressive fast-growing primary brain cancer which originate in the glial cells of the brain. Accurate identification of the malignant brain tumor and its sub-regions is still one of the most challenging problems in medical image segmentation. The Brain Tumor Segmentation Challenge (BraTS) has been a popular benchmark for automatic brain glioblastomas segmentation algorithms since its initiation. In this year, BraTS 2021 challenge provides the largest multi-parametric (mpMRI) dataset of 2,000 pre-operative patients. In this paper, we propose a new aggregation of two deep learning frameworks namely, DeepSeg and nnU-Net for automatic glioblastoma recognition in pre-operative mpMRI. Our ensemble method obtains Dice similarity scores of 92.00, 87.33, and 84.10 and Hausdorff Distances of 3.81, 8.91, and 16.02 for the enhancing tumor, tumor core, and whole tumor regions, respectively, on the BraTS 2021 validation set, ranking us among the top ten teams. These experimental findings provide evidence that it can be readily applied clinically and thereby aiding in the brain cancer prognosis, therapy planning, and therapy response monitoring. A docker image for reproducing our segmentation results is available online at (https://hub.docker.com/r/razeineldin/deepseg21).

Keywords: Brain · BraTS · CNN · Glioblastoma · MRI · Segmentation

1 Introduction

Glioblastomas (GBM), the most common and aggressive malignant primary tumors of the brain in adults, occur with ultimate heterogeneous sub-regions including the enhancing tumor (ET), peritumoral edematous/invaded tissue (ED), and the necrotic components of the core tumor (NCR) [1, 2]. Still, accurate GBM localization and its sub-regions in magnetic resonance imaging (MRI) are considered one of the most challenging segmentation problems in the medical field. Manual segmentation is the gold standard for neurosurgical planning, interventional image-guided surgery, follow-up procedures,

A. Crimi and S. Bakas (Eds.): BrainLes 2021, LNCS 12962, pp. 473–483, 2022.
https://doi.org/10.1007/978-3-031-08999-2_41

and monitoring the tumor growth. However, identification of the GBM tumor and its sub-regions by hand is time-consuming, subjective, and highly dependent on the experience of clinicians.

The Medical Image Computing and Computer-Assisted Interventions Brain Tumor Segmentation Challenge (MICCAI BraTS) [3, 4] has been focusing on addressing this problem of finding the best automated tumor sub-region segmentation algorithm. The Radiological Society of North America (RSNA), the American Society of Neuroradiology (ASNR), and MICCAI jointly organize this year's BraTS challenge [2] celebrating its 10th anniversary. BraTS 2021 provides the largest annotated and publicly available multi-parametric (mpMRI) dataset [2, 5, 6] as a common benchmark for the development and training of automatic brain tumor segmentation methods.

Deep learning-based segmentation methods have gained popularity in the medical arena outperforming other traditional methods in brain cancer analysis [7–10], more specifically the convolutional neural network (CNN) [11] and the encoder-decoder architecture with skip connections, which are first introduced by the U-Net [12, 13]. In the context of the BraTS challenge, the recent winning contributions of 2018 [14], 2019 [15], and 2020 [16] extend the encoder-decoder pattern by adding variational autoencoder (VAE) in [14], two-stage cascaded U-Net [15], or using the baseline U-Net architecture with making significant architecture changes [16].

In this paper, we propose a fully automated CNN method for GDM segmentation based on an ensemble of two encoder-decoder methods, namely, DeepSeg [10], our recent deep learning framework for automatic brain tumor segmentation using two-dimensional T2 Fluid Attenuated Inversion Recovery (T2-FLAIR) scans, and nnU-Net [16], a self-configuring method for automatic biomedical segmentation. The remainder of the paper is organized as follows: Sect. 2 describes the BraTS 2021 dataset and the architecture of our ensemble method. Experimental results are presented in Sect. 3. This research work is concluded in Sect. 4.

2   Materials and Methods

2.1   Data

The BraTS 2021 training database [2] includes 1251 mpMRI images acquired from multiple institutions using different MRI scanners and protocols. For each patient, there are four mpMRI volumes: pre-contrast T1-weighted (T1), post-contrast T1-weighted (T1Gd), T2-weighted (T2), and T2-FLAIR, as shown in Fig. 1. Ground truth labels are provided for the training dataset only indicating background (label 0), necrotic and non-enhancing tumor core (NCR/NET) (label 1), peritumoral edema (ED) (label 2), and enhancing tumor (ET) (label 4). These labels are combined to generate the final evaluation of three regions: the tumor core (TC) of labels 1 and 4, enhancing tumor (ET) of label 4, and the whole tumor (WT) of all labels. Also, the BraTS 2021 includes 219 validation cases without any associated ground truth labels.

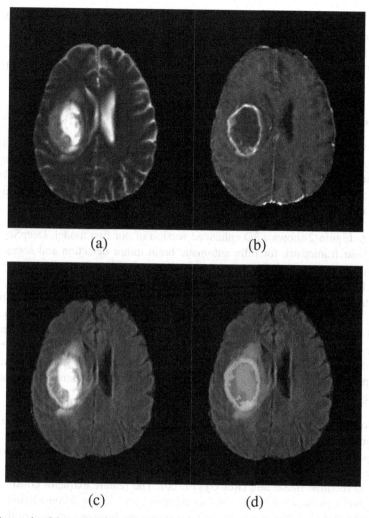

(a)   (b)

(c)   (d)

Fig. 1. A sample of the mpMRI BraTS 2021 training set. Shown are images slices in two different MRI modalities T2 (a), T1Gd (b), T2-FLAIR (c), and the ground truth segmentation (d). The color labels indicate Edema (*blue*), enhancing solid tumor (*green*), and non-enhancing tumor core, and necrotic core (*magenta*). Images were obtained by using the 3D Slicer software [17].

2.2 Data Pre-processing

The BraTS 2021 data were acquired using different clinical protocols, from different MRI scanners and multiple institutions, therefore, a pre-processing stage is essential. First, standard pre-processing routines have been applied by the BraTS challenge as stated in [2]. This includes conversion from DICOM into NIFTI file format, re-orientation to the same coordinate system, co-registration of the multiple MRI modalities, resampling to $1 \times 1 \times 1$ mm isotropic resolution, and brain extraction and skull-stripping.

Following these pre-processing steps, we applied the image cropping stage where all brain pixels were cropped, and the resultant image was resized to a spatial resolution of

$192 \times 224 \times 160$. This method effectively results in a closer field of view (FOV) to the brain with fewer image voxels leading to a smaller resource consumption while training our deep learning models. Finally, z-score normalization was applied by subtracting the mean value and dividing by the standard deviation individually for each input MRI image.

2.3 Neural Network Architectures

We used two different CNN models, namely, DeepSeg [10] and nnU-Net [9] which follow the U-Net pattern [12, 13] and consist of encoder-decoder architecture interconnected by skip connections. The final results were obtained by using the Simultaneous Truth and Performance Level Estimation (STAPLE) [18] based on the expectation-maximization algorithm.

DeepSeg. Figure 2 shows a 3D enhanced version of our first model, DeepSeg, which is a modular framework for fully automatic brain tumor detection and segmentation. The proposed network differs from the original network in the following: First, the original DeepSeg network was proposed for 2D tumor segmentation using only FLAIR MRI data, however, we apply here 3D convolutions over all slices for more robust and accurate results. Second, we incorporate all the available MRI modalities (T1, T1Gd, T2, and T2-FLAIR) so that the GBM sub-regions could be detected in comparison with the whole tumor only in the original DeepSeg paper [10]. Third, we incorporate additional modifications such as region-based training, excessive data augmentation, a simple postprocessing technique, and a combination of cross-entropy (CE) and Dice similarity coefficient (DSC) loss functions.

Following the structure of U-Net, DeepSeg consists of two main parts: a feature extractor part and an image upscaling part. Downsampling is performed with $2 \times 2 \times 2$ max-pooling and upsampling is performed with $2 \times 2 \times 2$ up convolution. DeepSeg uses the recently proposed advances in CNNs including dropout, batch normalization (BN), and rectified linear unit (ReLU) [19, 20]. The feature extractor consists of five consecutive convolutional blocks, each containing two $3 \times 3 \times 3$ convolutional layers, followed by ReLU. In the image upscaling part, the resultant feature map of the feature extractor is upsampled using deconvolutional layers. The final output segmentation is attained using a $1 \times 1 \times 1$ convolutional layer with a softmax output.

nnU-Net. The baseline nnU-Net is outlined in Fig. 3, which is a self-adaptive deep learning-based framework for 3D semantic biomedical segmentation [9]. Unlike DeepSeg, nnU-net does not use any of the recently proposed architectural advances in deep learning and only depends on plain convolutions for feature extraction. nnU-Net used strided convolutions for downsampling and convolution transposed for upsampling. The initial filter size of convolutional kernels is set to 32 and doubled at the following layers with a maximum of 320 in the bottleneck layers.

By modifying the baseline nnU-Net and making BraTS-specific processing, nnU-Net won first place in the segmentation task of the BraTS challenge in 2020 [16]. The softmax output was replaced with a sigmoid layer to target the three evaluated tumor sub-regions: whole tumor (consisting of all 3 labels), tumor core (label 1 and label 4), and enhancing

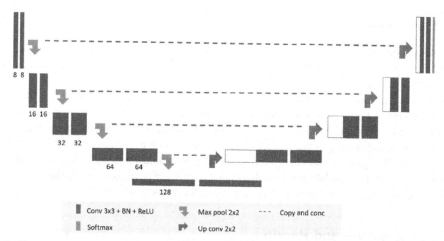

Fig. 2. DeepSeg network consists of convolution neural blocks (*blue boxes*), downsampling using maximum pooling (*orange arrows*), and upsampling using up convolution (*blue arrows*), and softmax output layer (*green block*). The input patch size was set to 128 × 128 × 128. (Color figure online)

tumor (label 4). Further, the training loss was changed to a binary cross-entropy instead of categorical cross-entropy that optimized each of the sub-regions independently. Also, the batch size was increased to 5 as opposed to 2 in the baseline nnU-Net and more aggressive data augmentations were incorporated. Similar to DeepSeg, nnU-Net utilized BN instead of instance normalization. After all, the sample dice loss function was changed to batch dice by computing over all samples in the batch. In our experiments, we incorporated the top-performing nnU-Net configuration on the validation set of BraTS 2020.

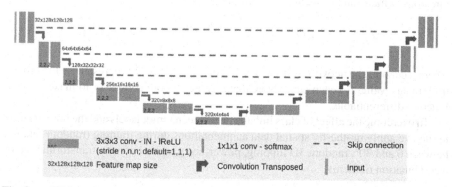

Fig. 3. nnU-Net network consists of strided convolution blocks (*grey boxes*), and upsampling as convolution transposed (*blue arrows*). The input patch size was set to 128 × 128 × 128 and the maximum filter size is 320 [16]. (Color figure online)

2.4 Post-processing

Determining the small blood vessels in the tumor core (necrosis or edema) is one of the most challenging segmentation tasks in the BraTS Challenge. In particular, this is clear in low-grade glioma (LGG) patients where they may not have enhancing tumors and, therefore, the BraTS challenge evaluates the segmentation as binary values of 0 or 1. Although if there are only small false positives in the predicted segmentation map of a patient with no enhancing tumor will result in a dice value of 0. To overcome this problem, all enhancing tumor output were re-labeled with necrotic (label 1) if the total predicted ET regions are less than a threshold. This threshold value was selected based on our analysis of the validation set results so that our model performs better. This strategy has a possible side effect of removing some correct predictions.

3 Experiments and Results

3.1 Cross-validation Training

We train each model as five-fold cross-validation on the 1251 training cases of BraTS 2021 for a maximum of 1000 epochs. Adam optimizer [21] has been applied with an initial learning rate of $1e^{-4}$ and a default value of $1e^{-7}$ for epsilon. Each configuration was trained on a single Nvidia GPU (RTX 2080 Ti or RTX 3060). The input to our networks is randomly sampled patches of $128 \times 128 \times 128$ voxels with varying batch sizes from 2 to 5 and the post-processing threshold is set to 200 voxels. This tiling strategy allows the model to be trained on multi-modal high-resolution MRI images with low GPU memory requirements. The DeepSeg model was implemented using Tensorflow [22] while nnU-Net was implemented using PyTorch [23].

For training DeepSeg, the loss function is a combination of CE and DSC loss functions, which can be calculated as follows:

$$L_{DeepSeg} = DSC + CE = \frac{2 * \sum yp + \varepsilon}{\sum y + \sum p + \varepsilon} - \sum y.\log(p) \qquad (1)$$

where p denotes the network softmax predictions and $y \in \{0, 1\}$ representing the ground truth binary value for each class. Note that ε is the smooth parameter to make the dice function differentiable.

To overcome the effect of class imbalance between tumor labels and the brain healthy tissue, we apply on-the-fly spatial data augmentations during training (random rotation between 0 and 30°, random 3D flipping, power-law gamma intensity transformation, or a combination of them).

3.2 Online Validation Dataset

The results of our models on the BraTS 2021 validation set are summarized in Table 1, where the five models for each cross-validation training configuration are averaged as an ensemble. Two evaluation metrics are used for the BraTS 2021 benchmark, computed by the online evaluation platform of Sage Bionetworks Synapse (Synapse), which are the DSC and the Hausdorff distance (95%) (HD95). We compute the averages of DSC scores and HD95 values across the three evaluated tumor sub-regions and then use them to rank our methods in the final column.

DeepSeg A refers to the baseline DeepSeg model, which has large input patches of the full pre-processed image, smaller batch size of 2. With DSC values of 81.64, 84.00, and 89.98 for the ET, TC, and WT regions, respectively, DeepSeg A model yields good results, especially when compared to the inter-rater agreement range for manual MRI segmentation of GDM [24, 25]. By using a region-based version of DeepSeg with an input patch size of 128 × 128 × 128 voxels, batch size of 5, applied post-processing stage, and on-the-fly data augmentation, the DeepSeg B model achieved better results of DSC values of 82.50, 84.73, and 90.05 for the ET, TC, and WT regions, respectively.

Additionally, we used two different configurations of the BraTS 2020 winning approach nnU-Net [16]. The first model, nnU-Net A, is a region-based version of the standard nnU-Net, large batch size of 5, more aggressive data augmentation as described in [16], trained using batch Dice loss, and including the postprocessing stage. nnU-Net B model is very similar to nnU-Net A model with applied brightness augmentation probability of 0.5 for each input modality compared with 0.3 for model A. nnU-Net models ranks second and third in our ranking (see Table 1) achieving an average DSC and HD95 results of 87.78, 87.87 and 9.6013, 10.1363 for each model, correspondingly.

For the RSNA-ASNR-MICCAI BraTS 2021 challenge, we selected the three top-performing models to build our final ensemble: DeepSeg B + nnU-Net A + nnU-Net B. Our final ensemble was implemented by first predicting the validation cases individually with each model configuration, followed by averaging the softmax outputs to obtain the final cross-validation predictions. After that, the STAPLE [18] was applied to aggregate the segmentation produced by each of the individual methods using the probabilistic estimate of the true segmentation. Our ensemble method is ranked among the top 10 teams for the BraTS 2021 segmentation challenge.

Table 1. Results of our five-fold cross-validation models on BraTS 2021 validation cases. All reported values were computed by the online evaluation platform Synapse. The average of DSC and HD95 scores are computed and used for ranking our methods.

Model	DSC				HD95				Rank
	ET	TC	WT	Avg	ET	TC	WT	Avg	
DeepSeg A	81.64	84.00	89.98	85.21	19.77	10.25	5.11	11.71	5
DeepSeg B*	82.50	84.73	90.05	85.76	21.36	12.96	8.04	14.12	4
nnU-Net A**	84.02	87.18	92.13	87.78	16.03	8.95	3.82	9.60	2
nnU-Net B***	83.72	87.84	92.05	87.87	17.73	8.81	3.87	10.14	3
Ensemble (*, **, ***)	84.10	87.33	92.00	87.81	16.02	8.91	3.81	9.58	1

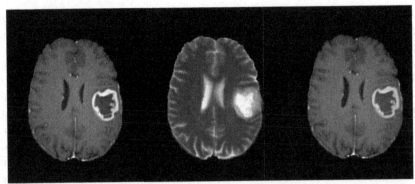

Best: BraTS2021_Validation_00153, EC (97.32), TC (98.77), WT (98.13)

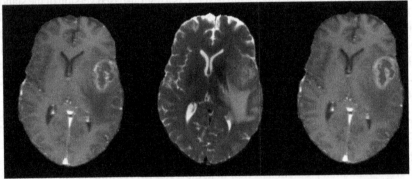

Median: BraTS2021_Validation_00001, EC (82.82), TC (91.04), WT (94.59)

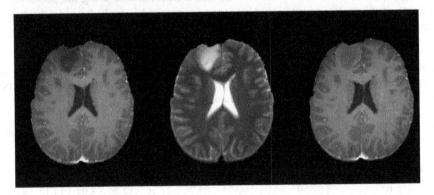

Worst: BraTS2021_Validation_01739, EC (0), TC (85.34), WT (95.72)

Fig. 4. Sample qualitative validation set results of our ensemble model. The best, median, and worse cases are shown in the rows. Columns display the T2, T1Gd, and the overlay of our predicted segmentation on the T1Gd image. Images were obtained by using the 3D Slicer software [17].

3.3 Qualitative Output

Figure 4 shows the qualitative segmentation predictions on the BraTS 2021 validation dataset. These outcomes were generated by applying our ensemble model. The rows show the best, median, and worse segmentations based on their DSC scores, respectively. From this figure, it can be seen that our model achieves very good results with the overall high quality. Although the worst case, BraTS2021_Validation_01739, has a TC of zero, this finding was not quite surprising as illustrated in Sect. 2.4 as a side effect of applying our postprocessing strategy. Notably, the WT region was detected with a good quality (DSC of 95.72) which could be already valuable for clinical use.

3.4 BraTS Test Dataset

Table 2 summarizes the final results of the ensemble method on the BraTS 2021 test dataset. Superior results were obtained for the DSC of ET, while all other obtained DSC results were broadly consistent with the validation dataset. In contrast, a substantial discrepancy between validation and test datasets for the HD95 is visible. Although our results were not state-of-the-art for the BraTS 2021 challenge, the proposed method showed better or equal segmentation performance to the manual inter-rater agreement for tumor segmentation [3]. The results confirm that our method can be used to guide clinical experts in the diagnosis of brain cancer, treatment planning, and follow-up procedures.

Table 2. Results of our final ensemble models on the BraTS 2021 test dataset. All reported values were provided by the challenge organizers.

	DSC			HD95		
	ET	TC	WT	ET	TC	WT
Mean	87.63	87.49	91.87	12.13	6.27	14.89
StdDev	18.22	24.31	10.97	59.61	27.79	63.32
Median	93.70	96.04	95.11	1.00	2.00	1.41
25quantile	85.77	91.33	91.09	1.00	1.00	1.00
75quantile	96.62	98.20	97.22	1.73	4.12	3.00

4 Conclusion

In this paper, we described our contribution to the segmentation task of the RSNA-ASNR-MICCAI BraTS 2021 challenge. We used an ensemble model of two encoder-decoder-based CNN networks namely, DeepSeg [10] and nnU-Net [16]. Table 1 and Table 2 list the results of our methods on the validation set and test set, respectively. Remarkably, our method achieved DSC of 92.00, 87.33, and 84.10 as well as HD95 of 3.81, 8.91, and 16.02 for, ET, TC, and WT regions on the validation dataset, respectively. For the testing dataset, our final ensemble yielded DSC of 87.63, 87.49, and 91.87 in addition to HD95 of 12.1343, 14.8915, and 6.2716 for ET, TC, and WT regions, correspondingly. These results ranked us among the top 10 methods for the BraTS 2021 segmentation challenge. Furthermore, qualitative evaluation supports the numerical evaluation showing a high-quality segmentation. Our clinical partner suggested that this approach can be applied for guiding brain tumor surgery.

Acknowledgments. The first author is supported by the German Academic Exchange Service (DAAD) [scholarship number 91705803].

References

1. Louis, D.N., et al.: cIMPACT-NOW update 6: new entity and diagnostic principle recommendations of the cIMPACT-Utrecht meeting on future CNS tumor classification and grading. Brain Pathol. **30**, 844–856 (2020)
2. Baid, U., et al.: The RSNA-ASNR-MICCAI BraTS 2021 Benchmark on Brain Tumor Segmentation and Radiogenomic Classification. pp. arXiv:2107.02314 (2021)
3. Menze, B.H., et al.: The Multimodal Brain Tumor Image Segmentation Benchmark (BRATS). IEEE Trans. Med. Imaging **34**, 1993–2024 (2015)
4. Bakas, S., et al.: Advancing The Cancer Genome Atlas glioma MRI collections with expert segmentation labels and radiomic features. Scientific Data 4 (2017)
5. Bakas, S., Akbari, H., Sotiras, A.: Segmentation labels for the pre-operative scans of the TCGA-GBM collection. The Cancer Imaging Archive. ed (2017)
6. Bakas, S., et al.: Segmentation labels and radiomic features for the pre-operative scans of the TCGA-LGG collection. The cancer imaging archive 286 (2017)
7. Ghaffari, M., Sowmya, A., Oliver, R.: Automated brain tumor segmentation using multimodal brain scans: a survey based on models submitted to the BraTS 2012–2018 challenges. IEEE Rev. Biomed. Eng. **13**, 156–168 (2020)
8. Kamnitsas, K., et al.: Efficient multi-scale 3D CNN with fully connected CRF for accurate brain lesion segmentation. Med. Image Anal. **36**, 61–78 (2017)
9. Isensee, F., Jaeger, P.F., Kohl, S.A.A., Petersen, J., Maier-Hein, K.H.: nnU-Net: a self-configuring method for deep learning-based biomedical image segmentation. Nat. Methods **18**, 203–211 (2020)
10. Zeineldin, R.A., Karar, M.E., Coburger, J., Wirtz, C.R., Burgert, O.: DeepSeg: deep neural network framework for automatic brain tumor segmentation using magnetic resonance FLAIR images. Int. J. Comput. Assist. Radiol. Surg. **15**(6), 909–920 (2020). https://doi.org/10.1007/s11548-020-02186-z
11. Russakovsky, O., et al.: ImageNet large scale visual recognition challenge. Int. J. Comput. Vision **115**(3), 211–252 (2015). https://doi.org/10.1007/s11263-015-0816-y
12. Ronneberger, O., Fischer, P., Brox, T.: U-net: Convolutional networks for biomedical image segmentation. Lecture Notes in Computer Science (including subseries Lecture Notes in Artificial Intelligence and Lecture Notes in Bioinformatics), vol. 9351, pp. 234–241 (2015)
13. Çiçek, Ö., Abdulkadir, A., Lienkamp, S.S., Brox, T., Ronneberger, O.: 3D U-Net: learning dense volumetric segmentation from sparse annotation. In: Ourselin, S., Joskowicz, L., Sabuncu, M.R., Unal, G., Wells, W. (eds.) MICCAI 2016. LNCS, vol. 9901, pp. 424–432. Springer, Cham (2016). https://doi.org/10.1007/978-3-319-46723-8_49

14. Myronenko, A.: 3D MRI brain tumor segmentation using autoencoder regularization. In: Crimi, A., Bakas, S., Kuijf, H., Keyvan, F., Reyes, M., van Walsum, T. (eds.) BrainLes 2018. LNCS, vol. 11384, pp. 311–320. Springer, Cham (2019). Doi: https://doi.org/10.1007/978-3-030-11726-9_28

15. Jiang, Z., Ding, C., Liu, M., Tao, D.: Two-stage Cascaded U-Net: 1st place solution to BraTS challenge 2019 segmentation task. In: Crimi, A., Bakas, S. (eds.) BrainLes 2019. LNCS, vol. 11992, pp. 231–241. Springer, Cham (2020). Doi: https://doi.org/10.1007/978-3-030-46640-4_22

16. Isensee, F., Jäger, P.F., Full, P.M., Vollmuth, P., Maier-Hein, K.H.: nnU-Net for brain tumor segmentation. In: Crimi, A., Bakas, S. (eds.) BrainLes 2020. LNCS, vol. 12659, pp. 118–132. Springer, Cham (2021). doi: https://doi.org/10.1007/978-3-030-72087-2_11

17. Fedorov, A., et al.: 3D Slicer as an image computing platform for the Quantitative Imaging Network. Magn. Reson. Imaging 30, 1323–1341 (2012)

18. Warfield, S.K., Zou, K.H., Wells, W.M.: Simultaneous Truth and Performance Level Estimation (STAPLE): an algorithm for the validation of image segmentation. IEEE Trans. Med. Imaging 23, 903–921 (2004)

19. Srivastava, N., Hinton, G., Krizhevsky, A., Salakhutdinov, R.: Dropout: a simple way to prevent neural networks from overfitting. J. Mach. Learn. Res., 1929–1958 (Year)

20. Ioffe, S., Szegedy, C.: Batch normalization: Accelerating deep network training by reducing internal covariate shift. In: 32nd International Conference on Machine Learning, ICML 2015, vol. 1, pp. 448–456. International Machine Learning Society (IMLS) (2015)

21. Kingma, D.P., Ba, J.: Adam: A Method for Stochastic Optimization (2014)

22. Abadi, M., et al.: Tensorflow: Large-scale machine learning on heterogeneous distributed systems. arXiv preprint arXiv:1603.04467 (2016)

23. Paszke, A., et al.: Pytorch: an imperative style, high-performance deep learning library. Adv. Neural. Inf. Process. Syst. 32, 8026–8037 (2019)

24. Tacher, V., et al.: Semiautomatic volumetric tumor segmentation for hepatocellular carcinoma. Acad. Radiol. 20, 446–452 (2013)

25. Visser, M., et al.: Inter-rater agreement in glioma segmentations on longitudinal MRI. NeuroImage: Clinical 22 (2019)

Author Index

Printed in the United States
by Baker & Taylor Publisher Services

Printed in the United States
by Baker & Taylor Publisher Services